THE ROUTLEDGE HANDBOOK OF LANGUAGE AND RELIGION

Edited by Stephen Pihlaja and Helen Ringrow

Routledge
Taylor & Francis Group

LONDON AND NEW YORK

Designed cover image: zpix, Getty

First published 2024
by Routledge
4 Park Square, Milton Park, Abingdon, Oxon OX14 4RN

and by Routledge
605 Third Avenue, New York, NY 10158

Routledge is an imprint of the Taylor & Francis Group, an informa business

British Library Cataloguing-in-Publication Data
A catalogue record for this book is available from the British Library

ISBN: 978-1-032-29353-0 (hbk)
ISBN: 978-1-032-29364-6 (pbk)
ISBN: 978-1-003-30127-1 (ebk)

DOI: 10.4324/9781003301271

Typeset in Times New Roman
by Newgen Publishing UK

CONTENTS

FIGURES

TABLES

CONTRIBUTORS

Paul Chilton (Foreword) United Kingdom – University of Warwick

Furzeen Ahmed United Kingdom – Aston University

Sharif Alghazo United Arab Emirates – University of Sharjah and Jordan – The University of Jordan

Amal Alhamazany Saudi Arabia – University of Ha'il

Samar Alkhalil Saudi Arabia – University of Ha'il

Iman Abdulrahman Almulla Saudi Arabia – Imam Abdulrahman bin Faisal University

Sharon Avni United States – City University of New York

Anastasia Badder United Kingdom – University of Cambridge

Melanie Barbato Germany – University of Münster and United Kingdom – Oxford Centre for Hindu Studies

Bene Bassetti Italy – Università di Modena e Reggio Emilia

Brian P. Bennett United States – Niagara University

Nevfel Boz Turkey – Social Science University of Ankara

Linda Sauer Bredvik United Kingdom – Edward Cadbury Centre for the Public Understanding of Religion

Gavin Brookes United Kingdom – Lancaster University

Clint D. Bryan United States – Northwest University

Isobelle Clarke United Kingdom – Lancaster University

Manar El-Wahsh Egypt – October University for Modern Sciences and Arts

Zehra Erşahin Turkey – Social Sciences University of Ankara and United Kingdom – De Montfort University

Mohamed Hassan United States – Ahmerst College

Manel Herat United Kingdom – Liverpool Hope University

Marwan Jarrah Jordan – The University of Jordan

Anthony J. Liddicoat United Kingdom – University of Warwick

Wei-lun Lu Czech Republic – Masaryk University

Marzena Makuchowska Poland – Opole University

Tony McEnery United Kingdom – Lancaster University

Charles M. Mueller Japan – Fuji Women's University

Clara Neary United Kingdom – Queen's University Belfast

Stephen Pihlaja United Kingdom – Aston University

Kate Power Australia – University of Queensland

Kumaran Rajandran Malaysia – Universiti Sains Malaysia

Peter Richardson Japan – Hokkaido Bunkyo University

Helen Ringrow United Kingdom – University of Portsmouth

Andrey Rosowsky United Kingdom – University of Sheffield

Fiona Rossette-Crake France – Université Paris Nanterre

Svitlana Shurma Czech Republic – Tomas Bata University

Simon Statham United Kingdom – Queen's University Belfast

Andre Joseph Theng United Kingdom – The University of Edinburgh

FOREWORD

Paul Chilton

The first signs of religion-like activity go back some 300,000 years. But religion in anything like its recognisable form probably emerged with the evolution of language in humans, going back 150 to 500 thousand years ago. For religious activity to emerge in a socially collective form, language must have already been developing. In written form, religious feelings appeared around 5,000 years ago. There is, therefore, a very tight link between language and religion—the subject of this enlightening new volume.

Religion is far from being irrelevant in the modern world, even though scepticism, agnosticism, and atheism are alive and kicking. For millions of individuals around the globe religion is a central element of everyday life, a key feature of social, political, and cultural bonding, and the very pivot of identity, not to mention religion's role as a source of personal solace and stability. That is not the whole story, however. There exist, and always have existed, extremely troubling aspects of religion, whether you are a believer or not. One need only think of the Christian Crusades of mediaeval Europe, the wars of religion following the Reformation, continuing in the death and destruction caused by the Thirty Years' War, and three centuries later in the violent Catholic–Protestant political conflict in Northern Ireland. Most obvious today is violent Islamic jihadism, and violent religious conflict in India. These negative aspects of religion also involve the use (or misuse) of religious language and concepts. They certainly deserve the attention of linguists and critical discourse analysts.

The term 'religion' is a relatively recent one in its modern senses. Its most likely etymology lies in the Latin verb *religare*, involving the idea of 'binding', physically or metaphorically. In Roman times the word *religio* meant something general, like moral and social 'obligation' (this word, too, contains the idea of binding and being morally bound), as well as 'reverence' and 'respect'. It was not at that time used to refer to organised religious systems. Its various meanings have developed since, in step with social and cultural change. A major development in the meaning of the term 'religion' occurred during and after the Renaissance and Reformation in Europe. From the Enlightenment on, it gradually became socially and culturally feasible to talk *about* religion, religions, and religious belief in an objective fashion, from outside of a religious framework. In other words, thinkers and writers began to work with a metalanguage. The new scholarly volume that Stephen Pihlaja and Helen Ringrow have so creatively assembled demonstrates exactly such an approach to making sense of the phenomenon of religion, advancing our understanding by introducing new methods of investigating the intrinsic role of language. Their volume offers novel ways of talking about, analysing, and understanding the relationship between religious feelings and religious language. Importantly, it also shows how new insights into these connections can be applied in a multi-cultural and multi-faith world, where secularity is also spreading. The overarching question is: what does the word 'religion' imply for us today?

To answer this, and similar questions about religion, the first thing that is needed is factual and impartial description. The collection of large amounts of data is now possible thanks to new digital technology. Compiling corpora, and refining methods of analysis, should be a multi-faith endeavour, both in terms of the diversity of faith traditions examined and in terms of the cultural and linguistic backgrounds of the researchers involved—a combination that the Pihlaja and Ringrow collection admirably exemplifies. The contributors provide a wide range of examples of religious texts, languages, and types of religious activity across a variety of settings. It is in newly emergent settings, produced by our increasingly globalised world, that new challenges for interfaith communication arise. This is particularly true for education, where different religious beliefs, customs, and languages coexist. Another problematic area is the teaching of English as a second language in societies that are often dominated by a particular religious system. Teaching of a national language necessarily involves introducing vocabularies that can carry underlying cultural assumptions and values that are not consistent with learners' own cultures and values. In these ways, the close relationship between language and religion has produced the contemporary need for new ways of thinking and talking about religion in the teaching and training establishments. There is an idealistic perspective in this kind of practical work since it holds the promise of overcoming the sorry histories of antagonism and violent confrontation that have been generated by religions.

Stephen Pihlaja and Helen Ringrow bring together not only scholars who address the crucial practical problems associated with religions in a diverse and interconnected world, they also bring into view the ways in which the linguistic sciences can begin to address fundamental questions about how, and perhaps why, religious feeling and thinking presents itself in the human mind. Consider just one of the areas that have troubled philosophers, anthropologists, sociologists, and others: do different religions have universal characteristics? A new focus on what may be the intrinsic connection between the religious mind and language has the potential to shed new light on religious mentation, religious practices, and religious institutions. There are at least two ways in which research into language and religion can move toward that goal. One is the application of research in cognitive linguistics, including but not overemphasizing the well-known theories of metaphor, and not forgetting that grammatical choices are also a cognitive process. If we think of cognitive linguistics as providing explanatory models for future testing, we enter the domain of neurolinguistics, which will over time provide closer evidence of the way in which language and religion interact in human brains. A second approach, already well advanced in linguistics and literary studies, is the study of genres and their distinguishing linguistic features. Many researchers in the various disciplines that examine religion and religions have noted the prevalence of particular genres that recur across numerous religious traditions. Well-known examples are rituals and rites, chanting and gestures, prayer and meditation, sermons and exhortations, sacred texts, exegesis, and hermeneutics—the list of genres that could be universal is long. What linguists can offer is far more detailed description of religious genres in different languages than has hitherto been available. In the process, new insights will emerge and more precise understandings of what kinds of languaging are universal to religion and what kinds mark differences among them. These are long-term goals for the field of language and religion research—theolinguistics might be one label for it or others may emerge—and they will doubtless change as the field develops.

Foreword

My own interest in the language of religion started when I was a doctoral student writing about a seventeenth-century French religious poet. As I had parallel interests in linguistics, I became intrigued by the peculiarities of religious language and the multi-faceted ways in which it engages thoughts and emotions. It was obvious also that religious language, though purportedly concerned with the eternal, was always rooted in the context of its historical present. Above all, it was clear that understanding religion's hold over human minds and societies was a task that would need many scholars from various academic disciplines, religious inheritances, and linguistic backgrounds. It was only much later that, with my co-editor Monika Kopytowska, we got around to bringing together several scholars who converged on the question of religious language. It seemed too much to hope at that time that this research path might develop further. This exciting new volume edited by Stephen Pihlaja and Helen Ringrow proves me wrong.

1

LANGUAGE AND RELIGION

Stephen Pihlaja and Helen Ringrow

Background

Religious belief and practice are deeply rooted in how we use language. These uses of language differ dramatically in different contexts, from the call to prayer from a mosque at dawn, to the chants of a monk in a monastery, to the recitation of a belief statement with a group of other believers. These kinds of religious contexts and the language that surrounds them are common in many cultures and belief systems. At the same time, language about religion and belief comes up in other contexts as well, when a friend says to another *inshallah* (if God wills it) when talking about their plans for the evening, or a person refers to a blessing in their life. These are ways of talking that implicitly orient towards a religious way of thinking about the world, often in ways that go completely unnoticed by the people interacting. And then there is the presence of religious language in otherwise secular institutions, when politicians subtly, or perhaps not so subtly, make use of sacred texts and recognisable religious language to imply the morality of their position, or sacred texts are used to reinforce otherwise secular governments. Telling where religious language begins and ends is rarely straightforward.

Religious identities are also important parts of how people see themselves and see the world, and consequently how they talk about themselves in this world. Like any other part of identity, consistencies can be seen across different groups, with specific registers relating to particular religions. Sacred languages can be an important part of how people connect with what they believe to be the divine and communities of believers can have shared ways of talking about the world around them. Belief itself and the path to joining a religion is often marked with the recitation of particular words, or ascension to particular beliefs using one's own language to describe an internal state of change. In the same way, language can be an important part of leaving a religious group, and marking a personal change, either to a different faith or to no faith.

Even in this small collection of examples, the breadth of possibility to investigate the relationship between Language and Religion becomes obvious. Religious belief and practice have had a deep and lasting effect on how humans communicate and organise our social world. How language has been and is being used to shape how people think and talk about spiritual experience, and organise beliefs around those experiences, is essential for understanding how social interaction works in many cultures. How it should be studied and, indeed, what it *is* exactly that is being

DOI: 10.4324/9781003301271-1

studied can be difficult to pin down. Language and Religion has long been of interest in different branches of philosophy, sociology, and theology, but has not always had the attention it rightly deserves within Language and Linguistics research.

Religion and religious language have had a consistent, if often somewhat backgrounded, presence in different strands of linguistic (and language-related) study. Most notably, 'Theolinguistics' has a long history (Crystal, 2018; van Noppen, 1981, 2006), as well as religion and spirituality in cognition (Downes, 2011; Richardson, Mueller, & Pihlaja, 2021), sociolinguistics (Omoniyi & Fishman, 2006), metaphor (Soskice, 1985, 2007), translation (Long, 2005; Rawling & Wilson, 2018; Wolf, 2015), social and new media (Bryan & Albakry, 2016), and media/news representations of people of faith (Baker, Gabrielatos, & McEnery, 2013; Bruce, 2017). The interest in a diverse range of approaches to language and religion has been growing in recent years, with OUP publishing *Language, Religion, and the Human Mind* (2018, edited by Paul Chilton and Monika Kopytowska) and de Gryuter's *Discourse Research and Religion* (Johnston & von Stuckrad, 2021), in addition to several journal special issues (Darquennes & Vandenbussche, 2011; Mukherjee, 2013; Pihlaja, 2017). Within linguistics and language-based research, there is a great diversity in terms of the tools, theoretical frameworks and methodologies used to examine the connections between language and religion. Lytra, Volk & Gregory's (2016) edited collection on *Navigating Languages, Literacies and Identities: Religion in Young Lives* is one great example of the myriad approaches used within this field.

Numerous journal articles and chapters on the topic have also appeared, including many from contributors to this book. Metaphor is a key theme of much of this research, especially in terms of how faith and religious concepts are conceptualised in different contexts (e.g. Richardson, 2012, 2017; Neary 2017). Increasing recent attention has been paid to the language of religion in digital spaces (e.g. Souza, 2017; Bryan & Albakry, 2016) in addition to more traditional contexts such as religious conventions (e.g. Warner-Garcia, 2016) and mainstream media outlets (e.g. Power, 2017; Bruce, 2017). In online and offline spaces (and the blurred places in between), the focus is often on how religious faith is discussed, contested, and (re)presented from within and without faith groups. Stephen's own monographs have also looked specifically at conflict in inter-religious dialogue and among people of faith, often in social media contexts (Pihlaja, 2014, 2018, 2021a, 2021b). Helen's research has examined how women from specific faith groups represent themselves and their beliefs in online communities (Ringrow, 2020a, 2020b).

Other work focusing on religious identity has considered how people of certain faiths communicate their beliefs, often through spoken language and conversation analysis (see for example Joseph, 2004 on the how national and ethnic identity intersect with religion) or how 'outsider' groups portray certain religions in contexts such as mainstream media (see for example Richardson's 2004 work on the (mis)representation of Islam in British news media). Outside of linguistics research, language is also a topic of discussion within theology and religious studies (see for example Hall, 1997 on religious discourse in North America; Malley, 2004 on Evangelical Christianity; and McGuire, 2008 on lived religious practices), but the focus is not often on empirical studies of language in religious experience or doctrine.

Although religion and religious identity are key elements of debates around nationality and nationalism, community, gender, sexuality, violence, and terrorism, linguistic research has not often adequately focused on religious discourse. Sociolinguistic research exploring language variation has often focused primarily on other identity markers over religion, such as gender, race, age, and so forth, but therefore there exists only limited body of work both exploring religion as a discrete identity marker of language variation and exploring how religion intersects with the other identity markers mentioned above. Building on the foundation of earlier work in theolinguistics and related work (not always explicitly under the 'theolinguistic' label), researchers have engaged with a broad range of approaches that focus on the lived experience of religion in community life.

There is little question that Language and Religion remains an important area of interdisciplinary research, with growing interest in the empirical study of language across different branches of linguistics, as well as theology, philosophy, sociology, and psychology. A comprehensive collection of research in the field, however, has until now been difficult to find, with researchers needing to draw on occasional books or articles that may have overlaps in terms of the topic covered, or the methodology used. The result has been an emerging, rich field of research that has not yet been able to be collected in a single volume, encouraging dialogue and curiosity across the different places this work has appeared.

Aims and Overview

Given the increased focus on the relationship between religion and language in various subfields of linguistics, our aim for *The Routledge Handbook of Language and Religion* is to establish a shared space for interaction among the various researchers working in the field. Specifically, this handbook:

1) further elaborates and defines Language and Religion as a distinct field of research within the study of language and linguistics;
2) provides a range of different approaches to the field from sociolinguistic, anthropological, ethnographic, and cognitive perspectives;
3) defines research priorities and suggests paths forward for students and scholars; and
4) makes explicit shared goals and interests across researchers looking at different religious traditions and employing different methods.

The common thread of interest in religion, broadly understood, is present in much of the research to date, but because the approaches have varied significantly—a sociolinguist's understanding and methods for investigating the relationship between language and religion differs substantially from a cognitive linguist's approach—a common way of talking about the field has not yet emerged. Even categorising the relationship between this work becomes problematic, as terms like *theolinguistics* may not encompass the broad range of research looking broadly at the relationship between religion and language. Likewise, the work goes beyond *religious language* as talk about religious belief or faith is explicitly religious. The point where talk is *religious* can be difficult to delineate.

At the same time, researchers have made useful connections across linguistic approaches, different understanding of religious practice and belief, and spiritual and religious experience, even if direct comparison and contrast might be difficult at times. This handbook is then an attempt to provide a broad and comprehensive overview of the subject of Language and Religion as it has developed across the subfields of linguistic investigations. These different approaches are collected in three key thematic areas: Religious & Sacred Language, Institutional Discourse, and Religious Identity & Community. The handbook is an introduction to an emerging field, with contributors from a wide range of different national and disciplinary contexts, including cognitive linguistics, linguistic ethnography, rhetoric, metaphor studies, and multimodality. For the purposes of this handbook, religion is viewed in its broadest conception as an organised set of beliefs and practices about the divine or supernatural. The goal is to allow for different understandings of language and religion and different approaches to be presented together, so that researchers can benefit from work done in adjacent fields and begin to make connections with methods and approaches they might not normally use.

This handbook does not focus primarily on theological or theoretical understandings of language but rather aims to explore how language and discourse about religious belief and practice affect the interaction in the day-to-day lives of religious believers and non-believers alike. Throughout the handbook, examples are taken from real-world discourses, where religious and sacred language are used in religious practice, or where religious and sacred language appears in otherwise non-religious contexts. Data includes papal statements, sacred texts, and language from religious rituals, but also includes conversational interaction where religious language emerges without any explicit discussion of religious faith, as in the use of so-called *Allah phrases* in Arabic conversation, or implicit references to religious metaphor in literature. The analysis in this handbook makes clear that language about religious belief and practice, far from being limited to religious contexts and religious people, permeates everyday life in many different contexts.

Taking this inclusive view of religious language and discourse, the handbook provides researchers in linguistics, sociology, theology, psychology, and religious studies with a comprehensive introduction to all the main issues in the empirical study of religious language and discourse. Our objective in compiling the handbook was to create an accessible resource for researchers at many levels of knowledge and experience in language analysis and beyond, from undergraduate students to senior academics, and we have encouraged contributors to write in a way that doesn't require specialist knowledge to understand and engage with an approach. Each chapter has the same core three sections: Introduction and Background, where the main issues and literature related to the chapter topic is introduced; Case Study, where the authors present an approach to and analysis of some specific language data; and Implications and Future Directions, where the authors discuss the key takeaway points from their case studies and suggest new avenues for research. Each chapter also includes four or five articles or books for suggested Further Reading to better understand the topic and approach taken in the chapter.

At the same time as we have ensured this consistency in structure, we recognise that differences in subfields, national backgrounds, and preferences means that not every chapter will be internally consistent, but differences in, for example, spelling conventions will be observed in the different chapters. The contributors for this handbook come from a variety of different backgrounds, from different countries, studying different religious contexts, with different, or no, religious beliefs and practices. In compiling the handbook and working with authors, we have worked to ensure that the presentation and analysis is agnostic in relation to religious belief but is respectful to all the different beliefs and practices that are presented. Contradictory positions, differing understandings, and outright disagreements between contributors should be as present in this handbook as serendipitous connections, shared understandings, and agreements. We recognise and celebrate this diversity, and believe we grow the most when we engage with and seek to understand people who differ from us, whether that difference is religious or academic, in theology or theory, or in religious practice or methodology.

The following sections outline the three main thematic groupings for chapters in the handbook and provide brief descriptions of all the research in the book.

Part I: Religious & Sacred Language

This section will provide an extended introduction to the concept of Religious Language and the different approaches to the study of language, religion, and the notion of 'the sacred' from a variety of perspectives. This section will consider the different ways that language has been treated within different disciplines, including theology, philosophy, and the sociology of religion. The section will also introduce the concept of 'sacred language' and how language from sacred texts comes to be viewed as divine (or from the divine), how those languages are protected and preserved, and the challenges of maintaining those languages within a myriad of societal and national contexts. Throughout this section, both religious and sacred language—and their translations—will be discussed critically in relation to how this language may be used to create and exercise power. 'Religious language' may be explicitly religious or more subtle, as some of the chapters argue. Particular themes addressed in this section also include the use(s) of language(s) within a range of religious traditions, spirituality outside of institutional religious contexts, and religious and moral issues within interaction in non-religious contexts. It will also discuss the increased presence of digital technologies and mediated communication in interaction around religion and in religious contexts.

This section opens with Bene Bassetti's *The Learning of Sacred Languages,* exploring the themes of the importance of language sounds, the importance of accurate pronunciation, and the emotionality of the language sounds within a case study reporting on learners of Quranic Arabic and Sanskrit.

Brian P. Bennett's exploration of *Sacred Languages* brings together discussions of culture, politics, art, technology, history, and faith from a comparative religious perspective, through consideration of the case of Church Slavonic in contemporary Russia.

Nevfel Boz and Zehra Erşahin carry on this theme of discussing sacred languages in different spatial and historical contexts in their chapter on *Digital Media and the Sacred,* where they employ Semantic Network Analysis to unpack the way in which institutional religious organisations in Turkey may be under pressure to conform to more secular discourses on social media.

Manar El-Wahsh considers how prayers can embody certain kinds of religious meanings in *Metaphors and Gestures in Prayers in Islam,* with particular reference to mental spaces and physical gestures in Muslim prayer rituals.

Mohamed Hassan's chapter explores *Religious Minority Representations in Arabic Language,* with a specific focus on how two Egyptian novels address the complex relationship between national and religious, and individual and collective, identities.

Marwan Jarrah and Sharif Alghazo consider *Pragmatic Functions of Religious Expressions* with a focus on the pragmatic messaging of these expressions in conversation, using the example of Jordanian Arabic to discuss the interplay between religion, culture, context, and prosody.

Charles M. Mueller explores the use of metaphor and metonymy in *Symbols and Icons in Buddhist Worship,* applying a cognitive linguistics framework to Buddhist iconography to consider how the viewer may bring their embedded experiences, cultural knowledge, and religious expectations to this multimodal context.

Also looking at the role of metaphor is Clara Neary in her chapter on *Analysing Metaphor in Religious Discourse in Literature,* exploring the (often implicit) religious language underpinning many literary texts through a specific analysis of figurative language in Hilary Mantel's novel *Fludd.*

Stephen Pihlaja examines *Language, Religion, and the Digital World,* with examples drawn from Christian and atheist YouTube videos to argue how tracing religious belief over time can be a useful way of showing how and why these beliefs might change with specific relation to the effects of the broader sociopolitical context.

Last, Svitlana Shurma and Wei-lun Lu's chapter on *Variation of Language in Religious Texts* considers the role of grammar in terms of translating Biblical scriptures into different languages, exploring language-specific styles of parallel religious messaging.

Part II: Institutional Discourse

This section focuses on the discourse of established institutions (both religious and secular) that develop and maintain explicit power structures and truth claims using language. This includes the language of interaction between religious institutions and the State, and the religious institutions within the State, and how contemporary governments and different societies and institutions have understood the relationship between the two. The discussion will include how religious institutions operate as governing bodies using language, both in the limited context of religious communities and in larger national contexts where religious and secular law are not separate entities. The section will explore the use how religious language is used within political, social national contexts (including the role religious language plays in political ideology), with a specific focus on contexts where religion is a part of both tacit and explicit political persuasion. We deliberately define 'institutions' in extremely broad terms in this section, as can be seen in the different chapter foci.

The chapters in this section include the following:

Furzeen Ahmed's chapter on *Religion, Literature, and the Secondary Classroom* sheds light on how students bring their religious beliefs and views into their educational reading practices, with a specific Text World Theory analysis exploring how a British Pakistani Muslim student engaged with issues of defiance and challenging God in a classroom discussion of Shakespeare's *Macbeth*.

Melanie Barbato continues this section with a focus on institutional religious greetings as political communication in her chapter on *Religious Greeting Messages as a Genre of Institutional Communication*, specifically examining the standardised patterns of religious greetings from the Vatican and the White House.

Gavin Brookes, Isobelle Clarke, and Tony McEnery also focus on institutional communication by investigating *Representation of Religion in News Media Discourse* through the application of corpus linguistic and critical discourse analysis tools to British newspaper data, drawing attention to how particular religious identities (specifically Islam and Muslims) might be legitimated or delegitimated.

Clint D. Bryan's chapter on *Pandemic Sermon Rhetoric and Evangelism* considers the rhetoric of Christian evangelical sermons during the COVID-19 pandemic, highlighting the blending of in-group and out-group language that pastors employed to reach live and virtual, and synchronous and asynchronous, audiences.

Anthony J. Liddicoat's chapter on *Language Policies and Religious Practice* addresses how different conceptualisations of the role of language influence how religions approach liturgy and proselytisation, discussing examples from Islam (Arabic) and traditional Catholicism (Latin).

Also exploring Catholic religious contexts is Marzena Makuchowska's chapter on *Politeness in Religious Discourse*, which unpacks the intersections between politeness and religious language through an exemplary analysis of papal speeches in particular relation to face-threatening acts.

Helen Ringrow and Simon Statham's chapter, *Religion in the Discourse of Abortion*, considers how the connections between religious institutions, political parties, and national governments shape the language of abortion rights, offering a particular focus on abortion in Ireland, where a constitutional prohibition on abortion was enacted in 1983 (the Eighth Amendment of the Constitution of Ireland) and repealed by a referendum in 2018.

Fiona Rossette-Crake's chapter on *Religious Oratory and Language Online* situates sermons within oratory specifically and within religious discourse more widely, using participant frameworks to consider how contemporary social media oratory takes on a 'quasi-religious' register as part of its technologically mediated performance.

In the final chapter of this section, Andre Joseph Theng also considers contemporary online spaces with *Catholicism and Social Media*, drawing attention to issues of authority and hierarchy in globalised media representations of Catholicism through analysis of official and lay social media accounts associated with the Catholic Church.

Part III: Religious Identity & Community

This section will engage with the role of language in creating and sustaining religious identity and community, in both national and diasporic contexts. The research encompasses work primarily looking at conversation and interaction, with perspectives taken from linguistic anthropology and linguistic ethnography, sociolinguistics, conversation analysis, and cognitive linguistics, among others. The chapters discuss the role of individual identity in religious communities and, in particular, the tensions inherent in heterodoxy, where individual identity is in conflict with traditional practices and beliefs. The chapters also investigate how particular diasporic communities understand themselves in relation to the larger social world, including the role of religious language and shared national languages in creating and sustaining certain identities. This includes analysis of how different languages and beliefs interact within diverse contexts, where believers from different national and ethnic contexts connect with shared belief and build communities of faith. The chapters discuss the different ways that languages become associated with particular religious identities, be they Arabic and Islam or Yiddish and Judaism. The relationship between ritual language and community is also a focus in several chapters looking at how the learning of ritual language builds and sustains communities, particularly in diaspora contexts.

The chapters in this section include the following:

Amal Alhamazany begins with a chapter on *Religion, Identity, and Second Language* which discusses how attitudes towards learning a second languages (primarily English) in the Saudi Arabian context are affected by perceptions of other languages and the relationship between one's language and one's religious identity.

Samar Alkhalil's work in the chapter *Selling English in an Islamic Society* builds on these ideas by discussing how English education is presented in the Saudi Arabian context and how Saudis understand learning English as it relates to their national and religious identity and how it can be accepted and resisted in different ways.

Iman Abdulrahman Almulla continues talking about the Saudi Arabian context in her chapter on *Narratives and Religious Identity* which looks at how religious identity emerges in and through conversations, exploring how individuals report on spiritual experience and divine intervention.

Anastasia Badder and Sharon Avni continue the discussion of religious identity and specific languages in their chapter on *Jewish Languages and American Jewishness* which describes the relationship between Jewish identity and language, with a focus on how different languages and language varieties are used in the American context for different functions and to index different identities.

Linda Sauer Bredvik then discusses *Multilanguaging in Interreligious Encounters*, looking specifically at conversations centered around religion between people who frequently don't share either a first language or the same religion. Creative use of multilingual resources serves to make meaning in spaces where differing linguistic and religious identities are the norm.

Manel Herat continues to look at the role of language in community in a chapter on *Ritual Language, Ritual Community* which shows how Buddhist ritual language in religious practice and in particular rituals around death, plays an important dual role in both reinforcing theological positions and in creating shared, affective experience.

Kate Power's chapter on *Religious Identity in Discourse* looks at how religious identity is understood in how people talk about their own religious identity, looking specifically at how people in rural Canada talk about their religious identity in relation to a majority Christian context.

Kumaran Rajandran continues looking at how people talk about their religious identity, and specifically changes in religious identity, in a chapter on *Conversion Narratives,* discussing how people talk about conversion to Hinduism and the resources they use to explain and justify changes in their religious identity.

Peter Richardson then takes a cognitive linguistic approach to conversion and religious experience narratives in his chapter on *Cognitive Metaphor and Religion* showing how people talk about these experiences using metaphors and explaining this metaphorical language using a variety of different cognitive approaches.

Andrey Rosowsky then discusses *Religious Ritual and Language in the Local Community*, drawing together several of the topical strands in the section, looking at how heritage languages in diasporic communities have shifted while liturgical language remains stable, showing how different languages and language varieties play a role in understanding and presenting religious identities in different ways, at different times.

Conclusion

Across this volume, the capacity for humans to find meaning in their lived experiences is striking. The chapters in this handbook show that religion is, at its best, about the human urge to understand our experiences, work with others to celebrate that meaning, and develop community with those around them. At the same time, the work in this handbook also shows how religious belief and practice, and religious institutions, can be tools for systematic and individual oppression and work to alienate and drive people apart. Language is central to both these sides of religion, and understanding both how community is fostered and thrives, and how division is seeded and fermented, is a central implication of all the research in this book. Analysis of language makes explicit the processes that lead to these different outcomes, and by identifying those processes and understanding how they work, practitioners can begin to encourage language that fosters community, and discourage and challenge language that underpins oppression.

Working through the different chapters, readers will be struck by the diversity of approaches to and understandings of Language and Religion. The field is growing and broadening beyond a niche interest in different linguistic subfields to an established, interdisciplinary subfield in its own right, with scholars bringing unique strengths and perspectives from the world of linguistics and language studies. In the various approaches to investigating the relationships between language, and religious belief and practice, the value of looking at the same phenomenon through different lenses and from different perspectives becomes readily apparent. A cognitive approach to the use of metaphor in religious language, for example, is not opposed to discourse analytic approach—the two complement one another. The handbook shows how interdisciplinary dialogue can be beneficial in helping researchers better understand how their contributions are unique and how they fit into a broader context beyond their own discipline's interests.

This handbook marks a significant milestone in the development of Language and Religion, but it is only the beginning. Across the chapters, we are struck by the potential for future work.

For scholars at every stage of their careers, the contributors offer new fields to explore and endless potential for collaborative and contrastive study. There is no right or wrong way to understand these relationships, and interaction between scholars taking different approaches or looking at different kinds of discourse and different religious traditions can produce more accurate and more complete pictures of religious belief and practice and how language shapes and is shaped by religion. We encourage readers to use the handbook to pique their curiosity and find connections where they might not normally look, and, at the same time, appreciate how religious belief and practice bring meaning in different ways to different people and recognise the hope that can be gained in the shared values humans find when they go looking for them.

References

Baker, P., Gabrielatos, C., & McEnery, T. (2013). *Discourse analysis and media attitudes: the representation of Islam in the British press*. Cambridge University Press.

Bruce, T. (2017). New technologies, continuing ideologies: Online reader comments as a support for media perspectives of minority religions. Discourse, Context & Media , *24*, 53–75.

Bryan, C., & Albakry, M. (2016). "To be real honest, I'm just like you": analyzing the discourse of personalization in online sermons. *Text & Talk, 36*: 683.

Chilton, P. & Kopytowska, M. (Eds.). (2018). *Language, Religion, and the Human Mind.* Oxford University Press.

Crystal, D. (2018). Whatever happened to theolinguistics. In P. Chilton & M. Kopytowska (Eds.), *Religious language, metaphor and the mind*, 3–18. Oxford University Press.

Darquennes, J., & Vandenbussche, W. (2011). Language and religion as a sociolinguistic field of study: some introductory notes. *Sociolinguistica, 25*, 1–11.

Downes, W. (2011). *Language and religion: a journey into the human mind*. Cambridge University Press.

Hall, D.D. (1997). *Lived religion in America: Toward a history of practice*. Princeton University Press.

Johnston, J., & von Stuckrad, K. (Eds.). (2021). *Discourse Research and Religion: Disciplinary Use and Interdisciplinary Dialogues*. de Gruyter.

Joseph, J. (2004) *Language and Identity: National, Ethnic, Religious.* Palgrave Macmillan.

Long, L. (2005). *Translation and religion: holy untranslatable?* Multilingual Matters.

Lytra, V., Volk, D., & Gregory, E. (2016). *Navigating Languages, Literacies and Identities: Religion in Young Lives*. Routledge.

Malley, B. (2004). *How the Bible works: An anthropological study of Evangelical Biblicism*. AltaMira Press.

McGuire, M.B. (2008). *Lived religion: Faith and practice in everyday life*. Oxford University Press.

Mukherjee, S. (2013). Reading language and religion together. *International Journal of the Sociology of Language, 220*: 1–6.

Neary, C. (2017). Truth is like a vast tree. *Metaphor and the Social World, 7*(1), 103–121.

Omoniyi, T., & Fishman, J.A. (2006). *Explorations in the Sociology of Language and Religion*. John Benjamins.

Pihlaja, S. (2014). *Antagonism on YouTube: Metaphor in Online Discourse*. Bloomsbury.

Pihlaja, S. (2017). Special issue on metaphor in religion and spirituality. *Metaphor and the Social World, 7*(1), 1–4.

Pihlaja, S. (2018). *Religious Talk Online: the evangelical discourse of Muslims, Christians, and atheists*. Cambridge University Press.

Pihlaja, S. (2021a). *Talk About Faith: how debate and conversation shape belief.* Cambridge University Press.

Pihlaja, S. (Ed.). (2021b). *Analyzing Religious Discourse*. Cambridge University Press.

Power, Kate. (2017). "Church trailblazer Rev Pat Storey on Weight Watchers, caffeine and how she named her dog after former New York Mayor": News representations of the first female Anglican Bishop in the UK and Ireland. *Irish Journal of Applied Social Studies, 16*(1), Article 6. DOI: 10.21427/D78T67

Rawling, P., & Wilson, P. (Eds.). (2018). *The Routledge Handbook of Translation and Philosophy*. Routledge.

Richardson, J.E. (2004). *(Mis)representing Islam: The racism and rhetoric of British broadsheet newspapers*. John Benjamins Publishing Company.

Richardson, P. (2012). A closer walk: A study of the interaction between metaphors related to movement and proximity and presuppositions about the reality of belief in Christian and Muslim testimonials. *Metaphor and the Social World, 2*(2), 233–261.

Richardson, P. (2017). An investigation of the blocking and development of empathy in discussions between Muslim and Christian believers. *Metaphor and the Social World, 7*(1), 47–65.

Richardson, P., Mueller, C., & Pihlaja, S. (2021). *Cognitive Linguistics and Religious Language: An Introduction.* Routledge.

Ringrow, H. (2020a). "Beautiful masterpieces": metaphors of the female body in modest fashion blogs. In H. Ringrow & S. Pihlaja (Eds.), *Contemporary Media Stylistics,* 15–34. Bloomsbury.

Ringrow, H. (2020b). "I can feel myself being squeezed and stretched, moulded and grown, and expanded in my capacity to love loudly and profoundly": Metaphor and religion in motherhood blogs. *Discourse, Context & Media, 37.*

Soskice, J.M. (1985). *Metaphor and religious language.* Oxford University Press.

Soskice, J.M. (2007). *The kindness of God: Metaphor, gender, and religious language.* Oxford University Press.

Souza, A. (2017). Facebook: a medium for the language planning of migrant churches. In A. Rosowsky (Ed.), *Faith and Language Practices in Digital Spaces,* 45–67. Multilingual Matters.

van Noppen, J.-P. (1981). *Theolinguistics.* Studiereeks Tijdschrift Vrije Universiteit Brussel.

van Noppen, J.-P. (2006). From theolinguistics to critical theolinguistics: The case for communicative probity. *ARC, The Journal of the Faculty of Religious Studies, McGill University, 34,* 47–65. McGill University.

Warner-Garcia, S. (2016). Rejecting exclusion, embracing inclusion: conversation as policy-making at a US Baptist conference on sexuality and covenant. *Language policy, 15*(2), 141–161.

Wolf, A. (2015). A Religious Ethics of Translation: The Love Command. *Journal of Translation, 11*(1), 61–73.

PART I

Religious & Sacred Language

2

THE LEARNING OF SACRED LANGUAGES

Bene Bassetti

Introduction and Background

Sacred languages are a category of languages that includes well-known examples, such as Quranic Arabic and Sanskrit, as well as less widely known ones, such as Pali and Ge'ez. According to Bennett (2018), a sacred language is characterised by a number (not necessarily all) of characteristics (here adapted for an audience of language researchers). It is typically:

- mythologised—associated with superhuman entities or events;
- specialised—used for specific religious or spiritual practices rather than interpersonal communication;
- learned—acquired through individual study and often instruction, not spontaneously like a native language; and/or
- considered sacred by a community.

For instance, Quranic Arabic was used by the Divine when communicating with the Prophet; is used for set prayers and for scripture reading; is usually learned in childhood from family, teachers and/or schools; and is sacred to all Muslims across time and space. I adapted Bennett's criteria, both to reflect the tenets and terminology of second language research (for instance, replacing 'mother tongue/not mother tongue' with 'acquired/learned'), and to include non-religious spirituality (adding 'spiritual' to 'religious', replacing 'divine' with 'superhuman'). However, a definition may be difficult and controversial, and different disciplines may need different ways to delimit the boundaries of this category of languages. For the purposes of second language (L2) research (research on second language acquisition/learning and sequential bi-/multilingualism), the most appropriate approach to the description and definition of sacred language is the emic one, namely a learner- or user-centred one. This is because the focus of L2 research is the language learner or user (see also Bennett's slightly different point that 'sacredness is in the eye of the believer', p. 9). A sacred language then is one the learner or user believes to have a special religious or spiritual value and learns and uses exclusively for religious or spiritual purposes. For instance, the yoga practitioners described below believe that Sanskrit has special effects on humans and the universe

DOI: 10.4324/9781003301271-3

and learn it in order to utter mantras and/or to understand ancient texts that have spiritual or philosophical meaning to them.

Sacred language learning is very diverse, with different types of learners learning in a variety of settings and at different times in life. Many learn at least the rudiments during childhood, but there are also late converts, who are first exposed to the language in adulthood; adult re-learners, who were first exposed in childhood but seek deeper knowledge later in adulthood; (trainee) faith-leaders; and silver learners, who engage with sacred texts or traditions later in life, often after retirement. Learning can start within the family, with or without the support of individual or group teachers, and there are a variety of religious and non-religious settings, both devoted to the language and offering the language within wider education, for both children and adults: supplementary schools, community schools, classes offered within the school system, courses offered at places of worship, further and higher education courses, summer schools, and many others. Independent study is also widespread, through written materials (bilingual texts, translations, textbooks) and new technologies (online interactive texts, synchronous or recorded courses, apps). Importantly, the objectives and scope of learning also vary, from the basic ability to utter short prayers without comprehension to complex exegesis of ancient texts.

Despite much diversity, sacred languages also share commonalities, so that they can be considered a category of languages (Bennett, 2018). Crucially for L2 research, a sacred language is always an additional language—one that follows chronologically after the acquisition of the native language(s)—which makes it a suitable object of language learning research. It is also always learned, meaning that it requires study and often instruction and is not acquired spontaneously like a native language, which makes it also a suitable object of language teaching research. It is learned to use it for religious or spiritual purposes, whether to perform rituals or to read ancient texts, so that its learning differs from the learning of non-sacred languages. This makes it an interesting object of research to expand knowledge about L2 learning and use.

Following applied linguists' recent interest in religion (discussed elsewhere in this volume), calls for research on religion and language learning and teaching appeared a decade ago (Dörnyei et al., 2013), and in 2018 Huamei Han called for the establishment within applied linguistics of 'the subfield of religion and language teaching and learning' (p. 436; see also responses by other scholars in the same issue). However, the proposed research agendas did not mention sacred languages specifically or any of their characteristics, and indeed only touched on issues of language learning, focusing instead on wider societal issues.

At present, empirical research on sacred language learning is scattered across disciplines, journals, and edited volumes. Sometimes it is found in publications about broader topics; for example, the learning of Quranic Arabic may be discussed in articles about Modern Arabic, and articles on sacred languages (for instance, Gregory et al., 2013a) can appear in special issues on language and religion. Yet, there has been at least one journal special issue devoted to Quranic Arabic literacy (Daugaard & Dewilde, 2019), and I am editing a special issue on sacred language learning that features articles on Quranic Arabic, Biblical Hebrew, and Sanskrit (Bassetti, 2024).

Some researchers have an interest in a specific language in a specific environment, as is the case with the extensive work of Rosowsky (2013, 2021a) on Quranic Arabic literacy in UK Muslim communities, and of Avni (2011, 2018) on Hebrew language and literacy in US Jewish communities. Other researchers extend previous research interests to investigate sacred languages. The BeLiFS (Becoming Literate in Faith Settings) group (Gregory et al., 2013a, 2013b; Lytra, 2020) benefitted from the principal investigator Gregory's previous extensive work on children's multilingual literacies in London; the world-leading researcher of language learning motivation Dörnyei co-authored an article on motivation in language learning among Bible translators (Lepp-Kaethler

& Dörnyei, 2013), within his wider interest in issues of Christian faith. My research on sacred languages builds upon two decades of researching linguistic relativism (the idea that the languages we know impact the way we think) in second language learners and users, hence my interest in the impact of sacred language learning on views of language and language learning (Bassetti, 2024).

Much research on sacred language learning is grounded in sociolinguistics. Indeed, 'language and religion' emerged as a research area within sociolinguistics 20 years ago (and sociolinguists were already reflecting on religion half a century ago), and the sociolinguistic approach is in line with current trends in second language research, where the 'social turn' of the mid-1990s brought to the fore social aspects of language learning. Because of its sociolinguistic orientation, research has mostly investigated issues of identity, language socialisation (learning to use language in socially appropriate ways), and other social aspects of learning. While research has investigated children's learning, or specific practices such as Quran memorisation and recitation, other types of learning and use have received little or no attention. Also because of the sociolinguistic approach taken, methods are qualitative, including ethnographic methods such as observation, as well as different types of interviews such as narrative interviews or focus groups, that aim at exploring language learners' perceptions, experiences, and beliefs. Research grounded in second language acquisition is as of yet underdeveloped.

Much has been written about the frequent absence of comprehension in sacred language learning and use. Sacred language users may decode, memorise, recite, chant, listen, and so on, without comprehending the language they perceive or produce, and indeed without feeling the need to comprehend it. Learners' primary, or even sole, goal can be accurate pronunciation of short oral texts, or the ability to decode a written text, or to recite a text from memory. Reception and production of speech without meaning appear incomprehensible to many, an issue well discussed in Chapter 6 of Bennett (2018). This is what Rosowsky (2021a), who began exploring this issue over a decade ago, calls 'ultra-lingual', namely a use of language that goes beyond semantic meaning. He argues for stronger respect for this use of language. It is indeed a matter of perspective, as what may appear as meaningless repetition to an outsider is a deeply meaningful experience to the language users themselves, as using the sacred language can be an act of religious piety, an important component of religious identity, a means to commune with the Divine or a community, or have many other layers of meaning.

However, far from always being secondary, the role of comprehension varies widely, ranging from the complete absence of comprehension of someone who recites a whole text without recognising the meaning of a single word, to the complex meaning-making of someone who translates or interprets a complex ancient text. This is not limited to faith leaders, as for instance learners of Biblical languages generally aim at an in-depth understanding of the text, or the ability to translate or to compare different translations. Some even learn their sacred language to read and interpret their scriptures by themselves, to verify and challenge the traditional interpretations of their community or their religious authorities. Attitudes towards the lack of comprehension also vary across individuals and time. While some English-literate Western children accept the absence of comprehension in their sacred language reading classes, others query or reject this approach (see articles by Badder and Avni and by Rosowsky in Bassetti, 2024). Among adults, the inability to understand a sacred language can result in negative attitudes towards one's faith, negative emotion, and even affect mental health. At least for some sacred languages, in Western environments, there may be a trend towards an increasing need to understand.

Various aspects of identity are important in language learning, but religious identity is paramount in sacred language learning. It indicates a compound of beliefs, practices, and sense of belonging, and it is central to many individuals and communities. The sacred language acts as a marker of collective religious identity, being the common language of the religious community, and its learning and use are central to religious and linguistic personal and collective identities. Using Quranic Arabic for prayer at the same time as all other Muslim worshippers gives a sense of being part of a worldwide community. Hebrew is a strong marker of Jewishness. This religious-linguistic identity has not been studied in mainstream L2 research.

The learning of sacred languages could be seen through a deficiency lens—communication is missing, production is missing—or more productively seen as a different form of language learning that can broaden L2 research. Some evident differences are discussed in this chapter—identity, emotion (see below)—but many others could have been mentioned, for instance attitudes towards the language and motivation to learn it. Sacred languages involve different language practices, such as cantillation, chanting, or calligraphy appreciation. The learning and teaching of sacred languages and literacy often reflects non-Western traditions, some of which are arguably better suited to learners' aims, which learners and teachers can adopt or syncretically integrate with mainstream education approaches. Many other interesting aspects will emerge as more research is conducted.

This brief overview can help answer two questions about the role of sacred languages in L2 research. First, is sacred language learning a legitimate part of research on language learning? Surely L2 research should include any form of language learning. The frequently remarked absence of comprehension and of communicative aims is only an objection if one assumes that language learning is about interpersonal communication, which is a circular assumption as it reflects the selection of languages currently being investigated. Crucially, learning is taking place, as there is a measurable difference between someone who has learned a sacred language and someone who has not. Second, can sacred language research contribute to mainstream L2 research? It appears that various aspects of sacred language learning differ from learners of non-sacred languages or are even entirely unattested among them. The next section explores this issue by means of an exploratory study, while some potential contributions of sacred languages to L2 research are then presented in the final section.

Phonology in the Learning of Quranic Arabic and Sanskrit

This section is an exploration of the learning of phonology (sounds) and spoken form across sacred languages. It discusses similarities and differences between two sacred languages—Quranic Arabic and Sanskrit— and compares findings from these sacred languages with the consensus in mainstream research on second language (L2) phonology. I argue that the field of L2 phonology research should include sacred languages, because studying the learning of sacred language phonology can extend and diversify the body of empirical evidence and contribute to theorising in L2 pronunciation research. The motivation for this is that:

1) phonology learning across different sacred languages is similar enough to warrant treating sacred languages as a category of languages within L2 research;
2) phonology learning across sacred languages varies enough that investigating different ones can contribute to the diversity of languages investigated within L2 research (something that is a major concern in an English-dominated discipline); and
3) crucially, phonology learning in sacred languages differs from phonology learning in non-sacred languages, including second, foreign, heritage/community, and classical languages. As such, this line of research can provide new perspectives to mainstream L2 phonology research.

16

Phonology was selected because it is an aspect of language learning where the realities investigated by mainstream L2 research differ widely from the realities of sacred language learners and users. The selected languages were Quranic Arabic (henceforth 'QA') and Sanskrit as a Sacred Language (henceforth 'Sanskrit'; not to be confused with spoken Sanskrit). These two languages are suitable in illustrating similarities and differences across sacred languages, because phonology and the spoken form of language are at the very core of the learning and use of both languages. There are however differences (discussed below) in learners' and users' perceptions of the sounds of the two languages, their aims in learning the pronunciation of the two languages, and the nature of the emotional resonance of the spoken forms of the two languages.

To identify similarities and differences in phonology learning in QA and Sanskrit, I re-analysed 16 interviews of Europe-based adult learners collected for previous studies: 12 semi-structured interviews of UK-based QA learners (Bassetti & Dewaele, 2018) and four narrative interviews of Italian learners of Sanskrit (Bassetti & Reinboldt, 2023; detailed information is found in the relevant articles). To identify learners' views of the phonology of their language, I first assembled all extracts that had been assigned codes related to language sound or pronunciation in previous thematic analyses using the software MaxQDA. Utilising this, I then re-read and annotated clean copies of all interviews to identify similarities and differences in talking about language sounds, before re-coding the 16 interviews again using MaxQDA and extracting themes. I used extracts from these interviews (marked with italics and quotes) to illustrate my analysis. To relate the themes to scholarship on sacred languages, QA and Sanskrit, I selected a general scholarly introduction to sacred languages (Bennett's (2018) *Sacred Languages of the World*), as well as three monographs for each language about its form, its sounds, and its aesthetic or emotional dimensions (Sanskrit: Beck, 1993; Pollock, 2006; Wilke & Moebus, 2011; QA: Gade, 2004; Kermani, 2015; Versteegh, 2014).

This chapter discusses three themes around sacred language pronunciation, selected from those that emerged from the analysis, each with three categories: Commonalities between the two languages, differences between the two languages, and differences between the two sacred languages versus mainstream L2 phonology research. To relate the findings to L2 research and L2 pronunciation research, I selected three recent overviews, one of L2 research (Ellis, 2021) and two of L2 phonology learning (Pennington, 2021; Derwing & Munro, 2022) using these criteria: a short English-language review; by one or more leading scholars; research-led but not aimed at specialists; published within the last three years. Unless a different source is specified, discussions of L2 phonology research are based on these sources.

The three themes are summarised in Table 2.1.

The first theme is the importance of language sounds. The sound of the language is fundamental to both learners of Quranic Arabic (QA) and Sanskrit (Sanskrit). The reasons for this centrality of pronunciation differ between the two languages, but this centrality is a major difference between learners of such sacred languages and of other languages.

In the views of both QA and Sanskrit learners within this study, the sounds of their sacred language are of paramount importance in and of themselves. Listening to and producing the language sounds is a fundamental and profound experience, regardless of comprehension. Listening to QA or producing the language (uttering prayers, decoding aloud the Quran) without understanding the meaning of the text is normal practice for millions of Muslims. A Sanskrit learner explains that '*the sounds of Sanskrit have power in themselves, ... even though you do not know the meaning*'.

The crucial importance of sound has different reasons for QA and Sanskrit learners, who at least partly reflect the views of language within their respective traditions. In Islamic traditions, QA is

Table 2.1 The three themes and their three categories

Theme	Similarities	Differences	L2 research
Importance of language sounds	The sounds of the language are fundamental	QA: The language of the Divine Sanskrit: The perfect and powerful language	L2 phonology is secondary
Importance of accurate pronunciation	Pronunciation must be perfect	QA: religious reasons Sanskrit: effects on body and mind	The goal is intelligibility
Emotionality of language sounds	Language sounds have aesthetic-emotional resonance	QA: religious emotion Sanskrit: positive emotion	Lack of interest in positive and sacred emotion

a unique language because it has divine origins. The Divine used this language to communicate with humans when transmitting the revelation to the Prophet Muhammad and then through the Quran. This has then been transmitted over the centuries, first orally and later also in writing. As the language the Divine chose to use, spoken and written QA partakes of the heavenly nature of the Divine. Indeed, the inimitable perfection of the Quran, which testifies to its divine origin as the verbatim reproduction of God's word, extends not only to its meaning but crucially to its phonological form (Kermani, 2015). Talking about reading aloud the Quran, a learner explained: '*we really believe that that's the word of God and created like Him.*'

In Sanskritic traditions, Sanskrit is unique because it is perfect, eternal, and has a supernatural power (Filliozat, 2000). Its vibrations resonate with the cosmos and manifest the ultimate nature of reality. It is believed to have a power that affects the human body and mind, as well as the super-human realm beyond it. Unlike QA, Sanskrit was not revealed by a Divinity, but was perceived by wise ancient men, and was transmitted as the language of the Veda (an archaic collection of hymns). Like the Quran, the Veda were transmitted first orally and then in writing. Unlike QA however the sacrality of Sanskrit pertains to its phonological form only, not the written form (Beck, 1995). This sound impacts Sanskrit learners and users: Something that among other effects '*gives you much joy... a really, really strong emotion of liberation*'. Learners' views also apparently reflect the traditions associated with their respective language. As previously noted (Bassetti & Reinboldt, 2023), learning a sacred language also involves internalising at least part of a novel, often radically different, view of language and language learning.

The centrality of phonology (language sounds) over and above semantics (meaning) is without doubt the most striking difference between sacred language learning and mainstream L2 research. This is often remarked and discussed in the literature on sacred language learning, because current views of language learning and use are centred around meaning and its transmission. The exclusion of sacred languages from mainstream L2 research is probably largely due to the frequent absence of meaning in their learning and use. Looking at L2 research, L2 phonology is a peripheral aspect of language learning. The main aim of language learning in the L2 phonology literature is interpersonal oral communication (transmission of meaning). The phonological form of the language is seen as a tool, needed for exchanging messages in oral interaction.

The second theme is the importance of accurate pronunciation. For learners and users of both QA and Sanskrit, pronunciation learning aims at perfection. As discussed below, the reasons are different—beliefs in the divine nature of QA and in the perfection and supernatural power of Sanskrit—and tolerance of imperfection differs in line with these views. The focus on perfect production contrasts strikingly with the tenets of L2 research, where the aim of L2 phonology learning is intelligibility within an interpersonal communication context.

Both QA and Sanskrit learners aim at perfect pronunciation. Learners resolutely agreed that pronunciation is central, with many QA interviewees spontaneously declaring that pronunciation is '*very important*' or '*extremely important*'. Indeed, learning pronunciation '*for us, really, it's the most important of all the things*' (with few exceptions: '*it's not my priority of my life actually*'). For Sanskrit learners too knowing the accurate pronunciation of sounds is '*essential*'.

Acquiring pronunciation is often a main aim in sacred language learning, or even the main aim. For some it is the only aim, although this seems limited to beginners, while more advanced learners can develop an interest in meaning. Accentedness (L1-influenced production) was not acceptable for interviewees, whether the QA production during communal prayers of Pakistani Muslim communities or '*the American version*' of Sanskrit *mantra*s (repeated sacred utterances such as *om*), because '*that sound is only in that way*'.

As was the case with the importance of sound (first theme), here too learners have internalised the views of the Islamic or Sanskritic traditions. These views are described in the literature. In both traditions, perfect production has been crucial for the survival of the sacred language. Transmission was oral, and error-less intergenerational transmission of a perfect and immutable body of spoken language was a main concern for many centuries, to avoid corrupting divine revelations or primordial insights. The crucial need for accuracy in transmitting the Quran and the Vedas led the Sanskritic culture to develop the most advanced science of phonetics in the ancient world, and the Islamic culture to create a sophisticated body of decoding and pronunciation rules for Quran recitation (*tajwīd*).

Learners of QA and Sanskrit aim at perfect pronunciation for different reasons, related to the different reasons for the importance of language sounds. QA learners seek perfect pronunciation for religious reasons, because the speech they perceive and produce is of divine origin. To these Muslim interviewees, QA is both the language the Divine used to communicate with humans, and the language humans use to communicate with the Divine, by means of set prayers and reading aloud and recitation of the Quran. Hence, accurate pronunciation shows respect to God: '*obviously we have a lot of respect*' and '*we don't mess around with the Quran*'. Learning correct pronunciation is also an act of piety, and it is worthy of religious merits. While learners acknowledge the limits of the quality of their current pronunciation ('*obviously we are not able to pronounce it perfectly and we pronounce it as we pronounce it*'), they agree that everybody should continue improving in an attempt to achieve perfection: '*That's everyone's own struggle, and someone might take a week to learn it, and other people might take years, but that's their own responsibility to do so*'. The religious implications of accurate pronunciation are evident '*because I wanna try to be the best Muslim possible and please God*'.

The Sanskrit learners in this study did not report a religious motivation (they were mostly yoga teachers and generally defined themselves as 'spiritual', but this may differ in other types of Sanskrit language learners). Yet, the speech they perceive and produce also has a sacred nature, as Sanskrit sounds and mantra impact the human body and mind and the universe. To these learners, the sounds of this language have a sonic power, but only if uttered perfectly. A mantra is only effective if pronounced perfectly, as its vibration '*is specific and fundamental*', and inaccurately produced sounds lose their efficacy: '*in Sanskrit pronunciation is the base of everything, the correct pronunciation of a mantra guarantees for its efficacy*'.

This difference between the religious and non-religious views of the sounds of language explains different levels of tolerance for imperfection. For QA learners, fluency and accuracy are not an issue '*as long as you put in effort and your intentions are pure and you want to please God*'.

For Sanskrit learners accentedness is not acceptable: '*it is not the case that there is a country that pronounces it in this or that way*'. The intention is irrelevant, as inaccuracy nullifies the sonic power of Sanskrit.

Whereas perfect pronunciation is central to sacred language learners, current L2 pronunciation research disregards accuracy. The aim is interpersonal communication and pronunciation is a tool to that aim, hence the goal is 'intelligibility' (being understandable to the listener, for instance not confusing *ship* and *sheep*). Intelligibility is a concern to QA learners too, but they are not worried about being misunderstood by their interlocutor. Intelligibility takes on a different meaning when the interlocutor is the Divine: '*you'll be saying the wrong prayer and asking for something else*'; '*for example if we want to say* God forgive me *and ... we pronounce* God forgot about me, *that would be bad*'. Crucially, intelligibility is not the aim, it is only a starting point.

When L2 scholars considered accurate L2 pronunciation as desirable (before the spread of the communicative approach in the 1980s shifted the emphasis on the transmission of meaning), the aim was nativelikeness (namely, similarity to native speaker norms). Nowadays L2 researchers consider nativelike production as unachievable for most, and pronunciation improvement can stop once errorless communication is achieved. This approach does not serve well learners whose L2 is a sacred language. The target of sacred language learners is not a native speaker. Their needs may perhaps fall within the category of so-called 'pronunciation for special purposes', but even then, would differ from the needs of other learners within this category (for instance, some categories of professionals), whose target is the phonology of a community of speakers (of a prestigious variety, or a global community of language users).

The third theme was the emotional resonance of the sounds of the sacred language. This was a widespread issue in both datasets, albeit the nature of the emotion was different in the two languages. L2 research on the other hand has a narrow focus on learning-related emotion, largely ignored positive emotion, and completely ignored sacred emotion.

Listening to and uttering the sacred language has profound aesthetic-emotional impact on learners. For them, the sound of the language '*is beautiful*' and '*really pleasing to hear*' and they have deep emotions: '*I love* [its] *sound*', '*I love it so much*'. This is a profound experience, and Sanskrit learners '*feel* [mantras] *in a really, really, really intense way*', and from the beginning felt '*an emotional, irrational aspect*' when '*that first contact with* [the sound of this language] *was really strong*'. This differs from the aesthetic pleasure deriving from artistic performance such as poetry, partly because it is unrelated to meaning, but mostly because it is linked to religious or spiritual experiences (see Kermani, 2015). Not only listening but also uttering or murmuring has emotional resonance '*when I ... have problems at work, inside me I hum a mantra*'.

The emotion induced by the sounds of QA is religious, as the language manifests the voice of the Divine. Listening to recitations (without understanding) has positive emotional resonance: '*it's very peaceful. ... it gives you a very nice feeling*', whether in the Mosque or listening to recordings at home. The literature confirms that the learners' views are the views of the Islamic and Sanskritic traditions: the unequalled, inimitable beauty that Muslim believers perceive in the language of the Quran is testament to the religious nature of this experience. However, apart from the pleasure deriving from the beauty of the spoken language, QA learners mostly reported negative emotions about their production. Many reported language anxiety (negative emotion associated with L2 speaking): Reading aloud the Quran '*is always nerve wracking*', uttering prayers causes '*fear of ... saying something wrong*'. They also feel guilt and regret for not having learned better. These emotional reactions are further evidence of the importance of sound.

The emotion induced by Sanskrit is not religious, at least in these spiritual-but-not-religious Sanskrit learners, but it is caused by a language whose vibrations resonate with and impact humans and the cosmos. Sounds are not only beautiful, but also beneficial to body and mind (*'it is a medicine'*, it *'does good'* to its listener) and emotional: *'So there is beauty, there is the benefit, the joy, it gives you a sense of joy,* ananda *means joy'*. This learner's use of the Sanskrit word *ananda* reflects her adoption of Sanskritic views that associate Sanskrit sounds with aesthetic pleasure, benefits, and positive emotion. Even when learners were less inclined to the spiritual side and had a more intellectual disposition, approaching *'the study of the sound'* as a scientific enterprise, still the discovery of sound resulted in *'fall*[ing] *in love with this language'*, another strong positive emotion.

While the emotional and aesthetic dimensions of language have always been central in QA and Sanskrit traditions, L2 research has generally disregarded these aspects. Research on emotion in L2 learning and use only began as late as the 2000s, and it is limited in scope, as it investigates few emotions that can impact language learning and use, usually language anxiety. QA learners indeed reported symptoms of language anxiety, but they were not worried about fellow believers' judgment, and the religious fear of addressing the Divine cannot be likened to the anxiety caused by speaking in front of a classroom.

Even after the very recent shift of interest towards positive emotion, research seems limited to those emotions that can impact language learning and use, such as enjoyment (of language classes). Indeed, none of the L2 phonology sources listed above mentioned emotional aspects at all, so that to discuss the issue here I had to add another L2 research source (Dewaele et al., 2019). The range of emotions related to sacred language sounds deserves more interest, particularly religious and spiritual emotion, which have not been investigated at all within L2 research.

Implications and Future Directions

The small-scale exploratory comparison of the learning of sacred language phonologies reported above was meant as an example of how researching sacred languages can contribute to L2 research. As Table 2.1 shows, this comparison revealed commonalities and differences. Participants raised other issues, but I selected the themes above as particularly fruitful for an exploratory and more general comparison of learning of sacred and non-sacred languages, and interested readers can find discussions of other issues in my other publications.

This exercise in analysis has limitations and issues with transferability (degree to which the analysis can be extended to other contexts), and of course pronunciation is not central to all sacred languages, and yoga teachers are not typical Sanskrit learners. Yet, two points can be made. Language learners' views of language sounds and of their learning were similar enough across the two languages (Quranic Arabic and Sanskrit) to allow for a discussion of phonology learning within sacred languages as a category of languages, and yet different enough to allow for distinctions within this category. The differences between the perceptions and experiences of these learners on the one hand and the consensus in L2 phonology research on the other testify to the important contribution research on sacred languages can make to L2 research. This becomes even more apparent if one compares the findings reported above with a recent authoritative state-of-the-art article, whose list of current concerns in L2 pronunciation consists of intelligibility, communication, meaning, and social factors (Pennington, 2021). The different views and needs of sacred language learners can help widen this narrow focus. In general, the inclusion of sacred languages can make a meaningful contribution to the body of evidence and theorising in L2 research.

This work has shown through a comparison of two languages that research on sacred languages can contribute to L2 research. The case study provides some indications for future directions. The first step should be to collect empirical evidence (see Han, 2018), from a variety of sacred languages, in different types of learners, in different contexts. Once a sufficiently wide body of evidence has been established, it will allow comparisons both among different sacred languages and with non-sacred languages.

There is a need to integrate the current focus on social aspects of learning and use with a more specific focus on learning. The leading second language acquisition scholar Ellis wrote that after the social turn of the mid-1990s all attention shifted to social aspects of learning, and "learning took a back seat" (2021, p. 9). He argued that L2 research should focus on learning development, its processes and outcomes, not just the social environment that surrounds it. The same applies to sacred languages. There is a strong need to put learning at the core of research on sacred language learning.

It will be fruitful to focus on those aspects of sacred languages that differ the most from mainstream languages. Emotion is certainly one, because emotion associated with sacred languages is qualitatively different from what is normally studied in L2 research, and in particular sacred emotion has not been investigated, but it could address current interest in positive emotion in L2 learning. Research on identity should continue, particularly religious-linguistic identity, and there is an evident need for research on motivation, as it differs dramatically from the current concerns of L2 motivation research. Pedagogy-oriented research investigating different approaches to teaching could be useful to practitioners as well as language teaching research.

To conclude, sacred language research could help L2 research achieve some of its current ambitions, in particular diversifying its knowledge base, and decolonisation. First, L2 research needs to increase the diversity of L2s it investigates, to validate and extend current theorising that is based on evidence from English and a handful of other mostly European languages. Sacred languages are not only different languages, they can also contribute different views of language learning and teaching. Second, applied linguistics is accused of having long prioritised some languages over others, and should better reflect the priorities and views of other language communities. The very absence of research on sacred languages has been at least partly attributed to the dominant secular approach of Western researchers. Investigating sacred languages could bring to the fore a large and largely understudied population of language learners. Taking their knowledge and needs into serious account could be a step forward in the decolonialisation agenda.

Further Reading

Bennett, B.P. (2018). *Sacred languages of the world: An introduction*. Wiley.
For a full introduction to sacred languages as well as Bennett's contribution in this volume.
Ellis, R. (2015). *Understanding second language acquisition*, 2nd edition. Routledge.
Much of Ellis's work on Second Language Acquisition will be interesting and useful for the reader, but this is a good starting point.
Avni, S. (2018). What can the study of Hebrew learning contribute to applied linguistics? *Modern Language Journal*, *102*(2), 446–448. https://doi.org/http://dx.doi.org/10.1111/modl.12487
Avni's writings (also in this volume) are good key texts for the learning of Biblical Hebrew, and this brief article presents her views of the contribution of research on Biblical Hebrew to applied linguistics.
Rosowsky, A. (2019). Sacred language acquisition in superdiverse contexts. *Linguistics and Education, 53*, Article 100751. https://doi.org/10.1016/j.linged.2019.100751
Rosowsky's work on the learning of Quranic Arabic as well as his chapter in this volume are good starting points on L2 and literacy learning and superdiverse contexts.

Bassetti, B. (Ed.). (2024). The learning of sacred languages. *International Journal of Bilingualism* [Special issue].

My own article on the learning of sacred languages and the other articles in special issue will also be useful.

References

Avni, S. (2011). Toward an understanding of Hebrew language education: Ideologies, emotions, and identity. *International Journal of the Sociology of Language, 208*: 53–70.

Avni, S. (2018). What can the study of Hebrew learning contribute to applied linguistics? *Modern Language Journal, 102*(2), 446–448.

Bassetti, B. (Ed.). (2024). The learning of sacred languages. [Special issue]. *International Journal of Bilingualism.*

Bassetti, B. & Dewaele, J.-M. (2018). *A first exploration of the use of a sacred language for prayer in Muslim believers.* 'Borders and Boundaries: "Religion on the Periphery", Joint Conference between the British Association for the Study of Religions and the Irish Society for the Academic Study of Religions, Belfast, UK. September.

Bassetti, B. & Reinboldt, R. (2023). Learning Sanskrit as a sacred language in the West: A narrative study. *International Journal of Bilingualism.* Online first. https://doi.org/10.1177/136700692311982

Beck, G.L. (1993). *Sonic theology: Hinduism and sacred sound.* Motilal Banarsidass.

Bennett, B.P. (2018). *Sacred languages of the world: An introduction.* Wiley.

Daugaard, L.M. & Dewilde, J. (Eds.). (2019). Faith literacy practices among Muslim children, youth and families in Scandinavia [special issue]. *Apples: Journal of Applied Language Studies, 13*(4).

Derwing, T.M., & Munro, M.J. (2022). Pronunciation learning and teaching. In T.M. Derwing, M.J. Munro, R.I., & Thomson (Eds.), *The Routledge handbook of second language acquisition and speaking,* 147–159. Routledge.

Dewaele, J.-M., Chen, X., Padilla, A.M., & Lake, J. (2019). The flowering of positive psychology in foreign language teaching and acquisition research. *Frontiers in psychology, 10.*

Dörnyei, Z., Wong, M.S., & Kristjánsson, C. (2013). Faith and SLA: An emerging area of inquiry. In M.S. Wong, C. Kristjánsson, & Z. Dörnyei (Eds.), *Christian faith and English language teaching and learning,* 291–296. Routledge.

Ellis, R. (2021). A short history of SLA: Where have we come from and where are we going? *Language Teaching, 54*(2), 190–205.

Filliozat, P.-S. (2000). *The Sanskrit language: An overview.* Indica.

Gade, A.M. (2004). *Perfection makes practice: Learning, emotion, and the recited Quran in Indonesia.* University of Hawaii Press.

Gregory, E., Choudhury, H., Ilankuberan, A., Kwapong, A., & Woodham, M. (2013a). Practice, performance and perfection: Learning sacred texts in four faith communities in London. *International Journal of the Sociology of Language, 220* 27–48.

Gregory, E., Lytra, V., Choudhury, H., Ilankuberan, A., Kwapong, A., & Woodham, M. (2013b). Syncretism as a creative act of mind: The narratives of children from four faith communities in London. *Journal of Early Childhood Literacy, 13*(3), 322–347.

Han, H. (2018). Studying religion and language teaching and learning: Building a subfield. *The Modern Language Journal, 102*(2), 432–445.

Kermani, N. (2015). *God is beautiful: The aesthetic experience of the Quran.* Polity.

Lepp-Kaethler, E., & Dörnyei, Z. (2013). The role of sacred texts in enhancing motivation and living the vision in second language acquisition. In M. Shepard Wong, C. Kristjánsson, & Z. Dörnyei, (Eds.), *Christian faith and English language teaching and learning,* 171–188. Routledge.

Lytra, V., & Ilankuberan, A. (2020). Syncretising ways of doing, seeing and becoming in children's faith-inspired text-making and conversations around texts at home. *Language and Intercultural Communication, 20*(5), 433–449.

Pennington, M. C. (2021). Teaching pronunciation: The state of the art 2021. *RELC Journal, 52*(1), 3–21.

Pollock, S. (2006). *The language of the Gods in the world of men: Sanskrit, culture, and power in premodern India.* University of California Press.

Rosowsky, A. (2013). *Faith, phonics and identity: Teaching in faith complementary schools.* Blackwell.

Rosowsky, A. (2021). *The performance of multilingual and 'ultralingual' devotional practices by young British Muslims*. Multilingual Matters.

Versteegh, K. (2014). *The Arabic language*. Edinburgh University Press.

Wilke, A. & Moebus, O. (2011). *Sound and communication: An aesthetic cultural history of Sanskrit Hinduism*. De Gruyter.

Acknowledgments

The research reported in the chapter was made possible in part by a grant from the Spencer Foundation (Award ref. 202100296). The views expressed are those of the author and do not necessarily reflect the views of the Spencer Foundation.

3

SACRED LANGUAGES

Brian P. Bennett

Introduction and Background

In this chapter religion is stipulated to be a cultural program that postulates the existence of super-human realities and provides ways for people to communicate or align with said realities for short- or long-term benefit (cf. Smith, 2019). Some religious programs, including Islam, Hinduism, Judaism, and certain branches of Christianity and Buddhism, have maintained an ancient, non-vernacular language for their core texts and practices. Examples include Pali, Avestan, Coptic, Ecclesiastical Latin, Sanskrit, and Classical Arabic. These are often called sacred languages. This chapter discusses the phenomenon from a viewpoint in comparative religion. The topic is immense; many important themes—like the manifold ways these ancient languages figure in the construction of contemporary religious identities (cf. Ringrow, 2022)—are skirted.

Language is central to both parts of the religious enterprise: namely, the postulation of, and the communication or alignment with, imagined superhuman realities. As Paden says, "Religious systems are topographies of language and practice in which humans construe the world as a place of engagement with superhuman beings and become actors in that culturally generated system" (2016, p. 70). Before trying to determine how sacred languages fit into this human activity, a few remarks about the term *sacred* are in order.

From a vantage point in the comparative study of religion, *sacred* is a cultural designation not a metaphysical one (Williams, 2008, p.125). To refer to such-and-such a language as sacred is really no different than saying the Qur'an is a sacred text for Muslims or the Ganges a sacred river for Hindus. Sacrality in this sense is something that can be observed in religious behavior and discourse. As Rudolph says about religion in general, we

> begin with encountering the specific appearances and expressions of the various religions as these can be seen and comprehended. ... all visible, cultic actions and places where these occur, with the persons who celebrate them. ... the specific forms of community we encounter, their functionaries, their sacred writings, laws, and songs. All of this is empirical evidence in the strictest sense of the word.
>
> (1985, p. 49)

DOI: 10.4324/9781003301271-4

From the perspective of an outside observer, then, sacredness is not inherent but imputed; it is a matter of sacralization (cf. Salverda, 2018), of beliefs and behaviors encompassing the language and elaborated over time. Languages like Pali and Classical Syriac could therefore also be called *sacralized, sanctified,* or *consecrated,* the "ed" suffix indicating the sedimentation of past sacralizing efforts (ritual, catechetical, etc.) by human agents.

Sacralization is a process. The sacredness of a language is not a *fait accompli* but something that can be increased, diminished, contested, altered, or reversed. The point can be clearly seen in the case of sacred architecture. Many churches in the Soviet Union were demolished, allowed to fall into disrepair, or repurposed as clubs, warehouses, or even museums of atheism. Except for the remaining elderly congregants, these buildings stopped being viewed by the populace as sacred places. Yet in the post-Soviet period, Russian society has changed, Orthodoxy has returned to a position of societal prominence, and many dilapidated structures have been renovated and rededicated—in short, resacralized.

Sacralization is a hierarchical process. It places one building or one language above others on a scale of religious values. Williams (2008, p. 127) refers to this as "sacred linguistic imperialism." The sacred language is valued above ordinary vernaculars, which may be tolerated or even encouraged for certain endeavors (e.g., missionary work) but not for the faith's most important texts and practices. There may also be an inner hierarchy, with different languages considered of "greater holiness and lesser holiness," as with Hebrew and Yiddish in some Orthodox Jewish communities (Fishman, 2006, p. 255).

Sacralization is a transitive process. Continuing with the architectural analogy, human acts of sacralization (siting, design, decoration, signage) differentiate mosques, temples, and wats from restaurants, apartments, and shopping malls. This ascribed sacrality can then act back on believers. Holding a funeral or a coronation in a church, as opposed to football stadium, solemnizes the occurrence. Paden puts it this way: "From the point of view of an analysis of cultural behavior, sacredness is therefore both a way of actively constructing or focalizing the world and a way that objects face back to the insiders of that world" (1999, p. 96). A language like Classical Arabic or Ecclesiastical Latin has been sacralized in countless ways over the centuries; for believers this sacredness is sedimented or deposited, as it were, in the very sound and appearance of the language. There is a kind of sacred 'charge' that can then be drawn upon to sanctify a person, place, or event.

Why is one language, and not another, deemed sacred? Being a *lingua sacra* depends on an interweaving over time of ideological, practical, and institutional factors. First, on the level of ideology, sacred languages are mythicized. Ecclesiastical Latin and Classical Arabic are extolled by devotees for their beauty, grandeur, and precision compared to everyday spoken languages. They are also lauded for their capacity to connect believers over time and space. However, similar ideologems may be expressed about vernacular languages (cf. Fishman, 1996). The most salient factor for sacralized varieties is, rather, that they are related to postulated superhuman forces and the concomitant means of communicating or aligning with those forces. Religious discourse assigns a sacralized language an important role in the community's salvation history and a place in its spiritual topography, with "other worlds, future worlds, higher worlds, parallel spirit universes, heavens and hells ..." (Paden, 2016, p. 71). The Saint Thomas Christians of South India have conserved Syriac, a form of Aramaic, because it is believed to be the language of Jesus as well as a special way of establishing proximity to God in prayer (Naumescu, 2018, p. 104). For Theravada Buddhists, Pali is commonly understood as the liberating word of the Buddha which resounds across all planes of existence. According to one devotee, "The Sanskrit language is said to put forth into human sounds, the language of the Gods, the great creative cosmic vibration" (Frawley, 1990, p. 75).

Second, in terms of practice, sacred languages are not used for interpersonal communication in the home or workplace but are "reserved for ritual or recitational purposes and usually associated with a text that is considered seminal and sacred by the adherents of that faith" (Rosowsky, 2022, p. 164). These purposes may be heuristically divided into scripture, cultus, and thaumaturgy (although not every sacred language is equally represented in these three areas).

- Scripture: The canonical texts of a religion may be preserved in a sacred language, as is the case with the Qur'an in Classical Arabic and the Tipitaka ("Three Baskets") in Pali. The languages are deemed holy "because of having been the vehicles of materia sancta" (Fishman, 2006, p. 253). In these cases, the language and the corpus of divine revelation are seen as a kind of monocoque entity—not two things, but one. The religious communities in question have built elaborate systems to safeguard, study, memorize, and recite their scriptures. This emphasis leads to several related practices. For example, sermons in Islam and Dhamma talks in Buddhism are often laced with, or expound upon, canonical words in Classical Arabic or Pali.
- Cultus: Sacred languages usually play a major role in cultus, in prayer, ritual, and cantillation, typically done in a designated place of worship such as a mosque, wat, or temple—the "natural habitats" of sacred languages. The sanctified variety will typically be treated by adherents as the preeminent—perhaps the only—verbal means for relating to the imagined superhuman realm. A restricted literacy is involved here: participants are not expected to be "fluent" in the ancient tongue, but to read, chant, or simply listen to a limited amount of predetermined content in the consecrated language, usually with some assistance from a local language like Thai, Polish, or Bengali.
- Thaumaturgy: Sacred languages may also be drawn upon for thaumaturgical (occult) practices (cf. Sharot, 2001). Snippets of sacred verses may figure in tattoos or amulets worn on the body or placed in a car, business, or residence to bring good luck and ward off dangers. Though sometimes condemned by religious leaders as superstitious or siloed by academics as "folk" belief, such practices and paraphernalia may in fact be the main ways that most devotees engage their sacred language. With reference to Theravada Buddhism in Southeast Asia, McDaniel notes that the Pali Canon is actually the esoteric phenomenon, whereas the use of bits and pieces of Pali for apotropaic purposes is commonplace (2011, p. 229).

Third, sacred languages are institutional varieties, not mother tongues. Languages such as Coptic and Avestan are typically not learned at home, but bookish varieties maintained and transmitted by seminaries, madrasas, faith-based supplementary schools, and similar institutions. Furthermore, sacred languages are often associated with clergies, the intellectuals and ritualists of the faith: monks, priests, imams, rabbis, and pandits. Pali for example is primarily preserved and promulgated by the Sangha, the Buddhist monastic order. Ecclesiastical Latin is not taught *en famille* but sustained by the Vatican as well as religious organizations like the *Fraternitas Sacerdotalis Sancti Petri* (Priestly Fraternity of Saint Peter) dedicated to its continuance.

It is helpful to distinguish two subtypes of sacred language which entail contrastive ideological, practical, and institutional profiles. Borrowing terms from Egyptology, these may be called the demotic (*dēmos*, the common people) and the hieratic (*hieratikos*, priestly). On one side, a language like Classical Arabic, which is understood as the untranslatable medium of divine revelation and a centerpiece of Muslim identity, is acquired to varying degrees by Muslims around the world. According to Haeri, "regardless of native language, a believing Muslim must know some Classical

Arabic in order to read the holy text, to perform the daily prayers and to carry out other religious rituals and obligations" (2003, p. 2). Consequently, given the size of the Ummah or Muslim community, it is one of the most widely known languages in the world (Rosowsky, 2008, p. 208)—demotic indeed. Pali and Ecclesiastical Latin present a different picture. Though Pali is also a language of scripture, it is primarily studied by monks and nuns, not laypeople. Theravada monks function as priests, insofar as they chant the Buddha's salubrious words and dispense blessings to "householders" during funerals and other occasions. Obviously, some Catholic laypeople study Latin, but it is not necessary for them to do so in the way it is for priests who continue to celebrate the Latin Mass.

Religions, of course, are neither stable nor monolithic. They may be affected by schisms, reforms, revivals, missionary endeavors, fundamentalist movements, cultural transpositions, technological innovations, political alliances, and much else. A religion of sufficient age and size will therefore be many different things to many different people—to paraphrase Walt Whitman, it will contain multitudes. Sacred languages usually shape and are shaped by these divisions and developments. For example, a study of Indonesian mosques shows a correlation between Arabic lettering and sectarian identity: traditionalist (Nahdlatul Ulama) mosques are characterized by "the massive use of Arabic inscriptions" while modernist (Muhammadiyah) ones have simpler, less decorated interiors (Yusuf & Putrie 2022). In American Catholicism, positive or negative views of Latin align with conservative and progressive factions of the Church and their associated politics (Johnson & Priestley, 2022).

When it comes to sacred languages, the question of intelligibility is a recurring and multifaceted issue. Many religionists, including members of the clergy, seem to have a poor understanding of the very language they claim is central to the faith. But there is more going on here than meets the eye. For one thing, it should not be assumed that a religious text or ritual is somehow inherently intelligible to believers just because it is couched in a vernacular language. Moreover, there are certain factors that may aid comprehension of a *lingua sacra*. In the cultic domain, for example, the sacred language "is often paralleled in the symbolic systems of those other media—the visual and tactile properties of the physical objects, the kinesthetic sensibilities of gesture and movement—which then serve to reinforce, enhance, or even complete the verbal meaning" (Wheelock, 1987, p. 443). Finally, Rosowsky's important discussion of "ultralingual" meaning demonstrates affinities between sacred language performance and secular phenomena such as opera, where the matter of comprehension is likewise neither simple nor straightforward (Rosowsky, 2021, pp. 48–61). In this connection Liddicoat speaks of two general orientations or *ethoi* in religious thought and practice: sacrality and comprehensibility. The sacral view emphasizes the "mysterious, numinous and transcendent" nature of engagement with the divine, whereas the comprehensibility position postulates a more immanent form of superhuman power amenable to direct communication (Liddicoat, 2012, p. 122). The tension between sacrality and comprehensibility is a recurring one in religious communities that have maintained a sacred language, and can be tracked across the levels of ideology, practice, and organization.

In terms of ideology, those who endorse a sacrality orientation often engage in linguistic apologetics, justifying the value of the sacred language over against vernacular options. The mythic, symbolic, and aesthetic associations of the language may be said to outweigh the semantic, just as the warm glow of a candle is more conducive to prayer and meditation than the bright light of a fluorescent lamp. Traditionalist Catholics, for example, may acknowledge that Latin is not entirely understandable to them, but still appreciate the language for its purported dignity and universality. In the realm of cultus, the dueling priorities of sacrality and comprehensibility are often navigated by means of bilingual prayerbooks, vernacular paraphrases, and in some cases, computer screens or projectors in the sanctuary, providing real-time translation during the ceremony. Although translation may be allowed in these limited measures, it may be frowned upon or forbidden if allowed to get too close to the tradition's canonical texts and rites, which may be deemed untranslatable (cf. Wilson, 2022). Finally, the *raison d'être* of faith-based schools and educational programs is precisely to preserve the sacrality of the ancient language while making it increasingly comprehensible.

The sacrality-versus-comprehensibility issue is manifested most dramatically in language ideology debates (cf. Blommaert, 1999). Long-simmering disaffection may erupt in public disputation, with different factions in the community putting forth competing values—intelligibility, spirituality, history, purity, accessibility, beauty—in support of, or opposition to, the sacred language. Such polemics usually take place against a backdrop of wider social, cultural, and political change. The most famous example of such a debate occurred at the Catholic Church's Second Vatican Council in the 1960s, which challenged the linguistic imperialism of Latin (*de facto* if not *de jure*) and promoted vernacularization of the Mass. This represented a colossal move from a sacrality to a comprehensibility ethos—one that has engendered a small but persistent reactionary movement within the Church that seeks to reclaim Latin and the sacrality it supposedly represents. Though less publicized, disputes have also taken place with regard to Hebrew, Sanskrit, and Avestan (Bennett, 2018, pp. 169–179).

Having outlined some of the ideological, practical, and institutional factors that contribute to sacralization, it is necessary to differentiate sacred languages from other varieties with which they are sometimes confused or conflated. A *lingua sacra* is not simply an elevated style or religious jargon. Sacred languages are named varieties ("Pali," "Church Slavonic") perceived, used, and taught by faith communities as self-standing languages. Just because an English prayer includes archaic features like *thee* and *thou* does not make it a sacred language. It simply represents a higher stylistic register. Scientology has developed a distinctive lexicon: Thetan, Org, Rundown, Tech, Exteriorization, E-Meter, Floating, etc. But this is a kind of jargon, not a complete language (at least not yet). As Fischer says, "Scientology-Speak is within English…" (2019, p. 79).

The category of *sacred language* should be distinguished from the much broader category of *religious language*, which includes phenomena like prayer and preaching but also some forms of discourse found in such unexpected domains as advertising, sports, and healthcare (Hobbs, 2021, p. 2). *Sacred language* should also be differentiated from the narrower category of *ritual* or *liturgical language*. While sacred languages are typically used in cultus, they are not alone in that capacity. Since the reforms of Vatican II, for example, vernacular languages from Vietnamese to Igbo have been authorized for use in the Catholic Mass—hence they are now ritual languages. Hebrew and English prayers may both be heard in a Reform Jewish service. That makes them both ritual languages, but only Hebrew is called the Holy Tongue.

Last, although sacred languages may not have native speakers, that does not mean they should be considered *dead*, even if some adherents accept that designation. Unlike (say) Etruscan or Sumerian, languages like Sanskrit and Ge'ez are still cherished, learned, and utilized for canonical texts, ceremonies, and even limited conversation (at least among some clerics). The Vatican publishes new texts in Latin every year and offers regular radio broadcasts in the ancient language: "*Hebdomada Papae: Notitiae Vaticanae Latine redditae*" (The Pope's week in review: Vatican news bulletin in Latin). Sacred languages should therefore be considered fixed, conserved, or curated. They continue to represent prestigious semiotic resources used in a variety of ways by religious believers and to intersect with other aspects of contemporary culture and society.

Case Study: Church Slavonic in Contemporary Russia

Church Slavonic is a sacralized variety maintained primarily among Orthodox Slavic communities (Russians, Ukrainians, Belarusians, Bulgarians, Macedonians, and Serbians), as well as some Croatian and Czech Catholics (Keipert, 2014, p. 1212). The focus here is on Orthodoxy in Russia. The Church Slavonic tradition is over a thousand years old. The language was originally codified in the ninth century as part of the mission to the Slavs associated with Saints Cyril and Methodius. Originally based on a South Slavic dialect, the language was first used to translate Byzantine Greek scriptural, liturgical, and other devotional texts for the newly converted Slavs of Moravia. The tradition then spread to Bulgaria and thence to Rus, the polity that modern-day Ukraine, Belarus, and Russia trace their origins to.

The designation Church Slavonic (or Church Slavic) covers several regional and chronological variants: Old Church Slavonic, the oldest known stratum, associated with the foundational texts of the Cyrillomethodian mission; Church Slavonic, a bookish language comparable in some ways to Latin in the medieval and early modern eras; and New Church Slavonic, a *lingua sacra* clearly demarcated from the vernacular and now restricted to the liturgy and associated devotional literature (Mareš, 1979, pp. 12–13). Marginalized during the atheistic Soviet era, Church Slavonic has been revitalized in post-Communist Russian Orthodoxy (Bennett, 2011).

In Russian Orthodox publications, Church Slavonic is often called a sacred or sacral (*sviashchennyi, sakral'nyi*) language. It is mythicized, being assigned a place in Russian salvation history and spiritual topography. Traditional discourse proclaims the language to have been created under divine inspiration and further hallowed by a millennium of prayer by both Russian saints and pious folk (*narod*) alike. It is said to unite Russians with their ancestors as well as with other Orthodox Slavs. A common trope is that it is impossible to be rude or vulgar in Church Slavonic. For devotees, the language is pure, rich, solemn, dignified, and numinous—set apart from, and above, colloquial Russian. One catechetical text refers to the

difference between daily, conversational speech and the language of prayer: it helps our consciousness step forward to the open door of heavenly reality. ... Church Slavonic is not a barrier, but a nexus, not only between past and present, but also time and eternity, earth and Heaven.

(Makarii, 2017, p. 154)

An interesting motif in traditionalist discourse is the repeated reference to Church Slavonic as a "verbal icon" (*slovesnaia ikona*). Obviously connected to the iconography for which Russian Orthodoxy is famed, the idea appears to be that the Slavonic language somehow embodies or manifests the truths it conveys, just as visual icons of Christ, Mary, and the saints, are considered to be not artistic portraits but heavenly portals (cf. Leonard, 2020).

Church Slavonic fits the profile of a hieratic sacred language. It is associated above all with cultus, and its "natural habitat" is an Orthodox church, often called a temple (*khram*). In the Russian Orthodox system, all "sacred servers" (*sviashchennosluzhiteli*)—i.e., priests and deacons—are required to know Church Slavonic to perform liturgies. Altar servers, readers, Sunday school teachers, choir directors, and icon painters may know the language to a certain degree. Laypeople are encouraged to study the language, and some do so in parish groups or on their own through conventional textbooks or online courses, but many simply pick up bits and pieces through repeated liturgical attendance. About 20 percent of regular churchgoers in the Moscow area say they have a good grasp of Slavonic (Leonard, 2021). Though most Russians self-identify as Orthodox, a small percentage (under 10 percent) regularly attends church services. The opacity of Slavonic is sometimes blamed for this.

A debate over the understandability of Church Slavonic has been going on for 150 years (Kravetskii, 2019) and has heated up on several occasions in the tumultuous decades since the collapse of the Soviet Union (Bennett, 2018). Here it is worth noting that Church Slavonic, though related to Russian, is not merely an older form of Russian; it is South Slavic in origin, whereas Russian is East Slavic. But the situation is quite complicated, as the two varieties have coexisted and influenced each other for centuries (Bennett, 2011). The language debate has many layers—theological, liturgical, pastoral, cultural, historical, sociological. Believers are divided on the topic: a 2011 poll showed that 37 percent favored a Russian-language liturgy, with 36 percent supported the traditional Church Slavonic services (Ponomariov, 2016). Different proposals for some degree of "Russification" have been intensely debated but then rejected by church officials as well as by the more traditionalist sectors of the community. And so, the controversy continues with no end in sight. Unlike Russian and Russians, or Bulgarian and Bulgarians, there are no native speakers of this sacralized language, no "Church Slavonians" (*Kirchenslaven*) (Keipert, 2014, p. 1213). Nevertheless, different individuals and institutions continue to mythicize, teach, debate, and develop the language. A closer look at the Church Slavonic script is a convenient way to demonstrate the ongoing relevance of this ancient religiolinguistic tradition.

The Church Slavonic script, called *kirillitsa* (Cyrillic), is similar to the Russian script of today, but has more letters, which are more angularly shaped (reminiscent of calligraphy pen strokes), as well as numerous diacritical marks. In the early 1700s, Peter the Great wanted an alternative to the ornate Slavonic script, which he found outdated and opaque. Since a simplified script would facilitate the publication of ostensibly useful secular and scientific literature, he pushed for the development of a "civil script" (*grazhdanskii shrift*), which represents a simplified and Latinized version of Slavonic writing. From that point on in Russian cultural history, a separation was made between the Russian and Slavonic languages and the corresponding "civil" vs. "church" scripts. The former became linked to modernity and secularity, while the latter's associations with faith and tradition were reinforced (Bennett, 2022, pp. 151–161). Later, the Bolsheviks removed several letters from the civil script, further distancing Russian writing from Slavonic.

Church Slavonic lettering is a part of the sacral aesthetics of Russian Orthodoxy. Slavonic writing is not only found in liturgical and devotional texts, but on icons, crosses, altar cloths, and other liturgical paraphernalia. The ornate lettering seems of a piece with the cultic appurtenances—the beeswax candles, silver-covered icons, golden liturgical vessels—that characterize an Orthodox place of worship. The space is marked and sanctified by the script, separating it from the outside world, where Russian (and Roman) lettering prevail. The past decade has seen developments in the area of Slavonic typography and calligraphy, exemplified by Unicode and *vyaz,* respectively, which have altered the religiolinguistic landscape.

Unicode is a system for encoding text. Unicode-compliant fonts are what enable words to be read across computers, phones, and other devices. The foundational goal of the Unicode Standard was to create a single way to encode the characters of the world's diverse writing systems, both ancient and contemporary. It comprises letters and ideographs but also punctuation marks and even emojis. The project is intended to serve diverse constituencies, including academic researchers and liturgical language users (Unicode Consortium, 2021). The Unicode Standard encompasses not only the familiar Latin, Greek, Arabic, Hebrew, and Devanagari scripts, but also the lesser-known Coptic, Avestan, Ge'ez, and Syriac writing systems.

A cadre of computer programmers, liturgists, academics, and religious devotees worked on rendering Church Slavonic in Unicode (see Andreev et al., n.d.). This has not a been an easy task.

With its multiple accents and diacritical marks, along with dozens of *nomina sacra* abbreviated with ligatures, the Slavonic script is complex. There have been ideological challenges to go with the technical ones. According to Aleksandr Andreev, a participant in this project, "Unicode has been hesitant to add a locale for Church Slavonic because it considers it a 'dead language', which it most certainly is not." There has also been some suspicion of Unicode in Russia, exacerbated by political tensions between Russia and the US (Andreev, personal communication). Despite these challenges, Unicode-compliant Slavonic fonts are now available, covering not only modern Church Slavonic but different historical eras (https://sci.ponomar.net/fonts.html). Thus, thanks to the Western secular technology of Unicode, a substantial library of Church Slavonic texts is now readily available to Russian Orthodox believers.

Ironically, however, although great progress has been made in the field of Slavonic typography, most prayerbooks for lay people are now printed in Russian transliteration, that is, using the plainer civil script as opposed to the more ornate Slavonic alphabet, which many Russians have trouble understanding. This trend represents a move away from the sacrality ethos toward one of comprehensibility, switching from a candle to a lightbulb, as it were. That makes it controversial. There are two camps that object to this publishing trend. Some traditionalists endow the Slavonic script with mystical meaning. Church Slavonic letters are considered to be "chariots" and "carriers of Divine energy" (Leonard, 2021, p. 153). Traditionalists may find the civil script objectionable due to its association with the secularizing reforms of Peter the Great and Lenin (Bennett, 2011, pp. 141–142). Meanwhile, educators typically disdain the contemporary Russian alphabet because it cannot convey all the grammatical information that the Slavonic can. On the other hand, some contend that the extra grammatical information packed into the Church Slavonic script puts visual and mental stress on readers who may already be struggling to understand the underlying language. One way to ameliorate this stress is to use of the civil script instead. Defenders of Slavonic complain that attempts to make the language more graphically comprehensible end up decreasing its sanctity and authority (Liudogovskii, 2015).

While Orthodox prayerbooks are being pushed in the direction of increased intelligibility, recent years have also seen a growth of interest in Slavonic calligraphy, especially a style known as *vyaz*, which emphasizes numinous beauty over legibility. *Vyaz*, meaning link or ligature, is a particular form of Slavonic writing mostly associated with ecclesiastical texts and contexts. It is commonly found on icons and is used for titles in scriptural and devotional texts. The letters are intertwined and sometimes set inside each other, often in an exaggeratedly condensed way, with letterforms stretched, stacked, pressed together, and interlocked. The end result may be described as iconotextual, blurring the boundary between word and image—a kind of Slavonic hieroglyphics. The effect can be visually powerful, but difficult even for experts to decipher. *Vyaz* seems to connote sanctity, medievality, and mystery. Its presence sacralizes the text, icon, or building where it is applied.

The past decade or so has seen a growing interest in *vyaz* calligraphy, as evidenced by a proliferating number of workshops, exhibitions, and tutorials (in-person and online). One common theme found across these settings is the idea of returning to a neglected ancestral art form. For example, the Museum of Calligraphy in Moscow described a workshop thus:

> gathered within its walls the lovers of one of the most beautiful forms of Slavonic writing–vyaz. Recently we have seen a growing interest in Slavonic writing, and many contemporary calligraphers are turning in their work to a rethinking of our lettering heritage. It becomes important not only to study and repeat the proven forms of writing of our ancestors, but to rethink, to breathe new life into traditional forms of writing.

Vyaz-style writing has become a prestigious semiotic resource used for diverse, sometimes contradictory, projects within and beyond the Russian Orthodox Church. It is now appearing in some unlikely places, including product packaging, jewelry, and advertising (Khakimova, 2022). Furthermore, a number of artists are doing what might be termed calligraphic performances of *vyaz*-inspired lettering in unexpected ways, which are then posted and circulated on YouTube, Instagram, VK (VKontakte, the Russian equivalent of Facebook), and other venues, contributing to the "banalization" of the ecclesiastical script (cf. Stähle, 2022, p. 163).

Yuri Vol'f is a "calligraphy artist" who works in what he calls Neorussian Vyaz. He applies this style in playful and provocative ways to objects far removed from any Orthodox cultic context—a bicycle, a cabinet, a pair of shoes, a pandemic mask. One piece is simply the word "freedom" written on a concrete wall beneath barbed wire; it seems to merge calligraphy with graffiti. Another involves a long quotation about sex taken from the Hindu guru Osho (aka Bhagwan Shri Rashneesh) and inscribed on a woman's naked body, blurring the lines between calligraphy and tattooing, the carnal and spiritual. Some projects are vast in scope and take up the side of a building or a city block or plaza. Photos of these projects are posted, "liked," and commented upon on Instagram and other social media sites. Overall, Vol'f's art subverts and secularizes the sacrosanct style of Slavonic *vyaz*.

Victor Pushkarev is a "multidisciplinary artist" whose calligraphy spans different languages, genres, materials, and styles. He was commissioned to do inscriptions for the Cathedral of the Resurrection of Christ, the main cathedral of the Russian Armed Forces and the third largest temple in Russia. Since the collapse of the USSR, there has been an increasing alliance between the Russian military and the Moscow Patriarchate. Army bases have chapels, priests regularly bless troops and weapons, and medieval warrior-saints are invoked for present-day operations (Adamsky, 2019). Dedicated to the 75th anniversary of the country's victory in the Great Patriotic War (as World War II is known), this building epitomizes the convergence of the Church and the military in contemporary Russia. The use of metal from Nazi tanks, the unusual style, "[c]lad in metal and glass, painted military green," and the incorporation of both Stalin and Putin in some of the iconography (later removed), generated a firestorm of publicity (Stähle, 2022, p. 1).

Pushkarev (2022) worked for six months on the project. Based on the "militaristic essence" of the cathedral's overall design, he first created a *vyaz*-based typeface called Arma, which was then expanded for the inscriptions on the façade. The inscriptions, which come from the Bible as well as Russian saints, are in both Church Slavonic and Russian. The work had to first be presented to representatives of both the Church and the military (Pushkarev, personal communication). In some cases, the style and location of these *vyaz* inscriptions would make them difficult or impossible to read, though that is actually typical of the style: when it comes to *vyaz*, perceived sacrality often supersedes intelligibility. Given its religious and historical connotations, the presence of this calligraphic style sacralizes the cathedral and what it stands for.

After Russia's invasion of Ukraine in early 2022, Pushkarev published a remarkable disclaimer (in English):

> This project was done in a period when I believed I was working for the good sake of my homeland and country. It was a great opportunity to prove my talents and determination, since the original idea behind this cathedral was the approval and praise of the defenders of country during history of Russia and all her historical epochs: Kievan Rus', Russian Empire, USSR. In my perspective this project was about union, not destruction. As an Orthodox Christian, I believed so, even though I had doubts. But current war and aggression is a truly tragic turn of events.

(2022)

Vyaz connotes Russian "history and holiness" (Pushkarev, personal communication). The incorporation of this iconic form of Slavonic writing in the Cathedral of the Armed Forces demonstrates how sacrality may blend with "webs of social power and political legitimation" (Paden, 2000, p. 205). And yet the artist's disclaimer shows that such blendings may be questioned. Indeed, the topics of religion in general and Russian Orthodoxy in particular are objects of ongoing discussion, critique, and mockery online (cf. Stähle, 2022).

This brief reconnaissance of the Church Slavonic script in contemporary Russia, from Unicode fonts to *vyaz* calligraphy, illustrates how one sacred language tradition is maintained and modified in relation to broader developments in culture, art, politics, and technology. Depending on where one looks in the overall religiolinguistic "ecology," the sacred script is being digitized, vernacularized, secularized, banalized, nationalized, or militarized. Though Church Slavonic may be a "language without a people" (*Sprache ohne Volk*) (Keipert, 2014, p. 1213), it lives on in the hands of priests, parishioners, painters, publishers, programmers, pedagogues, and polemicists. It could not be otherwise: no people—no sacred language.

Implications and Future Directions

References to *sacred languages* are common enough in the comparative study of religion (also known as the history of religions), though the category is often more assumed than explained. Bennett's *Sacred Languages of the World: An Introduction* (2018) is the first monograph to explore the phenomenon in detail.

The last two decades have seen a growing interest in sociolinguistics regarding the intersection of religion and language, including sacred languages. The terminology varies, with references to *holy languages*, *liturgical languages*, *religious classicals*, and *lingua sacras.* Much of this research has focused on issues of language acquisition and identity, for example, Rosowsky's research on Arabic liturgical literacy among Muslims in the UK (2008, 2021) and Avni's on Hebrew education in the US (2011).

It is necessary to investigate individual sacred languages and scripts in all their complexity, not only within religious programs, but more broadly in relation to art, education, technology, the media, church–state relations, and other factors. What Lincoln (2018, p. 21) says about religions applies *mutatis mutandis* to sacred languages: they should be studied

> as social and historical entities, within their proper cultural context. They must be studied not only as phenomena that change over time as the result of their own internal dynamic, but more importantly as expressions of broader conflicts and tensions within specific social and historical configurations and, what is more, as vehicles of change and conflict.

Haeri's study of Classical Arabic in Egypt (2003) and Bennett's examination of Church Slavonic in post-Soviet Russia (2011) represent two attempts along these lines. But huge gaps remain in our knowledge of sacred languages. Research is needed into the ideologies, practices, pedagogies, and organizations of other cases, including Coptic, Avestan, Ge'ez, and Classical Syriac.

At the same time, to understand the *lingua sacra* "genus" and not just individual "species," comparison is needed. The field of comparative religion has long struggled with reconciling cultural specificities and viable generalizations (Smith, 2004). The risks of comparison—including decontextualizing, essentializing, and universalizing—are well known (Freiberger, 2019). It is important to stress that all comparison is inherently limited and aspectual, heuristically highlighting certain elements while leaving everything else in the background. For example, the distinction between hieratic and demotic varieties discussed earlier primarily concerns *who* studies sacred languages, priests or the "people." Other taxonomies are possible, depending on the perspective and goal of the comparativist. As with a kaleidoscope or volvelle, each click of the comparative lens can illuminate different patterns of similarity and difference.

Interested in challenging certain entrenched conceptions in religious studies, Holdrege posits a spectrum of religions ranging from "embodied communities" to "missionizing traditions." In this ideal-typical scheme, brahmanical Hinduism and rabbinic Judaism are "paradigmatic species" of the embodied genus, since their identities are "defined in relation to a particular people (Indo-Āryans, Jews), a particular sacred language (Sanskrit, Hebrew), a particular sacred land (India, Israel), a particular corpus of sacred texts (Veda, Torah) and a particular set of sociocultural traditions" (2018, p. 4). Missionizing traditions like Christianity and Buddhism, on the other hand, claim to have a universal message relevant for all peoples. Of course, as is well known, these proselytizing traditions have been inculturated in different locations—hence Irish Catholicism, Japanese Buddhism, and so on. Holdrege suggests that Islam represents an intermediary case since, though missionary from the start, it nevertheless "has maintained deep ties with the particular ethnocultural complex—the Arab people, language, and culture—out of which it arose" (2018, p. 45).

Comparative categorization can provide an instrument of discovery (Paden, 2000, p. 186). Although Sanskrit served as a prestigious lingua franca in premodern South and Southeast Asia, some ideologues of Hindutva ("Hinduness") have seized on the sacred language as a narrower symbol of India's ethnocultural superiority (Truschke, 2020, p. 6). Meanwhile, supporters of the traditional Latin Mass contend that "a liturgical language common to us all reminds us that we belong to an institution greater than any nation, and one that binds the faithful all over the world" (Woods, 2008, p. 68). While according to the demotic/hieratic taxonomy, Sanskrit and Latin would be grouped together as priestly varieties, approaching the languages from Holdrege's vantagepoint highlights the ideological disjuncture between the two, with Sanskrit linked to the embodied tradition of Hinduism and Latin to the transnational program of Catholicism. As for Church Slavonic, Holdrege's model alerts the researcher to those discourses which connect the sacred language to the travails and glories of "Holy Russia," like the claim that Church Slavonic is the "soul of the Russian people" [*dusha russkogo naroda*] (quoted in Leonard, 2021, p. 154). Some discussions of *vyaz* take on a similarly nationalistic tone, as in the claim that it is a worthy calligraphic heritage for Russians to rediscover, lest they continue to live in a "cargo culture" dependent on Western products (Pushkarev, personal communication). Such tropes link the Church Slavonic language and script to the mythos of the mighty Russian nation, beleaguered but unbowed, with a historic spiritual culture, set in opposition to the disincarnate universalism of the West.

The analytic categories sketched in this chapter—scripture/cultus/thaumaturgy, demotic/hieratic, embodied/missionizing, and so on—necessarily require refinement and rectification in dynamic interplay with investigations of particular historical and cultural contexts. The comparative study of sacralized languages has only just begun. There is much work to do. To paraphrase the influential comparativist Jonathan Z. Smith (2004, p. 334), the antinomy of sacred and vernacular languages, the competing *ethoi* of sacrality and comprehensibility, their permutations and interactions within and between religious traditions—all of this constitutes an enduringly important theme in the study of language and religion.

Further Reading

Bennett, B.P. (2018). *Sacred languages of the world: An introduction.* Wiley.
The first comparative monograph on the phenomenon, based on nine specimens: Arabic, Avestan, Coptic, Ge'ez, Hebrew, Latin, Pali, Sanskrit, and Slavonic.
Fishman, J.A. (2006). 'Holy languages' in the context of societal bilingualism. In N.H. Hornberger & M. Pütz (Eds.), *Language loyalty, language planning and language revitalization: Recent writings and reflections from Joshua A. Fishman.* Multilingual Matters.
An insightful article by the sociolinguist who did more than anyone else to draw attention to the relevance of sacred languages.
Rosowsky, A. (2008). *Heavenly readings: Liturgical literacy in a multilingual context.* Multilingual Matters.
The first in a sequence of sophisticated works by the same author that explore the places, discourses, practices, and institutions of Classical Arabic literacy.
Salverda, R. (2018). Empires and their languages: Reflections on the history and the linguistics of lingua franca and lingua sacra. In J. Braarvig, & M.J. Geller (Eds.), *Studies in multilingualism, Lingua franca and lingua sacra*, 13–78. Open Access, Max Planck Institute for the History of Science. http://mprl-ser ies.mpg.de/studies/10/.
A stimulating historical and theoretical consideration of what makes something a sacred language compared to a lingua franca.
Wheelock, W.T. (1987). Language. In M. Eliade & C.J. Adams (Eds.), *Encyclopedia of Religion, 8*, 439–46. Macmillan.
An older but still worthwhile piece that outlines the sacred language phenomenon vis à vis religious language more broadly.

References

Adamsky, D. (2019). *Russian nuclear Orthodoxy. Religion, politics, and strategy.* Stanford University Press.
Andreev, A., Shardt, Y., & Simmons, N. (n.d.). Church Slavonic typography in Unicode. Unicode Technical Note #41. www.unicode.org/notes/tn41/tn41-1.pdf
Avni, S. (2011). Toward an understanding of Hebrew language education; ideologies, emotions, and identity. *International Journal of the Sociology of Language, 208*: 53–70. https://doi.org/10.1515/ijsl.2011.012
Bennett, B.P. (2011). *Religion and language in post-Soviet Russia.* Routledge.
Bennett, B.P. (2018). *Sacred languages of the world: An introduction.* Wiley.
Bennett, B.P. (2022). Petropolis. The place of Latin in early modern Russia. In A. Cattaneo & K. Bennett (Eds.), *Language dynamics in the early modern period*, 142–165. Taylor & Francis.
Blommaert, J. (1999). *Language ideological debates.* De Gruyter.
Fischer, B. (2019). "The Bridge" and the veiling of meaning: Investigating the possible linguistic effects of Scientology's unique lexicon. *International Journal for the Study of New Religions, 10*(1), 67–88. https://doi.org/10.1558/ijsnr.38937
Fishman, J.A. (1996). *In praise of the beloved language: A comparative view of positive ethnolinguistic consciousness.* De Gruyter.
Fishman, J.A. (2006). 'Holy languages' in the context of societal bilingualism. In N. H. Hornberger & M. Pütz (Eds.), *Language loyalty, language planning and language revitalization: Recent writings and reflections from Joshua A. Fishman*, 251–258. Multilingual Matters.
Frawley, D. (1990). *From the river of heaven: Hindu and Vedic knowledge for the modern age.* Lotus.
Freiberger, O. (2019). *Considering comparison: a method for religious studies.* Oxford.
Haeri, N. (2003). *Sacred language, ordinary people. Dilemmas of culture and politics in Egypt.* Palgrave Macmillan.
Hobbs, V. (2021). *An introduction to religious language. Exploring theolinguistics in contemporary contexts.* Bloomsbury.
Holdrege, B.A. (2018). Interrogating the comparative method: Whither, why, and how? *Religions 9*(2), 58. https://doi.org/10.3390/rel9020058
Johnson, D., & Priestley, J. (2022). A 'sanctified language': A sociolinguistic study of the perception of Latin and its role in the mass for American Catholics. *Interdisciplinary Journal of Research on Religion, 18*, Article 8.

Keipert, H. (2014). Kirchenslavisch-Begriffe. In K. Gutschmidt & S. Kempgen (Eds.), *Die slavischen Sprachen: Ein internationales Handbuch zu ihrer Struktur, ihrer Geschichte und ihrer Erforschung.* 2: 1211–1252. De Gruyter.

Khakimova, Y. (2022). Russian vyaz: This old Slavonic lettering is once again gaining popularity in Russia. *Russia Beyond.* www.rbth.com/education/335444-russian-vyaz-slavonic-lettering

Kravetskii, A.G. (2019). Problema iazyka bogosluzheniia: 150 let nazad i cegodnia. In R.A. Gogolev (Ed.), *Iazyk pravoslavnogo bogosluzheniia: istoriia, traditsii, sovremennaia praktika. Materialy I Mezhdunarodnoi nauchno-prakticheskoi konferentsii* 9–37. OOO 'Begemot-NN'.

Leonard, S.P. (2020). The Word as an icon: The embodied spirituality of Church Slavonic. *Suomen Antropologi, 45*(3), 30–48. https://doi.org/10.30676/jfas.v45i3.98011

Leonard, S.P. (2021). 'Secularisation of the world': The semiotic ideologies of Russian Orthodox bloggers. *Journal for the Study of Religions and Ideologies 20*(60), 141–158. https://thenewjsri.ro/index.php/njsri/article/view/106

Liddicoat, A.J. (2012). Language planning as an element of religious practice. *Current Issues in Language Planning, 13*(2), 121–144.

Lincoln, B. (2018). *Apples and oranges. Explorations in, on, and with comparison.* University of Chicago Press.

Liudogovskii, F.B. (2015) Graficheskaia obolochka sovremennogo tserkovnoslavianskogo iazyka. http://pravmisl.ru/index.php?option=com_content&task=view&id=391

Mareš, F.W. (1979). *An anthology of Church Slavonic texts of western (Czech) origin.* Wilhelm Fink Verlag.

Makarii, Ieromonakh (Markish). (2017). *Bogosluzhenia. Kniga dlia vsekh, kto prikhodit v khram.* Danilov stavropigial'nyi muzhskoi monastyr'.

McDaniel, J.T. (2011) *The Lovelorn ghost and the magical monk: Practicing Buddhism in modern Thailand.* Columbia University Press.

Naumescu, V. (2018). Syriac as a *lingua sacra*: Speaking the language of Christ in India. In S. Luehrmann, *Praying with the senses. Contemporary Orthodox Christian spirituality in practice*, 103–104. Indiana University Press.

Paden, W.E. (1999). Reconceiving the category of the sacred. In E.R. Sand & J.P. Sørensen (Eds.), *Comparative studies in history of religions. Their aim, scope, and validity*, 93–108. Museum Tusculanum Press.

Paden, W.E. (2000). Religion, World, Plurality. In T. Jensen & M. Rothstein (Eds.), *Secular theories on religion. Current perspectives*, 193–209. Museum Tusculanum Press.

Paden, W.E. (2016). *New patterns for comparative religion. Passages to an evolutionary perspective.* Bloomsbury.

Ponomariov, A. (2016). The Body of Christ online: The Russian Orthodox Church and (non-) liturgical inter-activity on the internet. In M. Suslov (Ed.), *Digital Orthodoxy in the post-Soviet world. The Russian Orthodox Church and Web 2.0*, 111–139. *ibidem*-Verlag.

Pushkarev, V. (2022). Cathedral of the Resurrection of Christ. www.behance.net/gallery/99221475/Cathedralof-the-Resurrection-of-Christ

Ringrow, H. (2022). Identity. In S. Pihlaja (Ed.), *Analysing religious discourse*, 276–291. Cambridge University Press.

Rosowsky, A. (2008). *Heavenly readings: Liturgical literacy in a multilingual context.* Multilingual Matters.

Rosowsky, A. (2021). *The performance of multilingual and 'ultralingual' devotional practices by young British Muslims.* Multilingual Matters.

Rosowsky, A. (2022). Community. In S. Pihlaja (Ed.), *Analysing religious discourse*, 162–178. Cambridge University Press.

Rudolph, K. (1985). *Historical Fundamentals and the Study of Religions: Haskell Lectures delivered at the University of Chicago.* Macmillan.

Salverda, R. (2018). Empires and their languages: Reflections on the history and the linguistics of lingua franca and lingua sacra. In J. Braarvig, & M. J. Geller (Eds.), *Studies in multilingualism, Lingua franca and lingua sacra*,13–78. Open Access, Max Planck Institute for the History of Science. http://mprl-series.mpg.de/studies/10/

Sharot, S. (2001). *A comparative sociology of world religions: Virtuosos, priests, and popular religion.* New York University Press.

Smith, C. (2019). *Religion: What it is, how it works, and why it matters.* Princeton University Press.

Smith, J.Z. (2004). *Relating religion: essays in the study of religion.* University of Chicago Press.

Stähle, H. (2022). *Russian Church in the Digital Era: Mediatization of Orthodoxy.* Routledge.

Truschke, A. (2020). Hindutva's dangerous rewriting of history. *South Asia Multidisciplinary Academic Journal* [Online] 24/25. https://journals.openedition.org/samaj/6636.

Unicode Consortium. (2021). The Unicode Standard. Version 14. www.unicode.org/versions/Unicode14.0.0/ch01.pdf

Wheelock, W.T. (1987). Language. In M. Eliade & C.J. Adams (Eds.), *Encyclopedia of religion*, 8: 439–446. Macmillan.

Williams, A. (2008). The continuum of 'sacred language' from high to low speech in the Middle Iranian (Pahlavi) Zoroastrian tradition. In N. Green & M. Searle-Chatterjee (Eds.), *Religion, language, and power*, 123–142). Routledge.

Wilson, P. (2022). Translation. In S. Pihlaja (Ed.), *Analysing religious discourse*, 109–125. Cambridge University Press.

Woods, Jr., T.E. (2008). *Sacred then and sacred now: The return of the old Latin Mass*. Roman Catholic Books.

Yusuf, K. & Putrie, Y.E. (2022). The linguistic landscape of mosques in Indonesia: Materiality and identity representation. *International Journal of Society, Culture & Language 10*(3), 2–21.

4
DIGITAL MEDIA AND THE SACRED

Nevfel Boz and Zehra Erşahin

Introduction and Background

The concept of the sacred, along with its utilization and connotations, relies upon sacralization activities and the significance of meaning-making processes that are grounded in the paradigms of thought established by belief systems. The term "sacred" is an anthropological construct applied to an extensive array of religious and non-religious cultural contexts. This term is frequently employed interchangeably with notions such as mystical, religious, divine, magical, and, most commonly, spiritual and religious. Nonetheless, it possesses shared attributes, contingent upon the manner in which it is comprehended by individuals and collectives. The notion of the sacred also diverges from the profane realm and articulates life's ultimate meaning, encapsulating an eternal reality. In the context of religious discourse, the sacred often serves as an ontological referent, underpinning its utilization and culture-specific semantics. A defining characteristic of religion is the duality between the sacred and the profane; sacredness pertains to elements that are proscribed or demarcated by society. As society delineates these sacred entities, the source of sacred power ultimately resides in society itself (Durkheim, 1915, p. 47).

The term sacred is used to distinguish between worldly things and concepts and those that are godly or have some connection to God. The term sacred is usually used to describe beliefs with a spiritual or divine significance. In general, the concept of holy objects is more abstract, whereas concrete objects are considered sacred. Although the terms sacred and holy are similar and sometimes used interchangeably, there are subtle differences. In general, the term holiness refers to people and relationships, whereas sacredness refers to objects, places, or events (McCann 2008). The term sacred has religious connotations, as numinous and sui generis (Lynch, 2012), which we can refer to as non-negotiable beliefs and values we hold. The sacred is distinct in both individual and collective meaning systems. It has been used as an attribute of circumstances related to religion or important life principles, such as love, freedom, equality, and justice. A sacred thing, place, time, or concept is something unique and non-negotiable that is separate from or protected from everyday concepts. It manifests itself both directly and indirectly through ideas and values held to be central or essential to identities and beliefs. (Anttonen 2000; Mellor, 2006). Therefore, the concept of sacredness has evolved from religious contexts to various forms of inevitable human values and beliefs that individuals and societies are non-negotiable.

DOI: 10.4324/9781003301271-5

Sacred is also a distinct quality in both individual and collective meaning systems. The paradigms provided by the belief systems to which they are committed, whether religious, national, or ideological, guide these sacred-making activities and signification processes (Anttonen, 2000). A key point to remember here is that the sacred can be found in both national and ideological belief systems, not just in religions. Certain things are made sacred by a group's beliefs and values (flags, leaders, state borders, ideological principles); the sacred is protected by taboos, though in modern society taboos may be constituted by law (Durkheim, 1915). However, in today's digital age, the concept of sacredness has taken on new dimensions

A society's belief system makes certain ideas sacred and non-negotiable for its way of life. Different forms of sanctification have occurred among those of the same religion, and the degree of sanctity attributed to religion's basic sanctities may differ between denominations. In contrast to the Sunni tradition, the Shia tradition attributes sanctity to the institutions of "Ahl al-Bayt" (the family of the Prophet) and "Wilayat al-Faqih" (the guardian Islamic jurist). Again, in Christian tradition, different denominations evaluate Jesus' positions at varying degrees of sanctity. It also enables us to comprehend how sacred values have evolved over time in light of changes in religion's place and role in contemporary society.

Furthermore, the concept of sacredness has undergone changes in contemporary society due to the influence of digital technologies. Since individuals and groups can now share their non-negotiable beliefs and values across the world in real time, this has led to new forms of sanctification. As religions lost control of politics, science, and art, each of these spheres developed a sacred status to find the essence of religion in things traditionally regarded as secular. Contemporary sacralization of the secular occurs in the cultural arenas of society. For example, nationalistic celebrations reflect the sacralization of the secular within politics (Demerath, 2001). Today, national holidays may sometimes be celebrated more widely than many religious holy days; national anthems are sung as if they were religious hymns, national flags are important symbols, and national heroes and monuments have replaced the widespread worship of religious saints and temples (Roberts, 1984; Rook, 1984).

The sacred can be present in all spheres of life. However, the religious understanding expressed in sacred myths and rituals focuses on time, place, and agents. Sacred refers to representations that go beyond routine activities. Conversely, commonplace and unexceptional things are referred to as profane. According to Durkheim, religion was the practice of maintaining a distance and drawing lines between the sacred and the profane. Because the sacred is exceptional and magnificent and is easily contaminated by the profane, it is essential to distinguish between the sacred and the profane (Durkheim, 1915). From the standpoint of the sacred–profane dichotomy, which assumes that the sacred is completely different from everyday existence but necessary for everyday existence. The sacred manifests in concrete forms, which could also be profane. Although every sacred system of thought and action distinguishes between what it identifies as sacred or profane, all men find sacred to not manifest in the same way, and what is profane to some is sacred to others. Because the secular and religious concepts are frequently intertwined, it can be difficult to draw a clear line between them (Cavanaugh 2009).

The concept of "secular" is embodied in the concept of religion, as it is defined as the opposite of religion, and the concept of religion is often associated with the concepts of sacred and transcendental (Chanour, 2021). What is considered secular in this context is sacred and transcendental. This does not mean that what is secular is not from religion, but rather that fundamental differences that represent the conceptual distinction between religion and the secular do not exist. Therefore, the distinction between religion and secularism is arbitrary (Horiii, 2022). Moreover, the concept of secularism is complex and multifaceted. It encompasses political, cultural, social, and legal dimensions.

Today, many people do not consider themselves part of any religious tradition (Meintel & Mossière, 2013). Traditional religious structures somehow lost their sanctity, new forms of religious sanctification emerged, and people have had new possibilities to create their own "sacred" phenomenon (Yip, 2002). Modern individuals, who place personal choice at the center of their secular cosmology, place hedonism and tangible beings that represent it at the center of their own sacredness. This is based on the cultural idea of using specific ritual strategies to distinguish one's physical and mental selves from daily social routines (Anttonen, 1999). The values that make us who we are no longer arise from religions, which are the absolute authorities in the world, but from other values that are the main sources of one's own identity. While sacred is used to draw categorical boundaries, it has also been used as a quality in which distinctions are expressed between things that have a special cultural value and where there are countless beings perceived as sacred—physical and non-physical. Some refer more to superhuman beings, while others are less openly religious marks such as the flag, for example, by which members of a nation enhance or preserve its value (Bell, 1997).

The issues with defining and studying religion are manifestations of changes in people's attitudes toward the sacred in the modern world. The physical and social sciences have both enabled modern man to better his circumstances and live a better life. Especially after the eighteenth century, the acceptance of rational and critical perspectives to judge the claims of religious authorities contributed to the secular affirmation of man. This shift in modern consciousness has led to new forms of understanding the sacred, no longer understood solely within traditional religious frameworks but as a culturally constructed phenomenon. It is now recognized that the sacred is not only a religious concept but also a cultural one. In this investigation of the sacred and how it affects human behavior, the emphasis is on sacred perceptions rather than the ontological reality of the sacred, which is accepted as a result of psychological, social, institutional, cultural, and situational forces (Pargament et al., 2017). Today, with digital media, the concept of the sacred has taken on new forms and meanings and digital media have provided new avenues for the expression and experience of the sacred.

The advancement of technology, particularly the proliferation of the internet, has influenced the representation of the sacred. From a historical standpoint, the interdependence between technological progress and religious beliefs is not novel. For example, the printing press revolutionized how information spreads, and consequently, how people respond to that information. The printing and distribution of scriptures have resulted in a decrease in reliance on institutional religious formations in the reading and interpretation of sacred texts. This process, called "mediatization," determines not only how messages are sent and received but also how messages are produced and consumed (Hjarvard, 2013). The increasing mediatization of contemporary society has transformed the way in which the sacred is experienced and represented, impacting not only how messages are disseminated but also conceived. Mediatization as a concept refers to the changes that occur with the mass media and their development (Hjarvard, 2017). As a result, mediatization attempts to explain the social and cultural changes that occur in any society as a result of mass media influence. Mediation is not the same as mediatization. While mediation refers to the transmission of messages, mediatization considers how media, on the one hand, produces the content of the messages conveyed and, on the other, intervenes and transforms social and cultural processes (Mazzoleni & Schulz, 1999).

Along with mediatization, globalization has also had profound effects on religious beliefs and practices. With globalization, openness to new forms of religiosity (Frunză, 2011) has become widespread and social and political consequences have emerged (Souza, 2016). The advancement of technology has had implications beyond digital contexts, and it has become impossible to discuss religious interactions without explicitly or implicitly considering the role of technology in these interactions (Campbell, 2017). The implications extend beyond a subset of people who use digital media and the presence of social media influences how institutions form themselves, choose topics to address in presenting themselves, and communicate. It also affects how public life and policy are determined, as well as individual beliefs and practices. The increased mediatization and globalization of contemporary society have had profound effects on religious beliefs, resulting in a widespread religious understanding with social and political consequences.

The use of religious content in combination with radio and television also illustrates secularization through the broadcasting of sacred rituals to profane places or times (O'Guinn & Belk, 1989). "Televangelism" has also secularized religion through its association with the secular medium of television (Frankl, 1987). By becoming more connected to the secular, religion may have undermined its own sanctity and opened the way for other possibilities. The implications of these changes have important consequences for the future of religious beliefs and practices, as they challenge the traditional structures and authority within religious institutions. The increased use of technology and digital media in religious interactions has contributed to the mediatization of contemporary society.

The underlying organization of social and existential discourse is now influenced by media. As communication techniques and media technology advance, our society undergoes changes in ever-deeper layers, as communication progressively supplements reality (Johnson, 2007). However, to what extent can we assert that the media is so crucial to the lives of modern people that it even succeeds in shaping reality? One compelling explanation is that media has a significant impact on how reality is symbolically constructed (Reese, 1991). In this sense, the significance of mass media in the formation of identity and meeting of numerous identities in public spaces has become increasingly clear. This plays a significant role in how reality is construed by society (Donsbach, 1996). The presence of the sacred in everyday life is also an indication of people's need for meaning, mythologization, and ritualization in modern society. In this context, the media is responsible for the formation and implementation of the symbolic construction of reality at both the individual and societal levels.

Today, when it is impossible to maintain traditional types of relationships, the channels through which individuals resort to meet their communication needs have also transformed. The situations that have arisen with technological developments have become factors that significantly affect an individual's understanding of life, and therefore, their relationship with the sacred. As McLuhan (1964) has shown, the media itself functions as formative content. One of the many reasons why the digital world has an impact on the individual is that it has caused human beings to be exposed to excessive data, as never before. As technology has evolved, our way of life has also transformed, and our interaction with it has led us to have a mindset that transforms our relationship with the sacred and transcendent.

Religion and new media studies investigate how technology and digital culture influence religious traditions, and how new conditions emerge for an individual's experiences, practices, and beliefs through websites, social networks, apps, and digital devices. As digital technologies have become an indispensable part of daily life, our lifestyle is also transforming. This situation also shows the extent to which we are exposed to information bombardment through information and communication technologies. It should be noted that at no time in history has access to information been so far outside of the small elite of this privilege (Shenk, 1997). Nowadays, we encounter more information than we would like, and we are dealing with an increasing amount of information every day, and we have difficulty coping. Although not all of us may have a desire to deal with so much information, the digital technologies we inevitably use force us to do so, resulting in exposure to more information than we can effectively process (Berghel, 1997; Kirsh, 2000). The overload of information caused by digital technologies not only influences our daily lives, but also forcibly transforms our relationship with the sacred.

Another explanation is that the use of digital technology also transforms mental processes and the functioning of the brain in certain ways (Osiurak et al., 2018). The use of digital media technologies transforms our focus, productivity, reading skills, and personal interactions, leading us to adopt new habits. If we consider how the habits we acquire and the new interactions we establish and the skills of thinking, reasoning, and imagining mutually affect each other (Anderson & Subrahmanyam, 2017), this transformative effect of digital media technologies will manifest itself in our relationship with meaning and the sacred. It is important to determine which information is more valuable. Considering that this mass of information is made up of advertising and manipulation, how this overload of information transforms our relationship with the sacred is vital to human existence. The transformative effect of digital media technologies has led to the adoption of new habits, which in turn affects our relationship between meaning and the sacred. Naturally, this is also a result of the absence of authority that determines whether the information being given is significant. Algorithmic procedures and advertising tactics have replaced authority.

Technology plays a significant role in religious life because it affects how knowledge is shared, standardized, and preserved as well as how the sacred is transformed. Another dynamic consequence is that new authorities have emerged thanks to digital technologies. These modifications occur in both the presentation of beliefs and how they are perceived. Aside from the religious sphere, new and social media are effective, especially in the political and social spheres, and they can be used to effectively challenge authorities in these fields. Direct discourse can now be produced in the public sphere easily, and informality has developed as a result of communication evolution. Public discussions occur because of the opportunities provided by mediatization has given rise to. Additionally, the capabilities of digital technologies allow for the emergence of fresh perspectives that are not supported by traditional institutions such as religion.

Today, how religious institutions retain their power is a crucial question, given the diffused forms of authority in the digital world. The production of media culture in general and its effects on news and various spheres of life in particular are referred to as the logic of media (Altheide & Snow, 1979). The term mediatization describes the process by which the media transforms into a semi-autonomous institution that starts to control the information that people receive in certain spheres of their lives. A "new social and cultural condition in which the power to define and practice religion has been altered" (Hjarvard, 2013, p. 83) is the outcome of religious mediatization in the context of the sacred. This new circumstance suggests that the media as a whole serves as the main conduit for religious information, rather than face-to-face confrontations between believers or authorities from religious institutions.

The effect of digital media on religions, particularly in what Habermas (2006) refers to as a post-secular society, has accepted the "secularization hypothesis" based on Enlightenment principles and has accepted religion's eventual decline in the face of modernization (Possamai-Inesedy, 2019). What is happening on digital platforms is a new type of collective consent, but one that allows for consensus due to the diverse group opinions generated by online discussions (Possamai-Inesedy & Nixon, 2017). Covering consensus is oriented to commonality among seemingly diverse belief systems. Along with opportunities for the exploration of various religious perspectives and showcasing the diversity of the communities, digital media has created a new kind of collective consent focusing on the more secular concept. Our research supports the notion that newly emerging forms of communal secularity maintain the traditional idea while elevating the significance of social functions, identity, moral substance, and normative outcomes of communal religious life. The following case study examines how the Presidency of Religious Affairs (PRA), Turkey's official religious institution, uses different sets of sacred topics in its Friday sermons and Twitter accounts. Contextualizing the sacred from khutbahs (Friday sermons) to digital media (Twitter account) or contextualizing the sacred into the public ("secular") or political sphere, can change contexts and spaces, allow for new processes of meaning attribution, form new identities, and thus change communities.

Digital Media and The Sacred: Khutbahs vs Tweets

In general, as an intersection between content analysis and network analysis, semantic network analysis informs us about the network's key concepts, level of connectedness, the existence of sub-communities, and the network's sphere of influence. In order to analyze and describe network structures, Sowa (1991) claims that semantic networks allow the modeling of semantic relationships that are represented in a graph with labeled nodes and edges. Semantic networks are an old idea that provided a foundation for knowledge modeling and representation (Helbig, 2006). In essence, semantic network analysis turns any given text into a network of words that are linked to one another. It can be useful to identify key words in the text and group them together to extract the meanings, the topics, the frames, the themes, and everything else that emerges from it. One may explore the word network to look for key words and word clusters. In the end, they provide a representation of information and associations. It can be used to represent factual knowledge about classes of objects and their properties; ultimately, they offer a representation of facts and relationships. Making associations between objects, which is actually an idea derived from representation, is essentially an attempt to incorporate the features of human cognition into a knowledge representation. The interaction of network structure quantitative and qualitative analysis supports the interpretation of semantic structures.

Using semantic network analysis as a network of connected words and a combination of structural measures, we provide an approach that proves valuable for a more comprehensive analysis of large and complex semantic networks of formal discourse of (PRA) to explore khutbahs and Twitter data from the PRA. The methodology is divided into three stages: data collection, data preparation, and data analysis. Each khutbah is one to two pages of text, which is frequently stored in pdf format on the PRA website. We scraped together all 120 Friday khutbahs publicly accessible from the PRA website between January 2021 and December 2022. Also, the official PRA Twitter account was used to collect data from January 2021 to December 2022 using an R Studio program that enables Twitter data retrieval. To visualize the network data and determine the metric findings, the Gephi application, which is a visualization and exploration tool for various types of graphs and networks, was used.

To be more concise, based on "betweenness centrality," semantic network analysis has developed a set of centrality measures. The number of relations maintained by a given node is the easiest way to understand centrality in terms of its degree. Betweenness centrality is a measure developed to determine the most related terms (vertices, or nodes) that connect different communities in a network. High values indicate that a node reaches other nodes in the network with a shorter path relative to other nodes. Betweenness centrality is an indicator of power and influence, and it gauges how well the node under investigation can serve as a central hub for communication. If a node in a network with a high betweenness level were to be removed, the network would

Table 4.1 Example of the text cleaning from khutbahs

Original text/sentences:
In the hadith I have just recited, the Prophet Muhammad (saw) says, "A sign of man's good observance of Islam (his piety) is to keep away from that which does not concern him."

After stop words and text cleaning:
hadith just recited prophet Muhammad says sign man's good observance islam piety keep away

After lemmatization and cleaning the text
hadith just recite prophet Muhammad say sign man good observance islam piety keep away concern

---

disintegrate into otherwise coherent clusters. Betweenness centrality is a measure of a relationship and how important a node has over the flow of information in a graph.

The khutbahs were initially subjected to topic modeling analysis. After evaluating the khutbahs, Twitter's Academic Research Application Programming Interface (API) was utilized to extract Twitter data that included all tweets sent between January 2021 and December 2022 (the same timeframe as the sermons). The search returned 2,343 tweets, which comprised the entire scope of the PRA official account (@diyanetbasin. Turkish stop words were removed from the Twitter data using a combination of the stop words from SWNetTR++ (Sağlam et al., 2019) and TurkishSentiNet (Özçelik et al., 2021), as well as words with negligible information content. The data was then lemmatized using the udpipe library package from R. Lemmatization is employed to reduce various forms of a word to a single state, facilitating their analysis as a single entity. These tweets constituted the outcome variables of the analyses.

Each document, in this case, a khutbah, was supposed to be composed of a variety of latent topics, each of which is linked to a particular set of words. The process ended with the creation of a word–topic matrix. We selected English khutbahs from a corpus of 120 documents comprising Friday sermons. As it is a common practice in quantitative text analysis, we removed words that had ignorable information content (Silge & Robinson 2017). These included common stop words in English (e.g., synonyms for "and," "but," "be"); the list of the stop words comes from the text mining package in R (tm package) for English khutbahs. We also removed words that appear in almost all sermons (for example, "date," "religious affairs"). Then lemmatize English khutbahs words using UDpipe library package from R.

This resulted in a set of 1,139 distinct words scattered throughout the sermons. Religion and specific theological topics are frequently addressed in sermons, such as Allah, the life of the Prophet Muhammad, faith, and prayer.

Table 4.2 highlights the topics in the network ranked by betweenness centrality, which is a measure of centrality. These topics may have acted as important bridges in the network. In terms of betweenness centrality, the most prominent node in the graph represents the most essential words in the semantic graph. Consequently, many words are associated with the most significant nodes.

These links, which display varying levels of co-occurrence frequencies, represent one another when they are present together. The most frequent cooccurrences are displayed in these links. These links appeared together in texts more frequently and mathematically as they got thicker. Figure 4.1 depicts the semantic network analysis of all Friday sermons (khutbahs) that were delivered to millions of people in thousands of mosques. Figure 4.2 depicts the semantic network analysis of 2,343 tweets sent by the official account of PRA. Semantic network analysis has been used to generate a map of conceptual words in literature (Levallois et al., 2012). In this

Table 4.2 Top 10 topics ranked by betweeness centrality

Rank	Top 10 Topics in Khutbahs	Top 10 Topics in Tweets
1	Allah	Islam
2	Prophet	Nation
3	Lord	Country
4	Almighty	Mosque
5	Life	Human
6	Heart	World
7	Family	Muslim
8	Faith	Friday
9	Human	Children
10	Islam	Allah

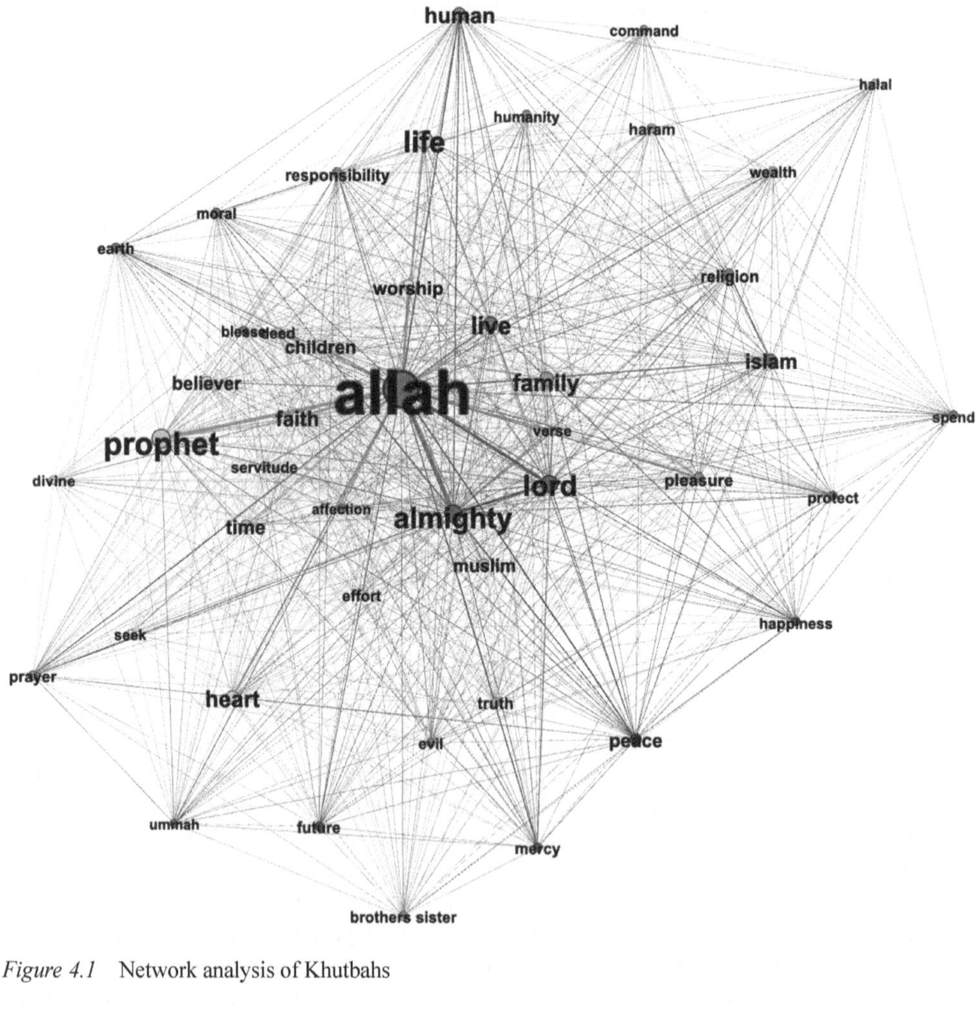

Figure 4.1 Network analysis of Khutbahs

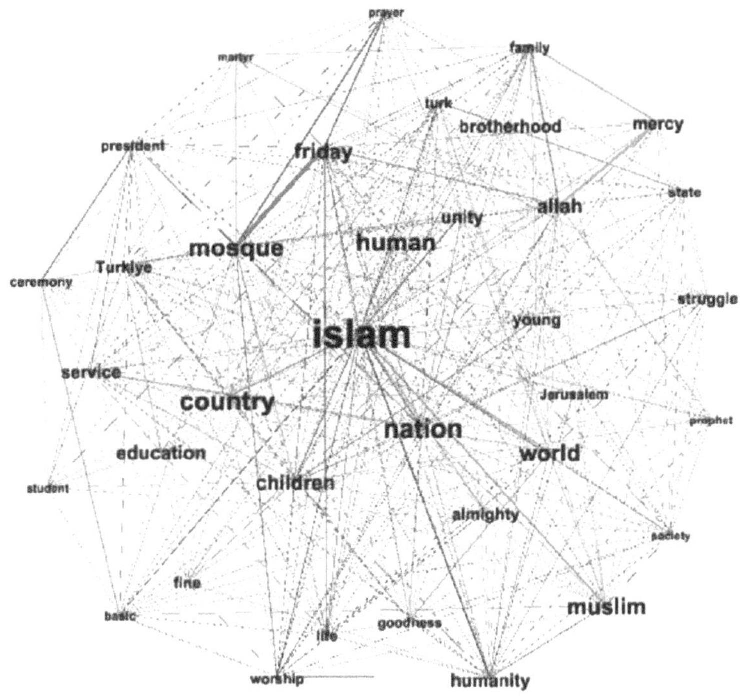

Figure 4.2 Network analysis of tweets

case semantic maps help us understand the meanings of khutbahs and tweets. From the khutbah (Figure 4.1), the word Allah is co-occurred with almost all words in the graph. Khutbahs generally convey messages to the individual, the believer who attends Friday sermons, with more affect-oriented transcendent concepts in creating a fulfilling, happy, and rewarded life by adhering to Allah's guidance. The central topics of khutbahs depict the sacred network of a person's relationship with the transcendent (Allah, the Almighty, and the Divine Lord), in the direction of his prophet (as believers to be a part of his ummah). In order to be corresponded with peace, wealth, mercy, blessings, and happiness both now and in the future, believers are instructed to live their lives and keep their hearts at peace with these qualities: servitude, good deeds and morals, and effort to embody truth, prayer, worship, effort in avoiding haram, and seeking a halal responsible life towards their children, families, brothers and sisters, and all humanity.

From the tweet graph (Figure 4.2), the word Islam is co-occurred with most of the words. Both Allah and Islam have important positions on the graph. From the word Allah, we can clearly see that in khutbah, the relationship we have is between humans and God or a vertical connection. However, in tweets, we noticed that Islam was the most prominent word. Furthermore, we find that the tweets of PRA include more than khutbahs to events of national importance and to the threats faced by the country. Nationalism in the tweets spikes more regularly than in khutbahs during the anniversaries of significant dates. Tweets use more institutionalized and society-oriented concepts of sacred in the creation of a religious national identity through the unifying practices of Islam, communicating messages to communities outside of just the individual believer and their social circles. The central topics of tweets portray the sacred network of a national institution's relationship with its audience and followers in providing Islamic-oriented services to its lands and beyond, calling for brotherhood, goodness, unity, worship, attending Friday rituals in mosques, and other such activities. Here, the relationship between Muslims and the Almighty is interpreted through the lens of social identity using secular conceptions of the state, nation, and country as well as of education for the benefit of societies in Turkey, including children and young people.

Overall, these findings suggest that, within the context of the PRA, digital religious activities exhibit a stronger association with secular topics in tweets as compared to khutbahs. But these does not allow us to interpret the data in a binary manner or as sacred or not-sacred. These concepts are always manifested intertwined. When we think about the khutbahs, we see a situation that is more focused on purification, nearer to a transcendence experience, and a struggle that affects daily life. The term secular is often considered anti-religious, but it would be better if the term secular was seen as the opposite of the sacred, not of religion. The sacred and the secular coexist in all contexts, and religions have both a sacred dimension (otherworldly) and an earthly dimension (Weber, 1966). This should not be seen as a dichotomy but as dualism. In the khutbahs, there is a more other worldly structure, which is a value-laden structure such as purification, contact with transcendence, etc. In the tweets, we have a worldly sacred as the image of the nation-state's effort to establish order in the world.

When we consider khutbahs, we can define Fridays as an activity that is presented to a specific group of believers and that a certain group of believers does within itself. In the case of tweets, there is a situation where everyone is open, his followers are diverse and unknown. At this point, while the same institution uses a value-oriented set of concepts in a religious activity (sermons) within itself, it prefers a more identity-oriented set of concepts when dealing with the other in digital media. The other in digital media is also a more amorphous and indecent mass and consists of plural individuals. To encompass this audience, at a more material level and in a way that refers to everyday experiences, the way is to maintain order and social control and to construct identity.

Additionally, it is anticipated that this research will contribute to the understanding of the interplay between religion and politics in Turkey. The findings also make a methodological contribution in using the "computational social science" methods to address long-standing questions in digital mediatization of the sacred. Here, we apply these tools to analyze hundreds of sermons and thousands of tweets, to the study of the mediatization of sacred in a non-Western context, and the findings have bearing on the secularization discussion.

Implications and Future Directions

From the perspective of traditional religious activities, the findings of the case study exemplify a form of mediatization and secularization of the message, specifically, in the representation of the sacred. Khutbahs typically deliver messages with more affect-oriented transcendent concepts to the individual, the believer who attends Friday sermons, about how to live a full, happy life by following Allah's instructions. The main themes of khutbahs portray the sacred network of a person's relationship with the transcendent (Allah, the Almighty, and the Divine Lord), under the guidance of his prophet (as believers to be a part of his ummah). Through the unifying practices of Islam, tweets help create a religious national identity by using more institutionalized and society-oriented concepts of sacred in communicating with communities outside of the individual believer and their social circles. It can be considered as an emerging tendency for established religious institutions to redirect their activities away from addressing the needs of individuals for internal growth and purpose, and towards more external forms or pursuits that are less related to spiritual life. It is also an effort by religious organizations to adjust to the norms of a secular society.

That is, the media not only transmits information but also actively produces and frames religious issues; therefore, what constitutes sacred. While this does not explain why individuals turn away from religion, it does suggest that the logic of media may have a partial secularizing effect. The relationship that people have with religious institutions and their decreased need for them are further implications of mediatization. In other words, the media offers a replacement and develops a new paradigm for "sacred" (Berger, 1990). Moreover, religious images that serve as popular narratives and standalone symbols are created and reproduced by the media (Hjarvard, 2012). For some people, these inadequately institutionalized, slightly personalized, and aesthetically enhanced forms also represent a new religious identity.

Religious institutions often strive to expand their influence in the public sphere by assuming responsibility for a portion of activities that the state can only partially support through its institutions, such as various social initiatives, environmental care endeavors, and healthcare system activities. This approach serves as a means of reclaiming diminished influence and power, both publicly and in individuals' personal lives. However, these trends aimed at revitalizing religious institutions do not align with an inclination to reevaluate theology and religious practices in a post-modern society to address the needs of individuals. The focus is not on rethinking religion or proposing a model for reconsidering the sacred. Nevertheless, it can be posited that this represents the case of Turkish official religious institutions' efforts to adapt to the conditions of a secular society.

The discussions in this chapter advance sociological knowledge of how a Muslim religious institution (PRA) handles the difficulties associated with existing pluralistic societies. This chapter's data, which is a snapshot of other potential religious venues, demonstrates that the PRA is actively seeking to strengthen its position in the public eye and is not a passive participant, as Beckford (2010) suggests. This procedure is related to Habermas's (2006) thesis that a strong foundation of religious neutrality must underpin any agreement regarding problems of public concern. Here, Habermas (2006) gives religious institutions the task of translating religious issues into universally acceptable "reasoned arguments" in the public sphere. The translation of religious-centric claims into reasoned arguments is a form of framing that resonates with religiously neutral discourses of the public sphere.

In the context of Turkish representation of the sacred, these frames show how Muslim discourse can be accommodated in a religiously plural and/or neutral discourse. Furthermore, the transformation of traditional religious discourse into profane discourse could be part of a post-secularization process in which secularization leaves religion as a versatile cultural tool. Moreover, the change in conventional religious discourses into profane speech can be a result of a post-secularization process in which religion is still used as a flexible cultural instrument (Fordahl & Ragnarsdóttir, 2021). According to the preferences of the audiences that are in contact with alternative spiritualities in the context of the growth of new religious representations, PRA social media accounts implicitly utilize more fluid interpretation. It is obvious that religion is not only fully mediatized in contemporary societies where the majority of our institutions, cultures, social networks, and activities are conducted and informed by digital media (Hjarvard, 2016), but that the mediatization, or rather the digitalization, of religion is also shaping and transforming religious discourse in the society at large.

From the standpoint of traditional religious activities, the findings of the case study illustrate a type of mediatization and secularization of the message, in this instance, the representation of the sacred. Established religious organizations are increasingly steering their activities away from meeting the needs of people for internal growth and purpose in favour of more external pursuits that do not have any connection to spirituality. Religious institutions frequently extend their influence in the public sphere, and this is a means to reclaim lost authority and influence, both in society and in people's private lives. In the context of sacred, the result of digital mediatization is a new power to define and practice religion in a new social and cultural context (Hjarvard 2013, p. 83).

Consequently, the notion of sacredness has evolved from religious contexts to encompass various forms of indispensable human values and beliefs. These implications extend beyond a subset of individuals utilizing digital media; the ubiquity of social media influences the manner in which institutions structure themselves, select topics to address in their self-presentation, and communicate. Furthermore, social media impacts public life, policy formulation, and personal beliefs and practices. The augmented use of technology and social media in religious interactions has contributed to the mediatization of contemporary society. Religion and new media studies explore the ways in which technology and digital culture affect religious traditions, as well as how novel conditions arise for individuals' experiences, practices, and beliefs through social networks, applications, and digital devices. The transformative impact of digital media technologies has precipitated the adoption of new practices, which, in turn, alters the relationship between meaning and the sacred.

Further Reading

Horii, M. (2022). *'Religion'and 'Secular'Categories in Sociology: Decolonizing the Modern Myth*. Springer Nature.
This comprehensive resource explores how "critical religion" in religious studies and postcolonial self-reflection in sociology approach the concepts of religion and the secular in social theory and sociology.
Campbell, H.A. & Tsuria, R. (2021) *Digital Religion: Understanding religious practice in digital media*, 2nd edition. Routledge.
Current edition of this book offers a thorough overview of religious engagement with a variety of digital media forms in a critical and methodical survey of the study of religion and digital media.
Isetti, G., Innerhofer, E., Pechlaner, H., & De Rachewiltz, M. (2021). *Religion in the Age of Digitalization.* Routledge.
This book examines how new media can affect and change faith and spirituality by giving a thorough overview of how they are currently used in religious engagement.
Faimau, G. & Lesitaokana, W. O. (2018). *New Media and the Mediatisation of Religion: An African Perspective*. Cambridge Scholars Publishing.
The use of digital media to produce and reproduce social, cultural, and religious practices has changed how religious meanings are expressed, and this book offers a novel analysis of how these processes work.
Sumiala-Seppänen, J., Lundby, K., & Salokangas, R. (Eds.) (2006). *Implications of the sacred in (post) modern media*. NORDICOM.
In the context of broader discussions about the sociology of religion, media representation, and contemporary secular values, this book examines how religion and the secular sacred are portrayed.

References

Altheide, D.L., & Snow, R.P. (1979). *Media Logic*. SAGE Publishing.
Anderson, D.R., & Subrahmanyam, K. (2017). Digital Screen Media and Cognitive Development. *Pediatrics, 140*(2), S57–S61. DOI: 10.1542/peds.2016-1758c
Anttonen, V. (1999). The Sacred. In W. Braun & T.R. McCutcheon (Eds.), *Critical Guide to the Study of Religion*. Cassell.
Anttonen, V. (2000). Space. In W. Braun & R. T. McCutcheon (Eds.), *Guide to the Study of Religion*. Cassell.
Beckford, J.A. (2010). The Return of Public Religion? A Critical Assessment of a Popular Claim. *Nordic Journal of Religion & Society, 23*(2), 121–136.
Bell, C. (1997). *Ritual: Perspectives and dimensions*. Oxford University Press.
Berger, P. (1990). *The Sacred Canopy: Elements of a Sociological Theory of Religion*. Doubleday.
Berghel, H. (1997). Cyberspace 2000: Dealing with information overload. *Communications of the ACM, 40*(2), 19–24.

Campbell, H. (2017). Surveying theoretical approaches within digital religion studies. *New Media and Society*, *19*(1), 15–24. DOI: 10.1177/1461444816649912

Cavanaugh, W.T. (2009). *The Myth of Religious Violence: Secular Ideology and the Roots of Modern Conflict.* Oxford Academic.

Chanour, F. (2021). A Comparative Study to Talal Assad and Charles Taylor's Approaches to Secularization. *The International Journal of Humanities & Social Studies.* Center for Promoting Ideas, 9(8), www.internationaljournalcorner.com/index.php/theijhss/article/view/165916

Demerath, N.J. (2001). Secularization Extended: From Religious "Myth" to Cultural Commonplace. In R.K. Fenn (Ed.), *The Blackwell Companion to Sociology of Religion*, 211–228. Blackwell.

Donsbach, W. (1996). Guided perception: characteristics and effects of media reality. *Ecquid Novi*, *17*: 106–111.

Durkheim, E. (1915). *The Elementary Forms of the Religious Life: A Study in Religious Sociology.* Macmillan.

Fordahl, C., & Ragnarsdóttir, B. (2021). When the Gods Fall: Varieties of Post-Secularization in a Small, Secularized State. *Politics and Religion*, *14*(2), 362–387. DOI: 10.1017/S1755048320000516

Frankl, R. (1987). *Televangelism: The marketing of popular religions.* Southern Illinois University Press.

Frunză, S. (2011). Does Communication Construct Reality? A New Perspective on the Crisis of Religion and the Dialectic of the Sacred (English version). *Revista De Cercetare Si Interventie Sociala*, *35*, 180–193.

Habermas, J. (1996). *Between Facts and Norms: Contributions to a Discourse Theory of Law and Democracy* (W. Rehg, Trans.). MIT Press.

Habermas, J. (2006). *Religion in the public sphere. European Journal of Philosophy*, 14(1), 1–25.

Helbig, H. (2006). Knowledge representation and the semantics of natural language: with 23 tables. *Cognitive Technologies.* Springer.

Hjarvard, S. (2012). Three Forms of Mediatized Religion: Changing the Public Face of Religion. In S. Hjarvard & M. Lövheim (Eds.), *Mediatization of Religion: Nordic Perspectives*, 21–44. Nordicom.

Hjarvard, S. (2013). *The Mediatization of Religion and Culture.* Routledge.

Hjarvard, S. (2016). Mediatization and the Changing Authority of Religion. *Media, Culture, and Society*, *38*(1), 8–17.

Hjarvard, S. (2017). Mediatization. In P. Rössler, C.A. Hoffner, & L. van Zoonen (Eds.), *The International Encyclopedia of Media Effects 3*: 1221–1241. Wiley-Blackwell.

Horii, M. (2022). *'Religion' and 'Secular' Categories in Sociology: Decolonizing the Modern Myth.* Springer Nature.

Johnson, M.K. (2007). Reality monitoring and the media. *Applied Cognitive Psychology*, *21*: 981–993.

Kirsh, D. (2000). *A few thoughts on cognitive overload.* Intellectica.

Levallois, C., Clithero, J.A., Wouters, P., Smidts, A., & Huettel, S.A. (2012). Translating upward: Linking the neural and social sciences via neuroeconomics. *Nature Reviews Neuroscience, 13*(11), 789–797.

Lynch, G. (2012). *The Sacred in the Modern World.* Oxford University Press.

Mazzoleni, G., & Schulz, W. (1999). 'Mediatization' of Politics: A Challenge for Democracy? *Political Communication*, *16*(3), 247–261.

McCann, C. (2008). *New Paths Toward the Sacred: Awakening the Awe Experience in Everyday Living.* Paulist Press.

McLuhan, M. (1964). *Understanding media: The extensions of man.* McGraw-Hill.

Meintel, D., & Mossière, G. (2013). In the Wake of the Quiet Revolution: From Secularization to Religious Cosmopolitanism. *Anthropologica*, *55*: 57–71. Canadian Anthropology Society.

Mellor, P.A. (2006). Religion as an Elementary Aspect of Society: Durkheim's Legacy for Social Theory. In J.A. Beckford & J. Walliss (Eds.), *Theorizing Religion: Classical and Contemporary Debates*, 3–18. Ashgate.

O'Guinn, T.C., & Belk, R.W. (1989). *Heaven on Earth: Consumption at Heritage Village, USA. Journal of Consumer Research*, *16*(2), 227–238.

Osiurak, F., Navarro, J., & Reynaud, E. (2018). How Our Cognition Shapes and Is Shaped by Technology: A Common Framework for Understanding Human Tool-Use Interactions in the Past, Present, and Future. *Frontiers in Psychology*, 9: 293. DOI: 10.3389/fpsyg.2018.00293

Özçelik, M., Arıcan, B.N., Bakay, Ö., Sarmış, E., Ergelen, Ö., Bayezit, N.G., & Yıldız, O.T. (2021). HisNet: A Polarity Lexicon based on WordNet for Emotion Analysis. In Proceedings of the 11th Global Wordnet Conference, 157–165. University of South Africa (UNISA).

Pargament, K.I., Oman, D., Pomerleau, J.M., & Mahoney, A. (2017). Some contributions of a psychological approach to the study of the sacred. *Religion*, *47*, 718–744.

Possamai-Inesedy, A. (2019). The study of post-secularization through the digital social. In *The Digital Social: Religion and Belief*. De Gruyter.

Possamai-Inesedy, A., & Nixon, A. (2017). A place to stand: Digital sociology and the Archimedean effect. *Journal of Sociology, 53*(4), 865–884.

Reese, S.D. (1991). Setting the Media's Agenda: A Power Balance Perspective. *Annals of the International Communication Association, 14*, 309–340.

Roberts, K.A. (1984). *Religion in Sociological Perspective*. Dorsey.

Rook, D.W. (1984). Ritual Behavior and Consumer Symbolism. In T.C. Kinnear (Ed.), *Advances in Consumer Research, 11*: 279–284.

Sağlam, F., Genç, B., & Sever, H. (2019). Extending a sentiment lexicon with synonym–antonym datasets: Swnettr++. *Turkish Journal of Electrical Engineering & Computer Sciences, 27*(3), 1806–1820. DOI: 10.3906/elk-1809-120

Silge, J., & Robinson, D. (2017). *Text Mining with R: A Tidy Approach*. O'Reilly Media, Inc.

Souza, A. (2016). Language and faith encounters: Bridging language-ethnicity and language-religion studies. *International Journal of Multilingualism, 13*(1), 134–148. DOI: 10.1080/14790718.2015.1040023

Sowa, J.F. (1991). *Principles of Semantic Networks*. Morgan Kaufmann.

Weber, Max (1966) [1922] *The Sociology of Religion*. Methuen.

Yip, A.K. (2002). The persistence of faith among nonheterosexual Christians: evidence for the neosecularization thesis of religious transformation. *Journal for the Scientific Study of Religion, 41*, 199–212.

5

METAPHORS AND GESTURES IN PRAYERS IN ISLAM

Manar El-Wahsh

Introduction and Background

Prayer is fundamental in many religions, and prayers are also highly cultural and even personal. People pray for varied reasons, either to conform to their religion, be part of a group, supplicate, or, perhaps most importantly, communicate their experiences. Experiences conveyed during prayer can be extremely emotional. This emotional connection speaks to the power of language and its crucial role in prayer execution. Prayer can be distinguished from other genres because it is highly symbolic and indicative of submission to a higher being, and it is based on an interaction between two quite different entities: God and humans (Corwin & Brown, 2019). According to FitzGerald (2012), prayer speaks to the psychological, social, and cultural aspects of human life. Its nature is multifaceted, so it takes place both within the body and is expressed by the body. Therefore, the relation between prayers, emotions, and language is very intricate.

Prayer is not only verbal, but it is also made of gestures. Gestures are overflowing in all cultures, and they are "culturally shaped" (Kress, 2010, p. 76). Gesture is a deliberate body movement, which demonstrates that embodiment plays a role in forming and expressing human thought. Gesture also expresses a metaphorical thought, and its physical nature further establishes that metaphors are embodied. Examining gestural metaphors illustrates that gestures are one of the grounds on which source domains rely (Cienki & Müller, 2012). In other words, "gesture attests to the metaphor passing from (a) something concrete to (b) the physical representation of something abstract" (Calbris, 1990, p. 194). Thus, a gesture is a bodily expression of an idea or a feeling, and it is done to achieve a purpose or deliver information, which can be metaphorical. The intended meaning behind prayers is engraved in our minds and bodies, and it affects our physical and social worlds. Thus, mental images are relevant to sensorimotor activities, which coat activities like prayers with a phenomenological nature (Gibbs, 2006). Like prayer bridges two worlds, gestures are brief and fleeting and they substitute handling something (physically) with imaginatively doing so. Gesture is vital to understand language and is viewed "as a critical link between our conceptualizing capacities and our linguistic ability" (Armstrong et al., 1995, p. 27). Therefore, the role of the body as it prays is crucial, as prayer's postures and gestures are parts of their "corporal grammar" (FitzGerald, 2012, p. 77). Gestures are meaningful on their own, yet they accompany language to add further, non-redundant meaning to it (McNeill, 2008). Meaning is understood to

DOI: 10.4324/9781003301271-6

be the result of mental representations; thus, an expansion to include all modes of meaning-making including gesture is crucial.

Religion is rich with metaphors. In many religions, a metaphor of love that governs the relation between God and humans exists, a metaphor that ties both an ephemeral life and a permanent, perpetual existence. For instance, Christianity depicts God's relationship with humans as one based on love (Szelid, 2012). Metaphors are thus used to paint a picture of God, stretching to include many different roles or even abstract notions (Tracy, 1978). The examination of metaphors including God and religious aspects in general is enlightening. More examples include: God (or virtue) is up (Lakoff & Johnson, 1980), and God, and deities in general, are up due to their sovereignty (Kövecses, 2012), and God is a guide (Kövecses, 2005).

Therefore, metaphor assumes a crucial role in understanding many aspects of human life through examining more concrete and easy-to-fathom domains (Lakoff, 1993). Lakoff and Johnson (1980) emphasize that metaphor arises from mapping a concrete entity into an abstract one, in other words, it is "understanding and experiencing one kind of thing in terms of another" (Lakoff & Johnson, 1980, p. 5). They also demonstrate that our conceptual system uses metaphor to deal with all aspects of the world around us (Lakoff & Johnson, 1999). Hence, metaphors are essential to understand the abstract notions that religions address through evoking concrete entities that we come about in our lives (Charteris-Black, 2004). This familiarity metaphors bring can significantly contribute to understanding religious discourse and practices including prayer, which can be applied to Islam as a religion and as a culture because metaphors are essentially "a matter if thought and action, and only derivatively a matter of language" (Lakoff & Johnson, 1980, p. 153). When these abstract and concrete domains combine (Kövecses, 2010), this hybridity, according to (Forceville, 2016) can be examined in blending terms since they create a new blended space that share characteristics from both domains. This blending "is another basic mental operation, highly imaginative but crucial to even the simplest kinds of thought" (Fauconnier & Turner, 2002, p.18). The blend acquires "conceptual materials that are new with respect to both the source and the target" (Kövecses, 2005, p. 7).

Religion provides "a set of mental representations with particular contents that underlie religious contents that underlie religious behavior" (Downes, 2010, p. 14). These representations or spaces are created constantly, regardless of the type of discourse (Fauconnier & Turner, 1998), and are advanced through religious practices. Using journey as a source domain (Lakoff & Johnson, 1980) is also prominent in Islam. Since prophet Muhammad took the Night Journey from Mecca to Jerusalem and ascended from Jerusalem to heaven to learn the composition of prayer, prayer's significance in Islam is made clear (*The Qur'an*, 2008, 17:1). In Arabic, the word prayer is translated to *salat*, and the word connection/being connected is translated to *sila* or *itisal*. All three words come from the same morphological root; thus, Muslims believe that prayers are indeed a connection with Allah. This is manifest in the physical activities as well as the linguistic expressions they use during prayer. Prayer connects us in our world to the sacred, spiritual one. Thus, it bridges a chasm between these two different realms. Unlike other practices in Islam, prayers are done five times every day. Therefore, its impact is emphasized repeatedly. It is constructed based on rituals that are both verbal and gestural.

An Examination of Prayers in Islam: Metaphors in Gesture

This chapter aims to examine metaphor in many gestures in prayer in Islam. Drawing upon conceptual metaphors (Lakoff & Johnson, 1980) and the blends (Fauconnier & Turner, 2002) that result from physical and spiritual practice, I aim to underscore that gestures involved in different stages in prayer are metaphorical; hence, they can be better understood in terms of conceptual metaphor. The analysis delves into the metaphors infused in many aspects of prayer in Islam, including its call for prayers, different phases of preparation, and its stages until its completion. This chapter's objective is to make sense of conceptual metaphors arising from the rituals and practices Muslims do as they pray. I aim to gain a deeper understanding of the construction of prayer and its influence by examining metaphor in gestures in Muslim prayer. This chapter seeks to offer a better understanding of the complex, symbolic nature of prayer in Islam.

Azan

Azan is the Islamic call for prayers, and it takes place five times a day. In Arabic, the word has two meanings: the plural form of *ear* and *permission* (*Almaany Dictionary*, n.d.). Therefore, azan's purpose is to notify people of the time of prayers and to invite them to pray, and this notification is auditory. Furthermore, azan is built on a deviation or repetition of many words (Leech, 2008), like *Allah*, *come*, and *prayer*, and it includes parallel declarative structures, creating a certain linguistic rhythm of connection and disconnection; as a result, it is very prominent and notable for Muslims.

Azan is metaphorical since the word itself carries two meanings: ears and permission, as previously stated. Thus, it creates a scene in which hearing it gives people permission. In this HEARING IS PERMISSION metaphor, the source domain originates from the perceptual process of *hearing* and stems from the sensory domain of perceiving sounds with ears. The target domain of this metaphor is the domain of permission or being granted permission to carry out an act. Therefore, the act of hearing azan is mapped into the act of being granted permission to pray. This metaphor is engrained in the Muslim culture because prayers do not commence unless people are granted this permission materialized in azan. Hence, hearing the azan creates a blend in the shape of an auditory permission, one that constitutes a connection between hearing the call for a prayer that takes place during a sacred time and being able to start the prayer. Thus, the permission concept manifests in the form of hearing the azan.

This also leads to another metaphor or highlights the metaphorical nature of time. Similar to Kövecses's (2005) TIME IS A MOVING ENTITY, with the azan, Muslims are called for prayers when the time "enters" or comes. This relates to the metaphorical nature of time, which is conceptualized as a person who comes or enters, with a group of people always waiting. This metaphor of time as a person includes mappings between a source domain of people and a target domain of time. Time is perceived as a person who invites and encourages people to pray. The resulting blend is a boundedness and urgency that characterize the azan and the fleeting nature of the time that it evokes. Thus, when the azan starts, the time comes or enters, which highlights mappings that not only coat time with qualities of humans, but it also indicates that it enters a place. This evokes another conceptual metaphor, which is viewing time as entering a place or space in which we exist, physically. This blend has characteristics of presence and relevance because time is not an abstract, distant notion anymore; it is a physical presence in our lives. Thus, time actively engages with us in our environment. Thus, this new blend takes time out of its isolated nature and brings it to humans, spatially, in a certain location.

Since time is a person who calls for prayers, it is like an invitation to meet with Allah, which highlights the metaphor of PRAYER IS A MEETING. For Muslims to perform the five obligatory prayers, the times must "enter" (TIME IS A PERSON) and from a mosque (more specifically a minaret), and a Mu'adhdhin (the person who calls for prayers) must raise their voice to call for prayers.

Like reciting the Qur'an, which calls for a beautiful voice akin to singing, azan also requires a harmonious, clear voice to call for prayers elegantly and eloquently. Muslims can pray additional prayers at nearly anytime, but the *written* ones, meaning obligatory, have times that are strictly related to the sun. The word 'written' is also an interesting choice of word because writing rather than orality makes the order more commanding and difficult to change. In the case of the Muslim five prayers, they are unchangeable. The metaphor of prayer as a meeting can be identified here. This maps the source domain of azan into a target domain of a call for meeting. Also, since prayers are "written" in certain times, azan is therefore mapped into the target domain of meeting minutes that are documented, so they are not lost. This blend between these domains prompts people to pray once they hear the azan because they are called for a meeting with Allah.

According to the prophet Muhammad, the Mu'adhdhins have the longest necks (*Sahih Muslim*, hadith 0750). This is an example of metonymy because "necks" serve to actually mean status or reputation. The source domain of necks is mapped into the target domain of reputation because the word neck is a word related to someone's reputation and status (HIGH NECKS ARE A GREAT STATUS). A long neck means high honor, as Mu'adhdhins are the reason people learn about this cornerstone of Islam and are invited to pray. Thus, there is a mapping between the physical characteristics of a long neck and its meaning is society, which is honor. The longer the neck (physical domain), the more honorable (target domain) you are.

Mu'adhdhins also carry this important task in a specific place, a minaret. A minaret shares morphological roots with the word *noor* or light in Arabic. Thus, a minaret is a place that emits light. This is especially important because it equates azan with light. Consequently, in terms of Muslim architecture, a minaret is symbolic of azan. Like the structure of churches, which includes tall buildings to lead its people to heaven metonymically (Evola, 2010), minarets are built with the same purpose: to lead people to mosques, especially in the dark to pray (physically) and to guide them to Allah's path (metaphorically). Akin to Kövecses's (2005) God's way which is a straight path, the minaret stands as a marker to find this path. The minaret is also a meronym of a mosque, as it is a part that guides people and delivers them to the bigger part, which is the mosque, and draws a comparison between the physical path and a spiritual path. There is a mapping between guiding people through the physical dark and the metaphorical dark, which is not being able to follow the path of God. The minaret is therefore conceptualized as a guide that leads people out of the dark, in both a literal and metaphorical sense.

Wudu

Wudu is the Arabic word for ablutions necessary for prayers, and it is also synonymous with beauty and light. It is a practice that involves cleaning specific body parts with water, and it is an obligation before commencing prayers. Wudu is therefore both a physical and a metaphorical cleanser in terms of the resolution of sins. This maps the source domain of cleaning into the target domain of sins resolution. Thus, pouring water on certain parts of the body is like getting rid of sins that can be cleansed by gestures that coat them with physical qualities, which are qualities of dirt (SINS ARE DIRT). Sins/dirt slip from all these body parts and from under the nails. The source domain in this metaphor is dirt, pollution or just being dirty, which is mapped to a target domain of spiritual cleanness (or lack thereof). Since sins are dirt, people who make wudu are people who clean themselves from dirt, and the act of making wudu is the act of ridding oneself of dirt, both physically and spiritually.

Getting Dressed

Awra is an Arabic word for something that must be hidden or should not be seen. The word also shares morphological roots with words that mean losing an eye, to blind someone, or ugliness (Al-Saqaf, n.d.). Thus, awrah dictates fashion choices in the Muslim world in general, but it is also a fundamental aspect in prayer. Prophet Muhammad advised his followers not to pray in the nude, and they are also prohibited from wearing see-through clothes as they pray. The act of covering oneself with clothes therefore corresponds to the idea of being modest in order to perform rituals (COVERING IS MODESTY). It also reinforces the idea that uncovering brings upon the person shame; thus, modesty in prayers, and rituals in general, is encouraged.

The concept of awrah can be traced to an ancient metaphor, which is our descent to earth. Muslims, like other Abrahamic faiths followers, see Adam as the father of humans. Since they lived in Eden, Adam and Eve's bodies were not like ours; they were heavenly, with no awrah to cover until they sinned. As the devil convinced them to eat from the forbidden tree, they knew shame for the first time and started to cover up. In the Qur'an, the word awrah can be translated as *shame*, *private parts*, or *nakedness* (*The Qur'an*, 2008, 7:22). In many aspects of prayer, the metaphor of God is up (Meier & Robinson, 2004) and humans are down is reinforced (Evola, 2010). Muslims believe in a heavenly God, who does not possess human nature, thus, he has no awrah to cover. However, humans are earthly; after Adam descended, humans acquired a body that can be naked and shameful, and to communicate with Allah who is up, humans who are "down here" on earth must cover up. This evokes the metaphor of vertical orientation (Landau et al., 2014), in which Muslims too place God in a higher position and place him in heaven while the devil is believed to occupy the opposite spatial domain. Because up is likeable and down is not (Meier et al., 2007), there is more respect to God who is up and must not be met with awrah exposed.

Furthermore, in terms of clothes, Muslims are advised to wear something beautiful as in the Qur'an, Allah advices Muslims to take their "adornment" or put in their "beautiful apparel at every time of prayer" (*The Qur'an*, 2008, 7:31). This preparation in terms of clothes is metaphorical, and it indicates that the meeting between Allah and humans is important. There is a lot of thought put into the outfit worn, as if one were meeting royalty at an official engagement. Thus, there is a metaphor in prayer before the prayers even begin: GOD IS KING (Vaivadaitė-Kaidi, 2018); when meeting him, one should follow a certain dress code. Thus, prayers require covering of sensitive places using beautiful clothes. This metaphor blends the act of getting dressed with the mental preparation to enter a sacred place in which serenity and reverence exist, which links to the coming part of prayer that is being in Mecca by body or by direction.

Direction

Muslims direct their bodies, heads, and gaze towards a specific direction, often referred to within Islamic traditions as the *qibla*. This direction is a fundamental cornerstone of prayers; they are not correct without it. The body must be positioned towards Mecca; to be more precise a smaller entity, *Kaaba* (The Cube). The word *qibla* shares morphological roots with the words *face* and *opposite*. Thus, the word literally means to face or align your body with Kaaba. This metaphor is akin to LOVE IS A JOURNEY (Lakoff & Johnson, 1980; Kövecses, 2010) in which a person who prays/travels (Charteris-Black, 2004) wishes to see or meet a beloved. Hence, this prayer is a journey metaphor that makes use of the source domain of journey to help understand the relation of long commitment that takes a person to pray. Hence, a comparison between praying five times daily for a person's lifetime and a long journey emerges, as both require commitment and effort towards what they love.

The journey towards Kaaba is not necessarily physical; Muslims think of Kaaba and try to visualize it as they execute their prayers. An orientation metaphor takes place here, in which the source domain is orienting the body towards a certain place while the target domain is orienting the soul towards Allah. Thus, qibla is seen as a correct place to be in, not just physically but also spiritually. Following qibla has been and still is a significant aspect in prayers and in Islam in general, because, in prayers, Muslims are united in rituals, time, and place.

In many verses of the Quran, Kaaba is called God's *bayt* or house. This metaphor shows that a person who changes places to visit another, or in this case Allah, activates a guest/host metaphor (Wiliński, 2015). Having a direction or being directed towards a certain place is such a prominent metaphor (Kövecses, 2010), which Kaaba and qibla emphasize. Thus, this metaphor borrows qualities from the source domain of home, which is populated by a host, visitors, and a relationship between them. The target domain is populated with the cube or Kaaba, Allah, and Muslims. This domain is the spiritual, abstract one. A mapping between Kaaba as a house takes place, which results in the conceptual metaphor of Kaaba as the house of Allah. There are also qualities that are blended between those who visit a host and people who pray; they are both in an intimate relation with Allah/the host. This metaphor seems to shed light on the fact that Muslims are visitors of Kaaba, in the presence of Allah. Allah is also mapped into the host role, the house owner role, who is gracious and accepts his visitor at any time. Thus, prayers are ultimately seen as an invitation extended by Allah to people to visit Kaaba (or direct their bodies towards it) and pray. Thus, praying is like an act of accepting an extended invitation from Allah, the host, and the host's guests.

Takbeerat Al-ihram

The previous sections are preparations for the prayer, but *takbeerah* is prayer's first cornerstone or *rukn*. Takbeerah means Allah is greater (than anything). Alongside this utterance, Muslims gesture a wave using both hands next to the ears or shoulders. This gesture indicates that when a person prays, they throw the world behind their backs. This gesture is synonymous with the phrase Allahu Akbar. Together, they emphasize that nothing is more important than praying and meeting Allah at a specific time of the day. This embodied metaphor means that through the hand gesture, the world is left behind: as prayers start, the whole world fades and becomes insignificant. This is another expression of ALLAH IS KING metaphor because when a king asks for a meeting (another metaphor explored earlier in the chapter), it cannot be postponed as everything else is insignificant in comparison.

The word *ihram* comes from the word *haram* (forbidden). This means that a person who starts their prayer with this opening is forbidden to eat, drink, talk, or engage in anything else that is outside prayers' scope. This part of the prayer is called *inekad*, which has morphological roots with the word *akd* or contract, which means the metaphor prayer is a contract. Thus, the source domain is a CONTRACT, which makes the target domain of PRAYER more vivid: people who pray are people who abide by a contract they signed. Their contract is with Allah, which means that the actions taken in prayer are mapped into signing and accepting the contract.

Furthermore, during this takberah, Muslims take a firm stance, and this prayerful posture is linked to an emotional state of humility (Corwin & Brown, 2019). Since prayer starts in an upward position with the first word *Allah* (with the previously mentioned gesture), a metonymy arises with the gesture during takberah. According to Evola (2010), gestures have metonymic relationships and can be polysemic in nature. This stance that people take while they pray is what constitutes a source domain; this posture is a body stance to arrive at the target domain which is complete devotion. Thus, a mapping exists between a physical stance taken during prayers and an emotional state of humility and devotion. This upward position, linked with the utterance, signifies a belief that prayer is of paramount importance.

The Opening (Al fatiha)

Known in Islam as *Umm al-Qur'an* (mother of the Qur'an), the opening chapter is obligatory in prayer; it is significant because Allah participates in prayers just as the people praying do. According to prophetic hadith, Allah divides the prayer into two halves—one said by Muslims when we recite the opening chapter, and the other half done by Allah (*Sahih Muslim*, hadith 41). This is another manifestation of the metaphor PRAYER IS A MEETING. This metaphor stems from the source domain of dialogue (which takes place in a meeting) and a target domain that includes a conversation with a higher being. Thus, reading a Quranic chapter is imbued with qualities from the domain of communicating and conveying a message. As in a normal conversation, which includes two people, prayers also take place between humans and Allah. Ultimately, this is an expression of devotion and a desire to speak to Allah to find spiritual guidance. This creates a blend that gives direct access to a conversation/meeting with Allah through prayers.

Ruku and Sujud

Bowing and kneeling have existed long before Islam. Manifest in many civilizations like ancient Egypt (Massey, 2014), ancient Asian civilizations (Ebrey & Walthall, 2013), and Christianity (Webber, 2009). *Ruku* is a bowing posture, in which Muslims glorify Allah (*Sahih Muslim*, hadith 20). This posture, in which hands are placed on knees and the back is straight, revives the metaphor Allah is king, which means that humans are his subjects. The word *rakaa* (a single unit or cycle of prayer) and ruku share a morphological root, which means to bow; thus, this position is essential to fulfill prayer. Here, the source domain which is the physical act of lowering oneself is mapped into a target domain of submission and humility. Thus, humans engage with Allah/king to whom they show respect by kneeling to indicate respect and reverence to this higher status in a way comparable to a king. Kings are people who exist in our experiential world, so it may make sense to use them as a source domain to understand an aspect of the relation between Allah and humans.

This visual/gestural metaphor clearly signals a twofold message: the first is that Allah is great, and the second is humans are in respect and submission to him. With this gesture, people bend their knees to Allah. Kneeling stresses the closeness of humans to earthly domain and stresses the existence of Allah in a heavenly domain, which results in a contrast. There is a division between the act of kneeling which emphasizes humility and the utterance glory be to Allah the most magnificent (literally translated to the higher). Here, prayers are divided into two acts: one is verbal (glorifying God verbally), and one physical, bowing by getting closer to the earth (glorifying God gesturally). By using this gesture, Allah is emphasized to be sovereign and all powerful. Not only Allah is king metaphor is evident here, but also the metaphor of ALLAH IS UP and HUMANS ARE DOWN is shown even in the physical form of this bow.

After ruku, Muslims do another type of bowing. In this part of the prayer, *sujud* or full prostration takes place as the climax of a cycle of positions that include a combined sitting and kneeling position. Muslims here lie prostrate with different parts of their bodies like the forehead, nose, hands, feet, and the extremities of the feet (*Sahih Muslim*, hadith 260). In social interactions, people hold their heads and foreheads high, yet in prayers these body parts are put on the ground. This is a paradox in which the most dignified part of the body is close to the floor to become closer to Allah.

During sujud, the two metaphors remain consistent as with ruku—ALLAH IS KING and ALLAH IS UP and HUMANS ARE DOWN. It is not only the role of language to express submission, but it is also the body's role because "bowing or lying prostrate is a gesture of humility" (FitzGerald, 2012, p. 77). To unpack the first metaphor which is Allah is king and people are his subjects, we need to understand the source domain of monarchy, in which a king is greeted with a bow or a courtesy; from this, the target domain of humility and submission arises. Praying is an act of submission, and prostration is seen as the embodied expression of humility and submission to Allah. This metaphor can be extended to another one which is ALLAH IS UP and HUMANS ARE DOWN in which prostration as a body movement constitutes the source domain. This is mapped into the target domain of humility and submission to Allah. As Muslims orient their body downward, they emphasize that Allah's position is upward. This paradox orients humans in a downward spatial position while simultaneously emphasizing Allah's high status. This maps a dual relation of supremacy and submission, the first to Allah and the latter to humans. This spatial metaphor creates an image of hierarchy, in which Allah exists at the top. This metaphor highlights that spatial orientation can deliver information about power dynamics and convey a symbolic meaning through gestures in prayer. This metaphor is based on the proposition that bowing and kneeling in prayer are imbued with spiritual meaning that ultimately highlights Allah's supremacy and authority. Therefore, the body, using gestures, can deliver feelings of submission and humility.

Tashahhud and Tasleem

As prayers come to conclusion, Muslims do what is known as *tashahhud* (testifying) and *tasleem* (blessings). While reciting tashahhud, Muslims take a seated position, pointing the index finger of the right hand. According to Kita (2003), pointing "is a communicative body movement that projects a vector from a body part. This vector indicates a certain direction, location, or object" (p. 1). During tashahhud, Muslims point the index finger of their right hand, an act they do towards the direction of another absent entity, which is Satan. This index pointing is metaphorical because it aims at preventing Satan from approaching the person who is praying. The person praying wants to escape Satan's influence, which is a spiritual need since Muslims believe that Satan's influence is destructive. Thus, this gesture works as a physical manifestation of the constant need devout Muslims have to repel or discourage Satan from being near them. This blend creates a connection between the physical world taking the shape of a gesture, and the spiritual world in which this gesture is meant to warn Satan from coming near those who pray, and it also works to belittle him.

Tasleem is the last step, after which life is resumed. This word shares morphological roots with the word *salam*, which means peace. With a nod from the head and uttering the words *assalamualaikum* (peace be with you), prayers come to end; it is like saying goodbye. It makes sense that this meeting ends with a form of goodbye that concludes the prayer and ends the previously mentioned state of ihram that prayer requires. The metaphorical image can be drawn from the source domain of social interactions, in which people end a gathering or a meeting with farewell. This leads us to understand the target domain better, which is a meeting between Muslims and Allah. This illuminates the nature of prayer because it is a metaphor including a communicative act (a meeting) with Allah. Muslims believe in the existence of angels, especially when they are in sacred places or are doing good deeds. Shaking one's head to the left and right is considered an acknowledgement or a nod to these angels. This reinforces the metaphor identified earlier of

PRAYER IS A MEETING , but this meeting does not only include Allah and people but also angels. This metaphor mixes the dynamics of social relations, interactions, and farewells with the abstract nature of prayers. This imbues gestures in tasleem with metaphorical elements that emphasize that ending a prayer is akin to ending a meeting.

Implications and Future Directions

As Muslims embark on this journey of prayers, many metaphors arise, and they vary between verbal and gestural metaphors. Therefore, the overall aim of this chapter is to reveal the different manifestations of verbal and gestural metaphors that can shed light on the unique nature of prayer and its multisensory experience. This shows that the body, too, prays. This experience of prayers is akin to experiences we encounter in other fields of life; thus, metaphors in prayers stem from a source domain related to life as we experience it.

We understand abstract notions metaphorically; it is how humans' conceptual system works (Lakoff & Johnson, 1980), and these metaphors create blended spaces. Such blends are crucial to understanding discourse in general (Fauconnier & Turner, 2002), including prayers, which draw on our existing knowledge of the physical world. It is apparent that the source domains here vary in nature, including meetings, guides, cleansers, kings, guests and hosts, houses, and a spatial relationship using up and down. All these source domains are used to describe prayer, which intensifies its metaphorical makeup. Thus, a metaphor arises in prayer between the seen, known, or familiar realm and the unseen or the metaphysical one, which concoct a complicated blend. This is because the blend does not only contain abstract ideas or domains to understand in terms of concrete entities, but it also contains different new realities with intended meaning manifested verbally and gesturally in prayers.

As Lakoff & Johnson (1980) put it, we think in metaphorical ways, and we pray in metaphorical terms as well. As previously mentioned, gestures in prayers do not point towards objects existing immediately in the environment, but they refer to an absent or imagined entity, a being we believe in. Hence, a gesture reifies a mental image. Experience, from which we borrow many source domains is thus a core requirement for the creation of gestures, and it is vital in the process of interpretation of gestures because they act as a physical expression of devotion Muslim display towards Allah. Experience therefore dictates the source domains in these metaphors are used to understand the target domain as well as the new blends arising in prayer; as a result, prayer becomes more relatable. Furthermore, using different source domains creates a multifaceted picture, as different sensory information is used to understand the elements that make up prayer, which can enhance the spiritual experience people go through as they pray.

Prayer is embodied since we do not only perform prayer in our minds, or even just verbally; it takes many actions synchronized with our words to pray. This spiritual experience in prayer in Islam is holistic and requires work both physically and mentally. This mental labor is made possible by our conceptual system that is based on metaphor. Understanding a complex activity like prayer, with many of its abstract notions, is facilitated when examined through metaphor. This metaphoric thinking gives us the opportunity to channel our knowledge and experience in the physical world into the meaning behind the construction of prayer. Metaphor also deepens our understanding of the many layers that make up an embodied daily activity such as prayer.

Future research can stem from this one, research that can answer more questions about the nature of gesture in prayer, more specifically the origin of gesture in Islam, whether they are related to other Abrahamic religions and other ancient religions or not. While many studies have addressed metaphor is Islamic discourse, examination of metaphor and gesture is needed to understand complex theological concepts that can be more relatable if deconstructed in terms of metaphor. It is also important to delve into prayer in Islam in relation to cultural or gender-related variations. While prayer is supposed to be executed in the same manner for all Muslims, it is different from one person to another: consider for instance, a person embracing Islam as an adult, who does not speak Arabic and does not understand the gestures that are culturally specific. Future research could address the difference between men and women in prayer. In mosques, they pray in different quarters, and they have different awrahs, which can influence their experience and offer different metaphorical images.

Since this study is an examination of metaphor and gesture in prayer to offer a better understanding of it, an examination of worshipers' experience upon understanding its metaphorical construction can be helpful. It can attempt to answer questions such as: does prayer make more sense or is less complicated if we understand its metaphorical content? Can it be more spiritually rewarding if worshipers became aware with these metaphors? Can understanding metaphor in religious discourse make the experience of praying, and other rituals, more apprehensible? Furthermore, an examination of the social aspects of metaphor around worshipers themselves, not prayer, can be illuminating. For example, when someone is branded a worshiper, they are regarded highly in society and more likely to be accepted as husbands or friends by many Muslims. Unpacking these metaphors and tracing them to their origins in society can be valuable.

Further Reading

Charteris-Black, J. (2004). *Corpus Approaches to Critical Metaphor Analysis*. Springer.
Addressing metaphors across different genres, the book examines metaphors from many angles. The most relevant part to this chapter is part four: Metaphor and Religious Discourse. It offers a thorough consideration of source domains constituting many metaphors in the Holy Qur'an. This section also addresses the domains The Qur'an uses that are similar to other holy books.
Cienki, A., & Müller, C. (Eds.). (2008). *Metaphor and Gesture*. John Benjamins Publishing Company.
This volume is significant because it offers an insightful exploration of the intricate relation governing metaphor and gesture. It examines how they intertwine to offer meaning, which helps in understanding the embodied nature of metaphor.
Downes, W. (2010). *Language and Religion: A Journey into the Human Mind*. Cambridge University Press.
The book addresses abstract notions such as God and spiritual feelings. It focuses on how the metaphysical world of religion plays an important role in relation to both thought and action.
Musolff, A., & Zinken, J. (Eds.). (2009). *Metaphor and Discourse*. Palgrave Macmillan.
In this work, the contributors introduce an intersection of metaphor and discourse. This volume addresses how metaphor functions in public discourse, utilizing a cognitive linguistic approach. The book also highlights the role of the study of metaphor, which can enhance our understanding of language use and interpretation.
Chilton, P., & Kopytowska, M. (Eds.). (2018). *Religion, Language, and the Human Mind*. Oxford University Press.
This collection addresses the complex relation between religion and language, and it also highlights how they relate to cognition. It illuminates how metaphorical expressions influence our understanding of different religious concepts.

References

Almaany Dictionary. (n.d.). *Azan*. Retrieved 10 January 2023, from www.almaany.com/ar/dict/ar-ar/%D8%A2%D8%B0%D8%A7%D9%86/
Al-Saqaf. (n.d.). *Awrah*. dorar.net. Retrieved 15 January 15 2023, from https://dorar.net/feqhia/874
Armstrong, D.F., Stokoe, W.C., & Wilcox, S.E. (1995). *Gesture and the Nature of Language*. Cambridge University Press.
Calbris, G. (1990). *The Semiotics of French Gestures*. Indiana University Press.
Charteris-Black, J. (2004). *Corpus Approaches to Critical Metaphor Analysis*. Springer.

Cienki, A., & Müller, C. (2012). Metaphor, Gesture, and Thought. In Raymond W. Gibbs Jr. (Ed.), *The Cambridge Handbook of Metaphor and Thought*, 483–501. Cambridge University Press. https://doi.org/10.1017/CBO9780511816802.029

Corwin, A.I. & Brown, T.W. (2019). Emotion in the language of prayer. In *The Routledge Handbook of Language and Emotion*, 325–343. Routledge.

Downes, W. (2010). *Language and Religion: A Journey into the Human Mind*. Cambridge University Press.

Ebrey, P.B. & Walthall, A. (2013). *East Asia: A Cultural, Social, and Political History*. Cengage Learning.

Evola, V. (2010). A Multimodal Analysis of Individuals' Beliefs and Metaphors in Words, Gestures and Drawings. *Form, Meaning, and Body*, 41–60.

Fauconnier, G. & Turner, M. (1998). Conceptual Integration Networks. *Cognitive Science, 22*(2), 133–187. https://doi.org/10.1207/s15516709cog2202_1

Fauconnier, G. & Turner, M. (2002). *The Way We Think: Conceptual Blending And The Mind's Hidden Complexities*. Hachette UK.

FitzGerald, W. (2012). *Spiritual Modalities: Prayer as Rhetoric and Performance*. Penn State University Press.

Forceville, C. (2016). Conceptual metaphor theory, blending theory, and other cognitivist perspectives on comics. In N. Cohn (Ed.), *The visual narrative reader*, 89–114. Bloomsbury.

Gibbs, J. & Raymond W. (2006). *Embodiment and Cognitive Science*. Cambridge University Press. https://doi.org/10.1017/CBO9780511805844

Kita, S. (Ed.). (2003). *Pointing: Where Language, Culture, and Cognition Meet*. Psychology Press.

Kövecses, Z. (2005). *Metaphor in Culture: Universality and Variation*. Cambridge University Press.

Kövecses, Z. (2010). *Metaphor: A Practical Introduction*. Oxford University Press.

Kövecses, Z. (2012). *Emotion Concepts*. Springer Science & Business Media.

Kress, G.R. (2010). *Multimodality: A Social Semiotic Approach to Contemporary Communication*. Taylor & Francis.

Lakoff, G. (1993). The Contemporary Theory of Metaphor. In A. Ortony (Ed.), *Metaphor and Thought*, 202–251. Cambridge University Press.

Lakoff, G. & Johnson, M. (1980). *Metaphors We Live By*. University of Chicago Press.

Lakoff, G. & Johnson, M. (1999). *Philosophy in the flesh: The embodied mind and its challenge to western thought*. Basic Books.

Landau, M.J., Robinson, M.D., & Meier, B.P. (2014). *The Power of Metaphor: Examining Its Influence on Social Life*. American Psychological Association.

Leech, G. (2008). *Language in Literature: Style and Foregrounding*. Routledge.

Massey, G. (2014). *Ancient Egypt—Light of The World, 1*, Jazzybee Verlag.

McNeill, D. (2008). *Gesture and Thought*. University of Chicago Press.

Meier, B.P., Hauser, D.J., Robinson, M.D., Friesen, C.K., & Schjeldahl, K. (2007). What's "up" with God? Vertical space as a representation of the divine. *Journal of Personality and Social Psychology, 93*: 699–710. https://doi.org/10.1037/0022-3514.93.5.699

Meier, B.P. & Robinson, M.D. (2004). Why the Sunny Side Is Up: Associations Between Affect and Vertical Position. *Psychological Science, 15*(4), 243–247. https://doi.org/10.1111/j.0956-7976.2004.00659.x

The Qur'an (translated by M.A.S.A. Haleem) (Reissue edition). (2008). Oxford University Press.

Sahih Muslim (translated by S. Abdul Hamid). (1976). Peace Vision.

Szelid, V. (2012). Set Me as a Seal Upon Thine Heart: A Cognitive Linguistic Analysis of The Song of Songs. In S. Kleinke, Z. Kövecses, A. Musolff, & V. Szelid (Eds.), *Cognition and culture: The role of metaphor and metonymy*, 180–191. EÖTVÖS University Press.

Tracy, D. (1978). Metaphor and Religion: The Test Case of Christian Texts. *Critical Inquiry, 5*(1), 91–106. https://doi.org/10.1086/447974

Vaivadaitė-Kaidi, E. (2018). The Network of Conceptual Metaphors of GOD and JESUS in the Fourth Gospel. *Respectus Philologicus, 34*(39), 35–47. https://doi.org/10.15388/RESPECTUS.2018.34.39.03

Webber, R.E. (2009). *Worship Old and New*. Zondervan.

Wiliński, J. (2015). Metaphoconstructions: Combining metaphors and construction. *Studia Anglica Resoviensia, 12*: 91–108. https://doi.org/10.15584/sar.2015.12.9

6

RELIGIOUS MINORITY REPRESENTATIONS IN ARABIC LANGUAGE

Mohamed Hassan

Introduction and Background

There has been a recent growing interest in media, fiction, and pop cultural discourses by sociolinguistic research (Androutsopoulos 2010, Bell & Gibson, 2011, Jeffe et al., 2015, Stamou, 2014, 2018). Stamou (2014) highlights the difference between fiction as a mirror of sociolinguistic style and fiction as construction of sociolinguistic style and a reproduction of the larger language ideologies circulating in society. She adds that "the former conceptualized fictional discourse as being non-authentic, while the later focuses on the role of fictional discourse in actively shaping particular versions of language and the world, rather than reflecting the sociolinguistic reality 'out there'" (pp. 122–123). Stamou (2018) called this emerging field of study "sociolinguistics of fiction" and she proposed the concept of "fictionalization" as a case of "mediatization" that includes "all representational and editorial selections, devices and resources involved for the making of sociolinguistic diversity into fiction" (p. 2). She argued for employing style-centered/ constructionist sociolinguistic approaches to pivotal points from which to engage with social meanings constructed in fictional texts and the ideological consequences of such constructions. In this view, fictional discourse as mediated public discourse is analysed employing constructionist, micro-level methodological approaches in its own right, exploring how it shapes readers' understanding about certain social groups or identities and constructs aspects of social reality instead of passively reflecting sociolinguistic realities. Within critical discourse analysis (CDA), various analytical categories have developed for the representation of social groups and collective identities such as discursive strategies for the representation of the self and the other (Reisigl & Wodak, 2014) and the socio-semantic social actor analysis (Van Leeuwen 1996, 2008). The fictional data in the present analysis stresses the interactional nature of the construction of identities.

There has only been a small group of Coptic Egyptian novelists since the beginning of the novel genre in Egypt. One of the reasons of this scarcity was the preoccupation of Copts in general with the church-focused and the ecclesiastical discourse, compared to the general Egyptian discourse (Fayez, 2020). Although the analysed discourse is fictional, Lewis acknowledges that most of his characters in the two novels represent real people he actually knew, or represent personality traits of actual people who lived around him in Egypt (A Conversation with Shady Lewis, 2019). In the prologue of *A Brief History of Creation and East Cairo*, Lewis writes "These events

DOI: 10.4324/9781003301271-7

actually happened, or at least, they could have possibly happened. Places and their names are all real. What connects one event to the other, or to a specific place is my creation" (p. 9). Social actors as a discourse analytical category will be a useful tool in reading the text of the two novels as being embedded in the contexts of their production, distribution, and reception (Fairclough, 2003). The analysis will try to reflect on the political and cultural contexts of the query that Lewis has posed: "what it means to be a Copt in Egypt" (Abraham, 2021). The main character in the two interconnected novels is the same person in different phases of his life, and each novel foregrounds an actual, almost-forgotten tragic incident in Egypt's modern history.

The religious, linguistic, and social histories of Christians in Egypt, their relationships to different institutions like the state and the church, and their national identities as Egyptians are themes investigated in the two texts analysed in this chapter. The contact between old Egyptian languages, the Coptic and Arabic languages, represented significant stages in the history of Egyptian languages that extended for over six millennia. Unlike the earlier Egyptian scripts of Hieroglyphic and Hieratic that depended on pictograms or hieroglyphs, or Demotic that used a script with fewer symbols, Coptic had an exclusively phonetic-based character system. Its alphabet system comprised elements from the two scripts that were used in administering Egypt during the first century AD: Greek and Demotic (Takla, 2014). Christianity was introduced in Egypt in the mid-first century by St. Mark. Nearly a century and a half later, the mostly Hellenized Christians of Alexandria worked on developing a new script for Coptic that utilized characters from Greek in addition to a few Demotic characters to record the Egyptian language and to introduce Christianity to illiterate and poor Egyptians who did not know Greek. The language continued to gradually gain ground due to the rapid spread of Christianity in Egypt in the fourth and fifth centuries AD. Coptic then became a core value that represented the identity and culture of the Copts. Greek, however, was also still used among the educated and affluent Egyptians.

The history of Christianity in Egypt was the main factor in the development of the Coptic language from its first and second centuries roots, to the abandonment of its use as an everyday language in the twelfth century, to its domain transformation to a liturgical and ecclesiastical language that continues to the present day. In tracing the history of development of the Coptic language in Egypt, Takla (2014) divided this history into stages that start in the late second and third centuries when it was mainly used as a translational tool for Christian literature, such as the Scriptures. The Golden age extended from the early fourth century to AD 451. This age witnessed accelerated conversion to Christianity and a transformation of the language from a translation tool to a fully literary language. This was followed by an isolation age after the Council of Chalcedon (AD 451) where the Coptic Orthodox Church of Alexandria went through two centuries of isolation from both eastern and western churches. In the sixth and seventh centuries, Coptic became a sign of opposition to the Melkite Church, that is the Imperial, Byzantine, and Chalcedonian Church, especially during the oppression of the anti-Chalcedonians in this period (Rubenson, 1996).

The Arab conquest of Egypt was completed in AD 642. It brought with it a new religion and a new language, and they were here to stay. At that time, Coptic in its six major dialects was the vernacular language for most Egyptians and enjoyed a prestigious literary status. Greek and Coptic were the main languages of administration that remained largely staffed by non-Coptic Greek-speaking pro-Chalcedonians or Melkites (Farag, 2014). More than 60 years later, the situation historically changed during the rule of Abd al-Aziz ibn Marwan. In 705, Abd al-Aziz implemented an Arabization of administration edict issued by his brother, the Caliph Abd al-Malik ibn Marwan (685–705) (Mikhail, 2014). Christian elites in the administration thus started to learn Arabic to maintain their government positions. At the beginning of the transition to the Abbasid rule

(750–1258), Coptic continued to be used by the population and remained the only language of the Orthodox Church for at least three more centuries. Rubenson (1996) maintains that, compared with the transition from Syriac and Greek to Arabic among the Christians of Mesopotamia, Syria, and Palestine that happened within a century after the Arab conquest, the Copts in Egypt did not fully adopt the use of Arabic for almost 300 years.

The new era after the Arab conquest witnessed a simultaneous use of Arabic and Coptic in sep-arate domains of the population's life. A translation movement from Coptic to Arabic started in the tenth century but flourished from the eleventh to the thirteenth centuries during the Fatimids (969–1171) and the Ayyubids (1171–1250) rules. The first Christian to write exclusively in Arabic was Eutychius (*Said ibn Batriq*), the pro-Chalcedonian Patriarch of Alexandria (d. 940). In the tenth century, Bishop of Ashmunin, *Sawirus ibn al-Muqaffa* (d. 987) wrote exclusively in Arabic, which he mastered as a scribe before becoming a monk, inaugurating a new genre: Coptic Arabic Literature that produced Christian texts translated or authored by Copts (Mikhail, 2014).

Translations of the Bible from Coptic into Arabic started in the tenth century. In these translations, the Copts benefited from earlier Arabic translations of the Bible made by Melkites (from Greek), Syrians (from Syriac), and Egyptian Jews (from Hebrew). The most important work in this field is the Arabic translation of the four gospels by *al-As'ad inb al-Assal*. The unpublished critical transla-tion was made from Bohairic Coptic in 1253 (Moawad, 2014). Arabic started gradually being used in liturgical texts. This was done in two different ways: as a reference column translation, and as separate Arabic books. As Coptic was in decline as a means of communication, the church started to teach Arabic, with Coptic in the beginning of the twelfth century (Takla, 2014). By the fifteenth century towards the end of the Mamluks era (1250–1517), the volume of Coptic Arabic Literature significantly decreased—older texts continued to be copied, but original compositions almost stopped. Hanna (2018) discussed the cultural and the social dimensions of translating the Bible into Arabic within the wider context of Arabizing Christianity and Christianizing Arabic. Among the numerous translations of the Bible referred to in the introduction, Hanna (2018) examined the two translations of Assobawi (1300) and AlBustani-van Dyck (1865). The purpose of Assobawi's translation was making the Bible accessible in Arabic in Eastern Churches. In his efforts to make his translation close to the "sacred" rhetoric, he used Qur'anic language in terms of vocabulary, syntax and direct and indirect intertextuality with the Qur'an. According to Hanna, this translation ceased to be publicized and the conditions of a "sacred" Christian language were being reassessed (p. 35). The other translation, still available to the present day, was that of AlBustani-van Dyck (1865). It was supported by the Protestant missionaries in the Middle East, and it created its own linguistic domain away from the Quranic stylistic devices so that readers would treat it independ-ently. It contradicted some Catholic convictions and was used in Coptic Orthodox Churches in Egypt. Still, the religious and ideological stances and representations of the Christian minority in Egypt were always inseparable from linguistic choices. In 1921, William Willcocks—a British civil engineer who worked in Egypt—translated the New Testament into the Egyptian vernacular (*ammiyya*), specifically the Cairene urban variety. This translation rechanneled the conceptual-ization of the sacred language that was preserved for the standard Arabic variety (*fusha*) with its history and its Islamic heritage. Hanna (2019) maintains that the sociocultural contexts in which Willcocks's translation was produced, disseminated, received and finally muted raise a few questions about the translation of the Bible in the Arabic vernaculars (p. 369).

Finally, from a historical perspective, the Ottoman period (1517–1798) was one of modest recovery for Copts. Despite restrictions, Coptic community leaders were able to spearhead important artistic, literary, and cultural products through constructing and repairing religious sites, supporting religious manuscript reproduction and funding religious festivals as a way of maintaining Coptic identity (Armanios, 2014). Encounters with European missionaries in Egypt was more notable in the late eighteenth century. The period between 1798 witnessed some reforms and redefinitions of the idea of Egyptian citizenship, national unity, and identity. In 1855, Khedive Said abolished the *(jizyah)* tax that non-Muslims had to pay, for the first time since the beginning of Arab rule in the seventh century and, in 1857, drafted Copts into the Egyptian army, which was previously forbidden (Hanna, 2014). Sectarian relations took a different turn after the 1952 Revolution in Egypt. Nasser adopted the rhetoric of Arab nationalism and made the church the official representative of Coptic concerns.

To establish the broader meaning of the analysed texts, we need an approach that connects textual and intertextual contexts to institutional, historical, and sociopolitical contexts. The Discourse-Historical Approach (DHA) developed by Ruth Wodak and her colleagues in the Vienna School of Discourse Analysis (de Cillia, Reisigl & Wodak, 1999; Reisigl & Wodak, 2001; Reisigl & Wodak, 2014) can offer this connection as an interdisciplinary model or approach in CDA. CDA in general maintains that "the interrelations between the social and the linguistic aspects of the discourse are manifested in a framework that incorporates text, discourse context and social context" (Fairclough, 2010, p. 9). DHA mainly deals with critique, power, and ideology and integrates diverse theories and methods to try to understand and explain complex social issues like identity from a sociolinguistic viewpoint. The historical context in this approach plays an important role in engaging with texts as instances of language use that communicate a certain meaning. Historical here does not meant diachronic but studying texts in a specific historical moment in terms of their production, distribution, and reception (Wodak & Meyer, 2014). The texts are looked at as separate units that also require knowledge of the contexts of their production, distribution, and reception, and of other previous discourses that they refer to. This approach analyses the relationships between discursive construction of national sameness and the discursive construction of difference leading to political and social exclusion of specific out-groups (de Cillia, Reisigl & Wodak, 1999). Wodak (2014) suggested that discourses about nations and national identities depend on at least four types of discursive macro strategies: constructive strategies (aiming at the construction of national identities), preservatory and justificatory strategies (heading to the conservation and reproduction of national identities or narratives of identity), and transformative strategies (targeting the disseminating of national identities). Depending on the context, one aspect or more connected with these strategies in brought into prominence (p. 18).

As a mediator between the producer and recipient, the text and its context reveal patterns of power distribution. The analytical aim of DHA is to uncover how power relations are expressed through the text and how this text can influence recipients to reassess the power relations at play. The discourse of the two novels is understood as a textually mediated social action, doing ideological work by representing and constructing society and by reproducing unequal relations of power (Wodak, 2008). To analyse the conditions of discourse production, distribution, and reception and its wider sociopolitical formation, eclectic analytical methods can be employed. In the present analysis, the parameters of social actor representation, intertextuality, and interdiscursivity will be used to show how collective identities are communicated through the texts. Intertextuality means that texts are linked to other texts, both in the past and in the present, through explicit reference to a topic or main actor or by the transfer of one argument through different texts. Interdiscursivity signifies that discourses are linked to each other in various ways (Reisigl & Wodak, 2014, p. 90). Social actor representation (van Leeuwen 1996, 2008), on the other hand, is a contextual parameter that enables the analysis of out-group and in-group constructions and power relations between different actors in certain discursive and social contexts. The two novels selected for analysis in this chapter are based on actual events that happened in Egypt and that the author himself has lived growing up in Egypt. They are seen thus as representatives the discursive practice of exploring the collective identity of the Christian minority in Egypt and, in Reisigl and Wodak's words, as "a segment of social reality which constitutes a frame of discourse" (p. 90).

In *Ways of the Lord* (2018), the protagonist, Sherif, dives into the social and political history of Egypt through narrating his own personal story as an Egyptian Christian middle-class young man. What he and his family members went through portrays a picture of the complexities that a middle-class Christian family in Egypt goes through as they deal with the individuals around them, the Church and the state institutions. In *A Brief History of Creation and East Cairo* (2021), the narrator, also Sherif, recollects a day in his life when he was a child in the late 1980s during violent clashes between extremist Muslims and the riot police. As the child runs with his mother through the streets of their district, Ain Shams, to escape the violence, the reader is introduced to the complex connections between this level of violence and wider historical, societal, religious, psychological, and political implications. The linguistic features of a text selection from each novel will be analysed at the micro-level, and connections to the macro-level of discourse practice and social context will be discussed. Connections between language, ethnic and religious representations, and nationalism in search of identity will be linked to the relative powers of discourse participants and their social and institutional positions. In the two novels, Lewis achieved the link between the individual and the collective experiences through interdiscursivity or interweaving different historical, religious discourses into the text. This linguistic feature contextualized the characters' experience and shapes their roles within a wider picture.

The Discourse-Historic Approach is three dimensional: after (1) having identified the specific *contents* or *topics* of a specific discourse, (2) *discursive strategies* are investigated, then (3), *linguistic means* (as types) and the specific context-dependent *linguistic realizations* (as tokens) are examined (Reisigl & Wodak, 2014, p. 93). Because of space restrictions, a representative extract in which the main social actors interact with one another from each novel will be analysed to show how the Christian individual and collective identities are represented and negotiated critically in the two novels in a way that exposes the unequal distribution of power between the individual, the Church as an institution, and the state in modern Egypt. In this critical analysis, features at the textual level are interpreted in the context of the production, distribution, and reception of the two novels as a genre of expression, which are in turn further illuminated in terms of the wider social and historical context. The analysis explores the concept of identity through the eyes of the Christian protagonist, and discusses the relationship between language and identity, and language and religion.

Analysing Identity in Christian Minority Representations in Modern Egypt

Shady Lewis, the author of the two novels, is an Egyptian Christian novelist and journalist who currently lives in London. He studied engineering, psychology, and political science. His first novel, *Ways of the Lord* (2018) is set in Egypt in 2006. Lewis describes the novel as a work that traces the official procedures necessary for the young Christian, Sherif Muris Bolos, to obtain mandated approvals to marry his German fiancée. In the course of the journey to secure these approvals, the novel sheds light on the social history of the Copts in Egypt, their relation to the State, the Church, the ecclesiastical authorities, and their fellow Egyptians (*Oh Lord! How Amazing Your Ways are!*, 2018). The novel realistically historicizes the transformations in this complex network of relations from the post-Nasserist era right up to the Egyptian Revolution in 2011. Some of the events in the novel are set in the German capital, Berlin. This, in Lewis's words,

Adds another dimension in the novel where eastern religions minorities experience an ongoing identity crisis: their fellow citizens look at them as strangers who are closer to the Christian West, while this West treats them as easterners, or Muslims—one way or another.

(Oh Lord! How Amazing Your Ways are!, 2018)

Most of the events, however, are set in Cairo when the opposition movement *Kifaya* (Enough) was active during ex-president's Mubarak's tenure and when Egyptian riot police reportedly killed at least 20 Sudanese refugees in the government's attempt to evict the refugees from their protest camp in December 2005 (Reed, 2005).

In Egyptian law, a Coptic man should get his church to testify that he has not been married before to register his marriage. Priests would not issue this certificate had they not known the man personally. This was the case with Sherif who had no ties to any church. As an alternative that would enable him to register his civil marriage to his German fiancée, Esther, and to get this certificate, Sherif had to go through a series of confessional sessions for almost a year with Father Antonius, a priest in a Coptic Orthodox church that happened to be closest to Sherif's home. The analysed text from *Ways of the Lord* (pp. 106–108), translated from Arabic, is narrated in retrospect in 2017 by Sheirf in the first person. It describes one of the final conversations between him and Father Antonius whose job was to testify that Sherif is a good citizen of the Church and that the Church has no objections to his marriage. The main discourse topics in this text are: the historical baggage of injustices against his Christian family that troubles Sherif, the confusion Sherif suffers regarding his identity and sense of belonging in terms of Church denomination, the language he identifies with, and how he feels about the authority exercised by the Church and the State on him as an individual and on his fellow Christians.

The most prominent social actors in this text are Sherif, Egyptian Christians as a group, Father Antonius who represents the Church, the State, represented in the Ministry of Education, and of course, the reader or the recipient of the text. Four types of discursive strategies are salient in this text: nomination, predication, argumentation and perspectivization, and framing or discourse representation. Nomination is a discourse strategy that aims at the discursive construction of social actors. As a social actor, Sherif directly addresses the reader or the text receiver, envisaged here as any Egyptian. Thus, the focus is solely on addressing the reader in a direct storytelling mode. Sherif always refers to himself in the deictic "I." This nomination reference denotes personalization and individualization. The discursive qualifications attributed to Sherif as a social actor are predicated in a way that represents him as an unwilling participant in the conversation with the priest, "The stories I prepared to tell Father in my meeting with him this day were my own stories … I started to explain things to the old man after I reassured him that there was some truth in what he just said" (Lewis 2018, p. 106). Sherif is someone who feels historical injustices against his forefathers, and who is continuously struggling to tell his own story. In his search for his own identity, he began his own journey of self-education away from the Church. One of the main reasons he feels he does not belong to the Coptic Church community is language. He tells the priest: "I found the Masses here boring and repeated. I don't comprehend why we have to listen to hymns in a language that no one understands or speaks" (Lewis 2018, p. 110).

While the Church uses Coptic language liturgically as a marker of its identity, Sherif doesn't feel that the Coptic Church affiliation reflects his own identity. In terms of in-group identity practices, to him as an individual, issues related to language use, identity, and the relationship with religion were often convoluted. Sherif tries to convince the reader, in the course of narrating the accounts of his conversation with the priest, that he is motivated to be a devout Orthodox, but he feels alienated by the practices of the Church and the State. He positions his ideological perspective of not being able to belong to the Church institution in his statement: "I was convinced that God will accept [my prayers] from me in spite of not being a church goer" (Lewis 2018, p. 106). The address term the priest uses to speak to Sherif is "Chief Engineer" which is a colloquial Egyptian variation of "Engineer." This term of address is impersonalized and collectivized and formal. It indicates the distance between the participants and an attempt at honorification at the same time.

The second main social actor in the sample text is the Church priest. The nomination strategies Sherif uses to refer to him are "Father," "Father Antonius," "the man," and "the old man." According to van Leeuwen's social actor categorization (van Leeuwen, 2008), "Father" and Father Antonius" as a nomination strategy are membership categorization devices that indicate impersonalization, even with the name mentioned after the title. They also indicate collectivization, categorization, and functionalization, which in this instance are connected with the religious duties of the priest. "The man" and "the old man" are also impersonalized, collective categorization devices, but they add some identification and classification in their discursive construction of the priest as a social actor in the text and in the discourse. As a social actor representing the Church institution, the priest is characterized in the text as someone who is trying to help Sherif, but he is not sure he can accurately understand his dilemma: "He asked me to confirm his conclusions up to this point" (Lewis 2018, p. 107). He is also represented as someone who wants to protect and guard the method and practice of his church. As a social actor in this discourse, the priest, and the Church he represents, is presented as someone who is trying to help—a bureaucrat who is doing his job, but is unable to strike the right tone and is therefore unable to achieve his goals. The State is the third social actor in the text. It's referred to as "the government's religious education curriculum" and "the Ministry of Education" (Lewis 2018, p. 107). In terms of argumentation strategies, the text claims that the State cooperates with the Church in limiting sources of truth since it "only preached the lessons of the classic Orthodox faith and limited the only source of truth to the First Council of Nicaea (Lewis 2018, p. 107). Sherif positions himself here as invisible and ideologically oppressed by the State as a social actor. He is subject to religious education decision-making that does not give him the right to express himself as someone who is neither a Muslim nor Orthodox Christian.

The social action and social actor analysis here tells us much about the ideological position being taken by the text. Sherif's agency positions him as an individual. His relations with the Church and the State highlight the unequal power dynamics between these social actors. The nominations, attributions, and arguments articulated from Sherif's perspective in the text represent Sherif's futile attempts to define his own identity and sense of belonging in the middle of theological, linguistic, legal, and administrative hurdles. He experiences almost all Christian denominations in Egypt in search of his individual identity. The language factor is a primary issue for him as he states: "In the small Evangelical Church, the sermons were given in a language I understand—in standard Arabic which was magical in my ears, exactly like the language of the holy books" (Lewis, 2018, p. 110). At home, his in-group membership is also a challenge due to the different attitude that his non-religious father had towards Arabic language. Sherif adds: "My father, who openly resented everything eastern, totally prohibited any Arabic books in our house. He only allowed translated books of western literature and history books" (Lewis 2018, p. 111).

Religion remains a crucial aspect of everyday social, political, and cultural lives of Egyptians. The discourses of religious affiliations in Egypt are very strong; even if some people do not practice rituals, they still identify in terms of religion and the values that Arabic and Coptic languages represent in this domain. Eventually, Sherif does not end up marrying Esther. Traumatized by the riot police's killing of the Sudanese refugees that she used to work with as a UN representative,

Esther leaves Egypt after she and Sherif break up. Sherif finally ends his relations with any activists and succumbs to the powers of the Church and the State. He marries a girl recommended to him by the Church and faithfully works to serve the Coptic Orthodox Church. As he tells his story of how he "came back" to the Church to random Church visitors, "they nodded—in pity, or in admiration and muttered: 'how miraculous the ways of the Lord are'" (Lewis, 2018, p. 191).

The second text, translated from Arabic, is excerpted from Lewis's novel *A Brief History of Creation and East Cairo* (2021), the setting of which is Ain Shams, a densely populated old district in east Cairo that witnessed violent clashes between the police, radical Islamist groups, and Copts in the late 1980s. The narration traces a short journey of a Christian child and his mother in 1980s' Cairo across this district against the backdrop of violence that shook Cairo and Egypt to the core at that time. The act of walking through the streets of Ain Shams interacts with the representational time and place for the mother and child as they continually try to resist, or cope with, different layers of violence. Lewis recounts that the memory he was left with after witnessing these violent events in his childhood was "a mixture of feelings of intimidation and liberation of the outside world at the same time" (*A Brief History of Creation and East Cairo*, 2021).

Implicit and explicit violence is one of the major themes in the novel. It exposes levels of psychological and institutional violence in family relationships, childhood interactions, and educational and social welfare institutions, all of which operate within larger and more direct spheres of violence created by religious groups or by the government. To the outsider, Sherif, his mother, and his father live a deceptively quiet and uneventful life as a middle-class Coptic family, while, they are continuously struggling with different forms of violence and oppression that impacts every aspect of their lives. In an interview with Lewis about Coptic identity, Church–State relations, and citizenship, he states that

> *A Brief History of Creation and East Cairo* aims to establish a parallel between Genesis and the history of language. I move to the Bible and its different translations, followed by the divisions that happened within the church because of the different interpretations of the Bible.
>
> (Abraham, 2021)

There are two main topics in the analysed text from the novel (Lewis, 2021, pp. 83–85): Sherif's reflections on the real meaning of words and the relevant teachings of the Church, and the historical and social roles languages and translations play in our lives.

As a social actor, Sherif speaks in the first person. He delves deep into how we think about language as a religious and a social construct and how we as human beings are shaped by it. He is represented personally and individually as a child fleeing a bombing in his neighborhood church as he and his mother seek shelter there. After his mother is beaten by his father, she decides to leave the house with her son Sherif, with nowhere to go. Sherif is also represented collectively as a member of the bigger Christian group with his invocations of verses from the Bible about the nature of the "word" and language in general. As a social actor, Sherif's identification is highlighted through classification as a Christian or through "belonging to an organization" (van Leeuwen, 2008, p. 24). Through the interplay between Sherif's representational strategies in the text as an individual and as a member of the Christian community, his ideas about language are foregrounded.

The other prominent social actor in the text is language itself as an entity. Functionalization would be the category that best describes language as a social actor in this text with the representation denoting what language does—its activity or role in the life of Sherif as an individual and as a Copt who is trying to make sense of the Church's teachings as it relates to language. In terms of its nomination strategies and discursive construction as a social actor, language is referred to as "the Word", "words", "languages", and "language" (Lewis, 2021, pp. 83–85). The predication devices used to refer to language as a social actor include tropes like "the mirrors of language can break," "they weaponized words," and verbs and nouns used to denote processes, actions and relational qualities: "Words now have their own bodies" and "The words were also preserved by reciting revelations over and over again" (Lewis, 2021, pp. 83–85). A prominent linguistic feature of this text according to the DHA method is the discursive qualification of language as a social actor. Examples of the explicit predication of language in the text are: "salvation is reverting to the original meaning of words," "this is what Genesis said: In the Beginning, was the Word," "the Word was God the Logos," "They have hands and legs punctured by nails and a loin stabbed with a spear," "Words have eyes that get tired and sleepy, that feel hunger and pain like us, but they never lie," "The holy among words are as sharp as knives' blades" (Lewis, 2021, pp. 83–85). Language here is represented as a religious vehicle to understand the divine and the holy—an entity that has a life of its own with almost all human qualities except they are more honest, an innate human quality that enables people to express themselves through words; a distortion by humans who changed its nature; something that may lose meaning when translated from one language to the other; a mirror reflecting the world; and as words, especially holy words, that can be manipulated and even weaponized to lead to violence.

Intertextual and interdiscursive relationships are prominent features in this text. Intertextual relations "can be established in different ways: through continued reference to a topic or main actors; through reference to the same events; or by the transfer of main arguments from one text in to the next" (Wodak & Krzyzanowski, 2008, p. 205). Biblical verses incorporated in the text, mostly without quotation marks or reported speech inverted commas, are weaved into Sherif's utterances in a way that presents extra-linguistic sociological variables. The history of the Church as an organization and the role of language as a social product are intertwined with Sherif's personal narrative in his journey across the neighborhood with his mother. Intertextual connections in the analysed text are mostly established through direct reference to Biblical verses and references like "The Word became flesh and made his dwelling among us" and "those words that the Lord gave to Moses on Mount Sinai, the two tablets of the testimony, tablets of stone, written with the finger of God" (Lewis, 2021, p. 4), and also through tracing the history of humans with language. The text invites the reader to think about the notion of language starting from Adam, the Babel Tower, human attempts to record what they feel and mean throughout the ages from writing on clay tablets to writing in jail cells. This type of historical analysis and interdisciplinary orientation is among the strengths of the DHA. The Biblical quotations are de- and re-contextualized, i.e., newly framed (Reisigl & Wodak, 2014). They refer the reader to new meanings at the level of text, genre, and discourse related to the context of the novel, rather than the original biblical references.

The interdiscursivity of a text is part of its intertextuality. Interdiscursive analysis has the crucial effect of constituting connections between linguistic analyses and relevant forms of social analysis (Fairclough, 1992). Sherif's narrative about the fleeing journey with his mother as a child through Ain Shams district and neighboring districts in Cairo continuously signifies larger geographical and historical biblical references. Sherif, the narrator in both novels, tells us his story in two simultaneous voices: as a child with very limited comprehensibility of what is going on around him, and as an adult reconstructing what he experienced as a child and who is still struggling to contextualize his experience with the larger sacred and the secular histories for Christians in Egypt. The text becomes interdiscursively complex in grounding this personal feeling of confusion and oppression in the recontextualized discourses of Bible teachings and Bible translations into Arabic as part of the history of linguistic and religious disputes: "One word, sometimes one letter of that word, a period or a punctuation mark would draw a line between life and death. The divine and the human … the 'and' between the two was the cause for horrible massacres" (Lewis, 2021, p. 85).

The models of individual and collective Christian and Egyptian identities represented in the two sample texts and the role language plays in the formation of these identities reflect the internal struggles of Sherif as a non-religious Christian in Egypt. In its own way, Sherif's unhappy state of mind expresses the struggle of the Copts in general within the Coptic community and within the hegemonic spheres of the Church–State relations. The title of the second novel, *A Brief History of Creation and East Cairo*, clearly, and ironically, establishes the interconnectedness between Sherif's identity crisis and the complex religious, social, and linguistic histories that led to this crisis. The reader is challenged to continuously reflect on the relation between the history of creation and East Cairo. The CDA vision and the DHA and social actor representation approaches applied to this text offered language-centered tools that may help the reader delve deeper into the ideological role of fictional discourse in the construction of individual and collective identities and representations of social groups. The collective Christian identity that Sherif reflects in the novels is a mixture of three factors. The first is feeling historically and socially oppressed as a member of the Christian community, which becomes clear through his own family history in the two novels that offer numerous examples of this suffering. The second factor is the national feeling that he shared with every Egyptian when he engaged in leftist political opposition groups in *Ways of the Lord*. In these moments, his identity as Egyptian was in the foreground. The third factor is Sherif's non-religious nature. He experimented with Protestant, Catholic, and Orthodox churches, but chose not to follow any church and his desire was to abide by civil, not religious laws. The laws of the land in Egypt forced him to adopt a stance he did not identify with and to go through the Church system to be able to register his marriage. There was no easy answer for Sherif as to how to position his religious Coptic identity withing the cultural Egyptian context. Both his in-group and out-group identities were negative and blurred.

The idea of "what it means to be a Copt in Egypt" has been linked to language in the two novels. Since identity is composed of a combination of religion and language working in tandem with each other, how language was used to represent religions and cultures was a consistent topic in the two novels. The Discourse-Historical approach enabled the analysis of the text from the language perspective. Lewis stated that in *A Brief History of Creation and East Cairo*, he examined language as a "hegemonic structure and as a tool for oppression, submission, isolation, hiding, division, or escape" (Books: Shady Lewis: A Brief History of Creation and East Cairo, 2021). One of the historical contexts that were used in the novel to approach this type of representation was the history of the Protestant Church in Egypt and the Protestant translations of the Bible into Arabic, which, in Lewis's opinion "shaped the way Copts speak" (Abraham, 2021). The two novels discuss the contexts of how the Christian minority in Egypt expressed their identity and attitudes to the Arabic Language in its two varieties—standard Arabic (*fusha*) and the Egyptian vernacular (*ammiyya*). The relationship between Arabic and Coptic: the domains, functions, spaces, participants, and the cultural values of each language is in constant play in the two novels. Suleiman (2003) argues that both the Arabic language and the religion of Islam are identity markers uniting people in the Arab World, despite their political and social differences. Hence, whenever religious differences occurred, the common language was used to bond the people, and, where there was a difference in language, Islam was used as a marker of identity. By the beginning of the *nahḍa*, or Arabic literary revival during the second half of the nineteenth century and the early twentieth century, there was a common field of literary productions in Arabic for Muslims, Jews, and Christians. With the ascendance of nationalist movements in the Arab World in the twentieth century, nationalists tended to increasingly endorse the role of Arabic as a unifying factor in Arab secular identity. As Bassiouney (2014) explained, the nationalists refused to accept the equivalence between the religious and national identities, as they considered the Arab national identity to be an ethno-cultural one encompassing both Muslim and Christian Arabs.

Implications and Future Directions

This section shows the mutual impact of religion and language through the critical linguistic analysis of two fictional works that are based on true events in Cairo, Egypt in the 1980s. The two works focus on the government and the Church's authority over Egypt's Christians. The ideas of the embedded Islamic religious and civilizational identity in the Arabic language and how this affects the national and religious identity of the Christian minority to the Arabic language in Egypt are at the forefront in the two works. The diaglossic environment of the Arabic language and the interaction of religious-based social and linguistic style shifting with social dynamics as the interference of Western thought, Arab nationalism and religious conservatism is an area that needs further research, especially with the political and national complexities that surround this issue in the Arabic-speaking world. In his comparison of the context and function of Christian Arabic with that of Christian Greek and Latin, Versteegh (2017) confirms that in contemporary sociolinguistic research, religion as a correlate to linguistic variation has received less attention than the four main variables: class, age, gender, and ethnicity. He confirms that the connection between denomination and language attitude is undeniable, and that the resulting language choice may serve as an identity marker. Stressing that analysing linguistic choices in written texts is different from the ones in speaking, Versteegh argues that historically, the variety of Arabic spoken by minorities may have functioned as communal dialect. In writing, he adds, Christians and Jews had more flexibility in their adherence to the strict rules of standard Arabic than Muslims, who leaned more towards the strict rules of the standard Arabic because of the prestige of the Qur'anic text.

In modern Egypt, however, Bassiouney (2014) asserts that the official view is that there is no linguistic difference between Muslims and Copts apart from specifically religious terms since they share the same linguistic practices and they have equal access to linguistic resources: "In Egypt, public discourse tackles the thorny issue of religious differences by using two strategies: foregrounding and backgrounding" (p. 183). While religion as a belief system is foregrounded as a concept that all Egyptian share, religious differences between Christians and Muslims in Egypt are backgrounded as trivial and not determinant in identity formation (ibid.). Germanos and Miller (2015) presented valuable findings and debates around the issue of language variation and religious affiliation in spoken Arabic vernaculars. They concluded that "religious affiliation participates in the construction of social boundaries, but its role varies according to each specific context and the evaluation of its sociolinguistic impact needs very careful investigation" (p. 96). They added that religious affiliation alone is not and has not been a key factor of major linguistic differentiation in the Middle East and North Africa region; it is always linked with other social factors. Sociolinguistic analysis that is based on micro and macro analyses of discursive practices can be extended to investigating more boundaries between the religious-defined language discourses and cultures, which may, in turn further stress the value of interreligious research from a sociolinguistic viewpoint.

More sociolinguistic studies in the intersectionality between religious affiliation and Arabic linguistic variation as a component of group identity are needed. There are currently few studies of how religious affiliation plays a role in the variation of linguistic production and in citizenship and national feeling in the Arab world. Future directions in investigating the network of relationships between language and religion in the Arabic language contexts may further research different Arabic texts written by Egyptian Christians from the seventh century to the present to analyse how language users historically indexed their varied identities and how their linguistic strategies changed, or not, over time due to various mediating social, demographic, political, or historical factors. Another area worthy of more research is investigating which mediating factor(s) had more noticeable influence on language variation and identity expressions than others along religious lines. This research could analyse language ideologies within the linguistic practices of different religious groups.

As the central notions of Christianity were translated into Arabic for centuries, Arabic theological and philosophical domains of the language were created. Christian writers were less constrained by the norms of Classical Arabic as Muslims in Middle Arabic texts. They had choices in expressing themselves in forms of Arabic that are not directly linked to Islam. The history of Bible translations into different varieties of Arabic and the identity politics associated with these translations and their influence on subsequent religion-based texts is another case in point, especially with newer translations that used media other than print, including audiovisual and social media which invites a multimodal analysis framework. Another area that is worth more investigation in this field is the process of replacing Coptic with Arabic in Egypt over almost five centuries and its sociolinguistic context compared to similar contexts in the Arabic world like Syria and Iraq. Studies of the Copto-Arabic literature, the Coptic-Arabic language contact, language shift, and language maintenance will offer insights into a broader historical and political context of the various ways Christian identity has been discursively constructed and represented in more texts. Finally, the results of such analytical efforts and their educational recontextualization may lead to more conversations in public spheres in Egypt about citizenship and identity.

Further Reading

Al-Wer, E., Horesh, U., Herin, B., & Fanis, M. (2015). How Arabic Regional Features Become Sectarian Features. Jordan as a Case Study. *Zeitschrift für Arabische Linguistik* 62: 68–87.
This study focuses on the role that religion plays in sociolinguistic stratification in Jordan. It provides information about the stages of the emergence of religious affiliation as a sociolinguistic variable. It also sheds light on the underlying causes of sociolinguistic re-stratification in line with sociopolitical and demographic change.

Blanc, H. (1964). *Communal dialects in Baghdad*. Harvard University Press.
This is one of the first comprehensive studies to focus on religion-differentiated varieties of Arabic. In this study, Blanc compares three Baghdadi varieties: Muslim Baghdadi, Christian Baghdadi, and Jewish Baghdadi in terms of phonology, morphology, syntax, and lexicon.

Hary, B. & Wein, M. J. (2013). Religiolinguistics: On Jewish, Christian–and Muslim-defined Languages. *International Journal of the Sociology of Language*, 220: 85–108.
This study investigates the impact of religion on language. It offers a model of Jewish-defined religiolects, or linguistic varieties analysed for their religious characteristics. It extends and applies this prototype to other religious settings like Christian–and Muslim-defined languages.

Holes, C. (2016). *Dialect, culture and Society in Eastern Arabia*, 3, *Phonology, morphology, syntax, style*. Brill.
This book is the third of three volumes that present an overview of Clive Holes's research on dialect, culture, and society in eastern Arabia. It extensively deals with linguistic variation in phonology, morphology, syntax, and style in eastern Arabia.

Miller, C. (2007). Arabic urban vernaculars: development and changes. In Miller, C., Caubet, D., Watson, J.C.E., & Al Wer, E. (Eds.), *Arabic in the City. Issues in Dialect Contact and Language Variation* (Routledge Arabic Linguistics Series 5), 1–30. Routledge,

This study analyses some key aspects of Arabic urban linguistics. It discusses the status of urban vernacular Arabic versus national vernacular and points to the problematic use of the concepts of standardization, prestige, and norms in the Arabic setting. It summarizes the main socio-economic characteristics of twentieth century urbanization trends in the Middle East and the various linguistic impacts of this population renewal.

References

A Conversation with Shady Lewis. (2019, 12 September). AlArabi A Jadid. Retrieved 5 May 2023, from www.alaraby.co.uk

Abraham, N. (2021, November). *Egyptian Novelist Shady Lewis on Coptic Identity, Church-State Relations, and Citizenship. Arablit & Arablit Quarterly: A magazine of Arabic literature in translation.* https://arablit.org/2021/12/07/egyptian-novelist-shady-lewis-on-coptic-identity-church-state-relations-and-citizenship/

Androutsopoulos, J. (2010). The study of language and space in media discourse. In Auer, P., Schmidt, J.E. (Eds.), *Language and Space: An International Handbook of Linguistic Variation*, 740–759. De Gruyter.

Armanios, F. (2014). The Ottoman Period (1517–1798). In Lois M. Farag (Ed.), *The Coptic Christian Heritage: History, Faith and Culture*, 54–70. Routledge.

Bassiouney, R. (2014). *Language and Identity in Modern Egypt*. Edinburgh University Press.

Bell, A. & Gibson, A. (2011). Staging language: An introduction to the sociolinguistics of performance. *Journal of Sociolinguistics 15*(5), 555–572.

de Cillia, R. & Wodak, R. (1999). The discursive construction of national identities. *Discourse & Society*, *10*(2), 149–173.

Fairclough, N. (1992). *Discourse and Social Change*. Polity Press.

Fairclough, N. (2003) *Analysing Discourse: Textual analysis for social research*. Routledge.

Fairclough, N. (2010) *Critical Discourse Analysis: The Critical Study of Language*, 2nd edition. Routledge.

Farag, L. M. (2014). The Early Christian Period (42–642): The Spread and Defense of the Christian Faith under Roman Rule. In Lois M. Farag (Ed.), *The Coptic Christian Heritage: History, Faith and Culture*, 23–38. Routledge.

Fayez, V. (2020). *Ways of the Lord*. The Copts are United. www.copts-united.com/Article.php?I=4156&A=586636

Germanson, M-A. & Miller, C. (2015). Is religious affiliation a key factor of language variation in Arabic speaking countries? *Language and Communication 42*: 86–98.

Hanna, S. (2018). إنتاج المعرفة وتشكيل الهوية في ترجمتين للكتاب المقدس إلى العربية / Knowledge Production and Identity Formation in Two Arabic Translations of the Bible. *Alif: Journal of Comparative Poetics*, *38*: 11–45. www.jstor.org/stable/26496384

Hanna, S. (2019). When Jesus speaks colloquial Egyptian Arabic: an incarnational understanding of translation, *Religion*, *49*(3), 364–387.

Jaffe, A., Koven, M., Perrino, S., & Vigouroux, C.B. (Eds.). (2015). Heteroglossia and performance. *Language Society* (Special issue). *44*(2).

Lewis, Shady. (2018). *Oh Lord! How Amazing your Ways are!* [Editorial, 14 November]. Qantara.de. Retrieved 5 May 2023 from https://ar.qantara.de/content/

Lewis, S. (2018). *Turuq Al Rab (Ways of the Lord)*. AlKotob Khan.

Lewis, S. (2021). *Tarikh Mugaz Lilkhaliqah wa Sharq Al Qahira (A Brief History of Creation and East Cairo)*. Dar AlAian. Editorial at Jadaliyya, 1 June 2021. www.jadaliyya.com/Details/

Mikhail, M. (2014). The Early Islamic Period (641–1517): From the Arab Conquest through Mamluk Rule. In L. M. Farag (Ed.), *The Coptic Christian Heritage: History, Faith and Culture*, 39–53. Routledge.

Moawad, S. (2014). Coptic Arabic Literature: When Arabic became the Language of Saints. In L. M. Farag (Ed.), *The Coptic Christian Heritage: History, Faith and Culture*, 224–236. Routledge.

Reed, B. (2005). 20 killed as Egyptian police evict Sudanese protesters. *The Guardian US*. www.theguardian.com/world/2005/dec/31/sudan.brianwhitaker

Reisigl, M., & Wodak, R. (2001). *Discourse and discrimination: Rhetorics of racism and antisemitism*. Routledge.

Reisigl, M., & Wodak, R. (2014). The discourse historical approach (DHA). In R. Wodak & M. Meyer (Eds.), *Methods of Critical Discourse Analysis*, 2nd edition, 87–121. SAGE Publishing.

Rubenson, S. (1996). The Transition from Coptic to Arabic. *Égypte/Monde arabe*, *27–28*: 77–92. DOI: https://doi.org/10.4000/ema.1920

Stamou, A.G.,(2014). A literature review on the mediation of sociolinguistic style in television and cinematic fiction: sustaining the ideology of authenticity. *Langlit*, *23*(2), 118–140. http://dx.doi.org/10.1177/0963947013519551.

Stamou, A.G. (2018). Synthesizing critical discourse analysis with language ideologies: The example of fictional discourse. *Discourse, Context & Media*, *23*: 80–89.

Suleiman, Y. (2003). *The Arabic Language and National Identity*. Edinburgh University Press.

Takla, H. (2014). The Coptic Language: The link to Ancient Egyptian. In Lois M. Farag (Ed.), *The Coptic Christian Heritage: History, Faith and Culture*, 179–194. Routledge.

Van Leeuwen, T., (1996). The representation of social actors. In C. Caldas-Coulthard & M. Coulthard, *Texts and practices: Readings in critical discourse analysis*, 32–70. Routledge.

Van Leeuwen, T. (2008). *Discourse and Practice: New Tools for Critical Discourse Analysis.* Oxford Studies in Sociolinguistics. Oxford University Press.

Versteegh, K. (2017). Religion as a Linguistic Variable in Christian Greek, Latin, and Arabic. In Nora S. Eggen & Rana Issa, *Philologists in the World: A Festschrift in Honour of Gunvor Mejdell*, 57–88. Novus Press.

Wodak, R. (2008). Discourse studies: important concepts and terms. In R. Wodak & M. Krzyżanowski (Eds.), *Qualitative Discourse Analysis in the Social Sciences*, 1–29. Palgrave.

Wodak, R. & Krzyżanowski, M. (Eds). (2008). *Qualitative Discourse Analysis in the Social Sciences*. Palgrave.

Wodak, R. & Meyer, M. (2014). Critical discourse studies: history, agenda, theory and methodology. In R. Wodak & M. Meyer (Eds.), *Methods of Critical Discourse Analysis*, 2nd edition, 1–33.

Wodak, R., Galasińska, A., de Cillia, R., Reisigl, M., & Liebhart, K. (2010). The Discursive Construction of National Identity. Translation by Angelika Hirsch, R. Mitten, & J.W. Unger. *Applied Linguistics*, *31*(1), 166–168. https://doi.org/10.1093/applin/amp052

7

PRAGMATIC FUNCTIONS
OF RELIGIOUS EXPRESSIONS

Marwan Jarrah and Sharif Alghazo

Introduction and Background

Pragmatic and discourse manifestations and uses of religious expressions (i.e., expressions that refer to religious entities such as God, The Prophet, Devil, or one of their conventional descriptions or affiliates) have attracted the attention of many researchers (Wharry, 2003; Ingold, 2014; Malmström, 2015). According to Verdonik and Kačič (2012, p. 267), religious expressions "function as a special group of pragmatic expressions, such as discourse markers, interjections, topic orientation markers, pragmatic deictics, general extenders, etc." Such expressions can also be used to express the speaker's inner state of feeling or emotion at the moment of speaking towards either the content of the conversation or the context (conversational situation) (Verdonik & Kačič, 2012; see also Rajan & Vaz, 2018). Therefore, they are multi-purpose expressions whose semantic meanings are pragmatically overridden by their dynamic conversational and salient contextual contributions.

This multi-functionality of religious expressions is in fact a commonplace observation in Arabic and Muslim discourse (Nazzal, 2005; Susanto, 2006; Clift & Helani 2010). Morrow (2006, p. 45) notes that "the Arabic language is saturated with a rich variety of expressions invoking Allah explicitly or implicitly … an Arabic speaker could scarcely conceive of a conversation where the name of God would not appear" (see also Piamenta, 1979 and Wikan, 1996 for discussions of the preponderance of religious expressions in Arabic discourse). Religious markers are hence productively deployed in a multitude of ways in explaining speaker meaning. Johns (1985) discussed evidence that the common religious marker *ʔinʃaːllah*, 'if God permits' in Arabic and Indonesian contexts, is mainly used when the speaker does not make a commitment, especially when they are not interested in the hearer's request or invitation. Johns (1985) proposes that *ʔinʃaːllah* is also used to avoid offending a hearer's feelings. Nazzal (2005) mentions that *ʔinʃaːllah* mitigates the speaker's rejection. This is expected as people in Arabic and Islamic cultures may feel awkward about saying 'no' to express disagreement. This interaction between the use of discourse markers and cultural norms is an obvious reason for carving out more interest in the study of religious expressions as a socio-cultural form of pragmatics.

Note that religious expressions, especially in Arabic discourse, are widely viewed as formulaic expressions that are apparent enactments of (linguistic) politeness given their religious flavour that is lexically rooted in their basic meanings (see Farghal, 1995). Religious expressions are a mixture

DOI: 10.4324/9781003301271-8

of both discourse and politeness which are exploited by the speaker to achieve an interpretation which is consistent with their intention, and therefore such expressions fall under the category of mitigators or expressions of deference (Badarneh, 2020; al-Rojaie, 2021).

Several studies have argued that some religious expressions are obviously used as discourse markers or speaker-based expressions which convey special meanings not related to their religious invocations. One remarkable example of such studies is Farghal's (1995) which explored the religious expression *ʔinʃa:llah* 'if God permits', mentioning that *ʔinʃa:llah* "has drifted extensively from its semantic import by acquiring a wide spectrum of illocutions, thus becoming a pragmatically multi-purpose expression" (p. 253; see Clift & Helani, 2010 and Masliyah, 1999 for more discussion on the pragmatic uses of *ʔinʃa:llah*. Farghal (1995) shows that this religious expression can be used as a directive, commissive or expressive marker. As a directive marker, *ʔinʃa:llah* is commonly used as a tag question that makes the accompanying utterance function as an "information-seeker" and "an exclamation-bearer". Please note that throughout the article, we use IPA system to transliterate examples as well as those from other sources.

An example of *ʔinʃa:llah* as a directive marker is given in (1) (Farghal 1995, p. 257):

Extract 1

> **ʔinʃa:llah** (ʔint) rasabit bil faħisˤ
> 'You didn't fail the test, did you?'

Farghal (1995) points out that *ʔinʃa:llah* as a directive marker is pronounced with a rising-falling intonational pattern on it, which, as we claim below, is one significant factor that gives rise to the secular uses of religious expressions. One important note that bears mentioning here is that *ʔinʃa:llah* is not glossed in the first example (1), a matter that points to the fact that *ʔinʃa:llah* has a discourse or speaker-related function that is associated with the whole utterance. Farghal (1995) states that the use of *ʔinʃa:llah* mitigates the driving force of the directive, making it less impositional on the addressee (cf. Brown & Levinson, 1987). Therefore, *ʔinʃa:llah* is classified as a 'directive mitigator'.

Furthermore, Farghal (1995) shows that *ʔinʃa:llah* can function as a commissive mitigator that weakly commits the addressor to do something such as offering or threatening. For example, in (2), the speaker tells the addressee that they can have dinner together tonight, yet with a lesser commitment in the sense that they might not have dinner together that night. Therefore, the use of *ʔinʃa:llah* makes the speaker's utterance a semi-promise. The following example comes from Farghal (1995, p. 261).

Extract 2

> **ʔinʃa:llah** bnitˤaʃʃa sawa ʔilleilih
> 'We'll have dinner together tonight.'

The use of *ʔinʃa:llah* as a commissive mitigator is one significant factor that generates the implicature that the speaker may not attend the dinner tonight. In Jordanian Arabic, the use of *ʔinʃa:llah* in the utterance is becoming a direct indication that the speaker is not committed to his utterance. Farghal (1995) presents evidence that *ʔinʃa:llah* can also be used as an expression of "hopes and indifference, and secondarily for the purpose of thanking, congratulating and apologizing" (p. 264). Consider the following example (Farghal, 1995, p. 264).

Extract 3

ʔinʃa:llah ʔaχu:k bindʒaħ bil faħisˤ
'I hope your brother will pass the test.'

ʔinʃa:llah in the extract expresses the speaker's hope that the interlocutor's brother would pass the test. Note here that prosody plays a significant role in articulating the intended function of *ʔinʃa:llah* as an expressive cue. For example, if *ʔinʃa:llah* is said with a rising intonation and a longer pause after it, the speaker might be understood that he doubts that the interlocutor's brother would pass the text. In almost all instances, *ʔinʃa:llah* is used as an expressive mitigator which is defined by Farghal (1995) as "expressing something to a lesser degree by coupling it with theistic agency" (p. 267).

Migdadi et al. (2010) provide a corpus-based investigation of the communicative functions of the religious expression *ma:ʃa:llah*, meaning literally 'What God wishes (has and will come true)' in colloquial Jordanian Arabic in light of Speech Act Theory, Gricean maxims, and Brown and Levinson's (1987) politeness theory. They propose that *ma:ʃa:llah* serves a number of pragmatic meanings which are an extension of its literal meaning of expressing divine will. These pragmatic functions include "an invocation, a compliment, an expression of gladness, an expression of modesty, a marker of sarcasm, and as a conversational backchannel" (p. 480). For instance, *ma:ʃa:llah* in the following example (4) is used as a compliment intensifier which can boost the positive semantic effect of the intended compliment (Migdadi et al., 2010, p. 488).

Extract 4

(A woman addressing her little niece)
ma:ʃa:llah hal dʒakeɪt ʕan dʒad ħilu: mi:n ʔiχta:ruh ʔinta walla ma:ma:
ma:ʃa:llah what a jacket! It is really beautiful! 'Who chose it? You or mum?'

Migdadi et al. (2010) argue that the use of *ma:ʃa:llah* in this has a social meaning in that the subject of the compliment is valuable that it might be negatively influenced by the evil eye whose presence is largely weakened when *ma:ʃa:llah* is used (see Al-Khawaldeh et al., 2023 for more about evil eye). *Ma:ʃa:llah* is hence a mitigating tool which softens any face threatening act including refusals, complaints, and criticisms. *Ma:ʃa:llah* in this example (4) should not then be regarded as an exclusively compliment intensifier because it makes available a sense of divine invocation; hence *ma:ʃa:llah* functions "as a compliment intensifier and invocation simultaneously" (Migdadi et al., 2010, p. 488). One important remark raised by Migdadi et al. (2010) regarding the (complimentary) use of *ma:ʃa:llah* in colloquial Jordanian Arabic is that this use constitutes a pragmatic change where the semantic meaning and structural uses of this expression are abandoned.

Migdadi and Badarneh (2013) examine the functions of religious expressions that include prophet-praise, such as *ʔalla:humma sˤalli ʕala sajjidina: muħammad* 'may God's blessings be bestowed upon our Prophet Muhammad', *bsˤala:t ʔinnabi* 'with blessings bestowed upon the Prophet', and the imperative *sˤalli ʕannabi* 'bestow blessings upon the Prophet' as they are used in colloquial Jordanian Arabic. Migdadi and Badarneh (2013) mention that these expressions "have drifted from their prototypical semantics into a variety of pragmatic functions, particularly in spoken discourse" (p. 63). They proposed that such expressions have passed through a process of "pragmaticalization" (Aijmer 1996) through which semantic expressions have developed into markers of discourse structure (Schiffrin, 1987). Prophet-praise religious expressions are found to function as place-holding devices. They are also used to seek protection from the evil eye, express success, terminate disruptive or undesirable activities, claim the floor, intensify the basic message of the utterance, and elicit involvement and agreement. For instance, in the following example (Migdadi & Badarneh, 2013, p. 78) *sˤalli ʕannabi* is used to claim the floor as its presence would notify the interlocutors that the speaker is going to speak his or her turn; therefore, the addressee is expected to grant him or her the floor.

Extract 5

(During a family visit, a woman states that her sons are stubborn, and her husband supports her statement)

Woman: hu: fi: ħada ʔaʕnad min ʔilli ʕindi:

'Is there anybody who is more stubborn than those I have got [her children]?!'

Woman's husband: ʔagullak **sˤalli ʕannabi** walla:hi ma: ʃufit ʔaʕnad min sajf wala baha:ʔ ma: btigdariʃ titħa:jal

'Let me tell you, I swear to God, I have never seen someone who is more stubborn than Sayf or Baha! You can't deal with them!'

Migdadi and Badarneh (2013) mention that the imperative formula of the religious expression *sˤalli ʕannabi* contributes to the participation framework of discourse; the speaker leads their interlocutors to pay attention to his input. Given that this input is marked by this formula, it is perceived as important for the interlocutors. In this example (5), the husband intends to clarify his wife's previous remark about their children's obstinateness; therefore, he turns "the focus of the exchange from a rhetorical question implying this stubbornness to an emphatic and explicit statement about their behavior" (p. 80). Therefore, *sˤalli ʕannabi* can be translated into English as 'May I have your attention, please?'

Migdadi and Badarneh (2013) note that prophet-praise religious expressions are representative examples of the process of pragmatic deployment of religious formula. This deployment results in a set of socially derived meanings, which are used as politeness formulas and validate one of the basic assumptions of politeness theory, namely "notions of face naturally link up to some of the most fundamental cultural ideas about the nature of the social persona, honor and virtue, shame and redemption and thus to religious concepts" (Brown & Levinson 1987, p. 13). Migdadi and Badarneh (2013) point out that pragmatically based interpretation of religious expressions (formulas) in Arabic discourse lies at the heart of advancing our understanding of cross-cultural communication, second or foreign language learning, and translation.

Similar findings pertaining to the pragmatic use of religious expressions in other Arabic dialects are drawn. For instance, al-Rojaie (2021) has shown that religious expressions in Najdi Arabic are multipurpose linguistic resources that are used to communicate specific functions including "signalling the end of a conversation, persuading, mitigating and hedging, showing agreement and approval, reinforcing emphasis, expressing emotions, seeking protection from the evil eye, conveying skepticism and ambiguity, expressing humor and sarcasm, and expressing respect and honor" (p. 22). For instance, the religious expression *ʕazz ʔallah* can be used express agreement with the interlocutor's point of view. al-Rojaie (2021) proposes that religious expressions in Najdi Arabic should be pragmatically interpreted as they are strongly affected by the conversational situation, a matter that presents strong evidence for their drifting away from their literal meanings or semantic values (as an essential expression of religious rituals or practices). The pragmatic uses of religious expressions demonstrate the interplay between religion, culture, and language use. The religious expression in this example (6) above acquires a meaning that is beyond its traditionally prototypical meanings.

Therefore, religious expressions are used in Arabic discourse to serve several pragmatically inferred interpretations and functions that have drifted away from their literal semantic meanings. Some studies have examined the functions of a specific religious expression (see Farghal 1995; Migdadi et al., 2010) while others attempted to draw a generalization to a set of religious markers with a common thread (Migdadi & Badarneh, 2013) or all of them as a whole (al-Rojaie, 2021). In all cases, religious expressions are culturally and socially pragmatic cues that the speaker uses, to maximally exploit contextual effects with no potential threat to the addressee's negative face (or the speaker's positive face). In the following case study, we discuss the pragmatic uses of *la: ʔila:ha ʔilla ʔalla:h* 'no god but Allah', which is the most frequently used religious expression in our Jordanian Arabic corpus.

la: ʔila:ha ʔilla ʔalla:h 'No god but Allah'

To identify the most common religious expression in Jordanian Arabic, we built a corpus consisting of naturally occurring utterances with the help of ten graduate students at the University of Jordan. The corpus is essentially based on recordings of domestic family gatherings, café and restaurant gatherings between friends and university students, and sessions of daily radio shows where inter-active conversations between radio hosts and the public take place, such as the Al-Wakeel radio show, a popular radio show in Jordan where the presenter Mohammad Al-Wakeel takes phone calls from the public on issues that they face in their daily life.

Three hundred and fifty sessions of interactive exchanges and conversations were collected with approximately one million words. Each session was heard by at least two people (the two authors or the graduate students) and relevant tokens of religious expressions were extracted and written down. Two thousand and eighty-three religious expressions were extracted from all sessions and discourse markers which are thought to be derived from the name of Allah or its derivation were excluded (such as *wallah* 'sure!', *ballah* 'sure!', and *yallah* 'come on!'). We focused instead on religious expressions which can still be used for their semantic values as religious invocations. Table 7.1 shows the most common religious expressions that appear in our corpus:

Table 7.1 shows that Jordanian Arabic deploys a multitude of religious expressions some of which are very common while others are only occasionally used. The number of tokens of *la: ʔila:ha ʔilla ʔalla:h* (4), *ma:ʃa:llah* (3), *ʔinʃa:llah* (1), and *sˤalli ʃannabi* (2) total more than 50 percent of the overall number of tokens. On the other hand, other religious expressions are used more restrictively. This variance can be attributed to the fact that the latter group of religious expressions are essentially used to convey very specific pragmatic meanings. For instance, the expression *gu:l ʔallah* is used by the speaker to encourage the interlocutor to perform the action intended. Consider the following dialogue as a representative example:

Extract 6

> (Father is talking to his nephew)
> Man: ʔismiʕit ʔinak tˤa:liʕ ʕal χali:dʒ
> 'I heard that you are moving to a Gulf country.'
> Nephew: fi: ʕindi ʕardˤ mawʕu:d w baʕidni bastana bas wallah mitradid
> 'I got an offer, and I am still waiting; but, by Allah, I am hesitant.'
> Man: **gu:l ʔallah**
>
> 'Say Allah.'

Table 7.1 Religious expressions in the corpus

	Expression	*Literal meaning*	*Tokens*	*n%*
1	?inʃa:llah	if God permits	520	24.96
2	sˤalli ʕannabi	bestow blessings upon the Prophet	301	14.45
3	ma:ʃa:llah	Oh my God	266	12.77
4	la: ?ila:ha ?illa ?alla:h	no god except Allah	204	9.79
5	?alħamdulilla:h	Thank God	160	7.68
6	?astaɣfirulla:h	I beg Allah's forgiveness	110	5.28
7	la: ħawla wala quwwata ?illa billa:h	There is no might nor power except with Allah	104	4.99
8	ħasbuna ?alla:h waniʕma ?alwaki:l	Allah suffices us, and He is the best disposer of affairs	89	4.27
9	?aʕu:ðu: billa:h min ?aʃajtˤa:n ?arradʒi:m	I seek refuge with Allah from the accursed Satan	85	4.08
10	sˤalla ?alla:h w ba:rak	God bless	78	3.74
11	biħja:t ?annabi	In the life of the Prophet	45	2.16
12	ʕala ʃa:n muħammad	Because of Muhammad	39	1.87
13	biħja:t ?allah	Because of Allah	32	1.53
14	?aʕu:ðu billa:h	I seek refuge with Allah	15	0.72
15	?allah jidʒi:rna	God bless us	10	0.48
16	?allah jirħamna w jiʕa:fi:na	May God have mercy on us and heal us	9	0.43
17	gu:l ?allah	Say Allah	8	0.38
18	ja: rab daχi:lak	Oh Lord, your mercy	8	0.38
		Total	**2,083**	**100**

Using *gu:l ?allah*, the man wants to inform his nephew to make his decision to go to work abroad as this would be the better option given the expected differences in terms of salaries between Jordan and the Gulf countries. The religious expression *gu:l ?allah* is not interpreted as the man ordering his nephew to mention the name of Allah, but to perceive the positive side of going abroad. In other words, *gu:l ?allah* identifies the speaker's encouragement of the hearer's decision; *gu:l ?allah* is better translated into English as 'go ahead and never hesitate'.

The expression *la: ?ila:ha ?illa ?alla:h* has a higher number of occurrences compared to the expressions already examined in the related literature as we discussed in the previous section and is a good example of an expression where religion, culture, politeness, and prosody meet. This expression appears to serve two expressive meanings (an expression of astonishment or surprise and an expression of disagreement or rejection) and functions as a turn-taking device and a request marker not to reveal information (or what we call an information-cancelling marker). Table 7.2 presents the number of tokens for each pragmatic use of *la: ?ila:ha ?illa ?alla:h*:

One important use of *la: ?ila:ha ?illa ?alla:h* is that it expresses the speaker's own astonishment or surprise towards the interlocutor's statement. Consider the following exchange as an example:

Table 7.2 Functions of la: ?ila:ha ?illa ?alla:h

Function	Tokens	%
An expression of surprise	82	16.3
An expression of disagreement	55	13.3
Turn-taking	50	12.3
information-cancelling	17	11.1
Totals	**204**	**100**

Extract 7

Speaker A

?iħna: ?issanih ha:j bilbaladijjih ma: fi: muχasˤasˤa:t li bina: mustaʃfaja:t ?aw ħatta mara:kiz sˤiħijjih ?ina btiʕrif zaj heık maʃa:ri:ʕ bidha: muwa:faqa:t min ʕala ?al?aqal ʕaʃar dʒiha:t

'This year in the municipality, there are no allocations for building hospitals or even health centres. You know that such projects require approvals from at least ten agencies.'

Speaker B

la: ?ila:ha ?illa ?alla:h

'Nno god except .Allah'

Speaker A

naʕam bina:? mustaʃfa miʃ ?aj kala:m biddak kawadir w ?ida:rah w muχasˤasˤa:t w ?abnijah w ?ara:dˤi w ɣeıruh

'Yes, building a hospital is not a word. You need staff, management, building allocations, land, and so on.'

Speaker B expresses his astonishment or surprise towards Speaker A's statement that building a hospital requires many administrative steps. This surprise is lexically expressed by the use of *la: ?ila:ha ?illa ?alla:h*. Note that Speaker A is aware of Speaker's B surprise; this is why he mentioned some of the administrative steps which are not known to Speaker B. This interaction between Speaker A and Speaker B reveals that *la: ?ila:ha ?illa ?alla:h* is not literally interpreted, but its pragmatic meaning is the one understood to be more relevant.

Note also that although Speaker B voices his surprise towards Speaker A's relevant statement, Speaker A does not consider this surprise as an impolite act. *la: ?ila:ha ?illa ?alla:h* is a surprise mitigator that allows the interlocutors to engage in the conversation while respecting the hearer's positive and negative face needs (i.e., acknowledging his need for respect and autonomy). The sense of politeness as a mitigator that accompanies the pragmatic use of *la: ?ila:ha ?illa ?alla:h* is due to its semantic value as a religious formula. Therefore, although *la: ?ila:ha ?illa ?alla:h* loses its literal religious meaning in everyday interaction and obtains a pragmatic meaning, it is still flavoured by its literal meaning that makes it a mitigator and hence more accepted by the interlocutors.

The next exchange is another example where *la: ?ila:ha ?illa ?alla:h* is used as an expression of surprise.

Extract 8

Speaker A

kul tˤa:liba:t ʔalʔadabi bi ʔalmadrasah ʔissanih ʔilma:dˤijih rasabu: bi ʔimtiħa:n ʔattawdʒi:hi: w ʔiħna bnitfarradʒ

'All the literary stream students at the school last year failed the Tawjihi exam, while we were watching.'

Speaker B

la: ʔila:ha ʔilla ʔalla:h kul ʔatˤaliba:t wala ħada nidʒiħ

'There is no God but Allah; all the students, and no one succeeded?'

Speaker A

wallah ma: ħada nidʒiħ w ha:j ʔalkuʃu:f ʔarrasmijih mawdʒu:dih w baʕdein maʕ hal mahzalih

'I swear by Allah, no one succeeded, and these are the official lists; what are we going to do about this farce!'

Speaker A clearly mentions that none of the female students who chose to study the literary stream passed the high-school exam whose mark is essential for entry to university. He intends to say that we do not want similar results this year, so the government is has to change the teachers and bring in others who are more proficient. Now the fact that no student had passed the exam is in fact a surprising statement given that the educational system in Jordan is governmentally supported, and the level of the teaching is high (in other schools, less than half of the students would fail the exam). Speaker B expresses his surprise using *la: ʔila:ha ʔilla ʔalla:h*, focusing also on the fact that all students failed the exam. Speaker B's utterance is significant here because it also presents evidence that *la: ʔila:ha ʔilla ʔalla:h* is not taken literally; otherwise, Speaker B would be irrelevant because this is not a situation when one can proclaim religious monotheism.

The second frequent use of *la: ʔila:ha ʔilla ʔalla:h* is as an expression of rejection of the interlocutor's statement. Under this use, *la: ʔila:ha ʔilla ʔalla:h* is used to pragmatically indicate that the speaker does not agree with the hearer's previous statement, a matter that encourages the hearer to provide more evidence to support their point of view or to question the information if they are informed by a third party. In the example below, Speaker B expresses his rejection of Speaker A's suggestion to rent a new house away from the city centre.

Extract 9

Speaker A

bisˤara:ħah beitna la:zim nɣajruh sˤa:r ʔiʔdi:m w ʔilmantiqah muzdaħimih kti:r w batˤalna niʔdar nitħammal miʃ ʔahsan nirħal la bara:

'Honestly, our house has to be changed; it has become old, and the area is very crowded, and we can no longer bear it. Isn't it better to move outside the city?'

Speaker B

la: ʔila:ha ʔilla ʔalla:h

Speaker A

tˤab leiʃ ra:fidˤ ʔiʃraħli

'Okay, why do you reject the idea? Explain to me.'

Speaker B

> ma: fi: ʔaħsan min ha:j ʔalmantiqah w ʔidʒa:rna rχi:sˤ

'There is wherenothing better than this area, and our rent is cheap.'

Speaker A suggests that they as a family should move house because their existing house is old and is located in a crowded district. Speaker B rejects this proposal using only *la: ʔila:ha ʔilla ʔalla:h*. Speaker A questions this rejection by requesting some reasons behind that response. Speaker B mentions that this district is satisfactory and that their monthly rent is low (as compared to a new house they would rent in the outskirts of the city).

In the next example, Speaker A rejects the school decision to work on Saturdays for a month to prepare for the high-school exam.

Extract 10

Speaker A

> mudi:r madrasitna: ħaka: la:zim nda:wim ʔalʔisbu:ʕ ʔildʒa:j jawm ʔilsabit la muddit ʃahar ʔiða: biddna nku:n bi lidʒa:n ʔattawdʒi:hi:

'The principal said that we must attend school next week on Saturday and for a month if we want to be in the Tawjihi committees.'

Speaker B

> **la: ʔila:ha ʔilla ʔalla:h** ʔana: miʃ mda:wim

'There is no god but Allah, I will not attend.'

Speaker A

> w ʔana: kama:n ʔasˤlan ma: fi:ha fa:jdih

'Me too; it is useless.'

Speaker B's rejection of their school principal's proposal to have them work on Saturdays in preparation for the upcoming high-school exams is clearly manifested by his sentence *ʔana: miʃ mda:wim* which literally means 'I will not attend such a preparation'. This rejection is intensified by the use of *la: ʔila:ha ʔilla ʔalla:h* which functions here as an expression of rejection. Although *la: ʔila:ha ʔilla ʔalla:h* is interpreted as an obvious rejection or disagreement of the interlocutor's proposal or statement, it does not, nonetheless, pose a direct threat to the hearer's positive face, although mitigation invoked by the use of *la: ʔila:ha ʔilla ʔalla:h* as an expression of rejection or disagreement is less clear than that invoked by the use of *la: ʔila:ha ʔilla ʔalla:h* as a surprise expression.

There are some instances in our corpus where the use of *la: ʔila:ha ʔilla ʔalla:h* can give rise to a breakdown of communication. This is shown in the following example:

Extract 11

Speaker A

> ʔalmasʔu:lijjah ʕaleɪk tiχta:r ʃarikat ʔattaʔmi:n ʔalʔafdˤal ʔilak w ʔalʔakθar ʔiltiza:man ha:ða: qitˤaːʕ χa:sˤ ʔiddawlih ʔilha ʕala:qah bas fi: ħdu:d

'The responsibility is on you to choose the insurance company that is best for you and the most committed. This is a private sector. The state can veneinterfere, but within limits.'

Speaker B

ʔila:ha ʔilla ʔalla:h

Speaker A

ja: ʔaχi ma: biddak tismaʕni ʔinta ħur

'Brother, you don't want to listen? It is up to you.'

Speaker B's utterance is an expression of disagreement of Speaker A's argument. Speaker A therefore ends the communication between them as he thinks that Speaker B does not want to listen up to his point of view. Upon analysing all tokens where the use of *la: ʔila:ha ʔilla ʔalla:h* causes a communication breakdown, it turns out that such breakdowns take place when the interlocutors are not family members or friends; therefore, the chance for such breakdowns is remarkably higher. This indicates that mitigation of threats to positive face (as a result of disagreements or rejections) is overridden by the effects of social distance between interlocutors whereby such threats are never a sign of solidarity or membership (see Kasper & Rose, 2001; Brown, 2017).

Another point that is worth discussing here is that surprise *la: ʔila:ha ʔilla ʔalla:h* and disagreement *la: ʔila:ha ʔilla ʔalla:h* are quite different from each other in terms of the accompanying prosody. Surprise *la: ʔila:ha ʔilla ʔalla:h* is characterized by a prominence on the word *ʔila:ha* while disagreement *la: ʔila:ha ʔilla ʔalla:h* is characterized by prominence on *la:* which literally means 'no'. The difference in prominence placement is a deciding factor that distinguishes the two functions. This is consistent with House's (2007, p. 369) statement that prosody functions to "guide the listener in how to proceed: how to access the relevant cognitive context within which to interpret the speaker's contribution, how to evaluate that contribution, and how to construct the interaction itself, to enable the communication to take place" (see also Wharton, 2012).

Religious expressions can also serve a purpose in helping manage turn-taking in conversation and mitigate loss of face. Enforcement of turn-taking (intentional interruption) is a face-threatening act across cultures (see Talbot, 1992; Gnisci et al., 2018), including the Arabic culture (El-Dakhs & Ahmed, 2021). *la: ʔila:ha ʔilla ʔalla:h* can be used as a turn-taking device that is essentially employed when the speaker enforces interruption, yet with no threat to face. Consider the following exchange as an example:

Extract 12

Speaker A

ʕuma:l ʔalwatʕan dʒama:ʕah ʔilhum kul ʔalʔiħtira:m w ʔiħna: la:zim nwafir ʔilhum kul ʃi mumkin ma:lijjan w ħata ʔidʒtima:ʕijjan w ʔana: baʕrif ...

'The home-workers [dustmen] are a group who deserve all the respect. We have to provide them with everything possible, financially and even socially. And I know ...'

Speaker B

ʔila:ha ʔilla ʔalla:h ja: ʕammi ʔana: ma: ħakeɪt ɣeɪr heɪk

'There is no god but Allah; my uncle, I did not say anything other than that ...'

Speaker A mentions that dustmen (called locally 'home-workers' as a socially accepted nickname for them) should be treated with respect, and the government is required to provide them with more financial and social support. He starts talking about something relevant but is interrupted by Speaker B who enforces this interruption through the use of *la: ʔila:ha ʔilla ʔalla:h.* Speaker B says that he agrees with Speaker A who seems to have misunderstood him.

In the next extract, we present another occasion where *la: ʔila:ha ʔilla ʔalla:h* is used as a turn-taking device.

Extract 13

Speaker A

ʔawla:di ma: biḥibu: ʔalmadrasih mʕalmit ʔarja:dˤija:t ma: bitdarris w kul ʔusbu:ʕ bitɣi:b jawm ʔaw jawmein w ʔalmuʃkilih ʕasˤabijjih kθi:r w ʔilmudi:rah ʃikilha ʃaχsˤijjitha dˤaʕi:h

'My children do not like school. The maths teacher does not teach, and every week she is absent for one or two days. The problem is that she is so nervous, and the principal seems to have a weak personality.'

Speaker B

ʔana: baʃu:f ʔilmadrasih kwajsih bas ʔinti: da:jman ɣeir

'I think the school is great, but you are always different.'

Speaker A

keif ɣeir ʔana: ʔawla:di ʔam ʃi: w ʔiða: ma: ʔihtameit fi:hum bmi:n biddi ʔahtam

'How am I different? To me, my children are the most important thing, and if I don't care about them, who do I care about?'

Speaker B

ʔila:ha ʔilla ʔalla:h ʔiḥna: mniḥki: ʕan ʔilmadrasih ma: mniḥki: ʕan raʔijk

'There is no god but God, we are talking about the school, we are not talking about your opinion.'

Speaker A complains about the school, especially in connection with the maths teacher and the principal. According to her, the maths teacher is indifferent while the school principal has poor management skills. Her husband has a different opinion, though. She then complains about her husband's opinion which is taken to be a criticism of her concern with her children. She starts explaining her opinion, but her husband interrupts her using *la: ʔila:ha ʔilla ʔalla:h*, complaining about his wife's focus on his opinion rather than her argument about their children who are encountering problems at school

Note here that turn-taking *la: ʔila:ha ʔilla ʔalla:h* is pronounced in a prosody that is different from that of the surprise *la: ʔila:ha ʔilla ʔalla:h* or disagreement *la: ʔila:ha ʔilla ʔalla:h*. Turn-taking *la: ʔila:ha ʔilla ʔalla:h* is said with a prominence on the last word *ʔalla:h*. The placement of prominence on *ʔalla:h* 'Allah' is significant because it makes the speaker stop speaking and give the floor to the hearer to deliver his turn. It is in fact one basic tenet in the Islamic world to give the word *ʔalla:h* 'Allah' due respect; one aspect of this is to stop speaking when the word *ʔalla:h* is pronounced with prosodic prominence. Although *la: ʔila:ha ʔilla ʔalla:h* is a turn-taking device which enforces interruption, the positive face of the interruptee is not affected because this expression is not interpreted as an impolite way to impose the speaker's turn-taking. This is supported by the fact that enforced interruptions in our corpus always give rise to communication breakdowns or tensions that make the ongoing conversation unfriendly. Consider the following exchange:

Extract 14

Speaker A

Ɂana: tqadamit lilwadʕi:fah min ʃahreɪn w ma: ħada raddilna: χabar birraɣim Ɂinuh Ɂilkull biʕraf fi: naqisʕ bildʒa:mʕah

'I applied for a job two months ago, and no one called me although everyone knows that there is a shortage of staff at the university.'

Speaker B

bas Ɂal Ɂaχ Ɂal ʕazi:z χali:na: Ɂawdʕaħ

'But, dear brother, let us be clearer.'

Speaker A

Ɂiða: samaħit la: tqa:dʕiʕni lamma: ħakeɪt ma: ħada qa:dʕaʕak

'Please, do not interrupt me. When you spoke, no one interrupted you.'

Speaker B

ja: radʒil mahu: Ɂina: btiħki Ɂaʃija:Ɂ mu: ħaqi:qijjah

'Man, you are saying things that are not true.'

This conversation takes place between a university job applicant and an official of the university. The former explains that he submitted his job application two months ago, but no one from the university has called him for an interview. The university official interrupts him, so he can explain the university procedures. This interruption is attacked by the job applicant who asks the official to wait till he is finished speaking.

Hamady (1960, p. 160) has previously noted that Arabic politeness is strongly marked by its religious character. Even though forced interruptions can result in a communication breakdown, the use of *la: Ɂila:ha Ɂilla Ɂalla:h* allows such interruptions to be tolerated by the interlocutors and can be viewed as a social lubricant in interaction, one that renders the interrupter's move to claim the floor polite and hence acceptable to the interruptee. Hamady (1960, p. 160) mentions that

Religion [in the Arabic world] is to a large extent the source of politeness. The terms of bienséance where God's name is either uttered or implicitly understood are numerous. The habitual consciousness of God in everything is so deeply rooted that He is always invoked even when His name is not pronounced.

(see also Bouchara, 2015)

The last use of *la: Ɂila:ha Ɂilla Ɂalla:h* that appears in our corpus is what we call information-cancelling. This use factors in a major way in the sessions from family gatherings and friend meetings: *la: Ɂila:ha Ɂilla Ɂalla:h* can be used as a request by the speaker to prevent the listener from talking about something specific. In other words, the information that the hearer is discussing or is about to reveal is sensitive from the perspective of the speaker and therefore should be kept confidential. Consider the following dialogue between friends:

Extract 15

Speaker A

ʔizzalamih ħabasu:h halaʔ w ma: ħada: ʕa:rif weɪn maka:nuh

'The man is imprisoned now, and no one owsknew where he is.'

Speaker B

ʔeɪʃ ʔalmuʃkilih ma: fi: ʔaxba:r bi ʔalfeɪs buk w ma: fi:h ʔaj maʕlu:mah

'What's the problem? Isn't there news on Facebook or any piece of information?'

Speaker A

fi: dʒama:ʕah biħku: ʔinha: qadˤʕajjit muxadara:t w ʔildʒama:ʕah ma:ski:nuh w fi: na:s θa:nijji:n biħku:

'There is a group of people who say that it is a drug case, and the police have caught him; and there are other people who say …'

Speaker C

la: ʔila:ha ʔilla ʔalla:h

Speaker A

xalasˤ ʔu:keɪh ma: baʕrif

'It's over, okay, I don't know.'

This exchange takes place between friends who are discussing the reason why somebody they all know is detained by the police. When one of them starts revealing some potential reasons for this detention, he is interrupted by another who uses *la: ʔila:ha ʔilla ʔalla:h* requesting him not to disclose the reasons; the true reason for his detention is still unknown. Note that Speaker A is aware of this communicative use of *la: ʔila:ha ʔilla ʔalla:h*, indicating that he agrees with Speaker C that such reasons should not be discussed because they are gossip and might speak wrongly about the man being detained.

The following exchange is also an example where *la: ʔila:ha ʔilla ʔalla:h* is used as an information-cancelling device.

Extract 16

Speaker A

ʔilbint ʔitˤala?at min ʃahri:n w sˤa:jrih kti:r mityajrih baħiss ʔinnuh ʕindha: maradˤ nafsi:

'The girl was divorced two months ago and has become a lot different. I feel that she has a mental illness.'

Speaker B

la: ʔila:ha ʔilla ʔalla:h

Speaker C

tˤajjib mi:n biʕraf ʔa:xir ʔaxba:rha:

'Well, who knows her latest news.'

This exchange takes place between three girls talking about their friend who was divorced two months ago. One of them assumes that their friend in question developed a psychiatric disease. However, she was interrupted by one of her friends using *la: ?ila:ha ?illa ?alla:h* which is read as a request for her to stop talking about their friend's mental status. This request is understood by the speaker who shifts the topic of the conversation through asking the interlocutors about any news relating to their friend in question.

What distinguishes this use from its other uses is the fact that the vowel of the first word *la:* is remarkably lengthened while word stress is placed on *Allah* which is prosodically prominent. This is expected as *la: ?ila:ha ?illa ?alla:h* is in such cases inherently a device to interrupt speech. The use of *la: ?ila:ha ?illa ?alla:h* in such situations is in fact compatible with its semantic value as an invocation expression where the ultimate and main focus is placed on Allah, not anything else. In other words, it is used as a device to remind the interlocutor that the mentioning of *Allah* is better than gossiping about others and saying bad or insensitive things about them. Therefore, *la: ?ila:ha ?illa ?alla:h* adds an emotional flavour to the utterance because of its underlying religious connotation, something also found by Migdadi et al. (2010) in their discussion of *ma:ʃa:llah.*

To summarise, *la: ?ila:ha ?illa ?alla:h* serves four main functions in Jordanian Arabic discourse; these functions include an expression of astonishment or surprise, an expression of disagreement (and rejection), a turn-taking device, and an information-cancelling marker. Under all these functions, *la: ?ila:ha ?illa ?alla:h* also acts as a mitigator given its semantic connotations. Additionally, *la: ?ila:ha ?illa ?alla:h* has variant prosodic manifestations where each function is affiliated with a special prosodic contour that helps identify the function that the speaker intends to express. Being the case, *la: ?ila:ha ?illa ?alla:h* (as is the case with other religious expression in in Arabic dialects) is a mixture of four major components: context, politeness, religion, and prosody. These components interact in a systematic way that makes religious expressions truly socio-cultural aspects of pragmatic expressions and interpretation.

This research has provided an argument that the religious expression *la: ?ila:ha ?illa ?alla:h* is used to express four major pragmatic and discourse meanings or functions that are not related to its semantic value as an invocational expression. However, we show that these functions are coloured with the semantic connotations of this religious expression, a matter that makes it a mitigator, and its use can be tolerated by the interlocutors even in situations that include a face-threatening act. Yet, we show that social distance (and power) can override the mitigating effects of this religious expression. Furthermore, we propose that pragmatic functions of *la: ?ila:ha ?illa ?alla:h* are prosodically marked in the sense that each function is accompanied by a distinct prosodic pattern that helps identify which function is intended. In other words, prosody constrains the set of possible and likely functions of *la: ?ila:ha ?illa ?alla:h*, hence effectively facilitating the interpretation of the utterance and characterizing any infelicity in discourse. Additionally, we show that *la: ?ila:ha ?illa ?alla:h* as an information-cancelling device is mainly used between family members and among friends. Therefore, under this function *la: ?ila:ha ?illa ?alla:h* represents a membership marker that communicates "to the listener that the speaker shares an understanding of what is socially appropriate and right and how the world works" (Migdadi et al., 2010, p. 498). The uses of *la: ?ila:ha ?illa ?alla:h* are thus a window into social aspects of Jordanian culture where people who belong to the same family or domain or membership (friends, relatives, etc.) are free to interrupt other member's speech specially when this speech is socially sensitive.

Implications and Future Directions

The current study provides implications for the research on the interaction between language and religion, particularly in Arab and Muslim countries where religion is found to play a significant role in shaping people's verbal and non-verbal behaviours. It is beyond question that language is effectively used to express one's thoughts and beliefs to others; it is a powerful tool that disseminates religious thoughts and meanings to a wider audience. Additionally, religion is found to make available a set of expressions (religious formulas), which express several discourse meanings, which are not religious but secular (discourse-bound) for the most part. The use of such expressions is indicative of the role of religion in certain discourse markers and their actual uses and functions in discourse. Additionally, the current study is an avenue for pragmatic research and work on grammaticalization processes which are majorly related to how the nature of the semantic content of lexemes can develop grammatical and pragmatic functions with a specific role in the discourse.

Therefore, the study of religious expressions and their pragmatic and discourse meanings is a rich resource to understand the underlying relation between religion, culture, and language. The semantic content of religious expressions is peripheral in terms of the utterance meaning while their pragmatic illocutionary force is salient. Yet, their pragmatic contribution to their utterance is relatively hard to explain or specify without appeal to the cultural manifestations of these expressions. This is why such expressions can be better viewed as socio-cultural pragmatic manifestations of their religious use and interpretations. Therefore, more investigation into the functions of religious expressions as pragmatic markers is required as they are true reflections of the intricate relation between culture and language. Furthermore, there should be more research on the performative act of religious language to explore the implicated meanings and illocutionary forces of religious expressions. In Arabic linguistic research, many studies have shown that grammaticalization processes result in expressions of language use with newly developed communicative functions (see Jarrah et al, 2019). Table 7.1 above includes several religious expressions that have not yet been explored in this regard. Additionally, exploration into how these religious expressions behave in various Islamic and Arabic contexts is beneficial, especially with a focus on contrastive studies of inter- and intralinguistic nature.

Further investigations into the linguistic practices of religious practitioners as well as the sociolinguistic variation of religious expressions could be valuable. According to our experience as native speakers of Jordanian Arabic, it is quite apparent that religious markers are much used as pragmatic markers by older people than younger ones. For example, an old man or woman remarkably uses the expression ʔinʃaːllah expressing different functions and meanings, which can be specified according to the context. On the contrary, the younger generation uses this religious expression in a very restricted manner. In a similar vein, the older generation uses multiple religious expressions in their speech, while the younger generation uses specific expressions. Therefore, the use of religious expressions is an apparent feature of old people's speech. However, the role of age in the use of religious expressions requires exploration which we leave for further research. Likewise, the role of other social factors, including gender, education, and region, is worth exploring. Although we have no conclusive evidence, it is evident that (younger) women prefer not to use these expressions in Jordanian Arabic, something that, if true, points to the fact that the use of religious expressions in Jordanian Arabic is socially constrained.

This study shows the importance of prosody in identifying various functions and meanings of a single religious expression. As we have shown above, different prosodic contours on a specific religious marker give rise to different meanings. Therefore, prosody should be regarded as a contrastive feature that significantly helps the interlocutor identify the intended utterance meaning as well as the speaker's viewpoint towards the utterance. As we have shown, the religious expression *la: ʔila:ha ʔilla ʔalla:h* maintains variant prosodic manifestations where each function is associated with a unique prosodic contour. For example, when *la: ʔila:ha ʔilla ʔalla:h* functions as an information-cancelling device, the vowel of the first word *la:* is remarkably lengthened while word stress is placed on *Allah* which becomes prosodically prominent under this function. However, one look at the related literature reveals that few studies have addressed the relation between prosody and the meaning of religious expressions in Arabic and Muslim contexts. Furthermore, although the observation that different meanings can be associated with unique prosodic contours is obvious and in fact well-investigated, we have no proper understanding of this mapping between prosody and discourse meanings as a phenomenon. Relevant research mostly consists of single studies that target specific languages where a collective perspective of this mapping is lacking. Therefore, we call for more exploration of the effect of prosody on discourse meanings and structure, especially when prosody is deemed important in identifying different functions and meanings of a single expression or a marker.

Moreover, this research provides evidence for the use of religious expressions as discourse markers which are flavoured by politeness. As we have shown above, the religious expression *la: ʔila:ha ʔilla ʔalla:h* can be used as a turn-taking device, which can be employed when the speaker enforces interruption, yet with no threat to face. This intricate relation between politeness and the discourse expression of religious markers is worth investigating in detail. Is it the case the politeness flavour of such expressions drawn on the semantic meaning of such expressions, which is nonetheless bleached in the discourse? We have suggested that politeness is associated with the meanings of such markers because they are religious formulas; however, more research should be done in connection to this point, especially in terms of native speakers' judgements and perspectives. It is also worth exploring whether the politeness flavour is associated with all religious expressions or a subset of them. The main politeness meanings associated with such markers are also worth pursuing. According to the literature available in this respect, such issues are still outstanding with no sufficient description or analysis of them.

Further Reading

Migdadi, F., Badarneh, M.A. & Momani, K. (2010). Divine will and its extensions: Communicative functions of *maašaallah* in colloquial Jordanian Arabic. *Communication Monographs*, *77*(4), 480–499.
This study explores the pragmatic functions of *maašaallah* (a religious expression in Arabic) adopting the pragmatic theories of speech acts and politeness.
Eikrem, A. (2013). *Being in religion: a journey in ontology from pragmatics through hermeneutics to metaphysics*, 67. Mohr Siebeck.
This work presents a systematic perspective of the link between philosophy and religious discourse by examining different philosophical models and analysing the pragmatic and semantic components of religious discourse.
Migdadi, F. & Badarneh, M.A. (2013). The pragmatics of prophet-praise formulas in Jordan. *Anthropological Linguistics*, *55*(1), 61–91.
This study examines the pragmatic functions of certain religious expressions from the Prophet's formulas as used in Jordan.
Molendijk, A. (Ed.). (2018). *The Pragmatics of Defining Religion: Contexts, Concepts and Contests*. Brill.
This book discusses problematic issues in defining religious discourse and shows the controversy in the conceptualisation of religion.
Pihlaja, S. (2018). *Religious talk online: The evangelical discourse of Muslims, Christians, and atheists*. Cambridge University Press.
This book shows the connection between social media figures talk about religion to create a novel avenue for discussions on religion.

References

Aijmer, K. (1996). *I think*—an English modal particle. In T. Swan & O Westvik (Eds.), *Modality in Germanic languages: Historical and comparative perspectives*, 1–48. De Gruyter.

Badarneh, M.A. (2020). Formulaic Expressions of Politeness in Jordanian Arabic Social Interactions. *Formulaic Language and New Data*, 151–170. De Gruyter.

Bouchara, A. (2015). The role of religion in shaping politeness in Moroccan Arabic: The case of the speech act of greeting and its place in intercultural understanding and misunderstanding. *Journal of Politeness Research*, *11*(1), 71–98.

Brown, P. (2017). Politeness and impoliteness. In Y. Huang (Ed.), *The Oxford handbook of pragmatics*, 383–399. Oxford University Press.

Brown, P. & Levinson, S.C. (1987) *Politeness: Some universals in language usage*, *4*. Cambridge University Press.

Clift, R. & Helani, F. (2010). Inshallah: Religious invocations in Arabic topic transition. *Language in Society*, *39*(3), 357–382. Cambridge University Press.

El-Dakhs, D.A.S. & Ahmed, M.M. (2021). A variational pragmatic analysis of the speech act of complaint focusing on Alexandrian and Najdi Arabic. *Journal of Pragmatics*, *181*: 120–138. Elsevier.

Farghal, M. (1995). The pragmatics of *'inšāllah* in Jordanian Arabic. *Multilingua, 14*(3), 253–270.

Gnisci, A., Graziano, E., Sergi, I., & Pace, A. (2018). Which criteria do naïve people use for identifying and evaluating different kinds of interruptions? *Journal of Pragmatics*, *138*: 119–130. Elsevier.

Hamady, S. (1960). *Temperament and character of the Arabs*. Twayne Publishing.

House, J. (2007). The role of prosody in constraining context selection: a procedural approach. *Nouveaux cahiers de linguistique française*, *28*: 369–383.

Ingold, R. (2014). God, the Devil and you: A systemic functional linguistic analysis of the language of Hillsong. *Literature & Aesthetics*, *24*(1).

Jarrah, M.A., Alghazo, S.M., & Al Salem, M.N. (2019). Discourse functions of the wh-word ʃu: in Jordanian Arabic. *Lingue e Linguaggio, 28*(2), 291–317.

Johns, Y. (1985). Politeness in the Indonesian language: Knowing the right thing to say. *Indonesia Circle*, 38: 2–14.

Kasper, G. & Rose, K.R. (2001). Pragmatics in language teaching. In K. Rose & G. Kasper (Eds.), *Pragmatics in Language Teaching*, 1–11. Cambridge University Press

Al-Khawaldeh, S., Jarrah, M., & Alghazo, S.M. (2023). Evil-eye expressive strategies between utterers and interpreters: A pragmatic study on Colloquial Jordanian Arabic. *Journal of Pragmatics*, *204*: 6–20.

Malmström, H. (2015). The "Other" Voice in Preaching: Intertextual Form and Function in Contemporary English Sermonic Discourse. *Journal of Communication & Religion*, *38*(2).

Masliyah, S. (1999). A cross-cultural misunderstanding: The case of the Arabic expression inshallah 'If God Wills'. *Dialog on Language Instructio*n *13*(1–2), 97–116.

Migdadi, F. & Badarneh, M.A. (2013). The pragmatics of prophet-praise formulas in Jordan. *Anthropological Linguistics*, *55*(1), 61–91.

Migdadi, F., Badarneh, M.A., & Momani, K. (2010). Divine will and its extensions: Communicative functions of maašaallah in colloquial Jordanian Arabic. *Communication Monographs*, *77*(4), 480–499.

Morrow, J.A. (Ed.). (2006). *Arabic, Islam and the Allah lexicon: How language shapes our conception of God*. Edwin Mellen Press.

Nazzal, A. (2005). The pragmatic functions of the recitation of Qur'anic verses by Muslims in their oral genre: The case of Insha' Allah, 'God's willing'. *Pragmatics*, *15*(2–3), 251–273.

Piamenta, M. (1979). *Islam in everyday Arabic speech*. E.J. Brill.

Rajan, B., & Vaz, E. (2018). Sacred Texting: A Study on Social Media Language Trends in New Delhi and Bengaluru Churches. *Amity Journal of Media & Communications Studies (AJMCS)*, *8*(1).

al-Rojaie, Y.I. (2021). The pragmatic functions of religious expressions in Najdi Arabic. *Saudi Journal of Language Studies*, *1*(1), 3–25.

Schiffrin, D. (1987). *Discourse Markers*. Cambridge University Press.

Susanto, D. (2006). Codeswitching in Islamic religious discourse: The role of Insha'Allah. The Second Annual Rhizomes: Re-visioning Boundaries Conference of The School of Languages and Comparative Cultural Studies, The University of Queensland.

Talbot, M. (1992). 'I wish you'd stop interrupting me!': Interruptions and asymmetries in speakers-rights in equal encounters. *Journal of Pragmatics, 18*(5), 451–466.

Verdonik, D., & Kačič, Z. (2012). Pragmatic functions of Christian expressions in spoken discourse. *Linguistica, 52*(1), 267–281.

Wharry, C. (2003). Amen and hallelujah preaching: Discourse functions in African American sermons. *Language in Society, 32*(2), 203–225.

Wharton, T. (2012). Pragmatics and prosody. In K. Allan & K.M. Jaszczolt (Eds.), *The Cambridge handbook of pragmatics*, 567–585. Cambridge University Press.

Wikan, U. (1996). *Tomorrow, God Willing.* University of Chicago Press.

8

SYMBOLS AND ICONS IN BUDDHIST WORSHIP

Charles M. Mueller

This chapter applies a cognitive linguistics framework to the analysis of imagery encountered within the context of Buddhist worship. The analysis shows how both metaphor and metonymy underlie depictions in religious iconography. Visual representations in this genre afford multiple layers of interpretation based on devotees' prior embodied experiences, cultural knowledge, and expectations related to religious contexts. The chapter suggests that primary metaphor is especially crucial as it provides a preliminary layer of affordances to religious devotees who lack deep cultural and doctrinal knowledge related to their local Buddhist tradition. More complex metaphors and metonymy afford further layers of semantic potential, which are often only accessible to more knowledgeable viewers. It is noted that imagery is typically encountered within multimodal contexts, and these other modes further disambiguate, modulate, and elaborate the conveyed meanings. The final sections of the chapter consider how visual metaphorical mappings are used for ideological purposes and how conceptual mappings with a strongly embodied basis may underlie the durability of specific iconographic motifs through time.

Introduction and Background

The cognitive linguistics (CL) framework (Lakoff & Johnson, 1980) has generally been applied to verbal communication, but recent work on multimodality (e.g., Forceville, 2020; Hart & Marmol Queralto, 2021) has demonstrated that it is also applicable to descriptions of symbolic expression within other modalities such as imagery and gesture. This chapter employs a CL framework to examine metaphor and metonymy in monomodal and multimodal Buddhist iconography as it appears in the form of statues, relief carvings, temple paintings, and other visual forms. The analysis will consider these mostly as monomodal representations (i.e., as images), but the final section will also examine such representations as they occur within multimodal contexts (for example, when encountered within religious rituals).

This chapter will tentatively put forth four claims. First, it will argue that visual representations in Buddhist iconography often afford multiple layers of interpretation which are constrained by genre-related expectations related to religious contexts. Second, it will show that these interpretations are often evoked through many of the same conceptual mapping principles used in verbal communication, to include metaphor (especially *primary* metaphor) and metonymy. Third, it will suggest that some of the conceptual mappings, especially those related to primary metaphor, ensure that a minimal initial layer of interpretation is available to most viewers regardless of their familiarity with particular Buddhist traditions. Fourth, it will argue that the conveyed meaning

DOI: 10.4324/9781003301271-9

of imagery is, within religious contexts, further enriched and disambiguated through multimodal forms of expression. The final sections of this chapter will consider the implications of these claims, particularly in relation to how metaphor is used to reinforce doctrinal positions and factors contributing to the endurance of religious motifs.

Prior to engaging in the main topic of this chapter, we should first note that the visual modality differs in some important ways from verbal language, and these unique features have important implications for patterns of conceptual mapping. Verbal language is linear, so CL analysis of written or spoken language often involves breaking a text down into sequential units that are then placed into the categories relevant to the analysis (e.g., metaphor, simile, metonymy, etc.) An image, on the other hand, is viewed holistically. While the viewer's eyes may move around, fixating on various facets of a work (a dynamic process that the artist may attempt to control through the manipulation of compositional patterns), many of the interpretive conceptual mappings afforded by an image are present simultaneously. To give just one example, an image in a temple may express the eminence of the Buddha through an image's size, vertical positioning, centrality, or bright golden color; yet these elements are all available as part of a single gestalt, and their symbolic affordances are presumably processed, mostly on an unconscious level, in tandem. Moreover, key components of the communication model applicable to the visual mode differ from those of the verbal mode. Speech often occurs between interlocutors who share extensive knowledge related to communicative intentions and the immediate situation, and misunderstandings can be addressed through ongoing interaction. In the visual mode, at least in the case of religious iconography, the communicator (i.e., the producer of the iconographic representation) often has only a vague and general understanding of potential viewers and must accommodate heterogeneous audiences.

Despite these obstacles, producers of religious iconography can create highly expressive works that often surpass verbal modes of communication in their ability to convey meanings and evoke sublime emotions. This is partly due to the ability of genre attributions to set up certain expectations that elicit the audience's encyclopedic knowledge, which then facilitates interpretation (Forceville, 1996, 2020). In the case of religious iconography, viewers typically encounter visual representations within the context of worship, and they consequently assume that the representations have religious significance. For example, Buddhists visiting a temple would presume that most of the depicted anthropomorphic figures are to be venerated, or at the very least, that they are supernatural entities that support or protect associated figures that are to be venerated. They can also assume that the images will sometimes allude to narratives that are intended to be edifying in some way.

It must also be noted that religious iconography differs in important ways from the visual works (e.g., modern paintings, advertisements, and comics) that have been the focus of much previous academic research that has used a CL framework to examine imagery. Unlike these works, iconography, as an expression of specific religious traditions, tends to be very conservative, repeating specific motifs through time (often through centuries or millennia). In addition, religious devotees who attend a specific temple or regularly visit a holy site may encounter the same work repeatedly (in the case of a home altar, even daily) and may spend considerable time viewing the same sets of images. Iconography also reflects institutional requirements regarding doctrinal coherence and consistency. Finally, religious images are often encountered in an established order, as when Catholics visit each station of the cross when visiting a church. In northeast Asia, Buddhists will similarly often encounter images in a set order, bowing before the main gates of the temple and then the main hall prior to visiting other buildings within a temple compound.

Since this chapter analyzes Buddhist iconography in terms of conceptual mappings related to metaphor and metonymy, it is useful to briefly review the work of Forceville, one of the most influential scholars using a CL framework to examine visual modes of expression. In his seminal book, Forceville (1996) adapts Black's (1962) interaction theory of metaphor to examine pictorial metaphors in advertisements. He classifies the images in the ads as being based on four types of mappings: metaphors with one pictorially present term (MP1s), metaphors with two pictorially present terms (MP2s), pictorial similes, and verbo-pictorial metaphors (VPMs). He notes that in MP1s, the explicitly presented "term" (i.e., domain) tends to be the target domain, in contrast with verbal metaphors, in which it is the source domain that is explicitly presented. MP2s and pictorial similes are similar in that both domains (target and source) are pictorially represented; however, the pictorial elements in similes can be differentiated in that the two elements do not form a single gestalt. Forceville gives the example of a swimsuit ad showing a woman gracefully diving into the water alongside a dolphin. Forceville's MP1 and MP2 distinction is similar to the distinction between "Symbolic Suggestive" and "Symbolic Attributive" structures in Kress and van Leeuwen's (2021) work (p. 102).

Forceville (2020) notes that some images may be accompanied by verbal (e.g., written) elements, which can clarify, augment, or expand on the visual message (cf. Kress & van Leeuwen, 2021). In VPMs, one of the domains is presented verbally (in writing, in Forceville's examples), and the metaphor cannot be understood without that element. Forceville's research also draws on Relevance Theory (Sperber & Wilson, 1995), especially, the idea that an image can contain explicatures (ostensively communicated assumptions) and implicatures (implicitly communicated assumptions). Communicative representations (to include images) containing a wide array of weak implicatures that require the addressee to work to derive plausible interpretations are said to produce a "poetic effect" (Sperber & Wilson, 1995, p. 222).

The examples of pictorial metaphor discussed in this chapter primarily involve MP1s. The lower occurrence of MP2s and pictorial similes in the examples probably reflects genre differences: unlike advertisements which work to establish a connection (often, a very arbitrary connection) between a product (which is nearly always the target domain) and a positive characteristic (usually the source domain), iconography generally employs metaphor to attribute positive features to a figure of veneration. Moreover, the repeated viewing of religious imagery allows for a rich array of metaphoric and metonymic associations that are only understood after multiple viewings or are understood solely by those with extensive knowledge of the Buddhist tradition (e.g., monastics). Verbal elements can occur in iconography when, for example, written titles, stanzas from a poem, or lines from a sutra accompany an image. Often, the hall housing an image will have a plaque or nameplate that identifies the key figure. Liturgical practices can also help in identification, as when a congregation turns towards a wall painting and then performs a devotional chant to the image's central figure.

Many of the metaphors that appear in Buddhist iconography are *primary* metaphors. These are deeply entrenched mappings from a source domain that is associated with sensory experience (e.g., verticality) to a target domain that is associated with our interpretations or response to the world (e.g., social dominance). Due to these metaphors' grounding in experiential correlations, they appear widely within lexical patterns across the world's languages (Grady & Ascoli, 2017). Ortiz (2011) argues convincingly that these basic metaphors, while thus far explored almost exclusively in research on verbal language, are also highly relevant to the analysis of monomodal *visual* metaphors. She examines various primary metaphors occurring in film and advertisements (many of which also occur extensively within religious iconography), such as CONTROL IS VERTICALITY, IMPORTANCE IS SIZE, and SIMILARITY IS ALIGNMENT. In this chapter, it is argued that primary metaphor, when used in monomodal images, plays an important role in rendering key elements of artistic representations readily interpretable by a wide audience regardless of the viewers' level of expertise or their cultural or temporal distance from the creator of the object (for similar findings related to political cartoons, see El Refaie, 2009).

Like metaphor, metonymy can also appear in nonverbal communication and expression. *Metonymy* has been defined as "a cognitive process in which one conceptual element of an entity (thing, event, property), the vehicle, provides mental access to another conceptual entity (thing, event, property), the target, within the same frame, domain or idealized cognitive model" (Kövecses, 2006, p. 99). In other words, metonymy is based on relationships within the same network of knowledge. It should be noted that this knowledge is often cultural and is not limited to physical reality or personal beliefs. Thus, a picture of Rudolph the Red-Nosed Reindeer would be sufficient to evoke the idea of Santa Claus or Christmas to most modern English-speakers even if they were fully aware that Rudolph is a fictional character.

Whereas metaphor involves a mapping across domains, metonymy involves mapping within the same domain. Metonymy achieves this by highlighting a salient feature of a domain, and for this reason, metonymy (like metaphor) can evoke specific construals of the target domain. For example, we could refer to workers as either *heads* or *hands* (e.g., field hands), but the former will promote a construal of the employees as intellectual workers whereas the latter will construe them as manual laborers. Metonymy's strong reliance on cultural knowledge can make it opaque to those who lack such knowledge or relevant experiences. Consider metonymic expressions for the concept of MEAL in various cultures. Chinese, Japanese, and Korean speakers all use words for *rice* metonymically to mean *meal*. This is likely to cause initial confusion for an English-speaker learning these languages since bread, instead of rice, is a more salient part of the Western diet. For this reason, Christians traditionally talk of "breaking bread" together during communal meals (e.g., Luke 24:35, Acts 20:7).

Within religious discourse, narrative plays an especially central role, and key stories and myths are often expressed through metonymy, which serves multiple functions. In the case of well-known stories, depictions of key scenes can evoke the entire story in the mind of the viewer. Visuals set off by framelines (e.g., comic strips) or by "white space" (Kress & van Leeuwen, 2021, p. 205) can also use metonymy to evoke key events of a story, leading the viewer to subconsciously fill in the missing scenes based on general schemas and expectations regarding coherence (Forceville, 2020).

In this chapter, the discussion of iconography primarily focuses on visual images, but religious imagery often conveys meanings through multiple modalities simultaneously. Linguistic research has generally focused on morphosyntactic or lexical features that are associated with monomodal verbal communication, so it is easy to lose sight of the fact that human beings have a wide range of means with which to convey their thoughts. These range from the nonverbal elements that accompany spoken language (e.g., gesture) and written texts (e.g., font design) to an extensive array of resources to include static images (e.g., painting and sculpture), dance, and music. All these modes can co-occur within religious ritual activities, which tend to involve relatively rich multimodal forms of expression.

Conceptual Mappings in Buddhist Iconography from an Embodied Perspective

Buddhist iconography frequently employs several primary metaphors in its imagery. One of the most common is IMPORTANCE IS CENTRALITY (cf. Arnheim, 1982). As part of the more general metaphor PROPERTIES ARE PHYSICAL PROPERTIES, the metaphor is deeply grounded in human-embodied perceptual and social experience and is therefore ubiquitous across cultures. In normal lighting, our vision is acute only in the center of our field of view due to the high density of cones in the fovea, a deficit that we overcome by moving our eyes three or four times per second (Snowden et al., 2012). We therefore learn, from a very young age, to place objects where they will be in the center of someone's field of vision if we wish to draw attention to them, and conversely, to place them in the periphery (or better yet, outside) of another person's visual field if we want to hide them. Within social interactions, an important speaker will tend to be positioned at the center of a group where she will be more easily seen and heard, and groups of people who are interested in a person will tend to gather around her. These embodied experiences have led to a metaphor that appears in iconographic depictions in the placement of the most revered figure in the center of a bounded frame (e.g., a picture frame, a carved figure, or an architectural structure). According to Kress and van Leeuwen (2021), the center is often presented as the core element with which other elements are associated and from which they draw meaning and coherence (p. 201).

Centrality, as a signal of importance, can also be used to incorporate figures from competing religious traditions while relegating them to peripheral status. From the onset, Buddhism has historically taken a syncretic stance as it adapted to new cultural milieus. While taking in indigenous elements, it has managed to maintain the doctrinal primacy of the Buddha by relegating competing figures to subsidiary status. This is reflected within the iconography of all the main Buddhist traditions. Consider a typical large Korean monastery as an example. The *Daeungjeon* (literally, "Hall of the Great Hero") occupies the center of the monastic complex, and the statue of the historical Buddha occupies the center of this hall. This main figure is immediately flanked by key bodhisattvas, while the walls of the hall often contain large paintings depicting throngs of minor figures (e.g., guardians, deities taken from Indian, Chinese, and Korean pre-Buddhist traditions, and so on.) This hierarchy also finds expression in the layout of the monastery. The halls devoted to more traditional Buddhist figures (e.g., bodhisattvas) appear near the *Daeungjeon*, while those devoted to indigenous deities such as the *Sanshin* (Mountain Spirit) or *Chilseong* (Seven Stars—spirits associated with the Big Dipper) tend to be small and are located on the periphery of the temple grounds.

Such central positioning of figures also hints at some interesting cultural differences between traditions. Japanese temples, compared to those of Korea, have a much greater tendency to place indigenous patriarchal figures at the center of their temples. Thus a wooden statue depicting Shinran, the Japanese founder of the Jodo Shinshu Sect, is the central figure in the *Goeido* (Founder's Hall) of Higashi Honganji, the head temple of one of the major Japanese Pure Land sects (cf. Dobbins, 2001). One is hard-pressed to find equivalents in Korean iconography. Some Korean Buddhist temples have a hall devoted to patriarchs of the order (*josadang*), but it is invariably a small structure located on the outskirts of a monastery.

In the examples discussed so far, centrality has been associated with a positive evaluation, but this does not appear to be a requisite feature of the metaphor. For example, Tibetan *bhavacakra* thangka paintings depict *saṃsāra* (the cycle of mundane existence) as a centrally positioned demonic figure holding a wheel. At the center of the wheel are a pig, snake, and bird (representing the three "poisons" of ignorance, aversion, and attachment). Moving out from the center, one finds other concentric layers of symbolic depictions of *saṃsāra* until finally coming to the enlightened buddhas or bodhisattvas which are positioned at the periphery of the painting as an indication that they have transcended mundane existence.

In addition to CENTRALITY, VERTICALITY is often used as a key source domain in primary metaphors due to its association with several key target domains that are common in religious discourse, to include CONTROL, POWER, and GOD. In our everyday embodied experience, verticality is highly relevant since it relates to our ability to apply force. This is perhaps most obvious in situations involving aggression in which one person wrestles an opponent to the ground. The person on top is able to use the weight of his torso to amplify his effective strength when striking the other person or holding the person's limbs to the ground. Even in situations in which we interact with objects or human artifacts, power and control are related to verticality. It is therefore easier to nail a large board to the floor than to the ceiling of a room.

The metaphorical construal of VERTICALITY has received solid support in empirical research. Schubert (2005), in a series of experiments, has demonstrated that judgments of a group's power is influenced by vertical position in space and that this affect is not driven by valence differences. Valenzuela and Soriano (2009) have similarly found, in psycholinguistic experiments, that their participants naturally associate VERTICALITY with CONTROL. As might be expected, these primary metaphors form the basis for conceptualization of powerful supernatural agents such as God. As an all-powerful being who is control of everything, God and other such powerful entities are naturally construed as occupying a higher spatial position (e.g. Meier & Fetterman, 2020; Meier et al., 2021. In numerous cultures, verticality metaphors underly social practices such as bowing (the lowering of the self on a vertical axis, accenting the power or worth of the object of devotion), and these practices have, in turn, become pervasive within many religious practices.

One of the most graphic portrayals of power and control as expressed through verticality can be found in representations of the Four Heavenly Kings, which often appear at the entrance to Buddhist temples in China, Japan, and Korea. These guardian figures are frequently depicted as stepping on grimacing demonic figures, who writhe in pain underneath their feet. These guardians are also often depicted as larger than the typical human. In this way, metaphorical entailments related to VERTICALITY are further augmented by conceptual mappings related to SIZE. The mapping of SIZE to IMPORTANCE or POWER also has a solid basis in embodied experience. Throughout the animal kingdom, size is closely linked to hierarchy, and consequently, many animals will manipulate visual or auditory cues to fool a potential aggressor or predator into thinking that they are larger than they really are. Size is also a salient cue for human society. From an early age, children are aware of a correlation between the size of agents (particularly, *human* agents) and a host of other properties such as strength, authority, and power. Humans associate size and power even in modern situations in which such a link would appear to represent an unwarranted bias or prejudice (Littlemore, 2019, pp. 108–109). For example, research shows that physical stature is linked to the perception that someone is more dominant, charismatic, intelligent, high in status, and leaderlike (Blaker & van Vugt, 2014). It is therefore unsurprising that height is positively associated with career success for both men and women (Judge & Cable, 2004). The association appears to be bidirectional, with more powerful people perceived as possessing greater physical stature (Higham & Carment, 1992).

As would be expected, the experiential correlation between size and power has led to the development of size-related cognitive metaphors throughout the world's cultures. For example, Yu et al. (2017), in an analysis of English and Chinese, found consistent mappings between the source domains of SIZE and WEIGHT and the target domain of IMPORTANCE. In both languages, these associations are lexicalized, an indication that the conceptual metaphor is conventional. Research by Meier et al. (2008) indicates that large size is also associated with positive valence.

Metaphorical links between size and power are perhaps one of the most pervasive image-related metaphors employed in sculpture from the ancient past to the present, ranging from the massive carved megaliths at Göbekli Tepe (c. 9500 to 8000 BCE) to the two 20-meter-tall bronze figures of Kim Il-sung and Kim Jong-il at the Mansu Hill Grand Monument in Pyeongyang. In Buddhism, massive sculptures have appeared in the Buddhist world throughout history. Two notable examples would be the 55-meter-tall Buddha (built around 570 AD) and 38-meter-tall Buddha (built around 618 AD) at Bamiyan in Afghanistan, which were destroyed by the Taliban in 2001. The continued prevalence of the IMPORTANCE IS SIZE metaphor in Buddhism can be seen from the fact that many of the world's tallest statues are figures of the Buddha that were erected in the last couple of decades. These include the 128-meter-tall Spring Temple Buddha in Lushan, China (completed in 2008), the 116-meter-tall Laykyun Sekkya Buddha in Khatakan Taung, Myanmar (also completed in 2008), and the 100-meter-tall Amitābha figure in Ushiku, Japan (completed in 1993).

Size-related metaphors are used even when they distort natural proportions of well-known entities. Tanaka (2015, pp. 34–37) discusses one such example: an early Indian statue of the Buddha and an elephant depicting an incident in which Devadatta, an evil monk who was the Buddha's cousin, tried to kill the Buddha by setting an intoxicated elephant loose. When the elephant saw the Buddha, it was so overcome by his loving kindness that it immediately calmed down and knelt before him. In the iconic depiction of the event, the Buddha is shown with his right palm turned outward in what is known as the Gesture of Fearlessness (*Abhayamudrā*) with an elephant to his right. The elephant comes up just past the Buddha's ankles and could thus be easily mistaken for a kitten or tortoise. To the Buddha's left, an attendant figure is also depicted as unrealistically small, coming up just past the Buddha's left knee. The image demonstrates how the sculptor has, through the manipulation of relative size, chosen to sacrifice naturalness to convey the Buddha's power, authority, and control.

The primary metaphors related to CENTRALITY, VERTICALITY, and SIZE discussed so far map onto related target domains (e.g., IMPORTANCE and POWER), and for this reason, they are often combined in depictions in which a key figure is centrally located, positioned above the viewer (often on a pedestal), and is large in size. Another primary metaphor, which creates mappings from the domain of PROXIMITY to the domain of SOCIAL RELATIONSHIPS, is used in iconography to establish affiliations between figures of veneration. Like other primary metaphors, this has a strong embodied basis. Human beings who are socially intimate tend to be in close physical proximity with each other, so if we see a group of people huddled together in a park, we assume that they must be part of the same family, club, or group of friends. The metaphor underlies various common expressions related to human relationship, such as *drifting apart* and *getting closer*, and can also be seen in hand gestures in which the distance between the hands indicates the degree of intimacy or estrangement (Winter & Matlock, 2017).

The PROXIMITY metaphor is commonly used in iconography. To develop greater organization and integration of figures within the vast Buddhist pantheon, figures associated with the same texts, narratives, liturgies, vows, or practices are often placed within the same bounded frame. Such portrayals of affiliation are used extensively within esoteric Buddhism (e.g., Japanese Shingon). Leidy (2008, pp. 123–125) gives the example of the Womb World Mandala, which symbolizes the possibility of enlightenment within the phenomenal world. The mandala shows 12 courts that contain 414 deities. The central court shows Vairocana (the primordial "sun" Buddha) sitting on an open lotus whose eight petals contain seated buddhas at the cardinal points of the compass and bodhisattvas at intermediate points. On the right is the "Vajra Holder's Court" (symbolizing the power of the intellect to destroy human passions) and on the left is the "Lotus Holder's Court" (symbolizing the inherent purity of all sentient beings). The mandala is in turn paired with the similarly complex Diamond World Mandala, which serves as a guide to the spiritual practices leading to enlightenment. The two mandalas are used during public ceremonies, while sections of the mandalas are used in more private and specialized rituals. The arrangement of figures within geometric shapes (in the case of the Diamond World Mandala, a square containing nine squares, which in turn contain symmetrically placed circles) undoubtedly serves as a mnemonic for liturgy specialists (e.g., Shingon priests) while also expressing a meta-message conveying intimations of a vast and intricate cosmic order (cf. the concept of "layering" in Sperber & Wilson, 1987, p. 751).

In addition to the metaphor examples discussed so far, metonymy is also used extensively in iconography. Some examples come from the early period of Buddhism, during which anthropomorphic depictions of the Buddha appear to have been avoided and metonymic elements used in their stead. These include the Buddha's footprint used to represent the Buddha, or the bodhi tree where the Buddha achieved awakening used to represent the Buddha's enlightenment. The explanation for the apparent absence of the Buddha's bodily image in early Buddhism is controversial. Many (e.g., Linrothe, 1993) have claimed that there was an initial period of so-called "aniconism" during which the Buddha's physical form was not directly depicted, while others (e.g., Huntington, 2015) have argued that depictions such as the Buddha's footprint, which can be classified as metonymic, were more likely popular alternative styles of representation. A typical example of an "aniconic" depiction is provided by Tanaka (2015, pp. 5–6), who discusses a relief carving on the Great Stupa at Sanchi in Madhya Pradesh, India. In the detailed and crowded relief (full of other human figures) that shows the night-time departure of the prince (soon to become Buddha) from the palace to become an ascetic, the prince's presence must be inferred based on a parasol on the back of the royal stallion. As Tanaka (2015, pp. 5–6) points out, the idea that members of the royal family would be shaded by a parasol in India's hot climate makes perfect sense, but the depiction is nevertheless unnatural since the departure famously took place at night when everyone at the palace was asleep and a parasol would not be needed to block the sun.

Metonymic associations also serve an important function in iconography in the identification of key figures. To the untrained eye (and sometimes for experts as well), the myriad figures appearing in Buddhist art are often difficult to distinguish, but they can be identified through the placement of accompanying attendants, objects, or motifs that are conventionally associated with the figure (cf. Kress & van Leeuwen, 2021). Some of these, for example, the use of lion figures to identify portrayals of Shakyamuni from early Buddhist art (Leidy, 2008), could be regarded as MP2s. Hand gestures (*mudras*) and postures (especially, positioning of the legs) can also function as metonymic elements that facilitate identification of figures, and, in some cases, the narrative event being portrayed. For example, the *bhūmisparśa mudrā* (the depiction of the seated Buddha touching the ground with his right hand) is associated with the narrative of the historical Buddha's temptation by Māra, the evil one (Spagnoli, 2005). With this gesture, the Buddha invoked the goddess of the Earth to acknowledge his past merit and right to attain awakening.

In many instances, metonymy can be used to evoke or convey a narrative through depictions of multiple scenes from a story. An example of this is a lacquerware depiction found on the Tamamushi Shrine in Nara Japan (discussed by Leidy, 2008, p. 113). The work shows Siddhartha, during a previous lifetime as a bodhisattva, throwing himself off a cliff so as to provide food to a starving tigress and her cubs. In the depiction, Siddhartha (in a former life) is shown multiple times (within a single image lacking framelines) at the top of the cliff, in the air after diving off the cliff, and at the base of the cliff being consumed by the tigress and cubs. The artwork thus shows salient scenes of the story in superimposed form to remind the viewer of the entire narrative, which would be familiar to Buddhists as part of a shared oral and textual tradition. For the modern viewer, the use of multiple scenes to evoke a narrative is familiar (e.g., in comics). Even so, the reappearance of the same figure (the Buddha as bodhisattva) within the same scene without framelines is confusing since this sort of portrayal is not part of our current "grammar" of visual communication in which narrative frames are typically separated by boundaries or repeated spatial dimensions.

Metonymy can also function to evoke inferences that give a static image a sense of temporal depth. An example of this is found in a relief carving from Pakistan (second to third century) showing Shakyamuni's final transcendence (Leidy, 2008, p. 41). The image shows the grieving monks gathered around the Buddha, who is shown lying peacefully on his side in the center of the work. As Leidy (2008) points out, minor elements in the work have been placed to hint at preceding and concurrent events. For example, monks' staffs with carrying bags on top are shown in front of the funerary bed, indicating that monks have come from far away to attend the funeral, while an incense burner placed on the bottom left indicates that rites have been performed. A leafy medallion with a female figure inside shows the deceased Queen Maya descending from heaven to visit her son one last time. The use of metonymy to evoke temporal depth has received support in empirical research. For example, Shen and Biberman (2010) have shown that naïve participants who are asked to view pictures showing a "pregnant moment" will tend to enlist elaborate narrative organization to make sense of pictures, organizing "visual information as a sequence of temporally and casually related events" (p. 191). They add that this tendency to seek narrative organization appears to hold true when people view isolated pictures irrespective of genre.

Implications and Future Directions

As the above discussion demonstrates, Buddhist iconography expresses meaning through conceptual mappings that are often realized through metaphor and metonymy. The examples suggest that the choice of mapping reflects some of the varied ways in which religious artwork is viewed. For example, the use of primary metaphors presumably reflects concerns that the iconography be accessible to a wide audience. This is apparent if we imagine a scenario in which a visitor from abroad with no prior knowledge of Buddhism visits a Buddhist temple. It is difficult to imagine that even such a naïve visitor, after walking around the temple grounds, would be unable to readily infer that the giant Buddha image seated high on a pedestal at the center of the compound is of central importance to the devotees of the religion and that the smaller figures on the side walls of peripheral halls represent more minor figures.

As our imaginary visitor gained greater familiarity with the tradition, they would realize that the iconography also evokes some less obvious meanings. Some of these would be based on mappings associated with more complex metaphors that may be associated with a specific Buddhist tradition. The visitor might learn, for example, that a specific hand gesture (Skt. *dharmachakra mudra*) shows the Buddha "turning" the wheel of the dharma and that the image of a wheel is associated with the Buddha's teachings and first sermon. The visitor may also learn a set of associations, perhaps images evoking key narratives and events, that are expressed through metonymy. In this chapter, a key conjecture then is that iconography uses a mix of conceptual mapping types to ensure that religious art affords interpretive possibilities ranging from those that are readily accessible to all viewers, to include neophytes, and those that are accessible only to more knowledgeable viewers.

A possible objection to this line of reasoning is that there is often a considerable temporal gap between the production of iconography and the viewing of these representations. In practical terms, why would creators of iconography work to ensure that their works are interpretable in specific ways (e.g., in ways that accord with their specific tradition) by later viewers who encounter the works decades or even centuries later? One possible response is to adapt Sperber's (1996) notion of an "epidemiology of representations." This is the idea that the successful transmission of beliefs relies on a constellation of psychological and ecological factors, such as people's ability to understand and recall a belief, the existence of institutions to record and transmit the beliefs, and so on. Along these lines, it might be argued that the producers of iconography are transmitting the more successful representational processes of their predecessors. When iconography successfully provides affordances for doctrinally relevant interpretations to both neophyte and expert viewers (often through masterful use of both metaphor and metonymy), the same styles and motifs are maintained with only minor modification. When they fail to achieve such effects, artists presumably strive to create alternative depictions that break more radically from previous artistic practices.

The less accessible elements in iconography may play a similar role as the weak implicatures that produce "poetic effects" in poetry and literature by providing rich possibilities for additional interpretations beyond those that are immediately obvious. While Sperber and Wilson (1995) view explicatures and sets of weak implicatures as *alternatives* related to different communication strategies, it can be argued that *religious* audiences will often continue to search for additional layers of meaning within representations (regardless of the mode) even after a plausible explicature has been identified. This is due to distinctive assumptions related to religious discourse: the notion that there are deeper layers of significance awaiting the religious seeker who is willing to pursue them (Richardson et al., 2021, p. 122). Moreover, religious texts and images can sometimes be the object of intensive study and reflection for centuries, a situation that virtually ensures that multiple layers of alternative meanings ("weak implicatures" in Relevance Theory) will eventually emerge as the texts' audience seeks interpretations relevant to their society and their individual needs.

When analyzing religious iconography, it should be kept in mind that these works, while often encountered in museums or books, are typically designed for use within a rich context that involves liturgical activities and ritual. Such activities often employ the use of multiple modes of communication to include imagery, sounds, and spoken language. A good example of this is the ritualized use of a wooden gong. Throughout northeast Asian temples, this instrument often takes the form of a carved wooden fish. In early tradition, the instrument was used to notify the monastic assembly of mealtimes or work details. The fish shape was purportedly selected since fish never close their eyes, and the fish-shaped wooden gong thus reminds meditation monks to minimize their sleep as they engage in spiritual practice. In more modern times, the wooden gong has continued to be used in Zen temples in China, Japan, and Korea, primarily as a percussion instrument that accompanies chanting.

In Korea, in addition to this small wooden gong, called a *moktak*, larger monasteries also have a large wooden gong called a *mogeo*, which hangs in a central pavilion (along with a large bell and other instruments) that is located at the center of a complex. As a prelude to the morning and evening service, the wooden fish is struck by drumsticks that are moved back and forth in the hollow inside of the instrument. If we consider the Korean *mogeo* in terms of its actual function within devotional services, it serves as a good example of a multimodal representation based on both metaphor and metonymy.

The fish shape creates a metonymic link to a traditional tale of a monk who violated the teachings of his master and engaged in improper activities (Richardson et al., 2021). According to the tale, when the wayward monk died, he was reborn as a fish, which (due to his bad karma) had a tree growing out of his back. One day the master saw the fish struggling as it swam through the river and realized that it was the reincarnation of his wayward disciple. Out of compassion, the master performed a "water and land" ceremony (an offering to spirits in water and on land), which allowed the wayward disciple to return to human form. The disciple, deeply repentant, carved the tree that had grown out of his back into a fish as an admonition to others. The dragon head, seen on many *mogeo*, links to traditions of a magical jewel (Skt. *cintā-maṇi*) said to be obtained from the dragon-king of the sea. The jewel is said to manifest whatever one desires and is regarded as a metaphor for the teachings and virtues of the Buddha.

Part of viewers' experience of the *mogeo* when it is used in ceremonies involves nonverbal sounds (the striking of the hollow interior of the wooden instrument at a dramatically accelerating tempo). The instrument is quite loud, as it is meant to be audible throughout the entire monastic complex, and it therefore serves the obvious function of attracting attention. The loud and accelerating strikes are also associated with wakefulness, which is metaphorically associated with *spiritual* awakening (an association reinforced, in the visual mode, by the folk notion of fish as animals that do not sleep). As this example shows, multimodal religious representations are often rich and layered, and often involve the use of both metaphor and metonymy in multiple modes.

This chapter has briefly explored the use of the conceptual mapping principles put forth in CL in the analysis of religious iconography. This framework has been under-explored in work on religious art and iconography, so many questions remain. For example, is there a relationship between the primary functions of religious icons and the conceptual mappings type (e.g., primary metaphor, complex metaphor, metonymy) employed? Are there systematic differences between icons that are prominently displayed to the public and icons that are designed primarily for use in the esoteric practices of specialists? What is the relationship between the conceptual mappings employed in visual art and those found in spoken and written language? Moreover, there is tremendous scope for multimodal research that examines religious iconography in authentic contexts. Buddhist iconography is typically encountered within worship and ritual activities that may involve multiple modes of representation to include the recitation of related texts, the use of musical elements (e.g., the striking of a wooden gong or ringing of a bell), bowing (done individually or in unison), visualization practices, and the lighting of incense. It is odd that this exceedingly rich source of multimodal discourse has been ignored entirely in recent edited volumes on the subject.

Further Reading

Forceville, C.J. (2020). *Visual and multimodal communication: Applying the relevance principle*. Oxford University Press.
This is a recent overview of Forceville's influential framework, which applies relevance theory (Sperber & Wilson, 1995) to the analysis of pictorial images.
Kress, G., & van Leeuwen, T. (2021). *Reading images: The grammar of visual design* (3rd edition). Routledge.
This provides another excellent introduction to the analysis of imagery. It is more comprehensive in scope than Forceville's theory and is based loosely on systemic functional grammar (Halliday & Matthiessen, 2014).
Pérez Sobrino, P. (2017). *Multimodal metaphor and metonymy in advertising*. John Benjamins Publishing Company.
Many of the recent studies applying metaphor theory to the analysis of imagery have employed multimodal approaches. This work provides nuanced insights into the interactions between metaphor and metonymy within the genre of ads.
Pinar Sanz, M.J. (Ed.). (2015). *Multimodality and cognitive linguistics.* John Benjamins Publishing Company.
Fahlenbrach, K. (Ed.). (2016). *Embodied metaphors in film, television, and video games: Cognitive approaches*. Routledge.
These two recent edited collections provide excellent examples of recent work on multimodality. The latter work is especially useful in its discussion of metaphors within the macro-structures of film, which is characterized by especially rich compositions that bring together imagery, sound, and movement within narrative sequences.

References

Arnheim, R. (1982). *The power of the center: A study of composition in the visual arts.* University of California Press.

Black, M. (1962). *Models and metaphors: Studies in language and philosophy.* Cornell University Press.

Blaker, N.M. & van Vugt, M. (2014). The status-size hypothesis: How cues of physical size and social status influence each other. In J.T. Cheng, J.L. Tracy, & C. Anderson (Eds.), *The psychology of social status*, 119–137. https://doi.org/10.1016/j.neuropsychologia.2009.09.029

Dobbins, J.C. (2001). Portraits of Shinran in medieval Pure Land Buddhism. In R.H. Sharf & E.H. Sharf (Eds.), *Living images: Japanese Buddhist icons in context*, 19–48. Stanford University Press.

El Refaie, E. (2009). Metaphor in political cartoons: Exploring audience response. In C. Forceville (Ed.), *Multimodal metaphor*, 173–196.

Fahlenbrach, K. (Ed.). (2016). *Embodied metaphors in film, television, and video games: Cognitive approaches.* Routledge.

Forceville, C.J. (1996). *Pictorial metaphor in advertising.* Routledge.

Forceville, C.J. (2020). *Visual and multimodal communication: Applying the relevance principle.* Oxford University Press.

Grady, J.E. & Ascoli, G.A. (2017). Sources and targets in primary metaphor theory. In B. Hampe (Ed.), *Metaphor: Embodied cognition and discourse*, 27–45. Cambridge University Pres

Halliday, M.A.K. & Matthiessen, C.M.I.M. (2014). *Halliday's introduction to functional grammar* (4th edition). Routledge.

Hart, C.J. & Marmol Queralto, J. (2021). What can cognitive linguistics tell us about language-image relations? A multidimensional approach to intersemiotic convergence in multimodal texts. *Cognitive Linguistics*, *32*(4), 529–562. https://doi.org/10.1515/cog-2021-0039

Higham, P.A. & Carment, D.W. (1992). The rise and fall of politicians: The judged heights of Broadbent, Mulroney and Turner before and after the 1988 Canadian federal election. *Canadian Journal of Behavioural Science*, *24*(3), 404–409. https://doi.org/10.1037/h0078723

Huntington, S.L. (2015). Shifting the paradigm: The aniconic theory and its terminology. *Southeast Asian Studies*, *31*(2), 163–186. https://doi.org/10.1080/02666030.2015.1094203

Judge, T.A. & Cable, D.M. (2004). The effect of physical height on workplace success and income: Preliminary test of a theoretical model. *Journal of Applied Psychology*, *89*(3), 428–441. https://doi.org/10.1037/0021-9010.89.3.428

Kövecses, Z. (2006). *Language, mind, and culture: A practical introduction.* Oxford University Press.

Kress, G. & van Leeuwen, T. (2021). *Reading images: The grammar of visual design* (3rd edition). Routledge.

Lakoff, G. & Johnson, M. (1980). *Metaphors we live by.* University of Chicago.

Leidy, D.P. (2008). *The art of Buddhism: An introduction to its history and meaning.* Shambala.

Linrothe, R. (1993). Inquiries into the origin of the Buddha image: A review. *East and West*, *43*(1), 241–256.

Littlemore, J. (2019). *Metaphors in the mind: Sources of variation in embodied metaphor.* Cambridge University Press.

Meier, B.P. & Fetterman, A.K. (2020). Metaphors for god: God is high, bright, and human in implicit tasks. *Psychology of Religion and Spirituality*. https://doi.org/10.1037/rel0000324

Meier, B.P., Fetterman, A.K., Hauser, D.J., & Robinson, M.D. (2021). God is up? Replication and extension attempts of Meier et al. (2007). *Psychology of Religion and Spirituality*. https://doi.org/10.1037/rel0000433https://doi.org/10.1037/0022-3514.93.5.699

Meier, B.P., Robinson, M.D., & Caven, A.J. (2008). Why a Big Mac is a good Mac: Associations between affect and size. *Basic and Applied Social Psychology*, *30*(1), 46–55. https://doi.org/10.1080/01973530701866516

Ortiz, M.J. (2011). Primary metaphors and monomodal visual metaphors. *Journal of Pragmatics*, *43*(6), 1568–1580. https://doi.org/10.1016/j.pragma.2010.12.003

Pérez Sobrino, P. (2017). *Multimodal metaphor and metonymy in advertising.* John Benjamins Publishing Company.

Pinar Sanz, M.J. (Ed.). (2015). *Multimodality and cognitive linguistics.* John Benjamins Publishing Company.

Richardson, P., Mueller, C.M., & Pihlaja, S. (2021). *Cognitive linguistics and religious language: An introduction.* Routledge.

Schubert, T.W. (2005). Your highness: vertical positions as perceptual symbols of power. *Journal of Personality and Social Psychology, 89*(1), 1–21. https://doi.org/10.1037/0022-3514.89.1.1

Shen, Y., & Biberman, E. (2010). A story told by a picture. *Image and Narrative, 11*(2), 177–197.

Snowden, R., Thompson, P., & Troscianko, T. (2012). *Basic vision: An introduction to visual perception* (revised edition). Oxford University Press.

Spagnoli, M. (2005). Searching for the origin of the "bhūmisparśa-mudrā". *East and West, 55*(1), 329–344. www.jstor.org/stable/29757652

Sperber, D. (1996). *Explaining culture: a naturalistic approach*. Blackwell.

Sperber, D. & Wilson, D. (1987). Précis of relevance: Communication and cognition. *Behavioral and Brain Sciences, 10*(4), 697–754. https://doi.org/10.1017/S0140525X00055345

Sperber, D. & Wilson, D. (1995). *Relevance: Communication and cognition*, 2nd edition. Blackwell Publishing.

Tanaka, K. (2015). *Bukkyō zuzōgaku* [Buddhist iconography]. Shunjusha.

Valenzuela, J. & Soriano, C. (2009). Are conceptual metaphors accessible online? A psycholinguistic exploration of the CONTROL IS UP metaphor. In J. Valenzuela, A. Rojo, & C. Soriano (Eds.), *Trends in cognitive linguistics: Theoretical and applied models*, 31–50. Peter Lang.

Winter, B. & Matlock, T. (2017). Primary metaphors are both cultural and embodied. In B. Hampe (Ed.), *Metaphor: Embodied cognition and discourse*, 99–115. Cambridge University Press.

Yu, N., Yu, L., & Lee, C.Y. (2017). Primary metaphors: Importance as size and weight in a comparative perspective. *Metaphor and Symbol, 32*(4), 231–249. https://doi.org/10.1080/10926488.2017.1384276

9

ANALYSING METAPHOR IN RELIGIOUS DISCOURSE IN LITERATURE

Clara Neary

Introduction and Background

As Pihlaja (2021) asserts, religious discourse is a difficult concept to define, both because discussion of religion takes many different shapes and forms, moulded by their varying purposes and consequences, and because discourse is itself a notoriously complex phenomenon. We can also differentiate between "explicitly religious discourse", that is, "where the speakers are focused on issues of religious belief and practice" (Pihlaja, 2021, p. 6) and implicitly religious discourse, where the religious message or connotations are considerably more subtle and reveal themselves only upon close textual and/or contextual investigation. Analysing religious discourse in literary texts is therefore somewhat distinct from its analysis in conventionally non-literary texts because while the latter's consideration of religion is largely more explicit, literature frequently engages with religious discourse at both the explicit and the implicit levels. Metaphor proves a particularly useful feature for analytical focus in the face of such narrative complexity. This is due, firstly, to metaphor's range: figurative tropes cover both the macro-textual (e.g. allegory, analogy, extended metaphor) and the micro-textual (e.g. simile, metonymy). Secondly, the cognitive approaches to metaphor which now dominate linguistic metaphor studies provide an analytical framework which enables detailed and fruitful investigation of metaphor at both the linguistic and conceptual levels. The cognitive approach dominated by Conceptual Metaphor Theory has some limitations and its usefulness is dependent upon the ways in which religious discourse is constructed in the text as well as the intentions of the analyst (see 'Implications and Further Directions'). However, as the central tenet of cognitive approaches to metaphor is that metaphor is both linguistically and cognitively constructed, both cognitive and non-cognitive approaches to metaphor can be drawn upon in analysing a single text, as is illustrated in the case study carried out in this chapter.

Metaphor is particularly important in the construction of religious discourse, being seen as "the natural language through which religious faith is communicated" (Charteris-Black, 2017, p. 68). Dorst more explicitly states that "[m]etaphor and religion go hand in hand, given the fact that our religious and spiritual experiences are highly personal, emotional, and abstract" (2021, p. 251). This chapter aims to illustrate the usefulness of metaphor as a focus for the analysis of religious discourse by focusing particularly on religious discourse construction in literary texts. It will do so

DOI: 10.4324/9781003301271-10

by first offering an overview of the most common approach to metaphor study within language and linguistics—that of Conceptual Metaphor Theory—before sketching some of the other types of metaphoric construction that can usefully capture how religious discourse is constructed. Having provided this background, the chapter will proceed to a detailed analysis of the ways in which metaphor informs upon the religious discourse in Hilary Mantel's 1989 novel *Fludd*, a novel thematically centred upon both religion and metaphor and, most tellingly, on the ways in which they are interlinked.

From the Greek to 'carry over', metaphor can be defined as "the practice of talking about one thing as if it were another, on the grounds that there are some notional similarities between the two entities" (Jeffries & McIntyre, 2010, p. 138). As such, metaphor use is motivated and meaningful in that the reader/listener is being encouraged to make sense of one particular concept by drawing associations between it and a second specified concept. Notwithstanding metaphor's key role in meaning-making, until the mid-twentieth century traditional approaches to its analysis were primarily formal, seeing metaphor as a marker of literary discourse and being largely content to limit its consideration to the level of description (Jeffries & McIntyre, 2010, p. 139). However, the "cognitive turn" in the humanities (see Hogan 2003; Stafford 2011) ushered in cognitive-informed approaches to metaphor which asserted that metaphor is neither simply a mode of language nor the sole preserve of literary discourse. Rather, metaphor is a way of thinking about the world which reveals itself through language use (as well as through other semiotic modes, e.g. Forceville, 1996). As such, Semino points out that "metaphors are seldom neutral: constructing something in terms of something else results in a particular view of the 'something' in question, often including specific attitudes and evaluation" (2008, p. 32). Therefore, identification of the conceptual mappings underpinning a metaphor can be particularly illuminating of the text containing the metaphor, revealing its thematic concerns and its ideological worldview (see Goatly 2011; Semino 2008). This is particularly evident where metaphors are employed systematically across a text or discourse situation; as Lakoff and Johnson note: "the very systematicity that allows us to comprehend one aspect of a concept in terms of another … will necessarily hide other aspects of the concept" (1980, p. 10). Effectively, certain aspects of a conceptual domain are foregrounded while others are concealed, a selective operation which influences how we perceive the event, person, action etc. being represented (see Semino, 2008).

For example, let us consider Romeo's description of Juliet as the sun in Act II, Scene II of Shakespeare's play:

> But, soft! what light through yonder window breaks?
> It is the east, and *Juliet is the sun.*
> Arise, fair sun, and kill the envious moon,
> Who is already sick and pale with grief,
> That thou her maid art far more fair than she:
> (II, II; 2–6; emphasis added)

This metaphoric comparison functions to highlight positive attributes of the sun which can be applied to Juliet, such as its dazzling quality, its brightness, and its warmth. But both the immediate linguistic and the immediate cognitive contexts are key: we comprehend Romeo's comparison of Juliet to the sun in the knowledge that he is in love with Juliet, so only positive attributes of the sun are likely to be appropriate to him, and therefore it is only positive attributes that will be activated by us in our search for meaning. However, at the end of the play, our interpretation of this metaphor may require modification: the sun is not only life-giving but also essential to life and, when he thinks Juliet is dead, Romeo sees no option for himself but death. The choice of the sun as source domain to describe the target domain of Juliet now appears portentous for both the "star-crossed lovers" (Prologue, 6) and their families: as the Prince concludes in the play's final scene, "all are punish'ed" by the meeting of this doomed pair (V, III, 305).

Expounded by Lakoff and Johnson in their seminal 1980 book *Metaphors We Live By*, Conceptual Metaphor Theory (CMT) is the most dominant cognitive theory of metaphor. It draws a distinction between the linguistic manifestation of a metaphor—often known as the metaphoric linguistic expression—and the conceptual metaphor which underpins it. A central tenet of CMT is that the conceptual metaphors that underpin a metaphoric linguistic expression "represent, reflect, and shape deeply entrenched ways of thinking about abstract concepts such as time, life, and death, or strong emotions such as love, and help us articulate otherwise inexpressible, elusive concepts" (Senkbeil & Hoppe, 2016). Conceptual metaphors are those "certain conceptual patterns we rely on in our daily living to think about aspects of the world" (Kövecses, 2017, p. 16). LIFE IS A JOURNEY is one such fundamental conceptual metaphor and not only does it capture the way we think of the abstract domain of 'life', but also structures our thinking about it. Analysis using CMT typically involves finding the conceptual metaphor underlying a metaphoric linguistic expression by identifying the conceptual domain, or "any coherent organization of experience" (Kövecses, 2002, p. 4), which has been targeted for description (the *target* domain) and the conceptual domain drawn upon to act as a comparator (the *source* domain) and then analysing the characteristics of the source domain which are being activated or 'mapped' on to the target domain, a process which tends to involve identifying commonalities between target and source domain. Depending on the purpose of the analysis, the next step in a CMT investigation may be to see if the conceptual metaphors identified reveal a conventional or novel representation of the target domain and, by extension, of the entity or situation the metaphor is depicting. Lakoff and Turner assert that, "[a]t the conceptual level, a metaphor is conventional to the extent that it is automatic, effortless and generally established as a mode of thought among members of a linguistic community" (1989, p. 55). In this way, CMT analysis can provide a tangible means of tracing the origins of the defamiliarisation which typically follows the processing of unusual metaphoric constructions. As noted by Kövecses, "[w]henever a new source domain is applied to a particular target, we see the target domain differently than we saw it before" (2017, p. 17); the result is a semantic foregrounding of the entity or concept being described which effectively defamiliarises it or makes it 'strange'.

Unlike traditional approaches, cognitive approaches to metaphor do not distinguish between the various tropes of figurative language, instead labelling them all as 'metaphor' due to their common concern with 'mapping' from one conceptual domain to another. However, there are instances in which it is fruitful to make a distinction, especially when considering the specific effects of the trope of *metonymy*. A common feature of everyday language, metonymy comes from the Greek for 'change', and is defined as a "rhetorical figure or trope by which the name of a referent is replaced by the name of an attribute, or of an entity related in some semantic way" (Wales, 2011, pp. 267–268). From a cognitive perspective, "a metonym is when one entity stands for another to which it is closely related in experience" (Charteris-Black, 2017, p. 26). Metonymy is distinct from metaphor because, as Simpson (2014, p. 44) points out, while metaphor involves mapping from one conceptual domain to another, metonymy involves a transfer within the *same* conceptual domain. This is evident in the following typical examples which involve the replacement of, respectively: a part for the whole (e.g. 'an old *head* on young *shoulders*') which is a special type of metonymy called *synecdoche*; the producer for the produced (e.g. 'Have you seen the new *Tarentino*?'); the location for the institution (e.g. '*Downing Street* refused to comment'); and the object for its associated occupation (e.g. 'I've hired a new *brief*'). In each case, the metonymy is underpinned by an 'X stands for Y' conceptual template, with 'X' and 'Y' being related concepts drawn from the same conceptual domain.

Stylistically, the importance of metonymy lies in its indexicality: as Wales notes, metonymic constructions invoke "a directly or logically contiguous relationship between the substituted word and its referent" (2011, pp. 267–268). As such, the choice of the substituted word is meaningful and creates textual effect. Simpson notes that, unlike metaphor which "assumes" a certain distance between source and target domain—and indeed, in the case of literary metaphors, often prizes such distance because it strengthens defamiliarization—metonymy assumes a closeness between the concepts it draws upon and "upgrades" the relevant mapped elements so that they come to "represent that domain as a whole" (2014, p. 45). An easy way to distinguish metonymy from metaphor, Simpson asserts, is to attempt to turn the utterance into a simile: attempts to convert some of the abovementioned metonymic constructions into similes—such as 'a worker is *like* a hand' or 'a solicitor is *like* a briefcase'—do not succeed (2014, p. 45). On the other hand, a metaphoric expression such as 'I don't know which path to take in life' can easily be converted into the simile 'life is like a path/journey'. Wales adds that a further difference between metaphor and metonymy is that in the latter there is no flouting of the Gricean maxim of quality: by stating that 'X *is* Y', metaphor effectively lies, whereas in metonymy, which posits that 'X *stands for* Y', truthfulness is "maintained" (Wales, 2011, p. 268). The semantic deviation inherent in metaphor, which serves to foreground it, is hence absent in metonymy; nonetheless, as Wales continues, like metaphor, metonymy works by substitution "of an expected word by the unexpected" (2011, p. 268). It is the 'unexpectedness' that foregrounds metonymy and underpins its stylistic and rhetorical effects.

Dancygier and Sweetser point out that, in the context of religion, metaphor does not simply add additional meaning to the literal, as is the case in certain other contexts. Rather, the many "transcendent" and "ineffable" aspects of religious doctrine cannot be articulated without recourse to metaphor so that some religious contexts rely on figurative language because "literal language is seen as *radically insufficient*" (2014, p. 208; emphasis in original). Lodge similarly asserts the importance of creative metaphors in enabling us to talk about experiences that seem to resist capture in "'literal' language" (2002, p. 13). Indeed, as Dancygier and Sweetser note, figurative language does not merely pervade religious discourse, but rather "certain metaphors (e.g. GOD AS SHEPHERD) may even be seen as defining characteristics of particular religious discourse genres" (2014, p. 209). In addition, doctrinally based differences across and within religions can result from alternating views on the value and application of figurative language: for some, the sacred texts and their contents are considered literally true (a *subrationalist* stance) while for others they are considered figuratively true (a *superrationalist* stance). Such views are not relevant to practitioners of CMT given that its central tenet is that metaphor is a mode of both language and thought, and indeed Dancygier and Sweetser (2014) note the extent to which religious discourse draws upon common conceptual metaphors, such as GOOD IS UP and POWER IS UP, which are applicable to the divinities of most religions.

Using CMT, Charteris-Black (2004) illustrates that the sacred texts of the Bible and Qur'an have several conceptual metaphors in common while also containing some interesting distinctions. He notes that while, in both texts, "journey, fire and light and weather metaphors are important and are based on conceptual metaphors such as spiritual knowledge is light, good is light, divine anger is fire and divine punishment is a hostile weather condition" (2004, p. 238), the Qur'an tends to highlight the power of divine retribution. He also points out that certain semantic domains—such as food, drink, and animals—are used metaphorically in the Bible and more literally in the Qur'an.

Charteris-Black (2017) investigates the role of specific conceptual metaphors of fire—those with fire as the source domain—in religious discourse. He reframes religious discourse as a 'discourse of awe' and compares it to the 'discourse of authority' found in political discourse as a means of illustrating the power dynamics which underpin and connect the language of both. Discourses of authority, both religious and secular, have, as Charteris-Black notes (2017, p. 6), a long history of study by those concerned with the linguistic strategies by which power can be both acquired and maintained, and metaphor has often featured strongly in such studies. Echoing Dancygier and Sweetser, Charteris-Black notes that religion is "largely a complex system of metaphors" and that difficulties arise during attempts to distinguish the metaphoric from the literal—particular in the case of fire metaphors—because religion often involves "different individuals perceiving different degrees of metaphoricity" (2017, p. 117). Of relevance to this chapter, and particularly to the case study contained herein, is how Charteris-Black draws similarities between fire as a conceptual domain and metaphor:

> Metaphor is …, metaphorically speaking, fire in language. Just as fire transforms the visible material world into something immaterial and less visible, so metaphor shifts the sense of words away from their visible, material senses towards invisible, immaterial senses. Fire is therefore the perfect model for how metaphor works …"
>
> (2017, p. 9)

While the nature and substance of literature continues to be interrogated and redefined, this chapter follows Caracciolo in considering literature to be "a practice involving written—and typically, but not necessarily, fictional—texts that are thought to have special value in a given community" (2017, p. 207). An emphasis on the commonality and fundamentality of the conceptual templates underpinning metaphor means that cognitive approaches see metaphor as contiguous across literary and non-literary discourse. As the same conceptual and linguistic resources are available to all text types, there is no such thing as literary language (Simpson, 2014, p. 43). However, metaphor use tends to differ across text types in terms of its volume, its visibility, and its form, with attendant variations in its effects. Novel metaphors are more typically found in literary discourse than in everyday discourse (see Goatly, 1997). Firstly, this is potentially because the split-discourse context of writing provides the extra processing time needed for both the authorial crafting and readerly processing of less conventional metaphoric mappings; secondly, it must also relate to the fact that defamiliarisation is a key concern of literary discourse (as well as advertising discourse) and metaphor is, as mentioned above, "the foregrounding device *par excellence*" (Caracciolo, 2017, p. 208). In literature, metaphors also tend to be more novel, or what Goatly refers to as "active" and typically contain more patterning which adds meaning by drawing attention to recurrent differences or similarities across a text (see Goatly 1997, 2011). Furthermore, Kövesces states that literary metaphors are "typically less clear but richer in meaning than either everyday metaphors or metaphors in science" (2002, p. 43), which points not only towards a lack of any obvious single meaning (*clarity*) but also a strategic ambiguity that creates a potential multiplicity of meanings (*richness*) (see Lakoff & Turner 1989). As Wales notes, the result of this "indeterminacy" (2011, p. 266) is that metaphor can play a particularly important role in literary texts.

Of particular relevance in the context of analysing religious discourse is the genre in which it is located—or, more accurately, *the reader's identification* of that genre. Research shows that readers will process and interpret metaphor differently depending on what they perceive the genre in question to be. Steen (1994), for example, found that readers respond differently to metaphors in literature versus in journalistic texts; in the case of metaphors in literature, readers are more likely to "focus on metaphors, identify them explicitly, evaluate them according to aesthetic criteria, interpret them by referring to authorial intentions, and 'refunctionalize' them later on in the act of reading" (Caracciolo, 2017, p. 210; see Steen, 1994, p. 142). The increased attention paid to metaphor in literary discourse makes literature the ideal text type for what Steen has labelled the "deliberate metaphor" (see Steen, 2008, 2017), defined as any metaphor which is "expressly meant to change the addressee's perspective on the referent or topic that is the target of the metaphor, by making the addressee look at it from a different conceptual domain or space, which functions as a conceptual source" (2008, p. 222).

Although this chapter is focusing on literature, making Steen's conclusions more easily applicable, the obvious importance of perceived genre raises an interesting question about the potential location of religious discourse on an imaginary literature/non-literature continuum. For example, it is not clear whether religious discourse is perceived as literary or non-literary, fiction or non-fiction. In many ways, the parameters of religious discourse as a genre lie both *outside* and *across* the typical boundaries of generic classification for a multitude of reasons connected to the reader's perception of that religion—allied to the *subrationalist* and *superrationalist* ways of thinking mentioned above—as well as that religion's sanctioned status in the place in which it is being read.

The case study that follows focuses on the novel *Fludd*, written in 1989 by the British novelist Hilary Mantel (1952–2022), who went on to become a double-Booker Prize winner (in 2009 and 2012). The novel's thematic concerns with religion and metaphor, and religion *as* metaphor, make it ripe for analysis in this chapter on metaphor and religious discourse. These thematic concerns are evidenced across all levels of the text, inviting a combination of macro and micro analysis that investigates how language, and metaphor in particular, can be used to both construct and deconstruct religious discourse.

Metaphor and Religious Discourse in *Fludd* (Hilary Mantel, 1989)

Hilary Mantel's novel, *Fludd*, is concerned with events that follow the arrival of an enigmatic stranger, named 'Fludd', to the parochial house of a fictitious village in the North of England in the mid-1950s. The novel's religious themes are foregrounded from the outset: the opening paratextual note states, "The Church in this story bears some but not much resemblance to the Roman Catholic Church in the real world, c. 1956"; the second paratextual note describes Sebastiano del Piombo's painting *The Raising of Lazarus* (1517–1519); and the novel proper commences with the visit of the diocesan bishop to the local parish priest, Father Angwin. The bishop, "a modern man, no patience with scruples, no time for the ancient byways of faith" (p. 24) has come to instruct Angwin to remove the "idolatrous" statues from the local Church of St Thomas Aquinas, decrying them as "frills and baubles" (p. 21), mere "fripperies" (p. 21). It is, the bishop maintains, time to "drag you and your church and your parishioners into the 1950s" (p. 21). The temporal setting here is significant, given the establishment of Vatican II in 1962, only six years after the novel is set; the bishop is a counterpoint to the traditional Angwin, who perceives the younger man as "a person right outside of my experience" (p. 9). Rather than destroy the statues or give them away, Angwin decides, given their significance to the lives of the parishioners, to bury them: "I shan't have a service," he says, "Just an interment" (p. 27). The act of burying the statues is the catalyst that sets the novel's main events in motion, commencing with the arrival, that very night, of the enigmatic stranger, Fludd.

However, the second part of the novel's opening paratextual note appears to problematise the novel's explicitly religious themes by drawing an association between the 'new curate' and the early modern alchemist Robert Fludd: "The real Fludd (1574–1637) was a physician, scholar and alchemist. In alchemy, everything has a literal and factual description, and in addition a description that is symbolic and fantastical". Upon admitting the curate into the parochial house from the "bluish wild darkness" of an unseasonably stormy night—"a tall, dim shape, a man wrapped in a dark cloak, holes for eyes and mouth" (p. 42)—the housekeeper Agnes Dempsey feels a portentous "whisper at the back of her mind, and only he could have put it there: I have come to transform you, transformation is my business" (pp. 54–55). And Fludd's arrival indeed transforms the lives of those around him: Father Angwin's galvanisation into action sees his long-lost faith restored; Sister Philomena, a "true daughter of the Irish soil" (p. 32) sacrificed to the religious life by her family, is transformed "out of all recognition" (p.149); and the meek Miss Dempsey, housekeeper at the parochial house, is energised out of a faith-induced stupor. To a less agreeable extent, Father Angwin's nemeses—the local convent's Mother Perpetua and "His Corpulence" (p. 7) the bishop—are also altered.

Metaphor in Fludd

Just as alchemy is concerned with the transformation of one substance into another, so the new curate proves to be an agent of change, like his namesake Robert Fludd. Fludd's latter-day transformations, however, are rather different: "these days, he no longer worked in metal, but practised on human nature; an art less predictable, more gratifying, more dangerous" (p. 104). This fusion of Fludd with Robert Fludd suggests the novel is operating figuratively at the macro level, as both *analogy* and *allegory*. As Hamilton notes, "[a]nalogies are created when at least two things appear to be conceptually parallel to one another" (2002, p. 9); the new curate is constructed as an analogue of Robert Fludd, a trope that itself recalls the ways in which early modern texts appropriated figures from antiquity into their contemporary world.

In a manner indicative of the figurative layering in this novel, this analogue simultaneously constructs an *allegory*, as the new curate is specifically represented as not only *like* Robert Fludd but an actual *revenant* of the medieval alchemist. The theme of resurrection is foregrounded from the outset, with the second of the novel's opening paratextual notes describing Sebastiano del Piombo's painting *The Raising of Lazarus* (1517–1519). Definitions of the trope of allegory (from the Greek 'allegoria' meaning 'other speaking') vary considerably. It has been defined both very broadly to include "any fiction that is subject to a continuous and consistent metaphorical interpretation" (Ritchie, 2017, p. 339) and very specifically to include only metaphoric language that avoids overt or direct reference to the target domain (see Crisp, 2005). There are, however, two features largely agreed as typical of allegory; these are the presence of "abstract personifications" and of "topifications", which are "conceptually laden landscapes ... within the frame of a journey or quest" (Harris & Tolmie, 2011, p. 112).

In its narrowest sense, then, allegory only relates directly to the source domain (see Crisp, 2005, p. 326), a definition which helps to mark the novel *Fludd* as allegorical, as well as analogical. Fludd-the-curate is the target domain, while Fludd-the-alchemist is the source domain; the naming of the former by reference to the latter foregrounds this allegorical relationship. Typically, allegory involves an abstract personification, such as the figure of Death stalking the land, but the personification here is concrete. Nevertheless, while Fludd-the-curate is a real man his supernatural status is foregrounded throughout: the food and drink he is given seem to disappear rather than be consumed and he has no need of sleep. Fludd-the-curate is a revenant of Fludd-the-alchemist; his status is simultaneously natural and supernatural, and his status as allegory is therefore uncertain, which is fitting given that allegory is itself a "fuzzy category" (Harris & Tolmie 2011, p. 112). Fludd can be seen, however, to represent the concept of Transformation, which further emphasises the figurative dimension of the character at the novel's core: Fludd is transformation; he does not merely stand for it, but allegorically embodies it.

The novel's twin concerns of metaphor and alchemy are themselves linked through a shared emphasis on transformation: just as alchemy creates new *material* from old, metaphor creates new *meaning* from old. The novel is effectively underpinned by the conceptual metaphor METAPHOR IS ALCHEMY, with the mapped element being their mutual capacity to transform. As detailed elsewhere (see Neary, 2023), the novel also weaves the metaphoric with the literal at the level of narrative by mapping the stages of the alchemical process on to the novel's key events—the burial of the statues, the meeting between Fludd and Sister Philomena in the allotments and the exhumation of the statues—to create a kind of 'narrative alchemy'. Once buried, the description of the statues as "mouldering under the ground" (p. 82) suggests a state of corruption, the first stage of the alchemical process. The next stage involves the introduction of fire, which is metaphorically and literally kindled during Fludd and Sister Philomena's meeting in an allotment; their rising passions ignite "a Mediterranean frenzy of heat" (p. 106) in what is a dilapidated and draughty shed on the moors in mid-winter. Tellingly, it is here that Fludd tells Philomena of the importance, in alchemy, of the catalyst, for "no scientist, however accomplished, can light the furnace himself" (p. 105). Fludd is the fire, a catalyst for change: "Since he came here, [Philomena] thought, a match had been put to her future. She did not think that she loved him, but still, something burned: a slow, white flicker of approaching change" (p. 105). Finally, the disinterring of the statues marks the final transformation of the human subjects of this metaphoric alchemy: Father Angwin's faith is restored; Miss Dempsey's youthful vigour reappears; and Sister Philomena has "melted away, and remoulded herself into some other woman" (p. 144).

The effects of this narrative alchemy are far-reaching. At the very moment she is about to stop Roisin's flight from the parish with Fludd, the convent superior Mother Perpetua, Angwin's "mortal enemy" (p. 155), becomes a victim of "spontaneous combustion" (p. 174) caused by "a low blue flame, creeping towards her over the grass" (p. 172). The perpetrator seems obvious: the bishop rightly fears "there must be some chemical reaction that caused it" (p. 174) and the reference to the flame's colour recalls the "bluish wild darkness" (p. 42) out of which the new curate first arrived. During their meeting in the allotments, Fludd had spoken of Origen's Doctrine of Larger Hope to comfort Philomena; "all men will ultimately be saved", he told her, as the "torment of Hell is a purifying process" (p. 104). However, even the purification of hellfire is not granted to Mother Perpetua: though it is clear "she had had a shock" (p. 173), she survives "not much disfigured" (p. 173).

By the end of the novel the bishop is a chastened rather than a changed man. Following Angwin's discovery—aided by Philomena—that this "modern man" (p. 24) had once edited a text on Catholic doctrine based on "the old faith in its entirety; the dear old faith, with no room for doubt or dissent" (p. 157), "[H]is Corpulence" (p. 7) is reduced to "a shadow of himself" (p. 170). While he and Mother Perpetua have been altered by their brush with Fludd, their transformation has been degenerative rather than progressive. Significance must be read into the fact that, of all the characters transformed by Fludd, it is only the bishop and Mother Perpetua, sole representatives of the Catholic hierarchy in the novel, whose change is degenerative. Both figures can be said to represent the state of institutional Catholicism in the world of the novel, an institution characterised by ignorance and abuse of power. As Funk notes, Fludd "transforms the people he encounters by helping them find their inner self ...; he is, in a way, the Philosopher's Stone he was after in his real historical identity as an alchemist" (2013, p. 155). The result of his intercessions, as Funk continues, is "self-knowledge, something that conventional Catholic doctrine does not set great store by", or as Sister Philomena puts it in the novel: 'Christ died to free us from the burden of our sin, but he never, so far as she could see, lifted a finger to free us from our stupidity' (p. 117)" (Funk, 2013, p. 155). Self-knowledge restores Father Angwin's faith to him at the very same time that it liberates Sister Philomena from the bonds of her own.

Metaphor as Fludd

Angwin had sought to change the bishop's mind regarding the statues by countering that they "are not idols" but "just representations" (p. 21). Far from mere "representations" (p. 21), the reverence with which the statues are treated—they are buried in consecrated ground by professional gravediggers, attended by members of the Men's Fellowship wearing "an aspect of mourning" (p. 33)—reveals the statues' roles in the religious lives of the parishioners. As Miss Dempsey observes, "They're like people, to me. They're like my relatives" (p. 27). Fludd later points out that "Symbols are powerful things" (p. 79), an observation that provides us with a meta-textual opportunity for reflection upon the importance of metaphor, as well as one that proves true in the context of the novel. The burial and exhumation of the statues proves transformative to the lives and faiths of Father Angwin and Sister Philomena. Theirs is a purer faith, harking back to a pre-Reformation church more connected with the people and their needs. While the failure of Mother Perpetua or the bishop to progress to a state of purity is an indictment of contemporary institutional Catholicism, the transformations of Angwin and Philomena herald the importance of individual liberty and freedom of belief. It is a turning away from the literal towards the embrace of the symbolic: as Angwin notes at the opening of the novel, "if you take away the statues, and next the Latin, next the feast days, the fast days, the vestments [...] they won't come any more. Why should they? ... They might as well be out in the streets" (p. 22). The result of this narrative alchemy is the kind of "powerful literary metaphor" that, according to Biebuyck and Martens, "opens the door to re-interpreting non-figurative utterances in the literary text [...] thereby allocating to them a surplus metaphorical dimension" (2011, p. 65).

Metonymy and Fludd

Throughout *Fludd*, Catholicism is construed as in need of purification via a return to the "old faith" (p. 157). The fact that Fetherhoughton's church is that of St Thomas Aquinas is highly significant. Aquinas was a Catholic scholar of considerable renown, known for his articulation of the doctrine of *transubstantiation*, among the most central doctrinal tenets to distinguish the two main denominations of post-Reformation Christianity. While Protestantism's view of the Eucharist is based on the concept of *consubstantiation*—that the bread and wine 'stand for' the body and blood of Christ—the Catholic notion of *transubstantiation* argues that the bread and wine *become* the body and blood of Christ during the ritual of the Eucharist prayers, in particular during the *epiclesis*, during which the Holy Spirit or Holy Ghost is called upon to transform the bread and wine into the body and blood of Christ. While consubstantiation denotes a 'stands for' relationship that can be figuratively represented by metonymy, transubstantiation represents an 'is' relationship figuratively depicted by metaphor.

As mentioned above, the figure of Fludd in the novel functions as both analogue and allegory. Symbols may be "powerful things" (p. 79), but Fludd himself is not 'merely' symbolic: he is not cast as a *representation* of the alchemist Robert Fludd but rather as an otherworldly *revenant* of Robert Fludd. Fludd *is* Robert Fludd. As such, Fludd does not occupy a metonymic 'stands for' role, but rather a metaphoric 'is' role which is both true and false simultaneously. It is true in that if he is a revenant of the alchemist, then arguably he *is* the alchemist but false in that he clearly is not the resurrected Robert Fludd. In her reference to the painting *The Raising of Lazarus*, however, Mantel suggests that the very process of death and resurrection has made Lazarus 'other', an 'othering' created by the altered perceptions of others. Their gaze upon him is "puzzled and mildly censorious" and his resemblance to "a boxer in his corner" foreshadows the fight he has ahead of him; his "troubles", we are told, "are about to begin again". Death has transformed him so that the resurrected Lazarus *both is and is not* the Lazarus who died. This, of course, could be more easily said of Christ, whose resurrection was promptly followed by an ascension into Heaven which suggests a less corporeal and more spiritual resurrection than that of Lazarus.

In her second Reith Lecture, "The Iron Maiden", Mantel (2017) applies the mythology surrounding the drowned village beneath the Derwent reservoir in Derbyshire to illustrate "that a myth is not a falsehood—it is truth, cast into symbol and metaphor". Fludd is also "truth, cast into symbol and metaphor". For Christians, Christ too fits this description. The same could be argued of the Eucharist and yet this fact captures the doctrinal schism at the heart of post-Reformation Christianity: for Catholics the Eucharist *is* the body and blood of Christ (truth) while for Protestants the Eucharist is that truth, "cast into symbol and metaphor". Mantel's articulation of this seeming paradox unites the sub– and superrationalist stances mentioned earlier, which underpin the very status of metaphor in religious doctrine.

Implications and Future Directions

Applications of CMT to literature have, thus far, largely identified metaphor as functioning in at least one of the three following ways: metaphor as a marker of mind style, be that authorial, narratorial, or character; metaphor as explicator of a text's thematic concerns; and metaphor as a narrative device and general tool for characterisation. In *Fludd*, metaphor can be seen to function in all of these ways; indeed, the narrative hinges on a central overarching conceptual metaphor which alone could be said to fulfil all of these functions. However, *Fludd* is not unusual in this respect, with the typically pervasive nature of religious discourse meaning it often permeates multiple levels of a narrative.

Religion also continues to be a key theme in literature, not least because the affordances of literature provide a unique context in which to engage with the ineffable. This is particularly facilitated by the centrality of fictionality and fictional-world construction in literature. In addition, fictionality enables relatively low-risk engagement with what can be a highly controversial as well as a highly personal theme. Critical and academic engagement with the joint themes of literature and religion tends to focus on how religious belief systems interact, overlap, reflect, and compete with the central concerns of literature at any given time, often emphasising the ways in which differing aspects of religious life and belief are foregrounded by a variety of texts and text types across wide-ranging historical periods. The all-encompassing, some might argue consuming, nature of religious thought is evidenced in the scope and variety of religious themes in literature, ranging from engagement with doctrinal theory and some associated nuance, to the nature of sin and the efficacy of confession, to aspects of the religious life and/or its associated culture, to name but a few. Such themes in turn have an impact upon the nature of literature, its form, its functions, and its place in society at any given time. References to religion also simultaneously evoke narratives of securalisation, just as considerations of literature prompt engagement with the non-literary.

With seemingly infinite variation and potential permutations in the study of religious discourse in literature, it can be hard to identify an initial viable focus for analysis, a foothold upon which further meaningful exploration can be commenced. The ideal in such cases is to locate a near-universal feature of all texts which concomitantly reveals the conceptual underpinnings of its textual ideology and use this feature as an analytical foothold. Metaphor offers such a foothold. Future engagements in the nature of religious discourse in literature could benefit immensely from not only the scope but the variety of tropes of figurative language which come under the umbrella of metaphor, while the ubiquity of figurative language across all text types means it is a truly inter-disciplinary tool which can be analysed in various differing discipline-specific ways.

Vermeulen (2021) points out that cognitive linguistics and cognitive stylistics, along with phil-ology, are the three areas of linguistic enquiry currently concerned with the analysis of religious discourse in sacred texts. Cognitive Stylistics is also concerned with the linguistic construction of religious discourse in literary texts, which often involves recursion to sacred texts. For example, Canning (2008) carries out a Conceptual Blending analysis—a model closely allied to CMT—of the metaphysical poet George Herbert's linguistic construction of Jesus; the poetry of Gerard Manley Hopkins is the subject of both Sobolev (2003), who illustrates how Hopkin's metaphor use enables a negotiation between "the material and the transcendent" while beyond the genre of poetry, Neary (2017) traces metaphor use in the English translation of Gandhi's autobiography, illustrating Gandhi's appropriation of Christian metaphor for both spiritual and political purposes. As can be seen, however, explorations into the linguistic interrogation of metaphor in religious discourse in literature are relatively few. This could be for several reasons, not least the numerous and multi-level ways in which religious themes are often constructed in literary texts, which can make analysis via CMT quite complex.

For example, and as elaborated upon elsewhere (Neary, 2023), the claims to conceptual uni-versality that underpin cognitive approaches to metaphor can cause problems in the context of metaphor analysis of literary discourse. Fludernik points out that one of the ways in which CMT has been "problematic" for critics of literature is because it "has tended to focus on the metaphoric nature of our thinking, moving away from surface structure textual analysis to universal, or at least language-specific, cognitive base metaphors, captured in formulas like LIFE IS A JOURNEY" (2011, p. 5). In so doing, textual applications of CMT have tended to emphasise the conceptual universality of metaphor, moving towards "universality or reductivism in opposition to textual specificity" (Fludernik, 2011, p. 6) at the expense of the insights that can be gained by focusing on the uniqueness of some metaphoric expressions.

In addition, while CMT provides a really useful analytical framework, its focus on individual metaphoric expressions has meant that its usefulness at the macro level has not been sufficiently exploited. For example, while cognitive stylisticians have used CMT to identify how individual manifestations of a conceptual metaphor at key moments in the text can build up to a textually salient extended metaphor, or what Werth calls a "megametaphor" (1999), few, if any, applications of CMT acknowledge that a megametaphor can be textually and discursively constructed without any explicit linguistic manifestation. This is particularly relevant in the context of religious dis-course, which can often be represented at the macro and/or narrative levels, such as via analogy or allegory, as well as at the micro level. In their development of the concept of the *paranarrative*, Biebuyck and Martens agree that the "narrative dimension" of metaphor has been a blind spot in the cognitive approach to literary metaphor so far" (2011, p. 72), and advocate for acknowledgement of the potential of "the network of metaphors and figures of speech in a literary text" to construct "an additional layer of narrativity" (2011, p. 64).

Finally, while metaphors in literary discourse have been shown to have more meaning potential and garner more attention from the reader (see Steen 1994), as mentioned earlier, it is perhaps the case that more attention needs to be paid to the 'fuzzy' boundaries inherent in both religious texts and in literature. Ontological status is key to the identification of metaphoric constructions—based on whether the utterance is literally or metaphorically 'true'—but this distinction is frequently undermined depending on both the religion in question and its reader (see earlier assertions re sub- versus superrationalism). While an emphasis on universality can be useful, not least in linking ways of thinking across religious boundaries, nuance is key to meaningful metaphor analysis.

Further Reading

Charteris-Black, J. (2017). *Fire metaphors: Discourses of awe and authority*. Bloomsbury.
A focus on how religious and political discourses are built upon metaphors of fire, coupled with plentiful examples from a broad range of texts, convincingly demonstrates the simultaneous breadth and specificity of metaphor use in discourse.
Chilton, P. & Kopytowska, M. (Eds.) (2018). *Religion, language, and the human mind*. Oxford University Press.
An important edited collection that provides oversight of current and emerging trends in the interdisciplinary analysis of religious discourse, with a focus on metaphor in Part II.
Dorst, A.J. (2021) Metaphor. In S. Pihlaja (Ed.), *Analysing religious discourse*, 235–255. Cambridge University Press.
A very accessible chapter-length overview of Conceptual Metaphor Theory and its usefulness in the analysis of religious discourse.
Hobbs, V. (2021). *An introduction to religious language*. Bloomsbury.
A contemporary introduction to the field of *theolinguistics* that demonstrates the current available methods for the analysis of religious language, including corpus-assisted approaches alongside the study of specific linguistic features including metaphor and intertextuality.
Lakoff, G. & Turner, M. (1989). *More than cool reason: A field guide to poetic metaphor*. University of Chicago Press.
This classic text demonstrates the applicability of CMT to various genres of literature in a manner which subtly illustrates its compatibility with formalist literary studies.

References

Biebuyck, B. & Martens, G. (2011). Literary metaphor between cognition and narration: The Sandman Revisited. In M. Fludernik (Ed.), *Beyond Cognitive Metaphor Theory: Perspectives on literary metaphor*, 58–76. Routledge.
Canning, P. (2008). 'The bodie and the letters both': blending' the rules of early modern religion. *Language and Literature*, *17*(3), 187–203.
Caracciolo, M. (2017). Creative metaphor in literature. In E. Semino & Z. Demjén (Eds.), *The Routledge handbook of metaphor and language*, 206–218. Routledge.
Charteris-Black, J. (2004). *Approaches to critical metaphor analysis*. Palgrave.
Charteris-Black, J. (2017). *Fire metaphors: Discourses of awe and authority*. Bloomsbury.
Chilton, P. & Kopytowska, M. (Eds.). (2018). *Religion, language, and the human mind*. Oxford University Press.
Crisp, P. (2005). Allegory and symbol—a fundamental opposition? *Language and Literature*, *14*(4), 323–338.
Dancygier, B. & Sweetser, E. (2014). *Figurative language*. Cambridge University Press.
Dorst, A.J. (2021). Metaphor. In S. Pihlaja (Ed.), *Analysing religious discourse*, 235–255. Cambridge University Press.
Fludernik, M. (2011). Introduction. In M. Fludernik (Ed.), *Beyond Cognitive Metaphor Theory: Perspectives on literary metaphor*, 1–16. Routledge.
Forceville, C. (1996). *Pictorial metaphor in advertising*. Routledge.

Funk, W. (2013) Ghosts of postmodernity: Spectral epistemology and haunting in Hilary Mantel's *Fludd* and *Beyond Black*. In S. Adiseshiah & R. Hilyard (Eds.), *Twenty-First Century Fiction: What Happens Now*, 147–161. Palgrave.

Goatly, A. (2007). *Washing the brain: Metaphor and hidden ideology*. John Benjamins Publishing Company.

Goatly, A. (2011). *The language of metaphors.* 2nd edition. Routledge.

Hamilton, C. (2002). Christine de Pizan's *City of Ladies*. In J. Culpeper & E. Semino (Eds.), *Cognitive Stylistics: Language and cognition in text analysis*, 1–22. John Benjamins Publishing Company.

Harris, R.A. & Tolmie, S. (Eds). (2011). Cognitive allegory: An introduction. *Metaphor and Symbol*, 26: 109–120.

Hobbs, V. (2021). *An introduction to religious language*. Bloomsbury.

Hogan, P.C. (2003). *Cognitive science, literature and the arts: A guide for humanists*. Routledge.

Jeffries, L. & McIntyre, D. (2010). *Stylistics*. Cambridge University Press.

Kövecses, Z. (2017). Conceptual Metaphor Theory. In E. Semino & Z. Demjén (Eds.), *The Routledge handbook of metaphor and language*, 13–27. Routledge.

Kövecses, Z. (2002). *Metaphor: A practical introduction*. Oxford University Press.

Lakoff, G. & Johnson, M. (1980). *Metaphors we live by*. University of Chicago Press.

Lakoff, G. & Turner, M. (1989). *More than cool reason: A field guide to poetic metaphor*. University of Chicago Press.

Lodge, D. (2002). *Consciousness and the novel: Connected essays*. Harvard University Press.

Mantel, H. (2017). Second Reith Lecture "The Iron Maiden". *BBC iPlayer*. Retrieved 10 February 2023 from www.bbc.co.uk/programmes/b08v08m5 .

Neary, C. (2017). "Truth is like a vast tree": Metaphor use in Gandhi's autobiographical narration. *Metaphor and the Social World*, 7(1), 103–121.

Neary, C. (2023). "[E]verything that is to be made whole must first be broken": Religion, metaphor and narrative alchemy in Hilary Mantel's *Fludd* (1989). *English Studies*. DOI: 10.1080/0013838X.2023.2233310

Pihlaja, S. (2021). *Talk about Faith: How conversation shapes belief*. Cambridge University Press.

Ritchie, D.L. (2017). Metaphor and Story-telling. In E. Semino & Z. Demjén (Eds.), *The Routledge handbook of metaphor and language*, 337–352. Routledge.

Semino, E. (2008). *Metaphor in discourse*. Cambridge University Press.

Senkbeil, K. & Hoppe, N. (2016). 'The sickness stands at your shoulder …': Embodiment and cognitive metaphor in Hornbacher's Wasted: A memoir of anorexia and bulimia. *Language and Literature*, 25(1). Retrieved 18 April 2023 from https://journals.sagepub.com/doi/full/10.1177/0963947015608084

Simpson, P. (2014). *Stylistics*. 2nd edition. Routledge.

Sobolev, D. (2003). Hopkins's rhetoric: Between the material and the transcendent. *Language and Literature*, 12(2), 99–115.

Stafford, B.M. (Ed.) (2011). *A field guide to a new meta-field: Bridging the humanities-neurosciences divide*. University of Chicago Press.

Steen, G. (1994). *Understanding metaphor in literature: An empirical approach*. Longman.

Steen, G. (2008). The paradox of metaphor: Why we need a three-dimensional model of metaphor. *Metaphor and Symbol*, 23(4), 213–41.

Steen, G. J. (2017). Deliberate Metaphor Theory: Basic assumptions, main tenets, urgent issues. *Intercultural Pragmatics*, 14(1), 1–24.

Stockwell, P. (2020). *Cognitive Poetics*. 2nd edition. Routledge.

Wales, K. (2011). *The dictionary of Stylistics*. Longman.

Werth, P. (1999). *Text Worlds: Representing Conceptual Space in Discourse*. Longman.

10
LANGUAGE, RELIGION, AND THE DIGITAL WORLD

Stephen Pihlaja

Introduction and Background

Language used in and around religious practice and belief, as religion itself, has been shaped by technologies that have emerged over time. The study of religion is closely related to the study of the impact of technology on spreading ideas, from the Medieval period (White, 1978) to the proliferation of digital technologies in the contemporary world (George, 2006). In many ways, these technologies have influenced how confessional beliefs are produced and held across communities, by providing a means to capture thought through language and tie those thoughts to enduring artefacts that can be shared across time and space. Consistency in belief and continuity over time and space is a subsequent result of the presence of technology, and the written word as an acceptable way of capturing thoughts about spirituality, supernatural experiences, and the divine, is now taken for granted in discussions of religion.

The technology of mass production of books is widely regarded as an important step in the development of Christianity, particularly in its influence in the emergence of Protestantism (Rubin, 2014), but was accelerated in the development of radio and electric technologies in the last 200 years. New interpretations of Islam have also been connected to various innovations, including books, cassette sermons, and satellite TV (Anderson, 2003). Every major religion has been influenced by the presence of radio and television in the last 100 years, with information about different religions being spread around the world, and an increase in interaction with people of different beliefs both through media and through increased mobility as transportation methods have also developed. The two, media and religion, are mutually constructed categories (Hoover & Lundby, 1997). Whereas interaction with people of different beliefs would have been historically more limited to who was present in one's physical location, increased travel and communication led to a proliferation of ideas and people, even before the internet. That said, the development of computing technologies and the Internet have had a radical effect the everyday lives of believers and how religious belief is viewed in the contemporary world.

The early internet as it was popularised in the nineties onward was marked primarily by written communication (Herring, 2003), but even early research focused on how the interaction between people online was unique, while still maintaining many of the same social interaction issues as offline spaces, particularly in the formation of social groups and presentation of self (Keisler,

DOI: 10.4324/9781003301271-11

1997). Many of the features of interest around language change, and the emergence of so-called 'Netspeak' (Fahey & Prevost, 1994) or 'Cybertalk' (Denzin, 1999) were also present at this time, with researchers interested in how language itself was being changed by online interaction. Looking back on this early research at the time, Herring (2004, p. 26) identified two questions as key for researchers in what was then called Computer Mediated Communication (CMC): how has CMC technology changed, conceptually and feature-wise, from previous technologies? And more importantly, is new CMC technology giving rise to new social practices, and if so, in what directions is it steering us?

With spread of technologies that allowed users to capture video and images cheaply and the increased availability of online publishing platforms, users became more engaged in the process of creating content to distribute, beginning what became known as Web 2.0 (Herring, 2004). As Web 2.0 became more prominent in the experience of the internet, more focus was placed on the interaction between people in places and the effects on social interaction of being present with individuals from a variety of different social contexts in place. For example, on Facebook, a user might be 'friends' with their family, work colleagues, and real-life friends, of all of whom may have different understandings of who that person was. This situation wherein users were expected to present 'authentic' versions of themselves to different audiences has been described as Context Collapse (Marwick & boyd, 2011), and had specific implication for religious believers for whom their social media spaces then became spaces where they had to manage how their religious identity was viewed, both to their own community, to people who were indifferent to their belief, and those antagonistic to them, something which was particularly complicated on platforms like YouTube where multiple audiences would be viewing, commenting on, and reacting to one's content (Pihlaja, 2014).

As users have grown more used to interaction with these different audiences in their online lives, new ways of limiting and targeting particular users can be seen in the process of Context Design (Tagg et al., 2017), wherein users can code certain messages for certain audiences, through use of different languages for multilingual users or through coded or insider language. Increasingly technologies have grown more adept at understanding user preference as well. As technology has developed, so has the ability of apps and platforms to cater to the interests of each individual user. The so-called 'filter bubble' first described by Pariser (2011) showed that a user's identity and physical location affected the information presented to them when they made a search on Google, with two people using the same search term getting returned very different results. This technology only increased in effectiveness throughout the 2010s, with search algorithms, which are processes and rules used in computation to provide results that are most likely to be of interest to the user, becoming more and more precise and including more user information from a variety of different inputs from their use of a digital device. These processes have moved beyond searches of Google to be used by apps and digital platforms in deciding what is presented to a user when they access a certain site or open a specific app. Information is ordered and presented depending on what is most likely to provide the outcome that algorithm has been optimised to produced—in the case of social media apps and platforms, this is primarily engagement.

The connection between changes in religion and digital technology has also been of interest to scholars, particularly as it relates to these questions posed by Herring about the extent to which 'new' media is really new (Campbell & Lövheim, 2011). This involves not only the awareness of positions and beliefs that might not have been available in the past, but also new ways of accessing and consuming information that, in turn, changes the relationship with the religious belief itself. For example, reading of sacred texts has also been influenced by the development of digital technologies (Allington & Pihlaja, 2016). An increased access to these texts and ability to search within them, for example, for particular words or phrases has changed how those texts are then used in different situations, with websites offering Christians a collection of Bible verses about issues like worry. This collection of verses or commonplaces together is not new (Kolb, 1987), but technology provides enhanced and easier access, resulting in users having new ways of reading those texts and subsequently new ways of thinking about one's religious belief.

The development of digital religion has also led to online religious communities. These have been of key interest to researchers in the internet age, including looking at the complicated inter-action between religious, ethnic, and linguistic identities (Rosowsky, 2017) with digital technology allowing minority communities to make connections and develop relationships despite not being present in the same physical location. Religious communities in these cases can be both formal and informal. Hutchings (2017) has shown this diversity in the development of online churches, where community norms and rules for interaction have emerged both in independent communities and in more established denominations attempting to be active in online spaces. At the same time, the physical distance between members of these communities has meant that technology, particularly mobile technology, has become increasingly important for how people interact with one another and with religious texts and rituals, as Campbell (2012) has shown. The technology becomes a central part of how people interact with every element of the religion, from praying and reading scripture, to taking part in virtual pilgrimages (Bunt, 2009).

Technology that then caters to specific people and provides insights that are specific for each user can be seen in the use of apps like 'Jesus Calling' (Trammell, 2015) which provides reli-gious devotions to individual users developed from information the user provides about their own interests and needs. The focus on feed-based content wherein users are given an endless stream of content based on an algorithmic calculation about what may interest a user has had consequences for both user experience and community engagement in online spaces. On platforms like TikTok, users are subject to what is presented to them by the platform with little input. These technologies have changed the way that users not only interact with apps, platforms, and websites, but also how these technologies are viewed, no longer as only responding to prompts given to them by users but delivering content with little or no effort on the part of the user.

The development of the newsfeed and the presentation of information that may be of interest to users have also fuelled a further engagement between religious belief and political ideology, most notably in the rise of the relationship between Evangelical Christianity and right-wing politics in the USA. The election of Donald Trump as president and the subsequent relationship between Trump and the Evangelical movement evidenced how engagement between interests, fed and sustained by misinformation (Ali & Zain-ul-abdin, 2021), has established new affiliations between political and religious organisations that would not have been made possible without social media platforms pushing particular content to particular users based on how engaging that information was. The result is the development of belief and positions that have emerged that have shaped the theological landscape in the US and changing priorities for users on social media.

Methods for studying online interaction have often followed the pattern of drawing on previous offline methods for discourse analysis and adapting them in online spaces. Herring's work on analysis of 'Computer-Mediated Discourse' (Herring, 2003) adapted ideas from offline discourse analysis and understandings of community to look at the language and interaction of users in online spaces. Over time, more emphasis was also placed on gathering data about online com-munities and understanding norms and practices, for example, in analysing and understanding texting between friends (Tagg, 2012). Building on linguistic ethnography (Creese, 2008), others went further, arguing for a need to do discourse analysis with an explicit engagement with the communities, for example in Discourse-Centred Online Ethnography (Androutsopoulos, 2014). These methods have emphasised the importance of finding meaning in online interaction in the same way as offline discourse. At the same time, with the development of corpus linguistic tools, more work has been done on gathering very large datasets, to understand phenomena like language shift (Grieve et al., 2018). Both ways of looking at data, and many other in between, have led to a very different understanding of digital discourse from the time of 'cybertalk', to now include a vast variety of different modes and means of communicating.

Shifts in the ethics of gathering data online have also played an important role in how religious language data, particularly data gathered in public spaces online, is used, with scholars like Mackenzie (2017) arguing that researchers can't assume that publicly available data can be freely used by researchers without considering the ethical implications of their choices. Different processes and procedures now exist, offering researchers clear guidance on how data can and should be gathered in digital contexts. Mackenzie (2023, p. 40) presents four principles that are particularly useful for researchers looking at language and religion:

1. Maximise benefits and minimise harm;
2. Be attentive to context, including informational norms and participants' needs;
3. Acknowledge and analyse [one's] own positionality as a researcher;
4. Integrate ethical considerations at all stages of the research process.

These issues become potentially more complicated when talking about religion and language, and where presentation of different beliefs is occurring, or where users are making claims that could cause potential harm. The researcher must think about the consequences and potential impact of analysis of the data they have gathered, and the potential harm or attention it might bring to the users, especially when the data is taken from online contexts where users can be easily searched and discovered. These concerns relate to users with followings of many different sizes, both small creators and larger ones, for whom attention from academic circles might not be expected.

The Development of Religious Discourse Online

My research into digital religion and interaction about social media began in 2008 by following a group of Christians and atheists interacting on YouTube, often in long threads of videos followed by response videos followed by further response videos. The interaction among users in this community developed out of long (at least in terms of internet interaction) histories of disagreements, sometimes theological or philosophical, but often personal, and 'drama' as a concept unique to online interaction developed in these interactions. Importantly, within these communities, my research often showed that affiliations could shift over time and disagreements did not always emerge around issues of theology. Instead, how issues were argued and what was relevant could be very different depending on how someone felt they were being treated and the extent to which their interlocutors were engaging them antagonistically.

For this chapter, and its focus on the development of internet discourse and its relation to the religious belief and identity, I will profile three users from my YouTube research, tracing their development as users and revisiting them in their current online personas, on Facebook and YouTube. The first user was known as Fakesagan in my previous research (Pihlaja, 2014), an atheist who re-emerged in recent years as an Orthodox Christian and is now known by his real name, Christopher Anderson. The second and third users are profiled in my book *Religious Talk Online* (Pihlaja, 2018). The second is the Amazing Atheist, now know just by his name TJ Kirk, who was one of the early YouTube atheist personas, with a large following, who became less focused on theological issues and more on social commentary. The third is Joshua Feuerstein, who was an in-your-face Evangelical pastor who posted regularly on Facebook and became increasingly politically active, eventually taking part in the 6 January 2021 protests that led to the invasion of the US Capitol following the 2020 presidential election.

The development of the users represents different paths through varying levels of internet celebrity and shifts in how they present themselves and their message, affected by the sociopolitical and technological context in which they emerged and the development of those contexts. Each represents a different way that positions can change over time: Anderson in a marked shift in religious belief, Kirk in a shift of focus in content, and Feuerstein in a shift in focus on outcomes. To analyse these changes, I will use positioning analysis following Harré and van Langenhove (1998) as well as my own adaptation of positioning analysis (Pihlaja, 2021, p. 36) to discuss how their positioning has changed over time.

For each user, I will refer to the work I have previously published on them, and then return to a more recent video made by each, two of which reflect on their own history on YouTube: Anderson's 'ye, alex and nick are based. elon is cringe' and TJ Kirk's 'How I Created The Anti-SJW Genre, And Almost Destroyed The World'. Feuerstein's video used in this analysis is taken from a post on the 'Slavic Votes' Instagram and shared on Feuerstein's Instagram (see Source Videos). Each of these videos was chosen as recent presentations of the users which included topics and positions that represented shifts from their historical work: Anderson in his talk about belief, Kirk in talk about how he has influenced internet culture, and Feuerstein in his objectives.

Fakesagan, now Christopher Anderson, was an atheist who regularly argued with Christian users on YouTube. In these early videos, Anderson positioned himself as an antagonist to Christianity in a context where he also positioned Christian faith as the dominant worldview in the United States. His positioning of himself, along with other atheists at the time (including the Amazing Atheist), was often about a challenge to the status quo, and seeing themselves as outside of the mainstream in their lack of religious belief. These arguments, at least in the context of the videos I looked at in my books on religious interaction on YouTube (Pihlaja, 2014, 2018) were limited in scope to the logic and effects of religious belief, with very little interaction about larger political issues, particularly in the early days of YouTube. Little discussion engaged with a specific political context, beyond at times discussions of 'free speech' as it related to what content was taken down by YouTube when it was shown to violate the community standards. Those arguments, however, were not aligned with religious beliefs and the YouTubers, both self-positioned Christians and atheists, often held the same position as opposed to content being banned from the site.

Anderson, in the time since he posted as Fakesagan, took a long break from YouTube, but emerged again in recent years, no longer an atheist but a Serbian Orthodox Christian. The shift in presentation is most notable in his new beginning to videos which used to begin 'Greetings Citizens of YouTube' and now begin, 'Greetings Citizens of YouTube. All glory and honor to the Lord and Savior Jesus Christ'. He also regularly records his videos in front of the Banner of Serbia, which is clearly visible behind him and—importantly for some of his content in which he discusses his relationship with Russia and the war in Ukraine, a sign of his own loyalties—his username also included, at the time the video was collected for this research on 5 December 2022, an emoji of the Russian flag following his name. This positioning as a Christian is evident in some of the content and the topics that he discusses, but it plays a particularly important role at the time of this video in his representation of his political position as it related to the Russian invasion of Ukraine in 2022, something he argued was subject to censorship and deplatforming on YouTube.

In discussing his position on YouTube and the relationship between the current state of free speech and censorship on the internet, and his previous experience on the site, Anderson says:

> Um like all these social media giants have been getting away with with murder forever and who called it out first by the way? [...] Who called it out before anybody? You're looking at them. I'm never gonna get the credit I deserve thanks to censorship but I like-I've been talking about this shit since 2006–2007. Um you know because-because back in the day we-we had a little thing going on-on YouTube called the pwnage wars uh where-where it was kind of like a mud-slinging war of all against all. And-and everybody was trying to like insult and put each other down. I happen to be very good at it and so I was constantly getting banded, censored by YouTube before Google even bought it, before you know—And I was-I was up here saying we need free speech on these-on these big social media platforms and everybody left right and center and I mean that in the strictest definition leftists and right-wingers were saying, 'Oh dry up your tears snowflake, it's their private company. They could do whatever they want. It's not censorship.' So-so I-I was dealing with these libertarian arguments way back in the fucking day and nobody not even Alex Jones was making the argument that I was, that these guys need to be regulated the same as the phone company. Um so you're looking at a pioneer of Internet free speech right here, not that I'll ever get the fucking credit I deserve.

Here, Anderson notes a continuity of thought across his time on YouTube, referring to his original presence on the site and arguing that he has been consistent across that time, in terms of his position on free speech. He doesn't, however, mention that his own position was that of advocating for atheism, but instead claims that his content was taken down because of his attacks on others and his position questioning that censorship was rejected by everyone, regardless of the political position. He uses this story and his positioning of himself within it to say that he was 'a pioneer of Internet Free Speech' and compares favourably compared to Alex Jones, someone also implicitly positioned as a proponent of free speech.

Anderson's positioning in this video and his recollection of his own time on YouTube shows the importance of storytelling in construction of identity in this kind of vlog. All of Anderson's original videos as Fakesagan have subsequently been removed and his own presentation of the past and his positioning of himself within a storyline of advocacy for free speech and against censorship may or may not comport with the focus of his videos at the time; indeed, in the research I did, although the censorship of users was an issue, the complaints were often about one's own videos being taken down in ongoing fights between users, rather than an advocacy that all content remain up. His own memory of the experience and positioning of himself creates an understanding of the past that comports best with the state of the world as he sees it now. By emphasising a particular part of the story of his experience, one that is not factually inaccurate, a storyline of him acting with consistency and prescience emerges from his self-positioning.

This storyline of consistency is also present in the second user I will discuss: the Amazing Atheist, now TJ Kirk. Kirk's video does not represent either a clear break in his positioning from his historical persona, nor a clear continuation of the 'Amazing Atheist' persona that dominated his video channel. Like Anderson, he too positioned himself as an antagonist to the status quo, but as he gained popularity and atheism grew more accepted socially, Kirk's positioning of himself also shifted into more political arenas, while still maintaining the position of antagonist and outsider fighting against the status quo. With the affiliation between conservative Christianity and the political right in the US, there was a complementary positioning of atheists as leftists and liberals.

Kirk, however, like several other prominent atheists, positioned himself as more of a libertarian than a leftist, and actively attacked so-called 'Social Justice Warriors' (SJWs), or users and people who were positioned as advocating on behalf of a 'woke' ideology. Reflecting on this, Kirk says:

> I never viewed that content as being particularly important. I never tried to lay out the case that it was the uh it was leading to the collapse of Western Civilization or that we we're in a culture war for our lives. I never spun that sort of narrative. For me, SJW content uh on YouTube or out there in the mainstream or wherever you might find it was nothing more than something ludicrous to be mocked and I enjoyed mocking it. And even to this day I will hear stuff that you know makes me roll my eyes uh and that I would you know back in the day I would have jumped on.

Here, Kirk's relationship with his past positions, like Anderson, is marked both by an appeal to authenticity and consistency, which Kirk believed at one point is the same position that he holds now, regardless of how much that position is reflected in the content that he regularly makes, that is, if it still interests him. This positioning of himself as losing interest in different content is also the reason he has regularly given for his movement away from the Amazing Atheist persona, stating that he has lost some interest in making the same content as little changed in the arguments for and against God over the time he was on the site. This shift in interest, and how it is reflected in the content that he produces is, however, importantly positioned as not reflecting any change in what he himself thinks on the topic. Consistency is an implicit value, even if the focus of the channel has changed.

At the same time, Kirk allows for some development in his thinking about his past experience being seen as an advocate against SJWs, saying:

> And you know I didn't really realize that I was a-a useful idiot for that. I was just trying to create entertaining content about you know a group of people that I felt were ridiculous and I still feel ridiculous. But now I realize that you know making that sort of content is um like […] I were to say if I were to make a whole video about how ridiculous it is that um there are people upset at *Wednesday* [a Netflix series] for depicting black people as bullies uh not depicting all black people's bullies but just depicting particular black people as being bullies. Um if I were to make a video about that it would inflame all sorts of weird racial tensions that exist out there in the world and uh certain people who are racist are going to use that content as a way to further their racist agenda.

Here, Kirk positions himself as not changing his opinion that who he perceives to be social justice warriors are 'ridiculous'. At the same time, he describes himself as understanding better that making a video on the topic positions him with a group of people that he doesn't necessarily want to be positioned with, even though his position on the topic hasn't changed. Kirk positions his development not as a change in his belief, but how he understands his own position as it relates to potential viewers of his videos, that he became a 'useful idiot' in a political message that he himself did not share. He positions himself as not wrong in his belief while still recognising that the outcome, and how he came to be viewed by others, was not something that he desired.

Feuerstein, in contrast to Anderson and Kirk, has not had an obvious shift in his belief or his overall approach. In my analysis of videos which he made in 2014 (Pihlaja, 2018), politics was largely absent, with his content focusing on religious and moral messages. At the same time,

Feuerstein was engaged in some political issues, including around homosexuality and advocating against laws which required all businesses to serve customers, regardless of their sexual orientation, most notably whether a Christian bakery could refuse to make a wedding cake for a gay couple, a political issue in the early 2010s that was a part of a larger social change towards the acceptance of homosexuality and the tension within Evangelical Christianity around how to engage with these changes. However, this was only a small part of Feuerstein's online presence, and he was, instead, known for his engagement around theology. In a video entitled 'Dear Mr. Muslim' posted on 17 July 2014, Feuerstein starts by saying:

> Mr Muslim. Now I must preface what I'm going to say by simply saying that my Muslim friends are some of the most kind caring compassionate, incredible individuals I have ever met and to be quite honest with you and sadly so, well your propensity towards prayer and dedication to your religion, puts most Christians to shame.

In this video, Feuerstein positions himself with his 'Muslim' friends, making a connection between Muslim religious practice and Christian religious practice, including the suggestion that Muslim religiosity, in many cases, 'sadly' exceeded Christian religiosity. The positioning of himself with others, though, is done to a particular end: in this case, the goal was challenging Islamic theology and asserting the deity of Christ, a recurring theme in Feuerstein's videos at the time. The move to position himself at the beginning as a friend of others and showing empathy with them allowed, in this video and in others, for Feuerstein to present his message as relevant to his audience, and in the case of the short videos he made for Facebook, also give the impression that he was speaking directly to the viewer in an intimate way. The positioning served the purpose of the message that followed, one which often included an appeal to accepting Christianity or an Evangelical Christian moral position.

Like Anderson, Feuerstein manages a consistency in his own style, but has shifted in his goals, from presenting a simple gospel message to advocating for very specific political outcomes. The video that Feuerstein posted on 5 August 2022 is ostensibly a 'get out and vote' video, meant to inspire members of the Slavic community to vote. The video starts with Feuerstein saying:

> Hi guys, Josh Feuerstein here. Look, some of my favorite people in the entire world are the Slavic community. I've been in your churches. I've eaten at your dinner tables, some of the most incredible and passionate people in the world.

Here, Feuerstein begins by positioning himself much the same way as he did in his Mr Muslim video, with an appeal to the viewer, this time talking about the 'Slavic Community' and praising them as the 'most incredible and passionate people in the world'. The language is strikingly like the Mr Muslim video and shows how a message of Evangelism can be supplanted by a political message, with the same language and approach used for both. The shift in political advocacy, from culture war issues to a more explicit call to action for a particular political party represents, in a small way, the change that occurred within Evangelical Christianity in the period of Donald Trump's rise to prominence and his appeal to Christian voters. The way of speaking about religious and political belief is ostensibly the same. The two videos show how political and religious messages can be present in the same manner, with little apparent differentiation made between religious and political goals.

In all three instances, the users' belief and/or focus has changed significantly in the previous ten years. Those positions related to larger shifts in the culture: Anderson's move to religion and political militancy, Kirk's shift away from atheism to a form of 'anti-SJW' content of which he is now critical, and Feuerstein's political shift to become a supporter of Donald Trump and taking more explicitly partisan political positions. The case study also shows in a small way how beliefs and positionings can be influenced by and subject to the past positions that users have taken. Even where shifts have taken place, users can come to view contrasting positionings as internally consistent, or new messages and focuses as part of the same overall message and positioning they previously used. By following users like Kirk, Anderson, and Feuerstein, and looking at how they have changed or not, there is an empirical path over time, one that provides clearer answers to larger questions like how Donald Trump came to power, to more individual ones, like how does an individual change their personal religious belief.

Implications and Future Directions

The case study shows how the tracing of religious belief over time, both in terms of larger trends and in the development of individuals, can be a useful way of showing how and why beliefs change over time and the effects of larger socio-political changes on the lives of individuals. Insights can be drawn on how the content they produce has an impact on how religious belief and politics are spoken about. A digital archaeology will be useful for understanding how beliefs change over time and may help people understand themselves and changes in their own belief. Researchers will need to first recognise that digital archives are incomplete, and interaction must always be placed in the context in which it originally emerged, with an understanding of digital interaction as historical, rather than occurring only in the recent past and present. Next, researchers will need to develop ways of reconstructing timelines and finding ways of representing where pivotal events have happened that haven't been retained. Digital spaces, as my research on YouTube drama has shown, are full of situations where key texts have been either removed by the user or removed or deleted by the site or app operator for any number of reasons.

How we understand current technologies and platforms will continue to be influenced by experiences of previous iterations of the same technology or platform, or technologies or platforms that can be understood in analogy to previous technologies. In the same way that Facebook was initially understood in relation to MySpace as an analogous early social networking platform, researchers will need to understand the historical nature of religious interaction and discourse in digital spaces as emerging out of a longer history of digital interaction. Younger users and increasingly middle-aged users will have grown up with digital technologies as part of their day-to-day life, and with it, their experiences of religious belief and social life. Any study of 'offline' or 'real world' interaction will now necessarily need to include how people interact with and through digital technologies as a part of their day-to-day interaction.

Once such digital technology is blockchain: decentralised, distributed, and public digital ledgers that are used to support cryptocurrencies like Bitcoin, by tracking ownership of digital items. Blockchain technology could become important in the development of language and religion as fidelity in the transmission of information or records over time has historically been important in religious traditions. These could be digitised on the blockchain, providing a public record of sacred texts, membership records, pilgrimages, or any other key information about a religious group or person. NFTs (non-fungible tokens), or digital artefacts that passed between users with a record kept in public blockchains, could also be used in tracing different elements of religious practice, particularly as that practice moves online, and different religious practices become digitised. An individual could, for example, acquire an NFT as a part of a commitment made to religious organisation and which would then include a public record of that commitment. These will allow religious organisations to create and trace digital objects that they sanction and can use to create value, such as digital amulets blessed by religious figures or recording pledges made to spiritual gurus in digital form.

Within digital technologies, user input from explicit, conscious actions like subscribing to a particular YouTube channel or choosing to view a particular news story is still an important part of how content is navigated. At the same time, user input particularly as it relates to seeking out and choosing content to watch has become less prominent. This is certainly not a novel development in digital spaces, as YouTube, X (formerly Twitter), and Facebook for example have delivered content to users based on a mix of their choices and what the platform algorithm thinks they might be interested in consuming, through features like automatic play and newsfeeds. Applications like TikTok have taken this further by developing a for you 'page' which doesn't require any user input for content to be delivered. The preferences of the user are still logged through explicit user interaction with the app when skipping a video, liking it, or commenting on it, and those actions feed into how the app delivers content in the future. The continued development and implementation of this technology may continue to require less user input and explicit choices about content could become even further backgrounded, with technology that more seamlessly interacts with user thoughts, either through technology embedded in the physical body or through technology that can make predictions about preference before a user consciously interacts with a device.

The consequences for language and religion of less conscious decision-making in choice about digital content which users consume may require more focus on how language input is processed in the mind and how that processing affects and is affected by technology. Individual preference and how that preference is made manifest to technological devices will also have more impact on what content with which users interact and more attention will need to be paid to how technology is creating affordances that favour certain ways of presenting oneself in discourse. This will become more important as digital interaction becomes increasingly a part of how individuals have grown up in society and the treatment of its influence as a novelty worthy of specific interest fades. The normalisation of the technology in daily life, like print, radio, and TV in the past, will result in less natural curiosity and suspicion about its effects in daily life by lay and non-specialist users. This will result in substantial changes to how digital technology is accepted in life and the extent to which users are aware of its influence on their communication.

Finally, the development of artificial intelligence in the production of language could potentially have effects on how religious belief is understood and practiced online. AI in the form of Chatbots like ChatGPT will continue to grow proficient in offering advice and presenting answers to questions posed by users. This could result in chatbots that are trained on language related to a particular religious belief, allowing users to ask for personalised, religious advice from technologies that track users' actions and language use and provides them feedback based on this information. AI could also be used in arguments about and between different beliefs and used by religious leaders to produce messages that are based on certain parameters and trained to focus on goals. The integration of technology and user's physical bodies could blur the line between articulation of individual beliefs and the text produced by AI for a user. Differentiating between these producers and recognising 'authentic' human interaction could become increasingly difficult to identify as these technologies become ubiquitous in day-to-day life. The result will be a blurring of a line between personal belief and technologically informed belief, a new iteration of a very ancient process of learning and repeating what one has learned as one's own belief.

Further Reading

Campbell, H.A. (2012). *Digital religion: Understanding religious practice in new media worlds*. Routledge.
A key text for research on digital religion, particularly from a Sociology of Religion perspective, providing an important theoretical and methodological background for the study of digital religion, particularly as it related to Web 2.0.
Hutchings, T. (2017). *Creating Church Online: Ritual, Community and New Media*. Routledge.
A long-form study of how Christian religious communities use online spaces in different ways to recreate the experience of 'church'. Particularly interesting for its treatment of different kinds of institutional approaches to faith online, from established Christian denominations to newer, emergent communities.
Pihlaja, S. (2018). *Religious Talk Online: The evangelical discourse of Muslims, Christians, and atheists*. Cambridge University Press.
An in-depth study of the TJ Kirk and Joshua Feuerstein, two of the users highlighted in this chapter, with examples of how people of different faith interact on social media and how drama impacts interaction.
Ringrow, H. (2020). "I can feel myself being squeezed and stretched, moulded and grown, and expanded in my capacity to love loudly and profoundly": Metaphor and religion in motherhood blogs. *Discourse, Context & Media, 37*, 100429.
A good example of research focusing particularly on close linguistic analysis of metaphor, a key topic in religious language, with relation to social and cultural norms, showing ways of talking about experience are influenced by religious contexts and sacred texts.
Rosowsky, A. (Ed.). (2017). *Faith and Language Practices in Digital Spaces*. Multilingual Matters.
A diverse range of studies and approaches to online communities from the late stages of Web 2.0, with a particular focus on the language practices as they relate to religious belief.

Source Videos

1. 'ye, alex and nick are based. elon is cringe' posted by Christopher Anderson; published and accessed on 5 December 2022 from www.youtube.com/watch?v=dopwhApFo0o
2. 'How I Created The Anti-SJW Genre, And Almost Destroyed The World' posted by TJ Kirk; published on 1 December 2022 and accessed on 5 December 2002 from www.youtube.com/watch?v=Yu6c1g9r-P4)
3. SlavicVote Instagram post, shared on Feuerstein's Instagram on 5 August 2022 and accessed on 5 December 2022 from www.instagram.com/reel/Cg5CuYGlARv/

References

Ali, K. & Zain-ul-abdin, K. (2021). Post-truth propaganda: Heuristic processing of political fake news on Facebook during the 2016 U.S. presidential election. *Journal of Applied Communication Research, 49*(1), 109–128. https://doi.org/10.1080/00909882.2020.1847311

Allington, D. & Pihlaja, S. (2016). Reading in the age of the internet. *Language and Literature, 25*(3), 201–210. https://doi.org/10.1177/0963947016652781

Anderson, J.W. (2003). The internet and Islam's new interpreters. In D.F. Eickelman & J.W. Anderson (Eds.), *New media in the Muslim world: The emerging public sphere*, 41–55. Indiana University Press.

Androutsopoulos, J. (2014). Potentials and Limitations of Discourse-Centred Online Ethnography. *Language@Internet, 5*. www.languageatinternet.org/articles/2008/1610

Bunt, G.R. (2009). *iMuslims: Rewiring the house of Islam*. University of North Carolina Press.

Campbell, H.A. (2012). *Digital religion: Understanding religious practice in new media worlds*. Routledge.

Campbell, H.A. & Lövheim, M. (2011). Introduction. *Information, Communication & Society, 14*(8), 1083–1096. https://doi.org/10.1080/1369118X.2011.597416

Creese, A. (2008). Linguistic Ethnography. In N. Hornberger (Ed.), *Encyclopedia of Language and Education, 2*, 229–241. Springer.

Denzin, N.K. (1999). Cybertalk and the method of instances. In S. Jones (Ed.), *Doing Internet research: Critical issues and methods for examining the Net*, 107–125. SAGE Publishing.

Fahey, T. & Prevost, R. (1994). *Net. Speak: The Internet dictionary*. Hayden Books.

George, S.E. (2006). *Religion and Technology in the 21st Century: Faith in the E-World: Faith in the E-World*. IGI Global.

Grieve, J., Nini, A., & Guo, D. (2018). Mapping Lexical Innovation on American Social Media. *Journal of English Linguistics*, *46*(4), 293–319. https://doi.org/10.1177/0075424218793191

Harré, R. & van Langenhove, L. (1998). *Positioning Theory: Moral Contexts of Intentional Action*. Blackwell Publishers.

Herring, S. (2003). Computer-mediated discourse. In D. Schiffrin, D. Tannen, & H. Hamilton (Eds.), *The Handbook of Discourse Analysis*, 612–634. Blackwell.

Herring, S. (2004). Slouching toward the ordinary: Current trends in computer-mediated communication. *New Media and Society*, *6*(1), 26–36.

Hoover, S. & Lundby, K. (1997). *Rethinking Media, Religion, and Culture*. SAGE Publishing.

Hutchings, T. (2017). *Creating Church Online: Ritual, Community and New Media*. Routledge.

Keisler, S. (1997). *Culture of the Internet*. Lawrence Erlbaum Associates, Inc.

Kolb, R. (1987). Teaching the Text: The commonplace Method in The Sixteen Century Luthern Biblical Commentary. *Bibliothèque d'Humanisme et Renaissance*, *49*(3), 571–585.

Mackenzie, J. (2017). Identifying informational norms in Mumsnet Talk: A reflexive-linguistic approach to internet research ethics. *Applied Linguistics Review*, *8*(2–3), 293–314.

Mackenzie, J. (2023). *Connected Parenting: Digital Discourse and Diverse Family Practices*. Bloomsbury.

Marwick, A., & boyd, d. (2011). I tweet honestly, I tweet passionately: Twitter users, context collapse, and the imagined audience. *New Media & Society*, *13*(1), 114–133.

Pariser, E. (2011). *The filter bubble: What the Internet is hiding from you*. Penguin UK.

Pihlaja, S. (2014). *Antagonism on YouTube: Metaphor in Online Discourse*. Bloomsbury.

Pihlaja, S. (2018). *Religious Talk Online: The evangelical discourse of Muslims, Christians, and atheists*. Cambridge University Press.

Pihlaja, S. (2021). *Talk about Faith: How conversation shapes belief*. Cambridge University Press.

Rosowsky, A. (Ed.). (2017). *Faith and Language Practices in Digital Spaces*. Multilingual Matters.

Rubin, J. (2014). Printing and Protestants: An Empirical Test of the Role of Printing in the Reformation. *The Review of Economics and Statistics*, *96*(2), 270–286. https://doi.org/10.1162/REST_a_00368

Tagg, C. (2012). *Discourse of Text Messaging: Analysis of SMS Communication*. Continuum/Bloomsbury.

Tagg, C., Seargeant, P., & Brown, A.A. (2017). *Taking Offence on Social Media: Conviviality and Communication on Facebook*. Springer.

Trammell, J. (2015). Jesus? There's an app for that! Tablet Media in the 'New' Electronic Church. In M. Ward (Ed.), *The Electronic Church in the Digital Age: Cultural Impacts of Evangelical Mass Media*. Praeger.

White, L.T. (1978). *Medieval religion and technology: Collected essays, 13*. University of California Press.

11

VARIATION OF LANGUAGE IN RELIGIOUS TEXTS

Svitlana Shurma and Wei-lun Lu

Introduction and Background

In Cognitive Linguistics, the study of viewpoint has received extensive scholarly attention (e.g., Verhagen, 2005; Vandelanotte, 2009; Dancygier & Sweetser, 2012; Dancygier et al., 2016; van Krieken et al., 2019, among others) over time. Cognitive Linguistics views viewpoint as a verbal expression of subjective categorization of the world and relates the role of viewpoint in story-telling to human beings' unique capacity to coordinate activities as a core characteristic of human social cognition (Verhagen, 2016, pp. 1–3). To viewpoint a stretch of discourse, language users select linguistic means available in a given language to report on other people's speech and thought depending on their communicative intentions, thus verbalizing the same idea differently: for instance, it is possible to describe something we do not like by saying *I can't stand it* or *I hate it*.

Additionally, language speakers use language in a way that reflects peculiar categorizations of the specific communities or cultures they belong to: for example, Christians and atheists would assess and discuss euthanasia differently. This means that language users tend to embed their viewpoint into the messages they produce. To analyze these viewpoints in grammar, discourses, and across modalities and media, such tools as image schemas, frames, blends, and others are used (Vandelanotte 2017). One of the most revered viewpoint models is based on Langacker's Cognitive Grammar (e.g., 2008) and involves (1) a conceptualizer, or a "virtual entity" (Langacker, 2008, p. 448) capable of viewpoint shift from one position of observation to another; (2) vantage point, or a spatial or temporal position from which some conceptualized entity is viewed, often represented by spatial and temporal deictics, such as *this*, *here*, *before*, etc.; and (3) subjectivity, or the way the conceptualizer is involved in the conceptualized scene which ranges from them being a mere observer to being an "implicit locus of consciousness" (Langacker, 2008, p. 77). Recent studies of viewpoint in Cognitive Linguistics take a more experimental turn, too.

As a linguistic and conceptual phenomenon, viewpoint is also analyzed in narratives, especially since the so-called polyphonic (Bakhtin's term referring to multitude of voices in the texts influencing the perspective from which events are narrated and narrative worlds are created) texts can have multiple narrative voices. The narrative viewpoint focuses on understanding the narrative distance as a cognitive connection between the linguistic representation and the way it determines some physical or metaphorical point or distance from which an entity, such as an object, event, or

DOI: 10.4324/9781003301271-12

situation is represented, as "[n]arratives are still commonly considered the most fertile ground for viewpoint studies" (Dancygier, 2016, p. 281). It is through the stories that we can access the mind and thought processes of other people (Palmer, 2004). In narratives, the point of view is "related to the position established by the teller of a story vis-à-vis the elements of the story itself" (Yamazaki, 2006, p. 90).

What it means is that when a story is narrated, the events and participants in the story can be presented to us through different perspectives: the words used to narrate the story allow the narrator to create impressions of seeing the event or character from different angles. For example, at times, readers or listeners can see events through the eyes of the character; at other times, they can see a broader picture as if from a bird's eye view. A story can be told in the first person, such as King Nebuchadnezzar's narration in Daniel 4, or in the third person when a distant and detached narrator provides access to the thoughts and feelings of other characters, as in Matthew 2:7–8 when the narrator outlines how Harrod sent the Magi to Bethlehem. Thus, two aspects are important: a vantage point or the point of presentation of events and objects, and orientation, the depiction itself from that point; both are dynamic in narratives but also point to the subjective nature of viewpoints (Eekhof et al., 2020, p. 2). The choice of perspective is very important in storytelling and helps to create interest and aesthetic faculty of the text.

Two more aspects are to be considered in narratives: who tells the story and who sees it (Simpson 2004, p. 27). For example, a detached narrator could tell a story, but it could be a particular character who sees the events described. Let us look at the passage from Matthew 2:7–8 (King James Version):

> [7] Then Herod, when he had privily called the wise men, enquired of them diligently what time the star appeared. [8] And he sent them to Bethlehem, and said, Go and search diligently for the young child; and when ye have found him, bring me word again, that I may come and worship him also.

The narrator here seems detached from the story told—they know what Herod said and did—and the narrative is heterodiegetic. On the other hand, Nebuchadnezzar's sharing of his dream in Daniel 4, makes the King both the one who sees and tells the events of the dream, and is thus a homodiegetic narrator. In the latter case, the readers are psychologically much closer to the character-narrator compared to King Herod in Matthew's narrative. In both cases, there is a restriction on what we get to know about the characters from the narrators, known as focalization (Genette, 1972). Depending on how much the readers can access the characters' minds and psyche, Genette distinguishes between zero, internal, and external focalizations. This term helps to differentiate between the narration per se and the character's perception of what is being narrated.

Traditionally, the point of view is studied along five planes—a model first introduced by Uspensky (1973) and later revised by Fowler (1996). The planes are ideological, temporal, spatial, psychological, and phraseological. The ideological plane reflects the system of beliefs about the world which can be associated with the author, narrator, or character(s). The temporal plane is analyzed through the way the text refers to or signals time: through tense or aspect forms of verbs, temporal deixis, stylistic use of repetitions, flashbacks, or flashforwards. "[T]emporal point of view seems to be less about focalization and viewpoint and rather about narrative structure; it does after all encompass the structural segments and sequential progression of the time-line of a narrative" (Simpson, 2004, p. 78). The spatial plane refers to the way the story positions the characters and action in space. It is often compared to the "camera angle" (Simpson, 2004, p. 78; Yamazaki, 2006, p. 92), the effect achieved through the use of spatial deictics and locative expressions, as well as the ways character's speech and thought are represented. Psychological plane is often analyzed through the focalization and partially through the spatial plane as internal focalization is associated with shorter perceived distance. And finally, the phraseological plane lies in the realm of register or speech styles shifting, when the subtle changes in the use of vocabulary or forms of speech can signal a change in the point of view from that of a narrator to that of a character.

Furthermore, point of view in narratives is closely related to the term "construal" in Cognitive Linguistics, which means how a situation or a scene is approached and understood by a conceptualizer. When a scene is verbally encoded, it can be interpreted by the receiver of the message. In such a process, specificity, prominence, perspective, and dynamicity are important for structuring a construal. For instance, the choice of verbalization may be based on the conceptualizations ranging along the concreteness/vagueness line. The prominence is achieved by linguistic salience or foregrounding. In Cognitive Grammar terminology, this way of drawing attention to some fragment of the text by means of linguistic expression is known as profiling. Just as the figure and background interplay when one is looking at the picture, foregrounded elements are profiled against the conceptual base. Dynamicity is connected to the ability of language to offer mental access to certain concepts or conceptual domains in the knowledge system. And finally, perspective identifies how conceptualized content and communicative context are mentally arranged. Uspensky's spatial and temporal planes in Cognitive Grammar terms become the ground, which conceptualizers assume as their vantage point.

One way to analyze the viewpoint in a religious text is by using multiple parallel texts (MultiParT), which allow the researcher to see the actual range of cross-linguistic and intra-linguistic variation of construal of a particular usage event mediated by the linguistic toolkit of a particular human language. Previous studies (e.g., Lu et al., 2020, among others) have used literary texts as study materials, but the method can certainly be applied to the religious domain. In such an approach, analyzing the linguistic representation of viewpoint and its shifts, sentence by sentence in parallel texts, allows analysts to identify intra-linguistic or cross-linguistic differences in viewpoint management within different representative (or influential groups of) text producers within the same or different languages when highly similar content is verbalized through the conventionalized linguistic toolkit available for a particular linguistic community, such as versions or translations of the Bible.

MultiParT can be applied by using the toolkit of Cognitive Grammar to tease out relevant and detailed linguistic and conceptual aspects of viewpoint construction through semantic and grammatical variation in the target language. MultiParT allows us to see how the linguistic choices influence the way the text communicates with the reader; in the case of viewpoint study, how the same content is told through the narrator's operation on the narrative distance. From the perspective of Cognitive Linguistics, variation in encoding reflects variation in conceptualization, which results in slightly different representations of the conceptual scene narrated. The shifts happening along the temporal, spatial, ideological, and psychological planes would have variation in the windows of attention, or a way of directing attention in discourse through verbal and conceptual foregrounding of different elements of event frames within narratives (Harrison, 2017, pp. 100–101), due to the choices of verbalization of the events narrated. As the choices that the text producers make to vary the same event or experience, inevitably so will the readings vary. Therefore, the variation of the encoding strategies creates an inevitable influence on the rendition of the same religious text in different languages and among different speakers of the same language.

Before we proceed to the sample case study, it is important to note that when working with parallel religious texts, a suitable theoretical framework is necessary. To this end, we consider

Cognitive Grammar (CG) (Langacker 2008, 2009) a useful theoretical tool. CG is a cognitive approach to language that epitomizes a constructional approach to language, where grammar does not work independently of meaning but is in itself symbolic and meaningful. Based on the symbolic assumption of grammar, CG has been applied to stylistic analysis that examines linguistic choices and patterns in literary works and has produced meaningful results (Giovanelli & Harrison, 2018; Harrison, 2018; Nuttall, 2018). The application of CG to studying religious texts (especially parallel religious texts) has been rare and is certainly a promising future track of research.

MultiParT in Biblical Viewpoint Study

Let us illustrate how MultiParT works in the analysis of viewpoint shifts in translations of the Bible. Due to space limitations, we give only a detailed analysis of a small passage from Luke 19:1–3 taken from the King James Version (KJV), New Catholic (NCB), New International Version (NIV), and New American Standard (NASB) Bibles. Focus is given to the intra-linguistic variation among the above versions. In addition to showcasing the variation of construals among those English versions, we also set the texts against Yamazaki's (2006) interpretation of the Greek version of the same passage to see how shifts in viewpoint occur on the linguistic level in different versions of the translations, using the previous published scholarly work as a reference point. Although Yamazaki analyzes the Greek version, the metalanguage he uses is English.

The choice of the versions is based on different approaches to the translation strategy. For instance, the KJV New Testament is used as the basis of the Orthodox Study Bible in English, and NIV and NASB are popular Protestant versions of the Bible. One of the most well-known English translations of the Bible is the King James Version, which dates back to the 17th century and is known as one of "the most important books in the English-speaking world" (Campbell qtd in Hunt, 2011). The New Catholic Bible is translated from Hebrew and Greek texts with the aim to "reflect the most current consensus of Catholic scholarship" (Catholic Book Publishing Corp., n.d.). New International Version is a product of around 100 translators representing several of the Protestant denominations working with Hebrew, Aramaic, and Greek texts and claiming "the very best combination of accuracy and readability" (Biblica, n.d.). Just as NIV claims to have worked with Hebrew, Aramaic, and Greek texts, the New American Standard Bible differs in its approach to translation and asserts that it adheres to "the formal equivalence translation philosophy", or "literal translation" (Lockman Foundation, n.d.). For this reason, both versions are included in the present study. And finally, Yamazaki's 2006 study, to which we allude, is a published scholarly interpretation of the Greek original, which we use to further testify the intra-linguistic variation of construal in another dimension.

In MultiParT, we set the texts in parallel for the purpose of contrastive semantic and grammatical analysis of the language of these texts that signal the shifts in viewpoints. We follow how the text producers render the viewpoint into the target language, which itself allows for several possibilities. The linguistic tools chosen by text producers may vary, and thus have a different impact on the reading of the target text.

To begin with, what strikes the readers of the English versions is the fact that three of the versions—NCB, NIV, and NASB—have titles to Luke 19 (see Table 11.1). The titles serve the function of foreshadowing (or foregrounding in the cognitive-functional term) parts of the scene to be narrated, as when the reader encounters the chapter title, that invokes an expectation in the reader's mind through the narration and can be considered a strategy of introducing the narrator's voice (rather than the character's).

Table 11.1 Titles from different translations

Version	Content of the title
KJV	Not available in 1987 version analyzed here
NCB	Jesus and Zacchaeus, the Rich Tax Collector
NIV	Zacchaeus the Tax Collector
NASB	Zaccheus (*sic*) Converted

For instance, in NASB, the character which is foregrounded and nominated (van Leeuwen, 2008) is Zaccheus. He is characterized through passivation: a past participle *converted* is used. Conceptually, participial form "designates a process in which a participant [Zacchaeus] undergoes a change of state" (Langacker, 2008, p. 122), from being a non-believer to becoming a Christian in the NASB title, thus, exhibiting a property which he did not have before. The title foregrounds the main motif of the chapter, the act of conversion, yet, the agent of the action is missing. The past participle indicates that the action is completed (temporal plane) and thus fastforwards the narrative action to the end: because of that, the reader is left to anticipate the who, when, and how of the narration. At the same time, the passivated character is presented as beneficialized (van Leeuwen, 2008, p. 279) in the wider context of the Biblical story.

NIV also focuses on nominating the character (or *profiles* the character, in the term of Cognitive Grammar), Zaccheus; however, the NIV's approach is to characterize by adding a postmodifier which functionalizes (van Leeuwen, 2008, p. 288) the character by pointing out his occupation, and given the biblical time, the social role and the public's view of Zaccheus naturally associated with his occupation. While NASB presents the event in the form of a summary, thus keeping a considerable distance between the event and the reader, the title in NIV positions the narrator along the phraseological plane (Uspensky qtd in Yamazaki, 2006, p. 92). The title itself also creates the bridge between Luke 18:9–14, or the so-called "parable of the Pharisee and the Tax Collector", and the events which are about to unfold in Chapter 19, where the story told by Jesus would turn real in front of the audience. The title thus foregrounds one of the characters about to be presented, yet uses the strategy of exclusion (van Leeuwen, 2008, p. 274) by removing the mention of Jesus, though keeping the anticipation of his role in the further text.

The NCB title, for that matter, does not only present the two characters of the upcoming Chapter, Jesus and Zacchaeus, but also functionalizes and identifies through a classification (van Leeuwen, 2008, pp. 288–289) of the latter character: in this title, Zacchaeus is presented not only as a tax collector, but also as a "rich" one. The point of view on the ideological plane is indicative of the narrator's evaluation, and therefore foregrounds the point of view that the narrator would like to present to the reader. In the context of Luke 18:24–25, entitled in NCB as "Danger of Riches" (New Catholic Bible, Luke 18:24), the reader can easily create the association. The title itself sets the scene and foregrounds the basis for a "dramatic" situation.

In verse 1 of each of the versions, we also see a diversified presentation of the narrative viewpoint. The verse in the parallel versions is presented below as Table 11.2.

The analysis of the titles above is also important in the view of the opening sentence of the chapter. Yamazaki, analyzing the first verse, reports that Lukan narrator (in the Greek text) chooses to omit nomination of the subject of the sentence, Jesus, thus positioning the audience at a distance and also distancing the audience from identifying the point of view early in the chapter, in order to set the background for the story (Yamazaki, 2006, pp. 96–98). However, none of the

Table 11.2 Contents of verse 1 from different translations

Version	Content of verse 1
Greek	Καὶ εἰσελθὼν, διήρχετο τὴν Ἰεριχώ
Yamazaki's tr.	And having entered Jericho, he was passing through it.
KJV	And Jesus entered and passed through Jericho.
NCB	Jesus entered Jericho and was passing through it.
NIV	Jesus entered Jericho and was passing through.
NASB	*Jesus* entered Jericho and was passing through.

four English versions shows an attempt to preserve this effect by thematizing *Jesus* as one of the focal points in the narration (NASB even uses graphical foregrounding by italicizing the subject of the sentence, *Jesus*).

Of the four analyzed versions, KJV does not have a title for the chapter; therefore, verse 1 alone does the job of setting the scene. This is a full narrative clause in past tense. Compared to the Greek text discussed by Yamazaki, the translator uses polysyndeton by repeating *and* and thus stylistically slowing the pace of the narration. The reason for this might be the need to compensate for the loss of the imperfect "background tense" (see du Toit, 2017). In Yamazaki's analysis of the Greek text, as chapter 18 finishes with Jesus approaching Jericho, verse 1 of chapter 19 works as the continuation of the story, and so Jesus' entrance to the city is backgrounded. Unlike the Greek version, KJV accentuates the events in a series—*entered* and *passed*. According to Langacker (2008, p. 124), such types of finite clauses profile a process, while the "tense marking grounds this process by relating it to the time of speaking". The version also chooses to put Jericho in the position of a rheme. This deictic used as a viewpoint marker sets and keeps the narrator at the distance of a bird's-eye view, as the events of the narrative are presented in a summary fashion.

As we examine NCB, the version places the name of Jesus in the position of a theme, just as the other four versions. The lexical unit *Jesus* in verse 1 of NCB anaphorically refers to the title where it is syntactically placed in the initial position. Placing *Jesus* before *Zacchaeus* in the two coordinate elements seems to follow both superiority and experiential closeness constraints of element ordering in binomials discussed in Renner (2014). Jesus thus becomes an " 'energy source' and the initial participant in an action chain" (Langacker, 2008, p. 365) as we move to the actual narrative.

Unlike KJV but similar to NIV and NASB, NCB uses a combination of simple past tense and progressive aspect, thus the pace of the narration can be compared to the slow one discussed in Yamazaki (2006). The perceived distance to the audience is short, as explicit reference to Jesus zooms in on his actions as the scene develops. Another narrative element worth mentioning is the representation of the spatial plane in NCB. While KJV places *Jericho* at the end of the sentence after the two coordinate verbal elements, NCB mentions it twice, as *Jericho* after the first coordinate unit *entered* and as pro-form *it* after the second one *was passing*. This practice serves the function of placing the location of the action more in "focus" (Harrison, 2017, p. 222) than NIV and NASB, which omit the reference to the background location altogether. Note that Jericho, in this way, can be argued to serve as a cognitive reference point (*sensu* Harrison, 2017, p. 20), since it is mentioned in the Bible several times, especially in the Old Testament, which also makes Jesus' presence therein symbolically significant. Not only does this narrative practice create a continuation in the biblical story world, but it also serves as a point of focalization. The spatial position of the observation of the scene creates a zoom-in effect by repeating the reference to the city where the main action is about to take place. A contrast worth noting is that NIV and NASB, by omitting

Table 11.3 Contents of verse 2 from different translations

Version	Content of verse 2
Greek	Καὶ ἰδού, ἀνὴρ ὀνόματι καλούμενος Ζακχαῖος, καὶ αὐτὸς ἦν ἀρχιτελώνης, καὶ αὐτὸς πλούσιος.
Yamazaki's tr.	And look, a man named Zacchaeus. And he was a chief tax collector and he was rich.
KJV	And, behold, there was a man named Zacchaeus, which was the chief among the publicans, and he was rich.
NCB	A man there, named Zacchaeus, was a chief tax collector and a rich man.
NIV	A man was there by the name of Zacchaeus; he was a chief tax collector and was wealthy.
NASB	And there was a man called by the name of Zaccheus; he was a chief tax collector and he was rich.

the pro-form, leave the reader's focus with the moving agent's action rather than the background location where the action takes place.

Verse 2 of the chapter also demonstrates vast intra-language variation. Table 11.3 showcases the different versions of verse 2.

In verse 2, Yamazaki (2006, pp. 98–99) points out the "shift to a more immediate point of view" on the spatial plane in the verse through the use of Greek particle meaning "behold, look", nominative of exclamation *man*, emphasizing pronoun *he*, and insertion of the details about Zacchaeus (see full text below).

In the four analyzed versions, only KJV contains the "focusing device" (Yamazaki, 2006, p. 99), linguistically realized as *behold*, as an element of addressing the audience and signal of the change in the point of view. For the reader of KJV, though, it is unspecified as to the exact physical location of Zacchaeus. On the one hand, the previous verse states that Jesus' trip through Jericho is over, indicated by the simple past form of the verb; on the other hand, *there* in verse 2 at the start of the clause could be read in two ways: as a deictic reference to Jericho of verse 1 or as an expletive subject referring to "an abstract setting" (Broccias, 2008, p. 85).

The introduction of the subject and predicate into the clause does not reduce the distance between the narrator and the reader the way it does in Yamazaki's Greek version but continues keeping it at the bird's-eye view, shifting the reader's attention from Jesus to Zacchaeus—for KJV a new character. Different from the other versions of English, KJV employs a non-restrictive relative clause to introduce additional information about the new character, contributing to the shift of a zoom-in, whereas Yamazaki, NCB, NIV, and NASB all use functionalization to elaborate on the character in this verse. KJV chooses the phrase *chief among the publicans* (cf. *chief tax collector*) as the way to characterize Zacchaeus. As the oldest version among the versions analyzed, KJV uses an archaic expression *publican* to refer to the Roman tax-gatherer (Online Etymology Dictionary, n.d.). Notably, at the time of publishing, the word *publican* had a second, more commonly recognized, meaning in English: that of a pub-keeper (Online Etymology Dictionary, n.d.). Following from that, we can see that the choice of the archaism contributes to the temporal distance between the narrator and the reader. The noun phrase, in which the reference to the character's occupation occurs, is emphatic, setting the character above the others of the same profession but also contributing to the spatial distance between the narrator and the reader. The narrator's comment on the status of the character, *rich*, appears as a coordinate clause highlighting it as a detail in focus, and, as we have mentioned earlier, bridging with Luke 18, and in the verse, this is the only indicator of the shift along the ideological plane of narration.

NCB version has a simple sentence where the occupation and status of Zacchaeus are in coordination: we see that "the conjuncts are equal in the sense that neither of their profiles overrides that of the other, as is usual in grammatical constructions" (Langacker, 2009, p. 350). Since the reader already knows from the title that Zacchaeus is a rich man and a tax collector, the two characteristics of Zacchaeus are of equal importance for focalization. This structure is somewhat different from that in the NIV: *he was a chief tax collector and was wealthy*. In NIV, the grammatical balance is not quite in place as we have a combination of N and ADJ as conjuncts. The nominal and the adjectival phrase both function as complements of *was*, repeated twice, while the trajector corresponds to the profile of *he*, Zacchaeus.

NIV chose not to include the ideological plane in the chapter title; and in verse 2 we see that the narrator hesitates in using a slightly more "judgmental" *rich*, as in the other versions. The NIV narrative approach also contributes to the distance between the narrator and the reader on the ideological plane, unlike in NCB, where the narrator's attitude is explicated at the beginning. In NASB, Zacchaeus is characterized via homogeneous clauses: *he was a chief tax collector and he was rich*. Instead of reducing the structure to "a more compact form" (Quirk et al., 1985, p. 859) via ellipsis into, for example, *he was a rich chief tax collector*, NASB keeps the "overlap of content and structure" (Quirk et al., 1985, p. 858). In this way, the line sets a window of attention (Langacker, 2009, p. 351): through the repetition of pro-form *he, Zaccheus* (*sic*) is shifted closer to the reader, maintaining the narrative distance we see as in the Greek version.

On the spatial plane, the use of deictic *there* creates intra-language diversity in the perception of viewpoints in the four versions: *there was a man* (KJV and NASB), *a man there* (NCB), and *a man was there* (NIV). Though in KJV, discussed above, the deictic *there* is in the same syntactic role as in NASB, its profile is different, as there is no ambiguity as to the phrase being an expletive subject. One of the reasons for this perception, we argue, is the absence in this version of interjection "behold, look", discussed in Yamazaki, which directs the reader's attention towards what is to be remarked on. The syntactic proximity of *behold* to *there* in KJV, on the other hand, leads to ambiguity in the interpretation of the passage, but with regard to narration, it engages the reader's attention. In NCB and NIV, *there* is purely deictic and thus keeps the point of view along the same spatial plane as in verse 1.

What is also worth noting regarding verse 2 is the fact that all the English versions contain a finite clause, which is different from the bare nominative of exclamation in the Greek text reported by Yamazaki. We argue that such choice is defined by the conventionality of the English language, where we witness a tendency for verbalizing the grounding elements, or the lexical expressions which relate the story to the speech event, participants, and their interaction as well as extralinguistic context. All the English versions have a highly schematic verb *be*, which "[w]hen added to an atemporal expression, [...] lends its processual profile to the latter's more substantial content" (Langacker, 2008, p. 125), in our case *a man*. If we proceed from the idea that "anything we might conceptualize is also something we might want to talk about, and if we want to talk about it, we need a way of referring to it" (Langacker, 2008, p. 276), the use of nominal makes good sense, as now "the interlocutors direct their attention to the same conceptual entity" (Langacker, 2008, p. 276) in order to restrict the viewing frame. Quite different from the English versions, the exclamation, used in the Greek version, is used to perform a social action by calling for action or attention, and only then to further ground an individual, Zacchaeus, by conceptually profiling him in the linguistic form of a nominal.

Table 11.4 Contents of verse 3 from different translations

Version	Content of verse 3
Greek	Καὶ ἐζήτει ἰδεῖν τὸν Ἰησοῦν, τίς ἐστιν, καὶ οὐκ ἠδύνατο ἀπὸ τοῦ ὄχλου, ὅτι τῇ ἡλικίᾳ μικρὸς ἦν.
Yamazaki's tr.	And he was seeking to see who Jesus was, and he was not able on account of the crowd, because he was short in stature.
KJV	And he sought to see Jesus who he was; and could not for the press, because he was little of stature.
NCB	He wanted to see who Jesus was, but since he was short in stature, he could not see him because of the crowd.
NIV	He wanted to see who Jesus was, but because he was short he could not see over the crowd.
NASB	*Zaccheus* was trying to see who Jesus was, and he was unable due to the crowd, because he was short in stature.

Yamazaki (2006, pp. 99–100) states that in verse 3 the "dynamic of drawing the audience in […] is [first] stalled", as summary material and the choice of imperfect "prevent[s] the audience from being drawn right into the midst of the action"; yet, the verse contains the shift on the psychological plane once Zacchaeus's intentions are revealed. Referring to verse 4, Yamazaki concludes that the shift in verse 3 establishes Zacchaeus as a point-of-view character.

This shift in point of view, as pointed out by Yamazaki, is captured in the four English versions differently, as in Table 11.4: the verbal representation and the dynamics are not the same. Unlike the Greek version, three English versions (KJV, NCB, and NIV) continue the narration with the use of the simple past *sought* or *wanted*, which profile the character's intention as a finished event. NASB is the only version using the progressive aspect—*was trying*,—providing a close-up look at the character's attempt. Semantically, the choice of the verbs changes the perception of the motivation for the intention of the character, and thus the distance with the reader. Langacker (2009, p. 130, also pp. 151–152) describes an idealized cognitive model, or a "control cycle", reflected in the verbalizations of similar kinds through the relation between an actor having control of dominion, with a target entering the actor's field for potential interaction. In verse 3, the actor is Zacchaeus and the target is Jesus, while the dominion is the intention of the tax collector significantly reduced by his physique and the crowd of people. Langacker (2009, p. 152) correlated the verb *want* (used in NCB and NIV) with the potential phase of the control cycle. On the other hand, following this logic, the verbs *sought* (KJV) and *was trying* (NASB) correspond to action phases, and therefore present Zacchaeus at the physical level (externally), compared to NCB and NIV, where the reader gets a deeper view of Zacchaeus's internal or metal state, invoked by the verb *want*. Therefore, we can say that the choice of the verb *want* in NCB and NIV creates a greater zoom-in effect than the other versions.

As we look at all the versions, we see that the titles added to some of the versions offer different focalization and thus interpretation of the texts that follow. Though it is not known which of the existing Greek versions (see e.g., SainteBible 2018 mentioned without the titles or Interlinear Bible (2012), which has a title, though only in English—*Jesus and Zacchaeus*) had been used as the basis of each of the versions, the titles and their verbalizations do influence the representation of the viewpoint. The attention windows of the three versions fluctuate in focalizing either one character, two characters, or the action performed thus establishing the text producer-as-narrator's stand on the interpretation of the plot. In this case, the linguistic strategy becomes a choice only partially rooted in the systemic linguistic phenomena, as for example, the order of conjuncts in a series of coordinative items. These kinds of preferences also put in question the declared statuses of translation in terms of their accuracy.

At the same time, we see that the versions tend to employ more typically accepted language community structures, even if the language allows some flexibility in staying close to the original. In our view, this is manifested by the choice of the so-called "narrative tenses", the past tense and the progressive aspect, for opening a scene of the narration in verse 1. In a similar manner, the order of conjuncts follows the order of experiences guided by embodied cognition, as in verse 3. One more example of conventionalization is the tendency to avoid ellipses, such as adding Jesus' name to verse 1, or avoiding the nomination of exclamation in verse 2.

However, along the cross-linguistic dimension, some linguistic choices, as we have discussed earlier, induce change in the viewpoint of the target text, such as the one induced by semantic differences of adjectives *rich/wealthy* in verse 2 or verbs *want/seek/try* in verse 3. Syntactic variation through the creation of different attention frames also contributes to the shifts in viewpoints which can vary from implicit to more noticeable ones.

Implications and Future Directions

From what we saw in the sample analysis, it is clear that religious texts do provide a promising pathway for studying the diversity of human language and cognition. At the cross-linguistic level, we see that the different languages involved (Greek and English) do exhibit different tendencies in verbalizing the same literary scene. Along the intra-linguistic dimension, we also see that the different versions of the same language (which is English) similarly present varying verbalizations of the same literary scene. At a conceptual level, the analyses of viewpoints in parallel texts show that linguistic choices and narrative planes are closely connected in the representation of narratives. Verbal and structural choices influence how the viewpoint perspective develops over the course of a narration in comparison with the source text. This conceptualization is also partially stipulated by the intrinsic linguistic patterns and understanding of those helps to understand how narratives can vary.

We propose future directions of research:

First and foremost, as we have argued elsewhere (Lu et al., 2020), the MultiParT method allows us to identify the points of untranslatability across the languages and shows us where the translators have to make their own decision as to how to approach the text. In the religious domain, for editors of religious texts, such analysis can help in identifying the weak points of translations along with the changes that could potentially influence the reader in the undesired ways, e.g., to determine the viewpoint shifts that might have an ideological or a perceptual ground. We believe that this method also has strong potential in studying the translation of religious texts, as this method can help to identify and to avoid cross-linguistic variation (if at all possible), on the one hand, and on the other, to help the translators make informed use of the linguistic conventions of the languages involved to achieve a higher extent of accuracy and equivalence in translations, especially where the narrative distance and viewpoint are of cognitive and stylistic importance. Additionally, using multiple translated versions into one language can help us tease out individual stylistic preferences (see Lu et al., 2020) and variations which could be indicative of idiolects and idiostyles, especially when authorship is concerned.

Another promising pathway of development is to use religious texts for the purpose of the investigation of linguistic features. The Bible translation in various languages has been used by various scholars in typological research (e.g. Cysouw & Wälchli, 2009) and in comparative corpus linguistic research (e.g. Christodouloupoulos & Steedman, 2015). However, it must be noted that such research in cognitive stylistics is still rare, and future research in cognitive stylistics based on biblical texts is methodologically commendable.

Following from the above point, we see two promising extensions. The religious text used for such research does not necessarily need to be Christian texts; as long as a religion is developed to an extent such that any one of its canons has been translated into multiple languages and also such that multiple versions exist within a particular language, we see immediate applicability of the MultiParT method. Moreover, with this method, under-investigated languages can also be studied in depth thanks to the translation work done extensively by missionaries.

In addition, the method can be used in ethnolinguistic and cultural linguistic studies of religious and sacred texts, as it could help in analyzing, for instance, the ideological plane of values, norms, and knowledge expressed through language. As values and beliefs influence how contents in the religious domain are categorized and conceptualized, the language used in rituals, for example, in lamentations during the mourning process for the deceased, can help in tracking how people's construal of an event is inevitably shaped by the linguistic means available to the speech community. The concept of viewpoint, as, for example, applied in ethnolinguistic and cultural linguistic studies by Bartmiński (1990), is a useful tool for analyzing how the hidden values and beliefs are profiled via categorization, naming conventions, and the selection of specific linguistic features, such as language formulas or metaphors, which involve creating a subjective representation of an event from a specific viewpoint across communities. Additionally, the analysis of how reality is profiled through the language and other elements of rituals, such as music, gestures, and arrangement of artefacts, could help us gain insights into the cultural and social dynamics that shape linguistic and non-linguistic activities of a specific religious community.

One future application of the parallel-text study could contribute to digital religion research, a burgeoning field of studying religion and the internet. MultiParT could be used in studying not only verbal exchanges online, but also points of view and religious identities represented through the other modalities ranging from religious garments, uses of emoticons, visual representations, and so on. The study of memes in religious discourses could help track the blending of pop culture with religious narratives and practices or help explain their meaning-generation within religious communities and outside them, or, for instance, the re-contextualization of memetic quiddities in religious discourses.

At the same time, we should bear in mind that although the MultiParT approach presents a methodological opportunity for us to investigate the verbalization and the conceptualization of multiple parallel usage events, the method needs to be complemented by theoretical approaches that allow us to analyze and compare the construals invoked by the verbalization of those parallel usage events. In the sample analysis presented above, it is the viewpoint analysis and Cognitive Grammar in Cognitive Linguistics that are involved as the theoretical apparatuses of the comparison, but we by no means need to exclude the possibility of involving other theoretical frameworks in Cognitive Linguistics such as Conceptual Blending (Fauconnier & Turner, 2002) or Conceptual Metaphor Theory (Lakoff & Johnson, 1980).

As a final note, let us point out that given the profound influence they have on human life and the extensive translation work done thus far as a natural consequence of the influence, parallel religious texts constitute exciting pathways of future research. Use of parallel religious texts in linguistic research has proved to fertilize the fields of translation, linguistic typology, comparative corpus linguistics, and comparative stylistics. The wide span of languages where multiple renditions of the same canon exist allows us insight into the diversity of how humans can verbalize the same scene. When parallel religious texts are scrutinized with a suitable theoretical linguistic apparatus, this reveals the plasticity of human conceptualization (mediated through language use) in encoding the same scene.

Further Reading

Dancygier, B. & Sweester, E. (Eds.). (2012). *Viewpoint in language: A multimodal perspective*. Cambridge University Press.

This text provides a better understanding of viewpoint analysis in Cognitive Linguistics. The introduction and Part I introduce the theoretical foundation of viewpoint in Cognitive Linguistics; Parts II–IV are applications that can be useful to the reader.

Lu, W., Verhagen, A., & Su, I. (2018). A Multiple-Parallel-Text approach for viewpoint research across languages: The case of demonstratives in English and Chinese. In S. Csábi (Ed.), *Expressive minds and artistic creations*, 131–157. Oxford University Press.

This chapter explains the methodology of MultiParT, in an easy-to-follow case study. In this chapter, the authors demonstrate how even seemingly identical viewpoint constructions may behave rather differently across languages.

Pihlaja, S. (Ed.). (2021). *Analysing religious discourse*. Cambridge University Press.

For more applications of Cognitive Linguistics to analyzing religious discourse (discussed in the last part of the current chapter) interested readers are especially referred to chapters 13, 14, 17 in this edited collection.

Giovanelli, M. & Harrison, C. (2018). *Cognitive grammar in stylistics*. Bloomsbury.

Giovanelli and Harrison offer a solid theoretical understanding of Cognitive Grammar (to be used in the analysis of authentic linguistic data), and an excellent read that introduces the application of Cognitive Grammar to analyzing literary reading.

Langacker, R.W. (2008). *Cognitive Grammar: A basic introduction*. Oxford University Press.

This text is an accessible introduction to the theory written in a more reader-friendly way than the two foundational volumes published in 1987 and 1991.

References

Bartmiński, J. (1990). Punkt widzenia, perspektywa, językowy obraz świata [Point of view, perspective, linguistic worldview]. In J. Batmiński (Ed.), *Językowy obraz świta* [Linguistic worldview],103–120. Wydawnictwo UMSC.

Bible Hub. (2012). Luke 19. In Interlinear Bible. Retrieved 10 February 2023 from https://biblehub.com/interlinear/luke/19.htm.

Biblica. (n.d.). *About the NIV Bible translation*. Retrieved 10 June 2023 from www.biblica.com/niv-bible/.

Broccias, C. (2008). Cognitive linguistic theories of grammar and grammar teaching. In S. De Knop & T. De Rycker (Eds.), *Cognitive approaches to pedagogical grammar: A volume in honour of Rene Dirven*, 67–90. De Gruyter.

Catholic Book Publishing Corp. (n.d.). *New Catholic Bible (NCB)*. Retrieved 10 June 2023 from https://catholicbookpublishing.com/new-catholic-bible.

Christodouloupoulos, C. & Steedman, M. (2015). A massively parallel corpus: the Bible in 100 languages. *Lang Resources & Evaluation*, *49*, 375–395.

Cysouw, M. & Wälchli, B. (2009). Parallel texts: using translational equivalents in linguistic typology. *Language Typology and Universals*, *60*(2), 95–99.

Dancygier, B. (2016). Concluding remarks: Why viewpoint matters. In B. Dancygier, W. Lu, & A. Verhagen (Eds.), *Viewpoint and the fabric of meaning: Form and use of viewpoint tools across languages and modalities*, 281–288. De Gruyter.

Dancygier, B. & Sweetser, E. (2012). *Viewpoint in language: A multimodal perspective*. Cambridge University Press.

du Toit, H.C. (2017). The function of the imperfect tense-form in the narrative discourse of John's Gospel: some remarks. *Neotestamentica*, *51*(2), 209–234.

Eekhof, L.S., van Krieken, K., & Sanders, J. (2020). VPIP: A lexical identification procedure for perceptual, cognitive, and emotional viewpoint in narrative discourse. *Open Library of Humanities*, *6*(1),18, 1–38. https://doi.org/10.16995/olh.483.

Fauconnier, G. & Turner, M. (2002). *The way we think: Conceptual Blending and the mind's hidden complexities*. Basic Books.

Fowler, R. (1996). *Linguistic criticism*. Oxford University Press.

Genette, G. (1972). *Figures 3*. Seuil.

Giovanelli, M. & Harrison, C. (2018). *Cognitive grammar in stylistics*. Bloomsbury.

Harrison, C. (2017). *Cognitive Grammar in contemporary fiction*. John Benjamins Publishing Company.

Hunt, A. (2011). 400 years of the King James Bible. *The Times/The Sunday Times*, 9 February. Retrieved 10 June 2023, from web.archive.org/web/20110617001812/http://entertainment.timesonline.co.uk/tol/arts_and_entertainment/the_tls/article7171739.ece.

Lakoff, G. & Johnson, M. (1980). *Metaphors we live by*. Chicago University Press.

Langacker, R.W. (2008). *Cognitive Grammar: A basic introduction*. Oxford University Press.

Langacker, R.W. (2009). *Investigations in Cognitive Grammar*. De Gruyter.

Lockman Foundation. (n.d.) NASB Bible Info. Retrieved 10 June 2023 from www.lockman.org/new-american-standard-bible-nasb/.

Lu, W., Shurma, S., & Kemmer, S. (2020). Delivering the unconventional across languages: A Cognitive Grammar analysis of "Jabberwocky" and its Ukrainian renditions. *Review of Cognitive Linguistics*, *18*(1), 244–274.

Nuttall, L. (2018). *Mind style and Cognitive Grammar: Language and worldview in speculative fiction*. Bloomsbury.

Online etymology dictionary. (n.d.). Publican. In *Online etymology dictionary*. Retrieved 26 January 2023, from www.etymonline.com/search?q=publican.

Palmer, A. (2004). *Fictional minds*. University of Nebraska Press.

Quirk, R., Greenbaum, S., Svartvik, J., & Leech, G. (1985). *A comprehensive grammar of the English language*. Longman.

Renner, V. (2014). A study of element ordering in English coordinate lexical items. *English Studies*, *95*(4), 441–458.

SainteBible. (2018). Luke 19:1: Text analysis. Retrieved 10 June 2023, from https://saintebible.com/text/luke/19-1.htm.

Simpson, P. (2004). *Stylistics: A resource book for students*. Routledge.

Uspensky, B. (1973). *A poetics of composition: The structure of the artistic text and typology of a compositional form*. Translated by V. Zavarin & S. Wittig. University of California Press.

van Krieken, K., Sanders, J., & Sweetser, E. (2019). Linguistic and cognitive representation of time and viewpoint in narrative discourse. *Cognitive Linguistics*, *30*(2), 243–251.

van Leeuwen, Th. (2008). The representation of social actors. In T.A. van Dijk (Ed.), *Discourse studies*, *5*, 268–302. SAGE Publishing.

Vandelanotte, L. (2009). *Speech and thought representation in English: A cognitive-functional approach*. De Gruyter.

Vandelanotte, L. (2017). Viewpoint. In B. Dancygier (Ed.), *Cognitive Linguistics*, 151–171. Cambridge University Press.

Verhagen, A. (2005). *Construction of intersubjectivity: Discourse, syntax, and cognition*. Oxford University Press.

Verhagen, A. (2016). Introduction: On tools for weaving meaning out of viewpoint threads. In B. Dancygier, W. Lu, & A. Verhagen (Eds.), *Viewpoint and the fabric of meaning: Form and use of viewpoint tools across languages and modalities*, 1–10. De Gruyter.

Yamazaki, G. (2006). Point of view in a Gospel story: What difference does it make? Luke 19:1–10 as a test case. *Journal of Biblical literature*, *125*(1), 89–105.

Luke 19:1–3

Yamazaki (2006, p. 96): [1] And having entered Jericho, he was passing through it. [2] And look, a man named Zacchaeus. And he was a chief tax collector and he was rich. [3] And he was seeking to see who Jesus was, and he was not able on account of the crowd, because he was short in stature. (Luke 19:1–3)

King James Version Bible (KJV)

19 And Jesus entered and passed through Jericho.

² And, behold, there was a man named Zacchaeus, which was the chief among the publicans, and he was rich.

³ And he sought to see Jesus who he was; and could not for the press, because he was little of stature.

New International Version Bible (NIV)

Zacchaeus the Tax Collector

19 Jesus entered Jericho and was passing through. ² A man was there by the name of Zacchaeus; he was a chief tax collector and was wealthy. ³ He wanted to see who Jesus was, but because he was short he could not see over the crowd.

New Catholic Bible (NCB)

Chapter 19

Jesus and Zacchaeus, the Rich Tax Collector. ¹ Jesus entered Jericho and was passing through it. ² A man there, named Zacchaeus, was a chief tax collector and a rich man. ³ He wanted to see who Jesus was, but since he was short in stature, he could not see him because of the crowd.

New American Standard Bible (NASB)

Zaccheus Converted

19 *Jesus* entered Jericho and was passing through. ² And there was a man called by the name of Zaccheus; he was a chief tax collector and he was rich. ³ *Zaccheus* was trying to see who Jesus was, and he was unable due to the crowd, because he was short in stature.

Acknowledgements

The authors thank Ondřej Pazdírek for comments on a working version of the chapter, with all responsibilities remaining ours. For comments or inquiries, please contact the second author at wllu@phil.muni.cz. The publication is associated with the project PID2020-118349GB-I00 (Spanish Ministry of Science, and Innovation, State Research Agency).

PART II

Institutional Discourse

12

RELIGION, LITERATURE, AND THE SECONDARY CLASSROOM

Furzeen Ahmed

Introduction and Background

In his speech on liberal education, the former UK Secretary of Education, Michael Gove (2011), advocated the canons (a body of texts considered to be the most important from a period and place), including the likes of Shakespeare, offer the richest literary, 'best knowledge' experience that no other can provide. This perspective influenced the subsequent curricular reforms in 2014 in the British educational system, including the introduction of the British Literary Heritage. This selection of texts consisted of works from Shakespeare's plays, poetry from 1789 onwards, 19th-century novels, and fiction/drama from the British Isles from post-1914. The way in which Western literature is conceptualised as superior, established, and perennial has raised concerns about the impact the reforms have had upon students' learning experiences, citing the need to encourage students to form critical yet meaningful relationships with texts, based on how interpretations are influenced by their cultural, religious, and social knowledge. Scholars have advocated for diversifying this monolithic perception of English literature, through different textual representations and also through foregrounding students' reading responses in the classroom (e.g. Shah, 2013; Ahmed, 2018; 2019).

Concerns about the impact of the reforms have been shared by those who are expected to conform to the changes implemented: English teachers. Although there are limited studies exploring the role of religion in the secondary English literature classroom, some literature does touch upon the impact of spontaneous discussions led by students' religious orientations on the dynamics of the literary experience for not only themselves but for their fellow readers. In her study documenting teaching *Macbeth* to her year 10 group, Cantwell (2014) reflects on the influence of the students' Muslim identities upon their reading of Shakespeare's play. For instance, after a drama lesson the group were asked to write down reflection on their allocated characters, such as Lady Macbeth and Macbeth, and Cantwell (2014, p. 25) noticed the reflections foregrounded the students' contemplations from a religious standpoint as well as concerns about Macbeth committing a sin against his faith. Such ethical judgements came to the fore for the students as Cantwell (2014, pp. 26–29) considered how the students used 'religious frames' as a 'prerequisite' of the students' learning rather than an extension of it. What became apparent, however, was the distinction between the teachers and students' socio-cultural and religious knowledge: the non-Muslim

DOI: 10.4324/9781003301271-14

teacher was positioned as being 'outside of shared reference' as a student explained 'our' religious 'teachings' (Cantwell, 2014, p. 28). This teacher knowledge gap is also highlighted upon by Turvey et al (2006, p. 59) when discussing a teacher's reflection on a British Muslim student-led discussion exploring Lord Tennyson's *Lady of Shalott* with reference to an Arab Muslim woman in purdah, a religious practice that was new to the non-Muslim teacher.

Here, teachers from other or non-religious backgrounds show either a lack of awareness or response to students initiating discussions on literature and religious beliefs. To note, the teachers do not respond or react to the scenarios but instead, Cantwell (2014) particularly contemplates the limitations surrounding her ability to 'bring' to her reading of the students' interpretations influenced by their socio-cultural and religious knowledge, due to being a non-member of the faith community. Cantwell's reflection on the lack of awareness of the students' shared references is also evident in Abby Carpenter's documented experience in extending her knowledge about the Lady of Shalott within the cultural frame shared by her student (Turvey et al., 2006). Students therefore take on the role of experts as they fill teachers' religious knowledge gaps, and this aspect is something which has not yet been explicitly explored in the existing literature on religion and the secondary school English classroom.

A point to consider is how teachers who do not have a faith influence classroom discourse with students' religious affiliations. The studies by Turvey et al. (2006) and Cantwell (2014) are from non-Muslim white-British teachers who do not identify whether they have a faith. These studies discuss classrooms consisting of students from ethnically, religiously, and culturally diverse backgrounds, who often entered these literary texts through avenues which were unfamiliar to the apparent authoritative figure in the classroom. However, Iffath (2020) provides an account of her teaching training experience as a British Muslim with roots in the same area as the students. Iffath (2020, pp. 373–374) shares that the discussions between students considering notions of colonialism in Conan Doyle's *The Sign of Four* to questioning the problematic stereotypes of Arabs and the narrow perception that Indians are only identified as 'Hindoo' (a term used by Conan Doyle to describe the first character of colour in the text, an Indian servant) highlighted issues that she was prompted to contemplate not only as a professional but as a member of the wider social, cultural, and religious communities she shared with the students. Although the studies, with exception of Iffath, consist of direct quotations from student-led interactions, the teachers have centralised their own anecdotes in the form of sharing their own reflections, thoughts, and conversations with colleagues on the students' contributions. As a result, there is limited critical exploration of how the students' initial responses on the text led by their religious affiliations in the social world challenge the funnelled perspective endorsed through the literature studied.

Echoing Iffath's (2020) reflection, the study of the British literary heritage unveils problematic, dated perceptions such as Hindus being considered as of Indian heritage as exemplified in Conan Doyle's text earlier, which can be challenged and clearly explained by teachers and students alike, as a student did so by explaining the religious diversity of the South Asian country. Shah (2014), as a British-Pakistani Muslim hijab-wearing teacher, critically reflects on how practitioners of ethnically, culturally or religiously diverse backgrounds understand through their own personal experiences the issues faced by students when they are not able to see, hear, or have their beliefs acknowledged. Shah (2014, pp. 219–220) details the tension which occurred when students attempted to build rapport with her as a Muslim woman through language, for instance, through greetings where blessings are exchanged in the form of 'Aslaam Alaikum Wah Rahmatullahi' (a form of greeting meaning blessings of Allah upon you shared between Muslims) and 'Khuda Hafiz' (greeting meaning may God be your Guardian upon leaving). These exchanges were met by other teachers reiterating the school policy for students to speak English only, resulting in

Shah providing an example of a student defying this policy by shouting the farewell greeting in Arabic and Persian. This example illustrates the fine line between enacting expectations upon students' linguistic repertoires and supressing multiculturalism in the form of policing cultural linguistic identities in the educational context.

Students' voices and perspectives are often in contention with texts, as we have just discussed, as well as in contention with teacher-led interpretations, and these interpretations are often privileged as they come from knowledgeable authoritative figures within the classroom. Such attempts to disempower students' contributions can be alleviated by 'interthinking' according to Mercer and Littleton (2007), who define this notion as a way for students and teachers alike to share, challenge, and develop thoughts and viewpoints together. The approach enables students to think and speak beyond teachers' expectations of how the learning should progress. This opportunity to share alternative perspectives is, to an extent, an example of presenting potentially conflicting understandings in a public sphere. Such dissemination of knowledge is enrichening by providing new or alternative information to fellow students and teachers that they may not have come across before. However, such sharing of information may not always be accommodated or understood (Mercer, 2000).

The variations in how individuals interpret a text being discussed are, according to Mercer (2000), not always understood and are considered negatively since they cause a sense of conflict and confusion. These 'misunderstandings' (Mercer, 2000, p. 5) can be considered as part of the learning process in acquiring new knowledge and bridging with the information already held. This 'working on understanding' is what is achieved through talk (Barnes, 2008, p. 1). Barnes's work (2008) involves reflecting on the joint construction between, in the case of the classroom, teacher and students, in producing talk. During this interaction, Barnes explains discourse participants actively construct knowledge and should recognise tension between variation in knowledge and experience as part of the learning process, rather than an obstacle to it. Such tensions occur when finding out new or alternative information, and as a result, students and teachers' roles can be considered fluid and dynamic, with their positions as learners and experts fluctuating during the learning process with each navigating it according to their knowledge and experiences.

The perception of teaching and learning roles as interchangeable moves away from the concerning idea that teacher's authoritative knowledge is considered valid at the expense of what students already know or are 'working' out to know, and independent interpretations become a form of 'manufactured student readings' in the English classroom (Giovanelli & Mason, 2015, p. 46). This perception of 'working' through interpretations that potentially do not conform to established or authoritative definitions is part of the learning process and the initial responses formed by students during first readings (Ahmed, 2018).

Students and teachers alike should acknowledge such conflicting engagement as part of the learning process that, if encouraged in a positive manner, can illustrate a sense of 'growth in thought' (Alexander, 2017, p. 26). Alexander's notion of dialogic teaching (2017) argues for students and teachers to not only exchange ideas by thinking aloud, but build upon them by critically evaluating the different perspectives shared. However, I would extend Alexander's argument and state that this strive for consensus in the classroom space can in turn undermine critical thinking, where students' voices are to an extent censored if they challenge the dominant beliefs or perspectives. This tension between student knowledge and schools is also explored in relation to religious views. Negotiation defines dialogic teaching and Ahmad (2021) discusses the role of dialogue in relation to religious educational context. Ahmad (2021) further explains that classrooms are dialogic spaces with more than one perspective existing at a time, and considers this nature of classroom discourse through *Halaqah*, an oral pedagogy consisting of a circle of learning. What would multiple perspectives in a classroom look like and how does conflict emerge through the negotiation of these perspectives? Although focused on Muslim students in the primary school context and being centred on religious education as a subject, Ipgrave (2010) explores the conflict in the inclusion of pupils' faiths in the classroom context. Ipgrave (2010, p. 20) explains that epistemological conflict occurs when students resist assimilation of new ideas, since the new knowledge has 'higher status than the old', resulting in feelings of alienation and disengagement when the students' own religious identities are to an extent not valued due to this hierarchy in knowledge. This hierarchy is evident in the interactions outlined in the case study and explores how faith-based identity inclusion consists of accommodating the differences rather than be considered a knowledge gap requiring correction.

Interrogating Faith in the English Literature Classroom

The case study derives from small-scale research I conducted exploring how students' diverse ethnic, cultural, and religious identities impact their study in the secondary English literature classroom (Ahmed, 2018). I aimed to address three research questions to centralise and understand the student literary experiences in the secondary English classroom:

1) How do students position themselves in relation to their cultural identities when studying literature?
2) How do students use language to convey their knowledges about religious affiliation and experiences to support their understanding of literature or related concepts studied?
3) How can Text World Theory be used to demonstrate the complex nature of the incrementation and development of knowledge about religious affiliations, experiences, and perspectives which challenge students' study of literature?

Methodology

I adopted an interpretivist approach (Emerson et al., 1995; Creese & Copland, 2015) by conducting a linguistic ethnographic study, where I was an active observer of participants' interactions in the research site, in this case the secondary school classroom. This mode of observation involved me interacting with the students and teacher about how they saw, heard, felt and talked (Creese & Copland, 2015, p. 149), linking to the notion of understanding how they experienced learning through their language use.

The context of my data collection was a British secondary school (students aged 11–18). I was interested in the impact of the curriculum reforms at key stage 4 level in the English subject, where students study towards obtaining their GCSE (General Certificate of Secondary Education) qualifications during their last two years of compulsory education at 15–16 years of age. The nine-month linguistic ethnographic study collated data from an inner-city secondary school, based in the East Midlands region, England, which ran from September 2017–June 2018.

The school consisted of an array of students of rich, cultural, ethnic, and religious backgrounds. This was reflected through the makeup of the allocated year 10 top-set (in the UK, students are usually grouped by ability in different subjects) in the subject English group for the research study, respectively. Figure 12.2 is a graph of not only 11 labels defining 32 students of the year 10 group: it represents the identities of the voices and perspectives reflecting certain positions students take up during their learning. In terms of the group's religious affiliations, around 69 per cent (20/32 students) identified as practising Muslims, while 28 percent (9/32 students) did not identify with a religious group. The white British female class teacher did not state she had a religious affiliation. Most of the students were British-Pakistani of Muslim faith.

The year 10 group was studying towards their GCSEs, an educational qualification obtained by students in the last two years of compulsory education in the UK, and were particularly focusing on Paper 1 of English Literature GCSE, where they studied one Shakespeare play, a 19th-century novel, and a poetry anthology. Since the students were minors, I completed the ethics process by first providing an information sheet detailing what the research study was about, its aims, the mode of data collection, clarifying that the data would be stored in a password-secure USB stick, and that the signed forms would be placed in a locked drawer, as well as the students' right to withdraw from the study at any time, plus a consent form which required the students' parent or guardian signature as well as the student's own signature permitting them to be part of the study. For those who volunteered to participate in the additional weekly group discussion, a separate information sheet and consent form were provided to be signed by student and parent or guardian. The consent form and information sheet were according to the guidelines provided by Aston University Ethics Committee. As minors, the students were provided with pseudonyms to conceal their real names.

The main focus of the study was to understand meaning from the speech of others (Creese & Blackledge, 2012) or, in other words, the interactions I had with participants and how they used their knowledge about the world in their meaning-making when conversing with others. As an emic observer, meaning someone who was part of the research site, I was able to have an insight of the relationship between social context and the experience unfolding in front of me. Through this focus, I captured the observations through video recording and keeping fieldnotes of each of the year 10's lessons for the nine-month period, with the observations consisting of exploring how students and teacher used language to develop ideas inside the classroom through experiences and knowledge being gathered outside the classroom space (Denzin, 1989). Extracts from the recordings which addressed the research aims would be transcribed, which joined together diverse experiences and understandings of the English classroom. The fieldnotes acknowledged voices of participants and enabled me to encapsulate the developing interactions, perspectives, and understandings which the students and teacher built on and against one another. In addition, I conducted weekly group discussions with six voluntary students (three male and three female students) to critically reflect on and discuss the week's lessons, in terms of what was said, done, written, and occurred. The recordings were grouped using the analytical software of NVIVO to examine emerging themes from the data collected. The students' active participation during discussions between themselves, with the class teacher or with me, demonstrated the notion of thinking together and involved exploring how individuals become critical reflectors regarding their own knowledge and understanding of other individuals shared in the classroom setting.

When considering the reading experience, as an individual reads a book, they begin to imagine the fictional place, people, actions, and emotions in their minds. This imagination leads to individuals creating a world in their minds. But this is an evolving process with these worlds becoming more intricate and complex as individuals continue to read. Text World Theory (Werth, 1999; Gavins, 2007) analyses the relationship between text and context based on the central idea, deriving from a metaphor A TEXT IS A WORLD (Gibbons, 2017), that explains how readers use language and background knowledge to construct, negotiate, and organise such worlds in their minds. In other words, the framework tracks how individuals create mental representations or pictures in their minds of what they read, or even see, listen, or talk—accounting for any type of interactions in which humans participate (Werth, 1999). When talking about context, this refers to the mental resources we use to help us understand an interaction. These mental resources or schemas (Fillmore, 1979) include our experiences, memories, emotions, thoughts, viewpoints, and

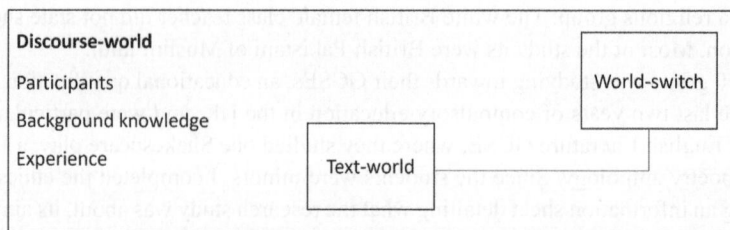

Figure 12.1 Text World Theory diagram

beliefs from which we cherrypick to make sense of a discourse situation in which we participate. Knowledge can be further categorised as individuals possessing cultural, experiential, perceptual, and general knowledge (Werth, 1999).

There are three levels to the conceptual model which shows the tracing of an individual's understanding of a language event as outlined below and illustrated in Figure 12.1.

Discourse-World: this is the immediate situation or the 'here and now' of a language-event. Individuals may share the same discourse-world, such as talking to a friend face to face or, it may be split such as when the reader may not share the same setting as the author. Individuals have access to their background knowledge, consisting of experiences, perceptions, and cultural knowledge which influence the way they understand language use.

Text-World: when processing language, individuals construct text-worlds that create mental representations of the interactions using the knowledge and experience they already have. Text-worlds are constructed when there is a change in time, place, and entities, or through actions such as speech and thoughts which move the interaction forward.

World-switches: Finally, world-switches occur when there is a shift from the initial text-world in time or space. These are triggered by metaphor, negation, or flashbacks/-forwards. World-switches can be categorised as the following when there is a change in point of view:

- Epistemic world-switch: modal verbs indicating level of confidence in a statement e.g. 'think', 'believe', 'feel';
- Deontic world-switch: modal verbs indicating level of obligation towards a statement e.g. 'must', 'world', 'will';
- Boulomaic world-switch: modal verbs indicating level of desire in a statement e.g. 'hope', 'wish'.

(Werth, 1999, pp. 81–86; Gavins, 2007, pp. 94–115)

Text World Theory therefore offers a rigorous framework to trace how students' thinking evolves and is valuable in exploring how reading works in the classroom. Students as readers build worlds in their minds and refer to these worlds through their own experiences as readers.

In the classroom setting, there is an amalgamation of experiences and cultural knowledge which form students' understandings of the world in which they reside. However, the intriguing question is how students negotiate and manage these differences and convey their comprehensions during conversations. Text World Theory is applied to the case study to examine a student's response in terms of how he manages new knowledge, by referring to his own stored knowledge (Werth, 1999), consisting of beliefs, general knowledge, and experiences.

By focusing on a classroom environment, it is possible to observe how students of an adolescent age manage and negotiate their way through conversations. This age group, when individuals are moulding their identity and adopting the beliefs, values, and customs of certain groups that they affiliate with and distancing themselves from others, are compelled to face challenges towards their developing identities, from the perspectives of other individuals, including their peers and teachers. The learning process prompts students' perspectives to change and mould by taking on alternative viewpoints in the form of their developing, enriching, and to an extent conflicting mental representations of the spoken discourse. Here, the moulding of identities consists of linguistically depicting affiliations with and distances from groups in the form of modal verbs demonstrating confidence in a belief or viewpoint. Text World Theory proves to be a significant analytical framework in demonstrating such use of modal verbs, since it examines how language use provides access to evolving conceptualisations. In the case study below, the student will be seen undertaking different conceptual activities from trialling new knowledge to challenging concepts which challenge his religious-based beliefs.

Extract 1: Questioning Philosophy

Far: Why would you quest–why would you do that? =
CT: = why would you do that because you are furthering academic study lik[e do
Far: [I'm not saying that I'm saying why like why would you want to question everything (.)
CT: well isn't that our role in life just to que[stion]
Awa: [so why are you questioning Miss though]
        [Some students laugh]
CT: inaudible

Extract 1 derives from a whole-class discussion during the second week of the year 10 group's study of Shakespeare's tragedy *Macbeth* and is an excerpt from the students' feedback for task 1. This task involved the students being provided with a summary of King James I's dissertation, *Daemonologie*, where, in the style of a dialogue, he explains the danger of humans forming relationships with the supernatural. As the class read the extract, the class teacher (hereby, CT), who identified herself as a white British female with no religious affiliation, asked students to share their initial responses to the notion of philosophy, a new term which was introduced and defined by Ie, a female student of British-Somali Muslim heritage as 'it's like questioning [.] religion and like why we are alive'. The definition was accepted by CT as being a 'brilliant answer'. This initial response on the definition of philosophy was met by an alternative perspective. During the feedback session, Far, a male British-Pakistani Muslim student, interrupted CT's definition of 'dissertation', another term which the students were introduced to, and the former responded as is documented in Extract 1.

After Awa's interruption, the discussion is halted and is not returned to during the remainder of the lesson. During the same week but, in a different lesson, I had a conversation with Far which explored his interrogative further which I shall discuss later in the chapter.

The exchange in Extract 1 begins with Far's reflection on the nature of questioning in the form of the interrogative 'why would you do that?' Although CT assumes Far is asking about the significance of completing a dissertation, Far clarifies that he is referring to the notion of philosophy and the previous student's definition. Here, the interesting aspect of Far's input

Classroom Discussion
(Discourse-World)

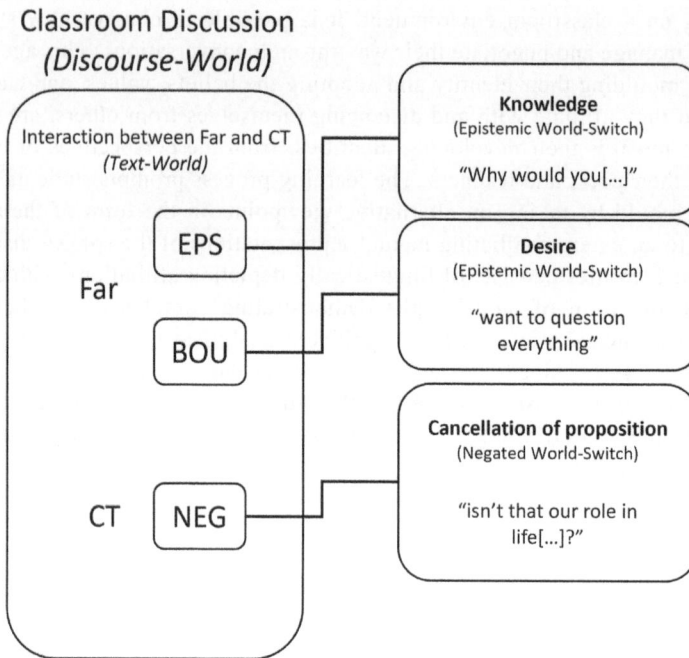

Figure 12.2   A Text World Theory diagram for Far's question 'Why would you want to question everything?'

is his use of the epistemic modal verb 'would', expressing a point of view, and boulomaic modal verb 'want', implying desire, which triggers a sense of challenge from the student against the notion being discussed. The use of the epistemic modal verb 'would' suggests that Far is questioning the essence of philosophy in relation to our being on earth as a remote idea from his discourse-world knowledge, which is storage of our experiences, memories, and beliefs mentally selected to use during discourse or interactions. This conflict is evident in Far's understanding of Macbeth's actions after hearing the witches' prophecies. Figure 12.2 illustrates this sense of impossibility for Far about questioning our existence. The epistemic modal world-switch distances the idea of questioning from Far's understanding of what philosophy means for him as a person with faith.

Far's interrogative becomes a starting point for the students' exploration of their own understandings of the term, philosophy, within the context of the text-world as well as the real world. The use of the boulomaic modal verb 'want' relates to this idea of an individual's voluntary desire to question rather than be prompted by others, placing the onus on humans for such decisions to challenge hierarchy. This perspective is further intensified by the second person pronoun 'you' that directs responsibility for the action towards other individuals, contrasting with the use of the collective pronoun by the student who initially defined philosophy as an act of questioning religion and 'why we are alive'. The students' use of the collective pronoun 'we' echoes a more unified and shared perception that all humans question their sense of being, whereas Far perceives this question as individually prompted and moving away from a consensus based on questionless faith.

158

Far's use of the second person pronoun 'you' shifts the focus onto the discourse-world by involving the discourse participants, such as the class and CT, who are comprehending the challenge posed by Far. The pronouns depict the differing positions the British-Somali female student, Ie, and Far are representing even though, as Muslims, they are associated with the same religious group. For instance, the use of the collective pronoun depicts to a degree broader affiliation between Ie and humanity. Far, however, distances himself from the act of questioning, aligning himself with the religious group his perspective is influenced by. The significance of the use of pronouns is further demonstrated by CT's use of the collective pronoun in the phrase 'our role' when responding to Far's question, shifting the focus onto the notion that such questioning takes place within the real world and suggests this questioning is part of human nature. CT identified herself as an atheist, therefore, the tension begins to occur on multiple levels, with CT's response challenging Far's notion that humans should not be questioning their being in the world based on one having a faith.

The classroom discussion provides an insight into the differences emerging from the initial definition provided. These differences are expressed in the form of questions, as discussed above, and will be further explored with regard to the use of negation, the use of 'not'. Hidalgo-Downing (2000a) examines the use of negation in discourse, particularly in literature, and proposes two types of negation: one stops flow of information (as well as forming a contradiction), and is not pursued further, while the other type offers an alternative viewpoint to be explored by other discourse participants. In particular, Hidalgo-Downing's discussion about negation 'rechannelling information by modifying information from the text-world' (Hidalgo-Downing 2000a, p. 198) in the form of contradiction, is interesting in relation to the scenario involving Far. Hidalgo-Downing (2000b, p. 219) believes 'negation plays a crucial role in this process of destabilisation', whereby the sense of disruption occurs at multiple levels in the form of the discourse participants' beliefs, values, perspectives, and emotions being queried and challenged.

CT's response in the form of the rhetorical question 'well, isn't that our role in life' is interesting to explore in relation to Far's comment. CT's question consists of a negated world-switch 'is [not]', creating a counterstatement which challenges Far's point of view regarding humans questioning their existence, and offers a differing viewpoint. Negation challenges Far and foregrounds CT's position within the classroom as the authoritative figure. In her response, CT destabilises Far's concept of questioning our being, and offers an alternative perspective, suggesting it is part of human nature to do so. This particular manner of offering an alternative viewpoint is because the information shared may not be definite or predictable for the listeners. When determining the predictability of a piece of information shared during an interaction, it is important to understand whether the contribution is in keeping with the context of the discourse. Far's comment presents alternative and challenging information which problematises the new knowledge shared, the term philosophy. CT's rhetorical question provides a hypothetical scenario which aligns itself to Ie, whose definition of philosophy resulted in Far's interrogative. Ie's definition is remote from Far's perception of the real world in which such a challenge raises issues with his faith or cultural discourse-world knowledge influenced by his Muslim identity.

However, CT and Far's contributions also reflect Hidalgo-Downing's (2000a, p. 198) argument that such scenarios consisting of contradictions should not be considered an issue requiring a solution but should rather be acknowledged as an 'unresolvable contradiction'. In this scenario, the epistemic world-switches depicted in Figure 12.2 exemplify what Hidalgo-Downing (2000a, p. 198) terms as a 'communicative block', requiring the discourse participants to interpret the two contradictory concepts simultaneously and in parallel with each other, and as should be the case here, where Far and CT hold distinct religious perspectives on the notion of philosophy. CT's use of the rhetorical question, '[…] isn't that our role in life just to question', suggests the answer is part of the discourse participants' shared knowledge; in other words, CT's question presupposes the class share the same discourse-world knowledge she is alluding to. Although CT's rhetorical question presupposes that participants understand that the answer is acknowledged, even if it is not widely accepted, it serves another purpose in the classroom context, which is to open Far's challenge to the rest of the class to respond to. Far's comment is held separately and, due to Awa's interruption, is not pursued further during the whole class discussion.

During the week, I was able to gain an insight into how Far's perspective developed over the course of the week's lessons, and have summarised discussion with the student in the fieldnote excerpt provided below in Week 3, Lesson 4:

> [..] Far develops his response by stating the characters 'question everything in this book' to which Mo expands on the former's answer by stating there is a sense of 'power-shifting' taking place in the play. When asking both Far and Mo what power shift is taking place, Far says 'Macbeth gets pulled into the storm' and then comments that if there was 'no phil-osophy, no questioning then no trouble fall on Macbeth. Everything would be calm'. [..] Far also says of 'questioning life and things' that 'we shouldn't question because it can bring the bad to me?' When asked how this comment links and reflects his own point of view on challenging religion, Far responds 'you shouldn't be a Muslim you're supposed to have in faith' and connects this to the text, saying 'she [Lady Macbeth] made him go against his own religion'.

The extensive discussion above enabled me to understand and develop my understanding of Far's perspective on Macbeth's position as the king, and the second most powerful entity after God. Here, the most significant aspect of the extract helping me understand Far's construction of his viewpoint considering his cultural discourse-world knowledge, was his and Mo's—a British-Pakistani Muslim student who sat next to Far at the time I began conversing with Far about his interrogative—discussion in the classroom setting on the power shifts taking place in the play. For instance, the following extract of the discussion demonstrates Far's understanding, influenced by this perspective of changes in power: Far says 'Macbeth gets pulled into the storm' and then comments that if there was 'no philosophy, no questioning then no trouble fall on Macbeth. Everything would be calm' First of all, Far's question—'why would you want to question every-thing?'—is extended in his contribution during this small group discussion. Here, Far explains that the power shift is due to the witches enticing Macbeth into believing he is the rightful heir to the throne, resulting in the protagonist being 'pulled into the storm'.

Lakoff and Johnson (1999) discuss how individuals utilise their perceptions to understand situations depicted either through written or spoken discourse. In particular, the type of percep-tion relating to the scenario above is the notion of 'imaginative perception' (Lakoff & Johnson, 1999, p. 38). To understand other people and the world, imagination enables an individual to comprehend how entities relate to each other. Lakoff and Johnson (1999) on how imagination is influenced by perception, in turn help construct understanding. Individuals become 'emotionally engaged' (Lakoff & Johnson, 1999, p. 15) with the process involving the fleshing out of informa-tion from knowledge, experiences, and imaginations as discourse participants. Far's metaphor can be understood as Macbeth's internal dilemma as he strives for kingship through unethical means. Macbeth's unethical approach to obtaining the kingship is due to his actions contradicting his reli-gious affiliations. The protagonist's internal dilemma of defying God's order and having the inten-tion to harm others to claim power can be understood as forms of 'non-physical experience[s]',

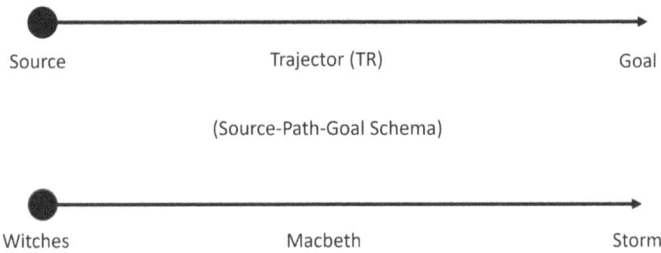

Figure 12.3   Illustration of Far's metaphor 'Macbeth gets pulled into the storm' as Source-Goal schema (adapted from Lakoff & Johnson, 1999, p. 40)

which can be 'mapped onto the physical by means of figurative devices' such as 'image schema' and metaphors (Werth, 1999, p. 36). In this scenario, the 'non-physical experience' of thinking and understanding is used to explain 'physical processes' (Werth, 1999, p. 36). To illustrate this point, Macbeth's downfall is described by Far through spatial relations by using the preposition 'into', demonstrating this situation as physical movements in a figurative sense. Macbeth is considered the trajectory or the figure which moves in front of the background.

Johnson (1987, p. 73) suggests that an 'image schema' should be understood as a metaphor since he argues that thought is constructed through the metaphorical formation of individuals' knowledge and experiences. The examples he provides focus on how concepts can be understood in terms of spatial relations: this relates to Far's contribution under discussion, since Johnson (1987, p. 29) states that individuals understand concepts through the notion of 'bodily movements through space'. Space is a defining factor in sharing perspectives as Far's comment can be comprehended using the notion of image schema, such as how objects move, physically and figuratively, across space. During the discussion, Far's metaphor reflects an important relationship between entities and space, as demonstrated in Figure 12.3 of the deconstruction of his perspective. The trajector (TR) in Far's metaphor, Macbeth, is the object being acted upon, as the diagram below illustrates.

Here, the preposition in the phrase 'pulled into' indicates the movement towards the 'storm', a metaphor depicting the turmoil Macbeth faces by accepting the witches' prophecy that he will become king. There is a sense of calamity as the metaphor shifts the attention in showing the consequences of defying the divine right of kings' rule, and Macbeth's belief in God. Far's metaphor reflects concern regarding the defiance against the Divine by following the supernatural pathway. This concern is represented through the dynamic past transitive verb 'pulled', reflecting the witches' influence and power over Macbeth. The metaphor represents the consequences the protagonist faces after deciding to heed the witches' prophecies. The object, or the target domain (Lakoff & Johnson, 1999, p. 417) of Far's utterance, the 'storm', depicts the chaos which ensues after Macbeth decides to follow the witches, the source domain (Lakoff & Johnson, 1999, p. 417). Far's utterance illustrates that the witches are the ones who have led the protagonist to disobey God's order, suggesting he has gone against the natural structure. Macbeth, the trajector in this example, becomes part of the landmark, in this case the 'storm', and is depicted as an inanimate object who is being acted upon and does not have the power to counteract or change this outcome. 'Storm' reflects Macbeth's catastrophic yet inevitable end where the notion of questioning the Divine's order once again is foregrounded. The position of 'storm' as a landmark implies the inevitable consequences prevalent in the background throughout the play, only to come to the forefront when Macbeth realises the outcome of his fateful decision.

Far's comment that if there was 'no philosophy, no questioning then no trouble fall on Macbeth. Everything would be calm', reflects the underlying theme of destruction in relation to the play's text-world. This theme can be treated as an example of an 'extended metaphor' (Gavins, 2007, p. 147) which runs through the spoken discourse specified and also in subsequent ones as the class continued to study the play, and discuss defiance and consequences of this challenge to God's order. This defiance is also focalised in Far's phrase from the comment above in 'no trouble fall on Macbeth'. Here, Macbeth is once again considered as the object, or the trajectory, who is facing the consequences of his actions. The power re-shift is depicted in Far's perspective, where Macbeth is considered punished for attempting to defy God's order. Far's phrase depicts this punishment through a metaphorical image, where Macbeth is positioned as the object who is receiving this chastening from the highest order.

This is not only depicted in the syntactical structure with Macbeth positioned as the object, or the target domain of Far's utterance, but also in the way his contribution is understood by the hearer. Lakoff and Johnson's (1999) discussion on the representation of metaphors through domains is also applicable in understanding Far's comment since Macbeth is illustrated as being physically positioned at the farthest and lowest point in the hierarchy. Here, Far's metaphor is most striking with the hierarchical order positioning the subject, or the source domain of the utterance, 'trouble', as an active agent. To explain further, the abstract noun 'trouble' is personified here as being sent by God to punish Macbeth for his actions. Far's explanation implies this action is initiated by a more powerful, higher source directed downwards to Macbeth. Macbeth is the target domain but also as someone not only physically, but metaphorically, situated at the lowest point of the hierarchy understood to be God's order. Here, the religious hierarchy is metaphorically enacted through Far's quotation, with the verb 'fall' indicating Macbeth falling from his status as a leader, and thus being a subordinate rather than a superior in the hierarchy. However, the negation immediately shows how Macbeth would have avoided such dire consequences if he had not defied the Divine Right of Rule.

The metaphor 'storm' is utilised to show the contrast between the 'alternative viewpoints' depicted at the beginning of Far's utterance, and at the end of the utterance with the use of the evaluative adjective 'calm'. The contrast is positioned as the use of the negation in 'no philosophy, no questioning' indicates the need to refrain from questioning to avoid such calamity. To situate Far's interpretation in the wider context of the discussion surrounding the theme of philosophy, the notion of questioning is once again foregrounded as the catalyst for Macbeth's downfall, implying that challenging religion results in the individual being punished. Far's hypothetical proposition triggers an epistemic world-switch due to the condition suggested. Once more, the use of negation depicts an alternative perspective, where the notion of philosophy is omitted, suggesting the concept of questioning the hierarchy of the divine right of kings is absent. The thought of questioning the hierarchical order formed by the Divine is somewhat difficult for Far to accept. The shift occurs using the epistemic modal verb 'would' which constructs an alternative perspective where Macbeth is not chastised for his actions by adhering to the Divine's status as omnipotent. By emphasising the negation, Far's emotional involvement influenced by his Muslim faith in the explanation is echoed in the repetition of this linguistic item, reiterating his previous challenge.

I conducted post-hoc analysis discussions, where I provided a summary of the analysis chapters for the participants and the extracts to read. The discussions provided the opportunity for the participants to provide feedback on what was included in the analysis sections and to reflect on the scenarios selected. CT shared her pensive response to the analysis, particularly to the scenario discussed above. Her reflection on the analysis made her 'pause' and contemplate her initial understanding that the student was 'trying to be funny'. CT's perception of Far's response as being somewhat disruptive, illustrates the tension that occurs in not understanding that the question masked a sense of ethical dilemma for the student during his learning of *Macbeth*, related to his religious background.

Implications and Future Directions

The case study revealed students' affiliations with cultural and religious communities to limit to some extent their exploration of the literature studied by how they are perceived in the classroom setting. Here, the exploration of discourse-world knowledge was significant in understanding how diverse perspectives can also be considered a form of tension or barrier, to a degree, between the students being able to connect with the text-world and their affiliations in the real world. Such tension was linguistically depicted in the form of negation in demonstrating the influence of affiliations in the discourse-world upon students' understandings of the text-world, even if they conflicted with the agreed interpretations in the classroom. Cultural discourse-world knowledge was also the essential element of diversity amongst the students' understandings. Far shared a distinct perspective which projected his affiliations with cultural and religious communities in the real world. His use of an interrogative depicted a division between the culturally and religiously distinct perspective shared and the debate it triggered surrounding the outcome of Macbeth challenging God's order. Far's interrogative demonstrates the significance of classroom discourse challenging the established interpretations advocated in the study of the British Literary Heritage. Here, the student's initial response reflected the development of his understanding of themes and topics, which raised issues in relation to his cultural, social, and religious affiliations. This was a prevalent situation in the scenario presented, as he was able to use classroom interactions as a platform to share advancing and evolving perspectives; however, he was not explicitly encouraged to further elaborate on them.

Rather than aiming for consensus, classroom discourse should recognise the differences in perspectives, particularly faith-based beliefs, and create the space for such exploration of diverse thinking and believing. Space refers to not only the physical surroundings, the classroom, but how the interactions within this setting amalgamate the diverse social spaces individuals belong to in the wider world, as well as make way for students to reflect on this encounter of conceptual spaces. The feedback by CT demonstrates this is an opportunity which seldom occurs due to the teacher's presumptions of what Far is saying. There need to be such platforms where students' voices are foregrounded, whether in harmony or contention with each other. This is where I would advocate for classrooms to be explored in the following ways through future research in the field of religious discourse and the English literature classroom.

Teachers should not presume students' orientation of the world will resonate with the learning. This is where finding out about students' beliefs or those who do not have religious beliefs will enable teachers to understand the alternative perspectives from which texts will be comprehended. As a result, teachers should treat students as experts of their own faith-based knowledge which they can share in the classroom. For instance, Far could have been asked to explain his positioning on the notion of philosophy as a practising Muslim. There needs to be extensive research dedicated to centralising students' learning processes in the form of the struggles or challenges they meet in forming meaningful interpretations that are influenced by their socio-cultural and religious experiences. Such studies should involve conducting discussions with students as exemplified by Shah (2013; 2014) and Iffath (2020) earlier in the chapter, in understanding how their religious orientations impact their perceptions of text-worlds that are distinct at a social, temporal, and spatial level.

There should be more research considering that sharing religious experiences in the classroom space may not be comfortable for all, and investigating opportunities for teachers to partake in CPD (career professional development) sessions which provide a platform to share experiences of managing such discussions. Such research can evaluate how teachers build confidence in adapting their teaching to understand and integrate students' religious experiences and how they influence their study of literature, thereby making such engagements more comfortable. Future studies can also critically explore teachers' roles in understanding how students engage with the literature. It is about acknowledging what students bring to the learning process by what they do know, rather than what they do not know, and teachers should not censor students' entry into texts based on what they feel uncomfortable in engaging with at a discursive level.

Further Reading

Ahmed, F. (2018). First love letter to conflicting marriages: exploration of ethnically diverse students' developing understanding during their reading of Romeo and Juliet using schema theory. *English in Education 52(2)*,1–15.
The article is based on my linguistic ethnographic pilot study which explored how students utilised their cultural and religious contextual knowledge to conceptualise abstract and tenuous notions such as love versus arranged marriages.
Elliot, V., Nelson-Addy, L., Chantiluke, R., & Courtney, M. (2021). *Lit in Colour: Diversity in Literature in English Schools*. Penguin UK/Runnymede Trust.
The report details the critical issue of diversity and inclusion in schools including identifying the barriers preventing texts from writers of colour from being taught in classrooms; the small number of studies which document the teaching of canonical literature in multicultural classrooms; and students' call for a more diverse English curriculum which mirrors the pluralistic society to which they belong.
Gavins, J. (2007). *Text World Theory: An Introduction*. Edinburgh University Press.
Gavins' book is an accessible introduction to the analytical framework Text World Theory which can be used by students, researchers, and academics alike who are interested in exploring the framework.
Littleton, K. & Mercer, N. (2013). *Interthinking: putting talk to work*. Routledge.
Littleton and Mercer's book provides an extensive insight into their coined term and concept 'interthinking' to discuss the importance of co-constructing talk and thought between students and teachers in the classroom. This is particularly useful in understanding how religious discourse can be integrated as part of a learning experience for the authoritative figure, the teacher, in understanding how students enter the literary worlds using their socio-cultural, religious contextual knowledge.
Shah, M. (2013). Reading Canonical Texts in Multicultural Classrooms. *Changing English 20*(2), 194–204.
Shah's article details the complexities which ensue in a multicultural English classroom, where teachers and students navigate between cultural, religious, and ethnic identities, knowledges, and experiences, and the British literary heritage to form meaningful interpretations which depict their evolving, meaningful learning experiences of the canon.

References

Ahmad, F. (2021). *Dialogue in different cultural contexts*. University of Cambridge.
Ahmed, F. (2018). First love letter to conflicting marriages: exploration of ethnically diverse students' developing understanding during their reading of Romeo and Juliet using schema theory. *English in Education, 52*(2), 1–15.
Ahmed, F. (2019). *An exploration of students' construction of knowledges and identities during the reading of literature using Text World Theory*. PhD thesis (unpublished). Aston University.
Alexander, R.J. (2017). *Towards Dialogic Teaching: rethinking classroom talk*. Dialogos.
Barnes, D.R. (2008). Exploratory talk for learning. In Mercer, N. & Hodgkinson, S. (Eds.) *Exploring talk in school: Inspired by the work of Douglas Barnes*, 1–16. SAGE Publishing.

Cantwell, J. (2014). Constructing Macbeth: Text and Framing in a Secondary Urban Classroom. *Changing English*, *21*(1), 24–31.

Creese, A. & Blackledge, B. (2012). Voice and meaning-making in team ethnography. *Anthropology & Education Quarterly*, *43*(3), 306–324.

Creese, A. & Copland, F. (2015). *Linguistic Ethnography: Collecting, Analysing and Presenting Data*. Sage.

Denzin, N.K. (1989). *Interpretivism Interactionism*. Sage.

Emerson, R.M., Fretz, R., & Shaw, L.L. (1995). *Writing Ethnographic Fieldnotes*. 2nd edition. University of Chicago Press.

Fillmore, C.J. (1979). On Fluency. In Fillmore, C.J., Kempler, D., & Wang, W. (Eds.), *Individual Differences in Language Ability and Language Behaviour*, 85–103. Academic Press.

Gavins, J. (2007). *Text World Theory: An Introduction*. Edinburgh University Press.

Gibbons, A. (2017). Building Hollywood in Paddington: Text World Theory, Immersive Theatre, and Punchdrunk's The Drowned Man. In Gavins, J. & Lahey, E. (Eds.), *World Building: Discourse in the Mind*, 71–91. Bloomsbury.

Giovanelli, M. & Mason, J. (2015). 'Well I Don't Feel That': Schemas, Worlds, and Authentic Reading in the Classroom. *English in Education*, *49*(1), 41–55.

Gove, M. (2011). *A Liberal Education*. University of Cambridge.

Hidalgo-Downing, L. (2000a). *Negation, Text Worlds and Discourse: The Pragmatics of Catch-22*. Ablex.

Hidalgo-Downing, L. (2000b). Negation in discourse: A text-world approach to Joseph Heller's Catch-22. *Language and Literature*. *9*(3), 215–239.

Iffath, H. (2020). 'Miss, What is Colonialism?': Confronting the English Literary Heritage in the Classroom. *Changing English*, *27*(4), 369–382.

Ipgrave, J. (2010). Including the Religious Viewpoints and Experiences of Muslim Students in an Environment that is Both Plural and Secular. *Journal of International Migration and Integration*. *11*(1), 5–22.

Johnson, M. (1987). *The Body in the Mind: The Bodily Basis of Meaning, Imagination, and Reason*. University of Chicago Press.

Lakoff, G. & Johnson, M. (1999). *Philosophy in the flesh: the embodied mind and its challenge to western thought*. Basic.

Littleton, K. & Mercer, N. (2013). *Interthinking: putting talk to work*. Routledge.

Mercer, N. (2000). *Words and Minds: how we use language to think together*. Routledge.

Mercer, N. & Littleton, K. (2007*). Dialogue and the Development of Children's Thinking: a sociocultural approach*. Routledge.

Shah, M. (2018). What does engagement with a text look like in an English classroom? LATE Conference. 10 March. UCL Institute of Education.

Shah, M. (2014). Solitary Reapers: Reading Cultural Interjections in a London School. *Changing English*, *21*(3), 215–222.

Shakespeare, W. (2005). *Macbeth*. Wordsworth Classics.

Turvey, A., Brady, M., Carpenter, A., & Yandell, J. (2006). The many voices of the English classroom. *English in Education*, *40*(1), 51–63.

Werth, P. (1999). *Text Worlds: Representing Conceptual Space in Discourse*. Longman.

13

RELIGIOUS GREETING MESSAGES AS A GENRE OF INSTITUTIONAL COMMUNICATION

Melanie Barbato

Introduction and Background

At the beginning of Ramadan 2022, British Prime Minister Boris Johnson appeared in a video message that did not only wish Muslims a blessed and peaceful holy month of fasting but also praised the efforts of the British Muslim community during the COVID-19 pandemic, from supporting the vulnerable to "helping people to get jabbed and spreading positivity about the vaccines" to Muslim "NHS heroes" (10 Downing Street, 2022). The video is a typical example for a seasonal greeting message that extends good wishes to a religious community on the occasion of a festival but also seeks to bring across points that are more political in nature and extend beyond the festival to inter-community relations.

Religious festivals provide an opportunity for institutions to invest in positive relations with faith communities. The institutions that send tailored greeting messages with good wishes on such regular occasions include state actors, NGOs, religious organizations and, although typically in a much shorter format, local administrations. This chapter will explore the genre of the religious greeting message as part of the communication of both religious and non-religious actors. Occasional messages are sent outside of festive seasons, for example condolences after the death of a religious leader, but here the focus will be specifically on festival-related greeting messages.

While religious greeting messages can be seen as a genre of its own, it is useful to place them into a bigger picture of institutional communication. Religious-to-religious greeting messages are typically seen to fall under the category of interreligious dialogue. The Vatican, for example, sends its greeting messages to most non-Christian communities through a dicastery with that term in the title: the Pontifical Council for Interreligious Dialogue (renamed the Dicastery for Interreligious Dialogue in June 2022). Interreligious dialogue is itself an umbrella term for many different forms of communication, from a joint search for metaphysical truth amongst theologians to pragmatic alliances that involve communicating for a concrete cause that is not particularly "religious". The most popular categorization of interreligious dialogue is taken from a Vatican document, *Dialogue and Mission*, which offers four forms of interreligious dialogue: the dialogue of life, the dialogue of deeds, the dialogue of theological specialists, and the dialogue of experience (Pontifical Council

DOI: 10.4324/9781003301271-15

for Interreligious Dialogue, 1984). With the exception of the last category, religious greeting messages share features of all these forms of dialogue, which must be thought of as ideal types and not in an exclusive sense: greeting messages seek to promote interreligious friendship, especially when they are shared on the grassroots level, they seek to motivate towards joint action of issues of the greater common good, and, at least in the case of religious-to-religious communication, they tend to be written by theologians and contain theological reflections or references.

To this standard fourfold distinction of forms of interreligious dialogue, Moyaert (2013) has added a fifth category: diplomatic dialogue, the dialogue of religious leaders. This can refer to religious leaders from different traditions shaking hands or signing declarations on a big stage. It can, however, also be used to refer to institutional communication that falls under the realm of public diplomacy. This makes sense particularly when religious-to-religious greeting messages and secular-to-religious greeting messages are viewed as both belonging to one single genre. The messages by heads of state to parts of the population or the whole nation on the occasion of special religious or secular dates (such as Christmas or new year) constitute a form of public diplomacy that has already received some academic attention, usually, however, without a specific focus on the religious dimension (Jiang et al., 2022). The messages by religious institutions do not necessarily have to be categorized differently. Both high-level secular and religious greeting messages can be viewed through the lens of public diplomacy aimed at increasing soft power. "Soft power" is a concept introduced by Nye (2004) that refers to the power that is not based on coercion but on winning hearts and minds through the power of attraction. Religious greeting messages help institutions to bring themselves to the attention of the members of the target audience, to cultivate an image as a friendly and reliable partner, and at times to assert influence on selected issues. Greeting messages are tools for cultivating a long-term relationship between an institution and a religious community. Greeting messages by both religious and secular institutions carefully negotiate language on the boundary of politics and religion. Much like in diplomacy, the possible gap between the explicit and the implicit is important in interreligious dialogue (Wolf, 2021).

The language of public diplomacy can be analyzed with the methods of politolinguistics (Posch, 2017). Politolinguistics is the study not of the language of politicians but of political language, which may refer to the standard realm of politics but also to religious actors (Niehr, 2014). Among the standard methods of politolinguistics is the analysis of metaphors and other rhetorical devices, polar structures, and vocabulary choices. Employing the tools of politolinguistics can help to understand the communication strategies behind individual greeting messages as well as the typical features of the genre "religious greeting message". The reading of such greeting messages as political communication does not deny that there can also be other motivations behind the issuing of such messages. It does, however, allow for drawing parallels with communication that is clearly political, such as the language of diplomacy. While very little scholarly engagement exists on religious greeting messages, the charateristics of diplomatic language have been studied in other contexts. Kleiner (2010), for example, has shown how diplomatic language differs according to setting and depends on whether communication includes a request or merely an expression of concern.

While one-to-one diplomatic discussions with the diplomatic counterpart can be quite frank, in speeches directed at the public, diplomats will "try to appear modest and display common sense, restraint and, if possible, humor" and "will stress common bonds or interests" (Kleiner, 2010, p. 372). Towards the media, diplomats will seek to display prudence and restraint, and when seeking to convince the public, diplomatic actors choose a language that is "less ambitious and sophisticated" in order to make the text "readily comprehensible" (Kleiner, 2010, p. 373). Also, a "dispassionate approach will also be the best solution, even in a case where the official statement is in response to emotional questions or accusations. Diplomacy by insult does not work" (Kleiner, 2010, p. 373).

All these elements of the strategic communication of politics and diplomacy can also be helpful for understanding the language of institutional greeting messages. Religious-to-religious messages may also contain theological elements that could be either motivated by the sincere interest in the search for truth and greater metaphysical understanding, aim to show communality despite difference, or, against the intention of the genre, reveal implicit views of superiority. The labels "political" and "strategic" also do not mean to deny that the institutions that send the messages may genuinely believe in what they tend to call for in the messages: justice, harmony, peace, respectful collaboration, and universal human flourishing.

Religious greeting messages tend to work with big concepts. They rarely limit their reflections to the respective community but call for an attitude that reflects the interconnectedness of all people, and sometimes beyond the human sphere to all life on earth. One goal of religious greeting messages is to motivate people of the target community to extend their band of solidarity beyond their own community. As Dorst (2021, p. 251) points out, "[m]etaphor and religion go hand in hand, given the fact that our religious and spiritual experiences are highly personal, emotional, and abstract." Bringing together the emotional and the communal, greeting messages often use images that relate to spatial extension, such as calls to expand, open, or widen the circle of trust and collaboration. The resources for this extension of solidarity are usually presented as implied by the religious tradition itself, and as not introduced from the outside. For example, the World Council of Churches (WCC), the world's biggest Christian ecumenical institution, sends greetings to the Hindus every year at Diwali, the festival of lights. The Diwali lamps, which Hindus light during this festival, are in these messages discussed as the light in the human heart that calls people, regardless of affiliation, to peace and righteousness. It is thus not the light of Western enlightenment but the Diwali lamp that is native in India that is used to visualize the goal of bringing about a better world with the help of the Hindu community. Polar structures in Christian Diwali messages sent by the WCC or the Pontifical Council for Interreligious Dialogue (PCID) are typically constructed not between the Hindu and the Christian side, but rather between the friends and enemies of dialogue and interreligious collaboration (Barbato, 2020).

A typical feature of religious greeting messages are standardized formulations. Institutional greeting messages often follow the same structure year after year, and often, the variation of content is only minimal. From many messages it is not possible to infer anything about the events of the last year, or the challenges for the relationship between the sender and the recipient community. As such, greeting messages tend to be predictable. There are some significant exceptions, when greeting messages raise sensitive issues or express criticism of the recipient community. A successful greeting message, will, however, always balance such sensitive elements with a majority of familiar, positive, and appreciative elements.

Authors of greeting messages often choose vagueness and standardized expressions to minimize communicational risks. Part of the explanation is simply that no one likes to be lectured on the occasion of their religious festival. The tone of a religious greeting message must cater to the festive mood of the religious occasion that offers the opportunity for making contact but at the same time also restricts the language choices by presenting a certain frame of convention. Joyful greetings and standardized good wishes to individual believers, families, and the community take a central position in almost all religious greeting messages. Often, the expressions of the festive greetings are used to bracket the remaining text, once at the beginning, once at the end of the message. The body of the message then provides space for engaging with other issues, although the contrast between joyful greetings and the rest of the message must not be too stark. While the predicaments of the current time are often referred to in religious greeting messages, the negative and worrisome aspects of existence must not be given the last word. Rather, they are presented as challenges that communities can master if working together, with a general attitude of optimism prevailing. Religious greeting messages encourage believers to dream big, and they encourage them to trust in their agency, especially when joining forces with other faith communities or other people of good will. They call communities to tackle local, regional, and global challenges, from social exclusion of vulnerable groups to religious radicalization to climate change.

Sometimes, the issues that are raised are more explicitly political. In 2016 and 2017, the Ahlulbayt Islamic Mission, a Shia Muslim organization based in the UK, sent a Christmas message to Christians, calling for increased support of the people in Palestine and an end to Islamophobia (Ahlulbayt Islamic Mission, 2016, 2017). The outspokenly political agenda of campaigning for the institution's own interest sets these messages apart from most other religious greeting messages, which tend to keep the tone light and are hesitant to call to intervene in concrete conflicts. In most other aspects, the greeting messages of the Ahlulbayt Islamic Mission conform to the standards of the genre: In 2017, the message starts and concludes with warm greetings on the occasion of Christmas, the recipient community is addressed cordially as "our friends from the Christian faith", there is emphasis on communality ("We have an entire chapter in the Quran dedicated to Mary and numerous passages that shed light on the great life of Jesus"), and the call for socially just action is backed up with a quote from the recipient community's sacred texts: "Learn to do good. Seek justice. Help the oppressed. Defend the cause of orphans. Fight for the rights of widows. [Isaiah 1:17]" (Ahlulbayt Islamic Mission, 2017).

Organizations that send greeting messages usually have a network of contacts to which the greetings are sent. Often messages are also made available on the internet, so that the readers of the greeting messages are not only partner institutions but potentially all members of the respective faith community worldwide, as well as others who take an interest in the institution's communication. A major challenge of this genre is that greeting messages must appeal to a wide range of people who may have little in common beyond identifying as members of the respective religious traditions, which in itself might be diverse and fraught by internal hostilities. When drafting religious greeting messages, institutions must keep these diverse audiences with potentially conflicting interests in mind. Consequently, greeting messages are often kept very general to appeal to everyone while alienating no one.

Among many other elements, the challenge of diverse recipient audiences includes the choice of authorities or "heroes" that are quoted or referred to. Drawing on an important person from the recipient tradition is a good opportunity for creating rapport, showing respect, and providing evidence for the effort of engaging with material from the recipient tradition. It can also balance the sometimes-abundant references to figures from the institution or sender community. However, in diverse recipient communities, the selection of a particular figure may come across as preferential treatment of some because it foregrounds a particular strand of the religious tradition while leaving others unmentioned and invisible. Greeting messages therefore tend for each tradition to refer to a small number of religious figures that are assumed to be beloved by almost all the religious community, most obviously the religious founders. This one challenge of selecting suitable references already shows that the art of writing a good greeting message lies in combining the general and uncontroversial with the specific and relevant.

When evaluating religious greeting messages, it is important to keep two distinct aspects in mind. One aspect is the text of the greeting message, in which certain propositions are made, issues are raised, a certain tone and style is chosen, elements of a shared past are recalled and omitted, and so on. The other aspect is that a message is delivered at all, either as a hard copy, a speech, by email, or on a website. The act of sending a festive message can be interpreted as a ritual of gift exchange, in which the gift is the message (Villar, 2006). Understood this way, the redundancy and use of clichés turns out not to be a flaw but a feature of this genre. Repetition is an important feature of ritual language (Yelle, 2012). As Tambiah (1985, p. 132) has pointed out,

> [r]ituals as conventionalized behavior are not designed or meant to express the intentions, emotions, and states of mind of individuals in a direct, spontaneous and 'natural' way. Cultural elaboration of codes consists in the *distancing* from such spontaneous and intentional expressions because spontaneity and intentionality are, or can be, contingent, labile, circumstantial, even incoherent and disordered.

Like a rose that is exchanged on Valentine's Day between lovers, communication can be more successful when it is less original, and therefore less open to interpretation that could lead to insecurity and misunderstanding.

A gift that contains the same content every year can be accepted without hesitation. This is important particularly when the relationship of sender and recipient is complicated or strained. Consistency in format, style, and content help to establish and maintain trustworthiness. When a greeting message deviates from the usual format, this may raise questions as to whether this change is meaningful, and if it is meant to signal a negative change in the relationship. This occurred in 2014 when *The Economist* noticed that Barack Obama's Ramadan greeting message was somewhat shorter than in previous years and "pointedly avoided any reference to Arab struggles for democracy" (B.C., 2014).

Religious Greeting Messages: Joe Biden's Ramadan Greetings and the Vatican's Vesakh Greetings

This section will look at two examples of religious greeting messages from the year 2022: the message sent by PCID to the Buddhists on the occasion of Vesakh as a case of religious-to-religious communication and the Ramadan message issued by US President Joe Biden as a case of secular-to-religious communication. Both messages will be discussed paragraph by paragraph.

Secular-to-Religious Communication: Joe Biden's Message on the Occasion of Ramadan

Greeting messages tend to be short and structurally limited to a few paragraphs. The body of the message from the White House (2022) has 343 words, which would take around two to three minutes to read. The message is divided into six paragraphs with uneven length. In appearance, Biden's Ramadan message is typical for the genre.

This message is framed by expressing good wishes on the occasion of the month of Ramadan in the first and the last paragraph. The senders are President Biden, who appears in the message only as "I", and his wife, "Jill". The use of his wife's first name might imply that Biden sends the message as "Joe". Greeting messages often combine official communication of a powerful institution with the personal touch and approachable self-presentation of an individual leader and this casual, warm tone is emphasized again in the final paragraph, where the greetings are extended "from the Biden family to yours, and from the People's House to your own homes". The Bidens present themselves here as a neighbourly family, and the next part of the sentence transfers this familiarity to the political level, in which the "People's House" is connected to ordinary people's family home. This can be a strategy to help people identify with the president and the country's democratic institutions. The US government is presented not as an abstract entity but is given the friendly human face of the Biden family. The recipients are, as the first paragraph states, the "Muslim communities here in the United States and around the world", showing that the White House is aware of its potentially global reach. As the message is available online on the website of the White House, potential secondary readerships also include non-Muslims in the United States and abroad.

The second paragraph acknowledges that Ramadan is for "many around the globe, including fellow Americans all across the country" an important month for spiritual reflection but also for communities to come together. In this passage, Islam is recognized as a religion of global importance. At the same time, Muslims are not the other but included in American society: Muslims are also "fellow Americans all across the country". The message thus furthers the vision of the US as a religiously plural country within a religiously plural world.

The third paragraph states that "this year" breaking the fast together will be "an even more poignant reminder of the joys of health, family, and community". Mention is also made of those families who have lost a loved one. The fourth paragraph explicitly names the pandemic as the cause of this upheaval, but already in an optimistic, future-oriented formulation: "As we continue to rebuild from the pandemic, we must also continue all of our efforts to stand with all those who are suffering and vulnerable around the world."

The Ramadan message of solidarity and mutual assistance is extended to all people, especially those who are vulnerable or are enduring hardships. The call is then grounded in a quote from the recipient community: "As the Holy Qur'an teaches, whoever does even an atom's weight of good will see its results." Through this quotation, Biden encourages Muslims to do good in the world but the call is not imposed from the outside but presented as a native concept that can be traced back to the holiest source of Islam.

The fifth paragraph is the longest. It reminds the reader of the "heartbreaking accounts of lost lives and the images of families and children struggling to survive". Death and suffering, put in general terms like this, are issues that all people can relate to. These tragedies, the message states, "remind us of our common humanity—and the common teaching of all great faiths, including Islam—that we should always do unto others as we would have done unto us." In this paragraph, the emphasis is on the universal: the shared experience of suffering, and the golden rule which is upheld in different wordings by many religions. Both point towards a common humanity that ultimately transcends all religious boundaries. This shows that while greeting messages are addressing particular communities, the appeal tends to be universal. The message emphasizes that all people are "equal in dignity and rights". This choice of vocabulary connects the religiophilosophical and the legal realm, affirming the equality of all.

So far in the message, the structural movement has been from the particular (Muslims celebrating Ramadan) to the universal (serving our common humanity). Now the movement is from the universal to the particular, as Biden states that "the United States will continue to speak out for human rights everywhere—including for Uyghurs in China, Rohingya in Burma, and other Muslim communities all over the world." For a religious greeting message, these are strong, concrete, and politically loaded statements. These are sensitive issues not because of potential for conflict with the Muslim community but because they address human rights violations in specific countries and are thus clearly directed against the governments of China and Myanmar. In this specific case, however, it is unlikely that the reference to these two cases will cause new diplomatic irritations. Biden has already been outspoken on the situation in both countries in other contexts. The inclusion of these cases in the greeting message sends a signal to the Muslim communities that human rights issues relating to Muslim communities are on the government's agenda. They serve to underline Biden's commitment to good relations also on a political and diplomatic level, beyond general good wishes.

The last, short paragraph repeats the good wishes on the occasion of Ramadan and closes with the Arabic greeting "*Ramadan Kareem!*" Arabic has a special status for Muslims because it is the language of the Qur'an, which is believed to be the word of God. Using a community's native concepts and language is always a powerful way of signaling respect and friendly intentions. It also shows that the sender has made the effort of learning about the recipient tradition and is willing to meet the community on its own terms. This adaptation, however, must not be overdone, otherwise it could come across as if the sender was attempting in a manipulative and inauthentic way to imitate the language of a community that he or she is not part of. Usually, community-specific foreign language terms are therefore limited to a few, which is sufficient to signal a positive intention.

In the Ramadan message of 2022, there are several references that emphasize respect and a positive attitude towards Islam. Ramadan, the Muslim month of fasting, is referred to as "blessed month", "sacred month", and "holy month", thereby acknowledging in religious language the special status of this month for Muslims. The Qur'an is referred to respectfully as the "Holy Qur'an", and the verb used in connection with the quote is that the "Holy Qur'an teaches", which marks the elevated and authoritative status of this text. The Golden Rule is said to be shared by "all great faiths, including Islam", which is a positive statement about Islam as belonging to an otherwise unspecified group of "great faiths". Ramadan is referred to as the month when "Muslims everywhere honor God's great mercy". While other formulations would have been possible, God is here referred to as a given, as a reality that exists also outside the religious imagination. Biden is a Christian, but here it seems that he subscribes to the view of the merciful God that is honoured by Muslims. Going by this passage, Muslims and Christians, and possibly others as well, venerate the same God. This could be read again as an attempt to unite Muslims and non-Muslims as one American people who are often thought of, as the Pledge of Allegiance states, as "one nation under God".

Religious-to-Religious Communication: the PCID's Vesakh Message to the Buddhists

The Pontifical Council for Interreligious Dialogue (now the Dicastery for Interreligious Dialogue) is the Holy See's institution for communication with people who are not Christians or Jews. Every year, the Roman Catholic PCID sends a message to the Buddhists on the occasion of Vesakh. This festival celebrates the birth, death, and enlightenment of the Buddha. In 2022 the body of the Vesakh message of the PCID has 609 words. Compared to Biden's Ramadan message, it is almost double in length, but it will still only take most people four to five minutes to read, which is typical as an upper limit for religious greeting messages. It is signed by both the president and the secretary of the PCID. This does not mean that this message has two authors while the Biden message has one. Religious greeting messages are usually a collaborative effort, with a person with some expert knowledge and dialogue-related job drafting the message, and others, such as communication department staff, checking and proof-reading the message. The actual signatory may give some instructions at the very start of this process or receive the message only at the last stage. The name on the message is of representative status and not necessarily identical to the main author. Like with other forms of high-level political communication, the signatories have the support of staff and institutional processes, without which the required quantity of communicative output, such as messages to several faith communities on different occasions, would not be possible.

The Vesakh message is divided into seven paragraphs that are numbered consecutively (Biden's Ramadan message had six paragraphs). Like the Ramadan message, the first and the last paragraph frame the message with greetings on the occasion of the respective feast.

After the "warm greetings" to the worldwide Buddhist communities at the start of the message, the second paragraph hits a sober note: there are "manifold crises": people are still "held hostage" by COVID, the ecological crisis "exposed our fragility" as shared citizens, and various conflicts "continue to shed innocent blood". This last crisis is connected with the topic of religions: "Sadly," the message states, "there are still those who use religion to justify violence." The paragraph closes with a recent quote by Pope Francis that laments how humanity has, despite its intellectual and scientific achievements, gone backward in terms of peace.

The reference to "those who use religion to justify violence" opens a dichotomy that is typical for religious-to-religious greeting messages: on the one side there are religious people who work towards peace and human flourishing, on the other side the people who abuse religion for division and selfish goals. The dichotomy that is constructed in religious greeting messages is thus typically not between religious communities, in this case between Catholics and Buddhists; rather, the members of the religious communities are called to unite on the right side of being religious, that is, to collaborate for peace and justice.

Building on this, the third paragraph invokes this solidarity and the duty to serve as role models in challenging times: "As Buddhists and Christians, our religious and moral sense of responsibility should motivate us to sustain humanity in its quest for reconciliation and resilience." The reference to the moral sense is particularly relevant for the dialogue with traditions with strong non-, a-, or trans-theistic strands like Buddhism, where some might object to the idea of following a "religion", and the common ground consists in a shared philosophical and ethical outlook that deems human flourishing and the avoidance of suffering as valuable goals.

The fourth paragraph then compares and brings together Jesus and Buddha as the two founders of the respective traditions. The message states that both taught "transcendent values, albeit in different ways". The Noble Eightfold Path is referenced as a core belief of Buddhism, and is illustrated with a quote: "It is the fading away and cessation of that very same craving with nothing left over; giving it away, letting it go, releasing it, and not adhering to it (*Dhammacakkappavattanasutta*, 56.11)" The *Dharmacakrapravartanasūtra*, which translates as "setting in motion the wheel of the dharma", reiterates the first teachings of the Buddha after he achieved enlightenment. While historically the text will not be a verbal repetition of the words of the Buddha, the text concerns the most fundamental teachings of Buddhism, or, according to Gombrich (1996, p. 62), "the very essence of the Buddha's Enlightenment". Due to the foundational content, the text will be acceptable to many different schools of Buddhism and is in line with typical source choices for religious greeting messages. Quotations from the recipient tradition are a strong signal for the willingness to engage in deeper dialogue, because here a learning process about the sources of the other tradition had to take place. The message also acknowledges that "[i]f practised, the teaching is a cure to the ceaseless grasping that leads to greed and power-plays." This means that the PCID accepts the value of a core teaching of Buddhism, at least in an inclusivist sense.

The message then shifts to Jesus and the gospel message. Instead of force, the gospel proclaims "spiritual values", and the beatitudes: "Blessed are the poor, blessed are the meek, blessed are those who mourn, blessed are the peacemakers" (cf. Matthew 5:1–12). The paragraph closes with the statement that despite all difficulties, the blessed "rely on God's promise of happiness and salvation". The reference to "God" in this sentence is interesting because it follows a Christian, not Buddhist logic. It shows that despite the openness towards the Buddhist moral teachings, the metaphysical framework that underlies the message is that of Christianity, and that Christian viewpoints are not always flagged with restrictive additions (such as expressions like "according to the Christian faith" or "as Christians we believe" would offer). This need not be a hindrance to dialogue, but rather shows that religious actors do not usually suspend their own truth claims when sending greeting messages to other communities.

The fifth paragraph ties the traditions' spiritual riches, compassion, and wisdom for the Eightfold Path, and hope for the gospel message, to the message's key theme, resilience: "We can help humanity become resilient by unearthing the hidden treasures within our spiritual traditions." This phrase includes a call to action that has an intra- as well as an inter-religious dimension. It calls first and foremost for delving into one's own tradition to bring resources of that tradition back into use. The paragraph closes with another quote by Pope Francis that emphasizes the importance of hope.

The sixth paragraph continues the same theme of hope, this time with an uplifting quote by Thich Nhat Hanh, the Vietnamese Zen Master and proponent of Engaged Buddhism who is well known in the West, particularly for establishing a monastery and spiritual centre in France. With Thich Nhat Hanh, the message references a bridge builder between Eastern and Western religion and culture that can serve as a role model for both sides. Thich Nhat Hanh's approach of Engaged Buddhism, a Buddhism that is not focused on renunciation but wants to make a positive difference in the world through activism, is an attractive dialogue partner for the PCID, which in its religious greeting messages also has a strong focus on getting together with people from other faith communities, not to dispute doctrinal matters, but to join forces on issues of common interest for the benefit of the whole world. In line with this outlook, the paragraph closes with the appeal to work together for a better tomorrow.

The seventh, final paragraph repeats the Vesakh greetings but also sums up the two central elements of the message: that there are crises and suffering in the world, and that the world needs hope and good actions: "Dear friends, we wish that your celebration of Vesak will keep hope alive and generate actions that welcome and respond to the adversities caused by the present crises." Addressing the Buddhist recipients of the message as "friends" echoes the "warm greetings" at the beginning of the message: Buddhists are not members of an alien tradition. There is a compatibility in teachings, as the message shows, and a personal closeness of the communities that follows from it. Both Christians and Buddhists are called to draw on spiritual riches for making the world a better place, each community on its own as well as together in interreligious collaboration.

The PCID's message does not have the explicitly political element that was present in the Biden message. This is not because the Vatican is not political. Rather, the Vatican is a hybrid actor that can play on different levels and in different roles, and that can adjust its language and self-representation strategies accordingly. The PCID seeks to stay out of daily politics and concentrates on the more general establishment of good relations with other faith communities. Unlike the White House, the Vatican dicastery can present itself as a religious and non-political entity, which gives it advantages in the field of interreligious dialogue, where the pope often presents himself as a primus inter pares who leads interfaith action for the benefit of religious people from many traditions and the whole world. A typical example of this strategy is the video of the pope's prayer network, where the pope's narration on interreligious dialogue is intersected by video sequences that show people of different religions who "believe in love" (The Pope Video: Pope's Worldwide Prayer Network, 2016). The US president, on the other hand, cannot be a religious equal but can at best appear as a legitimate political power that also defends the interests of the respective faith community.

Religious greeting messages are a form of friendly institutional communication. They are about establishing and maintaining good relationships, often across religious and cultural boundaries. They are, nevertheless, also displays of power and status. Institutions that send religious greeting messages to national or global religious communities by this very act assert themselves as high-status conversation partners that are relevant to such communities. Both Joe Biden and the Vatican are global players. US presidents and popes regularly feature on the Forbes most powerful list. Addressing the national and global communities of Muslims and Buddhists is the league in which they play, namely the highest level of global institutions. Other institutions will send religious greetings in media outlets compatible with their more limited reach, such as their social media website or a local newspaper. Such messages will often be shorter and less formal or limited to the greeting on the occasion of the religious festival. The language and placement of a religious greeting message are thus indicators of how institutions view themselves and their role in the world.

One recurrent question is if such greeting messages are even read, let alone appreciated by the recipient communities. Sperber (2018) discusses this issue in her study of the Vatican's engagement in Christian–Muslim dialogue. She enumerates the reactions that the PCID's messages to the Muslims have received, ranging from informal expressions of gratitude to corrections of typographic errors to offers to proofread future texts before publication, and mentions that, as the practice of sending greeting message was extended to Hindus and Buddhists, there had been a request by Sikhs to receive such a message, too (which led the PCID to send such messages from then). While religious greeting messages are primarily motivated by the sender's interest to further relations with the recipient community, the recipients are aware in the status that is conveyed with these messages and might therefore consider receiving (and responding to) such messages as beneficial. This shows that greeting messages, even when there is little novelty in the texts, can indeed be a means of enhancing a two-way dialogue.

Implications and Future Directions

Religious greeting messages sent by religious or secular institutions are a relatively recent phenomenon. Nevertheless, there has already been a development of recurrent conventions of writing such messages that justifies studying them as a separate genre of institutional communication: They are sent on the occasion of a religious festival with positive connotations; they are signed by an important person within the institutional hierarchy; they begin and end with reference to this festival; they are relatively short and usually consistent in length and format over the years; their style of language is polite; they are marked usually by medium-length sentences and medium-level but not difficult-to-understand language; they have (at least in the case of religious-to-religious communication) some theological content; they sometimes provide information about publications, speeches, visits, etc. that connect the sender and recipient groups; they occasionally address difficult issues between the groups, such as religious freedom or violence against one's religious community, and they make a strong call for solidarity and joint activism for the benefit of all humanity.

Religious greeting messages are a genre of writing that arises out of an increasingly interconnected world, which is also a world in which connections must be renegotiated and reaffirmed amidst deep and rapid change. In this sense, it also holds true for institutional greeting messages what Shank (2004, p. 245) has observed for greeting cards:

> Whether the card showed the red rooftop of an imaginary home, the parking lot of a business, or a candle, sleigh, or star, it said little, but simply embodied the objective need for

connection. The perfect card was one that allowed the receiver to see past it; in this way, all greeting cards are blank cards, empty tokens of fungible affection.

Religious greeting messages tend to have one primary and many secondary functions. The primary function is to establish connection between an institution or the people it speaks for and the faith community that the message is addressed to. Secondary functions, like the opportunity to address sensitive topics or even the issues that are typically presented as common goals that need to be addressed, from intergenerational respect to climate change, are ancillary to this ritualized gift exchange. "Connection" can of course be read through different lenses: as interreligious friendship in the language of interreligious dialogue or as soft power in the language of public diplomacy.

Since the 20th century, many big Christian institutions have shifted from confrontation to collaboration and from mission to dialogue. This is reflected in the language of how these institutions speak both of and to other religious communities. While other religious traditions were for a long time perceived in negative terms and studied with a mission focus in mind, at the Second Vatican Council the document *Nostra Aetate* famously spoke of the reflection of the ray of truth that should be appreciated in other religions, too (*Nostra Aeteta: Declaration on the Relation of the Church to Non-Christian Religions*, 1965). For the Catholic Church, *Nostra Aetate* is rightly seen as a milestone in the development of an open relationship with other religions. The expression of the reflection of the ray is nevertheless vague and limited and has also been criticized by religious thinkers of non-Christian traditions. Within that image, it is not clear how much light these other religions are supposed to possess, if they even possess any light of their own at all. Definite statements about the value of other religious traditions have still not been made by the Catholic Church, although Pope Francis's statement about the divinely willed plurality of religions in the *Document on Human Fraternity* appears to come close to a religious pluralism. Here the question is if Pope Francis's language strategy relates to the theological, doctrinal level at all, or if, very much in contrast to his predecessor Benedict XVI, he is focusing on expressing through his words primarily openness and interreligious friendship, accepting that this may lead to a blurring but not revision of doctrinal boundaries.

Like *Nostra Aetate*, religious-to-religious greeting messages often draw on the light metaphor but usually contain no clear indication of the doctrinal positioning of the sender community towards the recipient tradition. It is typically not the salvific value of the recipient tradition that is praised or even expressed but the religion's values and positive impact on the lives of believers and the world. This holds true also for secular religious traditions, where the metaphysical aspect is often (but as we have seen in the Biden message not always) bracketed out. Religious greeting messages are generally not about theological discussion and evaluation but about community building. This community can be one of religious people joining forces (sometimes explicitly against an increasingly secularizing trend in wider culture) or, in the case of secular-to-religious messages, the diverse community of secular and religious people who believe in the greater good for a country or the human family. The fact that institutions are sending religious greeting messages does therefore not automatically imply a greater openness towards their religious truth claims but is an acknowledgment that contrary to some predictions the power of religion has not disappeared from the public and private sphere, and that religious communities as well as the religious dimension of many individuals' identity must be taken seriously and to be integrated into institutional communication strategies.

Digital communication, one of the biggest changes of the last decade, also has an impact on the genre of religious greeting messages. One such implication is that messages that are shared online can be viewed indefinitely and by people outside the intended audience. While a worldwide availability brings advantages as messages can be distributed worldwide cost effectively and instantaneously, the wide reach can also be a disadvantage. For example, a religious institution's greeting message can not only be read by the recipient community but by the sender community, too, and while the recipient community is likely to welcome the greatest possible openness towards its tradition, parts of the sender community might object to what they view as a watering down of their own doctrine. In the case of Christian actors, who are still initiating a large part of official interreligious communication, this internal criticism would be the abandonment of proclamation in favour of an interreligious dialogue that is based on sharing one's own beliefs, without any attempt to motivate towards conversion. Also, especially where interreligious relations on the ground are tense and where the sender community is in a minority position, friendly messages can be perceived as abandonment or as collaboration with the oppressor. Both is the case, for example, in Hindu–Christian relations, where friendly interreligious dialogue with high-caste Hinduism is objected by Dalit Christians who expect a liberative engagement, not what they might perceive as an exchange of pleasantries with the oppressor (Barbato, 2020).

Digital communication often favours the image over the word. Written statements that take several minutes to read can in this context come across as a dated form of communication. In the age of Twitter, Instagram, YouTube and TikTok, greeting messages, too, might shift towards short texts, images, and videos. One example for religious greeting messages that seek to go with the time are the messages sent by M.D. Thomas from the Institute of Harmony and Peace Studies (*Institute of Harmony and Peace Studies—YouTube,* n. d.). In continuation but also as an alternative to the PCID's messages, Thomas sends video greeting messages on a wide range of religious and secular occasions. He came up with this project during the COVID pandemic, when interaction with people of other religions was restricted but when, at the same time, technological forms of communication received an unprecedented surge. The video messages seek to use a language that is accessible also to the public, and they inform the audience about the context of the feast day or commemorative occasion, and they are designed in a visually appealing way (underlaid with music, varied nature themed background sequences, and lively presentation of the message by Thomas himself). The current trend in digital communication will likely continue and greeting messages will be increasingly send on digital channels and with the use of image and video. The analysis of such greeting messages will require a more integrated approach that also takes the visual and auditory elements into account.

Religious greeting messages are only one strand of institutional communication. Some institutions invest regular resources into the writing and distribution of greeting messages, which shows that people with these institutions attribute some importance and effectiveness to this form of communication. Like with all forms of public diplomacy, it is difficult to measure their impact. The challenge of evaluating interreligious dialogue initiatives is increasingly discussed by scholars (Abu-Nimer & Nelson, 2021; Driessen, 2020). The rise of digital communication can offer a means for religious and secular institutions to measure at least to a certain degree the effectiveness of their interreligious communication strategies. It is, for example, possible to see how many times a message on a website has been viewed or how many times a message that is linked to an email has been opened. Like the way in which market research impacts on advertisement strategies, institutions might gather such information and adjust future greeting messages accordingly. This, of course, can only capture part of what the greeting messages are aiming to do. Friendship across boundaries remains impossible to measure and presents an irreplaceable long-term task.

Concerning topic shifts, environmental issues already play an important role in religious greeting messages. As religious actors are increasingly appreciated for their social capital, it is likely that secular-to-religious messages that highlight the importance especially of themes like climate change will continue to increase, as religious institutions and communities will be called to be part of the solution. This also may lead in general to an increased academic interest in the way that the communication of and to religious institutions and communities at the intersection of interreligious dialogue and public diplomacy works. As religious greeting messages are intersecting with a number of fields, I agree with Wolf's (2021) more general remark about interreligious dialogue communication that an analysis will benefit from linguists and theologians (and I would add political scientists and scholars of religion) working together to analyze the bridge between religious traditions.

Further Reading

Barbato, M. (2020). 'Dear Hindu Friends': official Diwali greetings as a medium for diplomatic dialogue. *Religion, 50*(3), 353–371.
In this article, I compare greeting messages that are sent by the World Council of Churches and the Holy See to Hindus on the occasion of Diwali, and discuss common features, differences and underlying motivations.
Charteris-Black, J. (2005). *Politicians and Rhetoric: The Persuasive Power of Metaphor*. Palgrave Macmillan.
This book raises stimulating points about the role of rhetoric in politics, including the role of establishing trust through familiarity.
Sauer, C. (2007). Christmas Messages by Heads of State: Multimodality and Media Adaptation. In A. Fetzer & G. Lauerbach (Eds.), *Political Discourse in the Media: Cross*-Cultural Perspectives, 227–274. John Benjamins Publishing Company.
When greeting messages are read out to an audience, not only the text but also the delivery is highly scripted. This chapter analyzes the materialities of Christmas speeches by European heads of state on TV.
Sperber, J. (2019). *Anthropological Aspects in the Christian–Muslim Dialogues of the Vatican*. De Gruyter.
Jutta Sperber's detailed study of the Vatican's dialogue with Muslims is one of the very few texts that explicitly discuss the function and features of interreligious greeting messages.
Pihlaja, S. (Ed.). (2021). *Analysing Religious Discourse*. Cambridge University Press.
This edited volume is a valuable resource on the broad field of religious communication. For thinking about greeting messages, the chapters on Interreligious Dialogue by Alain Wolf, Institutions by Kate Power and Metaphor by Aletta G. Dorst are good starting points.

References

10 Downing Street (Director). (2022). *Ramadan 2022—Message from Boris Johnson*. 4 April. www.youtube.com/watch?v=d9tfxTuLrtE
Abu-Nimer, M. & Nelson, R.K. (Eds.). (2021). *Evaluating interreligious peacebuilding and dialogue: Methods and frameworks*. De Gruyter.
Ahlulbayt Islamic Mission. (2016). *AIM's letter to the Church for Christmas 2016*. 25 December. www.aimislam.com/aims-letter-to-the-church-for-christmas-2016/
Ahlulbayt Islamic Mission. (2017). *AIM sends message to the Church for Christmas 2017*. 15 December. www.aimislam.com/aim-sends-message-church-christmas-2017/
Barbato, M. (2020). 'Dear Hindu Friends': Official Diwali greetings as a medium for diplomatic dialogue. *Religion, 50*(3), 353–371. https://doi.org/10.1080/0048721X.2020.1754599
B.C. (2014). The politics of good wishes: Anglophone leaders wish Muslim citizens good luck with their month of fasting. 30 June. The Economist. www.economist.com/erasmus/2014/06/30/the-politics-of-good-wishes
Dorst, A.G. (2021). Metaphor. In S. Pihlaja (Ed.), *Analysing Religious Discourse*, 235–255. Cambridge University Press.
Driessen, M.D. (2020). Evaluating Interreligious Dialogue in the Middle East. *Peace Review, 32*(1), 1–12. https://doi.org/10.1080/10402659.2020.1823560
Gombrich, R.F. (1996). *Theravāda Buddhism: A social history from ancient Benares to modern Colombo* (Repr., 1. publ. 1988). Routledge.
Institute of Harmony and Peace Studies—YouTube. (n.d.). Retrieved 12 August 2022 from www.youtube.com/

Jiang, X., Jiang, Y., & Hoi, C.K.W. (2022). Is Queen's English Drifting Towards Common People's English?—Quantifying Diachronic Changes of Queen's Christmas Messages (1952–2018) with Reference to BNC. *Journal of Quantitative Linguistics*, *29*(1), 1–36. https://doi.org/10.1080/09296174.2020.1737483

Kleiner, J. (2010). *Diplomatic practice: Between tradition and innovation*. World Scientific.

Moyaert, M. (2013). Interreligious Dialogue. In D. Cheetham, D. Pratt, & D. Thomas (Eds.), *Understanding interreligious relations*, 1st edition, 193–2017. Oxford University Press.

Niehr, T. (2014). *Einführung in die Politolinguistik: Gegenstände und Methoden*. Vandenhoeck & Ruprecht.

Nostra Aeteta: Declaration on the Relation of the Church to Non-Christian Religions. (1965, 28 October). www.vatican.va/archive/hist_councils/ii_vatican_council/documents/vat-ii_decl_19651028_nostra-aetate_en.html

Nye, J.S. (2004). *Soft power: The means to success in world politics*. Public Affairs.

Pontifical Council for Interreligious Dialogue. (n.d.). *Message of the Pontifical Council for Interreligious Dialogue on the occasion of the Buddhist Festival of Vesakh/Hanamatsuri 2022*. Retrieved 3 November 2022 from www.vatican.va/roman_curia/pontifical_councils/interelg/documents/rc_pc_interelg_doc_20220501_vesakh-2022_en.html

Pontifical Council for Interreligious Dialogue. (1984). *Dialogue and Mission: The Attitude of the Church Towards the Followers of Other Religions*. www.dicasteryinterreligious.va/dialogue-and-mission-1984/

Posch, C. (2017). Rhetorical analysis. In R. Wodak, & B. Forchtner (Eds.), *The Routledge Handbook of Language and Politics*. 247–261. Routledge.

Shank, B. (2004). *A Token of My Affection: Greeting Cards and American Business Culture*. Columbia University Press.

Sperber, J. (2018). *Die anthropologischen Aspekte in den christlich-muslimischen Dialogen des Vatikan*. Vandenhoeck & Ruprecht.

Tambiah, S. J. (1985). *Culture, Thought, and Social Action: An Anthropological Perspective*. Harvard University Press.

The Pope Video: Pope's Worldwide Prayer Network. (2016). January: Interreligious Dialogue. *January: Interreligious Dialogue*. https://thepopevideo.org/interreligious-dialogue/

The White House. (2022, April 1). *Statement by President Biden Marking the Occasion of Ramadan*. The White House. www.whitehouse.gov/briefing-room/statements-releases/2022/04/01/statement-by-president-biden-marking-the-occasion-of-ramadan/

Villar, C. (2006). *Le discours diplomatique*. L'Harmattan.

Wolf, A. (2021). Inter-religious Dialogue. In S. Pihlaja (Ed.), *Analysing religious discourse*, 197–216. Cambridge University Press.

Yelle, R.A. (2012). *Semiotics of religion: Signs of the sacred in history*. Continuum.

14

REPRESENTATION OF RELIGION IN NEWS MEDIA DISCOURSE

Gavin Brookes, Isobelle Clarke, and Tony McEnery

Introduction and Background

The media, in all its forms, presents information about the world to the world. It is not difficult to find religion(s) and people/groups identified in terms of their religion being discussed or shown, and thus represented, in contemporary media. As Mahan (2014, p. 14) puts it, '[t]here is a great deal of religion, or something that looks a great deal like religion, to be found online and in modern media'. Knott et al. (2014, p. 36) argue that the media operate as 'gatekeepers of public religious literacy and ethical debate', and can serve as a means through which religions can 'justify' their existence in post-traditionalist societies (p. 35). Furthermore, research has demonstrated the news media to be a powerful shaper of knowledge and social attitudes, including those towards social issues and groups (Lynott et al., 2019). Yet despite this, the media has been somewhat overlooked by sociologists of religion (Knott et al., 2014, p. 36).

In this chapter, we aim to address this general lack of focus by exploring how a prominent type of media—specifically, news media discourse—contributes to societal representations and understandings of religion, and thus how it can be studied as such. The broad approach to religion and language described in this chapter rests on three important concepts: representation, discourse, and the (news) media. These represent key foci in applied linguistic and discourse analytical studies of mediatized representations of religion, which will be discussed before a case study presentation of a recent corpus linguistic analysis of discourses used to represent Islam and Muslims in the UK press.

An important starting point for this chapter, as for much discourse-based research on language in the media, is the understanding that it is never possible for any event, social actor, or group to be described in a completely impartial, accurate, and comprehensive way (Fowler, 1991). And this includes, importantly, descriptions of religions and religious groups. Instead, the media offer representations of such phenomena. Hall (1997, p. 61) defines representation as

> the process by which members of a culture use language [...] to produce meaning. Already this definition carries the important premise that things—objects, people, events in the world—do not have in themselves any fixed, final or true meaning. It is us—in society, within human cultures—who make things mean, who signify.

DOI: 10.4324/9781003301271-16

This oft-cited definition highlights several important features of representation which are worth considering in more detail, not least because they are consistent with the kinds of assumptions which typically guide discourse analytical studies of representations of religion. The first point worthy of note is that representations are accomplished through 'language', defined broadly here by Hall as 'any system which deploys signs, any signifying system' (1997, p. 61). Hall's definition applies to forms of communication—or 'signifying systems'—that include language but also implies a broader focus, incorporating other forms of semiosis, such as sound, image, and so on (Machin, 2007).

Representations can be accomplished, then, through language (along with other modes of communication). Discourse analysts studying representation (of religion, but of other topics too) have tended to interpret such language use in terms of discourses. The study of 'discourse' constitutes a significant activity across a wide range of disciplines within the humanities and social sciences (Mills, 1997; Baker, 2006), particularly among those which involve some orientation to language and text, such as linguistics, psychology, philosophy, and cultural studies A corollary of this multi-disciplinary interest is that many definitions for discourse have been put forward, presenting those new to the field with something of a potentially confusing picture (Baker, 2006). As with many other topics that have been studied through the lens of discourse and representation, those interested in exploring media representations of religion have tended to adopt a broadly social constructionist view of discourse (Mills, 1997). According to this view, discourse is taken to have the power to constitute societal understandings and indeed experiences of the phenomena with which they are concerned (Burr, 2015). The historian Michel Foucault is a key poststructuralist thinker, and his ideas have found particular influence among those adopting social constructionist perspectives on discourse. Foucault (1972, p. 49) famously used the term discourse to refer to 'practices that systematically form the objects of which they speak'. Influential though it is, a criticism of Foucault's conception of discourse is that it is rather abstract. Since Foucault was more interested in describing the effects of discourse—particularly in terms of power and governance—than in describing their textual reifications, his writing does not provide much by way of a practical guide for discourse analysts.

As something of a remedy to this, discourse analysts working within a broadly social constructionist paradigm have supplemented theoretical perspectives on discourse, inspired by accounts such as Foucault's but also others', with a more practical orientation. This dual focus involves looking at discourse as two forms of 'practice' simultaneously: (i.) as linguistic practice i.e. 'contextually sensitive written and spoken language produced as part of the interaction between speakers and hearers and writers and readers' (Candlin et al., 1999, p. 321) and, in the social constructionist sense, (ii.) as a form of social practice ('as ways of structuring areas of knowledge and social/institutional practices' (Candlin et al., 1999, p. 323)). From this dual perspective, discourse can be studied both in terms of forms of text and the concepts that are referred to within texts.

To demonstrate such an approach with an example that is relevant to the media, press discourse involves both the language use and the social practices that occur in and around newspapers as a genre. Studying social practices here might involve exploring the role played by practices surrounding the creation and consumption of newspapers, ranging from the use of printing presses, the hiring of journalists, the use of investigative practices to gather information relating to stories, and procedures set up to handle complaints about articles. We could also consider discourse in relation to the texts that press journalists create—how articles are laid out in relation to one another to form an edition of a newspaper, how individual articles are structured (use of headline, leader, paragraphs, etc.) and how language, in terms of content and linguistic features, is used to 'create' news, and within that how news values (Galtung & Ruge, 1965; Bednarek & Caple,

2017 (introduced later)) may privilege certain topics or stances along with the use of linguistic conventions such as terms like 'exclusive'.

We may also conceive of discourses around a concept such as a religion. Again, this would involve both social practices and language use. Linguistic practices here might involve identifying the linguistic means (e.g. narratives, metaphors, etc.) by which a discourse is invoked to represent a religion. Consideration of social practices might then involve considering the context in which that representation was created and took place in order to understand why the text creator opted for that discourse. In the context of news media representation, this can involve investigating the news creator's aims and target or 'imagined' audience (Bell, 1984), as well as considering what the wider implications of that representation might be for society as a whole, and for the religious group in question in particular.

This view of discourse—as not only stretches of language use but also ways of structuring knowledge and practices—brings us to the next feature of representation highlighted by Hall; that is, that 'objects, people, events in the world [...] do not have in themselves any fixed, final or true meaning. It is us—in society, within human cultures—who make things mean' (Hall, 1997, p. 61). Put another way, there is no reality that is wholly independent of discourse, for our understandings and experiences of all things in the world are, to a greater and lesser extent, both enabled and constrained by the discourses that we use to represent them. In this way, the discourses powerful text producers such as news media organizations use to represent religions do not merely reflect how people understand and evaluate those religions but have the capacity to shape those very understandings and evaluations at a broad scale.

In the paragraph above, we began to consider the role of text creators in the creation and dissemination of discourse. This brings us to the third and final point regarding Hall's definition of representation that we want to highlight. In particular, Hall (1997, p. 61) attributes agency in the creation of representations to those 'members of a culture' who produce the language—the discourses—that are used to communicate about things in the world. The referent of 'members of a culture' is suitably broad, as the discourses used to represent things in the world are often contributed by a wide range of social actors and institutions—being created by one, and then moulded and recontextualised by many others. Religion is no exception to this. We regularly encounter discourses around religion(s) across a wide range of texts and contexts, including the focus of this chapter, the news media. Yet news media constitute just one site for such representations, and the discourses surrounding religion(s) are produced and consumed within a wide range of contexts, and these discourses are likely to be contextually, and indeed culturally, contingent.

The contextual contingency of the discursive representations of religion(s) that we encounter serves here as a useful reminder of a point we made at the beginning of this chapter—that media representations do not constitute a transparent 'window' on society. In other words, none of the representations of religion(s) that we encounter (or indeed, study) in news media provide an 'objective' account but instead provide decidedly partial accounts that are shaped by 'a number of competing forces of differing strengths and directions' (Iggers, 1999, p. 100). These 'competing forces' include contextual factors at the sociocultural and institutional level (e.g. editorial practices), as well as textual affordances and constraints, for example pertaining to the mode of the texts and the linguistic grammar of the language in which the discourses themselves are rendered (Fowler, 1991).

A key consideration in the creation of news media—and an important 'competing force' for analysts to take into account—is the audience. Reporters' and editors' understandings of who constitutes their audience informs the selection of what is presented as 'the news', as well as the tone and style of presentation, including how a story is constructed as being newsworthy (Richardson, 2007). Relevant to this process is the concept of news values, which can be defined as

> the criteria employed by journalists to measure and therefore to judge the "newsworthiness" of events. [...] News values are meant to be the distillation of what an identified audience is interested in reading or watching, the "ground rules" for deciding what is merely an "event" and what is "news". Journalists use these ground rules to select, order and prioritise the collection and production of news.
>
> (Richardson, 2007, p. 91)

While the 'ground rules' of news values 'may not be written down or codified by news organisations [...] they exist in daily practice and in knowledge gained on the job' (Harcup & O'Neill, 2001, p. 261). The most influential list of 'news values' was provided by Galtung and Ruge (1965), who identified 12 criteria which, they suggest, are employed by journalists to gauge the newsworthiness of events. These are usefully summarised by Richardson (2007, pp. 91–92) as follows:

1. frequency (daily news needs daily stories);
2. threshold (the scale or intensity of the event);
3. unambiguity (whether the event can be easily described);
4. meaningfulness (the cultural proximity to the story);
5. consonance (events people expect or want to happen);
6. unexpectedness (the scarcity or rarity of the event);
7. continuity (follow-up stories);
8. composition (a balance of stories across the paper);
9. reference to elite peoples;
10. reference to elite nations;
11. personification (about or directly affecting people);
12. negativity (if it bleeds it leads!).

The concept of news values has proven to be useful in some discourse-based studies on media representations of religions and religious groups. For example, in a large-scale study of discursive representations of Islam and Muslims, Baker et al. (2013) observed how distinctions between newspapers' formats and political leanings could indicate different perspectives on newsworthiness. They found that for the right-leaning tabloids, Muslims claiming social welfare benefit was deemed to be newsworthy, but this was not the case for left-leaning broadsheets.

More recent research on news values has highlighted their constructed nature (Bednarek & Caple 2017); that is, the notion that news values do not necessarily guide the selection of events for news reporting but can, in fact, also be applied to an event during the process of news creation. For example, returning to Baker et al.'s (2013) study of representations of Islam and Muslims, the researchers found that the tabloids were more likely than the broadsheets to 'construct' events as newsworthy through a marked use of terms such as 'revealed', which implied certain practices attributed to Muslim social actors to be secret.

Studies which explicitly explore the representation of religions and their adherents in news media are few in number (relative, at least, to the other contexts in which portrayals have been considered, such as religious texts, literary texts, films, and television; see Mahan (2014), for a review). Furthermore, studies that have focused on such contexts have tended to adopt content—rather than discourse-based approaches to studying representation. The focus of such approaches is on describing the religion-related content of such texts, as opposed to the linguistic and other semiotic choices through which those discourses and their attendant representations are entextualized (see, for example, Zeiler 2018).

Of the discourse-based studies that have been conducted on news media representations of religion, the overwhelming majority have focused on the depiction of Islam and Muslims. An early example of such a study is Poole's (2002) analysis of representations of British Muslims in two British broadsheets, *The Guardian/Observer* and *The Times/Sunday Times*, between 1993 and 1997, as well as stories in the tabloids, *The Sun* and *Daily Mail*, in articles published in 1997. Poole found that British Muslims were often represented as irrational and antiquated, as threatening liberal values and democracy, as being involved in corruption and crime, as extreme and fanatical, and as being influenced politically by Muslims in other countries.

Much of the research on news media representations of Islam and Muslims has taken an approach situated within critical discourse analysis (CDA). CDA is a form of discourse analysis that is concerned with identifying how power is enacted, negotiated, and challenged through discourse, with the emancipatory agenda of challenging inequality and power abuse (Fairclough, 2015). Richardson (2004) used CDA to examine the discursive means through which broadsheet newspapers (re)produced anti-Muslim rhetoric in articles published in 1997. He identified four common argumentative strategies deployed by the newspapers when reporting on Islam: as a military threat, as being associated with terrorists/extremists, as a threat to democracy, and as a sexist or social threat. Through such strategies, Richardson argues that British broadsheets engage in processes of separation, differentiation, and negativisation.

Crucially, Richardson's (2004) CDA involved investigating discourse not only at the textual level but also at the level of 'discursive practice'. In this way, Richardson could interpret the argumentation strategies—or topoi—that were used to represent Islam and Muslims in terms of the contexts in which they took place and of which they were constitutive (including journalistic practices and socio-political and economic contexts). A similar kind of context-oriented approach was adopted by Døving (2016) who also drew upon methods from CDA in order to analyse the representations of Judaism and the Jewish minority in contemporary Norwegian news media. Importantly, this study paid particular attention to how Jewish voices within the press were framed, arguing that a multicultural discourse enabled such voices to argue for cultural rights in a way that would not directly refer to Judaism (in the process, potentially inviting anti-Semitic responses).

In recent years, critical discourse analytical approaches have been increasingly combined with methods from corpus linguistics to study news media representations of religion(s). Corpus linguistics refers to a group of methods which involve the computer-assisted analysis of naturally occurring language, as represented in large bodies of digitised text (McEnery & Wilson, 2001; Brookes & McEnery, 2020). This work was initiated by Baker et al. (2008), who brought the techniques together to study representations of refugees, asylum seekers and immigrants in UK newspapers. Baker et al. (2013) fused corpus linguistic and CDA methods in a major study interrogating the representational discourses around Islam and Muslims in a corpus of UK national newspaper articles on this topic published between 1998 and 2009 (inclusive). The structure of their data allowed Baker and colleagues to look at change over time and compare between newspapers of different formats and political leanings. Following that study, in 2019 Baker and McEnery carried out a follow-up study of the period 2010 to 2014 (inclusive), sampling articles using the same search-terms and criteria as Baker et al. (2013) for data comparability. Baker and McEnery (2019) reported both stability and change across the two periods studied (1998–2009/ 2010–2014), though stability was the exception and more had changed than had remained stable. An important finding in both the 2013 and 2019 studies related to the influence of subregister. In both studies, the authors claimed that distinct subregisters were linked to particular discourses. For example, opinion columns represented 'one way in which more negative constructions of Muslims are legitimated' (Baker et al., 2013, p. 189), while overtly Islamophobic discourse was linked to readers' letters and texts, with these subregisters constituting 'effective vehicles for the spread of generalising, negative discourses' (Baker at al., 2013, p. 190).

Another recent, emerging feature of discourse-based studies of news media representation of religion(s) is a focus on intersectionality. The concept of intersectionality advocates a view of identity as a fluid interaction between various aspects (e.g. sex, age, ethnicity, social class, sexuality, and so on; see Crenshaw 1991). In Baker et al.'s (2013) study, for example, the authors examined how discourses around gender intersect with discourses around Islam in representations of Muslim women. Krotofil and Motak (2018) examined the intersection of discourses around migration and religion in a weekly magazine published by the Polish Catholic Information Agency. In another study, Bompani and Brown (2014) explored the role of religion in Ugandan print media discussions of sexuality. The authors argue that the rise of socially conservative Pentecostal-charismatic churches in the country had moulded the market for newspapers to the extent that such media were now being tailored to fit the anticipated moral stances of their imagined socially conservative readerships. At the same time, the role of the Pentecostal-charismatic churches in shaping public discourse more widely (i.e. beyond news media discourse) had created censure around topics such as sexuality which are viewed by the church as immoral and indecent.

Corpus Analysis of Representations of Islam in the UK Press

In this section, we report as a case study a recent corpus-based analysis of representations of Islam and Muslims in UK newspapers carried out by Clarke et al. (2021). The aim of the work is to refresh the aforementioned work on this topic by Baker et al. (2013) and Baker & McEnery (2019). We constructed a corpus of all national UK newspaper coverage of Islam and Muslims between 2010 and 2019 (inclusive), sourcing articles by using the same search-terms as Baker et al. (2013, p. 28, and later Baker & McEnery 2019). The resultant corpus contains 497,523 articles (395,930,045 words).

Our analysis was based on keywords. Keyword analysis is an established technique in corpus linguistic methodology which involves identifying words that are especially frequent in one corpus as compared against another (Baker, 2006). In this case, we obtained keywords by dividing our corpus into ten annual sub-corpora. We then generated a set of keywords for each year by comparing it against the previous one (e.g. we obtained keywords for 2011 by comparing this subcorpus against the 2010 one). We ranked our keywords using the log-likelihood statistic (Dunning 1993). This statistical measure indicates the level of confidence that we, as analysts, can have that our keywords are in fact statistically key and have not arisen as such due to chance or a sampling error. We discarded keywords that were assigned a log-likelihood value below 3.84. This ensured that our keywords had a p-value of <0.05 (we may interpret this as saying that there is a 95-per cent likelihood that the keywords are not the product of chance—an interpretation common in social science research (McEnery, 2006)). We then removed keywords which did not occur in at least 5 per cent of texts in the target corpus, as well as eliminating those which occurred in more than 95 per cent of texts.

We then aggregated our keywords into linguistically meaningful groups by using a new approach to keyword categorisation (introduced more fully in Clarke et al., 2021). Broadly put, the approach considers whether each keyword in a given set is present or absent in each of the texts of a corpus. It then uses multiple correspondence analysis (MCA; Benzécri. 1979) to determine statistically meaningful relationships between keywords based on patterns of text-level co-occurrence. The approach is grounded in two notions. The first is linguistic co-occurrence: frequent patterns of co-occurring linguistic features tend to reveal an underlying communicative function (Biber, 1988). The second notion is that keywords can point to discourses (Baker, 2006). Taken together, the approach aims to identify the most common patterns of co-occurring keywords across the texts of the corpus, which are subsequently interpreted, based on the two notions, for the underlying communicative function and/or discourse to which they point. For our analysis, we used a consolidated list of keywords which represented all the keywords obtained across all our annual subcorpus comparisons (described above). This gave a consolidated list of 567 keywords. By combining the keyword lists into a single list, we are actively investigating how all the keywords co-occur across all the texts in the corpus, rather than just a subset of the keywords in an (annual) subset of the corpus.

We then computed the patterns of keyword co-occurrence across all the texts in our corpus, using MCA. This produced a series of dimensions representing the most common patterns of co-occurring keywords across the texts and indicated the association of the newspapers with the dimensions. Using the MCA results, the next step involved interpreting the dimensions through *coordinates* and *contributions*. Coordinates reflect the nature of the association between the categories of the keywords in terms of proximity, where keywords distributed in similar ways in the articles have coordinates closer to each other on the same side of the origin, and keywords not distributed in similar ways are positioned on opposite sides of the origin (i.e. one will have a positive coordinate and the other a negative one). Looking at coordinates allowed us to see patterns of co-occurring keywords across the dimensions. Contributions, meanwhile, show which categories of keywords are the most important contributors to the dimensions. Keywords with positive coordinates are interpreted in opposition to keywords with negative coordinates.

We interpreted each dimension in turn, starting with the first and continuing until we encountered a dimension from which no coherent discourse could be derived. The first dimension represents the best fit of the data in the sense that this is the most common pattern of variation with respect to the variables examined, which in our case are the keyword co-occurrence patterns. Each subsequent dimension represents the next most common pattern of keyword variation. MCA also assigned each article in the corpus a coordinate and contribution for each dimension. This revealed which articles were most associated with the keyword co-occurrence patterns captured by the dimensions. To interpret the discourse associated with the dimension, we manually analysed the texts most strongly associated with that dimension. In total, ten dimensions were explored. However, the first simply reflected the distinction between short and long texts, while the tenth dimension was judged not to be coherent. This therefore gave us eight dimensions for analysis.

In the full analysis, we thus analysed eight dimensions. Because our corpus comprises UK national press articles mentioning terms related to Islam and Muslim, and because our feature set (i.e. the keywords) represents the most statistically frequent terms in each yearly subcorpus within this corpus, we interpret the dimensions of co-occurring keywords as reflecting common discourses of Islam and Muslims in the press. Notably, the dimensions comprise keyword co-occurrence patterns that are the most frequent in the corpus. The sheer frequency and consistency of use of these co-occurrence patterns in the texts in the context of terms related to Islam and Muslims is meaningful, as they can contribute to understandings of typical events and behaviours related to Muslims or Islam. Of course, other discourses may exist in the corpus, but the dimensions represent those that are most frequent across the texts.

We assigned to the eight dimensions the following thematic labels, which reflect the themes around which the discursive representations of Islam and Muslim cohered in the articles: (i.) War, conflict, and terrorism vs. reporting of everyday life and events; (ii.) Foreign Affairs vs. domestic affairs; (iii.) Western political conflict vs. overseas conflict; (iv.) UK policy versus US policy; (v.) Globalisation vs. tribalism; (vi.) Corruption and human rights vs. the aftermath of terror attacks; (vii.) The rise of the far right vs. the radicalization of British Muslims; and (viii.) Political processes and elections vs. political processes and security threats. Importantly, these interpretive labels were arrived at through a qualitative analysis of a sample of the most characteristic articles for the positive and negative sides of each dimension (as determined through the MCA). Our consistent finding was that absences of keywords associated with a particular pole of a dimension tended to have their presences associated with the other pole of the dimension. A full report of these dimensions can be found in Clarke et al. (2021), while in Clarke et al. (2022) we examine their variation in frequency over time. Here, we focus on just three of the dimensions—(i.), (iii.), and (vi.). We have decided to focus on these dimensions as they were found to provide insight into the effects subregister in the articles' representations of Islam and Muslims, and we were interested in comparing our findings with Baker et al. (2013) and Baker and McEnery (2019)—who, as noted, also identified subregister effects—and in seeing whether our approach to keyword analysis could shed new light on this feature of the discourse, or even allow us to access it more easily.

Perhaps the major finding of the results, which mirror those of the previous studies cited, is that, in aggregate, they show that the media focus on Islam as an identity, not a religion. Mentions of Islam and Muslims, are used to index a group identity, yet an explicit discussion of matters key to defining the identity—such as religious beliefs, different varieties of Islam and the institutions of Islam—are backgrounded in the discourse. As shown, for example, by Baker, Gabrielatos and McEnery (2013, p. 64), the religion is associated with conflict primarily, with further, typically negative associations, to civic society present also. The same is also true of the analysis that follows.

War, Conflict, and Terrorism vs. Reporting of Everyday Life and Events

This first dimension opposes keywords which, on the positive side, feature in articles discussing war, conflict, and terrorism with keywords which, on the negative side, feature in opinion pieces and/or feature articles which discuss everyday life and events. Keywords strongly associated with the positive pole of this dimension include those related to war (e.g. *fighters*, *soldiers*, *weapons*), conflict (e.g. *violence*, *murder*), and terrorism (e.g. *suicide*, *bombing*, *terrorists*), as well as people and places (e.g. *citizens*, *members*, *Mr*, *spokesman*) and times and dates (e.g. *Friday*, *November*, *yesterday*) that are tied to the events being reported. Other keywords denote and describe ongoing investigations (e.g. *investigation*, *emerged*, *involved*, *described*) and feature in articles reporting on news events related to war, terrorism and conflict, such as in the article, 'Armed police shoot man "carrying a bomb in a rucksack after he takes a woman hostage" at Brussels tram station as they swoop on terror suspects linked to "imminent attack in France"' (*MailOnline* 25 March 2016).

By contrast, keywords strongly associated with the negative pole describe entities and encode personal opinions and feelings (e.g. *love*, *kind*, *hope*). These keywords are not connected by a consistent topic. However, some are used to discuss politics (e.g. *Brexit*, *win*, *politics*,) and business (e.g. *job*, *money*, *business*). Overall, these keywords are used in the articles to encode personal opinions and stances on a range of topics. For example, a *Guardian* article entitled 'What is an Ideal Childhood?' (17 October 2015) asks five celebrities about their views on an ideal childhood. One, the poet Lemn Sissay, talks about the benefit of parents believing in something (politically or religiously), such as the Qur'an, as a way of getting children to think about who they are.

As the thematically coherent dimension with the best fit of the data, discourses around war, conflict, and terrorism can be viewed as being most commonly represented in the articles. This is consistent with previous research which found war and conflict to be the most common press discourse around Islam, while supporting Baker et al.'s (2013) finding that opinion pieces are an important subregister within which strong stances predominate. This dimension indicates that Islam is predominantly represented in the UK press as non-peaceful as its advocates and believers are frequently involved in conflict, war, and terrorism. The dimension also shows that religion is perceived by the press as a protected characteristic, as the discrimination towards Muslims and Islam generally comes from the opinions of individuals and not directly from the newspapers.

Western Political Conflict vs. Overseas Conflict

The positive pole of this dimension is characterized by reporting which links Muslims to Western political conflict. Keywords strongly associated with the positive side of this dimension focus on terror attacks (e.g. *attack, terror*), political processes (e.g. *meeting, response*) and legal actors/ actions (e.g. *court, police, prison*). Evaluation is apparent (*wrong*), as is reporting of speech and writing (e.g. *read, said, told*). The Muslim community, and often specifically the British Muslim community, is placed relative to the actors and actions discussed (*Muslims*), especially with respect to hate crimes and discrimination experienced and enacted by them. The political contexts in which these events are situated are Western, specifically the US (e.g. *Trump, White House*), Europe (*EU*) and UK (e.g. *Labour, Parliament,*

prime minister), and are often located in time (e.g. *Tuesday, yesterday*). Some keywords co-occur in articles covering the political far-right (*right*) and anti-Muslim bias expressed by such groups. Yet not all articles featuring these keywords focus on the persecution of British Muslims, as some are linked to cases where Muslims persecute other groups. For example, some articles associated with the positive pole of this dimension criticize political figures' links to Muslims (e.g. the article, 'Truly Disgraceful Day for the Labour Party' (*The Mail* 29 May 2019), which links UK politician Jeremy Corbyn to a group called British Muslims for Corbyn). The article claims that social media posts by the group are 'littered with anti-Semitic tropes', negatively framing both British Muslims and, by association, Jeremy Corbyn as anti-Semitic.

The negative pole of this dimension focuses on overseas conflict. Characteristic keywords refer to conflict, in terms of scale, the actors involved, and various associated actions, places and resources. Actions can be linked to conflict through explicit labelling (e.g. *battle, bombing, war*) and implicit labelling (e.g. *operation*), or by discussing the progress and sequence of actions linked to the conflict (e.g. *began, end*). Such actions are then linked to actors engaged in violence, both indirectly (e.g. [Saudi] *Arabia, ISIS, Syria, Russia*) and directly (e.g. *army, fighters, troops*). There is also a clear indication of where the actions being described occur within the area controlled by a group under focus (e.g. *border, city, streets*). Resources in those areas are also linked to the reporting (e.g. *food, oil*). Actions and actors involved are linked to words which vaguely indicate scale (e.g. *big, hundred, thousands*).

Overall, then, these keywords often co-occur in articles that report on the specifics of conflict overseas, principally in the Middle East. This relationship between actions, actors and places is demonstrated in the article, 'Life in the Shadow of ISIS: Inside the Terror-ruined Towns where Families Face Bombs, Poverty and Deadly Smoke; Families in Iraq are Facing Oil Well Blazes, Fatal Smoke and Hidden IEDs—Months after their Hometowns were Recaptured from ISIS' (*The Mirror* 3 January 2017). Here, an actor linked indirectly to violence (*ISIS*) is presented as operating in an area where resources (*oil*) are present and violent actions (*terror*) are impacting on a large yet imprecisely quantified group of people. However, many of the articles associated with the negative side of dimension 4 are travel guides and reviews which discuss the beauty and culture of destinations that have been impacted by both historical and ongoing conflict. Thus, keywords on the negative side of this dimension link to the newspaper subregister of travel guides and reviews.

Overall, this dimension indicates that the UK press often presents Muslims as involved in both verbal and physical conflict. When the conflict is of a terrorist nature, these perpetrators are depicted as security threats. When the conflict is related to western politics, these Muslims are represented as either criminal perpetrators that are anti-Semitic or victims of anti-Muslim bigotry. The representation of Muslims as victims in the context of warfare is at best implicit—the religious identity of Muslims is a keyword present on the positive side of the dimension, as opposed to the negative side, even though the victims of the violent acts described in articles on the negative side of the dimension are, presumably, predominantly Muslim. Through these common depictions of some Muslims as involved in conflict, the UK press indirectly presents Islam as an aggressive and prejudiced religion. Again, this illustrates that religion is a protected characteristic, as rather than directly refer to Islam negatively, negative behaviours of Muslims are instead foregrounded and consistently repeated across multiple texts.

Corruption and Human Rights vs. The Aftermath of Terror Attacks

Many keywords on the positive side of the dimension are associated with human rights and legal systems (e.g. *court, justice, life*). Other keywords refer to particular places and countries (e.g. *Arabia, church, university*), governments and leaders (e.g. *conservative, member*) and identities (e.g. *father, mother, Muslim, son*). We also find keywords referencing the economy, business, and trade (e.g. *business, company, economy*), temporal and quantity information (e.g. *December, July, years*), as well as keywords which draw contrasts and provide extra information (e.g. *despite, including, since, although, however*). Such keywords frequently occur in texts discussing human rights concerns from both a positive and negative perspective, such as gay rights, the death penalty, women's rights, and violence against women. For instance, some articles positively report progressive trends in Saudi Arabia, such as the lifting of the ban on women driving, whilst others negatively emphasize the intolerance of Islam and Islamic countries with reference to executions, corrupt and biased legal systems, and violence against women (such as genital mutilation).

Some of the articles associated with this side of the dimension are obituaries. These texts draw on the discourse of human rights and corruption to detail the lives of political leaders and their abuse of power. For example, the article, 'Iran: Seven Key Human Rights Challenges Facing President Rouhani' (*The Guardian* 4 March 2016) reports on President Rouhani of Iran following the success of his moderate allies in recent elections, which meant that Rouhani could focus on human rights violations. The article morphs into an obituary by reflecting on previous leaders who tarnished Iran's reputation, before leaving that subregister and discussing various human rights challenges that need to be remedied. Other articles are obituaries in a more explicit sense (e.g. 'Mohamed Morsi, Ousted President of Egypt—obituary (*The Telegraph* 17 June 2019)).

The keywords strongly associated with negative pole of this dimension are used to describe the aftermath of local terror attacks. Many keywords refer to terrorist groups (e.g. *ISIL, ISIS*), weapons, and methods of attack (e.g. *bombing, suicide*), investigations (e.g. *footage, incident, scene, suspected*) and war (e.g. *fighters, ground, Syria*). Other keywords relate to UK politics (e.g. *Cameron, MPs*) and US politics (e.g. *Donald, Trump*) and frame politicians' statements and comments (e.g. *added, comments, Twitter*). Such reporting often covers government statements and responses following terror attacks, including calls for missile retaliation, resignations, and new policies such as Trump's 'Muslim ban'. Keywords denoting mental, stance and perception verbs are used to report eyewitness accounts of terror attacks (e.g. *know, think, want*). Additionally, there is a curious mixture of imprecise keywords which suggest uncertainty around the events (*everyone, something, someone, thing, things, anything, everything, anyone*), with more precise keywords indicating certainty, such as verbs (e.g. *happened, let, stand*) and temporal information (e.g. *minutes, moment, morning*). Overall, then, these keywords co-occur in articles reporting on the aftermath of terror attacks, drawing upon eyewitness reports, government statements and details of the criminal investigation into the attack itself, as in the article 'Witnesses reveal moment armed officers stormed Tube station' (*MailOnline* 4 June 2017).

Taken together, then, the poles of this dimension indicate a pattern whereby Islam and Muslims are discussed in the national press in terms of being 'behind' on human rights (especially women's rights) or as having caused death and destruction to innocent victims.

It is through these frequent and consistent discourses when reporting on Muslims and Islam that the view that this is characteristic of Muslim behaviour becomes entrenched. In the same vein, by not mentioning explicitly that these behaviours are not carried out by all Muslims, and by not mentioning positive behaviours/events as consistently or frequently, readers of such articles might be more likely to develop a negative evaluation of the religion and its adherents, due to a mental association between Muslims and these actions which is forged through lexical priming (Hoey 2005).

Further, as discussed prior to the case study, the beliefs and values of Islam as a religion, are not used to identify Muslims, nor to define Islam. If media discourse is all that non-Muslims rely on to understand the religion, its adherents, and the behaviour of some Muslims, then it is hard to conclude that that understanding would be well informed. It would certainly not be an understanding rooted in theology, Islamic jurisprudence, or the social practices of the religion. Of course, what is judged by news producers to be newsworthy is a not insignificant factor here; the negativity of activities that are labelled as terrorism in news coverage likely means that news producers will view this kind of reporting as being more likely to sell their newspapers and/or generate traffic to their websites. Over time, this effect is likely to be compounded as news producers regard such coverage as being 'consonant' with what readers expect to read about this religious group (i.e. the association between it and terrorist violence). By contrast, ordinary religious practices associated with Islam and Muslims are likely to be regarded as less newsworthy (in that they tend not to satisfy the kinds of news values described earlier in this chapter), and so these sorts of practices rarely (if ever) make it into reporting. The result, then, is a distorted view of what constitutes religious identity and practice in the case of Islam.

Implications and Future Directions

In this chapter, we have explored what linguistic studies of discourse can contribute in terms of understanding how the news media represents religion(s). Although studies working from this perspective are few, studying the mediatization of religion(s) has much to offer. This is because, as Knott et al. (2014, p. 37) summarize, religious mediation and mediatization offer

> additional ways to think about interactions between religion, the media and society: (1) the media are a key part of the process whereby religion becomes more publicly visible; (2) the media may indeed become a primary source of information about religion; (3) media portrayals of religion have not been untouched by social change and may indeed have become secularized or banal; and (4) contemporary social transformations have changed the power relationship between religion and the media, and may account for the latter's quasi-religious role.

The analysis reported in the case study in Section 3, along with the other case studies discussed throughout this chapter, illuminate how discourse-based research can contribute better understandings of the role of language and discourse in the processes highlighted by Knott et al. above. Our case study, in concert with the wider analysis reported in Clarke et al. (2021), identified the major dimensions that characterize the discursive representations of Muslims in the UK press. These dimensions, and their associated discourses, indicate relative stability compared to those described by Baker et al. (2013) and Baker and McEnery (2019). Though recent years have witnessed the emergence of new social actors, groups, contexts, and events in news media reporting around Islam, representations continue to 'Other' Muslims, presenting them as especially violent and as adopting values and practices framed as 'behind' or different from those of the global West. This continuity arguably speaks to the power of these representations, such that they endure regardless of the specific people, places, and events that are newsworthy at a given time.

Our analysis did, however, highlight one area of significant change. Namely, the MCA approach to grouping keywords proved of value in accessing the intersection of subregister and discourse in a corpus in which subregister was not explicitly marked. In this way, we could link the presence of particular subregisters to representational discourses. As well as confirming a previously observed interaction between a subregister (e.g. opinion pieces) and discourse (see Baker et al., 2013), we also saw the use of the subregister obituary as a rhetorical strategy. Pieces which appear at first to be obituaries are, in fact, strongly evaluative and use the obituary subregister not to celebrate the lives in question, but to condemn them. In this sense, they can be viewed as delegitimation strategies. This is marked in the context of the obituary subregister, which otherwise typically serves to inform the public of a person's death and to celebrate the contribution that person has made to society. Yet the use of this subregister within coverage of Islam and Muslims can, as we have seen, reverse both of those purposes; such articles inform the public about the death of a Muslim person with whom they are unfamiliar while simultaneously condemning that person's contribution to society. The shift to the obituary subregister within such articles signals a change of purpose. The situated nature of that switch is likely to invert readers' expectations of what that subregister normally achieves, thus providing something of a 'back door' for anti-Muslim sentiment to be woven into news media discourses in contexts where readers are unlikely to expect to encounter it.

Future research should therefore aim, first and foremost, to address the relative paucity in discourse-oriented work on mediatized representations of religion(s). Such research can contribute significantly towards our understandings of the roles and perceptions of religions in contemporary societies, and understand the discursive means through which religious identities, specific faiths, and 'religion' itself as a belief system are legitimated and delegitimated in mass communication. Beyond this general call, future research should also aim to redress the imbalance in focus, whereby most discourse-based research in this area has focused on the representation of Islam and Muslims specifically. While we can locate studies exploring representations of other religions and religious groups—such as Christianity (Knott et al., 2014) and Judaism (Døving, 2016), for example—such studies are presently in a small minority. Regarding forms of news media, future research should also aim to explore the discourses produced by local as well as national news agencies. It is possible that regional news producers operate with different sets of news values, which may result not only in different types of stories but also more positive representations of groups such as Muslims. The case study we have presented in this chapter also makes the case for looking at variation not only *across* different types of news texts, but also *within* news texts, for instance by considering the effects of distinct subregisters on the kinds of discursive representations that emerge throughout a single text.

Further Reading

Fairclough, N. (1995). *Media Discourse*. Arnold.
This is a foundational book in the linguistic analysis of media language. It provides a detailed introduction to critical discourses analysis as part of that.
Knott, K., Poole, E., & Taira, T. (2014). *Media Portrayals of Religion and the Secular Sacred: Representation and Change*. Routledge.
This book explores the representation of several religions in media texts, including but not limited to a focus on discourse-based approaches.
Machin, D. & Niblock, S. (2006). *News Production: Theory and Practice*. Routledge.
This book provides a detailed account of the kinds of practices that sit behind news text production and considers how such insights can be utilized in (critical) discourse studies.
Mahan. J. (2014). *Media, Religion and Culture: An Introduction*. Routledge.
This book provides comprehensive coverage of the interaction between religion and mediatized representations of religion, and how these both shaped and are shaped by cultural context.
Poole, E. & Richardson, J.E. (Eds.). (2006). *Muslims and the News Media*. Tauris.
This edited volume presents an interesting collection of studies of news media representations of Islam and Muslims, including discourse-based studies.

References

Baker, P. (2006). *Using Corpora in Discourse Analysis*. Cambridge University Press.
Baker, P., Gabrielatos, C., KhosraviNik, M., Krzyżanowski, M., McEnery, T., & Wodak, R. (2008). A useful methodological synergy? Combining critical discourse analysis and corpus linguistics to examine discourses of refugees and asylum seekers in the UK press. *Discourse & Society, 19*(3), 273–306.
Baker, P., Gabrielatos, C., & McEnery, T. (2013). *Discourse Analysis and Media Attitudes: The Representation of Islam in the British Press*. Cambridge University Press.
Baker, P. & McEnery, T. (2019). The value of revisiting and extending previous studies: the case of Islam in the UK press. In R. Scholtz (Ed.), *Quantifying Approaches to Discourse for Social Scientists*. 215–249. Palgrave Macmillan.
Bednarek, M. & Caple, H. (2017). *The Discourse of News Values: How News Organizations Create Newsworthiness*. Oxford University Press.
Bell, A. (1984). Language style as audience design. *Language in Society, 13*(2), 145–204.
Benzécri, J.P. (1979). Sur le calcul des taux d'inertie dans l'analyse d'un questionnaire [On the calculation of rates of inertia in the analysis of a questionnaire]. Cahiers de l'analyse des données, *4*(3) 377–378.
Biber, D. (1988) *Variation Across Speech and Writing*. Cambridge University Press.
Bompani, B. & Brown, T. S. (2014). A "religious revolution"? Print media, sexuality and religious discourse in Uganda. *Journal of Eastern African Studies, 9*(1), 110–126. Routledge.
Brookes, G. & McEnery, T. (2020). Corpus linguistics. In S. Adolphs & D. Knight (Eds.), *The Routledge Handbook of English Language and Digital Humanities*, 378–404. Routledge.
Burr, V. (2015). *Social Constructionism*, 3rd edition. Routledge.
Candlin, C.N., Maley, Y., & Sutch, H. (1999). Industrial instability and the discourse of enterprise bargaining. In S. Sarangi & C. Roberts (Eds.), *Talk, work and institutional order: Discourse in medical, mediation and management settings*, 323–349. De Gruyter.
Clarke, I., McEnery, T., & Brookes, G. (2021). Multiple Correspondence Analysis, Newspaper Discourse and Subregister: A Case Study of Discourses of Islam in the British Press. *Register Studies, 3*(1), 141–171.
Clarke, I., Brookes, G., & McEnery, T. (2022). Keywords through time: Tracking changes in press discourses of Islam. *International Journal of Corpus Linguistics, 27*(4), 399–427.
Crenshaw, K. (1991). Mapping the Margins: Intersectionality, Identity Politics, and Violence against Women of Color. *Stanford Law Review, 43*, 1241–1299.
Døving, C.A. (2016). Jews in the News—Representations of Judaism and the Jewish Minority in the Norwegian Contemporary Press. *Journal of Media and Religion, 15*(1), 1–14.
Dunning, T. (1993). Accurate methods for the statistics of surprise and coincidence. *Computational Linguistics, 19*(1), 61–74.

Fairclough, N. (2015). *Language and Power*, 3rd edition. Routledge.

Foucault, M. (1972). *The Archaeology of Knowledge*. Pantheon.

Fowler, R. (1991). *Language in the News: Discourse and Ideology in the Press*. Routledge.

Galtung, J. & Ruge, M. (1965). The structure of foreign news: The presentation of the Congo, Cuba and Cyprus crises in four Norwegian newspapers. *Journal of Peace Research*, *2*(1), 64–90.

Hall, S. (1997). *Representation: Cultural Representations and Signifying Practices*. SAGE Publishing.

Harcup, T. & O'Neill, D. (2001). What is news? Galtung and Ruge revisited. *Journalism Studies*, *2*(2), 261–280.

Hoey, M. (2005). *Lexical Priming: A New Theory of Words and Language*. Routledge.

Iggers, J. (1999). *Good News, Bad News: Journalism Ethics and the Public Interest*. Westview Press.

Knott, K., Poole, E., & Taira, T. (2014). *Media Portrayals of Religion and the Secular Sacred: Representation and Change*. Routledge.

Krotofil, J. & Motak, D. (2018). Between traditionalism, fundamentalism, and populism: a critical discourse analysis of the media coverage of the migration crisis in Poland. In U. Schmiedel & G. Smith (Eds.), *Religion in the European Refugee Crisis*, 61–85. Palgrave Macmillan.

Lynott, D., Walsh, M., McEnery, T., Connell, L., Cross, L., & O'Brien, K.S. (2019). Are you what you read? Predicting implicit attitudes to immigration based on linguistic distributional cues from newspaper readership: A pre-registered study. *Frontiers in Psychology*, *10*, 842.

Machin, D. (2007). *Multimodal Analysis*. Bloomsbury.

Mahan. J. (2014). *Media, Religion and Culture: An Introduction*. Routledge.

McEnery, T. (2006). *Swearing in English: Bad Language, Purity and Power from 1586 to the Present*. Routledge.

McEnery, T. & Wilson, A. (2001). *Corpus Linguistics: An Introduction*, 2nd edition. Edinburgh University Press.

Mills, S. (1997). *Discourse*. Routledge.

Poole, E. (2002). *Reporting Islam: Media Representations of British Muslims*. Tauris.

Richardson, J.E. (2004). *(Mis)representing Islam*. John Benjamins Publishing Company.

Richardson, J.E. (2007). *Analysing Newspapers*. Palgrave Macmillan.

Zeiler, X. (2018). Digital Journalistic Uses of the Terms "Sacred" and "Trivial": Online Press Releases on Portrayals of Hindu Deities in the USA. *Journal of Religion, Media and Digital Culture*, *7*(3), 300–319.

15

PANDEMIC SERMON RHETORIC AND EVANGELISM

Clint D. Bryan

Introduction and Background

Preaching is essential to evangelical Christianity; each week pastors craft sermons geared to contexts that impose conditions on how these lexical elements function. Surprisingly, few scholars have studied how sermon content is packaged for online consumption by a larger population—leaving religious podcasts and online sermon videos, quickly becoming primary delivery systems of this content, insufficiently analyzed. The case study in this chapter, therefore, addresses the neglect of religious discourse in terms of constitutive rhetoric identified by Hill (2016). This study is particularly concerned with the ways that the language of contemporary American preaching is shaped by the demands and affordances of new media technology. Linguistics has not kept pace with technological advancements that American evangelicals have exploited for spreading the gospel—connecting people to the divine and to the devoted community. To interpret the ascribed meaning in evangelical preaching, researchers should locate a multidimensional framework that understands that "who we are to each other ... is accomplished, disputed, ascribed, resisted, managed and negotiated in discourse" (Benwell & Stokoe, 2006, p. 4). By closely analyzing representative sermon transcripts and applying the basic criteria of constitutive rhetoric (White, 1990; Charland, 1987), it is possible to extrapolate several salient features of contemporary American church culture from two practitioners' prevalent practices for preaching online. This chapter discusses evangelical preaching as a linguistic act, before moving on to considering the myriad ways that hosting a sermon on a webpage affects its rhetorical situation, especially for its various audience members and by its chief practitioners.

Preaching in today's church setting frequently requires performing verbal gymnastics. Relevance to a contemporary audience requires using updated diction and everyday idioms, yet evangelical churches are frequently aligned with entities that cherish conservative values, often encoded in speech and writing. Intertextual references to biblical texts often include translations replete with Latinate words. The discourse's register floats between a formal and an informal tone, depending on the moment in the sermon. For instance, a pastor may sound casual, connecting with parishioners before transitioning to a prayer composed of formal terms. The dominant liturgy of the church determines the pastor's word choices. Some employ slang for comedic, persuasive effect. For professional communicators who address hundreds in attendance weekly, diction is hardly

DOI: 10.4324/9781003301271-17

a random decision. The competency of matching one's vernacular to the occasion demonstrates intentional, interpersonal connection with in-person parishioners and online viewers. Moreover, the intermittent formal word adds a measure of solemnity to the occasion. The extent to which, however, this vacillation between formal and informal word choice translates on an interface to a virtual audience remains to be determined.

The internet offers access to spiritual content, thus pushing religious discourse into vistas outside church walls and beyond faith-based TV and radio channels. With a few mouse clicks, varied content (from neutral to negative, secular to sacred) appears on screen, scaled for optimal viewing on the respective device. The internet levels all content, situating the user as the final determiner of what to see and how to estimate its ultimate value. When it comes to religious content, however, especially digitized audio and video sermons originating from American churches, preachers grapple with political, authoritative power that influences (and is influenced by) the way Christianity is delivered online.

The internet homogenizes American evangelical preaching. Before the microprocessor, ministers rarely knew how their contemporaries preached. Pastors only heard various preaching styles while enrolled in seminary or attending ministry conferences. Today, they may access thousands of pulpits: hellfire-and-brimstone sermons, Catholic homilies, or messages from imams and rabbis, all from their devices. Online preaching is ubiquitous, although few linguists have analyzed digital ecclesiastical discourse until recently. From TikTok influencers who invite viewers to "share" their videos evangelistically (Pihlaja, 2020) to celebrity pastors who evoke a brand of "Cool Christianity" (Rocha, 2021) targeted to congregations that soar into the thousands, these popular preachers are easy to listen to via podcasts, allowing the rank-and-file minister to emulate their style.

Recently, traditional church attendance has declined precipitously, especially for American Catholics and mainline Protestants (Cooperman, Smith, & Ritchey, 2015). During this period, internet usage has skyrocketed. According to the Pew Internet and American Life Project, approximately 85 percent of Americans own smartphones (Perrin, 2021), prompting churches to use technology for "relational" rather than "informational" purposes to connect with those expressing spiritual interest (Bourgeois, 2013, p. 23). Those still interested in traditional worship formats often consult prospective church websites prior to their initial visits. Consequently, many American churches upload sermon content preached at their locations. These free, available sermons provide rich sources for linguistic analysis. A digital platform reinforces and subverts the power asserted by ministers delivering these sermons. Digital sermon content introduces thought-provoking questions about speakers' perlocutionary intentions (viz., the effects on listeners); implied performative speech acts (viz., the sense that these phrases enact something as they are stated); and rhetorical moves within a specific discourse community: evangelical users. Preaching online introduces new rhetorical attributes to the age-old discursive form of the sermon, what Yang (2021, p. 81) labels "new digital online traits: multilateral instant communication, holistic artistry, and shareability." It was this shareability that enabled me to devise a corpus of representative sermons from two suburban Seattle churches during the COVID-19 pandemic (described below) to analyze the language employed for indications of constitutive rhetorical patterns by contemporary preachers practicing religious communication.

Religion generally (and evangelical Christianity particularly) connects seekers to one another just as often as it purports to foster a relationship with God. Since it shapes interpersonal networks, the connectivity of social media has influenced how users interact with spiritual content and with like-minded users accessing the same streams. As Morgan (2011, p. 140) notes, nothing "seems essentially new" about religion's foray into mediatization; the faithful have marshaled new media since Gutenberg's printing press, but the "complicated relation" between media and religion results in "a culture in which consumption and media production are indistinguishable as forms of meaning making" (Morgan, 2011, pp. 140–141). Online users do not merely consume content; they shape posted content, recommending "viral" video clips that result in millions of "hits." Call-and-response preaching that used to garner a hearty "Amen!" from certain traditions now results in plentiful comments on social media and the chat section of a livestreamed video, even from more reserved factions (Mackin, 2020, p. 26). Now, sermon videos provide this platform for contentious debates in the comments section between devotees and their opposing counterparts, as "different communities of practice" clash over worldviews that might have never encountered each other in day-to-day dealings (Pihlaja, 2014, p. 11). Some note that new media forms carve out spaces that never existed—places users are eager to inhabit and transform.

Because they proselytize and count converts, evangelicals constitute a fruitful segment of the American religious populace for further study of their rhetorical praxis. Evangelical preachers often encourage their congregations to conceive of their "faith journey" as a narrative arc; so-called "testimonies" follow a structure of being "lost" then "found" or being bereft and abandoned before becoming part of a larger "family" or "the people of God." Stromberg confirms the hypothesis that retelling meta-conversion stories frames parishioners' "personal experience in canonical language … [,] recreating that experience in the telling" (1993, p. 3). The way the story is told—even in the language used—becomes a shibboleth, a litmus test for insiders to gauge whose testimonies sound legitimate to the trained ear.

Despite its banal nature, a sermon represents a "discursive art in which capacities central to our human experience with language come together with respect to supersensory, superordinate, supernatural reality, typically imagined in the form of culturally significant otherworldly audiences— divine beings with whom human beings enjoy rich, complex relationships" (FitzGerald, 2012, p. 2). The other public expression reserved mostly for the senior pastor in a public worship service, prayer, performs "an illocutionary act, one that through the force of utterance contributes to unfolding events perceived as action willed or permitted by divine beings and assented to or challenged by human beings" (FitzGerald, 2012, p. 56). As sociolinguists intent on noticing novel ways speakers employ language, preaching becomes a fruitful source for qualitative analysis. Burke's *The Rhetoric of Religion* considers religion a linguistic phenomenon rather than an ontological system, noting that "religious cosmogonies are designed, in the last analysis, as exceptionally thoroughgoing modes of persuasion, [composed of] … a body of spoken and written *words*" (Burke, 1961, pp. v–vi, italics in original). Clifford Geertz (1973, p. 90), building on Burke's seminal work, further defines "religion" as a "system of symbols which acts to establish powerful, pervasive, and long-lasting moods and motivations in men [*sic*] by formulating conceptions of a general order of existence." In simpler terms, one can spot an evangelical based on the lexicon they utilize in speech.

Preachers participate—even unknowingly—in larger cultural conversations through the language they employ to persuasive effect. Speakers always embed implicature (viz., implicit meaning of statements—often beyond the literal interpretation) in their public discourse—even in personalized sermon introductions. FitzGerald (2012) notes that even "acts of invocation … claim a measure of agency for oneself" (p. 56), thereby not always "count[ing] as prayer" per se (p. 57). That statement should not imply that speaking prayerful words while attempting to persuade an assembled audience seems rhetorically suspect. Instead, several things occur simultaneously in this speech act—a fact that becomes easier to recognize the more familiar a person becomes with preaching. As a hearer infers meaning and acts on it, implicature helps to predict how various audiences interpret given utterances. These evangelical preachers address multiple audiences weekly, often making strong requests of their parishioners by implying what they want churchgoers to do, to avoid appearing demanding.

Pandemic Sermonic Rhetoric

The COVID-19 global pandemic shuttered churches worldwide for months, requiring congregations to respond to an exigence not seen since the Black Death: a highly contagious virus precluded in-person gatherings. Coronavirus arrived in the United States during March 2020. King County, Washington, in suburban Seattle, where I live and teach, was hit early by the virus. Reticent or ready, ministers from Kirkland to Kalamazoo preached to cameras rather than pews; the digital space explored affordances of uploaded sermon videos, broadening parish boundaries exponentially. Even after the reopening of physical locations, online church remains. Lockdown conditions have forever altered ministerial appeals to their faith-filled audiences—especially those reluctant to visit a steepled building.

Sourcing local examples of pastors who pivoted quickly to the new normal of online preaching became key to this case study. Finding two larger churches linked by geography yet different in theological interpretation or ecclesiastical praxis seemed tantamount. With the first recorded case of coronavirus being a Seattle man who had returned from a trip to Wuhan, China, and the first outbreak occurring at a convalescent center for geriatric patients in the same vicinity—in Kirkland, Washington, the very town where my university is located just five miles (approximately eight kilometers) away, the Puget Sound region seemed an ideal case study. Metro Seattle does not boast of many churches—let alone large ones. Once the home of Mars Hill, a now-defunct church numbering 7,000 in attendance at multiple locations, King County also is the location of Churchome (formerly City Church), a nationally known church pastored by celebrity pastors Judah and Chelsea Smith. Because Churchome has led digital Christendom in streaming services, podcasts, and sightings of musician Justin Bieber, actor Chris Pratt, or basketball player Kevin Durant, it seemed less representative of standard experience of the churchgoing public in the Pacific Northwest (WBUR). Instead, it was vital to find smaller, active churches that adapted to the online model, necessitating a shift technologically and linguistically.

Western Washington State, a busy tech sector, provided an excellent test case area, given the restrictions enacted by Governor Jay Inslee's executive order, labeled as the "Stay Home, Stay Healthy" initiative (Office of the Governor, 23 March 2020). These stay-at-home orders extended from 23 March 2020 until 4 May 2020, one of the longest periods when houses of worship were forced to close their doors in the United States. Even after some restrictions were lifted, Seattle-area churches were required to de-densify seating arrangements in church sanctuaries and auditoriums, thereby limiting the number of in-person worshipers who were allowed to attend Mass or a worship service—albeit masked. It was not until 30 June 2020 that King County churches were permitted to open to all congregants wearing face coverings indoors under Governor Inslee's "Safe Start" initiative (Office of the Governor, 18 June 2020).

During this pandemic period, in the bustling Seattle suburb of Bellevue, sat two thriving congregations, situated just one mile (1.6 kilometers) apart. Bellevue Presbyterian, known by locals simply as "BelPres," has been pastored by Dr. Scott Dudley, a Stanford University graduate in English literature, for 20 years. The other congregation, Doxa Church, relocated from an original Mars Hill building to nearby Redmond in May 2022, not far from tech giant Microsoft's international operations hub. When the coronavirus shutdowns commenced in 2020, the Rev. Jeff Vanderstelt served as senior pastor at the Bellevue location. The Rev. Eddie Williams, a former National Football League player for the Seattle Seahawks, was installed as Doxa's pastor in 2022. Not only did both churches appeal to people in this affluent, ethnically diverse suburb with buildings just a few city blocks from one another, but their respective websites continue to feature an archive of computer-generated sermon transcripts that stretch back to the beginning of the pandemic. Such linguistic artifacts, ready for analysis, are rare discoveries on American church websites that often limit their "Media" tabs to sermon videos only months old.

Finding representative evangelical sermon content for research into this new trend of attending church digitally was straightforward. If famously "unchurched" Seattle demonstrates a preaching trend, then the practice is likely to be occurring elsewhere (Garnick, 2014). According to the Hartford Institute for Religion Research (Bird & Thumma, 2020), the pre-pandemic number of American megachurches (with over 2,000 in attendance) was roughly 1,750 (p. 2). The largest churches of that subset (842 Protestant congregations) gather over three million people on any given Sunday (Marcotte, 2 April 2021). However, the median Sunday morning attendance at an American church stands at 65 persons (Faith Communities Survey, 2020). That demographic fact alone indicates that many American evangelicals are familiar with sermonic discourse and the ways that ministers welcome their congregants as they gather in person. Furthermore, these opening sections of sermons provide the most pertinent content for interpreting how the minister seeks to build a cohesive connection between himself and the audience—even if as virtual "attenders," these online participants were cut off from others' responses and engagement in ways that an in-person service would afford them.

SketchEngine, an online text analysis software, compiled the sermons preached at BelPres between March 2020 and March 2022 into a corpus comprising 479,921 individual words. Of these 104 transcribed sermons, the corpus linguistics software isolated 14,455 unique lexical terms. Conversely, the Doxa corpus from the same time frame totals 341,927 individual words, with 11,854 unique terms appearing. The much smaller corpus can be explained by the total number of sermon transcripts uploaded to the church's website. Only 54 sermons within the two-year period were recorded in this verbatim way. Some videos came with a discussion guide or nothing in writing. Additionally, the Doxa sermon videos stretch longer (generally 30–45 minutes) than Dr. Dudley's typical sermons at Bellevue Presbyterian, which clock in usually under 25 minutes.

Once the corpus of transcribed sermon excerpts was compiled for the following case study, salient linguistic and rhetorical features of the introductory communicative moment when the preachers greeted the online and seated parishioners were isolated using key words in context (KWIC), such as "technology," "online," "pandemic," and "at home." These findings were coded with similar labels if it appeared that speakers were making analogous rhetorical moves. I annotated a representative sample of extracts from March 2020, March 2021, and March 2022, labeling the transcripts by identifying various terms relevant to how the sermon discourse and its preachers construct an identity for their audience out of their words (White, 1990; Charland, 1987). While the potential way(s) to organize and analyze the results obtained by critical discourse analysis of digital sermon/ prayer extracts emerged from the data themselves, examining greetings and opening prayers by the selected preachers, the rhetorical appeals used, and the myriad ways power and authority are enacted in preaching in an American evangelical church context surfaced as paramount. Moreover, this study examines how a digital platform both reinforces and subverts ministerial power as speakers try to connect with their audience(s). This study focuses on the lexical/rhetorical choices preachers make to conceptualize key doctrinal notions (e.g., what "worship" means) aimed at their different audiences—live and remote—all while asserting their personal power as the primary rhetor in the sacred space. The premise of this research was that the labels preachers prefer to call their online viewers (i.e., the customary phrase-frames used to greet the audience in the opening moments of a sermon) help constitute an audience, thereby constructing something that heretofore never existed in the evangelical church tradition.

Read together, these chosen sermon transcripts that follow yield insights into larger, discourse-level moves those evangelical preachers practice. How an individual minister riffs on recognized rhetorical patterns, especially in performing prayer, "makes explicit the relations that exist between speaker and addressee, while avoiding complicated matters of audience" (FitzGerald, 2012, p. 40). Despite preachers' contention that prayer constitutes a "conversation with God," the varied audiences whom they negotiate (the self, the "live" congregation, the divine, and the uncountable virtual participants) redefine intercession as a "complex auditory space" (FitzGerald, 2012, p. 40). FitzGerald responds to Burke (1970), building on his dramatistic notion of scene with "prayer as performance before multiple audiences" that always includes "overhearers" (2012, p. 40). When pastors pray into a microphone in a public worship service streamed online, their goal extends beyond merely engaging the Almighty. Sometimes they are simply mimicking communicative patterns that they have overheard on celebrity pastor podcasts with thousands of weekly downloads, without considering how fundamentally these greetings have altered evangelical preaching.

For example, Rich Villodas has served as senior pastor of the diverse, nondenominational, New York City-based New Life Church for ten years. What strikes the New Life Church podcast listener, however, is the ease with which the charismatic Villodas addresses multiple audiences simultaneously, a skill likely honed two years prior when the largest U.S. city found itself the epicenter of multiple waves of coronavirus infections, hospitalizations, and deaths, as well as mask mandates, stay-at-home orders, and church closures.

He greets his congregation(s) thusly:

Amen! Thank you to our worship team. Good morning, friends! Uh, what a gift it is to … uh. worship with you. Uh, for those of you watching online, on YouTube, newlife <dot> nyc, on Facebook, my name is Rich. I'm the lead pastor here at New Life Fellowship Church in Queens, New York City. And wherever you're joining from, uh … it's a gift to have you with us. And for those of you in the room, at the end of our service, I'll be downstairs in the lobby. If we've never met before, or we haven't seen each other in a while, uh… I'd love to connect with you, so make your way to me, and introduce yourself … uh, to me, before we head out.

(26 September 2022)

By attending carefully to the semiotic resources that two Seattle-based churches employed during the earliest weeks of the coronavirus outbreak and its ensuing months, clearly many preachers employed a somewhat similar greeting template as Villodas with little regard of the long-term implications to the way parishioners—in-person and online—would view attending church once pandemic-related restrictions eased.

By mentioning his emotional response to these unfavorable communicative conditions brought on by Washington's governor's orders to close church doors, Doxa's pastor at the time, Vandervelt, likely echoes the feelings of his bewildered flock:

Well, hello, family. I am sad that we can't gather together, but I'm glad that technology allows us to do this together, and I'm excited about the idea that we are going to get to experience the Lord work in us new ways. The Spirit of God is going to work on our hearts and change us and form our faith in new ways in this season, and we believe God's going to still do a mighty work in this area. So I'm continuing to be full of hope—I miss seeing you, but I'm glad that we get to be together in other ways. I'd love it if we could start with prayer before we talk about this text. Let's pray.

(23 March 2020)

By calling the people catching the livestream "family," Vandervelt evokes a powerful metaphor. Families regularly experience difficulties, but truly resilient households weather storms well. His tripling of the lexical term "together" in the same utterance indicates his intention to appeal for corporate unity, even though an online viewer does little to participate in the discourse as it is happening. Even by referring to the stay-at-home period as a "season," a common metaphor in evangelical parlance to explain the way devotees' faith grows over time, the pastor implies that it will last for a certain duration before transitioning to another one. At the time, certainly Vandervelt could not have predicted how long the season would last or what it would cost the church.

Similarly, early during the lockdown, Dudley equated turning on the computer screen with implied participation, even if he had few guarantees that the congregation was doing anything other than passively taking in the content. He highlights the sacrifice of the "small team" running the livestream, as if the staff's being in the church building constitutes superlative service:

> Well, thank you for participating in worship with us and joining us. We are grateful as we said at the beginning that the governor's mandate to stay at home does allow for an exception for us to have a small team of people here to live stream, so we're grateful for that and thank you. Thank you for joining us.
>
> …
>
> Senior adults, we want you to know that we are praying for you, and we are ready to help you in any way that we possibly can. You can let us know if you need help for something on the Together at Home banner on our webpage, just go there and click on that. We are with you. It is a hard time. It's a hard time for all of us … . This is like this whole stay at home thing, no people, like it's just killing me.
>
> …
>
> BelPres, BelPres, we are people of hope. We are people of courage, and we are the people who bring God's healing.
>
> Sermon from 29 March (Bellevue Presbyterian Church, 2020)

Despite his discomfort, Dudley offers calm assurance by calling those watching "people of hope." After attributing courage to those contending with the pandemic isolation, he places a definite article, "the," in front of "people." This slight semantic shift carries larger implications. He is calling his audience out as the ones who will adopt an other-centered perspective, showing compassion to those in need. This altruism becomes his expectation of the audience he is conjuring into existence as he utters the words. In this way, Dudley employs constitutive rhetoric: his audience comprises members of a given people group, not merely individuals making decisions that only concern themselves.

Once he has constituted an audience to receive his message, Dudley eases into his familiar role. Nonetheless, he uses an abbreviation of the church's name—"BelPres"—for those committed attenders who are soldiering on through the pandemic with him. Below, Dudley opens a 2021 talk entitled "The Lion and the Lamb":

> Well, hello, BelPres. Thank you for joining us. Special shout out today to Eloise who is celebrating her 100th birthday; happy birthday, Eloise. We are so glad you have joined us for worship. My name is Scott. I'm the lead pastor here, and we are happy that you are with us.
>
> Sermon from 21 March (Bellevue Presbyterian Church, 2020)

The informality of wishing a happy birthday allows Dudley to come across as winsome and warm. The deictic term "here" functions semantically in an interesting way. Clearly, Rev. Dudley stands behind a pulpit in Bellevue, Washington, as he utters the sentence, but do online parishioners conceptualize him as their pastor, let alone one tied to a specific geographic location?

A week later (21 March 2021), a few blocks away, Pastor Vanderstelt preached a message entitled "John: The One Who Can See," drawing from John 9:1–9. Here, he points to abuses of power in polarized American politics:

> You know, we saw this happen in the American church this last year with "evangelicalism" where evangelicalism became paired up, in fact, I'd say enmeshed with a political system to the degree at which people's responses look nothing like the kingdom of God. The way that we responded to COVID or racism or the election, it looked nothing like Jesus. It just was an aberration of what Jesus is really like. And, Family, we saw it here at Doxa. I mean I was personally surprised by how many people at Doxa were way more committed to their political party than to the kingdom that Jesus is in charge of … . Maybe that's some of you. Maybe some of you are going like, man, I have been mostly concerned about how I preserve my position, how I maintain power, how I continue to live as someone who's privileged at the expense of somebody else. Maybe you've been blind in that way.
>
> Sermon from 21 March (Doxa Church, 2022)

Even though he purports to put into words what an audience member may be thinking, Vandervelt uses first-person pronouns that render him "blind": "*I* preserve my position, how *I* maintain power" (*emphasis* added). Such explicit references to holding an authoritative position seem rare from a pastor, yet much of the discursive conditions of a sermon rely on such embedded power relations. Without an implied sense that the preacher has earned the right to stand behind the pulpit to address the congregation, the entire communicative arrangement collapses. Vanderstelt calls attention to the persona behind his preaching, which might have been a risky prospect for the online viewers. Thieme (2010, p. 37) posits that "texts imagine and situate different audience constituents and how they expect different audience groups to act in response." One can only conjecture how the virtual congregation responded to Vandervelt's blunt approach.

BelPres similarly leverages an honest articulation of recent challenges. Dudley's sermon from 13 March 2022, "Hope Producing Church," opens with a greeting to two distinct groups: "Well, I want to say hello to those of you here in the room, as well as those of you joining us online … ." Next, he extols the congregation's inner resilience by listing the obstacles—serious and comedic—that they have overcome in recent years:

> Doesn't that describe the last two years in some ways? Like the news is so bad, sometimes you don't even want to get out of bed, or I mean, like the pandemic is getting better, we think, but it's kind of still out there, it's still with us … .We all need some hope, and that comes from Jesus, but it also comes through His people, the community, the Bible calls Church. When the Church is being who Jesus intended us to be, and let's be honest, sometimes that doesn't happen, but when the Church is what Jesus intended, when we are a community of believers becoming like Jesus, on mission together to heal the world, there's nothing like it. Historically, when that has happened, that community of people has brought Jesus' hope and healing both inside the church and outside.
>
> Sermon from 13 March (Bellevue Presbyterian Church, 2022)

This phrase "inside the church and outside" signals two corporate objectives: fellowship between like-minded souls, evoking the Pauline metaphor of "the Body of Christ" (cf. Romans 12:4–5), and evangelism, reaching the unconvinced with the gospel. Dudley calls his audience a "community of believers," repeating "community" a second time to signal that they belong to a group committed to being "on mission together," itself another reference to sharing the gospel. Beitler (2019, p. 158) posits that "[v]iewing our worship practices as a Christ-centered constitutive rhetoric productively blurs the distinction that many Christians make between worship and witness." On the one hand, a church service that has moved online acts as a convenient way to stay connected with one's church, while on the other, the internet acts as a broadcasting beacon, sending the signal out much further than the typical reach of a local church with the resources of Bellevue Presbyterian. With every message free and publicly available for download after the fact, the church has broadened its outreach efforts beyond its postal code.

At times it seems that the preacher misses his rhetorical opportunity to reach a broader audience beyond those he can see from the stage right then. Occasionally, these constitutive rhetorical moves occur outside the initial moments of the sermon. For instance, as Pastor Williams draws Doxa's preaching time on 20 March 2022 to a close, he pauses:

> Oh, and by the way, if God is working in your heart right now, and you're like, you know what? I identified with the guy in the story, and I feel like God's doing something in me and I felt the love. You're not here by accident. In fact, we're doing baptisms in that tub in about four weeks on Easter. So, you can make a proclamation of faith to Jesus today. You can talk to me, talk to an elder. They'll be up here to pray with you after. Talk to someone in the back, we'll sign you up and we will baptize you in there as a proclamation of your faith. So, you can go love people, too. How does that sound? Let's pray.
>
> Sermon from 20 March (Doxa Church, 2022)

Clearly, Williams's words are directed solely to the people whom he can see during the live service. The word "here" clearly refers to the auditorium in Redmond; those individuals who drove themselves to the physical location to hear his challenge are not present "by accident."

It seems significant that by March 2022, Doxa Church and Bellevue Presbyterian speakers give only scant attention to the online congregation. Just because preachers neglect to mention the constituted audience explicitly, this evangelistic genie has left the bottle. If the New Testament Greek term *euangelion* means "good news," the tacit message received by many American evangelicals during the pandemic was something akin to: "*Good news!* You do not *actually* have to go to church in person for it to count! There's a new way, endorsed by the people who set the rules: Church Online." Hutchings (2017, p. 240) prophesied this new reality by studying the phenomenon of online churches before the pandemic, noting how these digital congregations "become transformative 'third spaces', [*sic*] safe places for the reconsideration of traditions and norms."

At least two caveats are in order. Watching a live church service disconnected from the discursive conditions of being there in person may cause certain viewers to form opinions of what is occurring that differ dramatically from the communicator's intention, yet the speaker ultimately bears the responsibility for how a message is interpreted. Further, the difficulty with quantifying accurately the number of times distinct users download and listen to an online sermon makes it even more challenging to estimate how many people who have not converted to Christianity (viz., the assumed audience for evangelistic appeals) are listening regularly to Christian content online.

The way that such content, however, is marketed and presented, it seems likely that the listeners are already converted.

Reconstructing the context in which these transcribed church services occurred required thinking deeply about how making these spaces accessible onscreen alters the rhetoric. Time ended up being a very significant aspect where the context differed dramatically between the imagined live church setting and the virtual version. Preachers regularly repeat phrases that lack significant meaning past the moment of their utterance: for example, any indication to the present moment relative to the speaker (e.g., "If you're here today and want to ask Jesus into your heart …"). Obviously, a person listening to an archived sermon podcast while running on a treadmill weeks later is not included in the communicative intent of the original message. Whether that inability to respond excludes the person listening online calls into question a fundamental principle of critical discourse analysis: "how we talk about the world influences the society we create, the knowledge we celebrate and despise, and the institutions we build" (Machin & Mayr, 2012, p. 21). It becomes challenging to determine whether religious media that exempt online listeners from complying with the most basic instructions given to accomplish speech acts constitute forms of institutional Christianity or are an abrogation of it.

For these new media evangelism opportunities to connect with virtual audiences unfamiliar with their nuances, evangelicals should define certain key ecclesiastical terms initially and often in each sermon. Preachers cannot assume that online listeners share their religious jargon. The internet is a leveling medium, available to billions worldwide with little regard to social class, ethnicity, or creed (albeit with inequality of access in some parts of the world due to infrastructure issues and censorship in other parts). In fact, many atheist forums online regularly watch, critique, and comment on religious content. One of their primary critiques—that American evangelicalism is out of step with contemporary times—is supported by abundant linguistic proof in the form of uploaded sermon videos composed in an idiom barely decipherable to the average American. The repeated references to space/time (e.g., "if you're here tonight and need Jesus"), as well as the portrayal of easy-believism ("now you are a Christian") belie the arduous process that some individuals undergo toward embracing Christianity or the personal cost that they may incur via persecution for adopting a particular faith.

Preachers who opt to marshal the internet for proselytizing purposes must, therefore, understand this tension and adapt their lexis (if not their entire public persona in their material churches) to fit a digitally saturated landscape where sermons are forever archived and exist as things to be viewed, traded, interrogated, downloaded, and discussed, rather than temporary speech events. The internet renders users as spectators, viewing religious services in progress in ways that used to require a visit to a church building. The problem with looking through stained glass (even via the flickering blue screen of a mobile device) is that the image is distorted and colored by the lens through which one views the experience.

Implications and Future Directions

Attendance in American houses of worship has not rebounded post-pandemic, even as the number of people choosing to worship online swells. Gallup reports that 31 percent of Americans say that they attend a church, synagogue, mosque, or temple "weekly or nearly weekly," despite more than twice that number—67 percent—admitting that they did as children (Jones, 2022). Ministers find themselves struggling to explain this decline and the rise of the "Nones" (Zuckerman, 2014), but perhaps ministers inadvertently created this situation—or at least contributed significantly to its viral spread—by their words. During the coronavirus pandemic, churches faced a choice: meet online or close their doors for an indeterminate period. Millions of devout churchgoers logged on and heard their familiar pastor welcome them to a new community: "Church Online." There, nearly every aspect of the typical religious service found its digital counterpart: music, preaching, offerings, and even "fellowship" in the form of Zoom chat conversations. Moreover, these pastors connected in other new ways: daily or weekly video calls and devotional lessons for download.

While lacking the interpersonal connection that a live service can provide, online church during the pandemic had features superior to being "in person." Further, online church allows the con-sumeristic viewer to skip parts of the service that they may dislike (e.g., loud music), tuning in for the "main event": the sermon. Therefore, when the opportunity came for churches to return to their buildings, researchers should not be surprised that many chose (and continue to choose) the digital option. After all, often leaders greeted them initially by a linguistic label that had never existed: *Church Online,* constituting a group to explain this newer, easier way to "do church" without leaving the comforts of home. Church Online became in a sense a new social medium—a way to customize spiritual content for delivery in the most convenient way possible. With the rise of artificial intelligence software, how long until American megachurches employ ChatGPT to send personalized sermons with frequent mentions of the recipients' names to their respective inboxes for download? The U.S. market has enjoyed Instacart for food delivery for years; perhaps the day is coming for Instasermon™ for iPhone and Android.

Most American teens and adults have led mediated lives for years. It has been estimated that pre-pandemic, many of us interacted with smartphones 2,617 times per day over 76 different sessions (Naftulin, 2016). Although media scholars from Boston University and elsewhere refute this statistic as overestimated (Groshek, 2018), this number certainly jumped precipitously when the boredom of enforced social isolation set in. Much of the two and half hours per day that users spend on smartphones (Naftulin, 2016), they spend time checking social media sites, mimicking the notion of relational networks by amassing "friends" or "followers." It can be difficult at times to discern the difference between connections made over a screen or over the back of a church pew. Therefore, when nearly every local church opened a livestreamed service accessible with a few taps on the screen, it is no wonder that devout churchgoers flocked to this new way to "attend," even to become a part of a nascent community called Church Online. If it looks like church, sounds like church, and feels relationally warm like church, then it must actually *be* church, right? After all, authoritative messengers whom parishioners had grown to trust kept calling it "church." Now, many parsons have changed their tune.

While this case study analyzed a corpus of messages by two pastors who boast a certain localized following in the Seattle area, their sermons hardly rank among the most downloadable variety. Sociolinguists should research how the pandemic accelerated the phenomenon of the celebrity preacher, and what the impact may be on followers' faith or church attendance when a minister with a meteoric rise experiences a publicized crash landing. When Carl Lentz, former hipster pastor of Hillsong New York City, was exposed in 2020 as having conducted a years-long affair with a woman who had been a co-pastor of Hillsong Boston (Tong & Cosper, 2022), the amount of media attention and vitriol on Twitter against evangelicalism increased, all while many self-described Christians continued to curate their sermon playlist of other polished communicators whose megachurches number in the thousands.

Following the end of the official lockdown, podcasts dedicated to pastoral audiences have featured a recurring theme: encouraging despondent ministers whose congregations have not returned to their buildings post-pandemic, preferring instead the slick videos of even larger megachurches. One such offering, John Mark Comer's "Rule of Life," puts the host in conversation with noted author and former *Christianity Today* editor Andy Crouch as the two discuss the online church phenomenon, prognosticating the future by urging preachers to emphasize intrinsic, analog benefits that can only occur when believers gather in person authentically:

AC: … *if* we show up on Sunday mornings [laughter] …

JMC: And *if* we show up in bodies …

AC: R-r-r-right. Totally. Let's just say Sunday morning and extend it to the mediated version. We show up looking for a sort of spiritual device. Like, I hope that the worship band plays in such a way that I feel that…connection to God that I felt at some key moment in my life. That's why I keep coming back—to find that magic again. But I'm not here to be formed through a difficult path of humble, patient, you know, development. I'm here for someone to hit the right button and start the smoke machine or start that chord sequence that arouses certain emotional response[s].

JMC: Or have the encounter moment or hear the brilliant insight …

AC: Or hear "the Word" …

JMC: Yeah, different traditions…

AC: And then, when you take away the embodied, uh, dimension of that and you're just looking on Zoom, no wonder people gravitate to the people who are the best magicians, the people who make things or who are the best at making things seem to happen through media. They have the charisma; they've got the just…they've got the whole panoply of people behind the scenes making the magic appear on the screen …

JMC: They've got the formulaic spirituality: "Do these three things … ."

AC: And if you actually tried to mediate the truly most formative movements in human history, like the monastic movement… You've hung out in monasteries?

JMC: Yes!

AC: Imagine trying to make a true video about what happens there? [Both men laugh.] It's the most boring …

JMC: Cannot be done.

AC: Cannot be done. And that's actually the most formative thing, but we turn on our screen, and we're like: "Boy, I hope my local pastor can at least do enough magic that I don't switch and go to some famous pastor like John Mark Comer and watch him instead. And every pastor is trying to do this thing that cannot be done, which is give people a device that makes them close to God."

                                                                        (Comer, 2022)

This conversation suggests another fruitful vein for further linguistic research: the reintroduction of ancient terms from church history into the lexicon of a growing number of contemporary, countercultural communicators. Borrowed from liturgical, High Church traditions, these words (e.g., "sabbath," "lectio divina," "spiritual formation," and a "rule of life") are arising more and more from a group more comfortable preaching in a pair of denim jeans and a T-shirt than a suit and tie. These vaguely familiar terms espoused by proponents of a slowed-down spirituality (Scazzero, 2017, p. 142) act as brakes to decelerate the careening pace of the evangelical church toward contemporary obsolescence.

Further Reading

Campbell, H.A. (Ed.) (2020). *Religion in quarantine: The future of religion in a post-pandemic world.* Digital Religious Publications.

This collection of brief essays from scholars in the Texas A & M Religious Studies department comprises different predictions made when the world found itself in lockdown, both anticipating cultural and religious trends and foregrounding perspectives that academics held mid-pandemic regarding the viability of online religious observance—a boon to researchers.

Huggins, N.J. & Djupe, P.A. (2022). Congregation shopping during the pandemic: A research note. *Journal for the Scientific Study of Religion, 61*(3–4), 726–736. https://onlinelibrary.wiley.com/doi/epdf/10.1111/jssr.12802

Huggins and Djupe analyze data from October 2020 surveys, surmising that the shakeup in established contemporary American religious practice brought on by COVID-19 led many churchgoers to investigate other congregations and preachers outside their denominational traditions, irrespective of political influences. This piece suggests a fluidity to American Christian allegiance.

Hutchings, T. (2017). *Creating church online: Ritual, community and new media.* Routledge.

Even though Hutchings mostly explores alternative faith communities on the internet, this book validates online churches as genuine congregations, especially for seekers who find themselves drawn toward the novelty of digital religion.

Pihlaja, S. (2020). The style of online preachers. In H. Ringrow & S. Pihlaja, (Eds.), *Contemporary media stylistics*, 297–315). Bloomsbury Academic.

This chapter highlights how digital sermons can be commodified and shared widely on social media platforms, especially when the self-proclaimed preacher knows the audience well enough to influence their spread.

Yang, S.A. (2021). The word digitalized: A techno-theological reflection on online preaching and its types, *Homiletic, 46*(1), 75–90.

Yang, a professor at an American Christian university, points out the theological dearth surrounding online homiletics—a gap he fills with Karl Barth's threefold definition of the divine Word. By providing this theological framework, Yang adds further legitimacy to livestreamed church for those faithful who may have questioned its merit.

References

Beitler III, J.E. (2019). *Seasoned speech: Rhetoric in the life of the church.* IVP Academic.

Bellevue Presbyterian Church. (2022). *Sermon transcripts.* BelPres. www.belpres.org/sermon-transcripts

Benwell, B. & Stokoe, E. (2006). *Discourse and identity.* Edinburgh University Press.

Bird, W. & Thumma, S. (2020). *Megachurch 2020: The changing reality in America's largest churches.* Hartford Institute for Religion Research.

Bourgeois, D. (2013). *Ministry in the digital age: Strategies and best practices for a post-website world.* InterVarsity Press

Burke, K. (1970). *The rhetoric of religion: Studies in logology.* University of California Press.

Charland, M. (1987). Constitutive rhetoric: The case of the *peuple Quebecois. Quarterly Journal of Speech, 73*, 133–150.

Comer, J.M.C. (Host). (2022). *Luminary interview: Andy Crouch.* Audio podcast 31 October. https://podcasts.apple.com/us/podcast/luminary-interview-andy-crouch/id1646299048?i=1000584495528

Cooperman, A., Smith, G., & Ritchey, K. (2015). *America's changing religious landscape: Christians decline sharply as share of population; unaffiliated and other faiths continue to grow.* Pew Research Center. www.pewforum.org/2015/05/ 12/americas-changing-religious-landscape/

Doxa Church. (21 March 2022). *Media library.* Doxa-Church. www.belpres.org/sermon-transcripts

Faith Communities Survey. (2020). Twenty years of congregational change: The 2020 Faith Communities Today overview. Faith Communities Today.

FitzGerald, W. (2012). *Spiritual modalities: Prayer as rhetoric and performance.* Penn State University Press.

Garnick, C. (2014). *Christians discuss life in 'unchurched' Northwest. Seattle Times.* 27 September www.seattletimes.com/seattle-news/christians-discuss-life-in-lsquounchurchedrsquo-northwest/

Geertz, C. (1973). *Interpretation of cultures.* Basic Books.

Groshek, J. (2018). No, you probably don't touch your phone 2,617 times per day: A rationale for the Journal of Communication Technology. *Journal of Communication Technology, 1*(1), 1–29. https://doi.org/10.51548/joctec-2018-001

Hill, T. (2016). (Re)Articulating difference: Constitutive rhetoric, Christian identity, and discourses of race as biology. *Journal of Communication and Religion, 39*(1), 26–45.

Hutchings, T. (2017). *Creating church online: Ritual, community and new media.* Routledge.

Jones, J.M. (2022,). *In U.S., childhood churchgoing habits fade in adulthood.* Gallup. 21 December. https://news.gallup.com/poll/467354/childhood-churchgoing-habits-fade-adulthood.aspx

Machin, D., & Mayr, A. (2012). *How to do critical discourse analysis: A multimodal introduction.* SAGE Publishing.

Mackin, R.S. (2020). Reimagining church after quarantine: Online worship at Friends UCC. In Campbell, H.A. (Ed.). *Religion in quarantine: The future of religion in a post-pandemic world*, 24–27. Digital Religious Publications.

Marcotte, A. (2021). Church membership is in a freefall, and the Christian right has only themselves to blame. *Salon*, 2 April. www.salon.com/2021/04/02/church-membership-is-in-a-freefall-and-the-christian-right-has-only-themselves-to-blame/

Morgan, D. (2011). Mediation or mediatisation: The history of media in the study of religion. *Culture and Religion: An Interdisciplinary Journal*, *12*(2), 137–152.

Naftulin, J. (2016). Here's how many times we touch our phones every day. Business Insider. 13 July. Springer.

New Life Fellowship. (2022). *The church at Smyrna.* [Video]. 26 September. https://youtu.be/kTzJ0gdukE0

Office of the Governor (23 March 2020). Proclamation by the Governor Amending Proclamation 20-05: Stay Home–Stay Healthy. www.governor.wa.gov/sites/default/files/proclamations/20-25%20Coronovirus%20Stay%20Safe-tay%20Healthy%20%28tmp%29%20%28002%29.pdf

Office of the Governor (18 June 2020). Inslee announces updated religious and faith-based services guidance. www.governor.wa.gov/news-media/inslee-announces-updated-religious-and-faith-based-services-guidance

Perrin, A. (2021,). Mobile technology and home broadband 2021. 3 June. Pew Research Center. www.pewresearch.org/internet/2021/06/03/mobile-technology-and-home-broadband-2021/

Pihlaja, S. (2014). *Antagonism on YouTube: Metaphor in online discourse.* Bloomsbury.

Pihlaja, S. (2020). The style of online preachers. In H. Ringrow & S. Pihlaja, (Eds.), *Contemporary media stylistics*, 297–315. Bloomsbury Academic.

Rocha, C. (2021). Cool Christianity: The fashion-celebrity-megachurch industrial complex. *Material Religion*, *17*(5), 580–602.

Scazzero, P. (2017). *Emotionally healthy spirituality.* Zondervan.

Stromberg, P. (1993). *Language and self-transformation: A study of the Christian conversion narrative.* Cambridge University Press.

Thieme, K. (2010). Constitutive rhetoric as an aspect of audience design: The public texts of Canadian suffragists. *Written Communication*, *27*(1), 36–56.

Tong, S. & Cosper, M. (2022,). *Hillsong megachurch faces scandals, uncertain future.* WBUR. 26 July. www.wbur.org/hereandnow/2022/07/26/hillsong-megachurch-future

White, J.B. (1990). *Justice as translation.* University of Chicago Press.

Yang, S.A. (2021). The word digitalized: A techno-theological reflection on online preaching and its types. *Homiletic*, *46*(1), 75–90.

Zuckerman, P. (2014). The rise of the nones: Why more Americans are becoming secular, and what that means for America. In A.B. Pinn (Ed.), *Theism and public policy: Humanist perspectives and responses*, 37–52. Palgrave Macmillan.

16

LANGUAGE POLICIES AND RELIGIOUS PRACTICE

Anthony J. Liddicoat

Introduction and Background

Language plays an important role in religious activities, and religious institutions therefore need to make decisions about which languages they will use for the various activities associated with the conduct of religion. It is in making such decisions that religious institutions engage in processes of making language planning and policy (LPP). In multilingual contexts, such decisions may be complex as competing possibilities may be available for religious use. However, religious institutions may also add further languages or language varieties to those used in the surrounding secular community as a further element of complexity. The study of language planning in religious contexts is also complicated by how a religion interfaces with other aspects of human life and society.

Firstly, religion is both a public and a private matter and so language choices in religious practice may involve both collective and individual choices. Private religious acts such as prayer and other devotions are personal and individual acts and decisions about language use are to some extent private and personal, but the language choices made may be influenced by both public and private language norms; for example, private prayer or scripture reading may be done in the language used for public worship or in the language one uses as part of daily life. While the public dimensions of religious practice are most easily observed, the ways that they influence and are influenced by more private practices are also important to consider (Avni, 2012).

Secondly, language-related work in religion extends beyond strictly religious practices and may influence wider societal norms of language learning and use. For example, substantial research has been done on the language planning impact of Christian missionary bodies as agents of European colonialism (Womack, 2012). Through their work in evangelisation and education, such missionaries have played a central role in the dissemination of the colonial languages and in codifying and standardising languages of those they have evangelised and educated. The focus of such studies is not specifically on the languages used for religion but rather on the work of religious actors in wider societal language planning and policy issues (Spolsky, 2003).

The scope of interactions between religion and LPP is thus wide and much of what happens in this sphere is not specifically focused on religious practice itself but extends into wider language issues. This chapter will focus on aspects of LPP in specifically religious practices, as these have been less widely researched. It will consider the ways that religious institutions make decisions

DOI: 10.4324/9781003301271-18

about language use in two main aspects of communal religious practice: public worship and disseminating knowledge of the religion. However, these two areas of practice represent only a part of the complex and diverse relationship between language and religion. The chapter will therefore begin by reviewing aspects of LPP to investigate the range of possible connections between religion and LPP work.

Studies in LPP involve the identifying, analysis, and critique of the language norms within social contexts that reveal decisions about which languages can be used in specific contexts; which forms of language are normalised for such use; the functions for which languages can be used in such contexts; which languages will be supported (or not) for development and teaching; and which languages will be considered of value in specific domains of use. While the general topic of the language of religion has been widely researched, issues related to LPP in religious contexts have to date not been as widely investigated, although work in the field of LPP often mentions religious language as an area of interest (e.g., Kaplan & Baldauf, 1997; Spolsky, 2009).

LPP involves interventions into linguistic ecologies to influence aspects of language use and several different aspects of language use are subject to such interventions. In LPP studies, four key areas of intervention are typically identified: status policy and planning, corpus policy and planning, language-in-education, or acquisition, policy and planning, and prestige policy and planning. All these activities can be seen in the work of religious actors, although they impact on religious practice in different ways.

Status policy and planning refers to the norms of language choice that exist within a society or institution. In any society or institution there may be multiple languages that could potentially be used for communication or other functions that exist in a society or institution. Status policy and planning involves determining which language(s) will be included and which will be excluded in the relevant domains covered by the policy. In the case of religion, status policy and planning mostly specifically relates to the choice of languages for public use within the public acts of the faith community (Liddicoat, 2012b). In some cases, religious institutions may simply replicate the policies of the society in which they are located, for example, by using the official language(s) of the society for religious work. However, in other cases, their status policy may deviate from the society's policies for part or all of their work, for example, when a language that is not normally used in the society is used in public worship, in religious education, or in other contexts. Such policies may be multilingual or monolingual depending on prevailing societal language practices and ideologies. Multilingual policies may be quite complex, reflecting different ways of using languages and different purposes for using a language for different aspects of religious practice.

Corpus planning refers to decision-making about norms relating to the form of a language, such as orthography, lexicon, and grammar and typically involves processes of codification and standardisation. Corpus planning is often a secondary activity of religious LPP actors, being required in order to undertake some aspects of religious practice but not being oriented specifically to religious use. Missionaries have often been involved in corpus planning as a result of their missionary aims, especially in the spreading of scripture-based religions. Such religions may require written texts to be produced for languages that previously lacked written norms and thus their use in literate practice requires the establishment of such norms. For example, St Cyril is credited with the development of the Glagolitic/Cyrillic script as a necessary tool for disseminating Christian worship among the Slavs (Hetényi & Ivanič, 2021). In addition, as educated members of their communities, religious figures have often played a role in the development of literate resources for vernacular languages, for example, the development of Ajami—the writing of African languages in Arabic script—by Muslim clerics in West Africa (Diallo, 2012), or the production of pedagogical grammars for use in schools by Christian missionaries as an adjunct to developing scriptural literacy in the local languages of their converts (Hernández Triviño, 2016).

Language-in-education planning refers to language decisions made in educational contexts, relating to literacy development medium of instruction, language programmes and content, and additional language learning. Religious institutions have often played a role in the development of education and have exerted an influence on language choices within educational contexts. In religions that place a strong emphasis on individual access to religious texts, education to develop forms of literacy in the language of these texts has been especially important and religious practice has often been accompanied closely with educational work: for example, the teaching of Arabic for Quranic recitation (Günther, 2020), the teaching of Hebrew in Jewish schools (Avni, 2012a), or the literacy promotion of Protestant Christian Churches (Boppart et al., 2014). Religious institutions have also been influential in wider forms of education and many religious institutions run education programmes covering both secular and religious content. In establishing educational systems, religious institutions have adopted a range of different language policies. In some contexts, religious schools have implemented the language policies of the wider society, adopting official languages as languages of education or disseminating colonial languages through education (Diallo, 2012; Pennycook & Makoni, 2005). However, religious schools have also been important for maintaining and supporting minority languages in education, especially where the minority language has important religious functions. In Australia, for example, the Greek Orthodox Church has promoted schools in which Greek is used as the main language of instruction, supporting language maintenance and facilitating students' involvement in the Greek-language liturgy, while also developing English for participation in the wider society (Tamis, 2005).

Prestige policy and planning refers to attempts to change perceptions of a language in a society and to influence how a language is valued by its speakers or learners. Religious institutions are not centrally involved in this form of LPP work, but their language-related decisions often have consequences for the prestige of languages. When a language is chosen by a religious institution for use in the religious domain, this can grant prestige to a language and enhance perceptions of it compared to languages which are not used in this domain. For example, Dunn (2005) notes that the selection of Roviana as the lingua franca language of the Methodist Mission on the island of Roviana in the Solomon Islands led to this language gaining considerable prestige over other languages of the island, which in turn led to the acquisition of Roviana by other groups and the marginalisation of other languages in the literate practices of the islands' diverse linguistic communities.

Within LPP studies, a research focus on LPP in religious organisations has emerged as the result of a changing focus in the field that has expanded research and scholarship beyond the study of the policy documents of governments and governmental institutions (known as macro-level LPP) to examine to examine a wider range of situations (meso- and micro-level LPP) and a wider range of ways of encoding decisions about language (Liddicoat, 2012a). The traditional view of language policy as the study of the textual products of macro-level institutions is quite constraining for understanding decision-making about languages in religious institutions, as such institutions range from supra-national bodies, such as the Catholic Church, to local, independent groups of worshippers, and, as a result, decisions about language use can be enshrined in many different forms from official documents to tacit understandings of linguistic norms. It has therefore been useful in studying LPP and religion to adopt a wide view of language policy that sees it as something that can be done at any societal level and as something that exists in different forms in different contexts. Moreover, when LPP is considered as spanning macro and micro contexts, examining the ways that policies are transmitted across these levels and how local contexts and actors influence the forms that policies take becomes possible.

Policy exists in both covert and overt forms and is often represented in less codified forms. Contemporary approaches to LPP view language policies as existing in three broad forms:

- Policies as texts—documents of varying degrees of officialness that exist to establish and communicate norms of language selection and language use. Policy texts are "textual interventions into practice" (Ball, 1993, p. 12) that construct representations of desirable norms of language use that are both overt and explicit.
- Policies as discourse—the prevailing thoughts, beliefs, and values that are communicated through dominant ways of speaking and thinking about languages and which construct a framework for understanding certain language practices as legitimate and desirable and others as deviations from desired norms (Lo Bianco, 2005). The norms about language selection and use in policies as discourse may be overt or covert, explicit, or implicit.
- Practised policies—the patterned practices of language selection and use that reveal usually tacit understandings of norms of linguistic conduct (Bonacina-Pugh, 2012). Practised policies are typically covert and implicit and may be adhered to unconsciously as common-sense assumptions about linguistic normality in a particular context.

The discussion above shows that the ways that religion is involved in LPP is complex and multifaceted, reflecting the complex ways that religions function in human life and society. This complexity is also influenced by the ways that religious institutions are organised; some may be highly organised and legalistic with strongly formalised decision-making structures, while others may have less formal, local, and fluid ways of making decisions. These aspects of context are always important for understanding how and why language decisions are made with any faith community.

Language Policies and Religious Practice

The following discussion will consider two central areas of religious practice—liturgy and proselytisation. These two dimensions have been chosen because they are core elements of religious practice and because their different foci reveal different contextual factors influencing multiple aspects of decision-making about languages and their use in religious contexts.

Language Policies for Liturgical Practice

Liturgical practice, that is, acts of public communal worship being a primary site where religious institutions need to engage with choices of language and such acts typically require highly marked and self-conscious uses of linguistic resources (Keane, 1997). For some religions, the selection of a language for communal worship does not initially appear to be the result of a decision-making process so much as a continuation of long-established linguistic practices that have become common-sense norms; that is, they represent practised forms of policy. The decisions that created the existing norms are thus part of a remote past that continues to exert influence over later practice. Examples of such linguistic norms include the use of Hebrew in Judaism, Classical Arabic in Islam, Sanskrit in Hinduism, Ge'ez in Ethiopian Christianity, and, until the 1970s, Latin in Catholicism (Liddicoat, 2012b).

One consequence of the entrenchment of historical linguistic practices in religious use is that over time the language used in religion and the language used in other societal contexts may come to differ. Such languages often have marginal places in the overall language ecology of the faithful, and although being a regular part of their religious practice, they are languages that are little known or used by members of the faith community. Where past linguistic practices have become embedded within religious practice, their use often acquires the status of an article of faith and so become naturalised as the common-sense practice of religion that is not open to further decision-making. In other religious institutions, the choice of language for communal religious practice is considered as something that can legitimately be decided by the faithful and is responsive to the conditions of contemporary language ecologies. For example, Protestant, Orthodox, and modern Catholic Christianity have adopted languages of local faith communities as liturgical languages for some, or all, of the liturgy. These two different approaches to the choice of liturgical language are part of a continuum between highly fixed, doctrinally sanctioned language choices and more fluid choices that respond to local linguistic needs. They also represent two different understandings of the role and nature of language within liturgical practice. Liddicoat (2012b, 2013) refers to these orientations as sacrality and comprehensibility.

The sacral orientation views language itself as a sacred artefact, the use of which contributes to the sacred nature of the liturgical event (Liddicoat, 1993). When a language is viewed as a sacred artefact, it may convey a sacred dimension to other aspects of its use. For example, Posner (n.d.) argues that particular ways of using Hebrew convey holiness even to mundane objects: "It is not proper to use the lettering used for writing Torahs, *tefillin* and *mezuzot* for mundane purposes. Anything written or printed with such lettering must also be treated as a holy object," and that such objects must be disposed of reverently regardless of their mundane content. When language is viewed as a sacred construct, it is seen as confirming the holiness of the act of worship by endowing it with reverent and often mystical features. In the sacral orientation, liturgical acts may be understood as communications between the performer of the act (e.g., a priest) and its divine recipient in which the remainder of the faithful are secondary participants, whose role and presence may be incidental the conduct of the liturgy itself. For example, in Orthodox Christianity the part of the faithful is usually undertaken by a choir acting on their behalf; in the traditional Catholic liturgy the role of the faithful was performed either by a server, in spoken services, or by a choir and servers in sung services; and in Islam the linguistic parts of the liturgy are performed by the Imam on behalf of the assembled faithful. In such contexts, the relationship of the faithful to the liturgy may be that of an observer, although this may be understood as active and prayerful participation and connected with significant liturgical actions, such gestures, body postures, etc.

The comprehensibility orientation sees language having its primary role in addressing the faithful, directly, or indirectly, and the aim of the liturgy is not simply to address a deity but also to communicate aspects of the faith to the participants and to allow the faithful conscious and informed participation in the act of worship. Liturgical action is therefore understood as a collective religious act, a form of instruction, and a way of propagating beliefs (Maltby, 1998). The choice of liturgical language therefore needs to allow for the participation of the faithful and this needs to be a language variety that is known and used in the community. The comprehensibility orientation was fundamental for the Protestant Reformation, which promoted the use of vernacular languages in public workshop. For example, Article XXIV of the 1563 Anglican Articles of Religion states: "It is a thing plainly repugnant to the Word of God, and the custom of the Primitive Church, to have publick Prayer in the Church, or to minister the Sacraments in a tongue not understanded of the people."

The sacral orientation focuses on liturgical action as an experience of the divine as mysterious, numinous, and transcendent. Understanding of the liturgy is a secondary concern—something that is desirable but not necessary for the efficacy of the liturgy. In sacral approaches some aspects of the liturgical action may not be intended to be heard by all participants, for example being said quietly or covered by other actions, such as choral chanting, as occurs in the Latin-language Tridentine Catholic liturgy. The comprehensibility orientation is located within an experience of the divine as immanent and personal and emphasises an intellectual communion that requires an understanding and participation in the language being used. The two orientations, however, can be seen as potentially relevant in a single context and should not be considered as mutually exclusive orientations.

The LPP dimensions of choice of liturgical language are most obvious where the views of religious institutions shift between the two orientations as the result of societal, theological, or other changes. In some contexts where a comprehensibility orientation originally shaped language choice, the language may become imbued with sacral features because of its use in religious events and this can give rise to linguistic conservatism and the maintenance of language varieties even when they are no longer fully comprehensible for the faithful. For example, in Orthodox Christian Churches, classical varieties have been maintained as liturgical languages, as in the case of the Greek and Armenian Churches, or a language has been maintained after it has ceased to be used for other functions, as in the case of the use of Old Church Slavonic in Orthodox churches in Russia and other Slavic language contexts, Coptic in Egypt, or Ge'ez in Ethiopia. The adoption of Latin in the place of Greek by the early Christian churches in Rome was motivated by a comprehensibility orientation (Lafferty, 2003), but afterwards solidified into a sacral orientation that perpetuated the use of Latin after it has ceased to be regularly spoken. Similarly, in some cases the language of the vernacular liturgies of the Protestant Reformation was not modified in step with language use in the community creating registers which are uniquely associated with religion (Spolsky, 2003). The emphasis on sacrality may also be seen in other manifestations of linguistic conservatism such as the deliberate selection of archaic varieties for liturgical use or using archaising forms of the language for aesthetic or other reasons (Wales, 2001).

Religious institutions that adopt a comprehensibility orientation may be involved in LPP work that is required to implement their orientation, but which may also contribute beyond the immediate context of religious use. For example, the work of Protestant missionaries and the shift towards vernacular liturgies in the post-Vatican II Catholic Church have led to the introduction of local languages into liturgical practice, which has sometimes required the development of orthographic and other language norms and has often been accompanied by the development of educational programs in these languages. In diasporic contexts, religious organisations with a comprehensibility orientation may decide to replace the liturgical language used in their place of origin with the language of the host country because of language shift in the community (Wigglesworth, 2008) or they may become sites for language maintenance by using immigrant languages as liturgical languages in the host country (Souza et al., 2012). In multilingual contexts, decisions about which language to select where multiple languages could possibly satisfy the comprehensibility criterion can reflect the underlying value system and language ideologies that are present in the local language ecology (Hoenes del Pinal, 2016), indicating that decision-making about languages in religious contexts is linked to wider discourses about languages in the society and is not restricted to purely religious concerns.

As argued above, these orientations can be seen as poles on a continuum and both orientations may coexist within liturgical events and different elements of the liturgy may be subject to different decision-making processes. In religions with a sacral orientation, some activities, especially those considered as adjuncts to the liturgy proper, may be done in the usual language of the congregation e.g., preaching and hymn singing, or elements done in the liturgical language may be repeated in the language of the congregation as an extra-liturgical act, as in the case of parallel scripture readings. Similarly, religious institutions with a comprehensibility orientation may use languages not generally known by the faithful in their liturgies for historical or aesthetic reasons, as in the case of singling Latin versions of liturgical texts in the liturgies of some Protestant churches. Decisions about such uses of languages are generally made locally and reflect the needs and values of the specific groups for which the language policy is designed.

Preaching within a liturgy is an important point for decision-making about language choice as the aim is to convey knowledge and understanding of the faith for the faith community. As the intended recipient is the congregation, a comprehensibility orientation would appear to be most effective in realising the goals for this element of a religious ritual. However, other considerations may play a role in how the choice of languages for preaching is planned (Liddicoat, 2012b). In liturgical traditions with a comprehensibility orientation, all elements of the liturgy would normally be done using the same comprehensibility criterion across contexts. In religious contexts where an archaic variety of the language is used however, preaching is most normally done in the contemporary variety unless religious texts expressed in the archaic variety are being referenced. In liturgical traditions with a sacral orientation to the liturgy, a comprehensibility orientation usually prevails for preaching, which is done in the usual language of communication of the congregation. In Judaism, for example, the sermon at weekly services is normally delivered in the language of the congregation and this has been an element of synagogue worship since the sermon emerged as a liturgical practice, with preachers using Aramaic in Palestine and Greek in diasporic Jewish communities, and is evidenced in early Talmudic Judaism (Joseph, 1890). The choice of language for preaching was also a language planning issue in the early history of Catholicism with the Carolingian reform synod of 813 requiring homilies to be delivered "*in rusticam romanam linguam aut theotiscam quo facilius cuncti possint intelligere que dicuntur*" [In rustic Romance or German so that those present can more easily understand what is said] (Jungmann, 1986 [1951], p. 584), which explicitly emphasises the need for comprehensibility for sermons, even though the use of Latin elsewhere was not questioned. Nonetheless, in religious traditions with a sacral orientation, other practices have also existed that reflect the privileging of the sacred language over community vernaculars. For example, in mediaeval Catholicism, Latin sermons continued long after Romance-speaking congregations had switched to local vernaculars and macaronic sermons mixing Latin and a local vernacular were also found (Constable, 1994). In Judaism there is evidence of vernacular preaching being replaced by preaching in Hebrew in the early modern period (Meyer, 1988). The selection of Hebrew appears to have been a marker of distinctiveness for Jewish communities in predominantly Christian societies in which vernacular preaching was the norm.

Language Policy and Proselytisation

Proselytisation, or the conversion of non-believers, is considered a religious duty in many religions, most notably in Christianity (evangelisation) and Islam (*da'wah*) but is also a relevant religious practice in other religions. The dissemination of religious belief is an act of communication, often across linguistic and cultural boundaries, and so decisions about language play a significant role in proselytising work. For religious institutions involved in disseminating their beliefs, there may be several possible languages that could be used including official languages of the areas in which the religion is being disseminated, other languages spoken by the communities in which the dissemination work is to occur, and the languages spoken by those who will disseminate religious teachings. Given the aims of proselytisation, it would appear on the surface that the appropriate language to be designated as the language of conversion work would be a language that is understood by the intended audience, but other factors also play a role in decision-making about language choices (Liddicoat, 2012b).

The various language issues confronted by religious institutions in disseminating their beliefs can be seen in the historical work of Spanish-speaking missionaries in Latin America. In the early history of Latin American missionary work, the Spanish government viewed proselytisation as part of the colonising project and intervened directly and explicitly in the language policies of missionary organisations. For example, Charles V ordered the Dominican order to include the teaching of Spanish as part of their missionary work. In his order, Charles V argued that Spanish was the most suitable language for spreading Christian ideas: "*parece que está es la forma más rápida para che estos pueblos sean capaces de tener una acabada comprensión del Dios verdadero y de ser instruidos en nuestra santa fe católica*" [it appears that this is the fastest form by which these people will be able to have a full understanding of the true God and to be instructed in our holy Catholic faith] (de Solano, 1991, p. 49). Underlying this order was both a colonialist project of disseminating Spanish as a means of political control and a belief that languages which are closely associated with the usual practice of a religion are better adapted to the expression of the concepts of that religion. The idea that religious concepts are better conveyed in one language than another resonates with the idea of languages as sacred and has also affected religious views of the untranslatability of sacred texts (Delisle & Woodsworth, 1995). The colonialising agenda of religious conversion was articulated more explicitly in the 1513 Leyes de Burgos, which required that missionary priests should provide the sons of local chiefs with four years of education in the Spanish language and the Catholic religion to prepare them to return to their own communities as teachers of language and religion. Proselytisation thus served to develop a local enculturated elite.

The language policy of the Spanish government did not however prove effective for religious aims of the Catholic Church and the use of Spanish as the language of proselytising work was largely rejected in favour of local languages. Individual missionaries had in fact used local languages from the beginning of their work in the Americas, but in the second half of the sixteenth century this became the official policy of missionary institutions (Sánchez, 1996). The First Council of Lima (1551) declared an obligation to use local languages in missionary work and supported the production of religious works in Quechua and Aymara. The Second Council of Lima (1567) explicitly recommended that missionaries learn Quechua and introduced a fine for missionaries who had not made sufficient progress in the language. It also banned the use of interpreters. The provisions were later ratified by the state; in 1578, Phillip II introduced a requirement for missionary priests to know local languages (Ordóñez, 2007). In the context of disseminating the Catholic faith, the adoption of local languages was limited to catechesis, preaching, and other forms of religious teaching and the liturgical language remained Latin, which was rarely taught to converts (Sánchez & Dueñas, 2002).

Other missionary groups have adopted a policy of using local languages in missionary work. This is the case for many Protestant missions, where the use of local languages is motivated at least in part by their comprehensibility orientation to collective worship (Liddicoat, 2012b). As Christianity is a text-based religion, part of the work of conversion of missionary organisations has often included the production of religious texts such as bibles, prayer books, and hymnals. As noted above, this work has been associated with corpus policy and planning and language-in-education policy and planning and this association between proselytisation and other LPP activities has had consequences for how local language ecologies have developed. Where multiple religious denominations have worked in the same region, there has been a tendency for each group to work in isolation from others and for each to adopt different policies in relation to the development of the language varieties of the areas. One consequence of this is for linguistic continua to be disrupted along religions lines. For example, Chimhundu (1992) reports colonial Zimbabwe, closely related language varieties became associated with particular branches of Christianity: Karanga with the Dutch Reformed Church, Ndau with the American Methodists, Manyika with the Anglican Church, and Zezuru with the Catholic Church and the Wesleyan Methodists. Missionary work has constructed differences in the forms of written varieties that minimise the similarities between spoken languages and emphasise differentiation, with the consequence that linguistic boundaries which were not salient before the arrival of the missionaries have now become reified (Pennycook & Makoni, 2005).

The experience of proselytisation in Latin America discussed above reveals a potential tension between differing goals that missionaries may face between strictly religious objectives and colonialist or nationalist objectives, especially where religious institutions receive state support. In part, this tension arises because bringing people into a new religion is both a religious and a cultural endeavour, as proper adherence to a religion is often understood as adherence to the wider cultural values and expectations of the societies from which the religion is diffused. This means that religious and nationalist objectives can be closely intertwined. For example, the work of the Dhammacarik programme, which aimed to disseminate Buddhism among the animist hill tribes in Thailand, was based on the idea that disseminating Buddhism was a way to integrate minorities into the Thai nation and to establish loyalty to Thailand in precarious border regions (Platz, 2003). The programme opted to use Thai as the language of proselytisation as this was consistent with their nationalist and assimilatory objects. Similarly, Protestant missionary groups, despite their comprehensibility orientation, have also spread their national languages as part of their work in colonial contexts, often with specifically colonial objectives or with the aim of introducing civilisation to the hitherto 'uncivilised' (Porter, 1997). Language policies for proselytisation can thus be influenced by ideologies and objectives outside the purely religious domain and different decisions about language can reveal underlying tensions between religious and non-religious objectives.

Implications and Future Directions

Religion as belief system plays a significant role in giving meaning to human experience and articulating the nature of that experience is a central part of the communal expression of faith. As a communal activity, religion is essentially connected with language as it is language that allows a faith community to function as a community. This means that decision-making about language is central to the conduct of religious practice and that all faith communities thus have a language policy, whether this is overtly expressed or not. Studying LPP and religion reveals significant ways in which religion is not only a context in which decisions are made about language but also a factor that shapes how language is understood by faith communities. When LPP is connected to aspects of religious practice, language is not simply a vehicle for practice but also a constituent part of that practice and subject to the theological understandings that shape religious practice itself. Studying LPP in faith communities therefore reveals the ways the community theologises language and its role in communal religious practice. It can also reveal potential tensions and conflicts between different theologies of language and its use, as in cases where theologies of language change over time, as has happened for example in the Catholic Church, and between theologies of language and other social phenomena, as happens for example when language shift within a faith community renders continued use of a language for communal religious practice problematic. Different faith communities will respond to such tensions in different ways and privilege different ways of understanding language, the languages present in the community, and the use of language for religious expression.

Despite the centrality of language in religion and the importance of decision-making about language for understanding religion as a social and linguistic phenomenon, LPP in religious contexts has not received consistent attention in the LPP literature and research with a focus on religious practice has tended to be sporadic. The most researched area has been on the impact of religious actors on the language use of communities, especially in contexts where missionaries have been responsible for the dissemination of colonial languages. There has been much less, and much less sustained, attention to religion itself as a site in which language norms are developed, implemented, and maintained or changed. This means that there is much more that needs to be known about how religious institutions engage with language questions, especially in complex multilingual contexts.

Most work to date has focused on macro-level LPP actors, such as national and supranational religious institutions, especially in historical contexts where the resultant change in language practices has been significant. Much of this work has been done within the field of the History of Religion rather than in the field of LPP and so the linguistic dimensions of such work have been less well explored than the theological and historical issues. This work has usually focused on religions with an identified sacral language (especially Islam, Judaism, and Catholic Christianity), rather than in religions that adopt a comprehensibility orientation. Where the latter have been considered, they have often been understood as domains in which the language policy of the dominant society is (unproblematically) reproduced in the religious domain, or as instances of the religious domain in relation to processes of language maintenance or shift. This treatment has usually been located within sociolinguistic studies of multilingualism rather than specifically in LPP. More explicit LPP refocused research has tended to focus on the roles of religious actors in other forms of LPP work (e.g. Avni, 2012), on the tensions between religious goals and language work (Varghese & Johnston, 2007), and on the dissemination of national and/or colonial languages (e.g. Pennycook & Makoni, 2005).

The result of the research foci of studies of language and religions means that there has been more research about language *use* in religious institutions than about *decision-making* about languages in religious domains. As a result, there remains much work to be done to understand how religious LPP actors influence language practices in religious domains and how decisions about language are made, understood, and implemented. In particular, there is a lack of research about how actors in micro-level contexts, such as local faith communities, exert agency in relation to language issues facing their communities. This work is most especially important in contexts where linguistic norms are being renegotiated as the result of social, demographic, theological or other changes in the community. For example, little is known about the decision-making processes that contribute to language change in religious institutions that exist within multilingual communities and how the agency of the actors involved can be theorised and understood within religious contexts.

Such work requires a close examination of the enactment and consequences of activism to promote particular language policy positions in contexts where there are competing possible options for religious use of languages. This may occur in contexts where immigration has influenced the ethnolinguistic composition of a local faith community bringing new, or new forms of, linguistic diversity. It may also occur in contexts where the original linguistic profile of a faith community changes as the result of language shift between generations, especially in religious institutions with strong ethnic attachments, such as the Orthodox churches in immigrant contexts. It may also occur in communities in which a sacral liturgical language constructs linguistic uniformity for underlyingly linguistically diverse faith community and the consequences of the co-existence of both unifying and dividing linguistic affiliations, as in the case of Muslim communities made up of immigrants from diverse Muslim countries with different linguistic traditions. It may also happen in contexts in which language policy stands as a proxy for other forms of contesting or opposition within a religious institution, such as the place of Latin in the Catholic liturgy, which is closely associated with theological cleavages between supporters of the Tridentine and Vatican II liturgies. Such issues have been little studied and there is a need for a more sustained approach to religious institutions as sites of LPP work as a part of the emerging focus on meso- and micro-level LPP in the field.

Further Reading

Hoenes del Pinal, E. (2016). From Vatican II to speaking in tongues: Theology and language policy in a Q'eqchi'-Maya Catholic parish. *Language Policy, 15*(2), 179–197.
This article examines some of the complexities involved in making decisions about liturgical language use in the movement from Latin to vernacular languages in the Catholic Church and the ways that different theological positions can influence language choice.
Liddicoat, A.J. (2012b). Language planning as an element of religious practice. *Current Issues in Language Planning, 13*(2), 121–144.
This article examines how the sacrality orientation and comprehensibility orientation influence language planning in a range of areas of religious practice and the ways in which religious practice and the religious associations of language influence language planning more broadly.
Liddicoat, A.J. (2013). Language planning in religious observance. In C.A. Chapelle (Ed.), *The Encyclopedia of Applied Linguistics*. Wiley-Blackwell. https://doi.org/10.1002/9781405198431.wbeal0640
This article explores the issue of the ways that sacrality and comprehensibility influence decision-making about liturgical language use across different religions.
Pennycook, A. & Makoni, S. (2005). The modern mission: The language effects of Christianity. *Journal of Language, Identity and Education, 4*(2), 137–155.
This article examines the impact of missionary work on languages and critiques the role of missionary work in promoting European languages for religious purposes and the role of missionary linguists in the construction and invention of languages around the world.

References

Avni, S. (2012). Translation as a site of language policy negotiation in Jewish day school education. *Current Issues in Language Planning, 13*(2), 77–89. https://doi.org/10.1080/14664208.2012.678976
Avni, S. (2012). Hebrew-only language policy in religious education. *Language Policy, 11*, 169–188.
Ball, S.J. (1993). What is policy? Texts, trajectories and toolboxes. *Discourse, 13* (2), 10–17.
Bonacina-Pugh, F. (2012). Researching 'practiced language policies': Insights from Conversation analysis. *Language Policy, 11*(3), 213–234. https://doi.org/10.1007/s10993-012-9243-x
Boppart, T., Falkinger, J., & Grossmann, V. (2014). Protestantism and education: Reading (the Bible) and other skills. *Economic Inquiry, 52*(2), 874–895.
Chimhundu, H. (1992). Early missionaries and the ethno-linguistic factor during the invention of tribalism in Zimbabwe. *Journal of African History, 33*, 255–264.
Constable, G. (1994). The language of preaching in the twelfth century. *Viator, 25*, 131–152.
de Solano, F. (1991). *Documentos sobre política lingüística en Hispanoamérica (1492–1800)*. Consejo Superior de Investigaciones Científicas.
Delisle, J. & Woodsworth, J. (1995). *Translators through history*. John Benjamins Publishing Company.
Diallo, I. (2012). Qur'anic and Ajami literacies in pre-colonial West Africa. *Current Issues in Language Planning, 13*(2), 91–104.

Dunn, M. (2005). Vernacular literacy in the Touo language of the Solomon Islands. *Current Issues in Language Planning, 6*(2), 239–250. https://doi.org/10.1080/14664200508668283

Günther, S. (2020). *Knowledge and education in classical Islam: Religious learning between continuity and change*. Brill.

Hernández Triviño, A. (2016). Tradiciones, paradigmas y escuelas: Una visión general de las gramátics misioneras mesoamericanas. *Historiographia Linguistica, 43*(1–2), 11–59.

Hetényi, M. & Ivanič, P. (2021). The contribution of Ss. Cyril and Methodius to culture and religion. *Religions, 12*(6). MDPI. https://doi.org/10.1484/J.ABOL.4.01603

Hoenes del Pinal, E. (2016). From Vatican II to speaking in tongues: Theology and language policy in a Q'eqchi'-Maya Catholic parish. *Language Policy, 15*(2), 179–197.

Joseph, M. (1890). About preaching. *The Jewish Quarterly Review, 3*(1), 120–145.

Jungmann, J.A. (1986 [1951]). *The Mass of the Roman rite: Its origins and development (Missarum Sollemnia)*, Translated by F.A. Brunner. Christian Classics.

Kaplan, R.B. & Baldauf, R.B., Jnr. (1997). *Language planning: From practice to theory*. Multilingual Matters.

Keane, W. (1997). Religious language. *Annual Review of Anthropology*, 47–71.

Lafferty, M.K. (2003). Translating faith from Greek to Latin: Romanitas and Christianitas in late fourth-century Rome and Milan. *Journal of Early Christian Studies, 11*(1), 21–62.

Liddicoat, A. J. (1993). Choosing a liturgical language: The language policy of the Catholic Mass. *Australian Review of Applied Linguistics, 16*(2), 123–141.

Liddicoat, A.J. (2012a). Language planning and religion. *Current Issues in Language Planning, 13*(2), 73–75.

Liddicoat, A.J. (2012b). Language planning as an element of religious practice. *Current Issues in Language Planning, 13*(2), 121–144.

Liddicoat, A. J. (2013). Language planning in religious observance. In C.A. Chapelle (Ed.), *The Encyclopedia of Applied Linguistics*. Wiley-Blackwell. https://doi.org/10.1002/9781405198431.wbeal0640

Lo Bianco, J. (2005). Including discourse in language planning theory. In P. Bruthiaux, D. Atkinson, W. G. Eggington, W. Grabe, & V. Ramanathan (Eds.), *Directions in Applied Linguistics: Essays in Honor of Robert B. Kaplan*, 255–264. Multilingual Matters.

Maltby, J. (1998). *Prayer book and people in Elizabethan and early Stuart England*. Cambridge University Press.

Meyer, M.A. (1988). *Response to modernity: A history of the reform movement in Judaism*. Oxford University Press.

Ordóñez, F. (2007). Echoes of the voiceless: Language in Jesuit missions in Paraguay. In N. Echávez-Solano & K. Dworkin y Méndez (Eds.), *Spanish and Empire*, 32–47. Vanderbilt University Press.

Pennycook, A. & Makoni, S. (2005). The modern mission: The language effects of Christianity. *Journal of Language, Identity and Education, 4*(2), 137–155.

Platz, R. (2003). Buddhism and Christianity in competition? Religious and ethnic identity in Karen communities of Northern Thailand. *Journal of Southeast Asian Studies, 34*(3), 473–490.

Porter, A. (1997). Cultural imperialism' and protestant missionary enterprise, 1780–1914. *The Journal of Imperial and Commonwealth History*, 25(3), 367–391.

Posner, M. (nd). *Proper disposal of holy objects*. Retrieved 10 November from www.chabad.org/library/arti cle_cdo/aid/475304/jewish/Proper-Disposal-of-Holy-Objects.htm

Sánchez, A. (1996). Los inicios de la enseñanza del español en América: ¿Por la lengua hacia el imperio o por la lengua hacia Dios? [The beginnings of Spanish teaching in America: Through language to empire or through language to God?]. In *ACTAS del I Congreso Internacional de AESLA: El Español, Lengua Internacional* (pp. 35–47). Compobell.

Sánchez, A. & Dueñas, M. (2002). Language planning in the Spanish-speaking world. *Current Issues in Language Planning, 3*(3), 280–305.

Souza, A., Kwapong, A., & Woodham, M. (2012). Pentecostal and Catholic migrant churches in London–The role of ideologies in the language planning of faith lessons. *Current Issues in Language Planning, 13*(2), 105–120. https://doi.org/10.1080/14664208.2012.678977

Spolsky, B. (2003). Religion as a site of language contact. *Annual Review of Applied Linguistics, 23*, 81–94.

Spolsky, B. (2009). *Language management*. Cambridge University Press.

Tamis, A. (2005). Greek education in Australia. *Études helléniques/Hellenic Studies*, *13*(2), 115–150.

Varghese, M. M. & Johnston, B. (2007). Evangelical Christians and English language teaching. *TESOL Quarterly*, *41*(1), 5–31.

Wales, K. (2001). Archaism. In J. F.A. Sawyer & J.M.Y. Simpson (Eds.), *Concise Encyclopedia of Language and Religion*, 239–240. Elsevier.

Wigglesworth, A.E. (2008). The role of language in religion and ethnic identity: A sudy of liturgical language use in the Ukrainian Orthodox Church of Canada. *The Canadian Journal of Orthodox Christianity*, *3*(2), 33–49.

Womack, D.F. (2012). Lubnani, Libanais, Lebanese: Missionary education, language policy and identity formation in modern Lebanon. *Studies in World Christianity*, *18*(1), 4–20.

17

POLITENESS IN RELIGIOUS DISCOURSE

Marzena Makuchowska

Introduction and Background

Since the 1970s, a great deal of research has been devoted to the phenomena of politeness in various areas of social life (e.g., Kádár & Haugh, 2013; Locher, 2012; see discussion and references). However, less attention has been paid to the religion-related sphere of communication, even though it is equally important both at the micro (in the local community of believers) and macro (in the relations between the world's major religions and confessions and in international relations) level. Furthermore, due to the nature of religion, politeness represents an even more interesting research problem manifesting itself in two ways: horizontally (a relation between one human and another) and vertically (a relation between a human and a supernatural being, such as the Christian God). This is because some humans believe that they can cross an ontological boundary and make contact with God.

Previous studies of Judeo-Christian prayers have shown that, due to an anthropological necessity, we imagine the supernatural world in the "image and likeness" of the natural and human world and shape our way of interacting with *Sacrum* according to the conventions developed in interpersonal interactions (Wierusz-Kowalski, 1973). If we call God a *king* or *father*, we are speaking to God the same way as to an earthly king or father, following the norms and conventions of the time and culture. The combination of politeness and religious discourse opens up a wide field for exploration that can enrich our knowledge, both of the nature, mechanisms, and factors behind politeness, and of the use of language in the sphere of religion-related life. The following sections therefore discuss the main theoretical and methodological ideas relevant to both politeness and religious discourse.

The core of the modern scientific understanding of politeness lies in the concept of face, developed by sociologist Erving Goffman (1967), adapted to linguistic pragmatics by Brown and Levinson (1978 and 1987), and used and developed to this day (O'Driscoll, 2017). Brown and Levinson see face as a social image that each human wants to maintain, trying to ensure that (1) no one interferes with their actions ("negative face"), and (2) they are accepted and treated with respect ("positive face") (Brown and Levinson, 1987, pp. 61–62). They believe that most speech acts are face-threatening acts and politeness is a type of behaviour intended to protect against loss of face and is thus reflected by certain principles (strategies) aimed at avoiding or

DOI: 10.4324/9781003301271-19

mitigating potential conflicts. Further research shows that people not only defend their face but are also actively involved for the benefit of the face of the recipient, for example, by offering congratulations and compliments. These acts are defined using various names, including face-boosting acts, face-flattering acts, face-enhancing acts, and face-giving acts (as cited in O'Driscoll, 2017). Some acts, such as compliments, are studied separately in detail (Holmes, 1986).

However, face, associated with a model of the rational individual, is not the only concept used to explain human communicative behaviour related to politeness. There is also an emphasis on collective values, such as maintaining social harmony (as emphasised mainly by scholars from Asian cultures e.g., Kádár and Mills, 2011); regulating social intercourse, including restoring power relations (Watts, 2003; Watts and Mills, 2005); bonding social ties; and restoring the moral order (e.g., Kádár, 2017). The essence of politeness and the reasons behind it are also meant to lie in the human disposition to respond to the needs of their interlocutor (e.g., Fukushima, 2015).

The concept of politeness itself has also evolved. The first wave of the study of politeness focuses on describing the social conventions (rules, strategies) to be followed by the sender. The second wave, however, assumes that (in the opinion of the participants themselves) the "polite" course of the act of communication is the result of joint work, which is why the term "facework" is used (O'Driscoll, 2017). The empirical research has developed to observe the interaction embedded in cultural and situational contexts (*in situ*) based on the factors that led to this effect (Watts, 2003; Mills, 2011). Politeness is not assumed to be inherent in linguistic forms but rather a contextual evaluation (e.g., Fraser & Nolan, 1981, p. 96). On the other hand, it is noted that the human mind associates certain repetitive situations (contexts) with the customarily accompanying linguistic formulas so that the latter are conventionalised and carry polite meanings even *in abstracto* (Culpeper, 2011; Terkourafi, 2015).

The third wave of the study of politeness reveals the phenomenon of impoliteness (face questioning, aggression, discrimination, etc.). This is not the direct opposite of politeness, which is why the general term "interpersonal relations" is often used (e.g., Locher, 2012; O'Driscoll, 2017; Terkourafi, 2008) and the assumption is made that participants in any given interaction evaluate their behaviour as positive, neutral, or negative according to some kind of normative scale (Haugh, 2014, p. 159). This scale can be determined by two types of criteria: expected behaviours (resulting from behavioural regularities or habits) and social "oughts" (authoritative injunctions to perform social actions) (Haugh, 2014). Both criteria, supported by religious or other morality, induce behaviour based on the principle of reciprocity (Culpeper & Tantucci, 2021).

The theoretical background for the study of politeness has also provided findings regarding the phatic function attributed to the marginal phase of the conversation. The case study presented in this chapter only deals with the opening phase, but the importance of the opening phase for phatic communion can be better understood by considering the closing phase (contact closing). Laver (1975) argues that the main function of the phases is to facilitate a comfortable transition from silence to interaction and then from interaction to silence. Therefore, the opening phase turns to the inside of the interaction and the closing phase turns to the outside of it. The opening phase establishes solidarity, and the closing phase consolidates and promises continuance of solidarity (Laver, 1975, p. 233). "It is as if the encounter is a transitory microcosm with an ephemeral existence within the macrocosm of the wider social experience of the participants. Each participant brings aspects of his wider *macrocosmic* social identity to the momentary encounter" (Laver, 1975, p. 233). It makes the phatic function and the related behaviour an extremely important psychosocial instrument as the repetition of the interaction sustains (and cumulates) the effect of consensus between its participants, strengthening their relationships (Laver, 1975, p. 233).

Religious discourse is often considered within communication studies research due to the subject's social practice functioning as an instrument of power (Foucault, 1981; Howarth, 2000; Neff-Van Aertselaer et al., 2004, and many others). In this regard, religious texts can be studied as a product of a given religious community—a certain discursive community built on the same type of rationality, the same vision of the world, the same set of beliefs and values, with the same goals, interests, etc. This creates a filter used by a given discourse community to draw on the general resources of language, giving its discourse a recognisable character. The discourse of a given religious community not only reflects its beliefs and values but also disseminates its views in the social space and, specifically, marginalises the discourses of other actors. For example, the discourse of the Catholic Church on abortion seeks to marginalise the discourses of other actors on abortion with a different approach to the issue.

Texts reflect a subjective interpretation of the world based on the point of view of a given discourse community. Religious discourse is the product (and tool) of a community that believes in the existence of a supernatural reality (*sacrum*) and the duality of the world, i.e. the earthly world in which the temporal life of the human takes place, and the eternal and sacred world of God (understood in a variety of ways), invisible but real, and having many relationships with the former. This understanding of *sacrum* is typical of the great monotheistic religions, such as Judaism, Christianity, and Islam. There are also religions in which deity is immanent; however, a sense of mystery and some level of inaccessibility is characteristic of virtually every religion (cf. Sztajer, 2009, p. 7).

Because religions attribute metaphysical nature to the object of faith (God, deity, the world of *sacrum*), they are considered not to be accessible to empirical cognition. Thus, as claimed by religious studies specialists, talking about them is necessary to make it imaginable and tangible for people (Sztajer, 2006 and 2009). In religion, language, understood broadly as a system of verbal and non-verbal signs (including symbols, paintings, sculptures, film, etc.) (Sztajer, 2009), is not a tool to describe *sacrum* (as it is not possible to describe something that cannot be seen). Instead, it serves to create and sustain the religious world. The (permanent) communication constructs and reproduces the symbolic universe of religion, both the religious image of the world and the communal forms of religious life. Communication is the primary medium for the objectivation of the religious world.

Language is thus the primary medium through which the religious world becomes something objectively given (the religious scientist's assumptions are not ontological but epistemological, since they recognise that whether the supernatural world exists, it is beyond the reach of a human being's cognitive capacities). Therefore, the statement that humans at the same time produce the religious world and encounter this world are complementary rather than contradictory (Sztajer, 2009, p. 9). For example, religious people perceive the Bible as something that comes from outside the human world; nevertheless, the Bible is also a product of culture and was created using (human) language.

Religious people, however, generally believe that religious language reveals the world of *sacrum* and describes it as a previously given reality, independent of the act of communication. In serving this purpose, human language, adapted to tasks in the ordinary world, is very imperfect, approximate, and indirect but is nonetheless able to make some reference to the transcendence. In a religious perspective, language thus relates to a reality that exists outside of it, i.e., it performs the so-called referential (or: representational) function of language (cf. functions of language according to Bühler and Jakobson, e.g., in Kortmann 2020, pp. 12–13). Therefore, religious discourse is the product (and reflection) of a belief in theticity, or a reference to the reality that exists beyond the subjective experience of the speaker and the empirical reality of the world (Dupré, 1991, pp. 159).

Thus, in examining the way politeness is manifested in religious texts, it can be assumed that their specific character is due to two fundamental facts: (1) they are present in the ordinary world and do justice to ordinary, interpersonal rules and standards; (2) they perform important religious functions: they create/reflect the religious world, confirm belief in its existence, reproduce a certain image of it, and sustain religious worship and religious explanation for morality. For example, the Pope, as a sender, is a human that speaks to other people. Like any human put in this kind of situation, he is courteous to them and uses the conventions of a given culture. However, he also speaks as the Vicar of Christ on Earth and is supposed to constantly bear witness to Christ. The Pope is the head of the Church, and the Church is the visible sign of spiritual reality. Thus, the visible is to make the invisible present, putting it within reach of human perceptions, beliefs, and values. Therefore, the Pope's statements refer not only to the temporal world and human life but also the religious goals; opening up the religious perspective and showing the two-dimensional nature of the world: the physical and metaphysical dimensions, and encouraging the acceptance of all the consequences, including the affirmation and worship of God, living according to His commandments, etc..

Analytically, there are two orders determining how politeness is manifested in religious texts: (1) the order of human-to-human discourses and the social conventions that govern them, and (2) the order of religious discourse with its specific type of rationality (belief in transcendence) and its specific purposes (creating/revealing the world of *sacrum* as well as sustaining faith and following its precepts). Papal speeches, the subject of this case study, are placed in the religious discourse of the Catholic Church, in its most official and widespread stream, as opposed to the discourses of the various particular churches operating in individual countries. The context of the texts studied and the criteria used to define linguistic means are based on, among others, the following parameters: belief in the supernatural world (resulting in the development of such concepts as God, Christ, and Divine Providence, as well as such genres as prayer and blessing); doctrine (the Catholic doctrine in this case, separating the Catholic community from other Christian denominations and other religions); the religious axiological sphere (based on divine commandments, the Decalogue, and the moral teaching of the Church); the role of the sender (defined in religious terms, such as the Vicar of Christ and the successor of St. Peter, and in institutional terms, such as the head of the Catholic Church, teaching authority, power, etc.); general and specific objectives of the Church, such as the dissemination of the faith (based on its doctrine); and moral education.

With respect to the latter, the Catholic Church is pursuing what might be called a communication policy, according to what was adopted at the Second Vatican Council (1962–1965), programmatically favouring a positive model of communication and breaking away from the pre-conciliar era dominated by a model of negative communication (isolation, discrediting heretics and pagans). The last council postulates an attitude of love and respect for every human person and states that Catholics should be involved in the life of the world and in solving its problems, which can only be done together with other people, in harmony and cooperation. The papal speeches can be seen as part of a consistent implementation of these postulates.

Face-Enhancing Acts in the Opening Phase of Papal Speeches

This case study aims to investigate the stylistic choices made for the implementation of affirmative (face-enhancing) strategies of the addressees appearing in the opening phase of the papal speeches. The analysis shows that the choice of linguistic modes of behaviour during the initiation of the contact not only does justice to commonly used conventions but also manifests specific features of this social practice of the Catholic Church and its overall strategy to seek to establish and sustain positive relations with all communities.

The study is based on the statements of the last three popes (John Paul II, Benedict XVI, and Francis) made from the 1980s to 2022. They include speeches and homilies, i.e., texts formally directed to someone to whom the reference is made explicitly in the address form. Further below, they will be collectively called speeches. These texts are published in several languages on the Vatican website (www.vatican.va) and in the media such as web portals, newspapers, and books of many countries. The study comprises 90 speeches; most of them are in English, and those for which English is not available are in German, Italian, and Polish.

The papal speeches studied are written texts detached from the original circumstances in which they were delivered or read and devoid of the physical participation of the interlocutors. Therefore, directly observing the course of the conversation and seeing the effects *in situ* or asking the recipients about their feelings is not possible. Nevertheless, the researcher can take the position of one of the recipients and make their evaluation. There are two reasons behind this. First, papal speeches represent the official teaching of the Catholic Church. They apply mainly to Catholics but are accessible to all, which is why they are widely disseminated. Significantly, the teaching element is not only the essential, theological content of speeches, but also their interpersonal layer, for the pope—by his own example—teaches the desired attitude towards "fellow human beings". Papal speeches have thus been prepared in such a way that the intentions of the sender are clear to everyone.

Second, while it is generally believed that politeness (and impoliteness) may be expressed in various ways and is not inherent in linguistic forms, it can also be observed that in typical, repetitive situations, people use established and conventionalised means, which are linked to a given situation by custom (Terkourafi, 2015). For example, they use conventionalized formulas, such as "good morning" or "goodbye", at moments when contact begins or ends. Papal speeches are intended for such typical situations in which greetings, thanks, farewells, etc. are expected as routine, standardised, and recognisable behaviour, doing justice to commonly accepted conventions.

Thus, politeness is set in a certain context through a relationship between the politeness behaviours and the situation for which they were developed. These situations are official, ceremonial, and solemn in nature; they take place in cathedrals, basilicas, synagogues, palaces (episcopal, presidential, and royal), other distinctive places, such as sites of special historical significance, as well as squares and stadiums gathering thousands of people, which gives the meeting special importance. The Pope addresses the communities represented by the clerical and secular dignitaries present and the highest representatives of churches, religions, and state authorities, including monarchs. He is the head of state received in accordance with diplomatic etiquette (cf., e.g., Chilton, 1990; Cohen, 1997), and the most eminent religious hierarch treated with the utmost respect and attentiveness.

Address Forms

The focus is first made on contact-opening address forms, or direct expressions to the addressee. The reasons that lie behind the choice of the terms or titles used in this study are rooted in the wider historical context that, by way of contrast, reveal the real measure of politeness in the utterances. Then, some of the manifestations of activities aimed at enhancing the addressee's face and image as a benefactor are explored. Special attention is given to the implementation of obvious conventions and the use of the sender's objectives and means, typical of religion and the religious way of defining situations.

Address forms are direct expressions to the addressee. Their primary role is to establish contact and call the addressee's attention, and make the addressee know that the sender is addressing them. This is the so-called phatic function in its classical Jakobsonian sense (Jakobson, 1960). This function encompasses the so-called definite descriptions, including, in particular, proper names (first names, surnames, cf., "Ignatius", "Zakka") or the names of social functions and titles of an individual (e.g., professional titles), provided that it is known, in general or in a particular situation, who holds them ("Mr. President", "Mr. Director General"). The choice of a particular description defines the type of contact between the interlocutors, e.g., intimate or official. This means that address forms also have a performative function (in the Austinian sense; Austin, 1962). Papal speeches take place in official situations. Meanings on the interpersonal level are defined mainly by the names of addressees' titles and functions as used by the sender.

Invocations may combine both types of descriptions (proper names and names of titles) and add conventional honorific expressions (in accordance with diplomatic etiquette) belonging to and enhancing the title, for example, "Your Beatitude Patriarch Ignatius"). They are accompanied by conventional address forms-extending terms, such as "Venerable", "Honourable", "Dear", "Distinguished", etc., reinforcing their polite character. The texts studied are characterised by multiple address forms (two to six) as the meeting is public and held in the presence of many people. The politeness in address forms is primarily reflected by distinguishing the key participants in the meeting from the whole population, which results in affirmation. Here are some examples:

[1] Your Holiness
Your Eminences
Your Excellencies, Beloved Brother Bishops

[2] Mr. President
Mr. Director General
Ladies and Gentlemen

[3] Distinguished Religious Leaders
Dear Friends

[4] Your Beatitude Patriarch Ignatius
Your Holiness Patriarch Zakka
Venerable Bishops and Representatives of the Churches
Ecclesial Communities of Syria

[5] Your Holiness
Your Beatitudes
Eminences and Excellencies
Brothers and Sisters in Christ

The order of address forms is governed by the principle of respecting the hierarchy of addressees. It can be assumed that this issue, particularly sensitive, is carefully considered by those who prepare the speech. This is because any slip-up, such as omitting an important person or getting their titles wrong, would put the face of both the omitted recipient and the sender at risk. At best, the former would feel embarrassed and, at worst, disrespected or even insulted. The latter, on discovering his mistake, would feel guilty about the awkward situation.

There is also a more *implicite* principle at work here: from singular objects (such as a particular person, cf. singularis of nouns, names of addressees) through to less defined objects (collectives such as "Bishops", "Eminences and Excellencies", "Religious Leaders", cf. plural of nouns), to completely unmarked (such as "Dear Friends" in [3] and the most conventional "Dear Brother and Sisters" or "Brother and Sisters in Christ", as in [5]). The address forms are meant to encompass all those who are present and those who are absent, that is, ecclesiastical, religious, and ethnic groups and communities represented by those who are present.

These rules are common conventions used, for example, in diplomacy (politics). The titles, such as "Your Eminence", "Your Holiness", "Your Beatitude", "Patriarch", "Archbishop", and "Bishop", are specific to religious discourse. These titles not only feature elegance and rhetorical appropriateness but also, more importantly, incorporate the addressee's own nomenclature. In the pre-conciliar era, it was forbidden to officially honour "heretics" or to publicly show them respect and attentiveness. For doctrinal reasons, the names of ecclesiastical functions and titles were intended exclusively for the Catholic Church ("the only true" one). The use of such names by "dissidents" was considered usurpation and yet another reason for condemnation and reproaching. Briefly and in general terms, the Second Council adopted a new way of defining the concept of the Church (the so-called ecclesiality; Latin *ecclesiae*) and recognised the so-called Eastern Churches, calling them sister Churches. Others, such as Protestants, are described with the name "Church" for reasons of politeness and to build friendly relations and not on a theological basis, respecting the way their members self-determine. For centuries, Catholics could only call their Pope "Your Holiness". All the names being now in use and other positive names, such as leader, brother, and friend, are a momentous act of affirmation, raising the importance of the non-Catholic addressee.

Furthermore, the use of plural names referring to a collective, such as "bishops" and "churches", introduces an inclusive meaning (I + you = we), which includes the sender and their community (bishops = I + all Catholic bishops + bishops of other churches; churches = Catholic Church + other churches; [1] and [4]). In the pre-conciliar language of Catholicism, the term "Church" belonged to *singularia tantum* nouns, or nouns occurring only in the singular without the plural form because it was believed that the Catholic Church was the only community in the world representing the true Church. The plural form is a post-conciliar innovation and its use in relation to Christian communities, which, in a strictly doctrinal sense, are still not considered to be the Church, is a gesture intended to sustain good relations with them.

A particularly inclusive meaning can be attached to the terms, "brother" or "brothers" and "sisters", but this term is less frequently used, particularly because the religious hierarchy is made up of men. These terms support closeness as a semantic category understood as emotional closeness in psychological and sociological terms. The metaphorical use of "brothers" and "sisters" evokes the image of family relations with such values as equal treatment by parents and the emotional bond in friendship, love, and inseparable ties. For example, the term "beloved" in "Beloved Brothers Bishops" refers to love [1]. The terms "brother" or "brothers" and "brothers and sisters" are most often, but not always, linked to the simple and intimate "dear". Similar feelings may be evoked by the term "friends".

The inclusive meaning also occurs in the address forms used at ecumenical meetings of various Christian confessions, such as "Dear Brothers and Sisters in Christ". In the religious interpretative framework, Christ embodies an idea of unifying or fraternising all Christians. The most typical invocation "Dear Brothers and Sisters" has now extended to include those who were previously meant to be treated with hostility and alienation. The calls or prayers to God introduce the figure of God the Father that unites Christians and adherents of Judaism and Islam into one category of children of the same father.

Enhancing the Image of the Benefactor

While the address forms described above enhance the face of the addressee, raising their social, ecclesial, and community-related status, the address forms discussed in this section represent, in a more or less overt manner, the following message of the sender, "You are my bene-factor". In ordinary everyday life, saying thank you is one of the most common and routinised behaviours of politeness. Every society and socio-cultural group seem to have their norms and values defining what acts require thanking and how "thank you" can be said. It is, therefore, not surprising that the verbal means used in such cases often show a high degree of routinisation (Coulmas, 1981).

The papal speeches reveal the routinised character in the conventionalised formulas, stylistic-ally different but pragmatically equivalent ("I thank", "I express my gratitude", "I am grateful", "I wish to thank"):

[6] I thank you for your warm welcome. In particular, I express my gratitude to His Beatitude Patriarch Gregory III for his kind words of welcome to his Patriarchal residence.

[7] I wish to thank you for your gracious invitation to celebrate this parish anniversary with you.

Every verbalisation of gratitude refers to some action (or actions) of the benefactor or its result; such an action is referred to as the object of gratitude (Coulmas, 1981). In the marginal phases of papal speeches, thanks are reactive in nature; they are a reaction to the meeting-related stimulus received from the communication partner. Accordingly, the sender can express thanks for the invi-tation, the meeting, coming to the Vatican, the presence, the words of welcome, the hospitality, the good reception, etc. As a result, papal speeches do justice to one of the most conventional rules of interpersonal behaviour, forming the habitus of the everyday. There are various means used to give the acts an unusual and festive character. They lengthen the expression making it seem even more polite as they suggest the increased attention of the sender towards the addressee and reinforced affirmation.

One of the means is the use of expressions that enhance the value of objects of grati-tude: "gracious: words of welcome/invitation/introduction"; "kind: welcome/letter"/attention"/ invitation"; "cordial and joyful welcome"; "fraternal hospitality". The repertoire of value-laden terms is conventional. The term "fraternal" is an already mentioned convention, embedded in the post-conciliar Catholic (and not only Catholic) discourse, like "brothers" and "sisters"; it takes a part in the construction of the metaphor of family.

The following text shows that forms raising the value of the object of gratitude (and extended forms of thanking) can be longer than single expressions. In [8], the whole sentence is about how the sender appreciates what the addressee has done for them:

[8] [...] Thank you, Your Holiness, for having welcomed me into your home. This sign of love eloquently bespeaks, better than any words can do, the meaning of friendship and fraternal charity.

Since participants in the interaction decide for themselves how they perceive their partner's behav-iour, the Pope equates the addressee's gesture with a "sign of love" and thus raises the significance of the act of his benefactor. Another passage shows how the sender adds information about the emotional effect of the host's gesture (emphasis added):

[9] I thank each of those who offered the kind words and we have just heard. Your words have edified me.

The Pope recognises the contribution of the benefactors. Reactive thanks, triggered by the prior action of the addressee, is governed by the transactional principle of equivalence or reciprocity such as in payment equilibrium and debit/credit logic (see Culpeper & Tantucci, 2021). In this regard, the opening words of thanks of the Pope can be seen as settling a score. However, given the social role of convention, this is not trivial behaviour. A specific quality of conventional behaviours is that they may be hardly noticeable (cf., Locher & Watts, 2005; Watts, 2003), but their absence can be quickly deduced and in extreme cases, the term "scandal" is used. If, in the history of mutual relations, the parties experienced hostile or cold silence and refused to contact each other, the exchange of ordinary conventions is a momentous act intended to build normal, consensual, and friendly interpersonal relations. The "ordinary" character of conventions, limited to hospitality values, creates a space for basic human relations. The sender tries to symbolically extend the relations of this type to a macrocosm of relations with the personalities they address and, above all, their communities.

Expressions of joy at the meeting, whether during the Pope's visit to another place or the reception of the delegation in the Vatican, play a significant role in the opening phase. As a rule, they follow immediately after the address forms and may, as a source of positive emotion, straightforwardly refer to the fact of attending a meeting prepared by the hosts or receiving guests at home. The following example shows how the Pope *explicite* verbalises the historical change in the mutual relationship:

[10] For me, it is a great joy and a truly graced moment to be able to receive all of you here, at the tomb of Saint Peter, as we recall that historic meeting forty years ago between our predecessors, Pope Paul VI and the late Pope Shenouda III, in an embrace of peace and fraternity, after centuries in which there was a certain distance between us. So it is with deep affection that I welcome Your Holiness and the distinguished members of your delegation …

The passage contains the conventional verbal formulas referring to pleasure and joy, i.e., "I am pleased"; "It gives me great pleasure"; "It is a great joy"; "with joy"; "with great/deep affection". Some statements are longer and more stylistically sophisticated, e.g., with quotes from historically important speeches of predecessors or quotes from the Bible that speak of the joy of being with brothers (Ps 133:1: *How good and pleasant it is when brothers live together in unity!*), and indicate an anticipation and a strong desire to meet:

[11] I have greatly desired to visit this beloved land […]

[12] I have greatly looked forward to this meeting […]

Note the use of first-person forms ("I am", "I have", "for me") emphasising the personal emotional involvement of the sender and their participation in the interaction as a human being and not just a representative of the institution. The sender seeks to transcend conventions and increase their contribution to interpersonal relations by exposing the sincerity and authenticity of their feelings.

Due to the religious nature of the discourse, it is also possible to use an indirect means, i.e., formally address an act of gratitude or praise to the deity and thus send a message to the human, for example:

[13] With profound gratitude to the Most Holy Trinity, I make this visit to the Greek Orthodox Patriarchate of Jerusalem, and I greet all of you in the grace and peace of our Lord Jesus Christ.

[14] I give heartfelt praise to Almighty God for the grace of this meeting.

[15] I am profoundly grateful to Divine Providence for this meeting […].

[16] For me, this is indeed a moment of true blessing from Almighty God […].

Perceiving the event in religious terms as a gift from God (grace, blessing) greatly increases the value of the meeting and attributes it to the one who is involved in the meeting as hosting or visiting the Pope. The hospitality of the host, or visit of the visitor, is the source of the sender's joy and prompts them to express "deep" and "heartfelt" gratitude to God. This enhances the image of the addressee as a benefactor. Its other role is to reinforce the image of the community by showing the basis of the bond (the common deity), as emphasised by the possessive pronoun "our" (Lord Jesus Christ, [13]). As a rule, the statements to Christians refer to Jesus Christ, while speeches to followers of other religions use the term "God the Father". This is due to the theological differences between religions and the need to emphasise what unites rather than what divides to sustain good relations.

To sum up, in the address forms, the sender indicates the addressee, recalls him from among those present, distinguishes him from the background, confirms his high social position, symbolically enters into his "world", honouring his perception of reality (using the ecclesiastical nomenclature of the addressee, even if it deviates from the strict norms of Catholic theology) and (symbolically) incorporates him into the community to which he himself belongs, defining it at the same time as a family, a circle of friend (i.e., a community based on equality of status, positive feelings and united by an indissoluble bond).

Expressions of gratitude and joy at the contact appear in the places provided for by convention; yet, the manner in which they are stylistically grasped strives to give them a unusual and celebratory character. The statements are elaborate, making them more prominent and significant to the message of the speech as a whole. They contain measures that emphasise the positive value of the addressee's actions and gestures, defining them as a gift to the sender. The popes also make use of the specific stylistic resources provided by religious discourse, such as passages sourced from the Bible and the introduction of deity figures, which changes the perspective in which events are presented. Thus, the object of gratitude gains in value, reinforcing the face of the addressee as the doer of good, and the figure of the common lord (Christ) or father (God) helps to create the image of community. The strategies described are only one of many that can be observed in the material studied, thus warranting further research and exploration.

Implications and Future Directions

This case study only shows a small part of the phenomena oriented towards interpersonal communication in papal speeches and papal speeches are only a small part of the Catholic religious discourse. This shows that the research field arising from the combination of politeness and religious discourse is very extensive, especially when considering the multiplicity of religions (and confessions) and their different embodiments in different cultures (countries, regions, societies, etc.) as well as historical religions. For example, Kim Ridealgh (2021) studies ancient Egyptian Late Ramesside Letters (c. 1099–1069 BCE), showing that rituals may have a certain influence on human bonds.

Another important conclusion from this case study is that the research is transdisciplinary, combining politeness/impoliteness studies (which are themselves interdisciplinary in nature) and research on religion (confession), including its doctrine, forms of life, organisational shape, institutional shape, history, etc. The linguistic studies of religious discourse (also referred to as religious language or religious style) should draw from various disciplines, such as theology, religious studies, anthropology, sociology, psychology, history of religions, churches, and communities, and neurolinguistics (cf., Chilton & Kopytkowska, 2018), for a better understanding of the nature of the research object and possible contextual factors affecting communication in religion.

This chapter has demonstrated the necessity to consider the many contextual factors that determine communication in the religious sphere. A factor that plays a specific role in terms of religion is the two-dimensional character of communication as discussed in the introduction (the vertical dimension corresponds to the relationship between people and deity and the horizontal dimension describes the communication between people). However, these combine with further conditions, such as the social status of the participants in communication (real or imagined), the social distance between them, their communicative roles, the nature of the communicative situation, and so on.

The first dimension is primarily reflected in prayer, a basic religious act addressed by the human directly to God and expressing faith in the existence of God. The conceptualisation of the deity as a person creates a relational aspect, which results in the inseparability of expressing the relationship of the sender to the numinous addressee. The type of the relation stems from basic religious assumptions, that is, the ontic superiority of God over the human and the human's dependence on God. Showing reverence, respect, and humility to God is the first principle that shapes how human speaks to God. Linguistic evidence in texts of prayers can reveal not only the human perceptions of God such as God's likes and preferences, etc., but also the models of politeness associated with a given culture and a given time. For example, the feudal image of God as a king seated on a throne in a palace and surrounded by armies of angels required great humility and lowliness in addressing Him as if He were an earthly ruler. The prayers included phrases such as "I fall to my knees before You in deep humility", "we fall to our feet", and "we beseech the Divine Majesty" and the term "deign" (e.g., "deign to hear our prayers/requests"). Nowadays, in cultures in which democratisation has changed social relations and considerably shortened interpersonal distance, the old names of deity and the old models of politeness are not applicable anymore. Therefore, detailed contextualised studies are required to see how human social relations and related models of politeness are reflected in the perceptions of deity and the conventions of speaking to them.

An important aspect of the study of prayer is that it comes in two forms (in Catholicism and beyond): (1) as a ready-made prayer for use by the faithful (e.g., liturgical prayer or private prayer published in a prayer book); and (2) as a spontaneous, intimate, and one-time prayer of the believer. In the former case, the texts of prayer are addressed both to a supernatural addressee (*explicite*) and the human audience (*implicite*) listening to them or using them in their act of prayer. These texts are produced by religious experts and are approved by Church authorities—a prayer book must be given permission for the publication (i.e., *imprimatur*) by the bishop, and liturgical texts—by the Holy See because they are a source of theological truths (*locus theologicus*) and the standard of faith. Therefore, the way a deity is addressed is an element of teaching about them. Speaking politely creates an image of a deity as someone who should be addressed politely because of who they are. Therefore, it can be assumed that politeness is a factor that co-creates the deity's image. If this is the case, politeness studies would reveal yet another function of politeness.

Texts of the second type are not an act of communication with other people, but only with the addressee from the sphere of the sacred. Personal, intimate prayer may be the so-called inner prayer, uttered in thought, but as such it is not observable to researchers. There are, however, spontaneous prayers of the faithful recorded in writing, such as prayers written in so-called books of intentions, laid out in many churches (e.g., on a table placed by the altar with a "miraculous" image or statue) or written on pieces of paper that are thrown into a special urn. In such a situation, people formulate their prayers in the way that they themselves consider to be applicable in their dealings with God (with Mary, with a particular saint), guided by their own intentions, feelings, and their religious knowledge—not always in accordance with the official teaching of the Catholic Church—and linguistic and communicative competence, depending on age, education, etc.

A comparison of the two types of prayers could show how politeness strategies depend, among other things, on factors such as formality/intimacy, formality/spontaneity, or the variety of purposes of the utterance (directed only at the deity or simultaneously at the deity and the human recipients). Questions may concern the influence of doctrine, ecclesiastical traditions, and patterns on the one hand, and on the other, patterns and conventions consciously or unconsciously drawn from everyday life and current realities. Previous research shows that "ordinary" believers carry over into their own prayers accounts of family life, talking to God or Mary as if they were a close relative (e.g., using the diminutives "daddy", "mummy" in address forms to deity and signing "Katy", "Eddy", etc.), as well as behaviours familiar from (secular) offices, approximating their prayer to an official petition in which one presents a case and asks for it to be dealt with (e.g., "My niece, seventeen-year-old Basia, is losing her sight. The doctors offer no hope for her recovery. I turn to you, Blessed Virgin, with a fervent request […] heal her)" (Wojtak, 2019, p. 63).

Horizontal communication is primarily determined by worship, social in nature and resulting from the action of a group. Worshipping requires the organisation and performance of ritual activities involving people with different roles and statuses. In this regard, the relationship between the priest and the worshipper is fundamental. The institutional nature of religious life, as in the case of the Catholic Church, introduces a wide range of hierarchies (pope, cardinal, bishop, "ordinary" priest, parishioner) and thus a variety of positions, statuses, and communicative conventions. How hierarchies and power relations affect interpersonal interactions is already being studied, however, based on observations in other spheres of life, e.g., in communication between various types of medical caregivers (Graham 2009), and the study of the sphere of religion—due to its specificity—could result in the development of knowledge on this topic. It is also specific that here the principles of politeness may have an additional source and motivation. The principle of respect for the other in religion is linked to the injunction to love one's neighbour (cf. the so-called commandments, the *Decalogue*) and to a religious sanction (sin). Theoretically, therefore, the individual who claims to be a religious person has all the more to defend in their social behaviour, both in terms of their own "face" and the "face" of the religious community they represent. The best example is the Pope, who bears responsibility for the "face" of the entire Catholic Church.

One of the fundamental roles of language in religion is to spread the faith and provide religious education such as during a sermon or a religion lesson. Again, the relational dimension of language use is truly important as it can affect the effectiveness of educational activities and measures to maintain and attract followers. The same applies to *ad extra* activities, outside the community, in contacts between other religions, denominations, and cultures, as discussed in this study based on a small sample. Research involving the religious sphere would reveal the history of the formation of politeness conventions in this sphere (e.g., the influence of feudal culture), its axiological background (the values designated as the object of thanks, compliments, or apologies), and its stylistic resources (quotes from the Bible, acts of prayer, blessings, a strictly religious repertoire of greetings and farewells, etc.). How the religious and secular spheres merge and how the former affects the latter is also an interesting area of research (e.g., Bouchara & Qorchi, 2016; Alsohaibani, 2017).

A variety of communicative situations, functions of language in religion(s), and factors shaping its use, encourage the use of different conceptions and research methods concerning politeness, i.e., those that test the conventional side of its nature, those embedded in the situation (*in situ*), looking closely at the given interaction, identified by researchers as facework (O'Driscoll, 2017) or relational work (Locher, 2012), and those that search for axiological dimensions of human behaviour (Kádár, 2017). On the other hand, due to the specific character of religion, studying religion can also yield entirely new methodological inspirations.

Politeness (or more broadly the personal and relational aspect of communication) is, as we have seen, deeply embedded in religion, which is realised both as a relationship with deity and as a relationship between people. Research from this side seems particularly promising as this aspect could significantly determine the use of language in the religious sphere and explain many phenomena present in it. At the same time, research on (im)politeness could also benefit as new material and new contexts would offer opportunities to verify and complement existing knowledge in this sphere.

Further Reading

Al-Khatib, M. (2012). Politeness in the Holy Quran: A sociolinguistic and pragmatic perspective. *Intercultural Pragmatics*, 9(4), 479–509. https://doi.org/10.1515/ip-2012-0027
The article is the first analysis of one of the so-called holy books in terms of politeness strategies implemented in both God–human and human–human relations.
Alsohaibani, A. (2017). *Influence of religion on language use: A sociopragmatic study on the influence of religion on speech acts performance.* PhD thesis. University of East Anglia. https://core.ac.uk/download/pdf/153534299.pdf
The work addresses a number of questions about the influence of religion on communicative behaviour and the ways in which it is linguistically realised in everyday language.
Bouchara, A. & Qorchi, B. (2016). *The role of religion in shaping politeness during greeting encounters in Arabic. A matter of conflict or understanding.* Anchor Academia Publishing.
This work shows the relationship of politeness to (specific) religion and its possible implications for intercultural communication.
Makuchowska, M. (2022). "*I look with deep gratitude and admiration…*"—praising and complimenting in papal speeches. *Journal of Politeness Research 19*(1). https://doi.org/10.1515/pr-2020-0048
The article shows the specificity of praising and complimenting implemented in religious discourse.
Ridealgh, K. (2021). Talking to God: conceptualizing an alternative politeness approach for the human/divine relationship. *Journal of Politeness Research*, *17*(1), 61–78. https://doi.org/10.1515/pr-2020-0027
Using a new approach—the "community-embedded" model—the author analyses the impact of religious rituals on relationship maintenance between humans.

References

Alsohaibani, A. (2017). *Influence of religion on language use: A sociopragmatic study on the influence of religion on speech acts performance.* PhD thesis. University of East Anglia. https://core.ac.uk/download/pdf/153534299.pdf
Austin, J.L. (1962). *How to Do Things with Words.* Oxford University Press.

Bouchara, A. & Qorchi, B. (2016). *The role of religion in shaping politeness during greeting encounters in Arabic. A matter of conflict or understanding.* Anchor Academic Publishing.
Brown, P. & Levinson, S.C. (1978). Universals in language usage: Politeness phenomena. In E.N. Goody (Ed.), *Questions and politeness: Strategies in social interaction*, 56–310. Cambridge University Press.
Brown, P. & Levinson, S.C. (1987). *Politeness. Some universals in language usage.* Cambridge University Press.
Chilton, P. (1990). Politeness, politics and diplomacy. *Discourse & Society*, *1*(2), 201–224.
Chilton, P. & Kopytkowska, M. (2018). *Religion, Language, and the Human Mind.* Oxford University Press.
Cohen, R. (1997). *Theatre of power: the art of diplomatic signalling.* Umi Books On Demand.
Coulmas, F. (1981). "Poison to Your Soul". Thanks and Apologies Contrastively Viewed. In F. Coulmas (Ed.), *Rasmus Rask Studies in Pragmatic Lingusitics. Volume 2: Conversational Routine*, 69–92. https://doi.org/10.1515/9783110809145
Culpeper, J. (2011). Politeness and impoliteness. In G. Andersen & K. Aijmer (Eds.), *Pragmatics of society.* Handbooks of Pragmatics. *5*, 391–436. De Gruyter.
Culpeper, J. & Tantucci, V. (2021). The Principle of (Im)politeness Reciprocity. *Journal of Pragmatics*, *175*, 146–164. https://doi.org/10.1016/j.pragma.2021.01.008
Dupré, L. (1991). *Inny wymiar. Filozofia religii* [*L'autre dimension. Essai de philosophie de la religion*; Another dimension of the Philosophy of Religion]. Znak.
Fraser, B. & Nolan, W. (1981). The association of deference with linguistic form. *International Journal of the Sociology of Language*, *1981*(27), 93–110. https://doi.org/10.1515/ijsl.1981.27.93
Foucault, M. (1981). The Order of Discourse. In R. Young (Ed.), *Untying the Text: A Post-Structuralist Reader*, 48–78. Routledge & Kegan Paul.
Fukushima, S. (2015). In search of another understanding of politeness: From the perspective of attentiveness. *Journal of Politeness Research*, *11*(2), 261–287. https://doi.org/10.1515/pr-2015-0011
Goffman, E. (1967). *Interaction ritual: Essays on face-to-face behavior.* Pantheon.
Graham, S. (2009). Hospitalk: Politeness and hierarchical structures in interdisciplinary discharge rounds. *Journal of Politeness Research*, *5*(1), 11–31. https://doi.org/10.1515/JPLR.2009.002
Haugh, M. (2003). Anticipated versus inferred politeness. *Multilingua*, *22*(4), 397–413.
Haugh, M. (2014). *Im/Politeness Implicatures.* De Gruyter.
Holmes, J. (1986). Compliments and Compliment Responses in New Zealand English. *Anthropological Linguistics*, *28*(4), 485–508.
Howarth, D. (2000). *Discourse.* Open University Press.
Jakobsen, R. (1960). Linguistics and Poetics. In T. Sebeok (Ed.), *Style in Language,* 350–377. Massachusetts Institute of Technology Press.
Kádár, D. (2017). *The Politeness, Impoliteness and Ritual: Maintaining the Moral Order in interpersonal Interaction.* Cambridge University Press. https://doi.org/10.1017/9781107280465
Kádár, D. & Haugh, M. (2013). *Understanding Politeness.* Cambridge University Press. https://doi.org/10.1017/CBO9781139382717
Kádár, D. & Mills, S. (2011), *Politeness in East Asia.* Cambridge University Press.
Kortmann, B. (2020). *English Linguistics. Essentials.* J.B. Metzler Verlag.
Laver, J. (1975). Communicative Functions of Phatic Communion. In A. Kendon, R. Harris, & M. Key (Eds.), *Organization of Behavior in Face-to-Face Interaction*, 215–238. De Gruyter. https://doi.org/10.1515/9783110907643.215
Locher M. (2012). Politeness Research from Past to Future, with a Special Focus on the Discursive Approach. In L. Fernández Amaya, et al. (Eds.), *New Perspectives on (Im)Politeness and Interpersonal Communication*, 37–60. Cambridge Scholars Publishing. https://edoc.unibas.ch/26954/1/2018050317102 7_5aeb266331d94.pdf
Locher, M. & Watts R.J., (2005). Politeness Theory and Relational Work. *Journal of Politeness Research*, *1*(1). 9–33. De Gruyter. https://doi.org/10.1515/jplr.2005.1.1.9.
Makuchowska, M. (2022). "*I look with deep gratitude and admiration…*"–praising and complimenting in papal speeches. *Journal of Politeness Research 19*(1). https://doi.org/10.1515/pr-2020-0048
Neff-Van Aertselaer, J., Van Dijk, T.A., Ammon U., Dirven, R., & Pütz, M. (Eds.). (2004). *Communicating ideologies: Multidisciplinary perspectives on language, discourse, and social practice* (Duisburg Papers on Research in Language and Culture). Peter Lang.
O'Driscoll, J. (2017). Face and (Im)politeness. In J. Culpeper, M. Haugh, D. Kádár (Eds.), *The Palgrave Handbook of Linguistic (Im)politeness*, 98–118. Palgrave Macmillan.

Ridealgh, K. (2021). Talking to God: conceptualizing an alternative politeness approach for the human/divine relationship. *Journal of Politeness Research, 17*(1), 61–78. https://doi.org/10.1515/pr-2020-0027

Sztajer, S. (2006). How is Religious Discourse Possible? The Constitutive Role of Metaphors in Religious Discourse, *Lingua ac Communitas, 16*, 49–54.

Sztajer, S. (2009). Język a konstruowanie świata religijnego [Language and the construction of the religious world]. Wydawnictwo Naukowe Wydziału Nauk Społecznych UAM.

Terkourafi, M. (2008). Toward a unified theory of politeness, impoliteness, and rudeness. In D. Bousfield & M.A. Locher (Eds.), *Impoliteness in Language. Studies on its Interplay with Power in Theory and Practice*, 45–74. De Gruyter.

Terkourafi, M. (2015). Conventionalization: A new agenda for im/politeness research, *Journal of Pragmatics, 86*, 11–18. Elsevier. http://dx.doi.org/10.1016/j.pragma.2015.06.004

Watts, R.J. (2003). *Politeness*. Cambridge University Press. DOI: 10.1017/CBO9780511615184

Wojtak, M. (2019). Do Boga..., o Bogu..., przed Bogiem... Gatunki przekazu religijnego w analizie filologicznej. Teolingwistyka 15. Biblos. [To God..., about God..., in front of God... Genres of religious communication in philological analysis].

Wierusz-Kowalski, J. (1973). Język a kult. Funkcja i struktura języka sakralnego. [Language and worship. The function and structure of sacral language]. *Studia Religioznawcze PAN,* R. IV. Sources List.

Source URLs

1. www.vatican.va/content/john-paul-ii/en/speeches/1999/november/documents/hf_jp-ii_spe_19991108_tbilisi-patriarch.html
2. www.vatican.va/content/john-paul-ii/en/speeches/1999/november/documents/hf_jp-ii_spe_18111999_fao.html
3. www.vatican.va/content/john-paul-ii/en/speeches/1999/november/documents/hf_jp-ii_spe_19991107_religioni-new-delhi.html
4. www.vatican.va/content/john-paul-ii/en/speeches/2001/may/documents/hf_jp-ii_spe_20010505_ecumenical-meeting.html
5. www.vatican.va/content/john-paul-ii/en/speeches/2001/may/documents/hf_jp-ii_spe_20010506_clergy-cathedral.html
6. www.vatican.va/content/john-paul-ii/en/speeches/2001/may/documents/hf_jp-ii_spe_20010506_bishops-syria.html
7. www.vatican.va/content/francesco/en/homilies/2017/documents/papa-francesco_20170226_omelia-visita-allsaints.html
8. www.vatican.va/content/francesco/en/speeches/2016/june/documents/papa-francesco_20160624_armenia-cattedrale-etchmiadzin.html
9. www.vatican.va/content/francesco/en/speeches/2015/june/documents/papa-francesco_20150606_sarajevo-incontro-ecumenico.html
10. www.vatican.va/content/francesco/en/speeches/2013/may/documents/papa-francesco_20130510_tawadros.html
11. www.vatican.va/content/francesco/en/speeches/2016/june/documents/papa-francesco_20160625_armenia-incontro-ecumenico.html
12. www.vatican.va/content/john-paul-ii/en/speeches/1999/november/documents/hf_jp-ii_spe_19991109_tbilisi-culture.html
13. www.vatican.va/content/john-paul-ii/en/speeches/2000/jan-mar/documents/hf_jp-ii_spe_20000325_jerusalem-patriarchate.html
14. www.vatican.va/content/john-paul-ii/en/speeches/2001/may/documents/hf_jp-ii_spe_20010506_omayyadi.html
15. www.vatican.va/content/john-paul-ii/en/speeches/1999/november/documents/hf_jp-ii_spe_19991108_tbilisi-patriarch.html
16. www.vatican.va/content/john-paul-ii/en/speeches/1999/november/documents/hf_jp-ii_spe_19991108_tbilisi-cathedral.html

18

RELIGION IN THE DISCOURSE OF ABORTION

Helen Ringrow and Simon Statham

Introduction and Background

The language around abortion is often viewed through a religious lens. Although there is no one unified definitive 'religious position' on abortion (and within specific religions, there may well be a myriad of positions), religious institutions tend to have certain stances on abortion related to morality and ethics and these may intersect with national identity and/or geographical location (e.g. see Adamczyk, 2022 for more on the multilevel relationship between religion and abortion attitudes across the globe). In jurisdictions where religion and the interests of religious institutions are strongly intertwined with those of political parties and national governments, religious positions on abortion often drive and define the law on, and broad social and cultural views of, abortion and reproductive healthcare. These positions are routinely manifested in the language surrounding abortion in a range of national contexts. One such context is Ireland, where the interests of Church and State have been intimately and problematically interconnected since the foundation of the Irish State; this will be explored in the case study (Section 2).

Section 1 will review some of the existing linguistic and communication-based research on the religious language of abortion but will also draw on research from other disciplines that has implications for exploring religion in the discourse of abortion. We want to emphasise that, to the best of our knowledge, there is not a substantial existing body of work on this area specifically from a *linguistic* or *language-based perspective*, although the discourse of abortion rights (especially through a religious lens) is a hugely relevant area for those interested in the role of language. The body of work referenced in this chapter has therefore often come from disciplines outside of linguistics and communication studies but considers how the role of language is paramount in understanding debates around, and representations of, abortion in religious contexts or related to religious belief. This chapter surveys key research in the field, focusing on Christian traditions within the Global North.

The language used to discuss abortion (especially within religious framings) may be contested, particularly in terms of 'pro' or 'anti' 'choice' framings. More generally, labels are of interest for language analysis, especially if these labels relate to religious positions and/or if these labels may be contested or otherwise controversial (cf. Ringrow, 2021). The terminology in this chapter often makes use of the monikers 'pro-choice' ('pro-abortion') and 'anti-choice' ('anti-abortion')

DOI: 10.4324/9781003301271-20

to describe certain groups, and the language used by them. This framing broadly follows the Association for the Study of Abortion, which suggested 'right to choose' should counter 'right to life' terminology used by those opposed to abortion, and also reflects our own ideological positions as authors (Statham & Ringrow, 2022; see also Siegel & Greenhouse, 2010):

> To be 'pro-choice' clarifies that those in favour of reproductive rights and bodily autonomy are not 'anti-life' and offers a counterbalance to the 'pro-life' label adopted by the anti-choice lobby, particularly after the landmark United States Supreme Court decision in Roe v. Wade (earlier uses of the term were more general and were used, for example, by anti-war protestors who conflated positions opposed to violence with those opposed to abortion)
>
> (Statham & Ringrow, 2022, p. 540)

Within the range of examples cited throughout this chapter, the 'life' in the 'pro-life' moniker often comes from Christian groups, especially Catholicism and Evangelism, who tend to emphasise a foetal rights framework focused on the unborn child, embedded in a particular religious framing of when 'life' begins (Combellick, 2021; see also Watson, 2018), as opposed to an (often more secular) women's rights framework (e.g. Koralewska & Zielińska, 2021, Hunt, 2021). The terminology does not always fully do justice to the reality of these framings when experienced by individuals: for example, those affiliated with Christianity *do* have abortions and the connection between deciding whether to have an abortion is often highly complex, although religious background and abortion stigma are frequently intertwined (Combellick, 2021).

Religion in Pro- and Anti-abortion Discourses

Abortion is an issue that is linked to 'intense polarisation' (Combellick, 2021, p. 1), especially (although not limited to) religious contexts. Researchers working in this area have tended to explore the ideological underpinnings of these opposing discourses, which often reflect dominant voices within faith traditions. Much research has focused on the *gendered* representations of abortion in religious contexts, especially around mothers and motherhood. Lowe and Page (2019), for example, explore the construction of motherhood in anti-abortion activism in England and Wales, looking at the discourse of (predominantly) Catholic groups (and some Evangelical organisations). Their thematic analysis of abortion clinic activism shows that these groups emphasised the religiously framed 'natural' and 'sacrificial' role of motherhood through the use of religious messages and iconography (e.g. pictures of the Virgin Mary). However, these groups also employed secular framings to get across their religiously motivated arguments, such as quasi- or pseudo-scientific claims positing a (disputed) link between abortion and breast cancer for women (Lowe & Page, 2019). This appeal to the less religiously oriented audience, Lowe and Page argue, speaks to Britain as a 'post Christian' environment in which the majority of their intended audience may not necessarily respond well to explicit religious messaging. Within an Irish context, Kreischer's (2019) cognitive-corpus exploration also looks at gendered discourses through an examination of the concept words *mother*, *woman*, and *church* in Irish news media discourse on abortion. Her research finds that the discourse of a mother and child as being one entity who need protection often co-occurs with *church*, as a functionally supportive measure to reinforce traditional Catholic ideology on the sanctity and importance of motherhood. However, the terms *mother* and *church* do not always interact in other contexts: news articles *without* the term *church* more frequently speak of mothers being in danger.

Although much of the work on the discourse of abortion and religion has looked at opposing sides, some research does explore more ambivalent representations of abortion. For example, Combellick's (2021) empirical research into abortion storytelling websites examines how women discuss the morality of their abortions in this online context. Some of the narratives she identifies point to how, in contrast to traditional abortion debates within religious contexts, subjects manage apparent contradictory views around abortion in which they reference Christian theology or positioning in relation to the decision *to* terminate a pregnancy, often (re)presenting this as the morally desirable choice:

> I prayed and lifted all that was weighing upon me to God. And with all the love in my heart, I gave the potential life growing within me back to our creator.
>
> (from January 2012, Combellick, 2021, p. 13)

Other examples of this combining of religious worldviews with having an abortion includes one in which the foetus is conceptualised as having its own soul (a Christian framing), but the abortion is framed as an appropriate decision:

> I am Catholic so I had to make up an elaborate miscarriage story to friends to keep from being judged but I don't regret my abortion. My baby went straight to heaven and I know God sees our hearts and loves me and knew my desperation and fear of dying or almost dying in childbirth.
>
> (from October 2014, Combellick, 2021, p. 13)

Combellick (2021) views these and similar examples as resisting abortion stigma. For these subjects, their moral choices are not presented in opposition to their religious worldviews but rather as part of them. In Hunt's (2021) comparative study of human rights language in news media coverage in Canada and Ireland, she finds that non-religious framings of foetal rights (i.e. framings that do not mention morality or religious faith) are actually more frequent than religious ones in Irish news media texts from 'pro-life' groups. Morality or appeals to religious ethics/ viewpoints do, however, often appear in other representations of discourses of abortion (e.g. Statham and Ringrow's 2022 analysis of social media campaigns from Irish pro- and anti-choice groups; Bergen's 2022 exploration of how the Irish Doctors For Choice group provided an alternative narrative to a mainstream medical profession based on conservative Catholic ideas of sexual morality). The next section brings some of these above issues into a certain particular geographical, social, and historical focus through a case study on the use of religious language in Ireland's two abortion referenda.

Religious Language in Ireland's Abortion Referenda: A Critical Discourse Analysis

Our case study focuses on the issue of abortion in Ireland, where a constitutional prohibition on abortion was enacted in 1983 and, after decades of campaigning by pro-choice activists, was repealed by a referendum in 2018. We analyse campaign discourse from two key time periods, offering a critical discourse analysis (CDA) of religious language in the campaign to adopt the Eighth Amendment, the clause which gave the foetus constitutional status equal to that of women who were pregnant, in the 1980s, and the apparently less forceful focus on religion in the language of the campaign to retain the amendment in 2018.

In this section we analyse the presence and use of religious language in Ireland's two abortion referenda. The constitutional ban on abortion imposed in 1983 followed a controversial campaign which has been referred to as the 'second partitioning of Ireland', a phrase coined by an editorial in *The Irish Times* (30 August 1983)[1] and adopted by Hesketh (1990) as the title for his definitive work on the Pro-Life Amendment Campaign (PLAC), the group which spearheaded the adoption of the Eighth Amendment. One of the most prominent groups that fought unsuccessfully to retain the amendment in the referendum of 2018 was Save the 8th. We will use critical discourse analysis to assess the role played by religious groups and religious language in each campaign, reflecting upon the prominence and eventual decline of religion itself in late twentieth- and early twenty-first-century Ireland.

CDA is a critically focused and methodologically diverse analytical approach to the discourse produced by powerful institutions in society, including religious and political groups, aimed at revealing the 'ideologies which underpin dominant discourses in the social world' (Statham, 2022, p. 10). A key principle of CDA recognises that language is at the centre of how institutions naturalise and legitimise their principles and values. CDA encompasses a wide range of models of analysis that are unified through a core focus on how language operates as text, discursive practice, and social practice, with each of these interrelated levels of analysis corresponding with description, interpretation, and explanation (Fairclough, 1995). Essentially, CDA recognises that, whilst description of textual features of language is crucially important, analysis must transcend the textual in considering processes of production and consumption as well as view the social context of discourse and assess the wider societal effects of its linguistic structures. Our account of religious language in the discourse of the dominant anti-choice groups in the referenda of 1983 and 2018 will therefore address prominent linguistic features and discuss the socio-political context of this discourse.

The Pro-Life Amendment Campaign was an umbrella group that brought together 13 institutions to, according to a founding discussion document, 'achieve a constitutional referendum to protect human life from conception'.[2] It is clear at the outset that the language used by PLAC would be deeply moralistic; indeed Statham and Ringrow (2022) argue that concepts of morality—points about what is *right*—are at the core of both anti-choice and pro-choice arguments in the Irish abortion debate. Despite the clear focus on moral argumentation, the relationship between PLAC and religious groups and specifically religious language was, at least on the surface, somewhat more ambiguous. PLAC was concerned from its foundation about accusations from the diverse and broadly left-wing anti-amendment lobby that it was controlled by religious institutions, specifically by the Catholic Church. For example, an infamous article in the *Sunday Tribune* (21 August 1983)[3] connected the campaign to a 'purple shadow government' of Catholic Bishops who wanted the 'return of Irish politics to pulpit politics'. John O'Reilly, a leading right-wing figure, the vice-chairman of the Council of Social Concern, co-founder of the Irish Responsible Society and Knight of Columbanus who called the first meeting of PLAC in January 1981, stated in a discussion document that PLAC could be 'suborned to serve other interests or deflected from its purpose' if it allowed the 'tactics, policies and methods of a pro-life amendment to be unduly influenced or controlled by the Church'.[4] The campaign therefore took on a 'medico-legal turn' (Hug, 1999, p. 147) in terms of much of its official language, largely as a result of the influence of its chairwoman, Dr Julia Vaughan.

Despite this seeming wariness of too close an association with organised religion, PLAC's relationship with religious groups was not quite so straightforward. Dr Vaughan represented the Irish Catholic Doctors' Guild, one of the 13 founding institutions of PLAC. The others were the Congress of Catholic Secondary School Parents' Associations, the Guild of Catholic Nurses, the Guild of Catholic Pharmacists, the Catholic Young Men's Society, the St Thomas More Society, the Irish Pro-Life Movement, the National Association of the Ovulation Method, the Council of Social Concern, the Irish Responsible Society, the Society for the Protection of the Unborn Child, the Christian Brothers Schools Parents' Federation, and the St Joseph's Young Priests' Society. In the same discussion document in which O'Reilly sounded a note of caution on direct Church involvement in PLAC, he states, 'In our own lives and all our actions we must take moral and doctrinal direction from the magisterium of the Church and this is possibly what has us in the pro-life movement in the first place'.[5] The Church, O'Reilly states further, should 'promote the tenets of the Catholic faith clearly in their churches and schools and institutions which they control'.[6] It seems hardly surprising that PLAC was viewed as closely connected to religion and specifically to Catholicism and it is here where much of the specifically religious language of the 1983 abortion referendum is manifested.

Hesketh (1987, p. 366) refers to 'covert appeals from PLAC to Church authorities' and, despite a statement from the Catholic Hierarchy which acknowledged the 'right of each person to vote according to conscience', there were very clear connections between PLAC and the Catholic Church in Ireland. Chief amongst these connections was the fact that the view of abortion taken by PLAC, and indeed the anti-choice groups up until 2018 and beyond, was theologically identical to that of Catholic doctrine. It is for this reason that the Protestant churches in Ireland, despite not being broadly pro-choice, denounced the sectarian nature of the Eighth Amendment and ultimately did not support a referendum which was absolutist in nature, and which sought to curtail the ability of the Oireachtas (the parliamentary system in Ireland) to legislate on abortion. The language of a range of senior clerics in the Catholic Hierarchy makes clear the link between religious obligation and the stance that should be taken on abortion.

Bishop Kevin McNamara addressed the conscience element of the seemingly balanced Catholic Church statement on the referendum in a pastoral to his congregation by saying:

> A responsible decision of conscience presupposes that one has asked God's enlightenment in prayer, that one has informed oneself of the issues at stake and that one has carefully listened to the moral guidance of those whose duty it is to instruct and enlighten conscience.[7]

The syntactic organisation of McNamara's statement is particularly noteworthy from a textual perspective here; the process through which 'one has informed oneself' follows the act of prayer and is dependent upon the 'moral guidance' offered by the clergy. There was some awareness within the Catholic Church at the time of 'appearing to intrude on the political arena' (Hesketh, 1987, p. 360) but the extent of this awareness in practice often went no further than euphemistic noun phrases like 'those whose duty it is to instruct and enlighten conscience'. The process 'enlighten' is repeated in this sentence and it is provided firstly by God and then by the clergy; one's conscience is therefore not one's own, as it were.

Other members of the Catholic Hierarchy were less abstract and much more explicit in their language, with Dr Dominic Conway, Bishop of Elphin, saying pointedly that the 'referendum is not political but the issue at stake is the right to life of the unborn child. Human life is sacred according to Christian tradition'.[8] 'Christian tradition'—or more specifically in terms of the language of the Eighth Amendment, Catholic tradition—is presented here as self-evidently more important than a 'political' issue. Conway echoes another section of McNamara's statement which says that the 'issue is quite literally one of life and death. At stake in the referendum is the protection of lives of unborn children in great numbers'.[9] It is through this type of explicitly religious language that the

Church 'promote[d] the tenets of the Catholic faith in [...] institutions which they control' and they constructed a strong connection between religion and abortion to influence the voting intentions of their congregations in what was a deeply religious society. We will comment further below on the consistency of terminology present in the language of the Catholic Church, PLAC, and later Save the 8th—particularly in terms of the lexical construction of the foetus as a living, conscious being, which is common in anti-choice discourse in general—but we should also note that the language of Catholic clerics in churches and elsewhere in the 1983 campaign, which resonated much more powerfully and consistently than the Church's official statement on the referendum, was not wholly theological and addressed other political and ethical arguments in the debate.

Dr Dermot Ryan was one of the most senior figures in the Irish Church and, as Archbishop of Dublin, commanded influence over the country's largest population centre. Dr Vaughan consulted with Ryan at the beginning of PLAC's campaign in 1981. Ryan specifically addressed the issue of women's health in a pastoral to be read to congregations at Mass only days before the vote:

> We are being told that this amendment could kill women. No convincing evidence has been advanced to support this allegation. On the contrary, it has been firmly and repeatedly rejected by legal and medical authorities of the highest quality [...] My advice to you is that a "yes" vote on Wednesday will protect the right to life of the unborn child; it will not create a threat to expectant mothers; it will block any attempt to legalise abortion in this country.[10]

This statement offers a number of categorical assertions aimed at dismantling the pro-choice position that the Eighth Amendment posed a clear and present danger to the health of women in Ireland. Voters are told by Ryan that the amendment '*will* protect the right to life' and '*will not* create a threat to expectant mothers'; his statements are unambiguous and leave no room for doubt. The 'legal and medical authorities of the highest quality' who attest to these apparent facts were drawn largely from the Catholic organisations that founded PLAC and were frequently challenged by the legal and medical authorities who spoke as part of the Anti-Amendment Campaign (AAC). Hug (1999) suggests that the strong medical and legal support from each side of the debate almost cancelled out one another.

The tragic irony of Ryan's assertions is that it was the reality that 'this amendment could kill women' which eventually helped to abolish it in 2018. The death of Savita Halappanavar from a septic miscarriage in University Hospital Galway in 2012 was a direct result of the prohibitions to treatment enshrined within the Eighth Amendment and gave renewed impetus to pro-choice movements in Ireland that resulted in the Protection of Life during Pregnancy legislation in 2013 and the Health Act 2018, which followed the repeal of the Eighth Amendment. Savita Halappanavar's name will be infinitely connected to the repeal movement but there are countless women whose names we do not know who suffered as a direct result of the explicit and religious linguistic intervention of the Catholic Church into the 1983 abortion referendum.

Perhaps the most explicit of this religious, and specifically Catholic, linguistic intervention into Ireland's abortion referenda was the wording of the Eighth Amendment itself:

> The State acknowledges the right to life of the unborn and, with due regard to the equal right to life of the mother, guarantees its laws to respect, and, as far as practicable, by its laws to defend and vindicate that right.
>
> (*Bunreacht na hÉireann*, Article 40.3.3)

The legislation subordinates the life of the mother to the unborn foetus and reduces the constitutional status of 'woman' to 'mother' from the moment of conception. Whilst critical discourse analysis is obviously focused on the lexico-grammatical construction of text, it also concentrates on what is omitted. For this amendment those omissions refer to any acknowledgment to pregnancies resulting from abuse, rape, or incest or to fatal foetal abnormalities. The absolutism of the Eighth Amendment reflected the absolutism of the Catholic position on abortion and rejected any notion of the role of individual conscience or circumstances, which was acknowledged by Protestant and some non-Christian groups in Ireland.

The exact wording of the Eighth Amendment was the subject of political wrangling in the months prior to the referendum with somewhat more pragmatic terminology being preferred by other Christian churches and political parties. The dominant Fianna Fáil party however had historic and close ties with the Catholic Church and their wording passed both houses of the Oireachtas 'after a two-month long preaching campaign on the part of Catholic churchmen' (Hug, 1999, p. 153). The amendment was the latest manifestation of Catholic Church influence on government which could be traced back to the foundation of the Irish State and which was itself enshrined in the constitution. Mary Robinson, later President of Ireland and in 1983 a Labour member of Seanad Éireann, condemned the Church for 'entering into the political arena' and prophetically stated in a historic two hour-long attack on the Eighth Amendment that 'historians, commentators and social scientists will comment on […] the forces of the Catholic Church moving in on a political debate'.[11]

Mary Robinson classified the absolutism of the Eighth Amendment as a 'Catholic way of doing things'.[12] Despite the fact that much of the discourse produced by PLAC was marked by a medico-legal register, it cannot be said that the campaign was not guided by religion and religious language. Much of the official campaign language lacked explicit religiosity but this was a strategic choice rather than one which reflected the deeply Catholic ideologies at the heart of the organisation. These ideologies are reflected in the institutional composition of PLAC, contained within the wording of the Eighth Amendment itself and are very clearly manifested in the actions and discourse of the Catholic Church throughout the campaign.

By 2018 what Statham and Ringrow (2022, p. 542) call an 'almost perfect storm of circumstance' had left the Catholic Church in Ireland in a much less powerful and influential position. The features of this storm included paedophile priest scandals, exposure of cruelty in Catholic institutions such as so-called mother and baby homes and industrial schools, and new methods of campaigning utilised to significant success by pro-choice activists. The influence of the Catholic Church that was so pivotal in establishing the Eighth Amendment was now viewed as a potentially significant impediment to its retention. In comparing the campaign of Save the 8th with PLAC, John McGuirk, a spokesperson for the anti-choice group, described the campaign as a 'much more secular battle' in which 'telling voters to vote in a particular way because God wants them to was never likely to be a winner for either campaign'.[13] We will comment below on the fact that, not unlike the scenario 35 years previously, religion was nonetheless not wholly absent from anti-choice rhetoric in 2018. First, we offer a CDA account of language produced by Save the 8th, specifically the statement issued by the group's campaign director Niamh Uí Bhriain to accompany its official launch. The statement is reproduced below:

On May 25th, politicians are asking the public to trust them in legalising <u>abortion on demand</u>. They are effectively seeking a licence to kill *preborn babies*, and to introduce an abortion model that is in many ways even more <u>extreme</u> than the British regime. We believe that this is <u>a step too far</u> for most Irish people and that the abortion proposal will be rejected on May 25th.

For five years now, a sustained campaign to remove all legal protection from the *unborn child* has been waged. This campaign has been funded from overseas, cheered on by journalists, and embraced by **spineless politicians**.

There have been more **flip flops in the Dáil** in the last three years on the abortion issue than there are at the average beach.

The public are now being told by Simon Harris that this legislation will be restrictive. This is the same Simon Harris who begged for votes in 2011 from pro-life voters in order, he said, to save the 8th amendment. He has already **broken promises** on abortion—why should anyone believe his promises on abortion now?

We are told by the Taoiseach that this legislation will be restrictive—but this is the same Taoiseach who said in 2010 that any restrictive legislation would lead to <u>abortion on demand</u>.

Then we have Simon Coveney, who has held **four distinct positions on abortion in the last year alone**, and who **does not trust** his own colleagues not to **shift their position** again. Simon Coveney has had **more positions on abortion in the month than most people manage in an entire lifetime**.

This referendum is happening because Katherine Zappone demanded it as a condition for her support of the Government. What will **people like** Katherine Zappone demand in the future? <u>Extreme</u> as this proposal is, will it be followed by an <u>even more liberal abortion regime</u>?

The electorate are being asked to hand over the right to life of *unborn children* to a political class that has **broken promise after promise on abortion**. Nearly every politician in this Government has **broken a promise** on abortion, some of them have **broken several**. And now they're making another promise—that this is restrictive abortion. The facts speak otherwise.

This is <u>abortion on demand</u>, for any reason or none, through the first three months of the *preborn baby*'s life. It is abortion because the *baby* is a twin, or is inconvenient, or has a disability or is a girl. It doesn't matter what the reason is.

Then, <u>the proposal goes even further</u>. It seeks to allow late-term abortion—the killing of *preborn babies* up to 6 months on health grounds. In Britain 98% of all abortions are carried out on health grounds. And it also seeks to allow abortion until birth where the *baby* has a severe disability.

This referendum is not about helping women—abortion doesn't help women, it hurts them. Rather, the referendum seeks to make the Irish people complicit in establishing a licence to kill *preborn babies*.

The public cannot trust politicians. Every single voter in this country knows that to be true. And we're not being asked to trust them with water charges, or property taxes—we are being asked to trust them with the right to life of *babies in the womb*.

This legislation is <u>already more liberal</u> than what was initially proposed in the UK in 1967, and we need only look to see how that turned out. One in every five pregnancies in the UK ends in abortion. It is not just a travesty but a shocking and enduring tragedy.

A yes vote is not a vote for choice. It is a vote of active approval. It is a vote to sanction every single abortion that becomes legal after the 8th amendment is repealed.

On this side of the debate, we believe that this is deeply wrong, and that a YES vote would be a horrible and tragic mistake. We are asking the Irish people to trust their guts on this. They are being asked to give politicians a power **they do not deserve and cannot be trusted** to wield.

They are being asked to sanction not just this abortion law, but every abortion law, and every abortion, in the future. This, for Ireland, is <u>going too far</u>.

So, we're asking people to say NO to <u>abortion on demand</u>. And they are responding. 100,000 marched in the Rally to Save the 8th and thousands are out canvassing every week to Save the 8th. The polls are turning in our favour, as the reality of the repeal slogan become more and more evident to voters.

This is a rising of the people against the **elites**, and on May 25th, it's time to join a rebellion, and reject both <u>abortion on demand</u> and the **untrustworthy political class** that wants to repeal the right to life of *children before birth*.[14]

Several key themes are retrievable from a CDA of this statement which demonstrate some of the key strategic narratives constructed by Save the 8th during their campaign. A core message here is that politicians in Ireland are untrustworthy. The statement constructs a strong lexical field through repetition of words and phrases, which are indicated in **bold** in the reproduction here, that condemn an 'untrustworthy political class' who have 'broken promise after promise' on abortion. There is of course something ironic about anti-choice activists claiming to be a 'rising of the people against the elites' when elite political and religious institutions were at the forefront of anti-choice movements since the foundation of the Irish State. Critical linguists have also commented frequently on how institutional discourse often constructs ideological positions as established facts and here the untrustworthiness of politicians is presented as a common-sense reality of which 'every single voter in this country' is already innately aware. Hence to 'trust their guts on this' by voting 'No' should be seen as the only common-sense course of action available.

The argument that the 'public cannot trust politicians' plays on the insistence of Save the 8th that, rather than be 'restrictive', to repeal the amendment would lead inevitably to an 'even more liberal abortion regime'. This well-worn 'floodgate trope' (Earner-Byrne & Urquhart, 2019, p. 126) relies on the presupposition that proposed new abortion regulations are too 'extreme' and that they equate to 'abortion on demand'. Both these arguments are constructed in Uí Bhriain's statement through the phrases that we have <u>underlined</u> here. 'Abortion on demand' is repeated on five occasions in this comparatively short statement, reasserting the floodgate trope that abortion will become a casual act of convenience. Whilst pro-choice activists often remind us that the reasons for seeking a termination should be a matter for individuals, the convenience option implied by the phrase 'abortion on demand' invokes strong judgements of moral impropriety in many conservative and/or religious societies. The ninth paragraph of this statement attempts to establish that women will pursue abortion on a whim—'it doesn't matter what the reason is'—and the tenth invokes even stronger moral condemnation by connecting abortion to disability discrimination. The phrase 'abortion on demand' is an example of negative social sanction: propriety according to the system of Appraisal (Martin & White, 2005), which provides a model to analyse how evaluation is constructed in language. Negative social sanction refers to the fact that this phrase invokes a strong moral condemnation. Even though pro-choice groups were persistently accused of pursuing abortion on demand, they strategically avoided using the phrase. Whilst it is quite semantically ambiguous, 'abortion on demand' conjures up images of an uncaring, dystopian society marked by a 'licence to kill preborn babies', a phrase which is also repeated in the statement.

Uí Bhriain's statement includes ten references to the foetus, which are *italicised* here, all of which operate to humanise the foetus through nouns like 'babies' and 'children'. The modifiers of these nouns, 'preborn' and 'unborn', and prepositional phrases like 'in the womb' and 'before birth' all augment the perception of the foetus as conscious, feeling, and vulnerable with an established 'right to life'. There is a clear consistency here between the language of Save the 8th and the Catholic Church's religious language in support of the PLAC campaign in 1983. Catholic doctrine recognises life from the moment of conception and phraseology of the 'unborn child' present in the language of PLAC, Save the 8th, and indeed anti-choice groups historically and globally, is a key feature of the religiosity of their language.

Despite the characterisation of John McGuirk of the 2018 campaign as a 'much more secular battle' and the fact that the agenda of Save the 8th was not set by the Catholic Church or its affiliate institutions that comprised PLAC, it is not quite the case that religion had no role to play in the campaign. In the same way that they did in 1983, the Catholic Hierarchy issued pastoral letters marked by moral language—the Bishop of Cloyne, William Crean, spoke of a 'great struggle between light and dark, between life and death'[15]—that called on congregations to reject repeal. In the run-up to the vote in May 2018, Catholic priests threw open their pulpits to members of Save the 8th in a clear expression of a connection between the group and the Church. Save the 8th responded to criticism of campaigning from the altar, including by the liberal group the Association of Catholic Priests, by saying they were 'delighted and honoured' to do so, noting that 'our campaign shares, and applauds the deep commitment of the Christian community to the values of respect for the life and dignity of every human individual'.[16]

The language of both PLAC and Save the 8th is perhaps more moral than explicitly religious and both were marked by a medico-legal register also used by pro-choice activists. Nonetheless, certain recurring language, particularly in terms of lexical items which humanise the foetus, is markedly Catholic in terms of doctrine. PLAC was formed by Catholic institutions, enlisted the help of the Catholic Church both covertly and overtly, most significantly in the absolutist wording of the Eighth Amendment itself, and its campaign was explicitly supported by members of the Catholic Church in Ireland. Despite the collapse of the moral authority of the Irish Church following decades of exposure that laid bare the 'myth of Church compassion' (Statham & Ringrow, 2022, p. 542), Save the 8th shared the same absolutist view of abortion as their predecessors in PLAC and openly embraced the role of the Catholic Church in attempting, unsuccessfully in 2018, to secure its prominence over responsible healthcare in Ireland.

Implications and Future Directions

Despite victory for change in the 2018 abortion referendum, anti-choice voices have not fallen silent in Ireland. In part spurred on by the fact that the Health Act 2018, the legislation that resulted from the repeal of the Eighth Amendment, includes several restrictions which have been criticised by some in the pro-choice lobby (de Londras, 2020), anti-choice groups continue to agitate to decrease the scope of reproductive rights. One of the largest anti-choice groups in Ireland is Pro Life Campaign, which describes itself with no intended irony as a 'non-denominational human rights organisation'. The language of groups like Pro Life Campaign operates across a range of discourse types, such as online, on political leaflets and through the use of multimodal resources like artwork on placards and is marked by the same features evident in the language of PLAC and Save the 8th, such as lexis and images that humanise the foetus. As well as attempting to influence the mandatory three-year review of the Health Act to impose more restrictions on the circumstances of choosing a termination, in terms of sections of the legislation that relate to waiting periods and compulsory medical consultations for example, one of the current 'projects' of Pro Life Campaign relates to the six counties that comprise the state of Northern Ireland.

Up until repeal of the Eighth Amendment both states in Ireland generally had equally oppressive abortion regimes that were propped up by political and religious traditionalism, and pro-choice campaigns to overturn these conditions operated on both sides of and across the border in Ireland. Repeal of the Eighth Amendment gave greater reproductive freedom to women in the Irish Republic but did not amend the legal conditions in the North. One of the most significant linguistic features of the victory of the repeal campaign was the categorical assertion in the prominent slogan 'the North is next', which referred to the apparent commitment of the pro-choice movement to ensure that Irish women across the island would eventually have appropriate access to abortion care. It was however a private member's bill in Westminster, taking advantage of one of the characteristic stalemates in devolved governance in the North, which secured abortion rights, at least in theory, for Northern abortion seekers. In October 2022 the British government committed to delivering services that politicians had continued to refuse to enact despite their statutory obligations. In the North, too, anti-choice voices continue to be loud. Precious Life, the prominent Belfast-based anti-choice group, has appropriated the slogan 'the North is next' on placards which celebrate the overturning of Roe v. Wade in the US to claim that growing international anti-choice sentiment could still turn the tide in terms of the reproductive rights of Irish women. The academic and activist Goretti Horgan (2009) reminds us that political dealing between Northern political parties and the British government, including during the landmark Good Friday Agreement negotiations, have been to the detriment of the right to choose on several occasions in the past. Rossiter's (2009) account of the support network in place in Britain for Irish abortion seekers, spearheaded by the Irish Women's Abortion Support Group (IWASG), demonstrates very clearly that women from both sides of the border in Ireland were in equal need of aid and assistance in seeking a termination. Irish women were helped in London throughout from the 1980s onwards regardless of what part of Ireland they travelled from.

It is particularly noteworthy that a group like Precious Life has been able to recontextualise so prominent and linguistically categorical a statement as 'the North is next', a move facilitated by the fact that, despite the photo opportunities availed of by nationalist politicians in particular, very little action—linguistic or otherwise—was taken to make the assertion a reality. Several academic works, prominent amongst them the comprehensive historical analysis of Earner-Byrne and Urquhart (2019) and Rossiter's (2009) account of London-based abortion support networks for Irish women, have addressed the situation in the North in terms of abortion but many more have addressed the Irish abortion question as if it relates exclusively to the Irish Republic. For example, a wide ranging issue of the journal *Feminist Encounters* (6:1, 2002) comprises 16 compelling articles in a special issue on Irish abortion activism whilst barely mentioning the Northern context. A very prominent activist publication by Mullally (2018) includes the North in its chronological introduction but it does not feature any further and Griffin et al. (2019) review the 'transformation of Irish society' by exclusively focusing on the Republic. Many of these and other prominent works are of course analyses of the Eighth Amendment and so perhaps it is unsurprising that they take a somewhat exclusive approach. Most of them are also approaches from politics, history, and sociology and point to an opportunity for linguistic research on abortion in Ireland to emerge alongside works such as those by Bergen (2022), Kreischer (2019), Statham and Ringrow (2022), and Strange (2022a, 2022b) that take a language analytic approach to the Irish abortion issue.

Our case study in this chapter focuses on a particular geographical and cultural context but can be situated within a broader global struggle for bodily autonomy, which has been brought into sharper focus since the repeal of the landmark Roe v. Wade ruling in the United States. Our study can be further contextualised by examining the comparative role of religious language in these international arenas. We predict more research looking at pro- and anti-choice positions in both state and federal contexts, and the presence or absence of religion in the discourse of abortion. For example, Evans and Narasimhan (2020) explore anti-abortion testimony and legislative debate related to Georgia's fetal 'heartbeat' (i.e. at the detection of possible embryonic cardiac activity, generally six weeks gestation) abortion ban. Perhaps somewhat unexpectedly, they report a lack of religious discourse in their data, arguably deliberately so and in conjunction with a misuse of scientific discourse: 'heartbeat' was not connected to religious conceptualisations of when 'life' begins, and references to 'God' and 'religion' were, overall, limited by legislators and community members providing testimony (Evans & Narasimhan, 2020). Looking beyond North America to the context of Poland, which implemented a ban on abortion except for in some very exceptional circumstances in 2020, research in a Polish context following the use of language around this ban, and subsequent media coverage, is likely to increase further (see, for example, Koralewska and Zielińska's 2021 exploration of how abortion was covered in the Polish right-wing press).

Beyond geographical contexts, we also expect to see more research focused on trans- and non-binary abortion seekers, especially in religious contexts in which they may already face exclusion or discrimination due to their perceived lack of conformity with some faith-based gender norms. Trans- and non-binary abortion seekers are also likely to face additional barriers to abortion care but may be under-represented in the existing literature (cf. de Londras, 2020).

Within language studies and applied linguistics, there is a growing body of research that is investigating the ethical implications of researching sensitive or potentially distressing data. Whilst much existing research has focused on avoiding possible harm to participants, increasingly, researchers have asked: what about avoidance of harm to the *researcher*, especially in cases when the researcher may be faced with data promoting xenophobia, racism, facism, misogyny, and so on (e.g., Fuchs, 2018; Massanari, 2018; Rüdiger & Dayter, 2016)? In researching religion in the discourses of abortion, the researcher may not (necessarily) be faced with neo-Nazi or similar ideologies. Nonetheless, they may be faced with different challenges by researching a sensitive subject, from encountering opposing ideological and religious standpoints to what could be categorised as extreme prejudice from their 'unlikeable subjects' (Rüdiger & Dayter, 2016), graphic imagery and even the possibility of being targeted by activist groups. Researchers may also have had their own personal experiences relating to abortion and religion, which calls for a thoughtful and reflective approach to ethics. There are additional complex issues relating to the positionality of the researcher, and consent with regards to online data (e.g. Mackenzie, 2017). We imagine future research into religion and the discourse of abortion will draw on, and add to, this increasing body of work and may adopt existing good practice within linguistics (and other disciplines) of advocacy and support groups for researchers.

Notes

1 'The second partitioning of Ireland' (*The Irish Times*, 30/08/1983).
2 John O'Reilly ('The need for a human life constitutional amendment', PLAC, 08/01/1981).
3 *Sunday Tribune* (21/08/1983).
4 John O'Reilly ('The abortion problem internationally', PLAC, 01/07/1981).
5 John O'Reilly ('The abortion problem internationally', PLAC, 01/07/1981).
6 John O'Reilly ('The abortion problem internationally', PLAC, 01/07/1981).
7 Dr Kevin McNamara, Bishop of Kerry ('A Conscience vote is a "Yes" vote—Bishop', *Irish Press* 02/09/1983).
8 Dr Dominic Conway, Bishop of Elphin (Knock Basilica, 21/08/1983).
9 Dr Kevin McNamara, Bishop of Kerry ('A Conscience vote is a "Yes" vote—Bishop', *Irish Press* 02/09/1983).

10 Dr Dermot Ryan, Archbishop of Dublin (Pastoral letter, 07/09/1983).
11 Senator Mary Robinson (Seanad Debates, col. 543, 04/05/1983)
12 Senator Mary Robinson (Seanad Debates, col. 543, 04/05/1983)
13 John McGuirk ('Church and religion take back seat as secular Ireland votes on abortion', *Reuters*, 10/05/ 2018).
14 Niamh Uí Bhriain (Save the 8th, www.save8th.ie/campaign--launch-vote-no/).
15 Dr William Crean, Bishop of Cloyne ('Church and religion take back seat as secular Ireland votes on abortion', *Reuters*, 10/05/2018)
16 Save the 8th ('Save the 8th defends the practice of referendum campaigners speaking at Mass', *The Irish Times*, 05/05/2018).

Further Reading

Johnson, G. (2003). *Abortion from the Religious and Moral Perspective: An Annotated Bibliography*. Greenwood Publishing.
A hugely comprehensive resource providing suggestions for further reading on religious and moral perspectives for and against abortion, especially in a North American context.
Ralph, D. (2020). *Abortion and Ireland: How the 8th Was Overthrown*. Palgrave.
An in-depth sociological exploration of the campaign to secure abortion rights in Ireland, with a focus on 'abortion talk', i.e. the significance of women's own voices and narratives in the Repeal the 8th campaign.
Statham, S. & Ringrow, H. (2022). 'Wrap our arms around them here in Ireland': Social media campaigns in the Irish abortion referendum, *Discourse & Society 33*(4): 539–557.
This article assesses the specific role of social media language in the Irish abortion referendum and explores how campaign groups appealed to issues of morality within a specific religious and national setting.
Watson, K. (2018). *Scarlet A: The Ethics, Law, and Politics of Ordinary Abortion*. Oxford University Press.
This book provides a comprehensive look at private, 'ordinary' abortion conversations within the United States, considering legal aspects, the role of language in shaping the debate, and conflicting approaches to ethics.
Strange, L. (2022b). The Intersection of Nation and Gender in the Linguistic Landscape of Ireland's Eighth Amendment Referendum Campaign, *Linguistic Landscape, 8*(1): 1–31.
This article explores the linguistic landscape of the Irish referendum, exploring issues of national identity in relation to gender, heteronormativity, and Catholicism.

References

Adamczyk, A. (2022). Religion as a Micro and Macro Property: Investigating the Multilevel Relationship between Religion and Abortion Attitudes across the Globe, *European Sociological Review, 38*(5), 816–831.
Bergen, S. (2022). 'The kind of doctor who doesn't believe doctor knows best': Doctors for Choice and the medical voice in Irish abortion politics, 2002–2018, *Social Science & Medicine, 297*, 114817.
Combellick, S.L. (2021). 'My Baby Went Straight to Heaven': Morality Work in Abortion Online Storytelling, *Social Problems, 00*, 1–17.
Earner-Byrne, L. & Urquhart, D. (2019). *The Irish Abortion Journey, 1920–2018*. Palgrave Macmillan.
Evans, D.P. & Narasimhan, S. (2020). A narrative analysis of anti-abortion testimony and legislative debate related to Georgia's "fetal heartbeat" abortion ban, *Sexual and Reproductive Health Matters, 28*(1), 1686201.
Fairclough, N. (1995). *Critical Discourse Analysis: The Critical Study of Language*. Longman.
Fuchs, C. (2018). 'Dear Mr Neo-Nazi, Can you please give me your informed consent so that I can quote your fascist tweet': Questions of social media research ethics in online ideology critique. In Meikle, G. (Ed.), *The Routledge Companion to Media and Activism*. 385–394. Routledge.
de Londras, F. (2020). A hope raised and defeated? The continuing harms if Irish abortion law, *Feminist Review 124*, 33–50.
Griffin, G., O'Connor, O., Smyth, S., & O'Connor, A. (2019). *It's a Yes: How Together for Yes Repealed the Eight and Transformed Irish Society*. Orphen.
Hesketh, T. (1987). *The Pro-Life Amendment Campaign, 1981–1983*. PhD thesis, Queen's University Belfast.
Hesketh, T. (1990). *The Second Partitioning of Ireland? The Abortion Referendum of 1983*. Brandsma.

Hill, S., Hoover, S., McAuliffe, M., & Side, K. (Eds). (2002). Special Issue on Repealing the Eighth: Irish Reproductive Activism, *Feminist Encounters*, *6(*1).

Horgan, G. (2009). Foreword. In A. Rossiter, *Ireland's Hidden Diaspora*, 17–23. IASC Publishing.

Hug, C. (1999). *The Politics of Sexual Morality in Ireland*. Macmillan.

Hunt, K. (2021). Exploiting a Crisis: Abortion Activism and the COVID-19 Pandemic, *Perspectives on Politics*, *20*(2), 396–411.

Koralewska, I. & Zielinska, K. (2021). 'Defending the unborn', 'protecting women' and 'preserving culture and nation: anti-abortion discourse in the Polish right-wing press'. *Culture, Health & Sexuality*, *24*(5), 673–687.

Kreischer, K.S. (2019). The relation and function of discourses: a corpus-cognitive analysis of the Irish abortion debate. *Corpora*, *14*(1), 105–130.

Lowe, P. & Page, S.J. (2019). Rights-based Claims Made by UK Anti-Abortion Activists. *Health and Human Rights*, *21*(22), 133–144.

Mackenzie, J. (2017). Identifying informational norms in Mumsnet Talk: a reflexive-linguistic approach to internet research ethics. *Applied Linguistics Review*, *8*(2–3), 293–314.

Martin, J.R. & White, P.R.R. (2005). *The Language of Evaluation: Appraisal in English*. Palgrave Macmillan.

Massanari, A.L. (2018). Rethinking research ethics, power, and the risk of visibility in the era of the "Alt-Right" gaze, *Social Media + Society*, *4*(2), 1–9.

Mullally, U. (Ed). (2018). *Repeal the 8th*. Unbound.

Rüdiger, S. & Dayter, D. (2016). The ethics of researching unlikeable subjects: Language in an online community, *Applied Linguistics Review*, *8*(2–3): 251–269.

Ringrow, H. (2021) Identity. In Pihlaja, S. (Ed.), *Analysing Religious Discourse*, 276–292. Cambridge University Press.

Rossiter, A. (2009) *Ireland's Hidden Diaspora: The 'Abortion Trail' and the Making of a London Irish Underground, 1980–2000*. IASC Publishing.

Siegel, R. & Greenhouse, L. (2010). *Before Roe v. Wade: Voices that Shaped the Abortion Debate Before the Supreme Court's Ruling*. Kaplan.

Statham, S. (2022). *Critical Discourse Analysis: A Practical Introduction to Power in Language*. Routledge.

Statham, S. & Ringrow, H. (2022.) 'Wrap our arms around them here in Ireland': Social media campaigns in the Irish abortion referendum, *Discourse & Society*, *33*(4): 539–557.

Strange, L. (2022a). Ní Saoirse go Saoirse na mBan: Stancetaking, Gender and the Irish Language in the Linguistic Landscape of Ireland's 2018 Abortion Referendum, *Language in Society*, 1–25.

Strange, L. (2022b). The Intersection of Nation and Gender in the Linguistic Landscape of Ireland's Eighth Amendment Referendum Campaign, *Linguistic Landscape*, *8*(1): 1–31.

Watson, K. (2018). *Scarlet A: The Ethics, Law, and Politics of Ordinary Abortion*. Oxford University Press.

19

RELIGIOUS ORATORY AND LANGUAGE ONLINE

Fiona Rossette-Crake

Introduction and Background

The category of religious discourse encompasses multiple types of communication, including those that coincide with a sub-category, that of "religious oratory". Religious oratory serves as a banner term to group together what has traditionally been referred to as "oratory of the pulpit", "homiletics", or "preaching". In its most prototypical form, it corresponds to the relatively stable discursive genre of the sermon. Defined as "a talk on a moral or religious subject, usually given by a religious leader during a service" (Oxford English Dictionary), a sermon typically sets out to move and convert, and/or to help the congregation understand religious doctrine and holy texts, and to lead lives that are compatible with religious demands. In this chapter, the sub-category of religious oratory extends to new forms of speech that either take place in a religious context and/or fulfil some type of religious purpose.

Religious oratory is located within the general practice of oratory, or "the art or practice of formal speaking in public", (Oxford English Dictionary) with which it is inextricably linked. Oratory is both performance *and* text: it is the activity of speech-giving, and can remain as a textual product after the event in the form of an "archive text" (Maingueneau, 2014, p. 34); as noted for instance by Constable (1994), sermons often survive in a form very different from the way they were preached, such as in collections of manuscripts. Historically, religious oratory played an important role in the development of oratory and occupies a predominant position in the rhetorical canon. In the contemporary context of scholarship on religious discourse, oratory occupies relatively little space, or, at least, is rarely an object of study per se (e.g. Downes, 2010; Mukherjee, 2018; Chilton & Kopytowska, 2018; Hobbs, 2021). If this absence can be explained in part by the poststructuralist focus on text as opposed to oral modes of expression (Yelle et al., 2019), it is also due to the emphasis placed on new forms of (written and spoken) interaction—those in which religion is discussed and "worked out" (Pihlaja, 2021a, p. 1), and which take place thanks to the digital medium. These new forms of religious discourse contrast with the category of "institutional" forms, including sermons.

However, if the digital medium has engendered various new forms of religious discourse, it is also transforming the sermon as a discursive practice. Indeed, whatever the communication type, the digital revolution has triggered major upheavals, including the widespread renewal, thanks to

DOI: 10.4324/9781003301271-21

the advent of online video, of public speaking practice, which has engendered a number of new formats (cf. "the New Oratory" (Rossette-Crake, 2019)). In the case of religious oratory, next to the (traditional) format of the sermon delivered live by a speaker to a congregation, both of whom are physically present in church ("face-to-face sermon"), and following on from sermons broadcast via electronic media (radio and television—including televangelism), sermons, as well as various types of messages delivered by religious figures, are now being uploaded and/or livestreamed to a potentially limitless congregation/audience.

Parallel to the other technological revolution with which it is often compared—that of the printing press, which allowed the Bible to be (the first book) disseminated en masse—, the digital revolution is not only changing the way faith is practised and affecting belief itself (Campbell & Lövheim, 2011), it is also expanding the religious platform: the stage or pulpit is being replaced by the screen, and the place of worship has shifted to the virtual space provided by Web 2.0—one of the "new contexts for faith" identified by Pihlaja (2021a, p. 4). These online sermons qualify as an example of "online religion" whereby user-generated content serves "to 'do' religion online", that is, to worship, pray and exchange online (Helland, 2000). They are indicative of "the mediatisation of religious discourse and the emergence of new ways to distribute one's message to a variety of audiences" (Pihlaja, 2021b, p. 184), and are exemplified by the prominent phenomenon of "digital evangelism" (Omoniyi, 2017).

These new forms of technologically mediated preaching are forcing us to redefine the sermon, which can no longer qualify as "a religious speech *delivered typically in a church building, usually from a pulpit or an ambo*" (Adam, 2008, p. 9) (my emphasis), or as "pulpit oratory" (for instance, "Oratory of the pulpit", defined as "church oratory", features alongside "Oratory of the Bar" (legal oratory) or "Oratory of the Senate" in the nineteenth-century taxonomy drawn up by Cox (1863))—for the simple reason that there is no longer a pulpit. Similarly, we now grapple with (earlier) definitions for "preacher", which can no longer be reduced to "a person who speaks publicly about religious subjects *in a Christian church or other public space*" (*Britannica Dictionary*) (my emphasis)—unless we accept as "public space" the virtual realm of the Internet. Indeed, the digital medium has thrown into disarray the distinction between "public" and "private", not only in terms of space but also in terms of time and the self (e.g. "professional" versus "private" self).

This crisis of spaces, which was accelerated during the COVID-19 pandemic, particularly conditions videos posted to social networks, and results in what can be described as "public speaking turned private" (Rossette-Crake, 2022): that is, speakers, who are no longer necessarily public figures, are taking to the virtual floor of the digital interface, and are making their voices heard as they speak from private, intimate spaces. Such intimacy is a gauge of the authenticity that specifically characterises speaker ethos on social networks (Marwick & boyd, 2011). The consequences of the collapse of the divide between personal and public/collective is particularly far-reaching when religious devotion is at stake. For instance, when a preacher such as Juanita Bynum (see case study below) films herself from her living room for a video that is livestreamed and/or uploaded to YouTube as she delivers an oral performance that resembles, in terms of its content, a sermon, can we still qualify this as a "sermon" and/or as "religious oratory"?

If such content is included within the new "faith and language practices" borne out of "digital spaces" (Rosowsky, 2017), what of other examples of social media content delivered by other types of social actors and which, if they are far removed from conventional formats of religious devotion, are recognised as fulfilling a quasi-religious function? Assigned the status of "virtual sermon" (Stein, 2021)—here, "virtual" can be understood as "very near to" and "digitally simulated"—, such content is delivered by speakers who are themselves endowed with a quasi-religious status—that of "religious influencer" (Ajibade, 2019) or "quasi-spiritual influencer" (Stein, 2021), also described as the "neo-religious leaders of our era" or "Instavangelists" (*ibid.*) Indeed, a prominent category of social media content creator is that of "personal growth influencers": because they represent "role models of How to Live Life" (Chen, 2021)—for instance, "while they don't brand themselves as faith leaders, this is the role they play in many of their secular fans' lives" (Stein, 2021)—, a certain "religiosity" can be posited for the discourses produced by these influencers. These discourses often showcase the term "spiritual" rather than "religious"; they fulfil a "religious" function in the broad sense (in keeping with that adopted for this handbook) which extends for example to "the way people deal with ultimate concerns about their lives" and "attitudes toward the broader human community or the natural world" (www.britannica.com/topic/religion). Content creators such as Gabby Bernstein (see case study below) constitute "a different kind of clergy" (Stein, 2021), with their subscribers becoming "digital disciples" (Carlson, 2021) (these last two expressions are coined by members of the Christian community who criticise the phenomenon).

Importantly, what these various commentaries omit to acknowledge is the role of *spoken performance* in generating such a function/power, which is also identified in other types of online public speaking. An iconic example of this is provided by TED talks. TED talks date back to 1984, but the format as we know it today began with the launch of the TED website in 2006. TED stands for "Technology, Entertainment and Design", which captures the focus of the first talks, but today they cover most subjects, with many relating to self-help topics, which match particularly well with the TED slogan to deliver "inspiring" talks. In the case of the TED speaker, they are sometimes conferred a sacred-like status, akin to that of guru or "digital shaman": "One of the first steps toward becoming a digital deliverer is becoming a digital shaman, one who can foster an interaction in which the audience and shaman-rhetor co-deliver (invent) a solution to their shared, unconscious problems" (Morey, 2016, p. 13). Similarly, a number of influencers are commonly associated with the term "guru" for instance: "health guru", "mental health guru", "sports/lifestyle guru", etc. Shaman status derives not only from the type of content addressed in the talks (cf. "a solution to their shared, unconscious problems"), but also from the fact that the speaker is cast as mediator rather than as originator of the message—akin to the figure of the "shaman" or "official soothsayer" described by Zumthor (1983, p. 214) in the case of ancient tribal song.

This ancient form of orality particularly highlights the power of spoken language which, unlike writing, which isolates, plays on the vocal resonance of meaning and the "interiority of sound", linking it intrinsically to human experience and making it "empathetic and participatory" (Ong, 1982). In other words, there are dimensions to spoken language which are inherently collective and transcending and hold clear stakes in the religious context. And we can posit a natural link between digitalised speech and discourse that fulfils a religious or quasi-religious function, by virtue of the close association between technology and religion. As Noble (1999, pp. 4–5) argues, there is not only a "religion of technology" in that "the technological enterprise has been and remains suffused with religious belief", whereby "scientists and technologists increasingly attest publicly to the value of their work in the pursuit of divine knowledge", but there is also a "technology of religion" in that "religious leaders promote their revival of spirit through an avid and accomplished use of the latest technological advances".

Extending the category of religious oratory to include these digital productions by new types of social actors raises the issue of speaker authority. In these instances, we are, again, far removed from the traditional sermon, where the preacher speaks in their capacity as an official member of the institution of the Church. Further definitions for "preacher" include "one whose function is to preach sermons: pastor, minister" (*Dictionary Merriam Webster*), or "usually a member of the clergy" (*Collins Dictionary*). As noted by Pihlaja (2021b, p. 89),

One of the features of religious discourse in the contemporary world is the presence of a diversity of opinions and authorities in decentralised contexts [...] A Facebook preacher may have two million 'friends' and speak directly to them on a day-to-day basis, with no oversight from a traditional religious institution.

Such "decentralised contexts" reflect the horizontal, participatory ecosystem of social media, where the crisis of spaces is also a crisis of places or positioning of participants. The crises of space and place/speaker roles are two aspects of what has been described as the "crisis of public discourses" in the post-truth era (Angermuller, 2023), and which is directly dependent on digital technology and social media. In the case of these digital speakers, legitimacy depends directly upon the ability to attract subscribers, which, as underlined by Pihlaja (2021b), who talks of the "popularisation of religious leaders in the market economy", brings into play, just like the televangelists of the television era, forces of marketisation; in the context of social media, these forces interact with the phenomenon of microcelebrity (Marwick & boyd, 2011), foregrounded by the "presentation of the self" (Jones & Hafner, 2021, p. 212).

Research into the language of religious oratory in the contemporary context therefore needs to focus notably on the specificity (or not) of the language of the various aforementioned online productions which are produced by very different types of social actors. For instance, if they differ in format and content, are there nevertheless linguistic similarities with respect to face-to-face sermons produced by preachers belonging to traditional religious institutions? Can a "religious register"—or registers—be identified? What is the ethos of the religious orator? Are digital preachers still talking the "same" language? How do they compare with other (e.g. clearly secular) forms of digital oratory? For instance, is the situation today comparable to that predating the advent of digital oratory, apropos of which Crystal and Davy (1969) affirmed that the language of sermons had more in common with other varieties of public speaking than with other types of religious discourse—

obviously they will share a great deal of vocabulary (with other types of religious discourse) [...] But when one considers the whole range of [...] liturgical language, it becomes clear that the differences which exist between this and the other kinds of religious language are more striking than the similarities

(Crystal & Davy, 1969, p.149, quoted in Adam, 2008, p. 9)

And finally, because we are dealing with language that is *performed*, what parallels can be established between linguistic and multimodal resources—the latter proving particularly significant in the case of religious discourse, notably sermons?

Contemporary studies about the language of religious oratory typically emanate—like studies of religious discourse generally—from the field of discourse studies (Wijsen, 2013), and, no doubt because they view religion as a "category" that is "discursively constituted and shifting" (Yelle et al., 2019), extend their analysis to a number of the previously listed online formats. In terms of linguistic forms, these studies highlight the place of rhetorical questions, first-person reference, and deixis, as well as, in terms of rhetorical phenomena, the use of metaphor, narrative structure, and intertextual references. For instance, in a corpus of sixteenth-century sermons, Garner (2007) analyses the role of questions, embedded dialogue, discourse markers, verbatim repetition, and paraphrase; sermons are analysed from a functional sentence perspective by Adam (2008), and in regard to forms of appraisal in Malmström (2018). Marone (2017) investigates the rhetorical structure of the sermon (including a live-streamed sermon), as well as rhythm, pausing, and collective and first-person reference; the latter is also highlighted in Bryan and Albakry's (2016) study of the "hyper-personalised" discourse of online sermons, as well as in the psycholinguistic analysis of "digital-televangelists self-help texts" by Claydon and Whitehouse-Hart (2018).

Much scholarship is conducted within the framework of critical discourse analysis, across cultures and across faiths (e.g. Muchnick, 2005; Eldin, 2014; Khakpour & Ag, 2018; Khan et al., 2021; Mansouri, 2023). For example, El Naggar (2018) examines the interactive forms and construal of "ordinariness" in YouTube videos of the American Muslim televangelist Baba Ali, and concludes by announcing "the changing face of religious discourse". Comparisons across faiths can be seen in Singh and Thuraisingam (2011), while James (2010) studies the forms of what he calls the "McDonaldisation" of Indian televangelism. However, what is interesting about all these various studies is that they focus on specific examples and specific linguistic phenomena and do not seek to identify a "religious register" that would be common to other sermons. The case studies that follow explore this question, which is articulated with respect to the issue of speaker authority in association with an appraisal of participant frameworks.

Modelling Language Choices: Some Examples of Contemporary Religious Oratory

Presentation of Examples and Theoretical Framework

I propose to follow in current scholarship by adopting a discourse analytical approach, drawing mainly on a systemic functional framework (e.g. Halliday & Matthiessen, 2014). Oratory constitutes a complex object of study, to which linguists have given relatively little attention. Traditional descriptions contrast the lexicogrammar of "spoken" language with that of "written" language (e.g. Halliday, 1985; Biber et al., 1999). However, oratory corresponds to a mode of production that has for instance been described as "spoken monologic" (Halliday & Matthiessen, 2014): it is language which is spoken, but which, unlike that of prototypical speech (that is, the turn-taking of conversation), is monologic, marshalling an asymmetrical, "one-to-many" relation that brings together one speaker and multiple addressees. The speaker has "speaking rights" (Kress, 1994, p. 20) and is endowed with authority, power, and the assurance that they hold the floor, cannot be interrupted, and are hence master of a considerable span of (synoptic) text. To this effect, it corresponds most often to planned rather than spontaneous speech, and hence enacts "elaborate orality" (Rossette-Crake, 2022, pp. 51–52).

In this section, I take several examples of religious oratory from online contexts, produced by decentralised voices, that is, preachers who emanate from "decentralised contexts" (supra), and attempt to model language choices in reference to a number of discursive setups, to be defined below. This exploration is synchronic and limited to contemporary examples of oratory; it is also limited to the American context, to the English language, and to the context of Christian faith.

American Christian evangelist Joel Osteen is one of the most well-known "digital televangelists" (Claydon & Whitehouse-Hart, 2018). According to his YouTube channel, which has 2.99 million subscribers, he is identified as "Senior Pastor" of the Lakewood Church (founded by his father). His preaching, which is broadcast on cable TV, uploaded to his YouTube channel, and features on his website, is conducted face-to-face to a live audience/congregation at Lakewood Church, Houston, Texas, a former sports arena with a capacity of 16,800, and an example of a "mega-church" that mixes worship and entertainment. His sermons are not officially styled as such (recordings feature on his website under "Inspiration" and are labelled as "messages").

Another example of a decentralised voice is that of Juanita Bynum, described as "the most prominent black female television evangelist in the country" (Dawan, 2007). Originally a gospel singer, she styles herself by the title of "Doctor" (by virtue of a doctoral degree in theology), and, in recent years, has turned to YouTube (with a channel of 109k subscribers) to conduct online, livestreamed sessions of teaching and praise, which can be included in the category of social media oratory (Rossette-Crake, 2022).

Finally, the example of Bynum's fully digitalised performance is briefly compared with an excerpt of a video by Gabby Bernstein, an "Instavangelist" (Stein, 2021) who embodies a voice that is further decentralised as she neither belongs to a religious institution, nor holds a PhD in theology, but instead styles herself, according to her YouTube channel (255k subscribers) as "Spirit Junkie on a mission to help you crack open to a spiritual relationship …" (www.youtube.com/watch?v=eRgOrK6C4os). The texts of the examples were fully transcribed from the online videos of the performances for the purpose of this enquiry.

Televangelism Performed in Front of an Audience

Joel Osteen's sermons are both performed in front of a live congregation and filmed for television and online audiences. However, here, the televangelist performs on a *stage* of a "megachurch" (cf. supra). The speaker is not dressed in priest's robes, but a suit and tie. He stands on the stage close to a lectern, which he moves around. And we are very conscious of the fact that the speaker is being filmed: the filming process takes as it were "centre stage" in that Osteen does not attempt 180-degree eye contact but looks directly in front of him, visibly at the camera. He is filmed, both for the face-to-face audience (via close-up shots projected on multiple mega screens), and for the television/online audience (e.g. the YouTube video mixes close-up, medium, and long shots).

Like other digitalised forms of public speaking that belong to the era of the New Oratory (Rossette-Crake, 2019), Osteen's performance is characterised by an embodied delivery and feigned extempore speech. He constantly smiles (so much so that it may appear forced or unnatural in parts), and his delivery is extremely embodied: he constantly moves his hands, and many of his gestures are mimetic, with him acting out certain movements mentioned in his discourse. There is no written script visible on the lectern; he uses a prompter, which can be glimpsed in long shots from the angle behind the stage.

Participatory Preaching

For his sermon "A Healthy Soul" (https://youtu.be/88CKi2i8t-M), Osteen begins not with a prayer summoning the Holy Spirit but with another type of ritual which he scrupulously follows in all his recent preaching, combining a blessing, a greeting, marketing/commodification, and a joke/funny anecdote:

> God bless you, it's great to be with you today, and I hope you'll stay connected with us during the week, to our daily podcasts and YouTube channel and social media, and you can come and visit us in person. Love to have you be part of one of our services. Now I'd like to start with something funny …

After the punchline to the joke, he immediately launches into a chant, repeated in unison by the congregation, who stand and hold up their bibles:

> Say it like you mean it. This is my Bible, I am what it says I am, I have what it says I have, I do what it says I can do. Today, I will be taught the word of God. I've only confessed. My mind is alert, my heart is receptive, I will never be the same. In Jesus's name. God bless you.

After these words have been uttered, the congregation sits down, and the speaker moves immediately to the theme of his sermon ("I want to talk to you today about…"). All these elements enact a religious register in what could otherwise be mistaken for a form of secular entertainment. The above sequence qualifies as a ritual in that it is a "prescribed sequence of verbal and nonverbal acts", which takes "a highly formalised and predictable communication mode" (Lu & Shurma, 2021). Here, the ritual includes a chant, which represents a formulaic and performative use of language, with prototypical use of the first person singular, the present tense, parallelism, and short clauses. The chant enacts a first type of participant framework to be distinguished here: the participatory model, whereby the congregation is called upon to participate, synonymous with Black American preaching (Rosenberg, 1970), and which can also be enacted by the practice of call–response, as well as singing.

Another ritual that informs the participatory setup appears at the very end of the sermon, this time in the form of prayer. The prayer takes place after a sequence of hortatory preaching which is followed by a performative sequence ("I believe and declare…") that, retrospectively, is turned into a first prayer ("in Jesus's name"; "can you say Amen today?"), a status enhanced by the fact that the preacher slows down his delivery (a rare moment of vocal variation in the sermon) and shuts his eyes. Audience participation takes the form of the "Amen" they are encouraged to repeat, as well as the applause that follows:

> It's time to get honest with yourself. Don't let another year letting something you have control over hold you back. Get your soul healthy. Pull up those bitter roots. Start turning things over to God. Release the worry, the heart, what didn't work out. Keep your heart pure. If you'll do this, I believe and declare, because your soul is healthy, you're going to have good success and good health. New doors are about to open. Opportunity is going to find you, healing is coming. [speaker closes eyes] Strength, energy, vitality, the fullness of your destiny, in Jesus's name. [speaker opens eyes] And if you receive it, can you say Amen today? [applause]

The speaker then moves to a second, final, prayer, composed of three short clauses. The change of tone is announced by praise music that begins to play in the background. The short prayer is then, rather uncannily, juxtaposed with a call to action connected to commercial interests:

> I'd like to give you the opportunity to make Jesus the Lord of your life. Would you pray with me? [music begins] Just say, Lord Jesus, I repent of my sins, come into my heart, and make you my Lord and Saviour. If you prayed that simple prayer, we believe you got born again. We'd love to send you some free information on your new walk with the Lord, you can text the number on the screen, or go to the website, but I hope you'll get into a good, Bible-based church, and keep God first place. [end]

In this excerpt, the sudden switch between prayer and a call to (commercial) action echoes the mode of juxtaposition that informs the sermon's macrostructure, which alternates between scripture/religious teachings and everyday examples. For instance, the first scripture is not quoted until minute nine of this 28-minute sermon; after the opening blessing and chant, the first nine minutes contain no religious elements or themes.

Rhetorical Staging and Dialogic Staging

In addition to the participatory model, several other participant frameworks are at play in Osteen's discourse. At specific moments, such as the moments of prayer quoted above, Rhetorical Staging (Rossette, 2017) confers the preacher with the status of superspeaker, presenting him as a go-between with respect to a third, higher, and spiritual entity, and producing a transcending effect for the audience. Superspeaker status is construed both textually, via patterning based on rhetorical figures (e.g. repetition, syntactic parallelism), and also by other, non-textual means, such as via the scenography, with the projection of the image of the speaker on mega screens (at least three screens are visible behind him, one on either side of the stage, and one—even bigger—screen above him) creating a "big brother-like" representation akin to that of a superspeaker. Another striking feature pertains to Osteen's vocal delivery: he maintains a regular intonation pattern built on a series of fall-rise tone units (assertive, falling intonation, just like pausing, is markedly absent), creating an incantatory rhythm, not unlike that of chanting or recitation of scripture, which moves the discourse to another, potentially more spiritual, plane.

However, Rhetorical Staging plays a relatively minor role here in comparison to the participatory model, as well as in comparison to a third setup, that of Dialogic Staging (Rossette, 2019). Dialogic Staging simulates an interaction, a dialogue, within the monologic setup of oratory. It is a rhetorical device that does not orchestrate a real dialogue and is, moreover, not likely to be confused with one, because it retains some components of formal style and devices typical of oratory. Despite their close affinity, and the fact that they often combine, we can distinguish between the concepts of participation (i.e. on the part of the congregation) and interaction (i.e. between the preacher and the congregation), and the discursive setups informed by each respectively ("participatory preaching"; Dialogic Staging"). Dialogic Staging is conditioned by a personalised speaker ethos (cf. "I") and its linguistic markers include first- and second-person pronouns, direct interrogatives, imperative forms, discourse markers, as well as greetings and terms of address. It is a setup that has developed in oratory generally, particularly digital oratory, and which reflects the wider trend towards the "conversationalisation" of public discourses that is linked precisely to the technologisation of discourse (Fairclough, 1993).

Because Dialogic Staging goes hand in hand with a personalised speaker ethos, in the case of online sermons, it reflects the "hyper-personalised" style which serves notably to "lessen any perceived barriers between the speaker and his virtual congregation" (Bryan & Albakry, 2016). And it testifies to the way technologically mediated formats, particularly televangelism, "proximise the spiritual reality" which is achieved by "reducing various dimensions of distance and providing the audience with a sense of participation and interaction", and which work to renegotiate sacred time and sacred space (Kopytowska, 2018).

"Vehement" Ethos

At certain moments, the interaction that is staged is particularly direct, and even forceful. This is illustrated in an excerpt already cited above, namely the sequence of hortatory preaching that precedes the closing prayer:

> It's time to get honest with yourself. Don't let another year letting something you have control over hold you back. Get your soul healthy. Pull up those bitter roots. Start turning things over to God. Release the worry, the heart, what didn't work out. Keep your heart pure.

This sequence begins with a reference to urgency ("it's time to…") and is built on a series of imperative clauses ("don't let…"; "get your soul"; "pull up"; "start turning…"; "release the worry…"; "keep your heart"). The injunctive tone is amplified by the concision of the clauses. These lines illustrate what can be described as a "vehement" ethos. "Vehement" ("forceful", "passionate", "intense") ethos is said to characterise American Protestant preaching style, realised notably by an embodied delivery style (Maingueneau, 2009, §19). However, it is also realised linguistically, and endorses a specific participant structure. It contrasts with the "inspired" ethos that informs Rhetorical Staging. Here, the focus is not on a higher voice of whom the preacher would be the echo. Instead, the focus is (re)placed on the speaker's own voice and on the duo formed by the speaker and the addressee—with the high rate of injunctions that call for an individual rather than a collective response leading us to interpret the second-person reference in the singular rather than the plural.

Interestingly, vehement ethos does not appear to be adopted by preachers whose authority is legitimated institutionally. Instead, the intense hortatory style serves to command authority when such institutional legitimation is lacking (for instance, when it has been self-proclaimed, as is the case for Osteen, who is the head pastor of his own church). Vehement ethos also reflects the steadfast belief of the speaker, both with respect to their faith, and the ideas they are expressing.

Online Televangelism

Joel Osteen's performance can be compared with the online performances of Juanita Bynum. Unlike the previous example, these do not take place in front of a live audience. Instead, they qualify as (purely) digital oratory, and, like most digital oratory posted to social networks, they orchestrate "backstaging" (Rossette-Crake, 2022), being filmed in intimate settings and creating a tension between intimacy and the "public" dimension of a performance that is accessible to a potentially limitless audience. The effects of backstaging are particularly interesting when the speaker is a preacher: one question notably concerns whether the online format is compatible with some of the transcendent effects associated with the figure of the preacher.

In a video series posted to her YouTube channel, entitled "Work with the warfare", Juanita Bynum conducts sessions which can be likened to sermons that mix didactic and horatory purposes. In these videos, there is no pulpit or stage; the speaker sits behind a desk, in what is probably a living room, and is dressed in a sweatshirt. The fact that she is sitting does not prevent an embodied delivery style: her discourse is continually punctuated by hand/arm gestures. A cosy atmosphere is created by a fire blazing in the fireplace located to the left of the frame. As is typical of social media oratory (Rossette-Crake, 2022), this construes authenticity and sincerity. However, unlike much digital oratory, the video is not filmed from the close angle of a selfie video and does not match the same level of intimacy. In addition, authority is construed via the central position of the speaker within the frame (Kress & van Leeuwen, 2006), and is enhanced via the symmetry of the background (the speaker is "framed" by the curtains and the picture frame behind her). And unlike the examples presented up until now, the speaker does not speak from a script; her production appears to be completely spontaneous (extempore).

The overall linguistic template in the video under analysis (https://youtu.be/J16yLTyXZ6c) bears a very close resemblance to the language of spoken conversation. For instance, the speaker opens with a sequence composed of a greeting, a question, an expression commonly used by (secular) digital speakers ("I'm excited to be here"), as well as, like Osteen, a plug at commercial interests (reference to T-shirts and merchandise she sells). Intimacy and authenticity (and the sense of going "behind the stage") are enhanced, rather surprisingly, by the way the speaker comments on her dry lips, puts on lip gloss in front of her audience/congregation, and then very casually says "I don't know what that looks like, but I don't care":

> Hello everybody. How are you today? I hope you are having a blessed, awesome day. I know that I am. And I'm excited to be here. And many of you have gotten your T-shirts and your sweatshirts and whatever it is you ordered. Hold on a minute, as my daddy says, my lips are dry, they feel dry. [speaker puts gloss on her lips] Sorry about that. Going to be an awesome lesson today. I don't know what that looks like, but I don't care.

This discourse could be that of any (secular) influencer: apart from the use of the adjective "blessed", there is no linguistic item to suggest any religious/spiritual stakes. Language echoing that of a one-to-one conversation continues throughout most of the video. For example, the speaker provides a long explanation about finding God by letting go of certain relations. The following lines are located early in the demonstration (launched by the explicit exhortation "I want you to go with me today on this one"). A rare rhetorical figure in the form of syntactic parallelism ("where you used to lay your left elbow is not there anymore. Where you used to lean and put your right hand is not there anymore") is not sufficient to elevate the discourse to that of a superspeaker who would summon a higher, spiritual entity. Instead, Dialogic Staging is enacted via the one-to-one conversation that is simulated by recurrent use of second-person reference, discourse markers ("you know"; "so"; "and so"), and informal lexis (e.g. "stuff"):

> When it's time for us to go into our new journey that is not a subscribed, the prescribed social pattern, um there has to be some restructuring. *And so* when that starts happening, where you used to lay your left elbow is not there anymore. Where you used to lean and put your right hand is not there anymore. *So you have to restructure yourself. And* from that, there is a season of mourning, and that is to be expected. *So don't trip on that. You know,* it's like breaking up with a boyfriend. *You know,* you love him so much, and you're my world baby and all that, and then when you break up, *you know,* you'll be crying and stuff like that, and then two years down the road, you'll be like please, bye … *So* it's the same thing, it's really the same thing. *You know,* you go through that little mourning period, when you do that, if that is not replaced by a cause, then what you're doing is you're still allowing yourself to be vulnerable to sabotage, to sabotage, self-sabotage …

Also reproduced in italics in the above extract are the markers of direct, forceful hortatory preaching, which enact a vehement ethos. In a similar tone to the forecited initial exhortation ("*I want you to* go with me today on this one"), the speaker directs an imperative ("*So don't trip* on that") and an obligation ("*So you have to* restructure yourself") to her viewers. Likewise, soon after this extract, the intensity of the one-to-one speaker/addressee relation is underlined by the quasi-phatic question "*You understand what I'm saying?*"

In addition to this vehement ethos and sporadic quoting of Scripture, a religious register is occasionally construed in Juanita Bynum's video via vocal variation, which is another character-istic of Black American preaching style, making for "an experience that is essentially metrical, not semantic" (Rosenberg, 1970, p. 139). Here, vocal variation comes to the fore in the closing moments of the video. Just like in Joel Osteen's performance, the fact that the speaker begins to wind down is signalled by the introduction of praise music playing in the background, which is the first element to appeal to the sensory dimension. The beginning of the music coincides with a prolonged vocal pause, as the speaker sighs, shuffles the papers in front of her, and then takes a moment to listen to the music herself, swaying her head to the rhythm—almost as if she is taking inspiration from the music. In contrast to the fast vocal pace of the rest of the video (typical of social media oratory), every subsequent clause complex is punctuated by a long pause (marked //), during which the speaker appears to be in deep reflection:

> [Music begins, speaker pauses] This therapy session has cost you nothing. // It's only going to cost you change. // It's only going to cost you change // This is powerful. // This is why we don't know who we are. / This is why we don't know up from down. // Because we keep being spent around and spent around.

Significantly, marked prosody combines here with the very few examples in the video of rhet-orical figures, mainly in the form of repetition. When the clause complex "It's only going to cost you change" is repeated, not only is it preceded and followed by a pause, but every lex-ical word is emphatically stressed, and the volume of the speaker's voice increases. The segment "this is (why)" is repeated, forming a short, three-part anaphora. The speaker continues to pause after each clause complex for several minutes up until the last moments of the video, which con-tain a two-part anaphora via the repetition of "And then", in conjunction with accumulation and polysyndeton ("strength and power and success"):

> So you can make some changes right now. // And those changes / will begin to strengthen your emotional state, and your emotional state will then begin to strengthen your spirit // *And then* your spirit will be in a position to hear what the spirit of the Lord has to say to it. // *And then strength and power and success will then become your state.* // Welcome back to yourself. // Got to go. God bless you.

In the discourse of this online video, which is informed mainly by the setup of Dialogic Staging, it is this sensory dimension, together with the construal of a vehement ethos, that make for a "reli-gious" register.

The "Instavangelist"

If we look briefly at the videos of Gabby Bernstein, a pertinent question is whether the label of "Instavangelist" can stand up to linguistic and discursive scrutiny—that is, whether her spoken online productions share any of the features identified in the previous examples. Bernstein uses her online videos (posted to both her Instagram account but also to her YouTube channel) to promote the books she publishes (which, like Scripture does for sermons, offer the authority of an original, written intertext). Posts include recordings of public speaking events in front of a live audience, as well as videos produced uniquely for an online audience. In the case of the latter, it is worth noting that, akin to Juanita Bynum's videos, Gabby Bernstein does not reproduce the close-up, selfie video format of many influencers, but adopts a medium-angle shot in which she occupies a central position of authority, sitting in an armchair, with a big microphone placed in front of her. In addition to these multimodal resources, some of her linguistic choices, which appear to be the result of extempore production, echo those of Juanita Bynum's discourse, as illustrated in the first lines of one video:

> What I think is that you need to feel into what's working, feel into what's thriving, feel into what makes you happy, feel into it. That's the true practice of appreciation and gratitude. Feeling into it. Not just talking about it or just saying I have a gratitude list that I say every morning, F that! Feel it. ("Play the appreciation game for an instant mood boost", https://youtu.be/BY18yYxn1sU)

These first moments of the video serve as a preview and a teaser, just before the introductory musical jingle and voice-over. The words reproduce the forceful style identified in some horta-tory preaching (cf. "you need to"; the exclamation "F that!", the imperative "Feel it"). We are far from the tone we would expect to find in influencers' "alternative scripture online" that promote "wellness and 'self care'" (Stein, 2021). Instead, there is a vehement ethos, which is reinforced by vocal intensity (at times, the speaker is almost yelling) and embodied delivery (emphatic hand/arm gestures later in the video). In addition, these lines feature a staging of the signifier via the figure of repetition ("feel(ing) into": five instances), initially in conjunction with syntactic parallelism, as well as the pairing of two nouns (accumulation) ("appreciation and gratitude"). In the absence of any minimal lexical signalling of religious or spiritual stakes (e.g. "blessing"; "God bless you"), the speaker's vehement ethos may provide some linguistic justification for the parallels drawn with respect to the sermons delivered by preachers.

Implications and Future Directions

The model presented here posits a cline between two prototypical types of discourse, each of which coincides with a very different type of social actor. At one end of the cline, we can locate the Rhetorical Staging and inspired ethos of a speaker who is not only a preacher but also the elected head of a religious institution and whose authority is symbolised by the elevated position of the pulpit. This is for instance the case of many sermons pronounced by the Archbishop of Canterbury, head of the Anglican Church. The other end of the cline coincides with the enact-ment of Dialogic Staging and the vehement ethos of a speaker who occupies a decentralised space (cf. supra), is not legitimated by a religious institution and whose authority is hence uniquely construed discursively, and who presents, from their position behind the screen, an alternative form of spiritual guidance——that of "digivangelism" (a general term that extends to all social media, including YouTube). Different variations and degrees of hybridisation are located between these two extremes, as illustrated for instance by televangelist Joel Osteen, who mixes Rhetorical and Dialogic Staging, and whose ethos is at times inspired and at times vehement, reflecting his dual status as head of his (own) church.

The two main examples of televangelists, whose performances cater principally to a remote audience via technological mediation, whether they are performed on a stage to a face-to-face audience in a megachurch, or from a private space for a video disseminated via social media, each present a combination of the three aforementioned setups, with Rhetorical Staging being superseded by Dialogic Staging as technological mediation intensifies; in addition, televangelist oratory gives way to a vehement ethos which, within the overall setup of Dialogic Staging, discursively enacts the self-proclaimed authority of a speaker who hones in on addressees via intense exhortation; moreover, vehement ethos may be one element of a "quasi-religious" register in other examples produced by speakers who are not preachers (cf. "Instavangelists").

These discourses reflect, to varying degrees, a certain "religiosity" within the current context of renewed faith and belief (Campbell & Lövheim, 2011, cf. supra), where digivangelists are developing new types of spirituality. The "religiosity" of these new forms of spirituality can be identified in the common transcendent function, which is fulfilled both by the pulpit preacher and the digivangelist, with the latter representing "religious role models" who present "their own woes and pains to teach people how to transform them into *something greater than themselves*" (Chen, 2021) (my emphasis). Thus defined, this religiosity finds a natural means of expression in the discursive practice of oratory, which engages with the inherently participatory and empathetic medium of spoken language, as well as the fundamental asymmetry of a one-to-many relation— two factors which, for the individual who is part of the audience, contribute to an intrinsically transcendent effect.

This model partly validates and partly invalidates Crystal and Davy's (1969) findings that the language of sermons resembles that of other varieties of public speaking. On the one hand, it cannot be claimed that religious oratory exhibits a completely distinct set of linguistic choices. For instance, Rhetorical Staging is not specific to sermons and is also found in political oratory; similarly, Dialogic Staging is common to much contemporary (secular) oratory. On the other hand, the phenomena briefly analysed in the above examples reflect configurations of choices which contribute to recognisable religious colourings and which tend to validate the concept of "register". This is for instance illustrated when vehement ethos combines with certain multimodal choices (medium angle; central position of speaker) in the videos of Juanita Bynum and Gabby Bernstein. The question of distinctive languages or registers—like that of discursive genres—needs to be set against the move towards less specialised discourses and the decompartmentalization of discourse communities engendered by the internet, which goes hand in hand with the way social actors are carving out new roles and are reinventing themselves in the era of personal branding (Rossette-Crake, 2020).

These initial observations call for a wider appraisal over extended corpora. Further examples of all types of oratory (pulpit oratory, New Oratory—i.e. delivered on a stage and filmed—and social media oratory) need to be compared and contrasted. This chapter makes the case for a discursive approach, which takes into account the social status of the speaker and examines the interplay between linguistic choices and multimodal aspects of the performance. Some specific aspects provide the basis for exciting future research agendas. For instance:

- A diachronic study is necessary in order to provide a fuller appraisal of the development of the language of pulpit oratory, including the influence in recent decades of the "renewed homiletic" (Wesley Allen, 2010);
- A quantitative study needs to compare pulpit oratory with the technologically mediated spoken performances by the new types of social actors who are replacing the traditional figure of the preacher;
- These technologically mediated performances require placing within the wider body of social media oratory, in order to define—and justify—the category of digivangelists (discussion here

is set against the backdrop of previous work on secular oratory (e.g. Rossette-Crake, 2019; 2022), but requires confirmation via quantitative studies);

- Similarly, the era of digivangelists can be compared with the early period of televangelism, to grasp the possible differences between mediation via electronic and digital media;
- Comparisons between these different categories and time periods need to integrate multi-modal analysis, systematically taking into account elements such as dress code, body language, filming choices, (camera angles, editing) use of music and/or voice-over, etc.;
- Further definition is required both for participant frameworks and for the various types of discursive ethos—for instance, next to inspired and vehement ethos, how may the ethos of digivangelists vary from the generic ethos of the digital speaker, which is typically embodied by the figure of the Anglo-American entrepreneur (Rossette-Crake, 2022)?
- How are these different parameters informed by cultural phenomena? Is there a link between specific Churches and national culture (e.g. American Episcopal versus Anglican)? And can the modelling presented here be extended to oratory performed in other languages and within the contexts of other faiths?

Finally, if this contribution initially aimed at filling a relative gap in current linguistic scholarship in regard to the iconic communication practice of the sermon, the necessity to take into account contemporary examples led to an expansion of the field of study, and to the adoption of the general concept of "religious oratory". This chapter participates in the wider, ongoing, and crucial discussion of what qualifies, in the present day, as "religious discourse".

Further Reading

Jones, C. & Connelly, S. (2011). *Behind the Dream: The Making of the Speech that Transformed a Nation.* Palgrave Macmillan.
This book provides an insight into a landmark example of oratory in the English-speaking repertoire, that delivered by Martin Luther King in Washington in 1963. Even though it does not officially qualify as a sermon, it was produced by a pastor, and contains all the features typical of Black American preaching style, some of which are mentioned in this study.
Ong, W. (1982). *Orality and Literacy: The Technologizing of the Word.* Methuen.
This is a seminal work on the distinction between spoken and written language, as well as the impact of technology. Moreover, the theory of Walter Ong can be seen to reflect his Jesuit background, and the role of rhetoric that is recognised within the Jesuit tradition.
Rosenberg, B. (1970). *The Art of the American Folk Preacher.* Oxford University Press.
This is a comprehensive study of Black American preaching style and its extensive impact in other contexts of oratory.
Rossette-Crake, F. (2022). *Digital Oratory as Discursive Practice: From the Podium to the Screen.* Palgrave Macmillan.
This study compares oratory past and present, and the impact of digital technology, and notably social media, on contemporary spoken communication practice.

References

Adam, M. (2008). Secondary religious discourse: Sermon as a distributional macrofield. *Discourse and inter-action*, *1*(2), 5–18.
Ajibade, K. (2019). How to get faith trending: the rise of religious influencers. 25 June 2019. www.theosthinkt ank.co.uk/comment/2019/06/25/how-to-get-faith-trending-the-rise-of-religious-influencers
Angermuller, J. (2023). Truth in Post-Truth Politics? Discourse as a practice of social and epistemic valu-ation. Plenary delivered at the International Seminar on Social Media Discourse Analysis (ISSMDA), 2 February 2023, University of Aix-Marseille.

Biber, D., Johansson, S., Leech, G., Conrad, S., & Finegan, E. (1999). *The Longman Grammar of Spoken and Written English.* Longman.

Bryan, C. & Albakry, M. (2016). "To be real honest, I'm just like you": analyzing the discourse of personalization in online sermons. *Text & Talk, 36,* 683–703.

Campbell, H. & Lövheim, M. (2011). Studying the online-offline connection in religion online. *Information, Communication & Society, 14*(8), 1083–1096.

Carlson, L. (2021). 'Instavangelists' are Making Disciples. Are You? 20 May 2021, www.thegospelcoalition.org/article/instavangelists-disciples/

Chen, T. (2021). Is there an invisible string between religious proselytizing and influencing? I asked some influencers. 12 March. www.buzzfeednews.com/article/tanyachen/religion-and-influencers

Chilton, P. & Kopytowska, M. (Eds.). (2018). *Religion, language, and the human mind.* Oxford University Press.

Claydon, E.A. & Whitehouse-Hart, J. (2018). 'Overcoming' the 'Battlefield of the Mind': A Psycho- Linguistic Examination of the Discourse of Digital-Televangelists Self-Help Texts. *Language and Psychoanalysis, 7*(2), 29–56.

Cox, E. (1863). The Arts of Writing, Reading and Speaking. In E. Cox (Ed.), *Letters to a Law Student.* John Crickford.

Crystal, D. & Davy, D. (1969). *Investigating English Style.* Longman.

Dawan, S. (2007) A Minister's Public Lesson on Domestic Violence. *The New York Times.* 20 September.

Downes, W. (2010). *Language and Religion: A Journey into the Human Mind.* Cambridge University Press.

El Naggar, S. (2018). 'But I did not do anything!'–analysing the YouTube videos of the American Muslim televangelist Baba Ali: delineating the complexity of a novel genre. *Critical Discourse Studies. 15*(3), 303–319. DOI: 10.1080/17405904.2017.1408477

Eldin, A. (2014). Critical Discourse Analysis of Religious Sermons in Egypt–Case Study of Amr Khalid's Sermons. *International Education Studies, 7*(11). DOI: 10.5539/ies.v7n11p68

Fairclough, N. (1993). Critical discourse analysis and the marketisation of public discourse: the universities. *Discourse & Society, 4*(2), 133–168.

Garner, M. (2007). Preaching as a Communicative Event: A Discourse Analysis of Sermons by Robert Rollock (1555–1599). *Reformation & Renaissance Review, 9*(1), 45–70. DOI: 10.1558/rrr.v9i1.45

Halliday, M.A.K. (1985). *Spoken and Written Language.* Oxford University Press.

Halliday, M.A.K. & Matthiessen, C. (2014). *Halliday's Introduction to Functional Grammar.* Routledge.

Helland, C. (2000). Online-religion/religion-online and virtual communities. In J.K. Hadden & E. Cowan (Eds.), *Religion on the Internet: Research Prospects and Promises,* 205–223. JAI Press.

Hobbs, V. (2021). *An Introduction to Religious Language: Exploring Theolinguistics in Contemporary Contexts.* Bloomsbury Academic.

James, J.D. (2010). *McDonaldisation, masala McGospel and Om economics: Televangelism in contemporary India.* SAGE. https://doi.org/10.4135/9788132106135

Jones, R. & Hafner, C. (2021). *Understanding Digital Literacies: A Practical Introduction.* Routledge.

Khakpour, H. & Ag, F. (2018). Sermon of Imam Muhammad Bagir: Critical Discourse Analysis Based on the Theory of Fairclough and Van Dyke. *Religious Literature and Art, 3*(9), 9–32. DOI: 10.22081/jrla.2018.50189.1169

Khan, M.A., Syed, A.F., Junaid, M., Shakir, S., Mehmood, & Shahid, S. (2021). Analyzing The Farewell Sermon of the Prophet Muhammad: A Critical Perspective. *International Journal of Linguistics Studies, 1*(1), 71–81. https://doi.org/10.32996/ijls.2021.1.1.6

Kress, G. (1994). *Learning to Write.* Routledge.

Kress, G. & van Leeuwen, T. (2006). *Reading Images: The Grammar of Visual Design.* Routledge.

Kopytowska, M. (2018). The Televisualization of Ritual. In P. Chilton & M. Kopytowska (Eds.), *Religion, language, and the human mind,* 437–474. Oxford University Press.

Lu, W. & Shurma, S. (2021). Rituals. In S. Pihlaja (Ed.). *Analysing Religious Discourse,* 217–234. Cambridge University Press.

Maingueneau, D. (2009). Le sermon: contraintes génériques et positionnement. *Langage et société, 130*(4), 37–59.

Maingueneau, D. (2014). *Discours et analyse du discours.* Armand Colin.

Malmström, H. (2018). Appraisal, preaching and the religious other: The rhetorical appropriation of interreligious positions in sermonic discourse. *International Journal of Practical Theology, 22*(1), 40–57. http://dx.doi.org/10.1515/ijpt-2017-0016

Mansouri, S. (2023). Discourse-Historical Approach to Religious Genre: The Case of a Persian Sermon. *Journal of Studies in Learning and Teaching English*, *12*(1), 83–97.

Marone, V. (2017). The discursive construction of meaning across texts and media. *Social Sciences and Education Research Review*, *4*(2), 42–77.

Marwick A., & boyd, d. (2011). I tweet honestly, I tweet passionately: Twitter users, context collapse, and the imagined audience. *New Media & Society*, *13*(1), 114–133.

Morey, S. (2016). *Rhetorical Delivery and Digital Technologies, Networks, Affect, Electracy.* Routledge.

Muchnik, M. (2005). Discourse strategies of Maxzirim Bitshuva: The case of a repentance preacher in Israel. *25*(3), 373–398.

Mukherjee, S. (Ed.). (2018). *The Languages of Religion: Exploring the Politics of the Sacred.* Routledge.

Noble, D. F. (1999). *The religion of technology*. Penguin.

Omoniyi, T. (2017). Digital Evangelism: Varieties of English in Unexpected Places. In A. Rosowsky (Ed.). *Faith and Language Practices in Digital Spaces*, 135–157. Multilingual Matters.

Ong, W. (1982). *Orality and Literacy: The Technologizing of the Word*. Methuen.

Pihlaja, S. (Ed.). (2021a). *Analysing Religious Discourse*. Cambridge University Press.

Pihlaja, S. (2021b). *Talk about Faith: How Debate and Conversation Shape Belief.* Cambridge University Press.

Rosenberg, B. (1970). *The Art of the American Folk Preacher*. Oxford University Press.

Rosowsky, A. (Ed.). (2017). *Faith and Language Practices in Digital Spaces.* Multilingual Matters.

Rossette, F. (2017). Discursive Divides and Rhetorical Staging, or the Transcending Function of Oratory. *Journal of Pragmatics*, *108*, 48–59.

Rossette-Crake, F. (2020). The New Oratory': Public speaking practice in the digital, neoliberal age. *Discourse Studies*, *22*(5), 571–589. https://doi.org/10.1177/1461445620916363

Rossette-Crake, F. (2019). *Public Speaking and the New Oratory*. Palgrave Macmillan.

Rossette-Crake, F. (2022). *Digital Oratory as Discursive Practice: From the Podium to the Screen.* Palgrave Macmillan.

Singh, P.K.H. & Thuraisingam, T. (2011). Language for reconciliation in religious discourse: A critical discourse analysis of contradictions in sermons explored through the activity theory framework. *Multilingua: Journal of Cross-Cultural and Interlanguage Communication*, *30*(3–4), 391–404.

Stein, L. (2021). The Empty Religions of Instagram. How did influencers become our moral authorities? *The New York Times*, 5 March. www.nytimes.com/2021/03/05/opinion/influencers-glennon-doyle-instagram.html

Wesley Allen, O. (Ed.). (2010). *The Renewed Homiletic.* Fortress Press.

Wijsen, F. (2013). Editorial: Discourse analysis in religious studies. *Religion*, *43*(1), 1–3.

Yelle, R., Handman, C., & Lehrich, C.I. (2019). Introduction. In R. Yelle, C. Handman, & C.I. Lehrich (Eds.), *Language and religion*. De Gruyter.

Zumthor, P. (1983). *Introduction à la poésie orale*. Seuil.

20

CATHOLICISM AND SOCIAL MEDIA

Andre Joseph Theng

Introduction and Background

The topic of social media in the Catholic world is best described as an emerging theme, espe-cially in religious-academic circles. While social media per se is certainly a well-explored area in sociolinguistic research, comparatively little attention has been paid to religious dimensions of social media. In this regard, Catholicism presents an interesting case in point, and the two-millennia-old Roman Catholic Church continues to be a global institution despite increased secularisation in a post-Christian world. The Church's (continued) challenge is to connect with its adherents as well as to spread its message, as it has historically relied on a variety of communications media to do so.

The arrival of the internet has been no exception, and in 1995 the Vatican launched its own website. Its communication strategy has extended to social media, and the Pope, the leader of the Church, has widely followed official social media accounts run by media professionals associated with the Vatican. The Catholic Church claims a membership of 1.3 billion worldwide in more than 200 countries and the Church is therefore a unique organisation worth considering in itself with regard to Wee's (2015) conceptualisation of 'organisation styling'. The role of the organisation is brought into question by Wee (2015, p. 9): the "organization's agency becomes more salient because each organization has to decide just what set of institutional myths it is prepared to select as relevant to its goals and identity." The prevalence of social media use in many parts of the world today has resulted in increased attention among scholars of both sociolinguistic and theology who are interested in its transformative effects for societies. The sociolinguistic tradition of studies involving the internet can be traced to the early use of the term "computer-mediated communica-tion" (see Androutsopoulos, 2006a; Herring, 1996) which explored contexts such as newsgroups or chatrooms and which was characterised by the nature of 'internet language' as blending written and spoken varieties of language. Yet other work has expanded beyond Anglo contexts to explore multilingual situations arising on the internet (Androutsopoulos, 2006b; Lee, 2017) as well as questions of identity and community (Seargeant & Tagg, 2014). Social media platforms have been described as "networked publics", publics that are simultaneously "constructed through networked technologies" and "the imagined collective that emerges as a result of the intersection of people, technology, and practice" (boyd, 2010, p. 39). As such they might be construed as a variety of

DOI: 10.4324/9781003301271-22

public space whilst having particular characteristics informed by the respective affordances of each platform.

Yet it is not just official sources who have a stake in the Catholicity of the social media world; Catholics (or otherwise) in different parts of the world have unsurprisingly looked to the internet in exploring their Catholic identity. As such a variety of evidently 'ground-up' social media pages serve as sites in which communities of Catholics can interact. I suggest two perspectives in broadly conceptualising Catholic social media activity—'top-down' and 'bottom-up', a heuristic not uncommon in sociolinguistic work. One sub-field where such a distinction is made is in the linguistic landscape (LL), originally interested in the study of the content and form of public signage, but which has since expanded to provide a theoretical lens into the "greater contextual (ethnographic) and historical understandings of texts in the landscape—who put them there, how they are interpreted, and what role they play in relation to space, migration and mobility" (Pennycook, 2017, p. 270). In Gorter's (2006) pioneering work on linguistic landscapes in Israel, he makes this distinction as an analytical starting point, where top-down refers to "LL elements used and exhibited by institutional agencies which in one way or another act under the control of local or central policies" and bottom-up referring to "those utilised by individual, associative or corporative actors who enjoy autonomy of action within legal limits" (Gorter, 2006, p. 10). In the context of Catholic social media, two similar perspectives can be observed: first, a top-down perspective covering institutional use of social media on the part of official groups associated with the hierarchy, and second, a bottom-up perspective covering accounts set up by individuals or groups who associate themselves with Catholicism.

In this chapter, I focus on online dimensions of 'religious language' associated with mediatised representations of Catholicism, highlighting the importance of studying Christian practices in online contexts which often function as extensions of offline communities and where religious language exists in secular spaces. My goal is to provide insight into how sociolinguistic theory might prove useful to the analysis of social media data in Catholic contexts, as well as to suggest how theologians might benefit from integrating a sociological view of language use into theological work; in short, how the intersection of the two fields could be a mutually beneficial process.

A starting point to a Catholic view on internet culture might be found in Spadaro's (2014) *Cybertheology: Thinking Christianity in the Era of the Internet* which as the title suggests is a theological statement on the implications of the internet for the Church; as much as "the Internet is changing our ways of living and thinking, does it not also change (and thus is already changing) our way of thinking about and living the faith?" (Spadaro, 2014, p. viii) and Spadaro writes in the preface that the book is his attempt to respond to these changes. Spadaro, as editor of *La Civiltà Cattolica,* a Catholic periodical based in Rome associated with the Vatican, and as someone known to be a personal friend of Pope Francis, provides us with insight into how the institutional Church understands the impact of digital culture. Defining cybertheology as "being the intelligence of the faith in the era of the Internet, that is, reflection on the thinkability of the faith in the light of the Web's logic" (p. 16), Spadaro primarily calls for theological reflection, drawing parallels between theological ideas and features of the internet.

Covering a disparate range of topics structured more as essays, there is some reference to the advent of social media. Reflecting on the move to Web 2.0, Spadaro writes: "Social networks are not an ensemble of individuals, but an ensemble of relationships between individuals...The key concept is no longer merely presence on the Web but connection" (p. 29) understanding the concept of connection with the biblical understanding of 'neighbour'. Also addressed is the role of digital technology in the administration of the sacraments. He writes, "It is enough to think, for example, of the experiment of sharing our own experience of God during Easter via Twitter, even while in church … the proposal would be very interesting, but the experiment to which I am referring does not foresee remote communion" (p. 76), suggesting a possible integration of digital practices in physical liturgies, while yet excluding the possibility of a sacramental life that takes place entirely online.

Little of the Church's official documents have addressed social media per se, and the most recent are a pair of 2002 documents released by the Pontifical Council for Social Communications called *The Church and Internet* and *Ethics in Internet*, expressing the Church's "longstanding interest in the media of social communication" which "do much to meet human needs and may yet do even more" (CI 1). The documents discuss how the internet, which is described as being "instantaneous, immediate, worldwide, decentralized, interactive, endlessly expandable in contents and outreach, flexible and adaptable to a remarkable degree" (EI 7), provides both opportunity and challenge for the Church—as a means for evangelisation, whilst noting some more nefarious uses of the internet such as 'hate sites', pornography, and violence. Of particular interest is a reference to how the "proliferation of web sites calling themselves Catholic creates a problem of a different sort" (CI 8). While "well-motivated, well-informed individuals and unofficial groups acting on their own initiative are entitled to be there [on the internet]", there arises the issue of "eccentric doctrinal interpretations, idiosyncratic devotional practices, and ideological advocacy bearing a 'Catholic' label from the authentic positions of the Church" (CI 8).

Two further sources worth consulting on digital questions in a Catholic context can be found in the work of Berger (2017), and Schmidt (2020). Berger primarily considers the effect of digital life on liturgical practices, beginning with a description of the role of technology in the 2015 Philadelphia Papal Mass of Pope Francis, where the mass was not only livestreamed on the internet, but also to a large screen along the street leading to the mass venue, as well to screens in local parishes. These are some of the 'signs of the times', to borrow from a line repeated in the Bible and in one of the Eucharistic Prayers for Various Needs—"that all the faithful of the Church, looking into the signs of the times by the light of faith, may constantly devote themselves to the service of the Gospel". Berger suggests that the faith practices are changing with the shift onto digital mediums, and online religion sites "have been among the fastest-growing sites in cyberspace" (p. 3). Berger taps on questions prevalent in liturgical circles and reframes them in light of digital culture, asking for example, what the "full and active participation" as proposed by *Sacrosanctum Concilium* looks like in light of internet liturgies, and the formation of communities which exist entirely online, a marked shift from the traditional system of organising Catholics into geographic, territorial parishes, and where the parish functions as the primary space in which Catholics are connected to the broader Church.

Schmidt (2020) builds on her doctoral dissertation (2016) in considering more broadly ecclesiological and sacramental questions vis-à-vis digital culture, working towards a "theology of the internet". In the introduction, she keenly points out the internet as a great opportunity for Christian living, where the internet is a space "necessary to the life of the church…and rather than lamenting the disappearance of their traditional iterations, I suggest that we pay close attention to their new residence in the digital context". Schmidt writes in response to theologians who critique virtual life as being 'merely' virtually mediated, disembodied, and decentralised in contrast to local churches which are seen as the ideal mediator between God and Catholics. She goes on to provide a taxonomy of five characteristics of the internet which give rise to theological reflection: "anonymity, vitriol, authority, access, and disembodiment". Particularly relevant is her discussion of authority where much of the internet is beyond the institutional Church's control, going on to suggest that "instead of traditional…ecclesial structures" providing the "hermeneutics and pragmatics for interpreting and acting upon magisterial teaching," consumer culture becomes the interpretive framework for such texts".

The subsequent chapters historicise Church teaching on the media communications (as outlined above) and engage closely with multiple examples of how the internet is transforming traditional Catholic practices. In Chapter 7, she provides some reflection on social networking platforms; Fr James Martin, a Jesuit priest and editor of *America* magazine is an oft-controversial figure in Catholic internet circles for his work with LGBT communities. Schmidt points out that amidst anti-LGBT vitriol posted in response to Martin's posts on Twitter, it has also provided Martin (and the Church) with the opportunity to speak to the LGBT community as evidenced by responses from openly gay Catholics to the same posts. Schmidt writes: "Virtual space has thus allowed for a moment so desperately needed in the church: Catholics (including clergy) speaking to one another in open and honest ways, and in a way that exhibits the love of Christ." Schmidt's work is theological (and to a lesser extent, sociological) reflection at the intersection of digital culture and the Catholic Church. Although written in a predominantly American context, Schmidt's ideas are worth exploring in a broader global context.

It is quickly evident there remains much room for a linguistic perspective to understanding Catholic social media use, or towards the study of instances of online iterations of Catholicism. In the next section I propose how a contrast between top-down and bottom-up perspectives might provide a starting point in this regard. I then provide examples from my case studies to illustrate how linguistic frameworks can be utilised in the analysis of religious data.

Two Perspectives to Understand Social Media Use

The top-down and bottom-up distinction as perspectives to understanding linguistic data is a common one in the field. This serves as a useful heuristic to conceptualising Catholic social media activity, where social media accounts can broadly be classified into these two categories, whilst acknowledging that there is much overlap where interaction between the institutional Church and lay Catholics might well occur on some pages. It is thus important to understand these two perspectives as being from 'creators', or describing the general nature of the respective accounts, although such a distinction is increasingly blurred on social media. While producers and audience are more clearly defined with traditional media, there is still an inherent hierarchy built into social media sites in which posters ("producers") and others who interact with the posts ("audiences") can be observed (Seargeant & Tagg, 2014, p. 3).

Top down: Institutional discourse

Wee (2015) introduces the notion of organisational styling and suggests that in the frame of the identity economy, or the commodification of identity, "the claimant organizations are aiming to exercise greater control over who gets to engage in the relevant practices, as well as what might count as the appropriate ways of engaging in such practices" (Wee, 2015, pp. 136–137). Wee points out why institutions are unique phenomena "ontologically distinct" from persons:

> Even if they are created by persons and even if they are often considered 'virtual' persons, organizations have properties that we will see carry significantly different implications for how they are expected to deploy the semiotic resources at their disposal, not least because they are constrained by institutional myths in ways that persons are not.
>
> (Wee, 2015, p. 13)

As compared to individuals who are born with particular characteristics they do not choose, "organizations are created with fairly specific organizational goals in mind... The ontological status of organizations therefore leads to different styling constraints than those that might be visited upon actual persons". There is thus a different understanding of agency in the styling of organisations, which often are largely dependent on their established goals.

The type of organisation that the Catholic Church is certainly bears discussion as it is a fairly unusual and unique one as far as organisations are concerned. While other Christian denominations, or other religious groups, might appear to have similar hierarchical structures, the dogma of papal infallibility, and Vatican centralisation renders special importance to its hierarchical structure. From an ecclesial and theological perspective, the Catholic Church is founded and headed by Christ (LG 9), but "brought into operation...through the sacraments and the exercise of the virtues that the sacred nature and organic structure of the priestly community" (LG 11). The Second Vatican Council's constitution of the Church, *Lumen Gentium* provides a kind of mission statement: "it desires now to unfold more fully to the faithful of the Church and to the whole world its own inner nature and universal mission" (LG 1). *Lumen Gentium* sets out the key role of the Church's hierarchy—the Pope, bishops, priests and religious, alongside the role of the laity in cooperating with the Church's mission. Practically speaking, the challenge of marking the boundaries of the organisation is that in many places, the Church's membership is not always clearly defined, where people who were baptised Catholic may no longer consider themselves to be part of the Church, or in the other extreme, where engaged members may in fact be unbaptised. Further challenges arise in considering individuals or groups who might consider themselves affiliated to the Church, but whom the Church does not consider to be Catholic, possibly for reasons of doctrinal disagreement. The internet has arguably given a platform for many to debate these boundaries, demonstrating the ambivalence of Catholicity of as a category. This poses a methodological challenge for researchers who employ the term 'Catholic', where it would be important to make some attempt towards defining and considering the context in which the term is used.

Other dimensions of Catholic social media remain unexplored from an organisational perspective; the phenomena of present-day 'religious influencers' appear to be a major force on social media, with a global following. These include personalities such as Bishop Robert Barron, Bishop of Winona-Rochester who founded Word on Fire ministries, which produces content for a YouTube channel counting more than half a million subscribers. The videos mostly feature Bishop Barron himself providing spiritual reflections. A second figure who rivals Barron in popularity is Father Mike Schmitz of Duluth, Minnesota, who also has a large YouTube following with his catechesis and spiritual content. In 2021, he completed a daily podcast series in which he provided reflections on the entire Bible, reaching the top of iTunes' United States podcast chart. Friar Casey Cole, an American Franciscan Friar has a following on his channel called 'Breaking in the Habit' and from further afield, Maltese priest Father Rob Galea has gained a social media following especially in Australia where he serves. The emergence of social media 'influencers' (Abidin, 2018) in the secular sphere has certainly inspired a generation of Catholic 'influencers' who exist in the shared space of social media platforms, and who are thus wont to build on popular aesthetic styles as a means of staking a place in the semiotically-mediated political economy (Gal, 1989) of influencer culture.

The internet has also given a platform to some more controversial Catholic figures who have more particular followings. These are often to do with Catholic issues which have had a strong mediatised dimension. One such example is the issue of the Traditional Latin Mass (TLM), a form of the liturgy that was largely replaced by a new text of the Mass in 1969 which featured major changes including allowing for Mass to be celebrated in vernacular languages and where the priest had now the option of facing the people during Mass. In 2007, Pope Benedict XVI provided concessions for the wider celebration of the traditional form, giving rise to a movement which suggested that the old form was in fact superior to the one commonly used at present, resulting in communities of people congregating around a shared attraction to TLM both online and in churches. This movement has become entangled with other socio-political standpoints, often identifying with (far-right) conservative politics and gender ideology. The movement has largely been facilitated by the internet; in the United Kingdom, early attempts to build such a following were facilitated by a LISTSERV page which contained information on when the next masses were happening (as they were only said occasionally).

In other places, community members often communicate via WhatsApp or other messaging applications. In the vein of religious personalities, certain figures are closely affiliated with the movement online, for example, Father John Zuhlsdorf, an American priest well known for his blog where he is known as 'Fr Z.' on which he provides commentary associated with the promotion of the TLM. In contrast to the other clergy mentioned earlier, Father Zuhlsdorf does not have a diocesan appointment, and his ministry and following can be said to be largely online. Traditionalism is an area warranting much further study, as much of its popularity can be attributed to its heavily mediatised nature. This extends to aesthetic dimensions of the traditional liturgy, and Instagram pages of collections of TLMs alongside TLM parishes' own social media pages commonly featuring masses celebrated in an ostentatious Baroque style have played a key role in ratifying an aesthetic-ideology dimension to traditionalism, playing into the performativity to which the politicisation of the movement can at least be partly attributed to.

Other dimensions of the complex nature of organisational communication arise when one considers how official church structures have their own social media pages, including local dioceses, diocesan organisations, and parish churches themselves, all of which function as variations of the 'public relations' work of the Church; known within Catholicism as 'social communications'. This confirms Wee's assertion that institutional environments are not homogeneous (Wee, 2015, p. 5). Related is the category of religious orders in the Church which exists alongside diocesan structures. Priests in the Catholic Church are typically of two kinds, the first of which are called 'diocesan priests' who serve under a diocesan bishop and who usually work in a parish church setting, and the second type are priests who belong to a religious order. Unlike diocesan priests, they usually live in community, with a spirituality based on their order's founder, taking solemn vows as a consecrated person. While they might be involved in parish work, their spirituality might also mean that they are devoted to some more specific mission, such as education, caring for the sick or poor, or evangelising through the Word of God and so on.

Bottom Up: Participant Discourse

A meaningful contrast to an institutional perspective to Catholic social media practices is how it might be understood from a 'bottom-up' perspective, considering that the affordances of social media allow for individuals to organise themselves on social media platforms alongside particular themes or points of commonality. Such practices can certainly be expected to be taken up by members of the laity who seek to participate in such online communities as part of their religious practice. This is certainly in line with *Lumen Gentium's* assertion of the role of the laity in the mission of the Church, where

> The holy people of God shares [*sic*] also in Christ's prophetic office; it spreads abroad a living witness, especially by means of a life of faith and charity and by offering to God a sacrifice of praise, the tribute of lips which give praise to His name.

(LG 12)

To date there has been some work studying these communities, especially from a sociological perspective. For example, Dugan (2022) looks at the case of a Natural Family Planning (NFP) Facebook group, in which members seek advice from more experienced or senior practitioners of NFP. The intimate nature of the interaction is enabled by the tension between anonymity and intimacy on the platform. Among other examples, she provides one post of a woman who had a negative experience with her medical doctor; despite it being a Catholic hospital, the doctor appeared to invalidate the effectiveness of NFP.

> Just had my six week postpartum checkup and my doctor brought up birth control, even though she knows my husband and I are practicing NFP. (This is a catholic [*sic*] hospital fyi). She said you can't practice NFP before you get your period again and I told her that you can. She smiled and said 'good luck, I'll be seeing you back here soon pregnant with your second!' I'm feeling very discouraged and worried. My husband and I are not in a position financially to have another child right now, nor am I physically in a position to be pregnant right now according to my Dr. Anyone else been in my shoes before? Needing some positive encouragement!
>
> (Dugan, 2022, p 56)

Dugan notes that the post was particularly popular and attracted many comments, with most communicating solidarity and sympathy. She suggests that the relative anonymity of the space allowed users to feel comfortable making such posts and its 'community' dimension unsurprisingly resulted in much support for the topic poster. At the same time, the Catholic affiliation of the site resulted in replies which Dugan calls "Catholic policing", where other group members suggested writing to the Bishop to lodge a complaint over the doctor's comments.

Work by Kołodziejska (2014, 2018) in the Polish context considers the use of Catholic forums, again a site where lay people can be found to congregate online which have been legitimised by the institutional Church, where they might be linked from official church websites. Yet other dimensions of online religious communities have been studied in varied contexts; Giorgi (2019, 2021) studies "religious masculinities" referring to LGBT+ Catholics who engage on Instagram in Italy, Brazal and Odchigue (2016) consider the use of Facebook among Filipino Christian migrants in the Philippines, Díez Bosch, Micó Sanz, and Sabaté Gauxachs (2017) examine the use of "religious webs and apps" among Catalonian youth and Neumaier (2020) the possibility of social media sites as a site of ecumenical encounter between Protestants and Catholics in Germany.

Ecclesial transformations are a common theme in much of this work; for example, in an edited volume by Rosowsky (2017), a chapter by Sawin (2017) looks at the concept of the parish, suggesting three Facebook groups or sites that form a kind of "digital Christian 'parish'" where

> such 'virtual parishes' created on social media platforms, while competing for engagement and affiliation with congregants' physical parishes by providing space where marginalized identities can be affirmed, also facilitate greater contentment within their physical parishes, since any unmet felt needs are met in the virtual ones.
>
> (Sawin, 2017, p. 19).

Attention to "religious language" among Christians (although not specifically Catholic) can mostly be found in work by Pihlaja (2018, 2021); in the 2018 volume he considers online, interactional context including data on interaction between Christians, atheists and Muslims online as studied from YouTube and Facebook videos. Other parts of the book utilise linguistic concepts of stories and 'storytelling' referencing Labov's (1972) narrative work.

In my empirical case of an online Facebook group of Catholics in Singapore, this has largely been a ground-up initiative among lay Catholics. Created in 2007, the page now has about 18,000 members and an average of 15 new posts every day, thus claiming more members than official diocesan social media channels. Having been a group member since October 2007, my long-standing relationship with the group suggests an ethnographic, emic perspective insofar as these terms can be applied to online contexts although I have posted only very infrequently whilst occasionally replying to others. I have thus been able to make observations about the group through this form of lay participation. For the purposes of my project, I systematically collected all the posts and comments made by users in a two-week period in 2023, resulting in a dataset consisting of 225 threads in the group. I analysed these first by classifying the functions of different posts into categories, as well as considering the interactional dynamics among members. Certainly, my consideration of the group as a source of data meant that my reading of posts in the group took on a more analytical flavour during the data collection period. I identify with Mackenzie's (2016) description as an "observer-participant", where I have spent much of my time in the group making broad observations of what is discussed in order to derive possible analytical categories and perspectives for this project.

The ethics of social media data collection is certainly an important issue to address, and a balance between the work of research and maintaining findings need be found and as such the question of the publicness of personas is left to be decided by several subjective criteria to determine the imagined audience of a particular post. The issue of privacy thus is an inverse relationship with the scale of imagined audience (Litt & Hargittai, 2016); where the audience is thought to be quite large, consent is relatively less important as when posts are seemingly "designed" (Bell, 1984) for a much more specific audience. Of the three areas of discussion which D'Arcy and Young (2012) raise, the more relevant issue that occurred in my research was "securing informed and ongoing consent". I adopted some principles which D'Arcy and Young propose. They note the importance of transparency, and Young used her real name on her Facebook profile in their research project. I do the same in my research on Facebook, maintain a single personal profile for posts on which my university affiliation is publicly available.

D'Arcy and Young (2012) also propose the setting up of a (new) Facebook group in which recruited participants join, and in which the name of the university and crest are clearly displayed. This however comes at the expense of capturing linguistic and social network data from existing groups, and thus I decided on alternative methods of obtaining consent. I had considered various options, including messaging individual members who had made posts or comments to ask for consent for their posts to be used for research. On further inspection I found this a thoroughly impractical option as it would greatly limit the number of posts I would collect due to the logistics of asking for consent for individual posts. In addition, regular posters would receive many repetitive messages asking for consent. Finally, sending the same message to many users in a short span of time will likely be constituted as spam by the platform. My eventual consent-seeking method involved first seeking the approval of group administrators, in which I explained the motivations for research. It was fortunate that I did not run into the issue which Johnson, Lawson, and Ames (2018) faced of a negative response on the part of the administrators, who felt that the researcher had gained access to the group under false pretences, negating the fact that the researcher was in fact part of the community of the group in question.

Upon obtaining approval from both the group administrators and from the university's ethical review board, I proceeded to make a post explaining my research goals and the data I would be collecting. I collected posts in a fixed span of time, in other words, not including posts retro-actively. In the post I asked members to inform me via message or email if they did not want their posts to be collected, thus adopting an 'opt-out' system of consent. I made clear that I would not be collecting any personal data or identifiable information as far as possible, and at the data collection process I did not collect usernames, names of people mentioned, names of churches or church groups. None of the members contacted me to opt-out, and many members commented, expressing enthusiasm, support, and interest in my project.

While most of the members would tend to be Mass-going Catholics, the particular space afforded by social media has created the semblance of a "joint enterprise", carving out a space across Singapore Catholic parishes for Catholics to express their faith within. The most significant insight from the data is how closely there can be observed a continuity between the offline Catholic world and the group space, suggesting an 'institutional effect' where lay conceptions of the Church as a hierarchical institution are mirrored in the online space. One example of a popular practice on the site is the sharing of image macros featuring Bible quotes, or the resharing of posts from popular devotional books written in the pre-Vatican II era, and the sharing of mediatised versions of prayer cards, analogous to the sharing of physical prayer cards once commonplace. There is a typology to the visual styles present in the examples; some such images are biblical quotes turned into images, others commemorate the feast of the day. These posts are commonly shared daily in a ritualistic way by particular members, and attract a smattering of comments (again, typically from the same people) who might comment "Amen" variously combined with the praying hands emoji, thought to represent a 'high-five' but which has become resemiotised as a symbol for prayers on the group. Yet another unusual practice is the reposting of images taken in churches; for example, instead of sharing a digital version of a poster advertising an event, some members would take a photo of a physical poster found and share it on the group. Members also commonly shared their personal experiences in churches, for example, posting photos from events in Catholic parishes. In this sense, the existence of the online group, and its predominant content is largely influenced by the offline experience of users, who adapt or extend their experience of offline church activity to the online group.

Another commonality with traditional church structures can be seen in the strong role the moderators played in the group. The moderators were all lay people and volunteers, who have the power to allow or disallow posts or to evict members. Over the years that I have observed the group, there have been instances where members disagreed or argued with the moderators' input or opinion, where especially the group's 'About' page states that posts should be sympathetic to orthodox Catholic, magisterial teaching. The moderators, alongside other frequent posters and commentors, thus give rise to the role of discursive expertise that results in the semblance of authority in online spaces. This expertise is performed, sometimes simply via frequent engage-ment, but especially through the mobilisation of church documents and other academic sources towards the ratification of theological viewpoints that point to a particular version of orthodoxy. One of the posts during the data collection period was a resharing of an article published on a Catholic news website, where one of the authors was also a member of the group. The article was a critique of the Catholic200SG celebrations in 2021 which consisted of events to mark the 200th anniversary of the arrival of French missionaries in Singapore, and the article argues that the cele-bration of a colonial milestone in some way ignores the pre-existence of Catholics in Singapore before the arrival of said missionaries. Members were quick to defend the event and the official narrative marking the beginnings of the Church in Singapore, pointing to sources which ratify that there is good reason to suggest 1821 as the 'beginning' of Catholicism in Singapore. The hierarchical structure of the Church thus both bears similarity and difference to the online iteration of Catholic life—while the moderators might be lay people in contrast to the priests and bishops who head dioceses and parishes, a strong sense of hierarchy remains evident in what is allowed to be discussed in the group.

A second example of a highly engaged-with post during the data collection period was one in which a member asked if it was "possible to be Catholic and Buddhist at the same time". This member utilised the anonymous feature of Facebook groups, which meant that their identity was only known to the administrators, and not other members. Again, the predominant message in the responses argued that it was not possible at all, doing so via the citing of Bible verses, and demonstrating knowledge associated with Buddhism to argue for its incompatibility with Catholicism. One member cited their qualifications in Buddhist studies before their conversion to Catholicism, while another explained their viewpoint via a constructed dialogue between 'Christianity' and 'Buddhism'. In such instances, the Facebook group can be observed to provide a space for such discussions that might otherwise be hard to come by in churches which do not always lend themselves to facilitating such interactions in an informal context.

Yet another feature of the group is the recounting of intimate, personal experiences, with the overarching message that these experiences are in some way a means through which God has spoken to them. This message allows for an intimacy that suggests a much more private and individual audience design, although the group's large size essentially renders it essentially a public space. The "semiotic ideology" (Keane, 2018) of the sharing of religious experience entails that an important dimension of religious language is how they are couched in a view of the world in which God is actively present, a God who is personally involved in the lives of Christians. In one post, a user, who appeared to be new to the group, recounted their experience attending a penitential service. These services are often held before Christmas and Easter, times in which Catholics traditionally avail of the Sacrament of Reconciliation, also known as confession. To accommodate the larger numbers of people wanting to make a confession at these times of the years, penitential services are organised where priests from other churches are invited to hear confessions as well. A penitential service can take various forms, such as a general absolution in which there would not be individual confessions. In the numerous comments which the post attracted, a high degree of alignment with the poster can be observed, with users affirming that her experience was indeed from God. The localities of these posts are demonstrated in various ways, including specific place references to an area in Singapore in the original post, and the name of a parish church. In the comments, group members utilised features of colloquial Singapore English, pointing to the multilingual nature of Singapore. These examples are but some of the ways in which space for religious practice is being extended onto online contexts, and where social media provides spaces for interaction and the narrative recounting of 'God-experiences' beyond those (un)available in face-to-face contexts. Social media sites are facilitating the creation of online communities fairly distinct, but not entirely unrelated to offline ones. Linguistic features used to structure these online communities can be observed to be heavily based on the affordances of social media platforms, from which the 'generic' spaces of social media are turned into spaces of intimacy in the context of religious and faith experiences. Religious language, and by extension, interaction, on social media can be said to be contingent on 1) continuity with offline church practice and experiences, 2) an interpretation of experiences as being associated as coming from God, and 3) a convivial affirmation demonstrating affiliation to the experiences of individuals.

Implications and Future Directions

As I have attempted to demonstrate, there remains much opportunity to explore a sociolinguistic dimension to mediatised religious practices. The impression that (Christian) religion has been relegated to a marginal position in society is perhaps an overly Eurocentric view, and in parts of the Global South there can be observed vibrant Christian communities both online and offline. I thus propose this paradigm of top-down and bottom-up as a heuristic to understand mediatised religious practices, whilst acknowledging that many spaces or case studies might feature a combination of the two.

Greeley proposed the existence of a 'Catholic Imagination'. He writes:

> This special Catholic imagination can appropriately be called sacramental. It sees created reality as a 'sacrament', that is, a revelation of the presence of God. The workings of this imagination are most obvious in the Church's seven sacraments, but the seven are both a result and a reinforcement of a much broader Catholic view of reality.
>
> (Greeley, 2000)

I suggest that a not unrelated Catholic digital culture can be observed online, characterised by several key features that look to transform our present-day understanding of Catholic ecclesiology. The emergence of global connections resulting from media technology appears to feed into Rahner's (1981) vision of the world church, and the online ministries which have especially boomed during the COVID-19 pandemic have demonstrated ways in which the geographic boundaries of Catholic life, traditionally divided into dioceses by territory, are becoming increasingly fluid. It has become easier than ever for Catholics in one part of the world to access content from another part, resulting in the transfer of both theological and aesthetic ideas. The emergence of the 'world church' is thus perhaps well observable on such online platforms discussed here, and future work will further reveal the consequences of social media on ecclesial practices.

Many connections can be observed with the research associated with the sociolinguistics of globalisation (Coupland & Blommaert, 2003), where global registers of language can be observed in urban city centres, and where a constant tension between the global and the local can be observed. This is true for both content, and forms of language—for example where English might be present in a rural village in the Global South, the form of English might take on local characteristics that point to this tension, and where big-name global brands are resemiotised and rescaled to local contexts, perhaps through handwritten signs referencing globality in this way. A global Catholicism across the English-speaking world can thus be observed to be emerging through these lenses, and a simultaneous alignment with institutional, Vatican-related and Diocesan-level discourses, as well as with local events relating more directly to Catholic life in specific places.

Several methodological challenges can be noted, especially more generally associated with the study of social media sites and online spaces. The use of theoretical concepts originally meant to describe offline practice pose a particular challenge, where there is often not a one-to-one correlation between the manifestations of such concepts; this is indeed the case for the two concepts I employ here, which largely have been interested in offline practice. An adaptation of these concepts is thus necessary to understand how both organisations and communities participate on the internet, considering how the affordances of social media sites facilitate or constrain interactional patterns. The ethics and practicalities of data collection on social media sites remain difficult, especially as terms of use often preclude the use of data for research, and that data is owned by social media sites themselves. The lack of application programming interfaces (APIs) means that 'scraping' of social media data is disallowed on many platforms; the often-intimate nature of religious discourse (for example, in the case of the NFP group) and the difficulty of obtaining informed consent are more considerations in conducting research on social media.

A balance between the work of research, maintaining findings, and approaching data ethically need be found. At the heart of the issue around social media is the demarcation of private and public spaces, a distinction that can be observed to be blurred in many examples of Catholic social media. The difficulty lies in part that pages belonging to organisations are not always clearly differentiated from those belonging to individuals, and it would not be immediately obvious by looking at a page in the first instance. Conversely there are options in the interface to switch between accounts, for example between a personal account and an organisational one that is administered by one or more people. Upon switching to the organisational account, one then 'speaks' on behalf of the organisation, with their comments bearing the name of the organisation instead. As such, the question of the publicness of personas is left to be decided by several subjective criteria in order to determine the imagined audience of a particular post. The issue of privacy thus is an inverse relationship with the scale of imagined audience (Litt & Hargittai, 2016); where the audience is thought to be quite large, consent is relatively less important as when posts are seemingly "designed" (Bell, 1984) for a much more specific audience.

Finally, the question of language seems to be increasingly central to understanding how Catholics experience their faith, where social media viewership is often organised along linguistic lines. This is to say that with global access to social media, linguistic difference appears to be the one limiting factor in the transmission of ideological and aesthetic ideas. In this chapter I have largely considered the social media output among Catholics in the English-speaking world, who can easily access and follow social media sites in another English-speaking country: for example, users in Singapore often follow American social media pages, including those belonging to American groups, priests, and bishops. In contrast, the Spanish-speaking Catholic world, which would certainly constitute a large part of the Catholic population, might well operate with a separate set of assumptions, and similarly for other languages as well. The role of language is once again brought to the fore, and as part of decolonising linguistic research a worthwhile first step is the acknowledgement of how research into spaces where English is not the dominant language entails that findings from English-language sites are not as generalisable as they can appear to be.

Further Reading

Campbell, H.A. (Ed.). (2012). *Digital Religion: Understanding Religious Practice in New Media Worlds.* Routledge.

Campbell has done much work into digital Christian practices more generally and much of it can apply to Catholic contexts. In this particular edited volume, questions associated with the field are presented thematically.

del Pinal, E. H., Roscoe Loustau, M., & Norget, K. (Eds.). (2022). *Mediating Catholicism: Religion and Media in Global Catholic Imaginaries.* Bloomsbury Academic.

This edited volume contains case studies into mediatised Catholic practices from varying contexts, providing insight into the use of media in Catholic contexts.

Kołodziejska, M. (2018). *Online Catholic communities: community, authority, and religious individualisation.* Routledge.

Kołodziejska provides a model for the study of online Catholic community in this volume, discussing questions of authority and hierarchy in an online context.

Schmidt, K.G. (2020). *Virtual Communion: Theology of the Internet and the Catholic Sacramental Imagination.* Fortress Academic.

Schmidt's volume proposes a "theology of the internet", providing a theological dimension into possibilities and constraints for a connected Catholicism.

Seargeant, P. & Tagg, C. (2014). *The Language of Social Media: Identity and Community on the Internet.* Palgrave Macmillan.

Seargeant and Tagg provide an excellent introduction to sociolinguistic approaches to studying social media, and the volume as a whole contains useful case studies applying sociolinguistic concepts to social media contexts.

References

Abidin, C. (2018). From Internet Celebrities to Influencers. In *Internet Celebrity: Understanding Fame Online*, 71–98. Emerald Publishing Limited.

Androutsopoulos, J. (2006a). Introduction: Sociolinguistics and computer-mediated communication. *Journal of Sociolinguistics, 10*(4), 419–438. DOI: 10.1111/j.1467-9841.2006.00286.x

Androutsopoulos, J. (2006b). Multilingualism, diaspora, and the Internet: Codes and identities on German-based diaspora websites. *Journal of Sociolinguistics, 10*(4), 520–547. DOI:10.1111/j.1467-9841.2006.00291.x

Bell, A. (1984). Language Style as Audience Design. *Language in Society*, 13(2), 145–204. www.jstor.org/stable/4167516

Berger, T. (2017). @ Worship: Liturgical Practices in Digital Worlds (1st ed.). Routledge. https://doi.org/10.4324/9781315163253

boyd, d. (2010). Social Network Sites as Networked Publics: Affordances, Dynamics, and Implications. In d. boyd (Ed.), *A Networked Self*, 47–66. Routledge.

Brazal, A.M. & Odchigue, R. (2016). Cyberchurch and Filipin@ Migrants in the Middle East. In S. Snyder, J. Ralston, & A.M. Brazal (Eds.), *Church in an Age of Global Migration: A Moving Body*, 187–199. Palgrave Macmillan US.

Coupland, N. & Blommaert, J. (2003). Sociolinguistics and Globalisation. *Journal of Sociolinguistics, 7*(4), 465–623. Wiley-Blackwell. DOI:10.1111/j.1467-9841.2003.00237.x

D'Arcy, A. & Young, T.M. (2012). Ethics and social media: Implications for sociolinguistics in the networked public1. *Journal of Sociolinguistics, 16*(4), 532–546. DOI: 10.1111/j.1467-9841.2012.00543.x

Díez Bosch, M., Micó Sanz, J.L., & Sabaté Gauxachs, A. (2017). Typing my Religion. Digital use of religious webs and apps by adolescents and youth for religious and interreligious dialogue. *Church, Communication and Culture, 2*(2), 121–143. DOI:10.1080/23753234.2017.1347800

Dugan, K. (2022). NFP Online: The Mutable Religious Space of Social Media. In E. H. del Pinal, M. Roscoe Loustau, & K. Norget (Eds.), *Mediating Catholicism: Religion and Media in Global Catholic Imaginaries*, 47–62. Bloomsbury Academic.

Gal, S. (1989). Language and Political Economy. *Annual Review of Anthropology, 18*, 345–367.

Giorgi, A. (2019). Mediatized Catholicism—Minority Voices and Religious Authority in the Digital Sphere. *Religions, 10*(8), 463. MDPI. Retrieved from www.mdpi.com/2077-1444/10/8/463

Giorgi, A. (2021). Religious masculinities: performing in/visibility on Instagram. *Mediascapes Journal*, (18), 67–79.

Gorter, D. (2006). *Linguistic Landscape: A New Approach to Multilingualism*. Multilingual Matters.

Greeley, A. (2000). *The Catholic Imagination*. University of California Press.

Herring, S.C. (1996). *Computer-Mediated Communication: Linguistic, social, and cross-cultural perspectives.* John Benjamins Publishing Company.

Johnson, A., Lawson, C., & Ames, K. (2018). *Are you really one of us? Exploring Ethics, Risk and Insider Research in a Private Facebook Community*. Paper presented at the Proceedings of the 9th International Conference on Social Media and Society, Copenhagen, Denmark. https://doi.org/10.1145/3217804.3217902

Keane, W. (2018). On Semiotic Ideology. Signs and Society, 6(1), 64–87. DOI:10.1086/695387

Kołodziejska, M. (2014). Religion on Catholic Internet Forums in Poland. A Memory Mediated. *Nordic Journal of Religion and Society, 27*, 151–166. DOI:10.18261/ISSN1890-7008-2014-02-04

Kołodziejska, M. (2018). *Online Catholic communities: community, authority, and religious individualisation*. Routledge.

Labov, W. (1972). *Sociolinguistic Patterns*. University of Pennsylvania Press.

Lee, C. (2017). *Multilingualism online / Carmen Lee*. Routledge.

Litt, E. & Hargittai, E. (2016). The Imagined Audience on Social Network Sites. *Social Media + Society, 2*(1). DOI: 10.1177/2056305116633482

Mackenzie, J. (2016). *The Discursive Construction of Motherhood Through Digital Interaction.* PhD thesis. Aston University. https://doi.org/10.1016/j.pragma.2013.12.003

Neumaier, A. (2020). The big friendly counter-space? Interreligious encounter within social media. *Religion, 50*(3), 392–413. DOI:10.1080/0048721X.2020.1754605

Pennycook, A. (2017). Translanguaging and semiotic assemblages. *International Journal of Multilingualism, 14*(3), 269–282. DOI: 10.1080/14790718.2017.1315810

Pihlaja, S. (2018). *Religious talk online: the evangelical discourse of Muslims, Christians and atheists.* Cambridge University Press.

Pihlaja, S. (2021). *Talk about faith: how debate and conversation shape belief.* Cambridge University Press.

Rahner, K. (1981). *Theological Investigations XX: Concern for the Church.* Darton, Longman & Todd.

Rosowsky, A. (2017). *Faith and Language Practices in Digital Spaces*: Multilingual Matters.

Sawin, T. (2017). Re-Parishing in Social Media: Identity-Based Virtual Faith Communities and Physical Parishes. In Rosowsky, A. (Ed.), *Faith and Language Practices in Digital Spaces*, 19–44. *Multilingual Matters.*

Schmidt, K.G. (2020). *Virtual Communion: Theology of the Internet and the Catholic Sacramental Imagination.* Fortress Academic.

Seargeant, P, & Tagg, C. (2014). *The Language of Social Media: Identity and Community on the Internet.* Palgrave Macmillan.

Spadaro, A. (2014) Cybertheology: Thinking Christianity in the Era of the Internet. Fordham University Press.

Wee, L. (2015). *The Language of Organizational Styling.* Cambridge University Press.

PART III

Religious Identity & Community

21

RELIGION, IDENTITY, AND SECOND LANGUAGE

Amal Alhamazany

Introduction and Background

The relationship between language and identity is reciprocal. Who we are can influence the way we speak, which in turn can portray parts of who we are. A very simple and direct example of this relationship is using language to identify ourselves. One more complex and indirect example is using a second language in a way that is similar to your first language to show aspects of your social identity and to distance yourself from L1 speakers of that second language; for example, transferring Arabic syntactic features into English such as copula deletion. This relationship between language and identity has been central to research in the field of sociolinguistics that views language use as reflecting aspects of speakers' identity. Language variation as an ingroup marker in particular has been examined in first language contexts (Milroy, 1980; Eckert, 1989; Drummond, 2018) and in second language contexts (Bayley, 2005; Drummond, 2012; Alhamazany, 2021). In these studies, language variation is examined in relation to the construction of speakers' social identity.

Tajfel's (1978, p. 63) social identity theory can be defined as "that part of an individual's self-concept which derives from his knowledge of his membership of a social group (or groups) together with the value and emotional significance attached to that membership". While it is called social identity, central to this theory is a person's sense of belonging to a group rather than the nature of the group *per se*. Additionally, emotional significance is another integral component of social identity (Joseph, 2004). This integral part of a social identity accounts for the reason a person may take a defensive and protective stance when their membership or social group is being challenged. Contrast is another aspect of the construction of social identity. Who the outgroup is opposes and defines who we are. The core psychological process of group categorization in social identity theory is based on intergroup behaviour, such as stereotyping, discrimination, and prejudice (Levine & Hogg, 2010). Defining and categorizing characteristics of outgroups helps in enhancing ingroup characteristics.

Building on social identity theory, Turner et al. (1987) proposed *self*-categorization theory which entails that conforming to attributes of social groups involves depersonalising *self*-perception. Categorizing ingroups and outgroups entails prototyping of ingroup members and stereotyping of outgroup members. In both cases, individuals become depersonalised versions of the general

DOI: 10.4324/9781003301271-24

characteristics of each group. What is relevant to this chapter is that in depersonalizing the *self*, a person may have to reduce or eliminate important personal behaviour or attributes which may contradict those of ingroups to which they belong, such as being Arab and speaking a 'Western' language (English) as a second language that is associated with a 'Western' outgroup.

Social identity and personal identity (or personality) can be viewed as separate types; the former is larger, and the latter has more defined characteristics. These two types of identity can be connected in that personal identity may derive some of its aspects from social identity. This argument is based on the fact that human beings are social creatures. We derive our personal attributes from socialising with groups in which we belong (Edwards, 2009). Therefore, personal identities are components of social identities, and the latter are "stereotypic in nature because of their necessary generality across the individual components" (Edwards, 2009, p. 20). Additionally, even though aspects of our personal identity might be derived from our social being, the *self* can be independent to the point that it can contradict our social identity. This argument echoes Schalk's (2011, p. 209) views regarding the *self* and the *other* relationship that it is not binary but lies on "a spectrum of relatedness". Schalk added to the *self* and the *other* categories a new term, the *other-self* that can "identify with or behave as an *other*" (Schalk, 2011, p. 209). On a spectrum between the *self* and the *other* exists several identity positions possible for the *self* to occupy and negotiate. Some of these identity positions might be closer to or resemble that of the *other*, which might also contradict the core perception of the *self* at the other end of the spectrum. Despite the different opinions regarding the distinction between personal and social identities, as Edwards (2009) explains, identity in general is central to all 'human' or 'social' sciences as they investigate how people understand themselves and others in social contexts. Indeed, in the field of sociolinguistics, the concept of identity has become a crucial factor in understanding language variable use (e.g. Drummond, 2012).

Religious identity is one of the many forms of social identity. It is a group identity because it relies on conforming to a group's belief. It contrasts with outgroups in the form of *disbelieving* their belief system; for example, Muslims vs. non-Muslims, particularly in communities that include diverse people of ethnic and linguistic backgrounds (Kulkarni-Joshi, 2015). In religious communities, religion may construct the core of individuals' sense of *self* as religion is "bound up with our deepest beliefs about life, the universe and everything" and not only defines who we are, but it may influence our biggest and smallest decisions (Joseph, 2004, p. 172). For example, in the case of Muslim communities, Islamic teachings along with social norms may dictate who members of those communities can and cannot marry, what they should eat and even how to dress. Religious identity may also contradict one's personal identity (for example, Muslim women who only wear a hijab for prayers). In this sense, a sinful *self* is a simple example of a contradiction between one's religious (social) identity and personal identity on a spectrum of the *self*, the *other*, and several possible identity positions of *other-self*. Speaking the language of other groups not associated with a person's religious identity might also be another example.

Religious identity in that sense can be viewed as being relatively restrictive of one's personal identity. Additionally, the influence of this restriction can vary among community members and according to the religion itself. It can be stronger for some individuals more than others because of social norms or expectations that enforce conforming to social/religious identity. For example, Saudi women are expected to adhere to social norms and social religious identity aspects more than men. Saudi women's social identity is a 'separate category' which is defined by social norms and expectations as being "pious and virtuous, modest, educated, financially comfortable, and devoted to her family" (Le Renard, 2008, pp. 610–614). The social pressure on Saudi women to adhere to certain social/religious identity formation can influence how women behave in a way that is different from men to reflect that identity, which can be viewed in their second language use, as I will discuss in the case study.

While religious identity can be independently viewed as a social identity in itself, it can also be part of a larger identity. For example, for Arabs, being Muslim is part of their *Arabness* as they speak the language of the Qur'an. In Lebanon, Muslims' religious identity is viewed as part of their Arab identity that is linked with being Arabic speakers (Joseph, 2004). Religious identity can also be independent of ethnicity or race, as is the case of African or any non-Arab Muslims. Both types of religious identity (ethnic Arab and non-ethnic/non-Arab Muslim identities) can oppose each other as one is racial and ethnic or has more linguistic association than the other. That is, in a larger and universal Muslim community, there are multiple Muslim identity formations that are seen as constituting opposing groups rather than one group, depending on how Muslims within each group represent their religious identity. An Arab Muslim might have stronger claim over being *ideal* or *prototypical* Muslim than a non-Arab Muslim by virtue of being Arab that is associated with the language of the Qur'an. However, there is a more complex social identity in Saudi Arabia which is not only associated with the language of Islam and ethnicity of being Arab but also derives its legitimacy from being associated with the scaredness of the place of Islam. This final form of Saudi Muslim identity opposes the previous two religious identities: ethnic Arab and non-ethnic/non-Arab Muslim identities.

The relationship between language, religion, and identity can be observed from different perspectives. Both religion and language are social constructs that can be ideologically motivated (Yaeger-Dror, 2014) and can be viewed as identity markers at individual and group levels. Both language and religion can influence each other (Omoniyi & Fishman, 2006). They can add value to and represent the value of the other. On one hand, religion sacralises language and raises its status to being holy. Additionally, religion can sacralise identity (Mol, 1976), which can be done through speaking a sacralised language. On the other hand, as Edwards (2009, p.105) notes, the ongoing debate about the first language God created (or God's language) to teach Adam the names of all things and creatures— 'And He taught Adam the names– all of them' وَعَلَّمَ آدَمَ الْأَسْمَاءَ كُلَّها (Sura 2, Al-Baqara, verse 31)—reflects the "continuing language- and-identity discourse". Religious language can unite multilingual and multi-ethnic communities. For example, Muslims in Kupwar, who are speakers of two local Indian language varieties (Marathi and Urdu), use the Arabic language to index their Muslim identity and show their membership of a universal Muslim community (Kulkarni-Joshi, 2015). A language with religious status can provide an authoritative and powerful status to people whose identity is marked by that language, so much so that it can grant monopoly of religion knowledge and the role of a prototypical devotee. Sacred sites along with religion may also add more sense of religiosity. The case study illustrates how this might be the reality for Saudis that their location and first language that are associated with Islam might have led them to claim a special 'Muslim' status or identity that differentiates them from other Muslims in other locations who are speakers of other languages (Alhamazany, 2021).

Languages that are associated with religion, such as Arabic, can be viewed as sacred and in need of protection from the influence of other languages, such as English. This fear of losing a religious language might not always be motivated by concerns to protect that language but by maintaining identity aspects that are associated with or indexed through the language or certain language features; that is, maintaining the status of the language as an identity marker. Edwards argues that "'language' movements are energized by the symbolic and identity-carrying aspects of language, and very rarely by the language *per se*" (2009, p. 101). So, when a Saudi English speaker, who is actively and willingly using the language, expresses their fear of the loss of Arabic, this fear might not be about Arabic itself but about losing the status of it that is associated with the Arabian or Islamic aspects of their identity.

The notion that the interaction between religion and language can be a way of indexing identity is now often prevalent in sociolinguistic research. Discourse analysis of everyday speech is one way of studying the construction of religious identity through language, for example, exploring how faith is represented through metaphor (Ringrow, 2021). Additionally, religion has been factored in studies of language choice and variation in first language contexts. For example, religious affiliation proved to influence vowel variation in the speech of people who self-identified as Mormons or non-Mormons (Baker & Bowie, 2010). Mallinson and Childs (2007) also found similar results that religiosity correlates with sound and morphosyntactic variation. In these studies, the concept of social networks (Milroy, 1980) was a primary factor that resulted in different linguistic behaviour. For example, variation was found in /u/ and /o/ fronting in the speech of 'church ladies' and 'porch sitters', two groups that differ in their religiosity (Mallinson & Childs, 2007). Social networks that are created based on religious affiliation can lead to variation in the speech of religious and non-religious speakers as a result of being members and non-members of those social networks. In such religious communities, close-knit social networks are constructed based on shared beliefs, sense of religiosity, and adherence to specific religious rules and teachings that must be maintained and protected from outside influences (Richardson et al., 2021).

In second language contexts, studies have examined the influence of religion on language choice in multilingual communities (e.g. Avineri, 2014; Kulkarni-Joshi, 2015), or on heritage language maintenance (Ding & Goh, 2020). In all the above studies, in first and second language contexts, religion or religiosity was assigned as a factor based on participants' self-reported affiliation or language use in certain domains including religious places. So, religion coding included either being Mormons or non-Mormons (Baker & Bowie, 2010), being Muslim, Christian, or Hindu (Kulkarni-Joshi, 2015), and using Yiddish for daily life activities or religious practices (Avineri, 2014). Even though religion and language in relation to identity have been the focus of some studies in second language contexts, it is important to note that in these contexts the second language under investigation is actually the language associated with speakers' religious affiliation.

Religion as a sociolinguistic variable has not been investigated in second language contexts in which the second language is not representative of speakers' religious identity, especially in more homogeneous contexts in which all speakers are assumed to affiliate with the same religion. For example, in Saudi Arabia, a Muslim country, where religion can be viewed as a more salient variable culturally and linguistically, every Saudi is assumed to be Muslim. Additionally, Arabic, the language associated with Islam, is the first and dominant language. Sociolinguistic inquiry should focus on contexts such as Saudi to examine the influence of religious identity on variation in a second language that is marked as the language of the *other*. Additionally, while the majority of studies concerning language and social identity focus on the distinctions between social identity or the *self* and the *other*, contradiction between the *self* (or personal identity) and social identity as reflected in language use and attitudes has not been examined, especially in relation to religion as a sociolinguistic factor. This contradictory relationship is explored in the following case study.

The Importance of Religion in Examining Language Use and Attitude in L2 Context

Saudi society is generally viewed as a homogenous country in terms of religion (Islam). Despite its important role in shaping Saudi society and education, religion as a social factor has never been considered in second language research in Saudi Arabia and has rarely been mentioned in general in relation to English. In the few cases in which religion is considered, it has been used as a justification for why English education in Saudi Arabia is important. For example, learning English can be used to spread Islam (Faruk, 2013). This justification has been exploited in several studies. Faruk (2013, p. 78), for example, claims that giving English "a prestigious status in Saudi official documents when it is stated that English can be used to spread 'the faith of Islam'" succeeded in getting Saudis' approval regarding teaching English. Saudis' religious identity has never been examined in relation to English as an international language or in relation to their language use. Speakers' identity in previous second language research in Saudi Arabia has not been considered in depth, as learners have been assumed to want to sound like *western native* speakers.

In the abovementioned studies, the spread of English in Saudi Arabia was given a religious purpose which shows how the English language might be negatively perceived as having Western associations. Education and research concerning English in Saudi Arabia are based on and reinforce ideologies such as 'native-speakerism' on one hand. On the other hand, there have been calls to preserve and protect Arabic as it may lose its status (e.g. AlJarf, 2008). When it comes to English in Saudi Arabia there are therefore two conflicting ideologies: an educational ideology that promotes English as the language of westernised native speakers which is reflected in English research (e.g. Alsamani, 2014), and a religious ideology that is prejudiced against any non-Muslim culture. Until 2005, religious education in Saudi Arabia has been characterised by intolerance towards non-Muslims (Al-Otaibi, 2020). Therefore, being Muslim and being an English speaker constitute aspects of Saudi identity, even though these aspects are at odds.

My research has looked at variation in English as a second language in Saudi Arabia (Alhamazany, 2021). It examined variation in the speech of Saudi English speakers as a reflection of aspects of their identity. Following studies such as Drummond's (2012; 2013), it is a second-wave variationist sociolinguistic study in which identity is seen to be indexed through certain linguistic variants as a result of interactions between language and social factors such as gender, tribalism, and age. Communicating identity through speech might not always be salient or direct. In such cases, the concept of identity might be observed through language attitudes or other social factors, both of which can be shaped by one's identity and can impact the way people talk (Drummond, 2013).

The study included Saudi participants from different social backgrounds and age groups. Interviews with the participants were conducted in English to gather data regarding English variation beside Saudi opinions and attitudes towards the English language and other topics such as religion in Saudi Arabia. Questionnaires were used to collect demographic information about the speakers, such as age, tribe, occupation, and English education experience. An attitudinal test was conducted to elicit information about their attitudes to English in Saudi Arabia which were compared with their opinions in the interviews. While I did not include 'religion' or 'religious identity' as a factor in the analysis, religiosity appeared to explain the influence of certain factors on language variation. In addition, speakers' religious identity was more evident in the thematic analysis (Alhamazany, 2021). In the following extracts, all speakers have been given pseudonyms to protect their anonymity.

Us, Myself and the Other

1. Ola: I'm actually working on this and hopefully, <u>hopefully, hopefully I become an English speaker as a native speaker,</u> but I know now, sometimes my grammar is not

good. Sometimes my accent is not good. But I still am looking forward to being as a native speaker.

Ola: When I was studying English, in the English classes, they told us 'You are not like a native speaker, you need to become like a native speaker'.

2. Ahmed: I think my accent is really poor.

    Interviewer: What do you mean poor?

    Ahmed: I mean it's not good I'm struggling with the accent.

    Interviewer: What's a good accent?

    Ahmed: I believe when you speak a foreign language, try to speak as good as native as possible.

    Interviewer: Who is a native speaker of English?

    Ahmed: English [British] people, American people, Australian people.

Wanting to be native-like and fearing the loss of their religious language is a contradiction that characterised many of the speakers' views in my study. Before discussing the findings concerning religious identity, it is important to talk about one important and general finding that will help explain the rest. The thematic analysis showed that speakers have established boundaries between the *self* and the *other*. The *self* which represents a social (Arab, Muslim, and Saudi) identity. The *other* includes any non-Saudis, especially western English speakers. This distinction can be seen as a product of the educational ideology that English is the language of (the non-Arab/Muslim *other*) *western* native speakers. This observation was clear in some of the speakers' opinions (for example, extracts 1 and 2).

3. Rami: I work at SABIC. I have people working under my organisation, English people and Saudis, our all communications are in English.

4. Aser: … English even in field of my work [hospital] we have more than eighty percent of the staff non-Saudis… non-Arabs and we speak and send emails in English.

5. Rahaf: …nowadays even universities, they started teaching English, they don't speak in Arabic. Even the teachers the doctors, they come from India, I think. In King Abdul Aziz University, they teach us in English because some words you can't explain them in Arabic.

6. Fahad: …now in college the main language used in colleges is English, so I think it is something that will benefit them in the future.

This distinction between the *self* and the *other* appears to be a result of misunderstanding of the concept of *multilingualism*. From the speakers' views it can be understood that 'good' second language use means approximating to 'native' speakers' use even though the participants admittedly have been fully participating in multilingual communities as English speakers. For example, Saudi English is widely used as a lingua franca at work (extracts 3 and 4) and as a language of education (extracts 5 and 6). Additionally, achieving the status of a 'good' English speaker entails substituting first language features with linguistic features of the *other* ('native' speakers' accent), as in extracts 1 and 2.

7. Interviewer: Is it important that they [Qala's children] stay bilingual?

    Qala: It is important, yes. Because they need to know the other language to get a job, to travel, or need to use the English language, specifically.

8.   Interviewer: Do you like that they are bilingual?

Maliha: I like that because I can see the difference between them and my niece and my nephew, they, they study at a private school [in Saudi], but I can see the difference, so I am proud of my kids.

The spread of English in Saudi has not happened despite Saudis but through them. The speakers in my study appeared to be well aware of their language use and of the reasons they chose to be English speakers. However, being an English speaker can be seen as a part of Saudis' personal identity which seems to contradict their religious identity. This is evident when religion is brought to the fore in discussions about English as a western or non-Muslim social construct. The conflict between personal identity, represented in personal English use, and social (religious) identity can be seen in justifying personal use of the language compared to criticising other Saudis' use. For example, Qala and Maliha explaining the reasons their children are bilingual speakers of Arabic and English (extracts 7 and 8).

9.   Qala: I do not think English is important. I don't think it's the policy of the country, you can see it from schools. If it was really important, they would have it from early age at school, everywhere, even in public schools, but it's not. So, I don't think this is the mission or the vision for them to have bilinguals.

10. Maliha: It should be in Arabic because our country's based on religion. So, when… This is the truth, because the law is based on religion, everything is, in my country, based on religion. Qur'an is a centre of our language. So, they [Saudis] kind of fear this big change to English.

On the other hand, Qala and Maliha did not have the same positive attitude towards English being implemented in Saudi education in general as they had when the focus of the discussion was on their own children's English education (extracts 9 and 10). Religion is foregrounded in Saudi speech when the context of the interaction is about the spread of English in society rather than about their own language use. The idea that the spread of English is out of their control might be the reason. They can control how western cultural associations can influence their lives, but how others might use English and how they might adopt western norms is out of their control, which seems to challenge aspects of their social identity, leading to invoking religion. When English is viewed in a social context in Saudi society, religion is brought up as a defence mechanism as in "the law is based on religion, everything is, in my country, based on religion" and "Qur'an is a centre of our language". Maliha, in saying that "they [Saudis] kind of fear this big change to English", might have been projecting her own fear of imagining Saudis as being English speakers rather than Arabic.

In this context, when English is viewed in relation to society, the speakers seem to have deactivated that personal aspect of their identity which is being an English speaker and activated their social identity as they might have felt it was being challenged or parts of it were being threatened. It is either the *Arabness* part of their identity which is associated with Arabic, hence projecting their fear of the loss of the language if substituted by English and bringing up religion to justify their fear, or the Muslim part of their identity which is also represented by Arabic. Either way, their fear and protective stance of the Arabic language might not be about the language per se but about "the symbolic and identity-carrying aspects of language" (Edwards, 2009, p. 101). Religion is central in both interpretations of the speakers' stance. In other responses it is more evident that religion could be the primary component of their social identity and being Arab is just one but integral part.

11. Zeyad: Yes, we could lose the language of our ancestors and it's in our culture it's the most used and like in religion. The holy Qur'an is in Arabic.

    Interviewer: But there are non-Arab Muslims.

    Zeyad: Yeah, but it's harder to communicate with us (Saudis) like when they come to perform Al-Hajj or to visit Al-Madeenah.

12. Reedha: I mean as Arab people as Muslims, you have to understand Arabic for you to understand the Qur'an.

    Interviewer: There are Muslims who can't speak or read Arabic.

    Reedha: But then I think also other Muslims should understand some Arabic language, at least the basic, to understand their religion.

13. Osama: we should secure our Arabic language because it's the most important to be honest it's important for us to read the holy book, the Qur'an is in Arabic.

    Interviewer: But there are Muslims who can't read Arabic? Islam is not only for Arabs, you know?

    Osama: No, but it's in [the] Arabic language, so if you are not… you can't read or write in Arabic, you will not understand it. Even for western people, they sometime, they need if they want to discover Islam, they have to read in Arabic.

In discussing the spread of English in Saudi Arabia and whether it could have any impact on the culture, the speakers seem to equate 'culture' with 'religion' as shown in the extracts from the responses of three Saudi participants in my study (extracts 11–13). Like the previous finding, when English is discussed in relation to society, religion is invoked as a defence mechanism to protect Arabic. All three speakers, Zeyad, Reedha, and Osama, first equated religion with culture and second they expressed their fear that English might undermine the status of Arabic. Third, they associated the Arabic language with the Muslim identity as all Muslims are expected to be Arabic speakers "to understand their religion" (e.g. extract 12). By doing so, Saudis in this study have positioned themselves as the ideal Muslims whose job is to protect the Muslim faith and identity, and the Arabic language which is a marker of that identity. All Muslims not only have to "understand some Arabic" but also should be able to "communicate with us [Saudis] like when they come to perform Al-Hajj or to visit Al-Madeenah". These examples show that Saudis' religion could be seen as a primary component of their social identity in addition to being Arab. Their first language (Arabic), ethnicity (Arab) and their location (where there are two holy mosques) seem to be crucial factors in legitimising Saudis' religious identity, not just as Muslims but as 'ideal' Muslims that other Muslims should be able to communicate with. A language that is presented as that of non-Muslim western native speakers, such as English, cannot be part of Saudis' complex social religious identity, even though it is a major part of their personal identity.

Overall, there are recurrent patterns that can be observed in some of the participants' responses. They seemed to have similar responses to the same triggers. Personal English use is perceived well but English in social contexts is not. This belief found in different individuals from different social backgrounds could be viewed as the result of their educational *systematic training*. These patterns could be seen as an example of the extent to which religious and English education ideologies in Saudi Arabia can contribute to shaping contradictory parts of Saudis' personal and social identities.

Religion and Second Language Variation

Religion and speakers' social (religious) identity appeared to be crucial in understanding Saudis' variable use of English. Their influence on language variation can be seen through the interaction between a host of social factors that constitute speakers' identity, as religion can be one of many social factors or even an aspect of one component that construct social identity. For example, religion can be considered as an element of ethnicity (Yaeger-Dror, 2014). Therefore, while the impact of religious identity on variation has not been examined directly through including religion as a factor in the analysis, it was evident in shaping social factors, such as gender and tribalism. Studies exploring gender in relation to language have found that gender-differentiated usage of linguistic variables is always motivated by other factors, often related to societal norms (Dubios & Horvath, 2000; Drummond 2012). In my research, gender appears to be a factor that can exert influence on variation in two grammatical features in the speech of Saudi women: third-person singular marker *-s* and verb *be*. In both cases women were more likely to use the 'non-standard' forms [no *-s*] and [no *be*], for example 14 and 15 (Alhamazany, 2021):

14. If we have good language skills that <u>mean</u> we can apply for better job.
15. Speaking English yeah, it's better than before but not too many <u>people ∅ speaking</u> English.

As in many conservative communities, social customs are more likely to be restrictive of women's lives. In Saudi, women more than men are expected to adhere to social, religious, and tribal norms (Le Renard, 2008). Until recently, Saudi women had limited freedom of mobility as they were not allowed to work, travel, or leave their homes without a male guardian's permission (Al-Asfour et al., 2017). This can be seen to have led women to have very narrow social networks. In my research, women reported that they used English less compared to men in different domains (at home, at work, with friends, and with non-Arabs). In contexts other than Saudi Arabia, several variationist studies have found that women are more likely to have limited social networks which can be seen reflected in their language use (e.g., Milroy, 1980; Dubois & Horvath, 2000; Drummond, 2012). It could be argued that having narrow social networks due to social and religious restrictions and less opportunities to use English and practise its 'standard' rules might have led Saudi women to rely more on their own linguistic system (Arabic). As a result, women were more innovative in producing new English forms. Men, on the other hand, had wider social networks and more opportunities to use English which is reflected in their adherence to English 'standard' rules (Alhamazany, 2021).

Another example of the indirect influence of religion or religious identity on language variation in Saudi Arabia can be seen in Saudis' use of the *definite article*. The 'Saudi' identity is complex in that it includes ethnic, religious, linguistic, and tribal components, which are interconnected. Saudis can identify as Arabs, speakers of Arabic, Muslims (extracts 16–18), and tribals or non-tribals.

16. Arabic is our language and it's our heritage.
17. We are Arabs, we have to speak Arabic.
18. As Arab people as Muslims, you have to understand Arabic for you to understand the Qur'an.

While the concept of tribalism may have a stigma of being pre-modern in western contexts, tribalism (Alqabalyah–القَبَلِيّة) in Saudi constitutes a major social status and hierarchy based on bloodline (Metz

1992). Although tribalism can be part of Saudis' national identity, it can also be viewed as a separate identity that differentiates several social tribal communities (Maisel, 2014). Tribalism in Saudi also differentiates between tribal and non-tribal Saudi communities, creating social hierarchy in which tribal Saudis might be considered more superior based on their origin (Asl اصل) and genealogy. On the other hand, non-tribal Saudis, while believed to be of tribal origins, cannot claim to be affiliated with any particular tribe (Maisel, 2015). For tribal Saudis, tribalism is a social identity that is partly constructed by adhering to traditional Arabian norms and affiliating with social networks of kinships (Maisel, 2015). Therefore, tribal communities can be characterised as more close-knit and less diverse compared to non-tribal communities which can influence language choice and use in each group. In tribal social networks, Arabic (or tribal Arabic varieties) is considered an identity marker as opposed to regional Arabic dialects that are mostly used by non-tribal Saudis.

In my research, tribal Saudis appeared to favour 'non-standard' use of the English definite article for generic reference in contexts which do not require *the* in standard English, such as the following:

19. [the] Arabs speak the same accent.
20. I think Arabic is more important in [the] social life.

In examining tribal Saudis' views regarding English, religion and religious identity were foregrounded to strengthen their rejection of English as it might undermine the status of Arabic; for example, the following extracts (21 and 22) from two respondents who are tribal and prefer non-standard use of *the*. Their views show the importance of Arabic in relation to their faith and identity. In this context, religion is used to justify their sense of fear that English might result in the loss of Arabic that is part of their social identity.

21. Taqreed: Nowadays, people just focus more maybe on English because it's like the spoken language all over the world but for me the most important thing is to teach my kids Qur'an and just to be to have the ability to read Arabic.
22. Reedha: I mean as Arab people as Muslims, you have to understand Arabic for you to understand the Qur'an.

    Interviewer: There are Muslims who can't speak or read Arabic.

    Reedha: But then I think also other Muslims should understand some Arabic language, at least the basic, to understand their religion.

Tribal Saudis seemed to distance themselves from what the English language represents (non-Muslim, non-Arab values) through not following its 'standard' rules. As a result, tribal Saudis more than non-tribals tend to use English in a way that is similar to the language with which they identify. In Arabic, the definite article (al—الـ) is used in contexts like that in 19 and 20, that is for generic reference, as in يتكلم العرب نفس اللهجة, [*the*] *Arabs speak the same accent*. To maintain their tribal identity and distance themselves from the *other* (western native speakers) with which English is associated, two strategies were used: first not adhering to English 'standard' rules (non-standard use of the definite article for generic reference), although subconsciously. Second, they used religion to justify their preference of Arabic and rejection of English. To reduce the inconsistency between one aspect of their personal identity (being English speakers) and a major aspect of their social identity (being Arab) resulted in tribal Saudis being innovative in using English through transferring features from Arabic into English.

The influence of religious identity on variation in the definite article could be seen as another example of how the impact of religion on second language can be indirect through other social factors. In this context while tribal and non-tribal Saudis' speech in English vary, religious aspects of tribal identity appeared to be the factor that differentiates tribal and non-tribal Saudis. That could also be viewed as another example of how in a society, that is assumed to be homogenous when it comes to religious affiliation, religious identity is actually more complex, and the degree of sense of that identity varies among members of that society.

Implications and Future Directions

The conflict between *the self*, *group identity* and *the other* can be resolved by presenting English through education as an international language and allowing speakers to imagine themselves as bilinguals in a multilingual world in which their social religious identity is not threatened and the *self* or the *other-self* can exist unchallenged. Problematic concepts such as *native-speakerism* should be substituted with concepts that help rid English of any western associations such as *World Englishes* (Kachru, 1992). More research should contribute to the new *bi/multilingual turn* (Ortega, 2013) in examining English in relation to local identities. In doing so, religion must be included in the analysis as it is a primary aspect that constitutes the Saudi society and is central to understanding Saudis' social identity.

In contexts in which religion categorisation seems to be salient, the degree of religious affiliation, especially in relation to other social factors, may influence language use, creating opportunities to explore language variation as a reflection of different identity formations. This is especially relevant in contexts such as Saudi Arabia in which the second language is perceived as the language of *the other* that might challenge speakers' perception of their religious identity. Religion should be factored in data gathering and analysis in conducting sociolinguistic research. It should be included as an independent factor through allowing speakers "to designate for themselves which of a possible multiple set of (religious) designations they affiliate with most strongly—and which other groups they also affiliate with" (Yaeger-Dror, 2014, p. 577) or in the case of Saudi Arabia where questions about one's faith might be sensitive, the degree of religiosity can be inferred. The latter can be done through asking indirect questions about religion, religious practices, or culture if it is perceived as a reflection of someone's religion. Beside coding limited religion categories, the degree of religiosity proved to be a primary factor that can influence speech (Yaeger-Dror, 2014). This is important in examining religious identity in relation to language use in contexts such as Saudi Arabia where people are believed to follow one religion. Even within one religious group, several religious categories are sometimes needed in research to code religion affiliations or degree of commitment.

In addition to interviews, questionnaires can be used to gather consistent and comparable information across many speakers from different social backgrounds. This would facilitate coding religious affiliation or degree of religiosity and would minimise the effect of sensitivity. Some speakers might feel less judged and might be more at ease answering sensitive questions in questionnaires. For example, in my research, some participants had different responses in the interviews and the questionnaires. Responding to questions about whether English is a westernised language, in the interviews, Saudis seemed to equate faith with culture and took a defensive position that English might result in the loss of Arabic. In the questionnaires, the majority of the same speakers did not agree that "learning English is an indication of westernization" (Alhamazany, 2021, p. 299). Having overt and covert attitudes or opinions regarding topics that might be considered sensitive is not uncommon. For example, in sociolinguistic studies it has been found that attitudes towards language varieties or use might not always be overtly expressed due to fear of social judgment (Milroy & Milroy, 1985). Discrepancy between what people say or do and their true opinions can be explored using two data-gathering methods, such as questionnaires and interviews, which could help collect more detailed information about faith affiliation.

In terms of data analysis, as identity is a complex concept, to explain identity production through language it is important to investigate methods, theories, and concepts from different disciplines. In my research, while the use of a variationist sociolinguistic approach revealed general aspects of Saudis' identity that are interconnected with broad social factors such as gender and tribalism, the use of a thematic analysis helped in understanding how Saudis position themselves as Muslim Arabs and as English speakers in a multilingual world. Additionally, I draw on theories from sociology, such as social identity theory and the concept of *self*-depersonalisation, to explain how variation in English reflects complex social identity formation. The use of third-wave variationist sociolinguistic methods can provide a new research opportunity to examine social identity in relation to language variation (Drummond & Schleef, 2016). This can be done through ethnographic observations of social interactions in which religious identity can be indexed directly or indirectly through first or second language.

Foucault's (1978) theorisation of power and knowledge can prove beneficial in understanding religious identity in relation to language. According to Foucault, power is productive in that it produces knowledge, common sense or truth, and discursive practices in which people construct themselves based on what is perceived to be truth. A Foucauldian discourse analysis focuses not on how meanings are constructed through interaction but rather on power-knowledge relations which produce knowledge or perceived truths that people rely on to define who they are and how they should behave (Khan & MacEachen, 2021); for example, Saudis positioning themselves as the ideal Muslims with whom other Muslims should be able to communicate and who cannot imagine themselves as speakers of the *others'* language. In this case, religion can be viewed as power that produces discourse that Arabic is a sacralised language and Saudi Arabia is a holy place and, by virtue, Saudis (in contrast to other Muslims who are from different countries or non-Arabs) gain more religious status. In this sense, the dominant Saudi Islamic discourse others any *other* Islamic discourse in addition to other religions which might explain Saudis' linguistic behaviour. This dominant Saudi Islamic discourse is the reason Saudi Arabia is often perceived as religiously homogenous and religion is usually overlooked in research concerning second language use and attitude. When examined closely, societies such as Saudi Arabia appear more diverse and complex which can provide fruitful avenues for further research in second language sociolinguistic variation.

Further Reading

Asprey, E. & Lawson, R. (2018). English and social identity. In P. Seargeant, A. Hewings, & S. Pihlaja (Eds.), *The Routledge Handbook of English Language Studies*, 212–225. Routledge.
This chapter provides an account of the introduction and study of identity in linguistic research concerning English with a focus on sociolinguistics. It discusses the shift of focus from micro aspects of identity to macro identities in the three waves of the field of sociolinguistics.
Dray, S. & Drummond, R. (2020). Mixing methods? Linguistic ethnography and language variation. In K. Tusting (Ed.), *The Routledge Handbook of Linguistic Ethnography*, 241–255. Routledge.
Dray and Drummond talk about their experience in implementing mixed variationist and ethnographic methods to gain more context-specific understanding of identity formation through language and social practices.
Pihlaja, S. (Ed.). (2021). *Analysing Religious Discourse*. Cambridge University Press.

This volume sets out different theoretical and methodological perspectives concerning the study of religious discourse such as institutional religious, media, and political discourse, and discourse around spirituality. Of particular relevance to this chapter is the use of conversation analysis to examine agency negotiation in interaction, the use of ethnography to study how faith is enacted through people's behaviour, and how metaphor is used to present faith and religious identity.

Souza, A. (2016). Language and religious identities. In S. Preece (Ed.), *The Routledge Handbook of Language and Identity*, 195–209. Routledge.

Souza provides an overview of the relationship between language and religious identity (particularly within the field of applied linguistics), discussing the roles of religion and language in indexing identity.

Yaeger-Dror, M. (2014). Religion as a Sociolinguistic Variable. *Language and Linguistics Compass, 8*(11), 577–589. Wiley-Blackwell.

This article reviews sociolinguistic studies and demographic studies that can inform research concerning language variation and religion. An argument is put forward for including more fine-grained religious coding and considering ideological positions in the study of language variation in religious communities.

References

Al-Asfour, A., Tlaiss, H. A., Khan, S.A., & Rajasekar, J. (2017). Saudi women's work challenges and barriers to career advancement. *Career Development International, 22*(2), 184–199.

Alhamazany, A. (2021). *Sociolinguistic variation in Saudi English: syntactic, morphological and phonological features* [Unpublished doctoral dissertation]. Manchester Metropolitan University.

AlJarf, R. (2008). The impact of English as an international Language (EIL) upon Arabic in Saudi Arabia. *Asian EFL Journal, 10*(4), 193–210.

Al-Otaibi, N. (2020, September). *Vision 2030: Religious Education Reform in the Kingdom of Saudi Arabia*. King Faisal Center for Research and Islamic Studies. www.kfcris.com/en/view/post/305

Alsamani, A. (2014). Foreign culture awareness needs of Saudi English language majors at Buraydah Community College. *English Language Teaching, 7*(6), 143–153.

Avineri, N. (2014). Yiddish: a Jewish language in the diaspora. In Wiley, T., Kreeft-Peyton, J., Christian, D., Moore, S.K., & Liu, N. (Eds.), Handbook of Heritage, Community, and Native American Languages in the United States: Research, Educational Practice, and Policy, 263–271. Routledge.

Baker, W. & Bowie, D. (2010). Religious Affiliation as a Correlate of Linguistic Behavior. University of Pennsylvania Working Papers in *Linguistics, 15*(2), 1–10. https://repository.upenn.edu/pwpl/vol15/iss2/2/

Bayley, R. (2005). Second language acquisition and sociolinguistic variation. *Intercultural Communication Studies, 14*(2), 1–13.

Ding, S., & Goh, K. (2020). The impact of religion on language maintenance and shift. *Language in Society, 49*(1), 31–59.

Drummond, R. (2012). Aspects of identity in a second language: ING variation in the speech of Polish migrants living in Manchester, UK. *Language Variation and Change*, 24, 107–133.

Drummond, R. (2013). The Manchester Polish STRUT: Dialect Acquisition in a Second Language. *Journal of English Linguistics, 41*(1), 65–93.

Drummond, R.,& Schleef, E. (2016). Identity in variationist sociolinguistics. In S. Preece (Ed.), *The Routledge Handbook of Language and Identity*, 50–65. Routledge.

Drummond, R. (2018). Maybe it's a grime [t]ing: Th-stopping among urban British youth. *Language in Society, 47*(2), 171–196.

Dubois, S. & Horvath, B. (2000). When the music changes, you change too: Gender and language change in Cajun English. *Language Variation and Change, 11*(3), 287–313.

Eckert, P. (1989). *Jocks and burnouts: Social categories and identity in the high school*. Teachers College Press.

Edwards, J. (2009). *Language and identity: An introduction*. Cambridge University Press.

Faruk, S. (2013). English language teaching in Saudi Arabia: A world system perspective. *Scientific Bulletin of the Politehnica University of Timişoara Transactions on Modern Languages, 12*(1–2), 73–80.

Foucault, M. (1978). *The History of Sexuality: An introduction, 1*. Pantheon Books.

Joseph, E. (2004). *Language and Identity. National, Ethnic, Religious*. Palgrave Macmillan.

Kachru, B.B. (1992). *The Other Tongue: English Across Cultures*, 2nd edition. University of Illinois Press.

Khan, T. H., & MacEachen, E. (2021). Foucauldian Discourse Analysis: Moving Beyond a Social Constructionist Analytic. *International Journal of Qualitative Methods*, 20, 1–9.

Kulkarni-Joshi, S. (2015). Religion and language variation in a convergence area: The view from the border town of Kupwar post-linguistic reorganisation of Indian states. *Language & Communication, 42*, 75–85.

Le Renard, A. (2008). Only for Women: Women, the State, and Reform in Saudi Arabia. *Middle East Journal, 62*(4), 610–629.

Levine, J.M. & Hogg, M. A. (2010). Self-stereotyping. In *Encyclopedia of group processes & intergroup relations*, 1, 740–741. SAGE.

Maisel, S. (2014). The new rise of tribalism in Saudi Arabia. *Nomadic Peoples, 18*(2), 100–122.

Maisel, S. (2015). *The Resurgent Tribal Agenda in Saudi Arabia*, Issue paper No. 5. Arab Gulf States Institute in Washington.

Mallinson, C. & Childs, B. (2007). Communities of Practice in Sociolinguistic Description: Analyzing Language and Identity Practices among Black Women in Appalachia. *Gender and Language, 1*(2), 174–206.

Metz, H.C. (1992). *Saudi Arabia: A Country Study*. Library of Congress.

Milroy, L. (1980). *Language and Social Networks.* Blackwell.

Milroy, J., & Milroy, L. (1985). *Authority in Language: Investigating Language Prescription and Standardisation.* Routledge.

Mol, H. (1976). *Identity and the Sacred: A Sketch for a New Social Scientific Theory of Religion.* Blackwell.

Omoniyi, T. & Fishman, J. (Eds.). (2006). *Explorations in the sociology of language and religion.* John Benjamins Publishing Company.

Ortega, L. (2013). Ways forward for a bi/multilingual turn in SLA. In S. May, (Ed.), *The Multilingual Turn*, 32–53. Routledge.

Richardson, P. Mueller, C.M. & Pihlaja, S. (2021). *Cognitive Linguistics and Religious Language: An Introduction.* Routledge.

Ringrow, H. (2021). Identity. In S. Pihlaja (Ed.), *Analysing Religious Discourse*, 276–291. Cambridge University Press.

Schalk, S. (2011). Self, Other and Other-Self: Going Beyond the Self/Other Binary in Contemporary Consciousness. *Journal of Comparative Research in Anthropology and Sociology, 2*, 197–210.

Tajfel, H. (1978). *Differentiation between social groups: Studies in the Social Psychology of Intergroup Relations*. Academic Press.

Turner, J., Hogg, M., Oakes, P., Reicher, S., & Wetherell, M. (1987). *Rediscovering the Social Group: A Self-Categorization Theory*. Basil Blackwell.

Yaeger-Dror, M. (2014). Religion as a Sociolinguistic Variable. *Language and Linguistics Compass, 8*(11), 577–589.

22

SELLING ENGLISH IN AN ISLAMIC SOCIETY

Samar Alkhalil

Introduction and Background

The English language has become one of the best-selling products in a world driven by increasing globalisation. It is viewed as having the potential to transform populations and qualify its speakers to cope with the requirements of the international labour market. The global role that the English language plays in various areas is the result of the 'neoliberal regime of human capital development' (Park, 2016, p. 453). Education in the neoliberal regime is assumed to be the production of self that possesses adequate skills and knowledge to be economically eminent (Gray et al., 2018). The study of English in many contexts has therefore changed from an inherently educational endeavour to a precondition for consumption: it is a commodity and a crucial skill that needs to be acquired by individuals and institutions to attain profitability. The position of English as a main form of linguistic power is a consequence of the expansion of the British Empire and the rise of the United States as the greatest economic force of the twentieth century (Crystal, 2003). British colonialism contributed substantially to the prestige of English recognised in many nations even if these nations were never colonised, as is the situation in Saudi Arabia.

The English language can also be viewed as a product of globalisation: a kind of 'good' that comes with a package of ideological messages that take the form of axiomatic assumptions. Ideologies pertaining to language refer to ideas, feelings and beliefs about language that are socially shared and link language and society in a dialectical framework (Piller, 2015). They are social representations that contribute to establishing, preserving, and changing the social relationships of power, domination and exploitation (Fairclough, 2003). In addition, ideologies have the power to regulate and control other socially shared beliefs and attitudes (Van Dijk, 2006). This trait of ideology involves the exercising of power and domination by a particular social group over another group to control their choices and decisions. These ideologies are rooted in different types of discourse genres, such as social, political, and promotional, which are reproduced by dominant social groups. As a consequence of this reproduction, the ideological orientation of this group becomes universal and natural. This naturalization of ideology is termed 'hegemony' (Gramsci, 1971)—a notion that refers to the pursuit of power not through coercion but rather through the propagation of tacit ideologies and the generation of consent (Fairclough, 2013). For subordinate groups to manifest assent, the discourses of the predominant group must seem to be genuine,

DOI: 10.4324/9781003301271-25

logical and tangible to the recipient (Mirhosseini, 2015); that is, the implied ideologies should be convincing in nature.

The supremacy of English brings about linguistic and cultural injustice. Several researchers, such as Pennycook (1994, 1998) and Phillipson (1992, 2009), have argued that the universal existence of English is a result of the British and American pursuit of political and economic superiority. This can be translated into a 'form of colonialism' (Al Hosni, 2015, p. 301) in which cultural and economic imperialism take place through the use of the unprecedented linguistic power of English. The term 'linguistic imperialism' was coined by Phillipson (1992) to signal the imposition of a predominant language, such as English, over other languages that ends in other forms of dominance, such as cultural, political, and economic. By normalising the dissemination of English, English-speaking countries have built a solid global English language teaching industry that transmits English not solely as a means of communication but also as a mechanism that eternises the ideologies of the Anglophone world. Such ideologies cannot be examined without referencing the educational circumstances and policies that can play a role in the circulation of these ideologies.

As the use of the English language is greatly embedded in globalisation, several institutions have promoted English language learning as a means of consolidating global society (Bacon & Kim, 2018). Nevertheless, English teaching involves more than familiarising students with new words and language systems, and the ideological dynamics of English policy and use comprise a permeating research problem (Pennycook, 2017). The imagining of English as linguistic capital arises from neoliberal theory diffused in the scope of the new economy. Neoliberalism is defined as 'the philosophy of economic and social transformation taking place according to the logic of free market doctrines that dictate the way economies and societies function' (Barnawi, 2018, p. 1). Such doctrines naturalise the consideration of English as the language of international competitiveness and academic distinction (Piller & Cho, 2013). By this rationale, the planning of the education system subjects to the economic protocol to provide the learners with adequate soft skills—a set of characteristics that is greatly valued in the job market and desired by people to become well qualified for corporate jobs (Ustinova, 2008). Speaking English is primarily an essential component of these soft skills, as it grants its users 'linguistic power' (Kachru, 1986, p. 1). This is also the case in some Islamic societies, such as Saudi Arabia, where investment in education, human capital, material resources, and economic diversification is becoming notably significant (Alkhalil, 2021). Therefore, it is unsurprising that English proficiency is considered a merit for those who command it.

In Saudi Arabia, a number of spiritual, economic, educational, social, and political factors have contributed to this prevalence of English. First, Islam which is the state religion of Saudi Arabia and a main cultural aspect, fosters learning new languages. It asks Muslims to call non-Muslims for Islam (Nouraldeen & Elyas, 2014). Knowing foreign languages enables people to understand other cultures and bridges social barriers that can be caused by miscommunication. Quran promotes learning languages as the following verse indicates:

(يَا أَيُّهَا النَّاسُ إِنَّا خَلَقْنَاكُم مِّن ذَكَرٍ وَأُنثَىٰ وَجَعَلْنَاكُمْ شُعُوبًا وَقَبَائِلَ لِتَعَارَفُوا)

O people! We created you from male and female and made you into nations and tribes so that you may know one another.

(Al-Hujurat Surah Verse 13)

Islam does not prohibit learning new languages since knowing foreign people requires knowing their languages. In addition, Saudi Arabia attracts millions of Muslims all over the world as it is home to Makkah and Madinah—holy cities for Muslim people. One of the Islamic pillars is pilgrimage to Makkah which entails considerable number of visitors to these holy places to fulfil this duty. These visitors speak different languages which necessitate learning English that serves as a lingua franca to interact with non-Arabic speakers.

Moreover, the oil discovery in 1939 caused a dramatic transformation in the politics and economics of the country (Elyas & Picard, 2019). The establishment of the Arabian American Oil Company, now called the Saudi Arabian Oil Company or ARAMCO, a petroleum and natural gas company known universally, has resulted in the widespread adoption of English in Saudi Arabia (Al Jumiah, 2016). Today, this company is owned by the Saudi government; however, initially, it was American, as evidenced by its name (Mahboob & Elyas, 2014). Therefore, a large number of employees in this company hailed from America, leading to the promotion of English education in the country. Despite the fact that the country has begun to move away from its dependence on petroleum, English continues to maintain its supremacy as an invaluable language for economic development and sustainable advancement (Alrabai, 2019).

The economic circumstances of Saudi Arabia and other Gulf countries supply the English language teaching industry with a profitable business entity and lead to its widespread adoption in the country (Karmani, 2005). As Karmani (2005) argues, English has been associated with industrialisation and Western-style modernisation, which has resulted in an increased demand for English learning. This indicates that English is perceived as a bedrock of prosperity and modernity or a form of linguistic power through which Saudi Arabia can compete on a global scale.

Currently, Saudi Arabia is celebrating remarkable transformations in its economic, social, and educational sectors. These changes are driven by a national plan called 'Saudi Vision 2030', launched by Crown Prince Mohammad bin Salman in 2016. This plan introduced a series of strategies and initiatives that address the current socioeconomic and political challenges facing the country (Barnawi, 2018). This strategic plan is designed to restructure the Saudi economy by reducing reliance on oil, creating a vibrant society, and placing the country at the forefront of the global market economy in all areas (Saudi-Vision-2030, 2022). According to this ten-year plan, education serves as a key tool to achieve these reforms that result in a consistent transformation for field of the economy. Therefore, improving the educational system is one of the exalted initiatives listed under this national plan. Because English is given significant importance in the discussion on the efficiency of teaching and learning in Saudi education (Alhawsawi, 2013), contemporary policy reforms to the education system involve incorporating more English courses into its curricula (Barnawi, 2018).

In the Saudi educational system, English teaching is compulsory in primary, secondary, and higher education, and English is the only foreign language taught in public schools. Earlier, English was taught to students at the secondary and intermediate levels. However, it has now been introduced to children in primary school due to its increasing importance (Alrashidi & Phan, 2015). Despite the status of English as a core school subject, students often arrive at higher education with low levels of English competency (Alrashidi & Phan, 2015; Habbash, 2011). This inconsistency can be explained by multiple factors. Historically, foreign language teaching was viewed as anti-Islamic (Elyas & Picard, 2019). In the Wahhabbi era (an Islamic conservative movement founded in the eighteenth century in Saudi Arabia that called for strict adherence to the Quran and the actions, sayings, and stories of Prophet Mohammad), the public were commanded to take their children to the Quranic school, where teachings were restricted to the memorisation and recitation of the Quran and Islamic ethics (Elyas & Picard, 2019). Arabic was the sole language of instruction, and the use of other languages was believed to inseminate foreign ideologies—a perception still held by some in Saudi Arabia (Mahboob & Elyas, 2014).

In the early twentieth century, Anglo-American trade and its political influence started to boost English teaching in Saudi Arabia, which was averse to the movement of Wahhabism (Elyas & Picard, 2019). During this period, education was deeply rooted in Islamic values and principles, despite being based upon a broader understanding than that in the Wahhabi period (Al-Ajroush, 1980). Subsequently, the growth of the petrochemical sector led to an increased number of foreign labourers entering Saudi Arabia (Hertog, 2012). The government responded by investing in secular education, including English teaching, and began to grant Saudi citizens scholarships to study abroad—a programme that continues (Elyas & Picard, 2019). However, English education in schools remained restricted, with more emphasis on Arabic and Islamic teaching. For example, until 2001, 21 out of the 30 hours of primary school instruction were devoted to Islamic-Arabic subjects (Mahboob & Elyas, 2014).

A major shift towards English teaching in Saudi Arabia occurred after the events of 11 September 2001 (Elyas & Picard, 2013). As Elyas and Picard (2010) illustrate, the United States developed certain prejudices and assumptions about Saudi people after the events of 11 September 2001. American officials and the media were trying to discover the motivation behind this attack carried out by the 19 hijackers, 15 of them from Saudi Arabia (Elyas, 2008). US media criticised the educational system, claiming that it had a role in producing Islamic extremists. The reason behind these claims is that these acts have been carried out in the name of Islam, the religion of Saudi Arabia. Saudi Arabia is indeed considered the heartland of Islam. Therefore, as the attack was committed in the name of Islam, Islamic religious people were surely the object of suspicion (Elyas, 2008). The religious educational system in Saudi Arabia was blamed for being partly responsible for motivating this act (Karmani, 2005). Several Anglophone countries solicited the Saudi government to include aspects of secular curricula in order to minimise extremism (Karmani, 2005). In addition to external compulsions, the private sector expressed its concerns regarding the failings of the existing educational system and called for educating Saudi citizens in a way that makes them capable of competing in the new era of globalisation (Barnawi, 2018). It took Saudi Arabia around five years after the act to acknowledge that there was a need to reform the educational system and transfer the nation to a new era (Elyas, 2008).

Consequently, the Ministry of Education implemented educational reforms that included the use of English as a medium of teaching at the university level, together with the enhancement of information technology and the improvement of educators' skills to support the pedagogical use of this technology in English teaching at the school level (Elyas & Picard, 2019). These developments were a part of accomplishing the Tatweer policy—a reform plan launched in 2007 that aimed to introduce an improved framework for learning and education that would foster citizens' development and national economic growth (Mitchell & Alfuraih, 2017).

English instruction has been a debatable topic in the past owing to the belief that 'more English' would result in 'less Islam' (Elyas & Picard, 2010, p. 140). The demand for more English language teaching is regarded as a threat to local culture and values as well as a means of persecution. A critical impact of English instruction on Arabic is the issue of identity and the concerns over losing it (Sulaimani & Elyas, 2018). The Arabic language has frequently been linked to Islam as it is the language of the Quran and Hadith (i.e. prophet Mohammad's sayings). This gives Arabic a certain gravitas and stamps it with cultural and historic resonance for Muslims. On the other hand, English is viewed as a language that is important for business and international communication but is also seen by some people as the propagator of foreign cultures. Socio-cultural ideologies and identities are perceived as unsteady due to the effect of English, and English learners who are exposed to resources and policy documents related to English language teaching are considered to be likely to change their beliefs and identity (Elyas & Badawood, 2015).

This viewpoint is evidenced by Clarke's (2008) study on ideologies and identity in the Emirates wherein people expressed concerns that foreign language learners may acquire the cultural values presented in textbooks. They also expressed fears about the possibility that minds and ideas are reshaped through exposure to different cultures. Despite the conception of English as a means that supplies learners with marketable skills significant in today's world, the marketisation of English in Arab-Muslim society is by no means innocuous (Mirhosseini & Babu, 2019). That is, the promotion of English instruction is mainly a promotion of beliefs that may not ultimately be in line with the national ones and that are structured around an 'us' (people who own the values of the Anglophones) and 'them' (people who own other values) (Mirhosseini & Babu, 2019, p. 11). National values such as collectivism, solidarity, and social coherence which distinguish Saudi society can be shifted towards Western modernisation, secularisation and materialism—a set of Western values that might impact the educational aspects and cultural tradition of the Islamic society.

Simultaneously, a Saudi English perspective might be arising in the materials used to teach English (Mahboob & Elyas, 2014). One characteristic of this perspective is the reliance on local culture, local religion, and local context in developing English language teaching material and content to address the concerns discussed above. Mahboob and Elyas (2014) conducted a content and linguistic analysis of textbooks used to teach English in Saudi Arabia. The texts investigated in Mahboob and Elyas's (2014) study naturalised the reading of English as an Islamic language. The textbooks included units that dealt with Islamic issues, e.g. 'Before Al-Hajj'. This term refers to the fifth pillar of Islam which means pilgrimage to Makkah. Other topics discussed in the textbooks were 'Ramadan' (i.e. a holy month in which Muslims fast from dawn to sunset) and 'The Early Spread of Islam'.

In addition, the textbooks were localised to the Saudi context as they included lessons on describing practices, life, and culture in Saudi Arabia. Although these textbooks are no longer used in the Saudi English language classrooms, it is still evident that English education and use in Saudi Arabia might not impose an alien standpoint, but instead entitle students to learn English by discussing issues that are related to the Saudi context and mirror local standpoints (Alshammri, 2020). Nevertheless, these arguments about the appropriateness of English and its impact on local values, cultural practices, and religious traditions may have resulted in 'sub-par English instruction' (Bunaiyan, 2019, p. 8), generating challenges for efficient language education in the country. This tension between the need to learn English to obtain a licence for today's labour market and the perspectives that are held around the suitability of English for an Islamic society results in duplicity in the way English is marketed, which is something that will be explored in the case study.

Islamic-Saudi Identity Representation in Advertisements Produced by Private English Language Teaching Schools

An emphasis on English has brought English language teaching services in Saudi Arabia that market English as a commercial product of national prominence. To accomplish their for-profit purposes, these institutions are inclined to overstate the advantages of English language learning (Alkhalil, 2021; Gray et al., 2018) by (re)producing ideologies that can influence people's beliefs (Mirhosseini, 2015). This section discusses how the English language is represented in Saudi Arabia using a corpus of 132 advertisements offered by eight English language teaching schools via their websites and Twitter accounts. The data were analysed using critical discourse analysis based on Fairclough's (2015) framework.

According to this approach, the analysis was conducted in three stages: description, interpretation, and explanation. Description focuses on the analysis of the linguistic features of the text. It indicates how language ideology moulds the contents of the oral, visual, and written texts that are produced by English language teaching schools. The second stage, interpretation, focuses on the ways in which participants understand text based on their cognitive, social, and ideological resources. In this stage, analysts draw on assumptions about the context and let the participants interpret a text with some context in mind, thereby influencing the way in which discourses' linguistic features are processed. Last, explanation leads to the final explanation of the underlying ideological messages by linking these ideologies with a wider social scope.

The advertisements represent English as a multifaceted language, that is, a language with Islamic and Anglophonic identities. The Islamic context affects promotional discourses through the use of Islamic-related discourses. Since Islam has significantly affected Saudi society and 97.1% of the population is Muslim (World-population, 2023), the targeted audience of the English language teaching institutes examined in the present study are mostly Muslims. As a result, the institutes' ads represent English as an Islamic language that complies with Islamic expressions and instructions. Simultaneously, Anglophonic identity is apparent in the ads that imagine native speakers of English as ideal teachers. In this way, English is presented as a Halal product (i.e. a product that is allowable and permissible according to Islamic law) that is manufactured by Western people which gives it popularity and authenticity. Accordingly, English can be consumed by Muslims since it does not contradict Islamic values. These representations are discussed below.

The Islamic identity of Saudi society is reflected in the ads examined in this case study through the use of Arabic language, Arabic calendar, and Islamic expressions, with less English usage. Arabic has often been associated with Islam, although not all Arabic speakers are Muslims (Raddawi, 2015). The Islamic community is diverse as Muslims come from different racial, cultural, and linguistic backgrounds. Since the Quran was revealed in the Arabic language and prophet Mohammad was an Arab, in addition to the fact that all religious terms as well as daily prayers are practised in Arabic only, the Arabic language becomes a unifying factor that links this diverse community. This fosters non-Arab Muslims to invest in Arabic learning in order to perform their religious duties (Selim, 2023). In view of this, Arabic serves not only as a form of Arabic identity but an allusion to Islam. Based on this religious connotation of the Arabic language, this has been taken into consideration in the data analysis of the current study.

In the analysis, I classified language choice of the ads according to the dominant language (Arabic or English), and the extent of language choice (Arabic only, English only, and minor or substantial use of either language). In the ads, Arabic was the predominant language, with a total of 115 (87.12%) ads out of 132 being predominantly Arabic. Of these, 7 (5.30%) ads mixed Arabic with substantial use of English such as a sentence or a question, while 34 (25.75%) ads were in Arabic only, and 74 (56.06%) ads included minor use of English such as numbers, word(s) and phrase(s) in the background. Concerning English language use, it predominated in 17 (12. 87%) ads. Of these, 5 (3.78%) were in English only, 6 (4.54%) included minor use of Arabic, and 6 (4.54%) were accompanied by Arabic translation.

This finding is unsurprising because the ads target Arabic speakers. The Arabic language is used to build rapport with the target audience and to introduce essential information about the promoted courses. It is used, for instance, to inform the reader about the 'باقات' ('packages') offered to the audience, the type of the course 'الصيف فرصة' ('summer is opportunity'), and the targeted audience 'جهّز ابنك/ابنتك للجامعة' ('prepare your son/daughter for university'), meaning that the course targets young people who are about to start university. Generally, it is used to tell the reader details about the course. In this way, Arabic is used for its communicative function or what Kelly-Holmes (2000) terms the 'utility value', where there is substantial information to convey (p. 67).

However, English is rare in ads compared to Arabic, and schools are conservative in using it. Code-switching into English is the most salient approach to ensuring the presence of English. Code-switching is the use of at least two codes of communication—Arabic and English, in this case—in a single text (Nashef, 2013). It is used at word, phrase, or sentence level to provide contact details, highlight the level of the course, or provide some secondary content. The ads use English as an instrument of symbolic communication. English numbers and weekdays would be easily recognised by most educated people in Saudi Arabia, even if they have no high level of English proficiency. Consequently, it can be inferred that schools 'decorate' their ads to associate the advertisement with the product (i.e. English) being advertised without influencing the utility function of the ad. English use serves as an index of the schools' skill in English language use and teaching.

In terms of the notion of presenting English as Islamic, there are local religious ways of communication used by advertisers to reach out to Saudis and attract their attention by utilising the Hijri calendar, which is an Islamic calendar system utilised in some Muslim countries such as Saudi Arabia for determining public, religious, and social events. Months in the Hijri calendar are in Arabic. The calendar is used by the schools to indicate the course duration. The English language here uses an Islamic mask to be accessible to Saudi people who predominantly use the Islamic calendar for dating important and daily occasions. The Islamic voice of the ads works to ensure the communication of information.

Moreover, Islamic expressions and adherence to Islamic values are marked in the ads. For instance, religious expressions such as 'بإذن الله' ('God willing'), which is used extensively in daily conversation, is included in the ads. In addition, the word 'الحكمة' ('wisdom') is frequently used in the ads:

Excerpt 1

معرفة اللغات يفتح لك أبواب الحكمة—روجر بيكون.

'Knowledge of languages is the doorway to wisdom.'—Roger Bacon.

This quotation shows that knowing a new language is desirable. The word 'الحكمة' ('wisdom') gives the ad a religious sense. It has a religious connotation, as it is mentioned in the Quranic verse in Luqman Surah Verse 12:

(وَلَقَدْ آتَيْنَا لُقْمَانَ الْحِكْمَةَ)

'And indeed we bestowed upon Luqmân Al-Hikmah [wisdom and religious understanding]'.

The quotation metaphorically depicts language learning as a gateway to wisdom. Although it does not highlight one language, it is presumed that the reader would figure out that 'English' is being referred to, as the school is marketing an English course. Simultaneously, the saying here is attributed to a Western leader, Roger Bacon, which evocates a sense of self-orientalism by which the school commodifies an Anglophonic cultural image, establishing the image of the 'superior Other' (Sihui, 2009, p. 279). The school is attempting to establish its affiliation with the Occident and show their familiarity with Anglophonic thinkers. By blending two identities in one ad, it can be assumed that the ad is inviting Muslim Saudis to a new culture by trying to mitigate any concerns of losing their Islamic self by associating English with Islamic words and traditions.

Another way of catering the English language to a religious society is through mimicking religious social norms. The ads replicate gender segregation, which is considered a feature of a religiously conservative society (see Excerpt 2). Advertisers indicate their compliance with Islamic norms to attract customers.

Excerpt 2

تواصل النساء/تواصل الرجال.

'Women's communication/men's communication'.

In addition, an Islamic tradition that is represented in the ads is Saudi women's Islamic fashion. The ads show pictures of Saudi women wearing abayas and covered by hijabs—Islamic black dresses commonly worn outdoors by Saudi women or in front of non-mahram (i.e. a man with whom marriage is permissible). When it comes to the issue of the hijab, many Saudi people believe that a woman must cover up her body with an abaya and her face with a cloak except the eyes. Although there is little guidance within the Quran with regards to whether women should be fully covered or not, Saudi women prefer to wear full cover except the eyes when they are outdoors (Macias, 2016). As explained in Macias's study, the reason for this preference is due to the women's religious beliefs and values and their desire to adhere to Saudi standards. In the ads examined in the current study, female students are wearing abayas but are showing their faces to invite Saudi women to a more flexible and secular classroom. Despite the fact that the ads show hijab wearing in a more secular way, such depiction reflects a form of religious expression and national identity. It indicates that English is a friendly language for Muslim women.

English as an Anglophonic Language

In contrast, the ads show female teachers wearing neither abaya nor hijab. The implicit assumption is that the teachers are native speakers of English as the notion of nativeness is indicated literally by mentioning that instructors are 'من أهل اللغة' ('native people'). In this way, English is conceptualised to be owned by Western people who do not necessarily adhere to Islamic norms. The female teachers represent a Western secular model of English language teachers who have the power to teach the language to female Saudi-Muslim students who abide by Islamic dress code and traditions. By doing so, these advertisements can create a seductive effect on what Sihui (2009) called the 'cultural other' (p. 268). This means that the ads seek to create a desire in the audience by associating English with Western culture. It can be inferred from the advertisements that English belongs to the Anglophones who own English and have the appropriate skills to teach students from other cultures. This is also clear from showing the UK and US flags and representing native speakers of English as ideal instructors. By doing so, the ads reproduce normative discourses that normalise the superiority of native-English-speaking teachers over non-native-English-speaking teachers, reinforcing that language and race are strongly linked as a means of discriminating Self and Other (Shrake, 2006). The ads carry a package of ideological messages that depicts English as the language of the Anglophones, on the one hand, and characterise Western women as liberal subjects, on the other.

Generally speaking, the English language according to the promotional discourses can cope with the Islamic society where it is advertised by means of revealing the Islamic identity. The ads seem to withstand any potential attitudinal resistance towards English which until recently was seen by some Saudis as a 'cultural defeat', 'an alienation' of the people and a frustration of the national culture (Alkhalil, 2021, p. 242). Other Saudis think that English undermines the salience of Arabic as the language of the Quran (Alhamazany, 2021). As Alhamazany (2021) argues, languages do not have religious and social values: people attach religious or social values to languages. English language learning does not make learners less Muslim and the same applies to its teaching and teachers. The common belief that more English equals less Islam can be seen because of religious ideologies that promote the idea that English is the language of non-Muslims.

The findings show a clash between the religious identity of learners and teachers of English. The dress code of the learners represents their Islamic identity, while teachers are not shown as Muslims. The identity of non-Muslims becomes a promotional tool that the institutes draw upon to attract English language learners. The promotional discourses invite individuals to study English with native speakers. This illustrates an implied hegemony granted to native-English-speaking teachers, which may be criticised as a kind of discrimination against non-native teachers of English. Despite certain hegemonic English discourses, English has never been 'owned' by a particular nation. The spread of English across the globe gives the right for teachers from different nationalities to teach the language.

Implications and Future Directions

The research discussed in the previous case study is important since it may help raise awareness among the English language teaching industry about its complicity in the obscuring of reality surrounding English and English language learning. In the context of this study, Islamic expressions serve as a marketing tool for attracting Muslim consumers who are interested in English language learning. The ads relate English to positive Islamic-desired characteristics, such as wisdom. This representation disguises any negative impact on the national identity of the Saudi people and might impact the public's views concerning their Arabic language and identity by means of associating English with desirable qualities mentioned in the Quran. As a result, learners' perceptions regarding their Arabic language might be influenced by the implied hegemony of English. It is true that the government, under the Saudi Vision 2030 programme, encourages English language learning and aims to enhance Saudi people's skills to better compete in the job market. Arguably, Saudi Vision 2030 can be successfully fulfilled through the collaboration of bilingual speakers of Arabic and English as well as through cooperation between qualified citizens with different capabilities (Alkhalil, 2021). Therefore, the country could gain a greater advantage by stressing the importance of the Arabic language in relation to the maintenance of the local identity, besides the significance of acquiring other languages in accomplishing the objectives of Saudi Vision 2030.

This chapter also has implications for remedial reforms that should be implemented by both the English language teaching sector and instructors. English language schools in Saudi Arabia predominantly show that English belongs to the West. However, since English is a *lingua franca*, no society can own it, and other varieties of English, such as Saudi English, spoken by Saudi teachers, should not be marginalised. This misconception—that Saudi English is somehow deficient—affects the hiring decisions of schools. It can also impact the audience's beliefs regarding the competence of English educators, specifically non-native-speaking teachers in state schools, as shown by Alkhalil's (2021) study which reveals negative attitudes towards Saudi educators. Therefore, the recruitment criteria implemented by private English language teaching schools must be reconsidered so as to align with Saudi Arabia's recent Saudisation policy, which stresses the hiring of Saudi nationals in the private sector, rather than sole reliance in state-owned enterprises (Picard, 2019). English language teaching schools should link their employment practices with the Saudisation policy and, where applicable, substitute their non-Saudi educators with Saudi citizens. Moreover, stakeholders in their hiring decisions should pay closer attention to traits that make an ideal teacher, such as personality, competence, experience, and qualifications.

In addition, this chapter may contribute to the body of knowledge on language ideologies in English language teaching schools. This study examined language ideologies in private English language teaching schools across a range of modalities (i.e. written, oral, static images, and videos). The language ideologies revealed were both transparently stated and implicit in the images. Critical discourse analysis is commonly employed in language and ideology research (e.g. Alkhalil, 2018). The case study in this chapter emphasises the suitability of this approach for future research; however, for an in-depth understanding of the ideologies underpinning the discourses of English teaching schools, a wider scope and integrated approach might be needed. Research methods such as interviews, questionnaires, or participant observations that involve the producers of the ads and the target audience could provide a broader basis of understanding. Furthermore, future research can widen the scope by collecting data from other sources, such as billboards, brochures, and posters, to reinforce the understanding of English language schools' ideologies.

Moreover, because this study found that the use of English is relatively limited in the ads compared with Arabic, further research is needed to closely explore the causes of this tendency and how language choice shapes the public's attitudes towards the advertised services. Future research could also investigate the impact of neoliberalism on how English language learning is perceived by both Saudi people and educational organisations and consider its potential influence on the cultural aspects and local language of Saudi Arabia.

Further Reading

Almayez, M. (2022). Investigating the place of religion within the professional identity construction of two Muslim English language teachers in Saudi Arabia. *Teacher Education and Development, 9*(1), 1–15. DOI: doi:10.1080/2331186X.2022.2091632

This article sheds light on the manner and extent to which Islam is interwoven with English language instructors' professional identity. Islam, according to this study, plays a significant role in shaping the teachers' relationships with their students and gives a sense of obligation to safeguard students' Islamic values. This study also highlights the contested relationship between English language teaching and Islam in Saudi Arabia. In relation to this chapter, this article adds more insight into how teachers' Islamic identities shapes their foreign language teaching practices.

Rohmana, W.I.M. (2020). Immersing Islamic value in English language teaching: A challenge for English teachers. *Journal of English Language Teaching, 4*(2), 47–50. https://journal.lppmunindra.ac.id/index. php/SCOPE/article/view/6404

This article considers the immersion of Islamic ethics and values in English language teaching in Muslim societies. The study seeks to mitigate the influence of foreign languages on local culture and identity by recommending the integration of Islamic content in English teaching. The article offers solutions for potential negative impacts on Islamic identity due to foreign language learning.

Moskovsky, C. & Picard, M. (2019). *English as a foreign language in Saudi Arabia: New insights into teaching and learning English.* Routledge.

This book provides a comprehensive discussion of essential aspects of English education in Saudi Arabia. It also increases readers' knowledge of the unique linguistic, historical, cultural, and religious context of English in the Saudi context. In conclusion, the book touches on the future of English and TESOL in the country and its implications for the field of English as a foreign language research subject.

Murray, D.E. (2020). The world of English language teaching: Creating equity or inequity? *Language Teaching Research, 24*(1), 60–70. DOI: doi:10.1177/1362168818777529

This study highlights the current trends towards English language learning and how the introduction of English within existing sociocultural, linguistic, and political practices and values can create tensions by challenging existing social identities.

Pennycook, A. (2017). *The cultural politics of English as an international language*. Routledge.

This book looks at issues related to the global spread of English and outlines how and why English has become an international language. It provides a critical look at how the promotion of English contributes to crucial social, political, and economic inequalities.

References

Al-Ajroush, H. (1980). *A historical development of the public secondary school curriculum in Saudi Arabia from 1930 to the present.* PhD thesis. University of Oklahoma. https://hdl.handle.net/11244/4833

Al Hosni, J. K. (2015). Globalization and the linguistic imperialism of the English language. *Arab World English Journal, 6*(1), 298–308. doi:10.24093/awej/vol6no1.23

Al Jumiah, A. (2016). *Language, power, and ideology in high school EFL textbooks in Saudi Arabia*. PhD thesis. University of New Mexico. Available from ProQuest Dissertations and Theses database.

Alhamazany, A. (2021). *Sociolinguistic variation in Saudi English: Syntactic, morphological and phonological features.* Manchester Metropolitan University. https://e-space.mmu.ac.uk/629861/

Alhawsawi, S. (2013). *Investigating student experiences of learning English as a foreign language in a preparatory programme in a Saudi university.* PhD thesis. University of Sussex. www.researchgate.net/publication/292869477

Alkhalil, S.F. (2018). *Promoting English in Saudi Arabia: A critical discourse analysis of advertisements for private English language teaching institutes.* Master's thesis. Macquarie University. http://minerva.mq.edu.au:8080/vital/access/manager/Repository/mq:72027

Alkhalil, S.F. (2021). *Ideaologies of English Language Teaching and Learning in Saudi Arabia.* PhD thesis. Macquairie University, Sydney.

Alrabai, F. (2019). Learning English in Saudi Arabia. In C. Moskovsky & M. Picard (Eds.), *English as a foreign language in Saudi arabia: New insights into teaching and learning English*, 102–119. Routledge.

Alrashidi, O. & Phan, H. (2015). Education context and English teaching and learning in the Kingdom of Saudi Arabia: An overview. *English Language Teaching, 8*(5), 33–44. DOI: 10.5539/elt.v8n5p33

Alshammri, A.F. (2020). *Representations of source and target identities and communities in English language textbooks used in Saudi secondary schools*. PhD thesis. Macquarie University.

Bacon, C.K. & Kim, S.Y. (2018). "English is my only weapon": Neoliberal language ideologies and youth metadiscourse in South Korea. *Linguistics and Education, 48*, 10–21. DOI: 10.1016/j.linged.2018.09.002

Barnawi, O.Z. (2018). *Neoliberalism and English language education policies in the Arabian Gulf.* Routledge.

Bunaiyan, W. (2019). *Preparing the Saudi educational system to serve the 2030 vision: A comparative analysis study.* PhD thesis. University of Denver.

Clarke, M. (2008). *Language teacher identities: Co-constructing discourse and community.* Multilingual Matters.

Crystal, D. (2003). *English as a global language*. Cambridge University Press.

Elyas, T. (2008). The attitude and the impact of American English as a global language within the Saudi education system. *Novitas-ROYAL, 2*(1), 28–48. www.researchgate.net/publication/26513299_The_attitude_and_the_impact_of_American_English_as_a_global_language_within_the_Saudi_education_system

Elyas, T. & Badawood, O. (2015). English language educational policy in Saudi Arabia post 21st century: Enacted curriculum, identity, and modernisation: A critical discourse analysis approach. *FIRE: Forum for International Research in Education, 2*(3), 21–33. DOI: 10.18275/fire201603031093

Elyas, T. & Picard, M. (2010). Saudi Arabian educational history: impacts on English language teaching. *Education, Business and Society: Contemporary Middle Eastern Issues, 3*(2), 136–145. DOI: 10.1108/17537981011047961

Elyas, T. & Picard, M. (2013). Critiquing of higher education policy in Saudi Arabia: towards a new neo-liberalism. *Education, Business and Society: Contemporary Middle Eastern Issues, 6*(1), 31–41. DOI: 10.1108/17537981311314709

Elyas, T. & Picard, M. (2019). A brief history of English and English teaching in Saudi Arabia. In C. Moskovsky & M. Picard (Eds.), *English as a foreign language in Saudi Arabia: New insights into teaching and learning English*, 70–84. Routledge.

Fairclough, N. (2003). *Analysing discourse: textual analysis for social research.* Routledge.

Fairclough, N. (2013). *Critical discourse analysis: The critical study of language.* Routledge.

Fairclough, N. (2015). *Language and power*, 3rd edition. Routledge.

Gramsci, A. (1971). *Selections from the prison notebooks.* Lawrence & Wishart.

Gray, J., O'Regan, J.P., & Wallace, C. (2018). Education and the discourse of global neoliberalism. *Language and intercultural communication, 18*(5), 471–477. DOI: doi:10.1080/14708477.2018.1501842

Habbash, M.M. R. (2011). *Status change of English and its role in shaping public education language policy and practice in Saudi Arabia: A postmodernist critical perspective.* PhD thesis. University of Exeter. https://ethos.bl.uk/OrderDetails.do?uin=uk.bl.ethos.549314

Hertog, S. (2012). A comparative assessment of labor market nationalization policies in the GCC. In S. Hertog (Ed.), *National employment, migration and education in the GCC: Economic development and diversification*, 65–106. Gerlach Press.

Kachru, B.B. (1986), The power and politics of English. *World Englishes*, 5, 121–140. https://doi.org/10.1111/j.1467-971X.1986.tb00720.x

Karmani, S. (2005). TESOL in a time of terror: Toward an islamic perspective on applied linguistics. *TESOL Quarterly, 39*(4), 738–744. DOI: doi:10.2307/3588534

Kelly-Holmes, H. (2000). Bier, parfum, kaas: Language fetish in European advertising. *European Journal of Cultural Studies, 3*(1), 67–82. DOI: 10.1177/a010863

Macias, T. (2016). *Saudi women studying in the United States: Understanding their experinces.* PhD thesis. University of the Incarnate Word. https://athenaeum.uiw.edu/uiw_etds/33/

Mahboob, A. & Elyas, T. (2014). English in the Kingdom of Saudi Arabia. *World Englishes, 33*(1), 128–142. DOI: 10.1111/weng.12073

Mirhosseini, S.-A. (2015). Resisting magic waves: Ideologies of "English language teaching" in Iranian newspaper advertisements. *Discourse: Studies in the Cultural Politics of Education, 36*(6), 1–16. DOI: 10.1080/01596306.2014.918462

Mirhosseini, S.-A. & Babu, S. (2019). Policies of English language teaching as part of the global "war of ideas". In A.S. Al-Issa & S.-A. Mirhosseini (Eds.), *Worldwide English language education today*, 18–34. Routledge.

Mitchell, B. & Alfuraih, A. (2017). English language teaching in the Kingdom of Saudi Arabia: Past, present and beyond. *Mediterranean Journal of Social Sciences, 8*(2), 317–325. DOI: 10.5901/mjss.2017.v8n2p317

Nashef, H.A.M. (2013). A, hello and bonjour: A postcolonial analysis of Arab media's use of code switching and mixing and its ramification on the identity of the self in the Arab world. *International Journal of Multilingualism, 10*(3), 313–330. DOI: 10.1080/14790718.2013.783582

Nouraldeen, A.S. & Elyas, T. (2014). Learning English in Saudi Arabia: A socio-cultural perspective. *International Journal of English Language and Linguistics Research, 2*(3), 56–78. www.researchgate.net/publication/269272686_LEARNING_ENGLISH_IN_SAUDI_ARABIA_A_SOCIO-CULTURAL_PERSPECTIVE

Park, J.S.-Y. (2016). Language as pure potential. *Journal of Multilingual and Multicultural Development, 37*(5), 453–466. Routledge. DOI: doi:10.1080/01434632.2015.1071824

Pennycook, A. (1994). *The cultural politics of English as an international language.* Longman.

Pennycook, A. (1998). *English and the discourses of colonialism.* Routledge.

Pennycook, A. (2017). *The cultural politics of English as an international language*. Routledge.

Phillipson, R. (1992). *Linguistic imperialism.* Oxford University Press.

Phillipson, R. (2009). *Linguistic imperialism continued.* Routledge.

Piller, I. (2015). *Language ideologies: Practice and theory.* Oxford University Press.

Piller, I. & Cho, J. (2013). Neoliberalism as language policy. *Language in Society, 42*(1), 23–44.

Picard, M. (2019). The future of EFL and TESOL in Saudi Arabia. In C. Moskovsky; & M. Picard (Eds.), *English as a foreign language in Saudi Arabia: New insights into teaching and learning English*, 157–177. Routledge.

Raddawi, R. (2015). *Intercultural Communication with Arabs: Studies in Educational, Professional and Societal Contexts.* Springer.

Saudi-Vision-2030. (2022). Message from Prince Mohammed bin Salman bin Abdulaziz Al-Saud. www.vis ion2030.gov.sa/v2030/leadership-message/

Selim, N. (2023). Adolescent non-Arab Muslims learning Arabic in Australian Islamic schools: Expectations, experiences, and implications. *Religions, 14*(1), 71.

Shrake, E.K. (2006). Unmasking the self: Struggling with the model minority stereotype and lotus blossom image. In G. Li & G. Beckett (Eds.) *"Strangers" of the academy: Asian women scholars in higher education*, 163–177. Stylus Publisher.

Sihui, M. (2009). Translating the Other: Discursive Contradictions and New Orientalism in Contemporary Advertising in China. *The Translator, 15*(2), 261–282. DOI: 10.1080/13556509.2009.10799281

Sulaimani, A. & Elyas, T. (2018). A glocalized or globalized edition? Contextualizing gender representation in EFL textbooks in Saudi Arabia: A critical discourse perspective. In A.F. Selvi & N. Rudolph (Eds.), *Conceptual shifts and contextualized practices in education for glocal interaction: Issues and implications*, 55–76. Springer.

Ustinova, I. P. (2008). English and American Culture Appeal in Russian Advertising. *Journal of Creative Communications, 3*(1), 77–98. https://doi.org/10.1177/097325860800300105

Van Dijk, T.A. (2006). Ideology and discourse analysis. *Journal of Political Ideologies, 11*(2), 115–140. DOI: 10.1080/13569310600687908

World-population. (2023). Muslim population by country 2023. https://worldpopulationreview.com/country-rankings/muslim-population-by-country

23

NARRATIVES AND RELIGIOUS IDENTITY

Iman Abdulrahman Almulla

Introduction and Background

While the study of narrative analysis dates back to the hermeneutic study of the Bible, the Talmud and the Quran the contemporary study of narratives has gone beyond the literary theories to include the humanities and social sciences (Czarniawska, 2004). Over recent decades, the emergence of what is called the 'narrative turn' in social sciences has taken into account the stories and narratives of both individuals and groups (Polkinghorne, 1988; Czarniawska, 2004; Goodson & Gil, 2011). Thus, it has been suggested that the world in which we live is shaped by stories (Sarbin, 1986; Somers, 1994; Bruner, 2002; Smith & Sparkes, 2008). Moreover, many scholars argue not only that people's lives consist of stories, but also that identity is narratively produced (Smith & Sparkes, 2008; Atkins, 2004; Burner, 2002; de Fina, 2003). However, due to the problematic nature of the concept of 'self' and 'identity', there has been disagreement in the field of qualitative research with regard to the meaning of these terms and their relevance to narrative analysis; yet, there is a consensus rejecting looking at these concepts from an essentialist standpoint to embrace a multidimensional view that takes into account social, historical, political, and cultural contexts (Smith & Sparkes, 2008).

Furthermore, the study of narrative identity in qualitative research has been tackled from different perspectives. For example, from a psychological perspective, even though life stories are produced through social interaction and that sociocultural elements influence a person's sense of self or identity, one distinguishing feature of the psychosocial perspective is that the individual is prioritized over the social. Consequently, there is typically a profound regard for the importance of one's own subjective experience, one's own 'inner' world, one's own autonomy as a maker of deliberate choices, and one's own role as a reflecting narrator of the events that make up one's life story. Thus, stories are often defined by their internal cognitive or psychological structures rather than the events that occur within them. According to the dialogic view of narrative identity, however, a stronger perspective on narratives as essentially social and relational arises as the individual aspect of narrative identities disappear almost completely. Yet another perspective, the one which is adopted in this study, is a performative one in which identities are the product of narratives in interaction. Here, conversational exchanges are seen as the place where both self and identity are constructed because of the central role language plays in their construction (Smith & Sparkes, 2008).

DOI: 10.4324/9781003301271-26

Peek (2005) argues that the topic of religious identity has not been considered as a distinct category in many studies focusing on identity theory. He notes, for example, that religion does not feature as an identity category—unlike gender, race, ethnicity, nationality, sexuality, age, physical and mental ability, and class, all of which are considered. Like Peek, Safran (2008) considers religion and language to be important markers of ethno-national identity that are connected to each other in both psychological and social ways and sees these as markers of group identity.

One of the earliest conceptualizations of religious identity can be found in the work of Mol (1979, p. 15), who argues that "religion in any of its forms favours the identity side of the dialectic". In his model, religion serves as a means of stabilizing individual and group identity since constant change is often resisted by religious traditions and institutions. Seul (1999) later claimed that religious meaning systems provide a framework for individuals to understand their place in the world and to make sense of their experiences. They offer guidance on how to live a meaningful life and provide a sense of purpose and direction.

Seul (1999) also highlights the role of religion in promoting the stabilization of individual and group. He, for instance, argues that one of the functions of religion is to maintain the psychological stability that its adherents require by providing them with a worldview that can provide a sense of purpose and direction in life, as well as a framework for understanding the world around them. It can also offer comfort in times of uncertainty or difficulty. Secondly, he draws attention to the role that religious texts play in religious identity construction, stating that they serve as part of "the community memory" (Seul, 1999, p. 561) and help to give religious group members a "cross-generational sense of belonging in time, as well as a sense of belonging with others in distant places" (Seul, 1999, p. 561). In addition, according to Seul (1999), these texts have socializing effects that contribute to the development of a shared identity and values within the group, which can further strengthen social cohesion and facilitate cooperation among members. Additionally, these texts may provide a sense of guidance and direction for individuals within the group, helping them to navigate complex social situations and make decisions that align with the group's goals and values. Both articles make the case that beliefs stemming from shared religious traditions can have a major impact on how individuals form perceptions of themselves and of the world.

Along similar lines, Joseph (2004, p. 165) observes that:

> Religious identities are like ethnic ones in that they concern where we come from and where we are going—our entire existence, not just the moment-to-moment. It is these identities above all that, for most people, give profound meaning to the names we identify ourselves by, both as individuals and as groups, and are bound up with our deepest beliefs about life, the universe and everything.

As in the field of identity studies in general, those researching religious identity have been influenced by a range of discipline and research traditions including psychology or cultural anthropology and interactionalism (Francis, 1988, 2009) which has influenced the development of ideas about boundary maintenance (Barth, 1981). Studies such as those by Jacobson (1997), Östberg (2000), Zine (2001) and Peek (2005) have highlighted the flexible nature of religious identities. These studies illustrate that religion is associated with other social factors, including race, gender, and ethnicity. Nonetheless, the clarity of the religious boundaries provides a means of navigating the ambiguities and contradictions present in the social environment. For many, the teachings of religion enable them to transcend the uncertainties of existence in a multicultural world as religion serves as an anchor against assimilation. Thus, the ability to engage in role performance is a source of religious identification. In addition, these studies demonstrate that the formation of religious identity is a dynamic and ongoing process that faces being defined, challenged, accepted, or rejected by other people, communities, and institutions, religious identities are actively constructed by individuals and groups in the social world. Strong religious identity requires increased self-reflection and self-awareness, individual decision-making, and acknowledgement of others. Basically, these studies emphasize the role that sociocultural contexts play in shaping religious identities, focusing in particular on how cultural and social processes influence their construction. In adopting this approach, these authors eschew essentialist psychological conceptions of religious identity that are built on the assumption of individuals' commitment to fixed beliefs and practices.

Omoniyi and Fishman's (2006) collection of studies provides some useful insights into the relationship between language, identity, and religion. Some of the contributions in the collection examine the influence of religion on language, such as Bolkvadze's (2006) study of the impact of the Eastern Christian tradition on the Georgian language. Other articles in the collection focus more directly on how language helps to shape aspects of religious identity, such as Chruszczewski's (2006) analysis of Jewish religious discourse which reveals how community incorporation can be facilitated by certain types of prayers. Rosowsky's (2006) contribution to the collection examines the links between language, religious identity, and liturgical literacy in Muslim communities in the UK, demonstrating how Qur'anic Arabic is given a higher status than the Pakistani community's own vernacular languages, Mirpuri-Punjabi and Urdu.

When it comes to investigating the relationship between Islam and identity construction, religious variation within Muslims around the world is important to note. Halliday (1999, p. 897), for example, observes that because "Islam may vary greatly", individuals who refer to themselves as adherents of this religion will not necessarily choose to live and see the world in the same way. Reflecting on the diversity and heterogeneity of the category 'Muslim', Modood (2003, p. 100) writes:

> Muslims are not […] a homogenous group. Some Muslims are devout but apolitical; some are political but do not see their politics as being 'Islamic' (indeed, [they] may even be anti-Islamic). Some identify more with a nationality of origin, such as Turkish; others with the nationality of settlement and perhaps citizenship, such as French. Some prioritise fundraising for mosques, others campaign against discrimination, unemployment or Zionism. For some, Ayatollah Khomeini is a hero and Osama bin Laden an inspiration; for others, the same may be said of Kemal Ataturk or Margaret Thatcher, who created a swathe of Asian millionaires in Britain, brought in Arab capital and was one of the first to call for NATO action to protect Muslims in Kosovo. The category 'Muslim', then, is as internally diverse as 'Christian' or 'Belgian' or 'middle-class', or any other category helpful in ordering our understanding.

Thus, in this chapter I use the term 'Muslim identity' instead of 'Islamic identity' to reflect the dynamic nature of religious identity that takes place in interaction and to be consistent with performative perspective followed in this study. This approach recognizes that Muslim identity is not a fixed or monolithic concept, but rather a complex and multifaceted one that is shaped by various factors such as culture, history, and personal experiences. By adopting this perspective, the study aims to provide a more nuanced understanding of how Muslim identity is constructed and negotiated in everyday interactions. It is also to acknowledge that no single individual or group can represent the entire religion and to avoid making generalizations based on the interactions of individuals accordingly.

Co-constructing a Collective Muslim Identity Through Collaborative Narrative Events

To investigate how people construct and co-construct a shared religious identity, I will present a sample analysis of data taken from naturally occurring conversations that were originally collected in a family setting in the Eastern Province of Saudi Arabia. My analysis will draw in part on the Labovian classical analysis of narrative "as a stretch of talk, usually produced by an individual, that conveys both a sequence of past events and the teller's perspective on what is reported" (Gordon, 2015, p. 311) and will partly highlight Labov and Fanshel's (1977, p. 100) classification of statements according to the shared knowledge involved as: A-events: known to A, but not to B; B-events: known to B, but not to A; AB events: known to both A and B; O-events: known to everyone present; and D-events: known to be disputable. However, it will be oriented more towards Blum-Kulka's analysis of narratives, which argues that it is important to consider tales not as "narratives produced, but additionally as *tellings*—or unfolding (often very collaborative) acts of narration—as these are produced by *tellers*" (Gordon, 2015, p. 312; emphasis in original). Accordingly, in this chapter, I will analyse narratives "not as stand-alone texts, but as co-produced *narrative events*" (Gordon, 2015, p. 312; emphasis in original). Consequently, this means that "what is said, how it is said, who says it and to whom, who responds and how, and so on are of interest" (Gordon, 2015, p. 312). My analysis focuses first on these three aspects of narrative which reflect the dimensions of collective religious identity construction: tales, tellers, and tellings (Blum-Kulka, 1993), and the stages of which any narrative event typically consists, namely, the opening, the body. and the discussion as well as considering two key functions of narratives in family discourse, namely, socialization and sociability (Gordon, 2015).

In this section, my analysis will focus on one of the extended interactions that I encountered in my data. This conversation revolves around the topic of divine interventions that happened because of using different types of religious language, and it originally took place at midday in the living room of family BF. There are four participants from a family I named family B in my data. In this extract: the father (BF), his eldest daughter (BD1), his brother (BU) and his niece (BN).

Extract 1

BF	2	انا بقولك على حاجة صارت معاي في هذي المعاملة/
		ana bagūlak 'ala ḥajah ṣarat ma'aī fī hadhī ilmu'amalah/
		I'll tell you something that happened to me with these papers.
BD1	3	/بابا شاي قهوة؟
		Baba … shay? gahwah?/
		Dad … Tea? Coffee?
BF	4	عطيني قهوة. في شاي هنا و لا كيف؟
		'atīnī gahwa … fī shay hina wala kaif?
		Give me coffee … is there tea here or anything else?
BD1	5	فيه شاي و فيه قهوة
		fīh shay w gahwah
		There's tea and coffee.
BF	6	عطيني شاي
		'atīnī shay
		Bring me some tea.

BD1   7   انشاالله

Inshallah
Yes of course.

BF   8   هذا امس في شي عندهم نسبة و عندهم امتار. و علق الكمبيوتر و يتمون يغلغلون فيه نص
ساعة مهب مطلعهم لازم يطلعون النسبتين مب مطلع الا وحده اما ذي او ذي ..سمعت؟ و يتم
يغلغل.. سمعت؟ و انا يمه و يم الكمبيوتر قلت له اسمع.. و قرأت و بصوت رفيع سمع (زوج
بنتي) و هذا جالس ..قرأت عليها ألم نشرح و لا و الله العظيم كملتها الى ان مع العسر يسرا
الا و ينفتح هذا الكمبيوتر

hadha ams fīh shai 'induhun nisbah w 'induhum amtar.. w 'alag ilcombutar w
yitmūn yghalghlūn fīh niṣ sa'ah muhub mṭaluhum lazim yṭlūn ilnisbitain mub
mṭali' ila waḥdah ima dhī aw dhī. sma't? w yitim yghalghil. sima't? w ana yamah
w yam ilcombyutar gilt lah isma'. w qar'at w biṣawt rafī' sima'a (zawj binti) w
hatha jalis qara't 'alaiha *alam nashraḥ*
laka ṣadrak wa la wallah ilaẓīm kamaltha ila *in ma'a al'osri yosra ila* winfitiḥ
hadha ilcombyutar/

Yesterday [I was in court] to get the land deed and it was either issued by
percentage or by metres but the computer froze and they kept trying to fix it for
half an hour, but to no avail. I needed to get the deed with both percentages and
metres but only one of them would appear on the screen, you know what I mean?
And the notary kept trying, you know what I mean? And I was next to him and
I said to him: "Listen," and in a very loud voice I recited, *"Have We not opened
your breast for you"* He [my son-in-law] heard me and the other man was sitting
there and, honestly, once I reached [the verse] *"Verily, along with every hardship
comes relief"* the computer unfroze.

BU   9   / إسبحان الله

subḥan Allah!/
Glory be to God!

BF   10   شوف هذا القراءة و الدعاء لا احد يستهين بيه

shūf hadha ilqira'a wil dua'a' la aḥad ystihīn bīh
See, reciting [the Quran] and *dua'a*! Never underestimate them!

The analysis of Extract 1 begins by examining the different roles played by the two participants
in this interaction. In this instance, BF is the initial teller, i.e. the participant who proposes the
opening to this narrative event. He introduces the story to be told by addressing BU: "*I'll tell you
something that happened to me with these papers*" (line 2), an intervention which marks a shift
from the previous discussion with BU about a land deed, signalling a narrative frame. Despite the
fact that he is interrupted by BD1 who offers him something to drink, he returns to the narrative
frame (line 8) and starts to narrate a story which involves an instance of divine intervention,
drawing on a personal experience in which he himself is the protagonist, i.e. the leading character.
The primary recipient of this narrative, i.e. "the co-narrator to whom a narrative is predominately
oriented" (Ochs & Taylor, 1992, p. 310), is BD1 (BF's eldest daughter), as marked in the Arabic
grammar. However, here, the other two family members (BU and BN) also seem to be "implicitly
ratified as audience" (Ochs & Taylor, 1992, p. 311).

After establishing the main participant roles in this initial interaction, it is useful to look at
the tale that is being told or the narrative itself. BF begins by presenting the main events of his

story (line 8), starting with the setting in terms of time (yesterday) and place (in court). This is followed by a complication (the computer froze), and then an apparent resolution (the computer unfroze after BF recited a Quranic verse). However, the narrative event does not, in fact, end here. BU (BF's brother) provides a ratifying response to the story that has just been told by BF (line 9), which is a characteristic of a high involvement style indicating participatory listenership. Typically, this is reflected in a lack of interturn pauses (overlap between speakers), an interruption to provide an evaluation, and/or the use of a raised pitch.

The narrative event then continues with BF providing a self-evaluation of the story that he narrated (line 10). His response—"*See, reciting [the Quran] and dua'a. Never underestimate them*"—formulates the purpose and the significance of his narrative as a moral construct. By doing this, the storyteller uses his narrative to help construct a shared religious identity. A point worth noting here is that BF's reference to the activity of reciting Quranic verses as a means of seeking divine intervention supports the interpretation that this practice is commonplace in the Saudi Muslim context.

Although this story of divine intervention told by BF can be considered an A-event (Labov & Fanshel, 1977), since it is one that only the teller himself knows, analysis of the participant interaction clearly provides evidence of the cooperative nature of the storytelling in this instance, since the narration of this story does not end here with BF's self-evaluation (line 10). As seen in Extract 1, the fact that the other family members did not share the experience that prompted BF's tale does not appear to stop them from actively participating in the storytelling. In this case, the other participants take advantage of their familiarity with similar narratives of divine intervention and draw on their shared background of these moral scripts to deliver their own personal accounts featuring a similar theme. This can be compared to the polyphonic type of storytelling that Blum-Kulka (1993) found, which was used by participants as a means of displaying high involvement.

In Extract 2, BD1 is the first to contribute to the narrative event, even though previously she does not seem to be addressed as the primary recipient of BF's narrative. She begins by responding to BF's self-evaluation of his account by offering her own evaluation: "*That's right*" (line 11). She then continues by providing her own account of how she used to pray for divine intervention when she was a young schoolgirl to avoid being picked by the teacher to answer questions in front of her classmates by reciting a specific *dua'a* (supplication). Just as BF did previously, she also starts her narrative account by establishing the setting in terms of time (when we were young) and place (at school). This is followed by the body: "*we used to recite dua'a such as 'And We have put before them a barrier ...' [laughs] so that the teacher wouldn't make us stand up*".

Extract 2

BD1   11   ترا فعلا! احنا من و احنا صغار و احنا فالمدرسة احيانا نقول ادعية مثلا و جعلنا بين /ايديهم سدا ‹تضحك› عشان المدرسة ما تقومنا

tara fi'lan! min wihna sghar w ihna filmadrisah ahyanan ngūl adi'a mathalan *w ja'alna min baini aidyahum sadan [laughs]* 'ashan ilmodarisah ma tgawimna/ that's right! ever since we were young, at school we used to recite *dua'a* such as ***"And We have put before them a barrier"** [laughs]* so that the teacher wouldn't make us stand up [to respond to questions].

Two points are worth noting in BD1's account. First, the Arabic prepositional phrase "*min wihna*" (line 11) is used here by BD1 to indicate continuity between the time introduced in the narrative (childhood) and the present. In other words, this is a long-standing personal practice that she *(and probably many others)* still engages in, conveyed here in the English translation by the use of the phrase "*ever since*". Her use of the plural form "we" in this context also suggests that this practice is very common among the group she is addressing, (i.e., Saudi Muslims). Second, it should be noted that although BD1 talks about "*reciting dua'a*", the example that she uses here is, in fact, the opening phrase of a Quranic verse from Surat Yaseen (36, p. 9): "*And We have put before them a barrier and behind them a barrier and covered them, so they do not see.*" The fact that she only recites the beginning of the verse is indicative of the fact that she assumes this is shared knowledge familiar to the other participants to whom she is telling her story, and that this verse is re-contextualised to serve a different purpose than the one used in the Quranic context.

In Extract 3, the high-involvement style of storytelling continues when BD1 is interrupted in the next turn (line 12) by BU who provides his own account of a related narrative of divine intervention prompted by prayer. As in the previous examples, BU is the protagonist when he relates his own personal narrative. However, this type of narrative is somewhat different to the previous ones, being what Labov and Fanshel (1977) refer to as an A-B event (i.e. it is known to the teller and to one or more other participants in the interaction, in this case BU and his daughter BN). BU establishes the fact that his daughter already knows this narrative, which could be interpreted as a way of obtaining more verification or serve as an invitation for his daughter to get involved, as he opens the telling of his story by specifically referring to her "*I told BN*" and then introduces the story with "*that there was something on my mind*" (line 12). He then proceeds with his own account of how his personal problem was solved after reciting (the Quran) and the *istighfar* (asking for God's forgiveness). Note here that BU repeats the phrase "*I told*" four times. By doing so, he emphasises that he considers BN to be a participant in his own narrative, implicitly prompting her to take part in the narration.

Extract 3

BU 12 قلت ل((بنتي)) قلت ((لبنتي)) هذا موضوع كان شاغلني هناك واحد مين يتوقع الساعة تثعش بالليل و انا اتكلم لها و اقولها تصدقين الموضوع الي كلمتش فيه الساعة يمكن سبع او ثمان اقول لها رحت انام الساعة تسع و قعدت اقرا انا قبل النوم الاستغفار يعني و الساعة ثنعش يدق التلفون الا ان المسألة محلولة

gilt il ()BN() hadha mawdhū' kan shaghlny hinak waḥid mīn kan yitwaqa' ilsa'a
ithna'ash bilail w ana atkalam laha w agūl laha tṣadgīn ilmawdhu' ilī
kalamtach fīh ilsa'a sabi'aw thiman agūl laha riḥt anam ilsa'ah tisi' w ga'adt
agra ana gabil ilnawm ilistighfar ya'ani w ilsa'ah ithana'ash ydig iltilifawn ila in
ilmasa'alah maḥlūlah.

I told BN there was something on my mind. I was expecting someone to ring at midnight and I told her ... Would you believe it? That issue that I told you about at seven or eight o'clock ... I told her I went to bed at nine o'clock and before I went to sleep I kept reciting, I mean, *istighfar* [prayers asking for forgiveness], and at midnight the telephone rang and the problem had been solved.

BD1	13	سبحان الله!

Subḥan Allah!
Glory be to God!

BU	14	شرايتش؟

shraich?
What do you think of that?

BF	15	سبحان الله!

Subḥan Allah!
Glory be to God!

BN	16	بابا عاد تجيله لحظات كذا .. ممكن يطلع له واحد قديم/

baba ʻad tijī lah laḥẓat kidha. momkin yiṭlaʻ lah waḥid gidīm/
Dad [referring to BU] has moments like this … an old acquaintance [of his] might turn up.

BF	17	لا يستهين احد بالدعاء و القرآن/

/la ystihīn aḥad bildu'a' wilqur'an
/no one should underestimate the *dua'a* or the Quran.

BU	18	الدعاء و القرآن فعلا

ildua'a wilquran filan
the *dua'a* and the Quran indeed

BF	19	ما في ابرك منه

ma fīh abrak minh
nothing bestows more blessings

BN	20	نعم الدعاء و الاستغفار الامور سبحان الله تتفتح

Naʻam ildua'a' wilistighfar il'imūr subḥan allah titfataḥ
Yes *dua'a* and *istighfar*. Glory be to God! Things work out for the best.

The collaborative storytelling style continues here when BD1 offers her brief but emotionally charged evaluation of his story, adding "*Praise be to God*" (line 13) using a raised pitch. BU then cooperatively prompts BN to respond by asking: "*What do you think of that?*" to elicit his evaluation of the story (line 14). Before BN has a chance to give her own evaluation, BF takes the floor, repeating the same phrase employed by his own daughter: "*Praise be to God*" (line 15). When BN finally gets the chance to participate, she starts by confirming that this is not an isolated incident "*It's true ... Dad* [referring to BU] *has moments like this*" and then appears to be about to recount another narrative as she continues: "*An old acquaintance* [of his] *might turn up*" (line 16). However, she does not succeed in telling her story as she is interrupted once more by BF who continues to formulate BU's narrative as a moral tale testifying to the power of divine intervention. His phrase "*No one should underestimate the dua'a or the Quran*" (line 17) is essentially a reformulation of his previous contribution (line 10), using very similar lexical terms.

As this interaction progresses, the discussion phase of each narrative event becomes ever more elaborate and is also characterized by frequent repetition by the participants. Thus, for example, "*Praise be to God!*" is proclaimed by three of the four participants (lines 13, 15, and 20) in Extract 3. In addition, the importance of reciting *dua'a* and/or the Quran is emphasised by repetition (lines 17, 18, and 20). BU himself repeats *istighfar* twice (lines 12 and 20) but is the only participant to mention this specifically.

Extract 4

BF	21	يوم من الايام/
		yawm min alayam/
		one day/
BU	22	/والله فعلا الامور تتيسر
		/w allah filan ilmoor tityasar
		/truly things work out for the best
BF	23	اسمع... اسمع... انت تشوف عندنا سفرة الطعام الي فوق؟
		isma'. isma'. int tishūf 'indina sofrat ilṭa'am ili fawg?
		Listen ... listen ... you know our dining table upstairs?
BU	24	القزاز؟
		il gizaz?
		the glass one?
BF	25	ايه. شفت القزاز كانت القزازة الي عليها اعرض من كذا و انا فاتح سورة ياسين تقرأ و (موجودة مين الي عليها؟)حفيدتي ١ جالسة
		eīh shift ilgizaz kanat ilgizazah ili 'alaiha a'raẓ min kidha w ana faitḥ sūrat yasīn tiqra' w mawjūdah mīn ili 'alaiha? Jalsah 'alaiha [Granddaughter 1]
		Yes ... You know the glass one, the sheet of glass that covered it previously was wider than this one and I was playing an audio tape of [Surah Yaseen] being recited on the recorder and who should be sitting on it [the table?] Granddaughter 1 [was sitting there].
BU	26	/ايه
		/eīh/
		/uh huh
BF	27	و امامها مين؟(حفيدتي ٢) و لعلها كانت جالسة على الطرف و تقوم و تنقلب ذيك القزازة و تتكسر و يوصل القزاز الى وين؟ الى الحجرة حقتي!
		wamamha mīn? [Granddaughter 2] w la'alha kanat jalsah 'ala ilṭaraf w tgūm w tinglib thīk ilgizazah w titkasar w ywaṣil ilgizaz ila wain? ila ilḥijrah ḥagtī
		and who should be in front of her? [Granddaughter 2] and she must have been sitting on the edge and suddenly the sheet of glass flips over and breaks and where do the pieces end up? In my room!
BD1	28	الي غرفتهم فعلا/
		/ila ghurfatihum fi'lan
		/honestly... in their [the parents'] room
BU	29	الله! الله! انتثرت/
		Allah! Allah! Intathrat/
		my God my God it shattered
BF	30	/و هي قاعدة عليها و انقلبت عليها و تكسرت و (حفيدتي ٢) و/ في وجهها
		/fi wajihaha wi hi ga'adah 'alaiha w ingalbat 'alaiha w itkasarat w [Granddaughter 2]/
		/she was in front of it and was sitting on it and it flipped over her and broke and [Granddaughter 2].

BU   31   /سبحان الله/

                    /Subḥan Allah/

                    /Oh, Glory be to God! /

Extract 4 provides further evidence of the extent to which the participants continue to contribute to what has become a collaborative narrative event on the theme of the power of religious texts in facilitating divine intervention. This time BF claims the floor and attempts to introduce a new story with the opening phrase "*one day*" (line 21). However, he is interrupted by BU who provides a further ratifying response to his previous narrative, declaring "*truly things work out for the best*" (line 22). BF then reclaims the floor and starts his narration with a double directive "*listen ... listen ...*" (line 23) to attract the attention of the recipient (BU) and then starts the body of the story by posing a question intended to attract the attention of the recipient. This clearly marks a change of story and teller: "*you know our dining table upstairs?*" The directives and the question are intended to indicate that what he is about to say is interesting and/or important and requires the careful attention of the recipient(s). BU's ratifying response "*the glass one?*" (line 24) indicates his participatory listenership.

In the next turn, after confirming that BU is correct in his assumption, BF starts narrating an A-B event-type story about an incident that was witnessed by BD1. The narrative focuses on his account of how one of his granddaughters escaped serious injury thanks to divine intervention, this time prompted by the fact that verses from the Quran were being recited on a tape recorder. As he narrates his story, there is overlapping talk with BU who provides a back-channelling "*uh huh*" (line 26) that illustrates his engagement as he follows the narrative and BF continues with his story (line 27).

BF adopts a specific narrative style, posing a question and then answering it immediately himself: "*and who should be sitting on it* [the table]? [Granddaughter 1] *was sitting there*" (line 25); "*and who should be in front of her?* [Granddaughter 2]" and "*and where do the pieces end up? In my room!*" (line 27). Since this is an A-B event, BD1's interruption serves to confirm that BF's account is true and partially echoes BF's own phrase "*honestly ... in their room*" (line 28). This is immediately followed by a ratifying response from BU (line 29) expressing both his surprise and concern: "*my God, my God it shattered*". BF reclaims the floor by offering what is essentially a summary of the whole episode: "*she was in front of it and was sitting on it and it flipped over her and broke and* [Granddaughter 2]" (line 30). Again, BU's turn overlaps, with an exclamation expressing his concern: "*Oh, Glory be to God!*" (line 31).

Extract 5

BF   32   /يعني شلون؟

                    /yaʻnī shlawn?

                    /so what did that mean?

BD1   33   عاد ((بنتي)) مسكينة جات في يدها

                    ʻad [my daughter] maskīnah jat fī yadha

                    My poor [daughter] it [the glass] injured her hand.

BF	34	لكن و شو جا في يدها شي بسيط
		لكن بفضل الله ثم بفضل بفضل سورة ياسين

lakin wishū ja fī yadha shay basīṭ lakin bifadhl Allah thuma bifadhl bifadhl surat yasīn

But it was just a very superficial wound thanks to the grace of God and the blessings of the Surah Yaseen.

BD1	35	الحمدلله.. ايه شي بسيط.. فعلا الحمدلله

ilḥamdu lilah.. eīh shay basīṭ. fi'lan *ilḥamd lilah*

thank God indeed … it was very superficial … truly *thank God*

BF	36	لأن سورة ياسين تقرأ بنية دفع البلاء

la'an surat yaesīn *tuqra' biniat daf' ilbala'*

because Surah Yaseen is recited with the intention of keeping danger at bay

BD1	37	لأنها فعلا تفتت القزازة تفتت

li'anha fi'lan ilgizazh tiftitat

because the glass really shattered, it scattered all over

BF	38	لاا سورة ياسين تقرأ إن شاء الله بنية دفع البلاء

la'an surat yasīn tuqra' *in sha'a allah* biniat daf' ilbala'

because Surat Yaseen is recited with the intention of keeping away danger, God willing

BU	39	تفتت القزازة

tiftitat ilgizazah

the glass scattered all over

BF	40	افتحها و لا هذا السورة و لا مستحيل ما يصابون

aftaḥa w la hadha ilsurah wila mustaḥīl ma yuṣabūn

If it wasn't for me playing this surah on the recorder there is no way they would not have been hurt.

BD1	41	صحيح فعلا

ṣaḥīḥ fi'lan

That's absolutely right.

BF	42	لان لو جايه شظية في عين وحدة فيهم

la'an law jayah shadhiah fi 'ain wḥadah fīhum

Because if a sliver of glass had gone into someone's eye …

BD1	43	خلاص ايه و لا قلبها و لا بطنها و اي مكان

khalaṣ eīh wala galbha wala baṭinha aw ay mikan

that would be it or into her or someone's heart or abdomen or anywhere

BF	44	لا هذا يهون في العين كل شي يتعالج جرح و يخلص لكن العين

la hadha yihūn fi il'ain kil shay yit'alaj jarḥ w yakhliḥ lakin il'ain

That's not as serious as the eye, a wound [elsewhere] can heal but the eye …

BD1	45	لا و الله يا بابا لو جا فالكلى و لا الكبد

la wallah ya baba law ja fililkila wala ilkabid

No, honestly, Dad, if it had gone into the kidney or the liver …

BF	46	القرآن لا احد يستهين به

ilquran laḥad yistahīn bīh

The Quran must not be underestimated by anyone.

BD1   47   فعلا فعلا لا القرآن و الدعاء يعني الله ييسر امور الواحد و يرد عنه اشياء واجد

fi'lan fi'lan la ilquran wil du'a' ya'nī allah yiyasir imūr ilwaḥid w yirid 'anah ashia' wajid

Absolutely, absolutely, the Quran and the *dua'a* Allah resolve one's issues and shield one from many things.

BU's ratifying response (line 31) is followed by a very long discussion of this narrative about the accident involving the glass table, with the participants displaying a high-involvement style as seen by the cooperative prompt (line 32). BD1's contribution (line 33) focuses on her daughter's injury, and threatens to shift the nature of the narrative, but BF immediately restores the divine protection motif in his turn by emphasising how much worse things could have been: "*but it was just a very superficial wound thanks to the grace of God and the blessings of the Surah Yaseen*" (line 34). Following her father's lead, BD1 shifts the emphasis of her contribution away from motherly concern and possible suggestions of scepticism to a wholehearted endorsement of BF's intervention: "*thank God indeed. It was very superficial ... truly thank God*" (line 35). BF reminds the other participants why his reference to this particular Quranic verse is relevant: "*because Surah Yaseen is recited with the intention of keeping away danger*" (line 36).

The participants then begin a more extended discussion about the narrative (lines 37–47), which includes BF and BD1 suggesting imaginary worst-case scenarios concerning what might have happened but for the divine protection provided by the Quran (lines 42–45). Here again, their interaction bears a strong resemblance to the polyphonic style that Blum-Kulka (1993) found. Slightly differing versions of what has already been said are repeated, sometimes several times, to connect the elements of the narrative and ensure everyone is following the key moral of the story: the power of the divine word should never be underestimated (lines 10, 17, 18, 46). When one speaker repeats what a previous speaker has said this also highlights their involvement, for example, BD1's "*the glass really shattered, it scattered all over*" (line 37), is echoed by BU "*the glass scattered*" (line 39). There is also extensive use of the Arabic word *fi'lan* throughout by various speakers (lines 35, 37, 41, 47), it can be used as an intensifier ("*really*") or to indicate emphatic support for what a previous speaker has said ("*absolutely*", "*indeed*"). All these features highlight the degree of involvement demonstrated by the participants.

Extract 6

BF   48   طيب هذا الدعاء الي تقرأه انا قلت (لبنت الاخ) اللهم لا خير الا خيرك و لا طير الا طيرك
كنت موجود مع واحد معي في المعهد و كنت احفظ قصيدة يقرأها و حفظتها و دخل من هو
ع و كانت في يدي بيالة شاهي

ṭaib hadha ildu'a' ili tiqra'ah ana gilt l(BN) *allahuma la khaira ila khairuk w ala ṭaira ila ṭairuk* kint mawjūd ma'a waḥid ma'ai fi ilma'ahad w kint aḥfidh qaṣīdah yiqra'aha w hafadhtha w dakhal minhu? [one of his old classmates] w kanat fī yad ī biyalat shahī

Right and this *dua'a* I told (BN) to recite it ***oh lord there is no good except your good and there are no omens but there is reliance on you*** I was once with a man at the institute [where BF used to study] and I was memorizing a poem, he was reading it and I was reciting it, and who should enter but X [one of BF's old classmates] and I had a cup of tea in my hand.

BU 49   >يضح<

    <laughs>

    <laughs>

BF 50   قال صرمتو قبل المطر؟ هي تجي من صالح و من طالح

gal ṣaramtū gabil ilmaṭar? hī tij ī min ilṣalaiḥ w mi ilṭaliḥ

He said "you packaged the dates before it rained?" [i.e. the student is making a sarcastic comment about BF's diligence in studying] it [the evil eye] comes from good guys and bad guys.

BN 51   >يضحك<

    <laughs>

    <laughs>

BF 52   صرمتو قبل الصرام؟ الغريب في يدي بيالة شاهي شارب يجي نصها و لا خذت الا القاعة حقتها تنزل

ṣaramtū gabl ilṣaram? ilgharīb fi yadī bialat shahī sharib yiji niṣha w la khadht ila ilgaʿah ḥagatiha tanzil

packaged them [the dates] before the packaging time? the strange thing is that I had drunk almost half of it [the cup of tea] and suddenly the base of the cup breaks and falls to the ground.

BD1 53   >يضحك<

    <laughs>

BU 54   اقوى جزء!

aqwa juz'!

the strongest part!

BF 55   لكن و هو داخل خطر في بالي الحديث ال ال ال الدعاء اللهم لا خير الا خيرك ابد و تنخرط

lakin whu dakhil khaṭar fi balī ilḥadīth il il il duaʿa **allahuma la khaira ila khairuk** w abad w tinkhrit

but before he entered the hadith the, the, the *dua'a* came into my mind **oh lord there is no good but your good** and all of a sudden it [the cup] just fell.

BU 56   سبحان الله

Subḥan Allah

oh Glory be to God!

BN 57   لا عاد هذا اقصى شي

la ʿad hadha aqṣa shay

oh no that's the most extreme.

BF 58   شوف كيف؟ سبحان الله

shūf kaif? **subḥan Allah**

see that? **Glory be to God**

Yet another narrative occurs in this interaction (Extract 6), with BF beginning his story by reminding BN about a particular *dua'a* that he told her to use. He then goes on to provide a personal account of how this *dua'a* protected him *hasad* (i.e. the evil eye or inflicting harm on whom it falls) when he was studying. Here, however, his narrative takes on a new humorous tone as seen by the response from the other family members (lines 49, 51 and 53), who continue with the same high-involvement style when discussing BF's narrative but in this case their interaction also takes the form of laughter. To a certain extent, this narrative acts as light relief in comparison to the potentially serious implications of the previous glass table narrative since the scenario here concerns nothing more threatening than a broken teacup. The discussion of this narrative and the topic of preventing the evil eye (line 50) continues. Due to the length of the discussion, the narrative event now moves towards a conversation frame. As Blum-Kulka (1993, p. 366) notes, "in oral story-telling, the realm of telling is embedded (in an open-ended fashion) in the realm of conversation, and the realm of tales within that of telling".

Extract 7

BU	64	بس المعوذات تنفع
		bas ilmu'awidhat tinfa'
		but the *mua'awithat* help
BF	65	الحين سبحان الله القدامى حتى عندهم
		alḥīn *subḥan Allah* ilqudama ḥata 'induhum
		now *glory be to God,* even ancient people had this))concept((
BD1	66	سبحان الله احس الناس تتفاعل
		Suḥan Allah aḥis ilnas titfa'al
		Glory be to God, I feel that people interact
BF	67	هو نوع من ال ال و لذلك ايش يقولن القدامى امسك الخشب
		hū naw' min il il wilidhalik aysh ygūlūn ilqudama imsik ilkhashab
		it's a kind of the, the … and that's why ancient people used to say knock on wood
BU	68	مممم
		Mmmmmm
		Mmmmmm
BN	69	صح
		saḥ
		Right
BF	70	و هذي مش موجودة بس في الحضارة المصرية حتى في اوروبا
		whadhi mush mawjūdah bas fi ilḥadhara ilmasriah ḥata fi awrwba
		and this [the evil eye] was not only known to ancient Egyptians but even in Europe
BD1	71	صح صح فعلا
		saḥ saḥ fi'lan
		right, right, absolutely
BU	72	الخشب؟
		ilkhashab?
		the wood?
BF	73	الخشب كانو يعتبرونه عازل
		the wood, they considered it to be a barrier
		ilkhashab kanū y'tabrūnah 'azil
BN	74	فعلا الاجانب يقولون طق عالخشب
		fiīlan iljanib ygūlūn ṭig 'al khashab
		true foreigners say knock on wood
BU	75	⟨ما في الا الواحد يمشي و في جيبه خشبه ⟨يضحك
		ma fī ila ilwaḥid yamshī w fi jaibah khshibah

the best thing for one to do then is to walk around with a piece of wood in one's pocket hehhhh

BD1   76   خشبة يحطها هنا او يعلقها

khishibah yiḥiṭha hina aw yaʻligha

A piece of wood that someone puts here or hangs it up.

BF   77   لا عاد بعدين الناس يتحول الى عقيدة

La ʻad baʻdain ilnas yithawal ila ʻakīdah

No, because then it could become a belief for people.

In Extract 7, the participants talk about the concept of the evil eye (i.e. the belief that a person can cause harm to another person or object by merely gazing upon them with envy or jealousy), with BF noting that this is an ancient concept (line 65). BD1 provides a ratifying response to show her agreement (line 66). BF then begins by attempting to clarify his claim but hesitates in describing the concept of the evil eye: "*it's a kind of the, the*" (line 67) and appears to change tack in mid-sentence, moving onto an apparently unrelated point: "*and that's why ancient people say touch wood*". Both BU and BN provide back-channelling devices (lines 68 and 69) which indicate high considerateness and mark reception of the message (Blum-Kulka, 1993), and BN provides a ratifying response showing agreement (line 69). BF continues to talk about the concept of warding off the evil eye, claiming that the idea of the protective qualities of wood was recognized in both Ancient Egypt and Europe (line 70). BD1 ratifies and displays high considerateness (line 71). BU asks a clarifying question about "[touching] wood" (line 72). BF responds by explaining that it is used as a form of protection, which BD1 confirms by noting "*true foreigners say knock on wood*" (line 73). When BU (line 75) jokes that people should walk around carrying a piece of wood to ward off the evil eye and BD1 joins in the joke (line 76), BF promptly dismisses this suggestion (line 77), warning that this might be thought of as something that runs counter to Islamic beliefs.

Extract 8

BD1   89   بس بابا هم ماقدرو يثبتونها علميا

bas baba hum ma qdarū yithbitūnha ʻilmian

but Dad they (scientists) couldn't prove it scientifically

BF   90   ايه العلم لا تقولين ما ثبت الي ما ثبت الان يثبت بعدين

eīh il ilʻilm la tgūlīn ma thibat ilī ma thibat alan yathbit baʻdain

No, don't say science has not proven it, what has not been proven yet will be proven later.

This discussion about the concept of the evil eye continues for several turns like the ones displayed above. When BD1 shows some scepticism (line 85) about the concept of the evil eye as something that cannot be scientifically proven, BF dismisses her claim by saying "*No, don't say science has not proven it, what has not been proven yet will be proven later*" (line 90). Between lines 90 and 159 the interaction continues with several shifts in topic that revolve around related topics such as the importance of modesty (lines 95–108) and of charity (lines 109–159). The discussion about religious matters then ends when BF shifts the topic back to talking about the land deed (line 160) when he addresses BU (line 160):

Extract 9

BF   160   انت الحين من رايك يكفي الي سويت و لا لازم اكلم الرجال؟

int alḥīn min rayik ykaffī ili sawait wila lazim akalim ilrajal?

Now do you think it's enough what I did or do you think I need to speak to the man?

In this section, I analysed an interaction recorded in my data in which participants displayed collaborative work in telling narratives about the divine interventions prompted by the use of liturgical language such as verses of the Quran, the Hadith or dua'a. I also demonstrated that the participants displayed a polyphonic style that is similar to one that Blum-Kulka (1993) found, and that the participants also displayed many instances of high involvement.

The findings indicate that accounts of divine interventions foster a sense of shared identity among participants. In this way, they confirm previous research indicating that narratives play a crucial role in the co-construction of identity in everyday interaction. Moreover, in the Muslim community where this study was conducted, narratives of this nature not only provide a shared sense of identity and belonging, but also reflect a profound connection to oneself and the way life events are viewed.

Using Blum-Kulka's model (1993), in this story-telling event, which is a social action taking place in real time and the text about several events at the discourse level, the storytellers provide the link between the two dimensions of tales (texts) and tellings (the act of narration). The textual content of the stories found in the data reflects the participants' beliefs of how liturgical texts (Quranic verses, Hadith, and instances of *dua'a*) have the power to summon divine interventions as a shield from the danger of everyday activities when/after God is willing.

The participants in the interaction, presented in the data as storytellers (performers), are responsible for the narratives of these divine interventions. Thus, they mostly fulfil the roles referred to as the principals, authors and animators by Goffman (1981, pp. 144–145). All three speaker roles (main character, author, and narrator) converged in these personal narratives of the relationship between liturgical language and divine interventions making the storytellers act as a link between their tales (texts) and their tellings (acts of narration). Accordingly, the narratives are transformed into narrative events of a religious nature since they include a number of stories that are co-narrated about divine interventions.

Implications and Future Directions

This study contributes to the investigation of how narratives play a role in the co-construction if religious identity. First, after the review of some of the fundamental ideas pertaining to identity research in general and religious identity, or Muslim identity, this study lends credence to the performative perspective of identity co-construction. This view places an emphasis on social interaction and social relations by demonstrating through a sample analysis that Muslim identity is a dynamic ongoing process that involves performance and negotiation. This study expands on the concept of performativity to suggest that within social interaction, participants do not only reflect or represent their beliefs, but also share, negotiate, and evaluate their beliefs through their shared experiences. This means that the social interaction is not neural or exists in a vacuum; rather, it serves a social function of shaping relationships and connect, or disconnect, participants from each other within the social interaction. To reflect this performative aspect of religious identity, I suggested using Muslim identity instead of Islamic identity to emphasize its dynamic aspect and how it reflects the people as individuals and as groups rather than the religion itself.

Second, the findings of the study also showed that individuals are able to develop a more profound connection with religious, as well as spiritual, beliefs when they tell stories about their shared experiences. The data demonstrated that when people listen to the experiences of others in their community, not only are they able to reflect on and interpret their own religious beliefs, but they also can connect with the experiences of those around them. Accordingly, through the act of telling stories to one another, the participants were able to cultivate a sense of shared Muslim identity. In this case study, the act of storytelling had the potential to not only bring people closer to the common ritualistic religious practices known to Muslims, such as the daily prayers or the fasting of the Holy Month of Ramadan, but also assisted in the formation of new types of religious identities through connecting the text to the divine experience. This suggests that when people talk about the ways in which they have experienced divine intervention in their everyday lives because of liturgical texts and share these experiences with others who are a part of their social interaction, they are able to generate a new religio-spiritual identity that gives new interpretations of the religious beliefs they hold.

Moreover, by listening to the accounts of others who have had similar experiences and held similar beliefs, the participants were able to establish not only a connection with God but also a sense of belonging with those individuals, which reinforces the religious identity at the personal level and the group level as well. Moreover, this study suggests that there is something that can be of utmost significance when trying to understand the religious experience and how people practise their religiosity not only through rituals but also through the experiences they have had in their lives. Here, I would like to raise the question of the blurred line between the religious and spiritual, as the shared stories do not reflect only religious ritualistic usage of instances of Islamic liturgical texts such as Quranic verses and *dua'a* but also a rather a religio-spiritual aspect since they connect the Islamic liturgical texts with spiritual divine experiences.

The narratives in the study have a variety of tones, ranging from serious to humorous. This suggests that humorous narratives could also contribute to the co-construction of Muslim identity as humour is a component of our social lives, despite the fact that it is customarily assumed that serious narratives will be associated with the process of jointly constructing a religious identity. These narratives were utilized by the participants to amuse, convince, and communicate the experience and played an important role in the construction and reinforcement of Muslim identity accordingly.

It is common practice in a wide variety of religious traditions to employ liturgical language and religious formulaic expressions. This practice can play a significant part in the development of an individual's sense of identity. In this chapter, I discussed how the use of liturgical language and religious formulaic expressions contributed to the formation of a new form of an individual's sense of religious identity. The tales described how specific phrases or words recited in a religious setting had the power to protect the participants from the dangers that they faced on a daily basis. This provides evidence that, within the context of this religious community, these expressions frequently take on a significant amount of symbolic weight other than carrying the quality of highly ritualized act. In addition, this demonstrates that one method through which individuals who are a part of a religious community can work to strengthen their sense of shared religious identity is by making use of religious formulaic expressions such as "glory to be to God," "thank God," and "God willing." Although these formulaic expressions are highly dependent on context and may have different pragmatic functions, they are used here as a commentary on the participant's own experience as well as the other participants' similar experiences in order to affirm and reaffirm the power of liturgical language.

The findings also suggested that interactions within the context of one's family play important roles in socialization and/or sociability. Since the family is an important component in the Saudi culture, interactions within the context of one's family can provide opportunities for socialization and sociability and a strong emphasis is placed on the role that the dynamics of the family play in the development of social behaviours and beliefs. However, these dynamics might play out differently in different societies and social groups. In this instance, narratives as well as other social factors such as the age and the status of the storyteller as the person who initiates the stories of divine intervention hints at the significance of how all these roles interplay in fostering religious socialization even after the participants become adults. In addition, the findings suggest that religious socialization may be achieved through and simultaneously with sociability. The findings also highlight how family members such as uncles, nieces, and daughters can also be part of the process of socialization, as well as how their interactions can shape a person's overall social development. In summary, the research places a significant amount of emphasis on the necessity of considering the intersectionality of various social identities when conducting an analysis of the dynamics of families and the outcomes of socialization.

Moreover, this research distinguishes itself from others on religious identity for two reasons. The first is that it pertains to Muslim individuals, where research on this topic is still scarce. The second is that it takes place in Saudi Arabia, a predominantly Muslim country. While there are other studies on Muslim identity in migrant communities, research on Muslim identity in Muslim countries in general and Saudi Arabia in particular is still extremely limited. One possible reason is that this kind of data is difficult to obtain and requires ethnographic background knowledge and skill. Research on the social aspect of religion in general and Islam especially in predominantly Muslim countries is particularly interesting and worthy of further investigation. The data I collected for this case study is original and rich. However, due to the qualitative nature of the case study and the limited amount of data collected in the research, it is difficult to make generalizations about the role of narratives in co-constructing Muslim identity. However, the theoretical model that was designed to analyse this data is transferable to other settings and can be utilized there.

Further Reading

Blum-Kulka, S. (1993). "You gotta know how to tell a story": Telling, tales, and tellers in American and Israeli narrative events at dinner. *Language in Society, 22*(3), 361–402.
The study highlights the importance of considering cultural diversity in analysing family conversations and the role of storytelling in maintaining cultural identity by suggesting a tripartite framework of telling, tales, and tellers.
Czarniawska, B. (2004). *Narratives in social science research*. SAGE.
This is an introduction to narrative methodology as an instrument for social science research and offers a practical foundation for the use of these instruments in qualitative research.
Joseph, J.E. (2004). *Language and Identity: National, Ethnic, Religious*. Palgrave Macmillan.
This book provides a comprehensive overview of the role of language choice in the formation of national, ethnic, and religious identity. It examines a wide variety of specific cases from different parts of the world to establish some general principles regarding the relationship between language and identity.
Pihlaja, S. (2021). *Talk about Faith: how debate and conversation shape belief*. Cambridge University Press.
This is an original study that explores a wide variety of texts from new media that look at how Christians and Muslims talk to people inside and outside their own groups about faith and how that impacts how they present themselves.

References

Atkins, K. (2004). Narrative identity, practical identity and ethical subjectivity. *Continental Philosophy Review, 37*(3), 341–366.

Barth, F. (1981) Ethnic Groups and Boundaries. In *Process and Form in Social Life: Selected Essays of Fredrik Barth, 1*. Routledge & Kegan Paul.

Blum-Kulka, S. (1993). "You gotta know how to tell a story": Telling, tales, and tellers in American and Israeli narrative events at dinner. *Language in Society, 22*(3), 361–402.

Bolkvadze, T. (2006). Eastern-Christian tradition and the Georgian language. In T. Omomiyi & J.A. Fishman (Eds.), *Explorations in the Sociology of Language and Religion, 60–67*. John Benjamins Publishing Company.

Bruner, J. (2002). *Making Stories: Law, Literature, Life*. Harvard University Press.

Chruszczewski, P.P. (2006). Prayers as an integrative factor in Jewish religious discourse communities. In T. Omoniyi & J.A. Fishman (Eds.), *Explorations in the Sociology of Language and Religion*, 278–290. John Benjamins Publishing Company.

Czarniawska, B. (2004). *Narratives in Social Science Research*. SAGE.

De Fina, A. (2003). *Identity in Narrative: A Study of Immigrant Discourse*. John Benjamins Publishing Company.

Francis, L.J. (1988). The development of a scale of attitude towards Christianity among 8–16 year olds. *Collected Original Resources in Education, 12*(3), A04.

Francis, L.J. (2009). Psychological type theory and religious and spiritual experiences. In M. de Souza, L. J. Francis, J. O'Higgins-Norman, & D. Scott (Eds.), *International Handbook of Education for Spirituality, Care and Wellbeing*, 125–145. Springer.

Goodson, I.F. & Gill, S.R. (2011). The narrative turn in social research. *Counterpoints, 386*, 17–33.

Goffman, E. (1981). *Forms of talk*. University of Pennsylvania Press.

Gordon, C. (2015). Narratives in family contexts. In A. De Fina & A. Georgakopoulou (Eds.), *The Handbook of Narrative Analysis*, 311–328. John Wiley & Sons,

Halliday, F. (1999). 'Islamophobia' reconsidered. *Ethnic and Racial Studies, 22*(5), 892–902. DOI: 10.1080/014198799329305

Jacobson, J. (1997). Religion and ethnicity: Dual and alternative sources of identity among young British Pakistanis. *Ethnic and Racial Studies, 20*(2), 238–256.

Joseph, J.E. (2004). *Language and Identity: National, Ethnic, Religious*. Palgrave Macmillan.

Labov, W. & Fanshel, D. (1977). *Therapeutic discourse: Psychotherapy as conversation*. Academic Press.

Modood, T. (2003). Muslims and the politics of difference. *Political Quarterly, 74*, 100–115.

Mol, H. (1979). The identity model of religion. *Japanese Journal of Religious Studies, 6*(1), 11–38.

Ochs, E.,& Taylor, C. (1992). Family narrative as political activity. *Discourse & Society, 3*(3), 301–340.

Omoniyi, T. & Fishman, J.A. (Eds.). (2006). *Explorations in the Sociology of Language and Religion, 20*. John Benjamins Publishing Company.

Östberg, S. (2000). Islamic nurture and identity management: The lifeworld of Pakistani children in Norway. British Journal of Religious Education, *22*(2), 91–103. DOI: 10.1080/0141620000220204

Peek, L. (2005). Becoming Muslim: The development of a religious identity. *Sociology of Religion*, 66, 215–242.

Pihlaja, S. (2021). *Talk about Faith: how debate and conversation shape belief*. Cambridge University Press.

Polkinghorne, D. (1988). *Narrative Knowing and the Human Sciences*. SUNY Press.

Rosowsky, A. (2006). The role of liturgical literacy in UK Muslim communities. In T. Omoniyi, & J.A. Fishman (Eds.), *Explorations in the Sociology of Language and Religion*, 309–324. John Benjamins Publishing Company.

Safran, W. (2008). Names, labels, and identities: socio-political contexts and the question of ethnic categorization. *Identities, 15*(4), 437–461. DOI: 10.1080/10702890802201743

Sarbin, T. (Ed.). (1986). *Narrative Psychology: The Storied Nature of Human Conduct*. Praeger.

Seul, J.R. (1999). 'Ours is the way of god': Religion, identity, and intergroup conflict. *Journal of Peace Research, 36*(5), 553–569.

Smith, B. & Sparkes, A.C. (2008). Contrasting perspectives on narrating selves and identities: an invitation to dialogue. *Qualitative Research, 8*(1), 5–3. https://doi.org/10.1177/1468794107085221

Somers, M. (1994) The Narrative Constitution of Identity: A Relational and Network Approach. *Theory and Society, 23*, 635–649.

Tannen, D. (2005). *Conversational style: Analyzing talk among friends.* Oxford University Press.

Zine, J. (2001). Muslim youth in Canadian Schools: Education and the politics of religious identity. *Anthropology & Education Quarterly, 32*(4), 399–423.

24

JEWISH LANGUAGES AND AMERICAN JEWISHNESS

Anastasia Badder and Sharon Avni

Introduction and Background

Across long and complex histories and wide-ranging ethnic affiliations, Jewish communities around the world have spoken languages that were different from their non-Jewish neighbors. The extent to and ways in which these languages were distinct from other local languages has varied, but all can be understood as Jewish languages. There exist several volumes (most recently, Hary & Benor, 2018) that outline the emergence, structural features, and specificities of dozens of historical and some contemporary Jewish languages. This plurality and attention to the details of each language has been critical in furthering our recognition and understanding of Jewish languages and the sociolinguistic fields in which they operate. However, this literature overlooks the ways in which multiple Jewish languages may be deployed in a single social field or region, especially in today's highly diverse and mobile world.

This chapter focuses on one such region—the United States. We argue that American Jews in the twenty-first century look to a range of languages to navigate and make sense of what it means to be Jewish in the modern world. Drawing on languages from Yiddish and its varieties, to Judeo-Spanish, to Modern Hebrew, to Jewish English, this diverse group not only engages languages to do Jewishness, but to define what Jewishness is. Though different in their trajectories, usages, and modes, these Jewish languages serve as key sites and means of boundary-making and identity formation. Unique to the American Jewish experience, language use among Jewish Americans is also a site of creativity and reimaginations of Jewish practice and values.

In many ways, Jewish language practices resemble those of other minority, heritage, and religious language users in the United States; from Muslim adults learning Arabic (Visonà & Plonsky, 2020) to Mandarin language use (Zhang & Slaughter-Defoe, 2009), these diverse religious and cultural groups engage specific linguistic repertoires to delineate boundaries, to define themselves as communities, and connect to other times and places with which they identify. In this way, exploring Jewish languages serves as a template for how individuals and communities look to language for religious expression. At the same time, Jewish languages do not fit neatly into categories like heritage, diaspora, or sacred/religious languages that are traditionally used to define the role of language for a religious group. As American Jews identify themselves (and are recognized by others) as a cultural, ethnic, and religious group, their mobilization of various

DOI: 10.4324/9781003301271-27

languages to express their Jewishness defies essentialized connections between language and identity.

Doing Jewishness with Language in the United States

Yiddish

Yiddish looms large as an ideological, symbolic, and communicative language for American Jews. Dating back to the ninth century, Yiddish emerged as a result of language contact between Jews and Christians in the Rhine Valley in the German region. Scholars identify Yiddish as a "fusion language" made up of Germanic, *lashon hakodesh* (holy tongue, composed of Biblical Hebrew and Aramaic), Judeo-Romance languages, and Slavic components (Harshav, 1990). Over the centuries, Yiddish speakers migrated eastward and southward, cementing its use as a defining feature of Jewish Ashkenazi secular culture across Central and Eastern Europe.

After the Czernowitz Conference in 1908, at which influential Jewish writers, journalists, activists, and intellectuals declared Yiddish as "a national language of the Jewish people," Yiddish asserted its legitimacy through language planning, standardization, and creation of belles-lettres. Consolidating the dominant position of Yiddish and Yiddish culture at the turn of the nineteenth and twentieth centuries, this conference reflected a collective sense that Yiddish was the marker of Jewish vitality, a linguistic unifier among Jews, and an effective weapon against the negative effects of the diaspora, assimilatory forces, and the minority status of the Jews in the host countries in which they lived.

Prior to the annihilation of much of the European Jewish community in the Holocaust, Yiddish served as a Jewish vernacular, with an estimated 11 million speakers, or 75 percent of world Jewry. Post-World War II, restrictive language policies against its use in the former Soviet Union and Israel led many to fear that Yiddish was a dying language with dim prospects for intergenerational vitality. "Yiddishland"—the locus of Yiddish use—moved to North America, as the United States, along with the new state of Israel, became the epicenter of Jewish life (Shandler, 2006a). Since then, with 370,000–500,000 speakers in the US, Yiddish has established roots in American soil and now serves as a form of Jewish practice and identification for disparate American Jewish communities.

The role of Yiddish in the US offers a fascinating case for thinking about the connection between language and religion, as it is used by varying Jewish communities with diametrically opposed orientations and belief systems. For members of Haredi Orthodox Jewish sects characterized by strict adherence to the traditional form of Jewish law and rejection of modern secular culture, Yiddish is the dominant home language and communal vernacular, particularly among men. Using Yiddish is one way in which Haredi members maintain boundaries from the outside, secular world. On the other end of the Yiddish-engaged spectrum are mostly secular Jews (and non-Jewish Yiddish enthusiasts), as well as Jews of other denominational affiliations. For many of these Yiddish users, the language represents a romantic, nostalgic, or sentimental desire to reclaim and return to a Jewishness of bygone days.

For many secular and non-Orthodox Jews, Yiddish exists in "postvernacularity"—a term that Yiddish scholar Jeffrey Shandler uses to captures the linguistic phenomenon in which the "language's secondary, symbolic level of meaning is always privileged over its primary level" (2006a, p. 22). Put differently, for postvernacular speakers, talk *about* Yiddish is as meaningful as talk *in* Yiddish. For this reason, the language is often woven into English interactions and texts with fragmented and isolated words that enable these interactions to signify an affective Jewish connection. Avineri (2014) further claims that the privileging of form over fluency enables these Yiddish users to constitute a "metalinguistic community" in which they can engage in "nostalgia socialization" into an imagined Jewish diasporic community that shares a linguistic past. This engagement ironically positions Yiddish as an endangered language despite its growing use in the Orthodox Jewish world as a home and community language.

For religious, secular, and cultural Jews—and everything in between—Yiddish provides the means of expressing Jewishness in all of its permutations. It is not a static, monolithic code, but rather an idiom that evolves to meet the needs of the Jewish communities engaging with it. In twenty-first-century American society, Yiddish is perceived as cool, hip, and trendy, particularly among the youth, leftists, the queer community, anti-Zionists, and others who see themselves on the fringe of mainstream American Jewish culture (cf. Fox, 2021; Shandler, 2006b). No longer solely associated with the enfeebled Jewish community living in the shtetls of the early twentieth century, Yiddish now includes translated books by popular authors, YouTube channels, podcasts, new Yiddish-language music, a Yiddish Duolingo course, online discussion groups and children's groups, new children's books and videos, a Yiddish meme platform, and Instagram, Facebook, and TikTok pages (Fox, 2021). Though Haredim cling to tradition in the face of modernity, their Yiddish continues to *also* evolve to include dialectical shifts and new calques from Modern Hebrew and English that distance the language from its Eastern European roots.

As a language that signifies Judaism, Jewishness, and diasporic Jewry, Yiddish complicates the traditional conceptualization of a religious language; it serves as a code which Jews and non-Jews use to express secular, cultural, and alternative religious identities. "Perhaps, in the end" as Shandler (2020, p. 188) suggests, "it is better not to speak of the life of Yiddish, but of its lives, as manifest in its multiple names, its geographic migrations, its shifting place within changing constellations of languages, its varied status as a language, and the range and dynamics of how it has been used."

Judeo-Spanish

Judeo-Spanish, a Spanish dialect (Zamora Vicente, 1985) that includes a range of influences from Aramaic, Hebrew, Romance, French, Italian, Turkish, Greek, and Arabic, has had many names across different post-expulsion communities: Ladino, Judezmo, (E)spanyol, Haketía, and more. In this chapter, for consistency, we will use the term 'Judeo-Spanish,' which typically refers to the vernacular as used for non-liturgical purposes (Schwarzwald, 2018). The language emerged amongst Jews in the Iberian Peninsula and spread across the Ottoman Empire and Europe as Jewish communities dispersed following the 1492 expulsion from Spain (Bunis, 2021). In the process, Judeo-Spanish changed, including shifting from Hebrew to Roman orthography, taking on more influences from French and Italian, and losing Turkish and Greek elements. Eventually, the turmoil of the twentieth century led many Sephardic (referring to Jewish individuals and communities who trace their lineage to the Iberian Peninsula region, especially pre-1492) Jewish communities to take up local languages and/or Modern Spanish, resulting in a decline in the use of Ladino texts and spoken Judeo-Spanish. Today, Judeo-Spanish is used by communities in the United States, Israel, France, and the Balkan region, but the number of native speakers continues to decrease and most of those remaining are elderly (Schwarzwald, 2018). Over the past several decades, some historians and linguists have even declared the Judeo-Spanish collectivity to be "dead" (Benbassa & Rodrigue, 2000).

Sephardic Jewish migrants began to arrive in places like South Florida, New York, and Los Angeles in large numbers in the early twentieth century. There, Judeo-Spanish-speaking migrants were confronted with large existing Modern Spanish-speaking communities. Though initially Sephardic migrants were not interested in establishing connections with the existent Spanish-speaking community, physical proximity and linguistic parallels eventually drew them closer together. For example, in New York, many Sephardim 'rekindled' their use of Judeo-Spanish through interacting and doing business with the Puerto Rican community (Harris, 2006). Additionally, as diverse Sephardic populations began to intermingle, those who spoke Judeo-Spanish built relations with those who spoke varieties of Modern Spanish (Kirschen, 2015).

Unfortunately, these interactions were not all positive; Kirschen (2020) found that some Judeo-Spanish-speakers reported being teased by Modern Spanish speakers, including Sephardic relatives, for their strange or 'unrefined' Spanish. Such uncomfortable encounters even led some Judeo-Spanish speakers to question the validity of their language (Harris, 2006).

Further, in the 1900s, many Judeo-Spanish-speaking migrants sought acculturation into American life (Kirschen, 2015). This often entailed making linguistic choices to present themselves as American to be able to participate in American social spheres. Judeo-Spanish speakers found that English provided a clear way to establish their American-ness, Yiddish and Hebrew were the most prevalent and recognized Jewish languages, and Modern Spanish varieties were the primary forms of Spanish in the country. Thus, facilitated by increasing interaction with Spanish and English speakers and the idea that these languages were vital to participation in American life, many Judeo-Spanish speakers chose not to prioritize socializing their children and grandchildren into Judeo-Spanish.

This had lasting effects on the use, linguistic elements, and knowledge of Judeo-Spanish amongst Sephardic communities in the United States. Today, remaining Sephardic communities maintain varying levels of familiarity and comfort with Judeo-Spanish and even those who report feeling competent in the language tend to exhibit significant levels of code-switching between Judeo-Spanish and varieties of Modern Spanish, as well as English (FitzMorris, 2014).

However, in recent decades, there has been a resurgent interest in Judeo-Spanish and Ladino text, song, and liturgy amongst Sephardic Jews. For instance, enabled by the internet, Sephardic individuals and groups from across the world are building online communities oriented around shared linguistic heritage. In virtual venues like *Ladinokomunita*, a popular cyber-community dedicated to the "maintenance, revitalization and standardization of Ladino," posters use Judeo-Spanish to debate the 'right' ways to speak and write the language, cultivate genealogical narratives for the language and its speakers, and construct a far-reaching community of speakers (Brink-Danan, 2011). On other sites, such as a Facebook group that describes itself as "a page for the people who feel passionate about the language, songs, culture, traditions, food and history of Judeo-Spanish communities," those who feel connected to Judeo-Spanish engage in conversations *about* the language, peppered with occasional Judeo-Spanish words and phrases (Brink-Danan, 2011).

Simultaneously, there has been a push for local 'in person' events, organizations, and classes dedicated to celebrating and transmitting Sephardic culture and Judeo-Spanish. For instance, since 2013, the University of Washington has hosted an annual 'Ladino Day,' a public event where scholars of Sephardic Studies and Judeo-Spanish give lectures, musicians and cantors perform, films are screened, and the *Ladineros*, a group of the last native Judeo-Spanish speakers in Seattle, share their stories. Also in Washington, the Sephardic Adventure Camp (SAC) has run an annual summer camp geared towards descendants of Judeo-Spanish speaking immigrants to the United States since the 1940s. The camp is conducted primarily in English, but counselors infuse Judeo-Spanish into their everyday activities. Through these various venues, Sephardic Jews and others with an interest in Judeo-Spanish build linguistic community through talk in and about

Judeo-Spanish, make Judeo-Spanish newly relevant in the contemporary world, and, critically, counter discourses that forecast the death of Judeo-Spanish.

Today, though few native speakers remain, Judeo-Spanish maintains a high symbolic value, as Sephardic Jews come together around narratives about historical Judeo-Spanish-speaking communities, engage in metalinguistic talk about the language, intersperse their speech with specific Judeo-Spanish words or phrases, and push back against narratives and histories that center a particular (Ashkenazic) Jewish experience in America. In this way, Judeo-Spanish indexes identity, resilience, and cultural preservation, linking those who relate to Judeo-Spanish across time and space, (re)constituting Sephardic community, and making up part of the growing push to better acknowledge and understand Jewish diversity in the United States (Kirschen, 2021).

Hebrew

Hebrew has always maintained a significant presence in Judaism and in Jewish life. Encompassing four varieties that represent different time scales throughout Judaism—Biblical, Mishnaic, Medieval, and Modern—the language has evolved due to language contact and the geographic dispersion of its users across the globe. Biblical Hebrew, the lingua sacra, is the language of divine revelation, the immutable language of the Hebrew Bible, and an icon of sacredness. Mishnaic and Medieval Hebrew (or Rabbinic Hebrew) varieties were widely used in the second and third centuries for rabbinic written texts and commentaries (i.e. Talmud). Modern Hebrew was revitalized by Jews of Central and Eastern Europe as a modern language in the late eighteenth and nineteenth centuries as an integral part of the Haskalah (Enlightenment)—an intellectual and social movement which sought a Jewish cultural renewal by promoting secular education and culture. Hebrew was later revernacularized by Zionist ideologues who saw Hebrew as an indispensable component of Jewish nationalism and sovereignty. This diachronic lens underscores the prominent role that it has held in the development of Judaism as a culture and religion across time and space. As each variety of Hebrew is linked to a distinct socio-historical period with specific religious and cultural significance, Hebrew is never far removed from the variable ways in which Jews have chosen to construct and sustain religious, ethnic, cultural, and national identification.

At present, Modern Hebrew is spoken by approximately nine million people in Israel and by approximately two to three million Jews and non-Jews around the world. However, these figures do not include many who may not speak Modern Hebrew but have varying degrees of proficiency in Hebrew literacy. This definitional characteristic is particularly apt for the vast majority of non-Orthodox American Jews, who attend after-school or weekend religious school programs where they learn to decode, recite, and chant sacred texts in order to participate in Jewish rituals, such as the bar/bat mitzvah ceremony (a rite of passage marking the transition between childhood and adulthood) and other synagogue practices (Benor, Avineri & Greninger, 2020). While some of these religious schools may also incorporate some Modern Hebrew, only a small percentage teach Modern Hebrew as a communicative skill. According to the 2013 Pew Center comprehensive study of the contemporary American Jewish community (2013), 52 percent of respondents stated they knew the Hebrew alphabet and could decode; however, only 13 percent said they could understand most or all of the words they could read. Only 10 percent of respondents could carry on a conversation in Hebrew.

Though American Jews have varying levels of literacy in textual Hebrew or communicative competence in Modern Hebrew, they ascribe great value to the language as a marker of Jewish identity. Indeed, many American Jews profess a profound and genuine attachment to Hebrew, and do not see their lack of fluency or an inability to comprehend what they decode as inimical to their desire to claim its ancestral value (Avni, 2012). Rather, American Jews claim Hebrew as an American Jewish language that is untethered to nationality, origin, or citizenship, creating a local variety that articulates American Jewish values (Benor, Krasner, & Avni, 2020).

This shift is seen in recent efforts to create a gender-inclusive form of Hebrew. Like many languages such as Spanish, Hindi, and French, Hebrew is a gendered language. That is, gender is embedded into the morphology of the language, conveyed through masculine or feminine verbs, adjectives, and adverb endings, and almost every other part of speech. For Orit Bershtling, a scholar of transgender identity, the extreme nature of the gendered Hebrew makes Hebrew "one of the most sex-manic languages out there" (Benaim, 2015). We can see American Jews articulating their communal values and priorities through their rejection of the gendered nature of Hebrew. Habonim Dror, a Jewish Socialist-Zionist cultural youth movement recently pioneered a gender-neutral form of Hebrew at its seven North American summer residential camps in 2016 (Zauzmer, 2016). This morphological change entailed changing the gendered suffixes in Hebrew nouns from *im* (plural masculine) and *ot* (plural feminine) to *imot*. As a result, campers were no longer called *chanichim*, but rather *chanichimot.* While the camp leaders hope "to set an example that Hebrew-speakers worldwide might someday follow," (Zauzmer, 2016)—itself an ideological move that challenges the centrifugal force of homeland-diaspora dynamics—their impetus for this linguistic change is connected to reimagining Hebrew according to their local interpretation of Jewish beliefs and values.

Another example of American Jews transforming Hebrew to meet their local conceptions of American Jewish values can be seen at Kehilat Hadar, an independent, egalitarian synagogue located in New York City's Upper West Side. Recognizing that members use gender-neutral pronouns in English, synagogue leadership undertook an extensive process of rethinking the language of the prayers used and issued guidelines for a gender-neutral Hebrew option (along with the traditional masculine and feminine forms) used for ritual synagogal practices. In their words, these efforts were intended to "be an important step towards the goal of making Kehilat Hadar a fully welcoming space to all" (Kehilat Hadar, 2018). Here again, we see a localized form of Hebrew being utilized to represent the progressive perspectives of the congregants.

What these two examples demonstrate is that Hebrew serves as a crucial language for American Judaism in all its manifestations. It is a central language of Jewish canonical texts that has evolved over the millennia and is now used as a vernacular in Israel and for Israelis living abroad. At the same time, it is also a means to articulate local Jewish priorities and positions. In this way, Hebrew serves as a language of boundary-making and identity formation for American Jews. It serves as a locus of tradition and collectivity, on one hand, as well as a site of local creativity and reimaginings of Jewish practice and values, on the other.

Jewish English

Jewish English is a dynamic language variety used by Anglophone Jews around the world. Like other Jewish languages, Jewish English emerged as Jews migrated, moving to new English-dominant areas where they picked up the local language and developed their own distinct variety. Jewish English is incredibly flexible: it can include a great variety of distinctive features, can be made more or less distinctive, can be deployed consciously by speakers based on context or aim, and can index a range of different identities and meanings depending on who is using it and how. Influenced by Yiddish, Hebrew, Aramaic, Jewish ritual, and community life and organization in the United States, Jewish English is a vibrant and increasingly visible Jewish language.

By the 1880s, millions of Jewish migrants began arriving in the United States from Central and Eastern Europe. Many of them were Yiddish speakers. Yiddish thus acted as the "primary substrate" through which Jewish English first developed and continues to play a major role in much Jewish English use today amongst Jews of all backgrounds (Benor, 2016a). With each period of immigration, migrant families formed communities and learned English, often with distinctive influences from their prior languages. Throughout the mid-twentieth century, a period in which American Jews focused on integration, Jewish migrants and their descendants used English with few, if any, distinguishing features (Benor, 2016a). Beginning in the early 1980s, while most Jews continued to speak English, they increasingly drew on distinctively Jewish features, including elements from Biblical and Modern Hebrew, and Yiddish, especially for in-group communication, a practice which continues today (Benor & Cohen, 2011). In its contemporary usage in the United States, Jewish English includes a great variety of distinctive lexical as well as tonal, discursive, and syntactical features, like Yiddish-influenced macro-rhythmic contours (Burdin, 2020), specific 'buzzwords' (Benor, 2016b), loanwords from Biblical and Modern Hebrew, Yiddish, and Yiddish-based grammatical constructions. These elements may be deployed more or less frequently, in varying amounts, and in different combinations, so that the distinctiveness of Jewish English from non-Jewish English operates along a continuum, with some speakers using only a smattering of choice lexical elements, while other speakers may be nearly unintelligible to those without knowledge of these language sources (Benor, 2009).

Interestingly, the linguistic elements of Jewish English are differently recognizable and index different things to American Jews of different religious backgrounds, levels of involvement in Jewish education, and Jewish socialization experiences in childhood and early adulthood (Avineri, 2014)—and to non-Jews. For instance, some Jews report being able to identify other Jews based on a particular rise-fall contour with its roots in Yiddish, while non-Jewish listeners associate that same intonation with Jewishness, Yiddish, and/or New York (Burdin, 2020). Similarly, several studies show that the overlapping argumentative discursive style characteristic of some individuals' Jewish English repertoires is perceived as Jewish, meaningful, and interactive by Jewish listeners, but aggressive, unpleasant, and 'New York-y' by non-Jewish listeners (Schiffrin, 1984). Much of the research on non-Jewish perceptions of Jewish English suggests that non-Jewish listeners link New York, Jewishness, and Jewish speech, or link specific Jewish English features to New York, but not necessarily to Jewish speakers. Burdin (2020) suggests that this could be related to a perceived relationship between New York-ness and Jewishness.

Jewish English can variously distinguish Jewish speakers from non-Jews, or connect Jewish speakers to other Jews, both those immediately present and those far away, both in space and time. For instance, Avineri (2017) describes non-Orthodox Yiddish-language learners in California who, by peppering their English speech with Yiddish and Yiddish-influenced lexical features, build a metalinguistic community. Through their language practices and ideologies, these speakers identify with and discursively and affectively connect to historical, 'authentic' communities, like those of Eastern Europe, and experiences, like that of diaspora (Avineri, 2014).

In other contexts, non-Orthodox Jewish English speakers attending a wide variety of summer camps "infuse" textual and Israeli Hebrew and other linguistic varieties into English to form a variety of English called "camp Hebraized English" (Benor, Krasner & Avni, 2020). While the degree and scope of the infusion varies among the summer programs, each camp deploys Jewish English to the same ends: to support strong Jewish identity development amongst campers and to cultivate a sense of a Jewish world united by language. While campers may not use this specific mode of Jewish English beyond camp, summer camps remain powerful spaces in which young Jews learn to use camp Hebraized English as a central part of feeling and behaving like an American Jew and connecting to other Jews locally at camp and beyond its geographic borders (Benor, Krasner, & Avni, 2020).

Many Orthodox and ultra-Orthodox deploy Jewish English as well, the specific linguistic practices of which are also variously named Hasidic English, Yinglish, or Yeshivish, all of which have different connotations and associations. However, their use of a distinctive English-based repertoire not only connects them to other Jews, but also *distinguishes them from* other Jews. For many Yiddish-speaking Hasidic Jewish communities, for instance, Hasidic English is a much-used Yiddish-inflected Jewish language (Assouline, 2018; Fader, 2009). Within these groups, variations such as more or less Yiddish inflection, are used to index greater or lesser observance, historical trajectories, and communal associations, marking boundaries amongst Jewish communities and traditions.

While all the Jewish languages in this chapter demonstrate the multiple, flexible, and polyvocal potential of Jewish language, it is arguable that Jewish English does so most emphatically. As a linguistic repertoire, Jewish English takes a huge range of forms, draws on a great variety of influences, and is deployed in countless ways, interactions, and contexts to widely various ends. Jewish English and its specific elements intertwine in complex ways with different ideas about religious observance, modes of morality, relationships to imagined pasts, and envisioned futures. Further, Jewish English maintains an osmotic relationship with Standard American English: just as Jewish English in the United States draws from Standard American English, so too have some common lexical elements of Jewish English, words like *klutz* and *schmooze*, made their way into Standard American English usage, where their Jewish language origins may not even be recognized by users (Benor & Cohen, 2011).

Implications and Future Directions

This thorough body of research illustrates that across the United States, Jewish communities engage a wide range of Jewish languages, understood as languages that are more or less distinctive from other languages spoken in the area and/or from other versions of the same language. In many locales, neighboring Jewish communities draw on different Jewish languages and, within a single Jewish community, individuals may deploy multiple Jewish linguistic repertoires. Further, individuals and communities engage these various languages in many ways, including proficiently for communication purposes, via 'ethnolinguistic infusion', and through metalinguistic talk about language.

Despite these multiple and various linguistic repertoires and modes of language use, many speakers deploy Jewish language to similar ends: to connect with other Jews and cultivate community. Their communities have very different textures and shapes, they reach across time and space in different ways, and they are perceived as having different qualities. For instance, the community constructed by Assouline's (2018) Jewish English speakers stretches from the United States to Israel and to a distant, idealized, and morally superior Eastern European past. In contrast, the community built by Benor's (2020) Judeo-Spanish speaking campers draws linkages between present-day Seattle and the far-off Iberian Peninsula as part of the process of constructing clear communal boundaries in the face of highly visible Ashkenazi histories. Yet both, like many Jewish communities across the United States, are working to build community by creating a sense of sharedness, and bridging temporal, spatial, and other gaps through their specific linguistic repertoires.

This simultaneous variation and powerful similarity remind us of the importance of attending to language use in practice and sidestepping debates over the precise definition of Jewish language or 'language variety' vs. dialect. Rather, asking productive questions about how Jews use language, in what contexts, and with what relational, ideological, and material consequences are fruitful directions for dismantling essentialist beliefs about language, religion, and identity. Further, that American Jews of different backgrounds have access to and deploy a repertoire of Jewish languages has direct implications for American Jewish identity. Scholarship in linguistic anthropology has amply demonstrated that becoming "a speaker of culture" (Ochs, 2002) entails individuals at various points across their lifespan being socialized through and in the use of communicative practices and language ideologies in the process of learning socially recognized ways of acting, feeling, and knowing of particular social groups (Ochs & Schieffelin, 2009). The wide range of languages American Jews mobilize in the process of signifying and practicing their Jewishness, in both its religious and cultural forms, suggest that becoming a speaker of American Jewishness is not limited to one particular linguistic code or way of speaking.

These new analytic frameworks have direct implications for how Jewish formal and informal educational contexts think and use various languages to educate Jewish youth and adults. Whereas in the past, the focus was strictly on learning decoding skills in Hebrew for liturgical and ritual participation or communicative competence, educators must also consider the ways in which individuals participate in metalinguistic communities in which the affective relationship to a language and talking *about* the language is as valuable as talking *in* the language. This is not to suggest that linguistic mastery is not a worthy pursuit or an achievable educational goal; rather, the idea of Jewish languages as a flexible signifier of different types or ways of being Jewish resonates with many, particularly younger generations of American Jews, who are questioning the pillars that have long defined Jewish beliefs and practices.

We go one step further to include teaching about Jewish languages as a way of centering language in the study of American Jews, their history as an ethnoreligious diasporic group in the US, and the ways in which language informs religious identification. In practice, this means expanding the formal and informal venues in which a range of Jewish languages are taught to Jewish youth and adults. One does not have to be a Sephardic Jew to learn Judeo-Spanish, nor does one have to hail from Eastern Europe to connect with Yiddish. Learning Jewish languages is also a means for less affiliated Jews, or those who have recently discovered Jewish ancestry through DNA tests, to connect with their heritage or Jewish culture, without taking on theological orientations. There are also pedagogical implications for non-Jews, who are active in learning these languages, particularly as they are being used in popular television and movies streaming into American homes. The popularity of streamed movies and television shows, such as *Shtisel*, about a Haredi family in Israel that uses a combination of Yiddish and Hebrew in their family and communal interactions, has led many non-Jews to take an interest in Yiddish, recognizing it as a window into understanding a religious community they have less familiarity with (Ambert Adler, 2021). As cultural products using Jewish languages reach beyond Jewish audiences, these languages move into new cultural spaces including streamed entertainment, websites, and mailing lists, turning them into virtual speech communities—what Sadan (2011) calls cybervernaculars—made up of individuals of varying ages and different religions and speech backgrounds who have access 24/7 to encountering, learning, and practicing Jewish languages.

As to the future direction in the field, there is an increasing interest to document and explore less commonly spoken or studied Jewish languages both abroad and in the US. In New York, for example, the Endangered Language Alliance focuses on Ladino, Juhuri, Bukharian, and Iranian

Jewish languages and there is a new joint initiative between Wikitongues and The Living Tongues to document all endangered Jewish languages. Finally, the Jewish Language Project is a repository of information about Jewish languages. The future in Jewish languages scholarship will also continue to ethnographically explore how Jews mobilize languages to 'do Jewishness' in varying ways within the political, social, and linguistics contexts in which they live (Badder & Avni, Forthcoming; Badder, 2022), and look to contribute to broader conversations in the fields of linguistic anthropology, language policy, sociolinguistics, and bilingual education around issues of language revival, endangerment, maintenance, and shift.

Further Reading

Ramati, I. & Abeliovich, R. (2022). Use this sound: Networked ventriloquism on Yiddish TikTok. *New Media & Society.* https://doi.org/10.1177/14614448221135159

This article is an example of two emerging trends in the research of Jewish languages. It is first and foremost an analysis of the affordances and nature of TikTok as a new media form. In theorizing new media through Yiddish language practices, Ramati and Abeliovich (2022) demonstrate the ability of Jewish language research to engage across disciplines and contribute to ongoing efforts to de-parochialize Jewish language studies. Further, this article offers an example of cutting-edge research into new modes, meanings, and networks emerging through and in Jewish languages shaped by the novel and specific affordances of new digital technologies, such as TikTok.

Benor, S.B. & Spolsky, B. (2020). Changes in the Sociolinguistic Ecology of Jewish Communities. In S. Brunn & R. Kehrein (Eds.), *Handbook of the Changing World Language Map.* Springer. https://doi.org/10.1007/978-3-030-02438-3_9

This chapter offers an analysis of Jewish communities maintaining Yiddish and Ladino for several centuries following migration, and enriching these languages with influences from the local languages in which they were in contact. This chapter applies a language lens to the history of Jewish migration and contributes to discussions about language contact and migration.

Margolis, R. (2021). Forays into a Digital Yiddishland: Secular Yiddish in the Early Stages of the Coronavirus Pandemic. *Contemporary Jewry, 41,* 71–98.

This text illustrates shifts and emerging patterns within Jewish languages and language communities, namely the 'cybervernacular' mode of Yiddish and its users, in the throes of the COVID crisis. In doing so, it invites readers to consider the ways that crisis both forces and affords space for linguistic change and provides a starting point for shifts in Jewish language and language communities in other crises.

Kirschen, B. (2020). Language Socialization and Intergenerational Transmission of Ladino: Three Generations of Speakers in the Twenty-First Century. *Heritage Language Journal, 17*(1), 70–91.

Kirschen's (2021) article zooms in on changes to ideologies, knowledges, and uses of Judeo-Spanish within a single family across three generations. In doing so, his work provides a rare, detailed portrait of Judeo-Spanish transmission practices and powerfully pushes back against the image of Judeo-Spanish as a dying language of little consequence or interest to younger generations.

References

Ambert Adler, R. (2021, April 15). Shtisel: How a TV Show on a Haredi Family has Enthralled Jews and Non-Jews. *Jerusalem Post.* www.jpost.com/israel-news/culture/shtisel-how-a-tv-show-on-a-haredi-family-has-enthralled-jews-and-non-jews-665223

Assouline, D. (2018). English can be Jewish but Hebrew cannot: Code-switching patterns among Yiddish-speaking Hasidic women. *Journal of Jewish Languages, 6,* 43–59

Avineri, N. (2014). Yiddish: A Jewish language in the Diaspora. In T.G. Wiley, J.K. Peyton, D. Christian, S.K. Moore, & N. Liu (Eds.), *Handbook of Heritage, Community, and Native American Languages in the United States: Research, Policy, and Educational Practice,* 263–271. Routledge.

Avineri, N. (2017). Contested stance practices in secular Yiddish metalinguistic community: Negotiating closeness and distance. *Journal of Jewish Languages, 5*(2), 174–199.

Avni, S. (2012). Hebrew as heritage: The work of language in religious and communal continuity. *Linguistics and Education, 23*(3), 323–333.

Badder, A. (2022). 'I just want you to get into the flow of reading': Reframing Hebrew proficiency as an enactment of liberal Jewishness. *Language & Communication, 87*, 221–230.

Badder, A. & Avni, S. (Forthcoming). The successful failure of decoding Hebrew: Reframing literacy in a religious setting. *International Journal of Bilingualism*.

Benbassa, E. & Rodrigue, A. (2000). *Sephardi Jewry: A history of the Judeo-Spanish community, 14th–20th Centuries*. University of California Press.

Benor, S.B. (2020). Ethnolinguistic infusion at Sephardic Adventure Camp. In R. Blake & I. Buchstaller (Eds.), *The Routledge Companion to the Work of John Rickford*, 142–152. Routledge.

Benor, S. B. (2016a). Jewish English. In L. Kahn & A Rubin (Eds.), *Handbook of Jewish Languages*, 130–137. Brill.

Benor, S.B. (2016b). On Jewish languages, names, and distinctiveness. *Jewish Quarterly Review, 106*(4), 440–449.

Benor, S.B. (2009). Do American Jews speak a Jewish language? A model of Jewish linguistic distinctiveness. *Jewish Quarterly Review, 99*(2), 230–269.

Benor, S.B., Avineri, N., & Greninger, N. (2020). *Let's stop calling it 'Hebrew School': Rationales, goals, and practices of Hebrew education in part-time Jewish schools*. Consortium for Applied Studies in Jewish Education. www.casje.org/HebrewEdPartTime

Benor, S.B., Krasner, J., & Avni, S. (2020). *Hebrew infusion: Learning and community at American Jewish summer camps*. Rutgers University Press.

Benor, S.B. & Cohen, S.M. (2011). Talking Jewish: The 'ethnic English' of American Jews. In E. Lederhendler (Ed.), *Ethnicity and Beyond: Theories and Dilemmas of Jewish group Demarcation*, 62–78. Oxford University Press.

Benor, S.B. & Spolsky, B. (2020). Changes in the Sociolinguistic Ecology of Jewish Communities. In Brunn, S. & Kehrein, R. (Eds.). *Handbook of the Changing World Language Map*. Springer. https://doi.org/10.1007/978-3-030-02438-3_9

Brink-Danan, M. (2011). The meaning of Ladino: The semiotics of an online speech community. *Language & Communication, 31*, 107–118.

Benaim, R. (2015). Does the Hebrew language have a gender problem? *Forward*, 9 November.

Ben-Ur, A. (2009). *Sephardic Jews in America: A diasporic history*. New York University Press.

Bunis, D.M. (2021). Judeo-Spanish (Judezmo, Ladino). *Oxford Research Encyclopedias: Linguistics*. https://doi.org/10.1093/acrefore/9780199384655.013.428

Burdin, R.S. (2020). The perception of macro-rhythm in Jewish English intonation. *American Speech, 95*(3), 263–296.

Fader, A. (2009). *Mitzvah girls: Bringing up the next generation of Hasidic women in Brooklyn*. Princeton University Press.

FitzMorris, M.K. (2014). The last generation of native Ladino speakers: Judeo-Spanish and the Sephardic community in Seattle. MA Thesis. University of Washington.

Fox, S. (2021). "The passionate few": Youth and Yiddishism in American Jewish culture, 1964 to Present. *Jewish Social Studies, 26*(3), 1–34.

Harris, T. (2006). The sociolinguistic situation of Judeo-Spanish in the 20th century in the United States and Israel. *Revista Internacional de Lingüística Iberoamericana, 4*(2),115–133.

Hary, B. & Benor, S.B. (2018). *Languages in Jewish Communities, Past and Present*. De Gruyter.

Harshav, B. (1990). *The meaning of Yiddish*. University of California Press.

Kehilat, H. (2018). *Kehilat Hadar gender inclusive ritual guidelines*. www.kehilathadar.org/gender-inclusive-ritual-guidelines

Kirschen, B. (2021). Spanish and Ladino in contact in the United States. *Studies in Hispanic and Lusophone Linguistics, 14*(2). https://doi.org/10.1515/shll-2021-2049

Kirschen, B. (2020). Language socialization and intergenerational transmission of Ladino: Three generations of speakers in the twenty-first century. *Heritage Language Journal, 17*(1), 70–90.

Kirschen, B. (2015). Judeo-Spanish as a Jewish language: Linguistic realities and ideologies. In B. Kirschen (Ed.), *Judeo-Spanish and the Making of a Community*, 2–49. Cambridge Scholars Publishing.

Margolis, R. (2021). Forays into a Digital Yiddishland: Secular Yiddish in the Early Stages of the Coronavirus Pandemic. *Contemporary Jewry, 41*, 71–98.

Ochs, E. (2002). Becoming a speaker of culture. In C. Kramsch (Ed.), *Language acquisition and language socialization: Ecological perspectives*, 99–120. Continuum.

Ochs, E. & Schieffelin, B. (2009). Language acquisition and socialization: Three developmental stories and their implications. *Linguistic anthropology: A reader*, *2*, 296–328.

Pew Research Center. (2013). A portrait of Jewish Americans: Findings from a Pew Research Center survey of U.S. Jews. Pew Research Center.

Sadan, T. (2011). Yiddish on the Internet. *Language & Communication*, *31*(2), 99–106.

Schiffrin, D. (1984). Jewish argument as sociability. *Language in Society*, *13*, 311–335. Cambridge University Press.

Schwarzwald, O. (2018). Judeo-Spanish. In B. Hary & S.B. Benor (Eds.), *Languages in Jewish Communities, Past and Present*, 145–184. De Gruyter.

Shandler, J. (2006a). *Adventures in Yiddishland: Postvernacular language and culture*. University of California Press.

Shandler, J. (2006b). Queer Yiddishkeit: Practice and Theory. *Shofar*, *25*(1), 90–113.

Shandler, J. (2020). *Yiddish: Biography of a language*. Oxford University Press.

Zamora Vincente, A. (1985). *Dialectología española*. Gredos.

Zauzmer, J. (2016). A camp tries to reinvent the Hebrew language, so transgender kids can fit in. *The Washington Post*. www.washingtonpost.com/news/acts-of-faith/wp/2016/08/11/what-does-a-gender-neutral-kid-call-themself-in-a-gendered-language/

Zhang, D. & Slaughter-Defoe, D. F. (2009). Language attitudes and heritage language maintenance among Chinese immigrant families in the USA. Language, *Culture and Curriculum*, *22*(2), 77–93.

25
MULTILANGUAGING IN INTERRELIGIOUS ENCOUNTERS

Linda Sauer Bredvik

Introduction and Background

In rapidly pluralizing societies, the role of religion is frequently questioned. Even if religion is deemed relevant, the focus is often on the challenges of talking with people who hold differing worldviews, challenges that are compounded by differing (and often unequal) distribution of linguistic resources and repertoires. This chapter will examine the role of mutilanguaging in intercultural and interreligious encounters where participants have a plethora of linguistic repertoires, but the dialogues and encounters are expected to take place in specific named and bounded languages. In today's superdiverse world, interreligious dialogues (broadly understood) are often seen as one means to contribute to the social cohesion of pluralizing societies in spaces and places where people who orient around religion differently may interact as equals. Frequently, however, participants must interact in a language for which they may not have full competencies. How do interlocutors use their varying linguistic resources to create and index a communicatively (in)effective encounter? (Using an ethnographic lens based on participant interviews, a communicatively effective dialogue is marked by non-contentious understanding, lack of a desire to change/convert others, all participants are heard and understood on their own terms, and each leaves with a better understanding of other worldviews). In what ways does unequal distribution of linguistic resources influence dialogue outcome? And how might some multilingual practices be masking systemic prejudice and privilege while perpetuating patterns of exclusion?

Multilanguaging is a speaker's use of the resources in their individual linguistic repertoire to create meaning in the moment with other interlocutors who may or may not share the same repertoires or the same degree of resources. It is an ongoing dialogical process between speakers and their language practices which falls on a continuum between fixed and fluid in ways that are highly context dependent. It is also descriptive of the linguistic attitudes of the speakers themselves, who view it as a quotidian occurrence.

This understanding of language as something that is active and co-constructed by speakers in the interaction began in the mid -twentieth century as a reaction against generativism. Languaging, as a verb, began to gain traction in 1988, when A.L. Becker borrowed the term from neurobiology in order to orient the study of language away from an understanding of language as a simple system of structures, independent of human actions, to languaging as a way of seeing "something

DOI: 10.4324/9781003301271-28

that is being done and reshaped constantly" (Becker, 1988, p. 25). As sociolinguists and linguistic ethnographers (across a spectrum of applied linguistics) began focusing on how multilingual speakers actually language in an increasingly diverse and pluralistic world, they began to move away from previous conceptualizations of how languages were used—speech communities and, later, communities of practice, for example. Instead, research began to focus on the individual speaker and their linguistic repertoire—the individual's collective resources that they can deploy at a specific point in time and space. These resources may be those of the speaker's L1 but they are often (or at least include) what Blommaert (2010, p. 12) frequently refers to as "truncated multi-lingualism," bits and pieces of language(s) that speakers stumble upon or strive to acquire over their own life trajectory.

From a Western, industrialized perspective, children acquire normative competency in one (per-haps two) spoken or signed language(s) at home. This is what linguists refer to when discussing a speaker's L1, or heritage language, and what is often expected when we say someone is "fluent" in a language or a "native speaker." Speakers acquire, in a linear fashion, the age-appropriate gram-matical and semantic skills in the standard variety of one named, bounded language. And yet in most spaces, *multilingualism* is the unmarked norm, particularly in Africa and Asia where children acquire multiple languages interdependently. Makalela (2019) calls this "ubuntu translanguaging;" children grow up speaking as many as six languages in contact zones where "it is inconceivable to use notions such as mother tongue or first language because in reality these do not exist from the **ubuntu** locus of multilingual development" (p. 240).

Yet speakers who have a traditional L1 "learn" a second (and a third) language. With mobility and the internet, people pick up pieces of songs and expressions from colleagues and friends. Even supposedly monolingual speakers will switch between varieties and registers of the same "language," for example from dialect to standard German or from street slang to British Received Pronunciation. What one sees in these cases are differential fluencies in and commands over various languages. Speakers use features or resources from whatever languages that they may "know" and then "blend them into hugely complex linguistic and semiotic forms" (Blommaert, 2016, p. 247). "These creative multilingual practices can cross what once were seen as imperme-able borders of languages, cultures, and nation-states" (Sauer Bredvik, 2020, p. 21) and represent a view of language "as a social resource without clear boundaries, which places the speaker at the heart of the interaction" (Creese & Blackledge, 2015, p. 21).

What has resulted from this more nuanced understanding of multilinguality is a poststructur-alist view that sees languaging as:

- a series of social practices and actions,
- embedded in web of social and cognitive relations, and
- a contested space constantly re-appropriated by actual language users with an emphasis on the agency of the speakers.

Several "languaging" terms have emerged in academic discourse space in the past two decades to highlight different aspects of people's multilingual practices and theoretical approaches to them—superdiversity (see Blommaert, 2016, 2013; Rampton, 2017, 2016), translanguaging (see Garcia, 2018; Blackledge & Creese, 2015; Li, 2018), polylingualism (see Jørgensen, 2016), metrolingualism (see Pennycook & Otsuji, 2015), and code-meshing (see Canagarajah, 2011). Of these terms and approaches, translanguaging has gained the most traction as first a descriptive label and, more recently, as a "practical theory of language" (Li, 2018, p. 10). It is the English translation of the Welsh *trawsieithu*, which Welsh educator Cen Williams used to define use of one language for input (teacher speaking Welsh) and another for output (students answering in English). Garcia's seminal research (2009, p. 45) calls it: "multiple discursive practices in which bilinguals engage in order to make sense of their bilingual worlds." In this sense, it continues to be highly relevant in second-language acquisition and EFL pedagogy.

The perspective has since been widened beyond the classroom to offer "a way of analyzing how the complex practices of speakers live between different societal and semiotic contexts" (Creese & Blackledge, 2015, p. 23). It does not deny the existence of named languages but seeks to transcend them, recognizing that they are "historically, politically, and ideologically defined entities" (Li, 2018, p. 27) that do not reflect multilinguals' language use in everyday life. Translanguaging puts the emphasis on the *trans*—the idea that meaning is beyond language (or even languaging) (Garcia, 2018, p. 4). As with metrolingualism, translanguaging typically focuses on settings where speakers, while having multi-layered competencies in various codes, still tend to be drawing from a co-negotiated set of repertoires and resources which are confined to a geographic space or a reoccurring group. (cf. Li's studies of New Chinglish and Singaporean Chinese, 2018; cf. Pennycook and Otsuji's studies in Sydney's marketplaces, 2015).

Multilanguaging shifts the focus from *trans* to *multi*, looking more closely at how speakers use multiple linguistic codes and resources in settings where local languaging practices have not been negotiated or where outside constraints (e.g., the use of a specific language) are imposed on an interaction. It is a lens through which to understand how multilingual speakers create meaning in one-off or intermittent settings. In these types of encounters, the pool of linguistic resources that interlocutors bring to the conversation frequently changes with each encounter, and the dialogue space must be re-appropriated by the language users in that encounter. In this vein, the interreligious dialogues investigated in this study frequently echo Wodak et al's (2012) extensive fieldwork inside European Union (EU) institutions where multilingual practices are co-determined by "specific contextual cues as well as on structural constraints" (p. 159). A wide range of conversations and interactions between people who orient around religion differently might be classified as interreligious dialogues, e.g., a casual conversation between work colleagues or parents at daycare, a scholarly debate, or a planning meeting for organized community activism. King (2011) defines an interreligious dialogue as "an intentional encounter and interaction among members of different religions *as* members of different religions" (p. 103). In this sense, I use dialogue and encounter interchangeably in this chapter. "Faith practices" or "worldviews" is used to indicate an individual's set of beliefs about the fundamental nature of Reality or God.

My research was multi-sited and focused on voluntary encounters and dialogues that were specifically organized to give participants a better understanding of the beliefs and perspectives of those who orient around religion differently. Within that broad framework, the groups I studied had a variety of goals and purposes with diverse institutional structures. Most were existing groups who allowed me to observe and record their ongoing encounters for varying lengths of time including: a Spiritual Reasoning group in the UK that had been meeting weekly for two years, participants in a British multifaith center's regular workshops and training seminars, an international association of intercultural and interreligious spiritual caregivers that meets annually for professional and spiritual enrichment, and a citywide network of representatives from various faith communities that has been meeting monthly for over a decade to raise awareness of the diversity of faith and culture in their city. The latter two are the main focus of this chapter and part of my continuing research. Participants' ongoing engagement in these two groups contributes to a sense of community and friendship. Relationships are sustained and negotiated, in part, by participants' multilingual practices. Two other groups met over a period of several months specifically for my earlier research.

While the topics of a meeting or workshop were not always necessarily "religious" (e.g., life after death, who or what is Jesus or Mohammed), interlocutors intentionally joined the discussion from the position of their specific faith practice or worldview. Some participants are vocationally religious—pastors, imams, rabbis—while others incorporate their faith practice into their job, such as spiritual counselors and chaplains. The dialogues I focused on are voluntary; participation is not part of the interlocutor's job requirements or duties (although some conferences where I collected data are beneficial to participants' work or education). Conversations might progress from an everyday topic—what instruments parents' children played—to the role of music in the worship of differing faith practices. But the "common denominator in all these forms of interreligious engagement is a mutual respect and openness to the possibility of learning from the other" (Cornille, 2013, p. xii) while maintaining their individual religious identities.

As noted, this research does not focus on either scholarly debate or institutional religious discourses—sermons, catechisms, or studies of sacred texts—but people meeting in places and spaces where their lived religious identities intersect. These are the everyday interactions that are "harder to track and trace," as Pihlaja (2021, p. 1) notes, but they are also those that are essential for understanding how people realize and implement their faith practices in contrast to their neighbors or co-workers who orient around religion differently.

I approach these dialogues as an ethnographer and interactional sociolinguist, relying heavily on Gumperz's work (2003, 1982) in Interactional Sociolinguistics as developed further by linguistic ethnographers like Rampton (2016, 2017) and Blommaert (2016, 2013). It is an approach to discourse analysis that "seeks as rich a dataset of naturally occurring interaction as it can get" (Rampton, 2017, p. 1). Multi-sited ethnography is one way of doing that. By collecting data from multivariate research sites (both temporal and spatial), I am better able to demonstrate how talk is constitutive of a specific social activity—in this case, interreligious encounters—and gain a more nuanced understanding of what speakers are indexing and inferring when they talk about differing worldviews while using varying linguistic repertoires. This approach investigates, rather than assumes, contexts for communication, knowing that meaning takes shape within specific places and activities that are "produced and construed by embodied agents with expectations and repertoires that have to be grasped ethnographically" (Blommaert & Rampton, 2016, pp. 33–34). Discourse "comes about when all the components of the system interact with one another, along with the time and space in which they occur" (Pihlaja, 2021, p. 3).

Many of these components are what Gumperz (2003, 1982) calls contextualization cues. They are non-verbal, prosodic, and pragmatic cues that index (point to) contextual or social phenomena outside an utterance and help achieve coherence by integrating these domains or meanings into the discourse while concurrently changing the process of the discourse (Sauer Bredvik, 2020, p. 32). At other times, these cues can also refer to the utterance itself, allowing the hearer to infer what the speaker intended. To identify these contextualization cues, as well as other multilingual practices, and determine how they might be affecting dialogue outcome, I observed encounters across a range of sites. Once the most relevant research sites were identified, I began audiovisual recording dialogues while continuing to take field notes. The recordings were then transcribed and analyzed both quantitatively and qualitatively. Depending on those findings, I conducted selected semi-structured interviews with the participants. What emerges is a very multi-layered view of participants' linguistic practices. It is very context dependent and occurs across a continuum of multilingual practices. Not all multilingual practices occur in all settings, so what follows is a cumulative case study taken from 55 hours of dialogue recordings and 11 hours of interviews.

Meaning-Making and Hospitality through Multilanguaging

The encounters I studied were representative of the multiplicity of cultures, languages, and faith practices and worldviews present in an increasingly secularized Western European context. Participants in these conversations identified with nine different faith practices or worldviews and reported 20+ L1s/home languages (resources from 11 languages occur in the recorded data). While almost all the interlocutors are multilingual, interviews showed they still maintain traditional concepts of named languages and grammar. What is relevant is that the speakers are educated—most with at least a master's degree—in Western-model educational institutions that perpetuate this understanding of language(s). At the same time, they invariably multilanguage (often subconsciously). At least one university professor emeritus, a most staunch defender of "proper" language use, freely mixes resources from three "languages" in one sentence.

How to code the multiplicity of linguistic resources for analyzation remained problematic. As noted when I began my initial research project (Sauer Bredvik, 2020), languaging theories look at the complexity of individual speaker's multilingual resources rather than named and bounded languages. But "the analysis of the features must involve if and how the features are associated with one or more 'languages' (Jørgensen et al., 2016, p. 139) if one is to gain a clearer understanding of the ways meaning is being co-created when speakers have differing linguistic repertoires. Eventually, a decision was made that the L1 for each dialogue was the predominant code and every occurrence of a switch from that code to any other (including the speaker's L1) was annotated as an L2, regardless of the number or truncated nature of the words in the second language. Note all participants have been anonymized and assigned pseudonyms designed to reflect their cultural and religious identities.

This multiplicity of linguistic resources and competencies in co-occurrence with diverse religious identities provides a unique opportunity to understand how speakers use language to index and negotiate their faith practices in conversation with others who orient around religion differently. The recorded data demonstrates that multilanguaging has several functions and forms. From a languaging perspective, speakers' use of their multilingual resources enables them to negotiate a code for the conversation, to co-construct shared meaning, to express and live out their individual religious identity, or to signal a change of interpersonal relations. At the same time, multilanguaging enables multifaith speakers to display linguistic hospitality. In the dialogues, as well as in the interviews, participants spoke of wanting to display respect and hospitality for those who believe differently. Many of these multilingual practices allow the interlocutors to infer that desire through a speaker's use of their shared linguistic resources.

Negotiating a Conversational Code

Each of these conversations took place within the parameters of an interreligious encounter. Each had a specific time, place, and purpose for the participants to join the dialogue and it was generally understood that there would be a specific "language" used to carry on the conversation. However, given the multilinguality of speakers in this data, the use of different "languages" was continually being negotiated. At times, language was assumed based on the prevailing resources of the group's participants or the physical location of the conversation (e.g., country or institution). It is often structural; the international spiritual caregivers association officially uses both English and German for all their seminars and publications. But even within these structural confines, language use can be explicitly negotiated at the beginning of the conversation, as demonstrated in the follow example.

A conversation between four chaplains began in German with "Sollen wir auf deutsche unterhalten oder auf englisch? Oder Mischmasch?" (*Shall we use German or English for our discussion? Or a Mischmasch?*) One participant (Abdul) is a Pakistani Muslim, born in Germany, whose L1 is Urdu and who is extremely uncertain of his English skills and strongly prefers German. One participant (Dirk) is a former Dutch military chaplain who was stationed in Germany, worked closely with British troops, and is equally comfortable in either English or German as an L2. The third participant (Peter) is German but has lived in the US for over 20 years where he teaches chaplaincy in a hospital setting, and he frequently switches to English for professional conversations. The fourth (Felix) works in a German care home and, like Abdul, prefers German. While the initial consensus is for German, what occurs is a multilanguaging *Mischmasch*. Abdul and then Peter use German but Peter frequently intersperses English words or phrases for professional aspects of his work (*chaplain, small group, chapel*). Dirk introduces himself and his work entirely in English, to which Abdul answers in German, followed by Felix, after which the conversation remains largely in German.

Even when the code for an individual conversation was not negotiated, the presence and impact of multiple languages on conversations was sometimes directly addressed. The caregivers' association often viewed their multilinguality as a hindrance to group dynamics and interactions. Aline, a long-time board member, referencing an earlier presentation of my research results to the stakeholders, noted that intentionally engaging the group's multilinguality was a way "to create community and contribute to intercultural understanding. Languages divide us but they bring us together. It is a chance to practice graciousness" (unpublished field notes, 21 October 2018).

These negotiations and discourses demonstrate the more fixed elements of multilanguaging. The ever-changing pool of linguistic resources, coupled with the structural constraints of more organized dialogues, requires interlocutors to re-appropriate the dialogue space with each encounter.

Co-constructing Shared Meaning

As just shown, one of the primary foci of multilanguaging is on how speakers use multiple linguistic codes to construct shared meaning in settings where they have not previously been negotiated (such as urban London schoolyards [Rampton 2006]), where use of a specific language is imposed or negotiated on an interaction (above), or where the pool of linguistic resources frequently fluctuates due the changing nature of the location or participants in an encounter. Not all the resources of a group are always available and languaging involves not only the speaker drawing from their own repertoire to communicate but also "involves shuttling between the languages brought by the other to co-construct meaning" (Canagarajah, 2011, 5), something that can demonstrate the more fluid aspects of multilanguaging.

An example of this occurred in a small group conversation during a caregivers' conference. Participants, mostly Christian, were asked to explain what their faith means to them personally and not just professionally. One French Alsatian Christian with more extensive French and German resources expressed his frustration at what he felt was an inability to express something so important to him in English. The Syrian Muslim moderator speaks Arabic, German and English but, to the surprise of those in the group who knew her, urges him to "say it in French" and, after some negotiation, he does. (See transcription conventions at the end of the chapter for all excerpts.)

Excerpt 1

1. Pierre: Uh . it would @be @ @ better t-_to say this in_in French uh @but uh @ @≅
2. Akilah: ≅S-_s-_sa-_say it_say it in_in_[in French.] Say it in French.
3. Pierre: <L2=FRENCH> c'est pour moi c'est une combinaison entre la la croix et la résurrection… dans la mesure ou la croix euh …montre bien que la souffrance euh la pei–la misère la peine fait partie de la vie. (*That is, for me, that is a combination of the the cross and the resurrection . in the measure or the cross uh shows well that suffering the misery and the pain are a part of life*)

He continued in French and when he finishes, Akilah says:

4. Akilah: <L2=FRENCH> merci beaucoup je suis tres [heureux …parce] que j'ai compris le la majorite … </L2> (*Thank you very much. I'm happy that I understood the majority.*)

Akilah here demonstrates Canagarajah's point that meaning making involves "shuttling" between the resources that are available at that particular moment in a conversation. Akilah was a participant in multiple dialogues across several research sites and **frequently** multilanguaged, using resources from Arabic (her L1) and German (her professional language), as well as English. However, until this encounter, she had no other interlocutor with whom she could co-construct meaning using her French resources, hence the group's surprise.

In other dialogue settings, participants are more aware of the group's pool of resources and meaning is co-constructed as the conversation evolves. The (predominantly) English encounter in Excerpt 2.2 occurred during a workshop at a caregivers' conference where almost all the participants were long-time members and aware of their collective linguistic resources—primarily Dutch and German.

Excerpt 2

1. Lise: <L2=DUTCH>… Wat zij segt? (*… what she says?*)
2. Jop: Of er neg andere … dergelije gebeden zijn (*whether there are other … of such prayers*)
3. Johanna: <L2=GERMAN> diese Art des Gebets ist sehr besonders gewesen, also sonst uh. uh nicht üblich gewesen unter den christlichen . </L2> (*this kind of prayer was very special so otherwise not so common among Christian …*)
4. Jop: <L2=GERMAN> ja, doch. um .
    Johanna: wait <L2=GERMAN> # # in der Christliche Tradition gibt es … die_ die Benennung von Gott eh mit viel Namen? </L2> (*in the Christian tradition, God is referred to by many names?*)

Johanna, an L1 German speaker, was one of the few participants who was new to the association and struggling to express herself in English, which resulted in the preceding multilingual exchange. Lise and Jop are L1 Dutch speakers who have been a part of the association for several years, and Lise (who does not always trust her own English) utilizes their shared resources to try to clarify what Johanna had just asked in English. Johanna seems to understand and responds in German, rather than English or Dutch.

In other conversations, there is deliberate translation, sometimes professionally and sometimes ad hoc among group members. This frequently results in some very fluid co-constructions of meaning. In one English workshop, for example, Beate (an L1 German speaker) was the designated moderator. After a few minutes in English, a few older L1 German participants asked her to translate a phrase and, after completing the translation, Beate continued in German. At this point, a British woman who has lived in Germany for 50 years seamlessly stepped in and began translating back into English.

As conversations moved online due to the 2020 COVID pandemic, I began observing and recording existing groups to determine how, or if, their linguistic practices changed in the digital environment. Observation of the recordings showed that multilanguaging practices essentially ceased. The caregivers' group, which previously displayed the most prolific and multifaceted multilanguaging practices, switched to either monolingual English or German conversations and divided the Zoom rooms accordingly. In a limited number of instances, a code was negotiated at the start of a breakout room, like the previous in-person examples, but the choice of language was then closely observed and lacked any spontaneous multilanguaging that is emblematic of their in-person seminars.

This again parallels Wodak et al. (2012), who note the different layers of multilingual practices and language choices in an organizational setting. The caregivers' association, while loosely organized and whose members are often long-time friends, is still an "official" association for the "practice, education and research" of intercultural and interfaith care and counseling (their website). Unable to duplicate the informal, spontaneous small group discussions that occurred in person, the organization prioritized the stated educational and research aspects of their association in conducting online seminars during the pandemic. The result was "discursive practices" that followed "particular genre-inherent sets of rules" (Wodak et al., p. 160), that is, the normative give-and-take of an online professional dialogue conducted in a lingua franca setting.

The exception to a lack of online multilanguaging was one discussion of the intercity forum. Again, this is a loosely organized association that works to build interfaith awareness and cooperation with voluntary and governmental organizations in their community. Unable to host community events or advocate politically, the group continued meeting online once a month simply to maintain their interpersonal relationships. This, in contrast to the caregivers' association, prioritized the informal, rather than the formal, aspects of their interactions, and resulted in a multilingual exchange that created a site of narrative overlap; Hill Fletcher (2007, p. 548) describes these as places in our everyday lives where the "multiplicity of our stories" intersect and allow for points of communication in spite of complex religious differences. A Bahá'í participant excused himself early for his Irish lessons, which everyone seemed to be aware he was taking. A Jewish woman cheerfully asked if he had made progress in learning Irish during the pandemic, and he responded with a few words in Irish that several others in the group seemed to understand. He then noted he also spoke a "bit of Hebrew," and a lively back-and-forth ensued between the two of them and the Catholic priest in both Hebrew and English.

Metaphorical Code-Switching

Gumperz's (1982, p. 61) concept of metaphorical code-switching is frequently contested since code-switching is still seen as being too essentialist, implying that speakers have separate, discrete languages with completely grammatical competencies in all. However, speakers in these encounters did use language—often language varieties such as Arabic, Hebrew and Sanskrit that are associated with a specific faith practice—in ways meant to communicate "metaphoric information about how they intend their words to be understood;" that is, their use of a religious language worked metaphorically to draw on the social and religious associations these varieties have (Parkin, 2016). Thus I take what Hall and Nilip (2015, p. 615) call a "holistic understanding of code-switching as social practice," a juxtaposition of *features* associated with different codes that are seen in terms of all possible varieties of a "named" language (Sauer Bredvik, 2020, p. 24).

One example of this comes from a lunchtime conversation between two Christians—one Palestinian (Amir) and one Argentinian/American (John)—a British rabbi (Eli), and Akilah (Syrian Muslim). The conversation centered around an earlier lecture where the professor was talking about the concept of "sacred," which Akilah was struggling to understand both from the perspective of Islam and in English. Amir, also an L1 Arabic speaker, was trying to explain it in Arabic to Akilah, and the rabbi asked him to repeat the word. Note Akilah's use of both Arabic and German resources (the latter of which she shares only with the researcher):

Excerpt 3

1.	Eli:	In Arabic?
2.	Amir:	<L2=ARABIC> muquaddas (*holy*)
3.	Akilah:	Eh, there is [₁there is nothing in] Islam [₂as as sacred] or <L2= GERMAN> heilig. </L2> (*holy*). No! Just_just God!
4.	Eli:	[₁What is the word?]
5.	Amir:	: [₂ muqaddas </L2>]
6.	Akilah:	<L2=ARABIC> SubuuH-un *qudūs rab almalaa'ikati warruH </L2> (*sacred god, the god of angels and souls*)
7.		It's *just* God!

Later, the conversation continues between the rabbi and Akilah, and the rabbi uses Hebrew to clarify what Akilah has just said in Arabic:

8.	Akilah:	[But this is_this] is a attribute that just came in the Qur'an . for God. For Al*lah.* [<L2=ARABIC> SubuuH-un qudūs: rab almalaa'ikati warruH </L2> That's all.] (*sacred god, the god of angels and souls*)
9.	Eli:	[Only God is <L2=HEBREW> Kadosh. </L2> Yeah. . Yeah.] (holy)

In attempting to come to a shared understanding of the concept, the participants are using their shared resources, as well as noting the similarities between the two Semitic languages. Throughout the longer conversation, Akilah was conversing back and forth in Arabic with Amir to ask for clarification of the Christian understanding of "holy" and "sacred" while also appealing to his knowledge of their shared culture in the Levant region to corroborate her point that only Allah is holy. The rabbi asks Amir, as someone familiar with both Judaism and Hebrew, if the Arabic and the Hebrew term have a similar meaning. At the same time, the ways that they use their linguistic resources also index their differing religious identities as Christian, Jew, and Muslim.

In many other conversations, Jewish and Muslim participants would use words from their own "religious language" that their conversation partners did not understand (and then offer an English or German clarification) because "the practice and the language are so closely intertwined that use of any other linguistic resources is too difficult or seems insufficient to the speaker" (Sauer Bredvik, 2020, p. 13). Abigail, a young Jewish student, explained (interview 2018):

> It may be self-conscious but I think I sort of reflect on what it actually **is**, what it means [to use specific Hebrew words.] If you only use English terms, of course you can translate … but maybe these words are common in English and they're used in many different contexts. Of course many of them can be used by Muslims or by Bahá'í to describe their religious concepts. I think it's more distinct to say: 'Okay. That's the concept **I have** and of course yours may be similar' but I think it's to really make a distinction, to say: 'it's not just any word you would use.'

An example of this is taken from a conversation where Abigail is clarifying Jewish mourning rituals in which one prays for "your seven closest relatives" upon death every day for 11 months before transitioning to "normal life" in the twelfth month:

Excerpt 4

| 1. | Abigail: | you um (1.051) you have (1.25) uh three prayers every day and they all begin with <L2=HEBREW> Kaddish </L2> and then you should say <L2=HEBREW> Kaddish </L2> for (1.034) your beloved ones. But uh . well in fact it doesn't always work because <L2=HEBREW> Kaddish </L2> is a prayer you can only say if you've got a <L2=HEBREW> minyan </L2> (*quorum of 10 Jewish adults*) |

In other instances, interlocutors would use words or scriptures from their conversation partner's faith practice as a way to seek sites of narrative overlap, places where their practices and identities might converge. Amir, for example, quoted excerpts from the Qur'an (in Arabic) in conversations with Akilah. "If it's not patronizing, it is a way to connect with people, to start a conversation" (Emre, Muslim scholar, interview, June 2021).

> When people use my language—'inshallah' or 'Allah'—it's not like they are converting but they are relating to me. When people use your language, it gives that kind of hospitable feeling.
>
> (Arzu, Muslim psychologist, interview, May 2021)

Less frequently, speakers used shared religious linguistic resources to delineate differences and to pinpoint points of debate between differing faith practices. In one conversation, three of the four participants share a subcontinental Indian background and some linguistic competencies in Sanskrit and Tamil. One participant is Hindu (Raji) and two (Gordon and Alfred) are Protestant

Christian pastors. The conversation became factious at multiple points, particularly in relation to the caste system and Gordon's perception of institutionalized Hindu support for it. His use of linguistic resources associated with Hinduism infers that he has an understanding of the faith practice and wants to demonstrate the aspects he disagrees with. Note Gordon's use of German, as well as Sanskrit.

Excerpt 5

1.	Gordon:	<L2=SANSKRIT> Brahmā Paramātma, nuh? (*the universal that stems from self-sacrifices of primordial man)*
2.		ātma para[mātma] ≅ </L2>
3.	Alfred:	<L2=SANSKRIT> [ātma paramātma] </L2>
4.	Rahi:	≅Yes.
5.	Gordon:	And but then how can we wa-_have this contradiction between the: <L2= SANSKRIT> Bra-_Brahmin </L2> (*head*) soul <L2=GERMAN> und auch </L2> (*and also*) the <L2=SANSKRIT> śūd-_śūdra </L2> (*soles of the feet, or lowest caste*) soul or #not. #Un-_Untouchable
6.	Raji:	The s_soul itself . is not <L2=SANSKRIT> Brahmin </L2> [or <L2= SANSKRIT> śūdra </L2>] or man or woman≅

Multilanguaging must clearly be understood as an agentive act; as Gumperz (2003, p. 221) points out: "Codes-switching … serves as a communicative strategy to achieve specific interpretive effects," in this case, drawing boundaries between "my" religion and "your" religion. Throughout the conversation from which Excerpt 5 was taken, the Christian speakers were using their shared resources in Sanskrit and Tamil to query Raji about his position, as a Hindu, on topics they found problematic, specifically the caste system and the Hindu understanding of monotheism. While the conversation was not hostile or completely inhospitable, it was adversarial at times. Other speakers (Akilah, Abigail, Eli) most often used resources from a language associated with their own faith practice to create a hospitable space for discussion, but speakers in this conversation used resources from the other's faith practice, which created borders. The following examples demonstrate another agentive facet of code-switching: speakers with the same L1 (German) choose opposing linguistic resources to index their interpersonal, rather than religious, relationships.

One regular participant in the caregivers' conferences (Claudia) often makes statements that are seen as insensitive or completely inappropriate. She is an L1 German speaker who is comfortable using English but, at times, struggles for specific English words. At a conference focusing on spiritual care for migrants and immigrants at the height of the 2016 European refugee crisis, she spoke of *die schweigende Mehrheit* (the silent majority), a politically loaded term used pejoratively in conversations about immigration in German-speaking countries. The use of German resources in combination with what was seen as a very poor choice of words from various historical and political contexts was provocative at best and inflammatory at worst. Field notes (and later analysis of the transcript) focused on not only the overall group reaction, but also the interaction that followed. Christiane, another L1 German speaker who had demonstrated a clear preference for German throughout the conference, began rebutting Claudia's comments in English. Christiane refused to use their shared L1, even when Claudia attempted to answer her in German, instead using English to distance herself personally from Claudia.

An online interaction in 2021 demonstrated the same pattern. Claudia was in a workshop about gender diversity and sensitivity being led by Israel, a binary Jewish convert who is completing their certification as a spiritual caregiver. Israel was sharing the details of an emotionally distressing interaction as a counselor with a patient in the hospital who was anti-Semitic in his comments and antagonistic in his reaction to Israel's binary gender. In the group discussion that followed Israel's presentation, Claudia began her comments (in English) with:

Excerpt 6

1.   Claudia: I will not uh pardon the patient's anti-semitism but I will try also to um to take his position …

Claudia continued at length, referencing the generation of the patient (a Baby Boomer), his feeling of suffering and confusion over Israel's name and (perhaps) appearance, as well as the fact that the patient was not "an academic" and that Israel, as "the professional" was in a better position to respond. Claudia's comments were seen as inappropriate and, again, a fellow L1 German speaker responded. Gabi, unlike Christiane in the earlier conversation, is quite comfortable in English and prefers to use it during the conferences. Immediately prior to this excerpt, she talked extensively in English about reactions and feelings she shared with Israel. But in this setting, like Christiane, she refuses to identify personally or culturally with Claudia by using the same linguistic resources. Instead, she uses metaphorical code-switching to create difference and distance at a level of inter-personal interaction.

2.   Gabi: <L2=German> ich sagt zuerst auf deutsch. Es gibt ein Unterschied zwischen "verstehen" und "Verständnis." Verstehen bedeutet: ich kann die Situation nachvollziehen aber ich habe kein Verständnis für Verhalten. </L2> (*I'm going to say it first in German. There is a difference between comprehension and agreement/empathy*)

Linguistic Hospitality

Ricœur posited the concept of "linguistic hospitality" in *On Translation* (2006), arguing that translation means both welcoming another language into one's own while also exiling oneself to inhabit the other's language in order to understand them. He went on to suggest that this type of mediation between identity and strangeness could also serve as a model for interactions with other religions (pp. 23–24). Participants' multilanguaging practices in these dialogues, while serving other functions, also functioned to co-create hospitable encounters.

The exchange in French between Akilah and Pierre (Excerpt 1) allowed them to co-create meaning from their shared pool of resources but it also enabled Pierre to express something very close to his heart in a code he felt more comfortable using. The earlier Irish and Hebrew exchange in the intercity forum created a space where their multilingual resources forged a friendly bond of understanding. Speakers also sought sites of narrative overlap when they used linguistic resources from another's faith practice or used their own religious language to demonstrate a meaningful aspect of their beliefs—Amir's use of a verse from the Qur'an, for example. Two Jewish rabbis used Hebrew resources in multiple conversations to show how specific Jewish concepts and beliefs are relevant to universal calls for human justice and environmental care.

Discussion

What emerges from the data is a multi-layered continuum of multilanguaging practices. Speakers are drawing on their linguistic resources in creative ways that make sense "under specific social circumstances" (Jørgensen, 2016, p. 142). The genre of the encounters (voluntary but organized multilingual interreligious dialogues), the need for a lingua franca, and a dynamic pool of linguistic resources influenced speakers' linguistic practices. Given these parameters, there is more fixidity in these conversations than in more casual interactions in schoolyards and marketplaces. At the same time, fixidity and fluidity are not dichotomous but, rather "symbiotically (re)constitute each other, a dynamic emergency in the form of a spiral as people move between fixed and fluid understandings and uses of language and identity" (Pennycook & Otsuiji, 2015, p. 111). One could see more fluidity in the ad hoc translations of a workshop or online interactions between friends in the intercity forum or during coffee breaks at the caregivers' conferences.

While the use of a lingua franca is acknowledged, speakers still negotiate, sometimes explicitly and sometimes implicitly, within those boundaries to find the most productive ways of co-creating meaning. Data also demonstrate how multilanguaging, in an interreligious encounter, works metaphorically. Speakers join these conversations with the goal of gaining an understanding of other faith practices and how those worldviews affect the adherent's assumptions about the topic of discussion. Nevertheless, participants also maintain their own religious identity while they interact. Using languages typically associated with specific faith practices is one means to establish their own identity while recognizing their interlocutors' differing worldviews.

Multilanguaging can also work to signal interpersonal relations and how the speaker wants those to be understood, particularly when questions of shared identity could be inferred based on a shared linguistic code. This use of multilanguaging also points to speakers' conscious desire to display respect and hospitality, particularly toward those who orient around religion differently. Overall, this quantitative analysis of qualitative data provides a more nuanced understanding of encounters between people who want to understand one another's differing worldviews but who often do not share a common cultural background nor first language.

Implications and Future Directions

Organized interreligious dialogues, as noted earlier, are increasingly viewed as a means to create social cohesion in rapidly pluralizing societies, particularly in Western Europe. Moreover, from an Interreligious Studies perspective, they are seen as a way to create and increase understanding and respect. Research models based on hospitality (Moyaert, 2019, 2018; Sauer Bredvik, 2020) demonstrate these dialogical spaces do enable, in many ways, a more peaceful interreligious coexistence. Continuing research and observations show, however, that some multilingual practices can also be masking systemic prejudice and privilege while perpetuating patterns of exclusion.

Participants have frequently observed that, while necessary, the choice of a dialogue code (e.g., English as a lingua franca) immediately privileges some while preventing others from participating fully in the conversation. Moreover, the worldview of those determining dialogue agendas (even informal ones) influences the topics and how they are framed for discussion. During COVID, when dialogues were forced online, one could observe that a Eurocentric view of the world affected actual scheduling of the meetings, i.e., at times convenient for those in Western Europe but at the periphery of the day for participants in Indonesia and India. Lastly, observation is also showing that societal assumptions about what constitutes "good" religion—apolitical, personal, and private—versus "bad"—exterior and group-oriented—religion (Moyaert, 2018, p. 3) often perpetuate inequality through unseen language practices.

Talk is incomplete—speakers do not explicitly convey everything they mean through spoken or signed language—and creating meaning is a multi-faceted process in which one can detect interlocutor's assumptions and biases through their linguistic practices. As noted earlier, speakers index and infer meaning through cues that are often non-verbal or non-denotative and which rely on a listener's (assumed) shared understanding of the context surrounding a conversation—culture, religion, and gender. When that background knowledge is not shared—or one viewpoint is privileged—the dialogue outcome can be ineffectual or even hostile. One such example occurred between long-time colleagues—one German Protestant and one Turkish Muslim—who were discussing various aspects of chaplaincy and spiritual caregiving. The conversation was clearly frustrating both participants until the German realized he had been relying on his cultural and religious understanding of spiritual caregiving which was not shared (or understood) by his Muslim colleague.

My work approaches these conversations as happening *in medias ras*—participants are speaking from their own embedded and embodied identities while assuming a dialogical space of reciprocity. The challenge with this equalizing tendency is that it can downplay the reality that some participants in a conversation deviate more strongly from the group norm (Moyaert 2019)—be it linguistic or their specific worldview—and that these prejudices are then reflected in use of contextualization cues. If, for example, the encounter takes place in a Global North setting where private, apolitical religion is considered the norm, the words of participants from a faith background that is embodied and visible are often not judged to be as credible. Moyaert (2019, p. 8) uses an example from her classroom in which two liberal Protestant females challenge a young female Muslim who is both a feminist and wears a hijab. They continue to argue from the privileged Dutch viewpoint—a historically Christian culture that now values pluralism—that "good" religion is apolitical and private. Thus, an exterior sign of a person's faith—a hijab—is "bad" or "oppressive" religion and she does not fit their understanding of a feminist.

A more nuanced understanding of the role of multilanguaging in interreligious encounters can be gained by employing a more *critical* ethnographic analysis to interreligious dialogue research. This is not to dispute the strengths of a model of hospitality but a call to identify how it overlooks structural and societal power imbalances and prejudice. Assuming equality and equity does not always make it so. To do this, future research needs to first identify the dominant sociocultural norms in the places and spaces where dialogues are happening. These will clearly differ based on the structure of the dialogue, i.e., which faith practice or worldview tends to be setting the agenda, what language(s) are chosen for the dialogues and how they are chosen, and how does the dominant group in that setting view the role of religion. This can be done initially through observation and in-depth interviews with dialogue participants. Based on that information, an in-depth analysis of dialogue transcripts can identify how multilanguaging practices are indexing and inferring not only the individual speaker's stance toward the dialogue and dialogue partners, but also structural and societal stances toward diverse worldviews.

As demonstrated by the preceding examples, speakers' willingness to draw on various pools of shared—and sometimes unshared—linguistic resources frequently enabled them to co-create meaning in ways that demonstrated respect and linguistic hospitality. Multilanguaging is a way for people who orient around religion differently to gain an understanding of other faith practices and the ways in which those worldviews affect the lived identities of neighbors and co-workers. But, as can be seen in Excerpt 5, shared languages can also be used to draw boundaries and borders between "us" and "them" rather than create a space of equality. Multilanguaging can also reveal unspoken societal prejudices about linguistic, as well as religious, practices. Two different interview participants, both professors with PhDs, noted that their "non-standard" English (one is Cuban American and one is subcontinental Indian) had often marked them as "uneducated" or even mistaken for being cleaning staff.

Taking this more critical approach to interreligious encounters will allow researchers, as well as dialogue participants and practitioners, to identify and better understand how multilanguaging practices are influencing dialogue outcome in ways that can also contribute to better socio-political debates surrounding religious diversity in society.

Transcription Conventions

(based on DT2, University of California, Santa Barbara, DuBois et al, 2014)

General

.	final contour
?	appeal final contour
,	continuing contour
?,	continuing appeal
#	unintelligible, one symbol per syllable
#word	uncertain word
..	short pause, untimed, < one second
(1.023)	timed pause > one second
wor-	truncated word
_	linking, no break
:	lag, prosodic lengthening
<L2=CODE>	start of code switch
</L2>	conclusion of code switch
"	rush start, anacrusis
[words]	overlap, marked for each speaker
≅	latching
&	discontinuous IU, used only when 2nd speaker intervenes
* *	stress on enclosed word or syllable

Arabic Transliteration

7	ح
3	ع

Further Reading

Arnaut, K., Blommaert, J., Rampton, B., & Spotti, M. (Eds.). (2016). *Language and superdiversity*. Routledge.

A synthesis of the current sociolinguistic research around superdiversity with a focus on complexity, rather than plurality.

Moyaert, M. (2019). Interreligious Hermeneutics, Prejudice, and the Problem of Testimonial Injustice. *Religious Education*, 1–10.

An overview of how research from an Interreligious Studies perspective can move beyond the hospitality model to recognize how hospitality can also mask systemic prejudice and privilege while perpetuating patterns of exclusion.

Pihlaja, S. (Ed.). (2021). *Analysing religious discourse*. Cambridge University Press.

An overview of contemporary research on religious discourse from a variety of theoretical and methodological perspectives.

Rampton, B. (Ed.). (2022). *Linguistic Practice in Changing Conditions.* Multilingual Matters.

A collection of essays that traces the development of sociolinguistic and linguistic ethnography as an approach to understanding social change through the prism of everyday communicative practices.

Sauer Bredvik, L. (2020). *Discussing the Faith: Multilingual and metalinguistic conversations about religion.* De Gruyter.

A more explicit treatment of the contextualization cues mentioned above that affect the creation and outcome of interreligious encounters, including the roles of silence, disfluency, and pragmatic markers.

References

Arnaut, K., Blommaert, J., Rampton, B., & Spotti, M., (Eds.). (2016). *Language and superdiversity.* Routledge.

Becker, A. (1988) Language in particular: A lecture. In D. Tannen (Ed.), *Linguistics in Context*, 17–35.

Blommaert, J. (2016). From mobility to complexity in sociolinguistic theory and method. In N. Coupland (Ed.), *Sociolinguistics: theoretical debates*, 242–259. Cambridge University Press.

Blommaert, J. (2013). *Ethnography. superdiversity and linguistic landscapes: Chronicles of complexity.* Multilingual Matters.

Blommaert, J. (2010) *The sociolinguistics of globalization.* Cambridge University Press.

Blommaert, J. & Rampton, B. (2016). Language and superdiversity. In K. Arnaut, J. Blommaert, B. Rampton, & M. Spotti, (Eds.), *Language and Superdiversity*, 21–48. Routledge.

Canagarajah, S. (2011). Translanguaging in the classroom: Emerging issues for research and pedagogy. *Applied Linguistics Review*, 2(1), 1–28.

Cornille, C. (Ed.). (2013). *The Wiley-Blackwell companion to inter-religious dialogue.* Wiley-Blackwell.

Creese, A. & Blackledge, A. (2015). Translanguaging and identity in educational settings. *Annual review of applied linguistics*, 35, 20–35.

DuBois, J.W. (2014). *Representing discourse* (working manuscript). Linguistics Department, University of California, SB.

Fletcher, J. H. (2007). As long as we wonder: Possibilities in the impossibility of interreligious dialogue. *Theological Studies*, 68(3), 531–554.

García, O. (2018). The multiplicities of multilingual interaction. *International Journal of Bilingual Education and Bilingualism*, 21(7), 881–891.

Gumperz, J.J. (1982). *Discourse strategies.* Cambridge University Press .

Gumperz, J.J. (2003) Interactional Sociolinguistics: A personal perspective. In D. Schiffrin, D. Tannen, & H.E. Hamilton, (Eds.), *The Handbook of Discourse Analysis*, 215–227. Blackwell Reference Online.

Hall, K. & Nilep, C. (2015) Code-switching, identity, and globalization. In D. Schiffrin, D. Tannen, & H.E. Hamilton, (Eds.), *The Handbook of Discourse Analysis*, 597–619. Wiley & Sons.

Jørgensen, J.N., Karrebœk, M., & Møller, J.S. (2016). Polylanguaging in superdiversity. In K. Arnaut, J. Blommaert, B. Rampton, & M. Spotti, (Eds.), *Language and Superdiversity*, 137–154. Routledge.

King, Sallie B. (2011). Interreligious Dialogue. In C. Meister (Ed.), *The Oxford Handbook of Religious Diversity,* 103–114. Oxford University Press.

Li, Wei. (2018). Translanguaging as a practical theory of language. *Applied linguistics*, 39(1), 9–30.

Makalela, L. (2019). Uncovering the universals of ubuntu translanguaging in classroom discourses. *Classroom Discourse*, 10(3–4), 237–251.

Moyaert, M. (2018). Inter-worldview education and the re-production of good religion. *Education Sciences,* 8(156), 1–15.

Moyaert, M. (2019). Interreligious hermeneutics, prejudice, and the problem of testimonial injustice. *Religious Education, 114*(5), 609–623.

Parkin, D. (2016). From multilingual classification to translingual ontology: A turning point. In K. Arnaut, J. Blommaert, B. Rampton, & M. Spotti, (Eds.), *Language and Superdiversity*, 71–88. Routledge.

Pennycook, A. & Otsuji, E. (2015). *Metrolingualism: Language in the City.* Routledge.

Pihlaja, S. (2021). *Talk about faith: How debate and conversation shape belief.* Cambridge University Press.

Rampton, B. (2017). Interactional Sociolinguistics. *Tilburg Papers in Culture Studies*, Paper 175, 1–14.

Rampton, B. (2016). Drilling down to the grain in superdiversity. In K. Arnaut, J. Blommaert, B. Rampton, & M. Spotti, (Eds.), *Language and Superdiversity*, 91–109. Routledge.

Rampton, B. (2006). *Language in Late Modernity: Interaction in an urban school.* Cambridge University Press.

Ricœur, P. (2006). *On Translation.* Routledge.

Sauer Bredvik, L. (2020). *Discussing the faith: Multilingual and metalinguistic conversations about religion.* De Gruyter.

Wodak, R., Krzyżanowski, M., & Forchtner, B. (2012). The interplay of language ideologies and contextual cues in multilingual interactions: Language choice and code-switching in European Union institutions. *Language in Society, 41*(2), 157–186.

26

RITUAL LANGUAGE, RITUAL COMMUNITY

Manel Herat

Introduction and Background

Buddhism in Sri Lanka has a wide variety of sects. Buddhists in Sri Lanka practise "Theravada Buddhism", which translates as "the perspective of the elders" (Tilakaratne, 2012, p. xxiii). The senior Buddhist monks are the elders. Since the Buddha's initial teachings were recorded in Sri Lanka in the first century CE, Sinhala Buddhists feel that their practice is the most closely aligned with these teachings (Williams & Tribe, 2000). They are referred to as the Tripitaka, or "three baskets", and were written in Pali. The *Vinaya Pitaka,* which contains the rules for monastic life, the *Sutta Pitaka*, which contains the Buddha's teachings, and the *Abhidamma Pitaka*, which consists of supplementary philosophy and religious teaching. Since these books have not been altered since they were recorded, Sri Lankan Buddhists believe it is crucial to memorise certain portions of these scriptures so that they can be utilised in Buddhist ceremonies (Williams & Tribe, 2000, p. 31). Crosby (2003) writes that the main characteristics of Theravada Buddhism consist of the use of Pali as a sacred language and the recognition of the Pali scriptures as the highest textual authority, and the prominent role given to celibate monkhood that follow a unique monastic code (*vinaya*).

The languages of Buddhism utilised by the Sri Lankan Buddhist community are mainly Pali and Sinhala, and to a lesser extent, English. Pali is the sacred language of Buddhism and the language of the Buddhist scriptures. Sinhala is the language of the Sinhala people in Sri Lanka, which is an Indo-Aryan language, believed to have originated in North India. It is a diglossic language, with distinct spoken and written forms (Gair, 1968, 1998). While the written form is more formal and archaic, the spoken variety includes both formal spoken Sinhala and colloquial Sinhala used in everyday discourse (Gair, 1998, p. 216).

The origin and development of Sinhala culture and literature is considered by scholars to have commenced with the arrival of Buddhism in Sri Lanka. The influence of Buddhism on the development of Sinhala "for creative and aesthetic purposes" is described by Ludowyke (1956, p. 91). This is corroborated by de Silva (1981), who sees Buddhism as the main catalyst for literary output among the ancient Sinhalese. He further notes that many languages, especially Pali, the liturgical language of Buddhism, and Sanskrit, the ancient literary language and the sacred language of Hinduism, had a significant impact on Sinhala (de Silva, 1981). Consequently, the

DOI: 10.4324/9781003301271-29

Sinhala language consists of a huge number of equivalent forms from both Sanskrit and Pali, for example, *nirvana* (Sanskrit), *nibbana* (Pali), *karma* (Sanskrit), and *kamma* (Pali). The word stock in Sinhala demonstrates the language's substantial Pali and Sanskrit lexical impact, particularly after Buddhism was introduced to Sri Lanka. Senaratne (2008) writes that all Sri Lankans at all socioeconomic levels speak the spoken variety of Sinhala, which is an amalgamation of Pali, Sanskrit, Tamil, and former colonial languages, such as Portuguese, Dutch, and English, which have contributed vocabulary to the word stock of Sinhala.

Samarin (1976) observes that religious communities are linguistically distinct and that it is fascinating to 'reveal' the particular ways in which they use language for rituals. Du Bois (1986) identified the following linguistic forms as being characteristic of the language of religious rituals:

- use of a ritual register
- archaistic elements
- elements borrowed from other languages
- euphemism and metaphor
- semantic opacity
- semantic-grammatical parallelism
- marked voice quality
- stylized and restricted intonation contours
- unusual fluency of speech
- gestalt knowledge
- personal volition disclaimers
- avoidance of first and second person pronouns
- speech style attributed to ancestors
- use of mediating speaker

(Du Bois, 1986 cited by Keane, 2003, p. 437)

Keane (2003, p. 437) observes that these characteristics are interdependent and that following Wittgenstein (1953) must be understood in terms of "'family resemblances' to the extent that they do not constitute necessary and sufficient conditions for membership in a set but instead group together in connected clusters such that no one family member must have every characteristic". Du Bois' (1986) list can be divided into performance and textual features. Features which relate to performance include marked voiced quality, unusual fluency of speech, stylised and restricted intonation contours, gestalt knowledge (learning whole texts rather than parts), and personal volition disclaimers (crediting a traditional source for one's words). The performance aspect of ritual language reinforces the textual elements such as the use of a ritual register (different lexical item for the same word in ritual and colloquial language), archaic language, borrowed words from other languages, euphemism and metaphor, semantic opaqueness, and semantic and grammatical parallelism (see Keane, 1997; 2003). Likewise, Thompson (2003), who has also examined the prevalence and linguistic characteristics of religious language, highlights the existence of a particular use of language to express or describe religious experiences, practices, or beliefs.

Feuchtwang (2010, p. 282) on the other hand, identifies rituals broadly as a "prescribed sequence of verbal and nonverbal acts", having a highly formalized and predictable communication mode. This is corroborated by Lu and Shurma (2021), who emphasise the importance of the use of formulaic language associated with the practice of some traditionally regulated and symbolic behaviours. They reiterate how both religious and non-religious rituals permeate our daily lives, illustrating the importance of ritual language within communities.

As followers of Theravada Buddhism, Sri Lankan Buddhists see their use of ritual language as fostering their religious convictions, moral principles, and charitable deeds, which are an important component of the *Sutta Pitaka*, the long discourses of the Buddha's teachings. De Barry (1972) specifically mentions how the Pali Canon's *Sigalovada Sutta* urges every devotee to uphold family traditions, to honour their ancestry, and to make offerings to the deceased. Although in Buddhism rituals can be performed during any occasion such as a birthday or a full moon day *(poya)*, the most common occasion where chanting (reciting *gatha*), ritual, and preaching occurs together is during a funeral.

Buddhist funeral rituals involve a combination of chanting, preaching, and ritual activity, where the Buddhist monks play a central role (Langer, 2009). Buddhist devotees invite monks to chant in the house on the days leading up to and after the funeral to conduct the rituals. Unlike many other religious traditions, Buddhists typically hold multiple services during the mourning period: preaching on the sixth day, offering *dana* (alms/food) on the seventh day, offering *dana* after three months, and at yearly ceremonies of remembrance. These rituals are conducted according to a certain sequence: on the sixth day one monk is invited to preach, on the seventh day several monks are offered food (usually lunch), then they give a short sermon after which they recite *bana* for transfer of merit to the deceased and to the gods that offer protection (Langer, 2009; Gombrich, 1988). The data discussed in this chapter are the funeral rituals used on the sixth day and the sermon given at this preaching event. As Gombrich (1988, p. 125) notes, "death is the perfect occasion for preaching on impermanence and the inevitability of suffering". He further states that the transfer of merit is especially important in Theravada practice. This is because the purpose of the rituals is to transform people's lives by persuading them to engage in good deeds. The merits from these good deeds are then seen as being transferred to the deceased, the family, relatives, friends, and the gods.

Although, as Langer (2009) observes, chanting, preaching, and ritual cannot be separated as all are equally important, this chapter will primarily focus on preaching, as that is where language plays a pivotal role together with chanting, as the rituals also involve nonverbal aspects and the use of artefacts such as a tray with betel leaves, ornamental elephant tusks, an alarm clock, a jug of water, and a bowl. The language used by monks for chanting is Pali, the sacred language of Buddhism, but the language used for preaching (giving sermons) in Sri Lanka is Sinhala interspersed with mainly Pali words and quotations as well as Sanskrit and occasionally English words. Sri Lankan Buddhists refer to preaching as *bana* or *dharma deshana*. Deegalle claims that the word *bana* refers to "devotional activities of giving Buddhist sermons" (2006, p. 182) However, this is debated by other Buddhist scholars (Kent, 2008) who disagree with him. Kent (2008, p. 79) states that "sermons share properties with performance utterances; statements with meaning extending beyond the information contained in the language". He disagrees with Deegalle that Buddhist sermons are simply about doctrinal content, which de-emphasises performance aspects and argues that *bana* is "shaped by a dialectic between performance and content" (2008, p. 82).

According to Deegalle (2006), *bana* encompasses elements of "public speaking" as well as "religious instruction" and is a method through which Buddhist philosophy is disseminated among the community, especially during the performance of rituals. However, this is not altogether accurate, as during the occasion described, the *bana* appeared to be used as a means of providing comfort to the family and giving them solace rather than merely disseminating knowledge of Buddhism, although there was a didactic element in the sermon. Some of the content for the preaching used by Buddhists monks is drawn from *banapoth* (preaching texts) that are either in Pali or in Sinhala and consist of Buddha's teachings often referred to as *jathaka* stories. These texts are interspersed in the sermon and discussed in order to actively engage listeners with Buddha's teachings.

A noticeable feature is that the entirety of the sermon is structured with no written notes. In order to elaborate certain points, the priest will draw on Buddha's teachings or *jataka* stories or use analogies or metaphors. According to Janowitz (1989), the words of some Jewish mystical texts are identical to those sung by angels, so the human reciting them joins the angelic chorus. In Buddhist rituals too, *Buddha vachana* (Buddha's words) or the use of words from sacred texts blur the distinction between the original words and the context or the person employing them.

Funeral Rituals on the Sixth Day After a Death

The language discussed in this chapter comes from the rituals performed during a sixth-day mourning ceremony. The people are seated reverently on the floor with their hands together in prayer and heads bowed and are mostly wearing white clothes with one or two people wearing light colours. The ceremony begins with the priest formally requesting permission (*avasara* in Sinhala) to speak from the Sangha (*maha sangarathnayangen avasarayi*). The priest then greets the audience and formally addresses the assembly as *pinvathuni* (meritorious devotees) and refers to the deceased as *swaminwahansa* (priest—formal).

In Sri Lanka, Buddhist monks are especially revered and special lexis is used for talking about activities associated with Buddhist monks, such as coming in (*vadinawa*), eating (*valadinawa*), sleeping (*sethapenawa*), and dying (*apawath wenawa*) (see Herat, 2015). Likewise, as seen here, the Buddhist monks also use different lexical items for the same word when addressing the audience than would be used in ordinary conversation such as referring to the assembly as *meritorious devotees* and the deceased as *swaminwahansa* rather than *hamuduruwo* and using other words not used in normal Sinhala discourse; for instance, in Sinhala, the word for gods is *deva* but the priest uses the word *brahma;* similarly, instead of *avasanaya (cessation),* the word *niruddha* is used and for *maranaya* (death), the word used is *viyova*.

After that the priest starts chanting some well-known Pali stanzas shown in Extract 1. Every sermon starts with Pali *gatha* and these stanzas can be seen as Pali formulae that are used to create a connection between the audience and the Buddha's teachings.

Extract 1

Anicca vata sankhara, uppadavayadhammino.
Uppajjitva nirujjhanti tesam vupasamo sukho.

(Impermanent alas are formations, subject to rise and fall.
Having arisen, they cease; their subsiding is bliss.)
(Kariyawasam, 1996, Chapter 2)

The words in the Pali stanzas, as seen from the translation, have no connection that relate them specifically to an offering; the only connection is the ritual itself. As Langer notes (2013), the stanza is so well known and distinctive that it immediately draws comparisons between the current event and previous funerals one may have attended. Once the chanting is completed, the deceased's family offers what is referred to as *pansakula;* this is the offering of *mathaka vastra* (new robes) to the priests. The people in the audience touch the offering with both hands before it is offered to the priest. After the *pansakula* is offered, the immediate family of the deceased are instructed by the priest to begin the ritual of pouring water into a cup that is on a plate till it overflows. Kariyawasam (1996) mentions that the purpose of this ritual is to transfer merit from the living to the dead as "a kind of *dakkhina* or offering". While pouring the water, the following Pali stanzas (*gatha*) in Extract 2 are chanted.

Extract 2

> Unname udakam vattam yatha ninnam pavattati
> evameva ito dinnam petanam upakappati.
> Yatha varivaha pura paripurenti sagaram
> evameva ito dinnam petanam upakappati.
>
> (Just as the water fallen on high ground flows to a lower level, what is given from here accrues to the departed. Just as the full flowing rivers fill the ocean, what is given from here accrues to the departed.)
>
> (Kariyawasam, 1996, Chapter 2)

Here, the language of these two stanzas suggests a connection between the transfer of merit and the pouring of water with reference to bodies of water such as the flowing river filling the ocean. During the water-pouring ritual, the immediate family are gathered close together around the water jug and touch it as the water is being poured. The touching of the offering and the water jug are regarded as a symbolic blessing.

The priest concludes the ritual by summarising the meritorious acts performed in memory of the deceased since their death (keeping *bodhi puja*, inviting the sangha to say *bana*, the offering made to the *sangha*), and drawing attention to the meritorious nature of the event. Then at the end he chants verses that bestow blessings on those assembled. Up to this point, the occasion is mostly to do with performing the ritual and chanting rather than preaching. The language used is mostly Pali. People's behaviour also indicates familiarity with the ritual and the chanting, as people join in the chanting and are attentive to the priest's instructions (for example, *sadhu, sadhu, sadhu kiyanna* [*say*], *...kiyala prarthana karanna* [*make this wish*]*...den pin anumodan karanna* [offer merit]. The audience responds with "*sadhu, sadhu, sadhu*" in acknowledgment to the priest's directive.

Kent (2008, p.124) notes that the term *sadhu* serves "a similar function to the Christian term 'amen,' and is the stock response given by listeners to the words of a preacher". The use of explicit "stage instructions" (Langer, 2013, p. 87) is an interesting aspect of the ritual. Langer (2013, p. 87) notes that these instructions are not a "concession to outsiders" but a part of the proceedings and that they make Buddhist rituals easy to follow without any awkwardness. Once the blessing is concluded, the audience is instructed to remain seated and contemplate for a few minutes before the commencement of the sermon.

As the priest is not using any written notes throughout the sermon, this can be seen as unusual fluency of speech, particularly as the preaching has a structure and the thematic focus is not lost throughout the sermon. This could be because the theme is familiar even if the sermon is not the same on every occasion. As memorisation of scripture is central to monastic education; oral recitation comes naturally for most Buddhist monks. One of the ways in which the unusual fluency of speech is demonstrated is through the large number of rhetorical questions and trigger responses used throughout the sermon. These question-answer adjacency pairs are highly effective as they enable the priest to maintain the topic of the sermon. The priest uses the strategy of question-answer pairs on 68 occasions, as in Extract 3:

Extract 3

What makes the consciousness turn good? Good qualities.

In this way, the priest not only organises his own thoughts but also gets the audience to think about the content of the sermon. The priest is able to influence the audience's hearts through this question-answer style of storytelling and instruct them on what to think. Simply put, the priest's words extend agency to the listeners to transform themselves by providing inspirational doctrine which enables contemplation and introspection. In other instances, he uses his voice in a rhythmic manner as well as lengthening the vowel sounds of certain words at the end of an utterance to affect the audience. This can be compared to the highly rhythmical and repetitive linguistic patterns used by American folk preachers when "filled with the spirit" (Pitts, 1993 cited in Keane, 2003, p. 442).

Another performance technique that is used is three or four part lists. The use of a three or four part list is a common rhetorical device that is used in public speaking, as it is appealing to the listener and allows the speaker to convey a sense of wholeness and completion. In Extract 4, the interrogative form is used with a conditional in a three-part list to appeal to the hearts and minds of the audience:

Extract 4

If we plant a mango seed, what grows? A mango tree will grow.
If we plant a kohomba seed, what will grow? A kohomba tree will grow.
If we plant a coconut what will grow? A coconut tree will grow.

One of the key aspects of the textual use of language in Buddhist preaching is the use of multiple languages. Once the chanting is completed, the monk begins what is referred to as *mathaka bana*: the preaching of the sermon. The language used for this is Sinhala often interspersed with Pali, Sanskrit, and a few English words (*trip, lead, accident, engine*). The sermon lasts for about one hour and the first part of the sermon centres on the teachings of the Buddha and is a discourse on consciousness and karma, whereas the second half of the sermon is about reinforcing the virtues and good qualities of the deceased and why the family should rejoice in their remembrance of the deceased. The final part of the sermon is transferring merits to the deceased, the deities, the doctors, family members, relatives, and friends (see Extract 5).

Extract 5

Therefore by the power of these merits may you all have the opportunity to follow the path of the Supreme Buddha and achieve happiness and well being. Likewise may all these merits be beneficial for all of us to be free from the woeful samsaric journey and find eternal happiness by realising the true path.

In general, Buddhist sermons tend to capture the attention of the audience through drawing on stories from the *Dhammapada*, which are incorporated into the narrative and contain discourse where the characters in the story speak. The language used in Extract 6, illustrates how the *jathaka* story is used to explain the concept of *karma* and to draw attention to the inevitability of death and the endless consequences of unwholesome actions (*akusala*) such as killing animals.

Extract 6

> There is a *jathaka* story about a Brahmin who wanted to sacrifice a goat to please his god. He summoned his servants and said, "I have bought a goat which I wish to sacrifice to our god. Take the goat to the river and bathe it well." Once the servants bathed the goat and got it on to the shore, the goat began to laugh loudly; then in a moment, it started crying. The servants recognised the different sounds the goat made as it laughed and cried. They went back to the Brahmin and told him what had happened and wanted to know why the goat behaved as it did. The Brahmin ordered the servants to bring the goat before him. Then he asked the goat "why did you laugh?" The goat replied, "I was slaughtered in 499 past lives, and this is the 500th, so I shall be free. That is why I laughed." "Then why did you cry?" he asked. The goat replied, "I cried because I felt sorry for you. Although I shall be finally free from my predicament, by cutting off my head, you shall begin yours. That is why I cried." "No, no, no, I will not slaughter you. I will release you," cried the Brahmin. But the goat said, "It's no use. I can't be freed. This is my last day. My life ends today." "Then I will not sacrifice you. I will set you free."

> The Brahmin informed his men that no one is to touch the goat. So the Brahmin and the servants left taking the goat with them. On the way, the goat halted to eat some grass grown on a rock. With its front legs resting on the rock, the goat began nibbling the grass. Suddenly, at that moment the skies darkened and a stroke of lightning hit the rock. A splinter came off the rock and severed the goat's neck and he died instantly.

> Do you know what karma is? The supreme Buddha explained. 500 lifetimes ago the goat who was released from death had been born a human. He had invited some friends home for a party and he had killed a goat to prepare a feast for his friends. He had killed the goat 500 lifetimes ago. The nature of karma is that it never ceases to follow you until it has borne fruit.

As preaching is used as part of Buddhist ritual, we expect a sermon to contain lexis that is "extremely distinctive" and "archaic" (Crystal & Davy, 1969, p. 165). As in a Christian sermon, we expect several theological terms, which according to Crystal & Davy, 1969, p. 165) "provide the verbal basis for the formulation of a person's belief'. In the Buddhist sermon given by the monk on the sixth day, the archaism that Crystal & Davy (1969) refer to come from the use of ancient languages such as Pali and Sanskrit; however, unlike in Christian sermons, the words that are used can be understood and interpreted by an average person, for example, *karma*. The sermon includes the statement that "our samsaric life is based on the cause and effect phenomenon" and explains that "a doctrine of cause and effect means that when there is a cause there is an effect". The priest uses the words *samsaric journey* 13 times. He also uses words that relate to *karma* such as *chethana* (intention), *kusala* (wholesome), *akusala* (unwholesome). There is also a detailed exposition on how birth and rebirth happen and the word *vingnanaya* (consciousness) is used 70 times and it is explained as a *biijaya* (seed). The word *biijaya* is used 25 times.

Extract 7

> When we died in our past lives our consciousness passed away (*niruddha wenawa*). There are several reasons for consciousness to pass away. Consciousness passes away only if it was in the form of a seed. What is a seed? A seed is something that grows. If consciousness does not exist in the form of a seed, it ceases to exist. Cessation of consciousness is experienced by the Arahants. *Vingnanaya niruddha wenawa* We call this passing away—*nibbana piri niwan peewa*—the end of suffering.

In Extract 7, consciousness is said to pass away if it exists as a seed. The key idea behind conditional sentences is that the main clause's action is only possible if the particular circumstance in the if clause is fulfilled. The use of the conditional here suggests that a certain state can be achieved only if the condition in the if clause is met, for example, if consciousness does not exist, then it ceases to exist. The priest also explains that this state can only be achieved by *arahants*. An *arahant* is someone who has achieved liberation from all sorrow, someone who is worthy. In addition, words which relate to aspects of rebirth, such as *aathma* (lives) *apaya* (hell), *devaloka* (heaven) and *bhutayo* (ghosts) are also used. The performance aspect of the ritual is also reinforced through the lengthening of the final word *peewa* using special intonation in Extract 7.

Another aspect of lexis use is the use of *Buddha vachana* (Buddha's words). In Extract 8, the Buddha's words are quoted in the sacred language Pali when the nature of *arahants* is being described. None of the Pali words quoted are translated into Sinhala, suggesting the authority of the words. As in Janowitz's (1989) work, the use of *Buddha vachana* here obscures the distinction between the original words and the speaker.

Extract 8

> Khinam puranam (old karma was abolished)
> Navam naththi sambhavam (no new karma is created)
> Viratta citta ayatike bhavasmim (there are no attachments that bring about rebirth)
> Te kina biija (they have not the seed of consciousness)
> Avirulhiccanda (craving has been rooted out)
> Nibbhanti dhira (just as an oil lamp blows out the noble ones pass away to nibbana)

Du Bois (1986 cited in Keane, 1997; 2003) notes the avoidance of first- and second-person pronouns in religious language. Keane suggests that in most ritual activity, the speaker is decentred, with limited "volitional agency", so that the words come from some source beyond the present context which may be the reason for the lack of first- and second-person pronouns. This, however, does not appear to be the case here. In the sermon discussed, the first-person plural pronoun *api* (we) is the most frequently used pronoun with 98 occurrences, closely followed by the first-person possessive pronoun *ape* (our), which is used 90 times. The second person pronoun *oba* (formal) 'you' is used 54 times. Whereas we would expect the priest to distance himself from the content of the sermon, the priest uses an inclusive 'we', which includes himself in the theological exposition. This could be because the deceased is also a young monk. Tauzchik and Pennebaker (2010) observe that group cohesion can be improved through the use of 'we' as a marker of interdependence and this may be one of the reasons as to why the monk uses the first-person plural pronoun 'we'. It emphasises the message that death is an inevitable fact of life that is common to all.

Another linguistic feature that appears often is the use of semantic and grammatical parallelism. According to McIntrye (2010, p. 32), parallelism is "unexpected regularity" in the use of language and is a means through which ideas can be foregrounded. The foregrounding effect in parallelism comes about because of the repeated structure. There are a number of examples in the sermon that show semantic and grammatical parallelism.

Extract 9

> Those who are rich in merit are the ones who have the chance to change their fate. The rest have to go on the same journey. This journey is so long that one day 39 monks, who lived in the forest approached the Supreme Buddha. The Supreme Buddha thought "I should show these monks what sort of samsaric journey they had been undertaking." He started preaching.
>
> "Monks, the amount of blood you have shed in your long journey of samsara when you have been born as animals and have been slaughtered is more than the water of the ocean.
>
> "The amount of blood you have shed when you have been born as thieves and being killed is more than the water of the ocean.
>
> "The amount of blood you have shed when you have been born as pigs, cockerels, goats and cows is more than the water of the ocean.
>
> "Therefore each and every one of us had a history of shedding more blood than the water of the ocean."

In relation to the interpretation of parallel structures, Leech (1969, p. 67) explains that every instance of parallelism "sets up a relationship of equivalence between two or more elements: the elements which are singled out by the pattern as equivalent". In Example 9, there is semantic parallelism in the use of animals such as "pigs, cockerels, goats and cows" which refers to the number of times a human may have been born as an animal in a previous life as well as syntactic parallelism in the word combinations (i.e. "the amount of blood you have shed when you have been born" and "more than the water of the ocean"). In addition, as mentioned, the parallel structures have equivalent phonology and syntax and are given in a four-part list, which makes it appear complete and influences the audience—what Samuels (2010) refers to as "attracting the heart" (*hita adaganima*).

Du Bois (1986 cited in Keane, 1997; 2003) suggests euphemism and metaphor are common linguistic features used in religious rituals. In the Buddhist sermon analysed, the more common features are the use of metaphor and analogy rather than euphemism. The difference between the use of metaphor and analogy is subtle. According to cognitive metaphor theory, the use of metaphor is not merely a linguistic element; it is also a fundamental aspect of our conceptual framework and the way we interpret the world (Jeffries and McIntyre, 2010). In cognitive metaphor theory, the way a metaphor is understood is by mapping the source domain onto the target domain. An analogy, on the other hand, compares the degree of resemblance between two items and whether they are similar in ways that are pertinent to the argument being made. Unlike simile or metaphor, which typically focus on one point of resemblance, an analogy draws a comparison between two dissimilar items that have a number of characteristics or points of similarity. In the sermon, both metaphors and analogies are used. Metaphors are used to illustrate how a concept is conceptualised, i.e. life is a journey, whereas analogies are used to explain the concept in more detail, i.e. the journey through *samsara* is an engine that works nonstop. By using analogies, a concept that is unknown is explained through a concept that is known.

In Extract 10, the priest talks about *karma* as a travelling companion taking consciousness from place to place, indicating that life is conceptualised as a journey that is going from one place to another.

Extract 10

Karma is the force that takes the consciousness from place to place.

Like Lu and Shurma's work (2021), this metaphor is used because death is a painful experience to demonstrate that death is not the end and that a person's actions determine their life. The use of the term *samsaric* journey (*samsara gamana*) is used 13 times during the sermon, reinforcing the LIFE IS A JOURNEY metaphor.

The linguistic features described in this chapter, give a flavour of the preaching through the use of examples. The way language is used by the priest illustrates that in performing the ritual, the goal is not only to disseminate Buddhist doctrine but to bring comfort and to effect some kind of transformation in the audience. The analysis has shown that ritual language and community are closely connected, and the two must be considered together when analysis of one or the other is done.

Implications and Future Directions

Conducting research on the language of Buddhist sermons in Sri Lanka given during the performance of death rituals such as the sixth day, carries several significant implications that highlight the beliefs, practices, and wider cultural and social aspects of Sri Lankan Buddhism. The sixth day after a death holds particular significance for the family and community of the deceased, and studying the language used in Buddhist sermons provides valuable insights into the ways in which Buddhists in Sri Lanka cope with the death of a loved one. One of the key implications of this research is the opportunity to delve into Buddhist beliefs and practices related to death and rebirth and the acquisition of merit. In Buddhism death is seen as a natural part of the cycle of rebirth, and the sixth day after a death is believed to be a particularly important time for the deceased's spirit as it transitions from one life to the next. This research therefore highlights the beliefs and practices that underpin this understanding of death and rebirth, as well as reveal how Sri Lankan Buddhists understand and conceptualise life after death.

Likewise, studying the language of Buddhist sermons provides a deep insight into the beliefs and practices of the Buddhist community in Sri Lanka, as the *bana* given by Buddhist priests on the sixth day as evident from the data analysed, are a rich source of Buddhist religious language that encompasses different languages and styles, from Pali chanting to *jathaka* stories, to the use of metaphors and analogies to *buddha vachana*. Thus, by conducting research on Buddhist sermons, scholars will gain insights into the type of language used in sermons relating to death and gain knowledge of the complex beliefs and practices of Buddhism in performing the rituals of death. Another impact is that it illustrates the role of ritual language in Buddhist practice, particularly in the use of the sacred languages Pali and Sinhala, which illustrates how language is used to con-struct and reinforce Buddhist cultural identity, and the ways in which these ritual practices are appropriated by the priests giving the sermon according to the occasion.

Similarly, another research implication is what the sermons illustrate about the central role of Buddhist priests in Sri Lankan society; by having an impact in bringing about transformation in people's lives and not just providing solace to the family of the deceased, they have a more thera-peutic function. Through studying sermons, scholars, therefore, discover more about the central role of Buddhist priests in society: how they interpret Buddhist teachings related to Buddhist phil-osophy, such as the concepts of *karma,* death, and rebirth and how they utilise these teachings to bring about behavioural changes at the same time as providing comfort to the bereaved.

The way language is used in Buddhist sermons also has implications for understanding how Buddhism intersects with other fields of inquiry, such as psychology in the use of metaphors and analogies to describe concepts of Buddhist thought to transform the heart. Metaphors are often used in messages that encourage people to make changes to lifestyle behaviour, for example, health messages. This process of creating mental imagery is closely related to cognitive theories of emotion and behaviour, where metaphors are used to help people to understand their thought patterns and to develop new ways of thinking and acting; metaphors are generally perceived as giving individuals an 'emotional jolt' to urgently make changes to their behaviour. By researching how metaphors and analogies are used in Buddhist sermons to enable the audience to visualise and experience psychological concepts in a tangible way, scholars can discover how Buddhist priests employ these linguistic devices to convey complex ideas and concepts. On a practical level, how Buddhist priests use language to bring about changes in personality to 'transform the heart' and how individuals use this knowledge in their own transformation is also valuable in fields such as counselling, where many chaplains and therapists incorporate the practice of mindfulness to change people's behaviour.

Additionally, this research has implications for cross-cultural communication, as the beliefs and practices of different cultures and religions help to promote greater empathy and tolerance between different groups of people. It can be useful in challenging stereotypes and misconceptions about different religions and promote a more nuanced and complex understanding of cultural diversity. Furthermore, the comparative analysis of Buddhist death rituals and those of other religions, such as Hinduism, Christianity, and Islam, can also have impact through revealing differences and com-monalities among religious traditions in mourning the death of a loved one.

Given the cultural and social impact that research on Buddhist sermons can have as discussed above, building on this case study, and in general, future research could explore the following topic areas further: first, in transcribing the sermon, I manually counted the number of times cer-tain words were used. In future work, a study could be conducted using corpus software, for example, Lancsbox, to examine a collection of Buddhist sermons used during different funeral rituals, such as a funeral sermon, a sixth-day sermon, and the sermon on the seventh day, to inves-tigate whether there are any common trends in the use of regular expressions and lexis or whether the style changes depending on the ritual event. Secondly, future research could explore the lexis used in Buddhist sermons in contrast to a general reference corpus to see what words are key in Buddhist sermons. It could also investigate how the concepts of 'heaven', 'hell', 'evil', 'wicked-ness' and 'good' are used in Christian and Buddhist preaching. This study could focus on the use of collocates and examine concordance lines to see how the search word is used in context. Finally, it would be interesting to carry out fieldwork and to collect both written and spoken texts (including sermons) from different ritual events—for example, *Wesak, Kathina, Bodhi Puja,* and *Pirith* ceremonies—to investigate how multiple languages including English are used depending on the ritual context and what role is played by different languages. Further research could also focus on the role of Buddhist priests in specific migrant contexts, particularly in relation to how they use language during different occasions such as giving advice, performing rituals, and conversing with different generations. Additionally, research could examine the language used by Buddhist priests during sermons and compare it with the linguistic devices used by chaplains or therapists during counselling sessions to investigate whether there are any similarities between the two practices in the way language is used in bringing about transformation.

Further Reading

Herat, M. (2015). Functions of English vs other languages in Sri Lankan Buddhist rituals in the UK. *Acta Linguistica Asiatica*, 5(1), 85–110. https://journals.uni-lj.si/ala/article/view/3023/3114
This work examines the functions of English and other languages in the performance of Buddhist rituals during *kathina* (this is an important ceremony in which monks move residence during the rainy season) and the New Year ceremony (Sri Lankans celebrate the New Year in April when the sun transits from Aries to Pisces according to the astrological calendar) by investigating language samples and looks at the instances where English is sanctioned by the Buddhist clergy.
Kent, D.W. (2008). *Shelter for you Nirvana for Our Sons: Buddhist Belief and Practice in the Sri Lankan Army* (especially, Chapter 3). PhD thesis. University of Virginia, https://thecarthaginiansolution.files.wordpress.com/2011/08/buddhist-belief-practise-in-sl-army.pdf
This work examines how Buddhist monks preach to soldiers who are preparing for war and discusses how the concept of *karma* is interpreted in relation to actions on the battlefield and the impact it has on soldiers and their families through interviews with Buddhist priests, soldiers, and their families.
Langer, R. (2013). *Sermon Studies and Buddhism: a case study of Sri Lankan preaching*. Studia Philologica Buddhica monograph series. International Institute for Buddhist Studies.
Using an ethnographic approach, this pioneering work investigates the context of three sermons given by two Sri Lankan Buddhist monks: the first at the funeral; the second, on the evening of the sixth day; and the third one on the seventh day after the alms giving. The final part of the book provides the Sinhala transcripts and the English translations of the three sermons.
Kariyawasam, A.G.S. (1996). *Buddhist Ceremonies and Rituals of Sri Lanka*. Buddhist Publication Society. www.accesstoinsight.org/lib/authors/kariyawasam/wheel402.html
This text investigates the different Buddhist rituals and practices observed in Sri Lanka such as rituals of Worship, Almsgiving and Funerals and Monastic Ceremonies.
Keane, W. (1997). Religious language. *Annual Review of Anthropology, 26*,47–71. https://sites.lsa.umich.edu/webbkeane/wp-content/uploads/sites/128/2014/07/religious_language.pdf
This work explores how the marked uses of language in religious contexts leads to tensions in how participants interact with religious language, due to distinctive beliefs about the religious context, where there are different assumptions about the workings of language.

References

Crosby, K. (2003). Theravada. In Robert E. Buswell Jr. (Ed.), *Encyclopaedia of Buddhism, 836–841*. Macmillan Reference USA.
Crystal, D. & Davy, D. (1969). *Investigating English style*. Longman.
De Bary, W. T. (1972). *The Buddhist Tradition*. Vintage.
De Silva, K.M. (1981). *A history of Sri Lanka*. Oxford University Press.
Deegalle, M. (2006). *Popularising Buddhism: preaching as performance in Sri Lanka*. State University of New York Press.
Du Bois, J.W. (1986). *Evidentiality: The Linguistic Coding of Epistemology*. In W. Chafe & J. Nichols (Eds.), *Self-Evidence and Ritual Speech*. Ablex.
Feuchtwang, S. (2010). Ritual and Memory. In S. Radstone & B. Schwarz (Eds.), *Memory: Histories, Theories, Debates*, 281–298. Fordham University Press
Gair, J.W. (1968). Sinhalese diglossia. *Anthropological Linguistics, 10*(8), 1–15.

Gair, J.W. (1998). *Studies in South Asian linguistics-Sinhala and other South Asian languages*. Oxford University Press.

Gombrich, Richard. (1988). *Theravada Buddhism: A Social History from Ancient Benares to Modern Colombo*. Routledge & Kegan Paul.

Herat, M. (2015). Functions of English and other Languages in Sri Lankan Buddhist rituals in the UK. *Acta Linguistica Asiata*, 5(1), 85–110. https://journals.uni-lj.si/ala/article/view/3023/3114

Janowitz, N. (1989). *Poetics of Ascent: Theories of Language in a Rabbinic Ascent Text*. SUNY Press.

Jeffries, L. & McIntrye, D. (2010). *Stylistics*. Cambridge University Press.

Kariyawasam, A.G.S. (1996). *Buddhist Ceremonies and Rituals of Sri Lanka*. Buddhist Publication Society. www.accesstoinsight.org/lib/authors/kariyawasam/wheel402.html

Keane, W. (1997). Religious Language. *Annual Review of Anthropology*, 26, 47–71. https://sites.lsa.umich. edu/webbkeane/wp-content/uploads/sites/128/2014/07/religious_language.pdf

Keane, W. (2003). Language and Religion. In A. Duranti (Ed.) *A Companion to Linguistic Anthropology*. Blackwell.

Kent, D.W. (2008). *Shelter for you Nirvana for Our Sons: Buddhist Belief and Practice in the Sri Lankan Army*. PhD thesis. University of Virginia. https://thecarthaginiansolution.files.wordpress.com/2011/08/ buddhist-belief-practise-in-sl-army.pdf

Langer, R. (2009). Preacher and ritualist: the role of theravada Buddhist monks. Retrieved 12 July 2022 from www.bristol.ac.uk/news/2009/6542.html.

Langer, R. (2013). *Sermon Studies and Buddhism: a case study of Sri Lankan preaching*. Studia Philologica Buddhica monograph series. International Institute for Buddhist Studies.

Leech, G. (1969). *A linguistic guide to English poetry*. Longman.

Lu, Wei-lun & Shurma, S. (2021). Rituals. In S. Pihlaja (Ed.), *Analysing Religious Discourse*, 217–234. Cambridge University Press.

Ludowyke, E.F.C. (1956). *The footprint of the Buddha*. Buddhist Cultural Centre.

Pitts, W.F. (1993). *Old Ship of Zion: The Afro-Baptist Ritual in the African Diaspora*. Oxford University Press.

Samarin, W.J. (1976). *Language in religious practice*. Newbury House Publishers.

Samuels, J. (2010). *Attracting the Heart: Social Relations and the Aesthetics of Emotion in Sri Lankan Monastic Culture*. University of Hawai'i Press.

Senaratne, C. (2008). *Sinhala English code mixing in Sri Lanka*. Lot Publications.

Tausczik, Y.R. & Pennebaker, J.W. (2010). The psychological meaning of words: LIWC and computerized text analysis methods. *Journal of Language and Social Psychology*, 29, 24–54.

Tilakaratne, A. (2012). *Theravada Buddhism: the view of the elders*. Hawa'i University Press.

Thompson, M. (2003). *Philosophy of Religion*. Hodder Arnold.

Williams, P. & Tribe, A. (2000). *Buddhist Thought: a complete introduction to the Indian tradition*. Routledge.

Wittgenstein, L. (1953). *Philosophical Investigations*. Translated by G.E.M. Anscombe. Macmillan.

27

RELIGIOUS IDENTITY IN DISCOURSE

Kate Power

Introduction and Background

Language is a significant component in any religion and even relatively private, mystical forms of spirituality retain a public, discursive dimension when associated with institutionalized religion. Lincoln (2000, p. 416) observes, for example, that religion is constituted by four different components that might interconnect in disjointed or contradictory ways:

1. A discourse that claims its concerns transcend the human, temporal and contingent, while claiming for itself a similarly transcendent status.
2. A set of practices informed and structured by that discourse.
3. A community, whose members construct their identity with reference to the discourse and its attendant practices.
4. An institution that regulates discourse, practices, and community, reproducing and modifying them over time, while asserting their eternal validity and transcendent value.

Regrettably, the social sciences often focus on "reactive forms of religion, notably fundamentalism" to the neglect of "the myriad forms of religion in the modern world that are an integral part of everyday life for millions of people" (Davie, 2006, p. 139). In the process, various "labels" are assigned to religious people that may or may not align with their own sense of—or preferred way of representing—their religious identity. This chapter, by contrast, focuses on Lincoln's third component of religion, namely how individuals represent their own religious identities in (and in reference to religious) discourse.

The predominant Western understanding of the person has long been that of "a bounded, unique, more or less integrated motivational and cognitive universe, a dynamic center of awareness, emotion, judgement, and action organized into a distinctive whole" (Geertz, 1979, p. 227). This traditional, realist conceptualization of the unitary "self" with its inherent qualities existing independently of either context or language is a view of human personhood now widely critiqued as "essentialist." Identity-related research that challenges this understanding has proliferated during the past four decades in linguistic anthropology, discursive psychology, queer linguistics, conversation analysis, critical discourse analysis, and language and gender studies. Identity is now

DOI: 10.4324/9781003301271-30

more commonly regarded by discourse analysts as created by, rather than pre-existing and determining, social and linguistic practices. Antaki & Widdicombe (1998, p. 2, emphasis original), for example, deny that individuals "passively or latently *have* this or that identity which then causes feelings and actions," arguing instead that individuals "work up and work to this or that identity, for themselves and others, there and then, either as an end in itself or towards some other end."It is important to remember, however, that post-essentialist conceptualizations of identity such as this differ significantly from those held by many religious (and non-religious) individuals, for whom essentialism serves as a resource for organizing and understanding their own identities. It is also worth recalling Rambo's (1993, p. 19) observation that "the scholar's own point of view […] is not intrinsically superior to the one being analyzed."

Relatively few discourse analytic studies have paid serious attention to religious identity, although it is emerging as a growing field of inquiry with real-world relevance. Baron's (2004) analysis of evangelical discourse in Mexico, for example, illustrates the liberating potential of claims (i) that context and audience influence discursive constructions of identity, and (ii) that where multiple constructions of identity are seen to be possible, individuals (and groups) become free not only to contest the identities assigned to them but also to forge new, and potentially more advantageous, identities. Baron's work examines how a socially disadvantaged Protestant woman increased her social influence by strategically drawing on evangelical discourse. Talking to and about God with her neighbours, she highlighted her religious identity, rather than her gender—and, in doing so, not only succeeded in overcoming "gender as a factor of primary relevance" (Baron, 2004, p. 253), but also materially altered circumstances for her family, opening opportunities for her son to marry against the social customs of her village.

Like discourse analysts, Religious Studies scholars have largely neglected discursive constructions of religious identity, perhaps because religious affiliation has traditionally been regarded as something which is "received or bestowed" rather than chosen (Woodhead, 1999, p. 59). Religious studies inquiries have largely focused on

1. how religious identity is construed as either *private* or *public* (i.e., conflated with membership in particular religious groups), and thus used to bolster opposing positions in the debate over secularization theory; or
2. how particular notions of religious identity facilitate the analysis of religious conversion.

From the second half of the twentieth century onwards, however, Religious Studies scholars began to recognize the contribution of personal choice to religious affiliation—and, in doing so, paved the way for a new line of inquiry into the nature of religious identity.

Zimmerman's (1998, p. 90) theoretical distinction between "discourse identities", "situated identities", and "transportable identities" provides a useful framework for analysing religious identity. In Zimmerman's usage, the term *discourse identities* refers to such identities as might be assumed by individuals in "the moment-by-moment organization" of a particular interaction. These include, for example, "current speaker, listener, story teller, story recipient, questioner, answerer, repair initiator, and so on" (Zimmerman, 1998, p. 90). *Situated identities*, by contrast, are "brought into being and sustained by participants engaging in activities and respecting agendas that display an orientation to, and an alignment of, particular identity sets" (Zimmerman, 1998, p. 90). Last, Zimmerman (1998, p. 90) defines *transportable identities* as those—such as gender, race, age, and religion—which "travel with individuals across situations and are potentially relevant in and for any situation and in and for any spate of interaction." None of Zimmerman's identity categories are conceptualized as "something static that people *are* or that they *have*", however, but rather only as "something that they can orient to and use as a resource in the course of interaction" (Wodak, 2004, p. 99, emphasis original). Therefore, in conceptualizing religion as a "transportable identity", it is not my intention to argue that religious identity is a fixed or immutable category. On the contrary, individuals both can and do own markedly different religious identities in different settings and timeframes, both associating with and dissociating themselves from various religious discourses and groups via their own language choices.

Because individuals "collectively identify themselves and others" in terms of religion and "conduct their everyday lives in terms of those identities", religious identities have "practical consequences" and might, therefore, be regarded as "intersubjectively real" (Jenkins, [1996] 2004, p. 87). Consequently, it is important to distinguish between "construal" and "construction" (as advised by Fairclough, 2003, p. 8), the latter being the term most often used to describe the discursive representation of social identity. On the one hand, religious and other discourses can both shape and be shaped by those who use them—and, in this way, religious and other social identities might be said to be "constructed" in talk. On the other hand, however, it is important to recognize that "the material and cultural resources used in identity making" are unequally distributed (Grad & Martín Rojo, 2008, p. 17). For this reason, Fairclough (2003) critiques social constructionism for tending to conflate *construction* and *construal*. Sayer (2003, p. 20) argues further that this tendency reveals both a confusion of "mediation and interpretation with production," and an erroneous supposition "that creativity or 'construction' can occur out of nothing, and regardless of the properties of the materials used in construction."

Social (including religious) identities can be both a "label" assigned by individuals to themselves, as well as a label assigned to them by others (Wetherell, 1996, p. 34). As Baron's (2004) study (mentioned above) implies, however, material and structural realities both influence and constrain social agents and social phenomena—and their disabling by talk is by no means guaranteed. On the contrary, as Fairclough (2003, p. 8) points out,

> [...] we may textually construe (represent, imagine, etc.) the social world in particular ways, but whether [or not] our representations or construals have the effect of changing its construction depends upon various contextual factors—including the way social reality already is, who is construing it, and so forth.

In short, *construal* (interpretation) does not equal *construction* (fashioning); neither are all construals adequate, nor all attempts at construction successful. In this chapter, therefore, I use the term *construal*—rather than the more popular *construction*—so as to highlight that "the processes of identity rest not simply on the claims made, but on how such claims are received, that is validated or rejected by significant others" (Bechhofer et al., 1999, p. 530). The case study later in the chapter focuses on religious self-categorization, without reference to how those construals might be received, but the analysis does show that religious self-categorization sometimes involves interacting with (accepting, nuancing, and/or rejecting) religious identity labels received from others.

Membership categorization analysis (MCA) is an ethnomethodological approach, informed by Harvey Sacks's (1979, 1992) work, which explores how people are categorized in specific contexts. MCA views category membership as a discursive accomplishment and prioritizes what "*the parties to the interaction being examined* [...] demonstrably orient to as relevant (as best we can establish it, to be sure)" (Schegloff, 1999, p. 579, emphasis original). Thus, the use of MCA is proffered as a corrective to commentaries that "deny [religious] persons their usual 'first person authority'" (Godlove, 2000, p. 165), such as scholarly and media commentators on religion (as noted above). First among the resources of membership categorization is the notion of "members' categories" (Sacks, 1992, p. 40), which refers to classifications describing people. Schegloff (2007, p. 477) provides the following examples:

[…] men, women, Protestants, minors (or miners), professors, goalies, adults, cellists, conservatives, vegetarians, merchants, murderers, 20-year olds, cat-people, technicians, stamp collectors, Danes, 'looky-loos' (people who slow down on the highway to stare at an accident), lefties (both politically and handedly), surfers, Alzheimers, etc.

These are all lexicalized categories—that is, representations that take the form of a single word or phrase. They are all also noun phrases capable of functioning as the subject of a sentence. However, a wide variety of nonlexicalized, *ad hoc* categories can also be "created spontaneously for use in specialized contexts"—"-and these, too, may be properly understood as members' categories (Barsalou, 1983, p. 211).

A second membership categorization resource emerges from the observation that (i) members routinely organize categories into sets or *collections* (such as sex, race, religion, and occupation), known as "devices"; and (ii) that the pairing of such collections with population members is governed by "rules of application" which, together with the relevant set or collection, constitute "membership categorization devices" (Sacks, 1992, p. 246). Several types of membership categorization devices (MCDs) have been identified in the relevant literature, including "standard relational pairs" which categorize any two persons (Sacks, 1992) as having mutual obligations towards one another by virtue of their respective category memberships, e.g., parent/child, vicar/congregation (Watson, 1987, pp. 278–279). None of these devices inhere in specific words or phrases but rather are accomplished discursively in specific contexts. For example, "Protestant" may be treated as either a "category" (i.e., a type of faith or church), or a "device" (i.e., collection of categories) including, for example, vicars, curates, members of the congregation, etc. (Watson (1978, p. 107). Last, a third membership categorization resource derives from the fact that members routinely (explicitly or implicitly) endow both categories and devices with specific "predicates" (Watson, 1978)—and, in doing so, display their own understandings about those categories and/or devices (Watson, 1978).

Together, these three resources of membership categorization analysis provide a framework within which to understand how people categorize themselves and each other—as social types, as social types related to other social types, and as social types stereotypically associated with certain characteristics and/or behaviours.

The presence and interaction of multiple "voices" within a single text—now broadly considered to be a fundamental property of all texts—is usually addressed by discourse analysts under the rubrics of *intertextuality* and *interdiscursivity*. The former involves the intermingling of a speaker's words with the specific words of another party, with reported speech being its most frequent realization (Fairclough, 2003, p. 219). In religious discourses, for example, *intertextuality* is commonly forged through quotations of sacred scripture or other religious authorities. In her study of Rev. Jerry Falwell's language and politics, for example, Harding (2000, p. 12) found that

Church-people … borrow, customize, and reproduce the … speech of their preachers and other leaders in their daily lives. Preachers appropriate each other's sermons piecemeal and wholesale, while church people assimilate their preachers' language at the level of grammar, semantics and style.

Interdiscursivity involves the combination of different genres, discourses, and/or styles within a single text. For analytical purposes, interdiscursivity is often regarded as a two-way street in which a given discourse is said either (i) to *appropriate* (that is, to take up and rework) another discourse, or (ii) to *colonize* it (Fairclough, 2003). For example, religious leaders from diverse faith traditions routinely address social, political, and cultural concerns in concert with, and through the strains of, their own religious discourses, and religious people routinely take up and rework public sphere discourses in prayers and casual conversations. The resulting interpenetration of religious and public sphere discourses constitutes a fertile, but hitherto largely neglected, site for the analysis of religious identities.

One of the most interesting ways in which interdiscursive links are forged between religious and other public sphere discourses is via attitudinal stance-taking on matters other than religion. Stance-taking is defined by Du Bois (2007, p. 146) as "a public act by a social actor, achieved dialogically through overt communicative means, of simultaneously evaluating objects, positioning subjects (self and others), and aligning with other subjects, with respect to any salient dimension of the sociocultural field." Ochs (1992) similarly observes that stance-taking can be indirectly constitutive of particular social identities within specific communities. For example, given the conventional associations that pertain between particular attitudinal stances on (some) social issues and particular (stereotypical) religious identities, stance-taking on those issues can be symbolically important in terms of signalling one's own religious identity. Indeed, religious identities can be discursively construed via stance-taking not only on religious issues, but also on matters other than religion. This type of religious self-identification is particularly salient in relation to issues such as abortion and same-sex marriage, where negative attitudinal stances are both widely and publicly "bound" to "traditional" forms of religious expression (Sacks, [1972] 1986, p. 335). Thus, people who publicly express negative stances on these issues effectively position themselves (whether intentionally or otherwise) as members of a "topic-opinion category" (Fitzgerald & Housley, 2002, p. 592) stereotypically associated with conservative religion. (Interestingly, in western public discourse, positive stances on these same issues are less widely "bound" to "progressive" religious identities.) In some (but not all) cases, speakers will offer or imply different forms of "support" to persuade their interlocutor of "the validity of the claim inherent in" their stances (Chandrasegaran & Kong, 2006, p. 377)—and this support can also be a resource for religious self-identification.

Before considering specific examples Claresholm residents' religious self-identification, it is important to clarify two points. First, the above propositions do not mean that people project specific stances because they "have" particular religious identities; rather, that some stances are conventionally associated with recognizable religious identities, which people can discursively enact and/or recast via stance-taking. Second, this case study reveals that religious self-identification via stance-taking can be indexed very subtly, not only via the (positive or negative) attitudinal stances people project on various social issues, but also via (1) their precise choice of stance "object" (Du Bois, 2007, p. 146), (2) the linguistic resources with which they project those stances, and (3) the different forms of "support" (Chandrasegaran & Kong, 2006, p. 377) offered or implied for those stances.

Discursive Construals of Religious Identity in Rural Canada

This case study explores how rural Canadians discursively construe their own religious identities, both more and less directly via self-categorization and indirectly via stance-taking on topics other than religion. By focusing on individuals who either are currently, or previously have been, personally involved in religion, this case study examines the discursive construal of religious identities in everyday interpersonal communication, rather than either discourses *about* or *of* religion produced by religious and other social élites—or the stereotypical/idealized subject positions proposed for religious individuals by the media, academics, or organized religion. This focus is inspired by Hervieu-Léger's (2000, p. 29) prioritization of popular manifestations of religion, which is an approach that, Lyon (2000, p. 12) argues, warrants:

> [...] caution about generalizing about religion in Canada from the views of certain mainstream denominational theological seminaries or the *Globe and Mail* newspaper, and a willingness to listen to persons from one of the prairie Bible colleges or to read stories in, say, the evangelical periodical *Christian Week*, and to talk with the diverse clientele of Christian bookstores.

Adopting Hervieu-Léger's (and Lyon's) approach problematizes some of the connotations stereo-typically associated with religious labels and reveals that rural Canadians' religious identities are complex discursive accomplishments. For, as Droogers ([1995] 2006, p. 29) points out, "Believers simply do not behave in a consistent manner, despite the official, more or less homogeneous and integrated version of their religion, as represented by its religious figureheads."

I conducted 31 individual qualitative interviews and two focus groups in Claresholm—a small town in rural Western Canada where I had lived for two years, prior to undertaking this research in 2005. I chose Claresholm as the location for this case study for several reasons. First, southern Alberta is commonly regarded as Canada's "Bible belt," suggesting a population interested in and potentially willing to discuss religion. Second, Claresholm exemplifies Bibby's (1999) depiction of the Canadian religious demographic as "a culturally diverse Christian monopoly." For, despite being home to just over 3,500 people, Claresholm boasts considerable diversity of Christian and related religious expressions, with ten churches representing different denominations and three Hutterite colonies. My third reason for selecting Claresholm was its integrity as a community in its own right. Situated approximately halfway between two mid-sized cities, Claresholm is suf-ficiently removed from each of these centres to make regular commuting difficult—particularly on Canada's icy winter roads, through hazardous snowdrifts. Consequently, far from being the bedroom community that many of Canada's rural towns have become, Claresholm is a dynamic municipality boasting a variety of business, social, and health services that attract both town and country residents from the surrounding area. At the same time, its clear geographic boundaries provided both logical and practical limits to my research: all the participants in this study either lived, worked, or worshipped in Claresholm at the time of their interviews.

In conducting this research, I adopted two core features of grounded theory. First, I sought "to discover [the] categories and their properties" (Glaser & Strauss, 1967, p. 62) used by my informants to construe their own religious identities—rather than attempting either to predict or to test for categories of my own choosing. Second, I determined to generate a theoretical account of how participants construe their religious identities on the basis of ongoing, reflexive data gen-eration and analysis (Glaser & Strauss, 1967). I did, however, begin the study with "an initial hunch" (Bauer & Aarts, 2000, pp. 33–34) that discursive construals of religious identity might be shaped, at least in part, by (i) individuals' religious or denominational affiliations; (ii) their differing relationships to organized religion (e.g., clergy/lay, core member/marginal adherent/non-participant); (iii) their gender; and (iv) their age. I drew on purposive, volunteer and snowball sampling to recruit diverse participants. I also anticipated that discursive construals of religious identity might be produced in conversations about important social issues, such as the legalization of same-sex marriage (which was a prominent issue in Canada at the time)—and this expectation provided me with a line of questioning that I used in my research interviews.

Religious identity can be just as much a matter of differentiation as of belonging and this case study discusses some of the ways in which rural Canadians discursively present themselves as *affiliated with* and/or *different to* particular religious groups. However, religious identity is more complex than a simple matter of belonging/non-belonging. Indeed, religious studies scholars have long identified various models of religious *half*-belonging (e.g., Day, 2009). Therefore, the distinction between discursive strategies that encode belonging and non-belonging is made chiefly for analytical purposes and should be read as indicative only.

Belonging

Claresholm residents routinely use category "labels" to identify themselves as "belonging" to particularly religious identities. Following Hester (1992, p. 158), who observed that speakers commonly categorize persons other than themselves as "deviant" using "deviant membership categories"—that is, by describing them via "culturally available names, types, or 'category concepts' of persons, such as 'bully,' 'slow learner,' 'nuisance,' 'menace,' and 'thief'"—I have dubbed the labels used for religious self-categorization "*religious* membership categories" (RMCs). As Table 27.1 below illustrates, RMCs can be quite direct individual religious categories, including ad hoc individual descriptors (Extract 1), particularized religious group identifications (Extract 2), religious job descriptions (Extract 3), and theological perspectives on church governance (Extract 4). They can also be collective categorizations, shared with one's family members (Extract 5), religious group, and/or the entire human race.

RMCs have several noteworthy features. First, whether lexicalized or ad hoc, RMCs are typically realized by noun phrases, although adjectival phrases based on the proper names of religious/denominational groups can also function as RMCs (e.g., Extract 2). Second, some RMCs indicate the "criterial feature" of the category "*in* the category name" (Jayyusi, 1984, p. 21, emphasis original) (e.g., Extract 1), while others may require specialist knowledge and/or elucidation by the speaker to be understood by their interlocutor (e.g., Extract 4). RMCs are routinely particularized via references to time and/or place (e.g., *right now*, Extract 3), pre-modifications (e.g., *baptized and confirmed*, Extract 2), and/or post-modifications (e.g., *in sacred space*, Extract 1). They may also be used in conjunction with either the definite, indefinite, or zero article, such that members can categorize themselves as the sole incumbent of a particular RMC (e.g., *the Bishop*, Extract 3) or one among many (e.g., *a Congregationalist*, Extract 4). They may refer to individuals (e.g., Extracts 1–4) or groups (e.g., Extract 5).

Table 27.1 Direct self-categorization (religious belonging)

Discursive realization	Example
1. Religious membership category (RMC)—ad hoc individual descriptor	1. *I'm a firm believer in sacred space*
2. RMC—group with a proper name	2. *I am baptized and confirmed Roman Catholic*
3. RMC—religious job descriptions	3. *my involvement is fairly heavy right now **I'm the Bishop** of the church of Claresholm*
4. RMC—theological perspectives on church governance	4. *because **I'm a Congregationalist** I would see that God communicates His will to all of His people and that I'm not to be leading it myself*
5. collective RMC (CRMC), shared with e.g., family, religious group, human race	5. *we started going to church our whole family when we moved here partly because **we were Nazarene** um when we lived in Calgary*

In each of the above cases, Claresholm residents produced explicit RMCs when asked about their religious identities. However, several participants conveyed a sense of their own religious identities by interacting discursively with—sometimes nuancing, at other times overtly rejecting—category labels assigned to them by others. Sacks (1979, p. 8) observed that some categories are used differently by incumbents and non-incumbents of the category in question. For example, categories such as "the Hebrew" are characteristically "used by nonmembers of the category and not by members of the category except when members are identifying themselves to nonmembers" (Sacks, 1979, p. 8). In Extract 6 below, for example, Tracy depicts the RMC *Mormons* as a non-members' category, preferring the RMC *members of the Church of Jesus Christ of Latter Day Saints* (lines 13–14).

Extract 6

1   Kate: *if someone said to you oh what religion are you // would you say I'm a Mormon?*

3   Gail: *//I would say sure*

4   Wendy: *sure I would say //I'm a Mormon*

5   Nola: *sometimes*

6   Leisl: *when I was growing up I always said that*

7   All: *yeah*

8   Leisl: *we were Mormons*

9   Tracy: **actually I taught my kids to … tell people that they are a member of**

10   **the Church of Jesus Christ of Latter Day Saints and when they get**

11   **the blank look then you say the Mormons**

12   Kate: *and why did you teach them that?*

13   Tracy: **because we aren't Mormons we are members of the**

14   **Church of Jesus Christ of Latter Day Saints**

For Jehovah's Witnesses in Claresholm, by contrast, members' and non-member's categorizations are distinguished not so much by the use of *different* RMCs, but rather by the different ways in which *the same* RMCs are combined with different parts of speech, to differing effects. For example, the RMC *a Witness* (line 3, Extract 7)—along with both *the Witnesses* and *Jehovah's Witnesses* (not shown)—was used exclusively in my Claresholm data by people who claimed membership in that religious group. Claresholm residents who did not claim such membership, by contrast, used the following categorizations: *a Jehovah Witness* (not shown), *the Jehovah Witness[es]* (not shown), and *the Jehovah's Witnesses* (lines 1–2, Extract 7). In short, by combining the RMC *Jehovah's Witnesses* with the definite article, category non-incumbents seemingly depict category members as belonging to a specific religious group (i.e., *the Jehovah's Witnesses*), whereas those using the RMC *Jehovah's Witnesses* without an article represent category members as people entrusted by God to perform the task of "witnessing" (i.e., *Jehovah's Witnesses*).

Extract 7

1   Kate: *maybe you could tell me how you first became involved with the*

2   ***Jehovah's Witnesses***

3   Charlie: *well she's been **a Witness** since 1949 I have since 1952 [...]*

People also discursively construe their own religious identities in relation to the categorizations of others, including by comparing themselves with specific religious others and/or a religious "mainstream," and by implicitly categorizing themselves through explicit categorization of one or more others.

Extract 8

1	Neil:	*I've had my life tested severely since I've been a Bishop [...] um much*
2		*the way that ah that many of the apostles of Christ had a nasty time*

Extract 9

1	Ernie:	*I believe in the I guess like what I would call the mainstream*
2	Kate:	*can you pin down could you kind of encapsulate what do you believe*
3	Ernie:	*well I think I believe in God um ... I think God is forgiving and I think if you*
4		*know if you lead a decent life or you know you're not out killing and*
5		*pillaging and whatever you will get to heaven*

Extract 10

1	Mark:	*I had prayed earlier on that **the Lord** would heal my back because I used to*
2		*have a lot of lower back aching problems*

In Extract 8, for example, Neil uses the phrase *much the way that* (lines 1–2) to equate his experience as *a Bishop* (line 1) with the *nasty time* had by *the apostles of Christ* (line 2). In Extract 9, Ernie explicitly construes his religious convictions as aligned with *the mainstream* (line 1). In Extract 10, Mark categorizes God using both a divine reference form and the definite article (*the Lord*, line 1). In doing so, he portrays God not merely as his own *Lord*, but rather as the *[one and only] Lord*—thereby implicitly categorizing himself as party to a "standard relational pair" (i.e., a relationship of mutual obligation) which might be rendered "the Lord / human subjects."

Religious self-categorization is not always this direct or explicit, however. Table 27.2 below illustrates that religious identity can also be construed less directly, without explicitly owning or responding to particular RMCs.

In Extracts 11 to 15, for example, various people discursively construe their own religious identities by describing attributes and/or behaviours that appear implicitly bound to RMCs—either instead of (e.g., Extracts 11–13, 15) or in combination with (e.g., Extract 14) explicit mentions of specific RMCs. The attributes that my informants claimed "either *to be* or *to have*" (Hester, 1992, p. 159, emphasis original) included, for example, being *straight-laced* (Extract 14) and having *a relationship [with God]* (Extract 11). The behaviours they report engaging in include both overtly religious actions (*anointed, prayed*, Extract 12) and actions made religious by context (*converse [with], follow [guardian angel's] guidance*, Extract 13), as well as both habitual actions (e.g., Extract 13) and actions taken on a specific occasion (e.g., Extract 12) (Hester, 1992, pp. 161–162).

Not (or Partial) Belonging

Claresholm residents use various discursive strategies to depict themselves as not belonging to specific religious groups, as shown in Table 27.3 below. The most direct of these strategies

Table 27.2 Indirect religious self-categorization (belonging, via attributes and/or behaviours)

11. Descriptive statement of religious attribute	11. *I wouldn't say I necessarily have a belief system it's more of a relationship* you know I know who God is and I know Him
12. Descriptive statement of religious behaviour	12. I'm just going to go to the bathroom and *I like anointed her kitchen [laughter] with the cooking oil [laughter] and prayed over her house*
13. Descriptive statement of non-religious behaviour (in a religious context)	13. Daniel is my guardian angel [...] and I yeah *we converse more or less and I follow his guidance*
14. Binding attributes / behaviours to RMC	14. *that's why I make a good Anglican we're very straight-laced*
15. Collective attribute / behaviour	15. with *people like myself who believe in a creator* the best that we can think of is that we would go back into some kind of a ether

Table 27.3 Direct self-categorization (religious non-belonging)

Discursive realization	*Example*
16. Owning a religious "non-belonging" RMC	16. *I* can't know what the great truth is and so for that the use of that word *I'm an agnostic*
17. RMC non-incumbency claim (denominational group)	17. I can no longer accurately regard myself as *a conservative Protestant*
18. RMC non-incumbency claim (ad hoc RMC)	18. I'm not um like *a heavy duty pray-er*
19. Religious Type Category non-incumbency claim (rare)	19. I wasn't Mormon bit of a reputation for you know ... *not exactly the church-going type*
20. RMC ambivalence	20. *I'm not an atheist [...] I guess I'm a Lutheran a little* but I'm not definitely not *even that's going a step beyond for me* anyways *I can't really say what I am*
21. Hypothetical conditional statements	21. *if it wasn't so late in my life I would actively consider take action to leave the church* but to join another church

involves owning/disowning RMCs by (i) explicitly claiming incumbency in a "non-belonging" RMC (e.g., Extract 16), or (ii) claiming non-incumbency in a "belonging" RMC—whether that be a denominational grouping (e.g., Extract 17) or an ad hoc RMC (e.g., Extract 18). The strategy of disowning membership in a religious "type category" was rare, but did appear, in my dataset (e.g., Extract 19). Claresholm residents also presented nuanced and complex construals of their religious non-belonging via RMC ambivalence (e.g., Extract 20) and hypothetical conditional statements (e.g., Extract 21).

In Extract 20, Ernie answers a question about his religious identity by claiming non-incumbency in a "non-belonging" RMC (I'm not an atheist). This kind of double negative religious self-categorization suggests a measure of discomfort on Ernie's part in assigning an RMC to himself, which is also evident in both his hedged self-categorization (*I guess I'm a Lutheran*) and subsequent retraction (*even that's going a step beyond*). Also, in this same part of our interview, Ernie seems to "try on" various grounds for categorizing himself in terms of religion, including both the religious identities of his parents (*my parents were United*) and partner (*cause that's what she is*),

Table 27.4 Indirect religious self-categorization (non-belonging)

Discursive realization	*Example*
22. (Dis)avowal of religious attributes	22. *I wouldn't say I'm all that religious*
23. (Dis)avowal of religious behaviour	23. *I mean **I'm not going to worship the Virgin Mary** I'm not going to*
24. Contrasts with religious others within one's own group	24. *so still Anglican but **the traditional Anglican instead of the Anglican Church of Canada***
25. Negative evaluations of other religious groups	25. *when we went to the Pentecostal church here... and they started you know [mumbling] and the hands were in the air and I always **every time I see those hands go up I hear sieg heil sieg heil***
26. Positive evaluations of other religious groups	26. *I got involved with that ... church and since I have left that and so ah **I miss those things** you know*
27. Negative evaluations of one's own religious group	27. *I believe that the Catholic Church is **stuck in the Dark Ages** pure and simple it has not evolved it is yeah **it is so archaic it's pathetic***
28. Reported speech accounts	28. *she said are you Catholic and **I just looked up and lied and said yes***
29. Hypothetical constructed dialogue	29. ***I didn't kind of say "Well is she saved? Is she?"** [laughter] "Have you tried this? I notice she hasn't been in church, maybe that's why"*

and his own religious behaviour (*I attended a Lutheran church more than anything*). Yet neither of these provide him with sufficient warrant to categorize himself as belonging to any religious group (*I can't really say what I am*). His unsuccessful search for such grounds does, however, construe religious identity per se as neither inherited from family members or life partners, nor the product of one's own religious praxis. Rather, Ernie's claim not to be an atheist—on the grounds that *I think I believe in a a higher being*—casts religious identity primarily as a product of belief.

In Extract 21, by contrast, Charlie uses the subordinator *if* with the modal auxiliary verb *would* to mark his religious belonging as provisional and contingent upon another of his "transportable identities" (Zimmerman, 1998, pp. 90–91), namely his age. After describing a hypothetical change to his age (*if I wasn't so old*), Charlie presents the potential consequence of such a change (*I would actively ... take action to leave the church*). By portraying this consequence as unfulfilled, Charlie positions himself as still affiliated with a specific church, but, by hypothesizing about such a change, he also displays a measure of disaffiliation with that church.

Further strategies used by participants to construe their own religious non-belonging are illustrated in Table 27.4 below. These include disavowing religious attributes (e.g., Excerpt 22) and/or behaviours (e.g., Extract 23), explicitly contrasting oneself with other sub-groups within one's own religious group (e.g., Extract 24), evaluations of other religious groups (e.g., Extracts 25–26), and/or one's own (e.g., Extract 27), actual (e.g., Extract 28), and/or hypothetical (e.g., Extract 29) speech reports.

Stance-Taking

Finally, rural Canadians discursively construe their own religious identities via attitudinal stance-taking on matters other than religion. Because I have discussed religious self-identification via stance-taking at length elsewhere, I provide here only a summary of three key findings from my Claresholm case study.

First, participants in my study often conveyed a sense of their religious identities by stance-taking on both multiculturalism (Power, 2016) and same-sex marriage (Power, 2014). The first of these issues is particularly interesting in the Canadian context because—although some religious groups have opposed multiculturalism on the grounds that it threatens the "shadow establishment" of Christianity in Canada (Martin, 2000, p. 23)—stances on multiculturalism have not polarized as clearly along religious lines as they have for same-sex marriage. Consequently, it is initially more difficult to see how attitudinal stances on multiculturalism might function as "predicates" of any particular religious identity. Yet, this is precisely where the value of close linguistic analysis (including paying attention to each speaker's specific stance object) becomes evident. Second, attitudinal stance-markers form a cline ranging from the explicit (e.g., evaluative lexis) to the relatively implicit (e.g., narrative, reported speech, disclaimers, apologies, self-repair, vague talk)—and rural Canadians simultaneously project attitudinal stances on social issues and construe their own religious identities using this full range of discursive resources. Third, attitudinal stance-taking can function as a resource for the discursive construal and critique of speakers' own religious identities. And, fourth, attitudinal stance-taking on social issues does not occur in a discursive vacuum; on the contrary, rural Canadians seem very cognisant of social norms and motivated to present a "positive self-image" by (i) demonstrating that they (and/or their religious groups) know and care about Canadian social norms, (ii) dissociating attitudinal stances that run counter to those norms from the religious groups and/or roles with which they affiliate, and (iii) hedging or otherwise downgrading their discursive commitment to those stances. Extracts 30, 31, and 32 below illustrate most (but not all) of these findings.

Each of the speakers in these excerpts project attitudinal stances on aspects of Canadian multiculturalism, but their conceptualizations—and hence their precise stance objects—differ. In Extracts 30 and 31, both Charlotte and Tanner were invited to respond to a quotation attributed to former National Chief of the Assembly of First Nations in Canada (1991–1997), Ovide Mercredi, but whereas Charlotte frames multiculturalism in terms of *cultural diversity* (lines 5–6, Extract 30), Tanner's response focuses on Canadian social policies (lines 10–11, Extract 31). In Extract 32, by contrast, Pat's stance object is Canada's public response to religious diversity.

Extract 30

1 Charlotte: […] I guess the sixth one here it's very talking very much about
2   multiculturalism and growing up in a Canadian society um I don't
3   know *I like multiculturalism* maybe just cause *that's something I've*
4   *grown up with* I actually I've noticed that in a small town like rural
5   Claresholm *I miss some of the cultural diversity that I had in*
6   *Calgary* […]

Extract 31

1 Tanner: Ovide Mercredi yeah [laughter] um that that's a problem we've had
2   is *we've tried to assimilate and that hasn't worked* and then we've
3   *we've tried to promote diversity and that doesn't work either* eh um
4   democracy [pause] don't have anything useful to say on that
5   Kate: okay

6 Tanner: that's political

7 Kate: okay

8 Tanner: it ah *I don't like what we have //[laughter] in Canada now*

9 Kate: //[laughter] what what is it that you don't like

10 Tanner: well *the kind of everybody's allowed to have their rights and*

11 *even if the religious rights of one impinge on the other*

Extract 32

1 Kate: and do you think there's a space for that range of beliefs in public life like do

2 you think religion is um an accepted part of public life

3 Pat: I think Canada's working their way through that ah I think that you know *it's*

4 *a whole pendulum shifting thing* ah I think ah it has it's been swung pretty far

5 towards not having any like example is when the Swiss Air flight crashed and

6 um they asked the the Christian chaplain they had representatives from

7 different faiths and they told the Christian chaplain that they couldn't mention

8 Jesus I think

9 Kate: mhm

10 Pat: which you know is *retarded* because //if you're asking==

11 Kate: //[laughter]

12 Pat ==other people and he obliged *of course he was a United Church minister*

13 *what other denomination would oblige that one* um what but *to me* that's just

14 *ridiculous the whole point of having different representatives of different*

15 *faiths is that you have representatives of different FAITHS*

Charlotte projects a positive attitudinal stance towards multiculturalism by combining the attitude verb *to like* with the first-person pronoun *I* (line 3, Extract 30). Tanner also uses *to like* with the same pronoun (line 8, Extract 31), but negates the verb to project a negative stance. In doing so, both speakers position themselves "along an affective scale" (Du Bois, 2007, p.143): Charlotte's stance is more positive than Tanner's. Yet, by negating *to like*—rather than selecting a more expressly negative verb, such as *to dislike* or *to disapprove of*—Tanner retains some of the positive connotations associated with *to like*, and thus positions himself closer to the middle of the affective scale. By contrast, Pat projects an extremely negative stance, using the adjectives *retarded* and *ridiculous* (lines 10 and 14, Extract 32) to attribute properties of mental deficiency to Canada's public handling of religious diversity. By using evaluative adjectives rather than attitude verbs, Pat's commentary seems designed to "adhere" the negativity of her stance to multiculturalism, rather than to herself. However, this strategy appears unsuccessful: her choice of the overtly pejorative retarded is met with laughter by her interlocutor (line 11), which suggests that this evaluation is heard as somehow inapposite (O'Donnell-Trujillo & Adams, 1983, p. 182). Pat in turn responds by using progressively milder adjectives (*ridiculous*, line 14; *dumb, silly*, not shown) and relativizing all further stance-taking on multiculturalism (*to me*, line 13; *I mean, I think*, not shown). She thus seems to downgrade both the attitudinal and epistemic stances projected in her initial response, which itself is an exception in my corpus.

Charlotte and Pat both go on record as respectively affirming and critiquing multiculturalism. By contrast, Tanner's use of the explicitly vague phrase "what we have [...] in Canada" now enables him (at least partially) to avoid going on record as overtly opposing this cherished Canadian social norm. Pat also uses a vague formulation ("a whole pendulum shifting thing," line 4), which both implies a negative evaluation of her stance object and implicitly invites her interlocutor to reconstruct and, in doing so, to corroborate her stance. For, in contrast to more descriptive head nouns, placeholders such as "thing" communicate stance "only weakly" (Jucker et al., 2003, p. 1750), and therefore invite collaborative stance-taking.

Last, these three speakers also provide different forms of stance support: Charlotte's positive stance appears grounded in her personal experience of having grown up with (line 4) cultural diversity in the city of Calgary (lines 5–6), before relocating to Claresholm. Tanner supports his negative stance with further negative evaluations, firstly of two key Canadian social policies (lines 2–3), and secondly of the potential that competing (religious) rights have to impact other people (lines 10–11). Pat's negative stance, by contrast, is both supported by and contributes to a critique of her own religious group (lines 12–13; note: Pat's explicit self-identification as a United Church minister is not shown here). She also recruits key principles of multiculturalism (i.e., diversity and inclusion) to support her critique of Canada's implementation of multiculturalism (lines 14–15).

Implications and Future Directions

The research presented in this chapter underscores the fact that religious identity is more complex than a simple matter of belonging/non-belonging and enumerates both the relatively direct and indirect ways in which it can be discursively construed. The symbiosis between categorization and particularization, and interdiscursive attitudinal stance-taking, are shown to be especially salient resources for this construal. This study also shows rural Canadians to be considerably more reflexive about, and self-critical of, their own religious identities than stereotypes of religious adherents might lead one to expect—and, in doing so, it challenges some common, derogatory notions of what it means to be "religious." This study also found that rural Canadians appear acutely aware of how their religious self-representations might be perceived by others and repeatedly seem to avoid claims that might subject them to charges of claiming to be better than religious others. One can only speculate, of course, as to why they do so—but this study suggests that this pattern is likely to be informed by social norms of modesty (within religious circles) and respecting diversity (within the Canadian context).

These findings have both research and practical implications. For research, they demonstrate the relevance of close linguistic analysis to religious studies inquiries, while contesting the stereotypical association of majority religious discourses and oppression and inviting more nuanced analyses of both religious identities and faith-based stances on controversial social issues. They also potentially contribute to Christian ecclesiology—which often conceptualizes the category "Church" not as an institutional or organizational entity, but rather as a collection of people—by revealing that one way in which individuals constitute the Church is by talking their belongingness to and/or disaffiliation from it.

Practically, this research has implications for people interested in better understanding religious family members, friends, and neighbours, as well as the news media. In particular, this study highlights that there are important differences between (i) inviting a person's own construal of their religious identity and (ii) assigning to others religious categorizations and the attributes or behaviours commonly thought to be "bound" to those categorizations (Sacks, [1972] 1986, p. 335). It follows that there is value in both paying attention to other people's religious self-representations and reflecting critically upon one's own a priori assumptions about religious categories before assigning them to others.

The research presented in this chapter paves the way for a wide range of further research addressing discursive construals of religious identity, just some of which I will propose here. First, three analytical categories emerged from my sampling strategy: (i) people who are *willing to discuss religion* when invited to do so, (ii) people who are *unwilling to discuss religion* when invited to do so, and (iii) people who demonstrate an *active interest in discussing religion*. These are potentially interesting categories around which future research into both religious discourses and religious identities could be organized. One might fruitfully study, for example, how different individuals respond to, avoid, and/or initiate religious talk in various discursive contexts, including the workplace, higher education, and neighbourhood conversations.

Second, this study shows that individual religious identities are commonly construed in terms of collective or shared identities—whether as a form of belonging, differentiation, or some combination thereof—and that these construals can take place in various conversational settings. Two important questions that emerge from this finding are (i) whether/how the discursive construal of individual religious identities differs between conversational settings, and (ii) whether/how *individual* and *collective* religious identities might be construed separately from one another.

Third, this study also highlights the intersection of religious and other social identity categories, such as gender, age, relationship status, sexuality, and occupation. Further research could explore this intersectionality with a view to developing a more complex, multi-faceted and nuanced model of religious identity which accounts for how these and other categories are construed simultaneously—and for their relationships to one another to be better understood. There is also considerable scope for examining both the similarities and differences between discursive construals of religious and other social identities, and the recruitment of diverse matters other than religion in such construals.

Fourth, this study found that—in addition to cooperating with my goal of conducting a research interview—rural Canadians seem to use discursive construals of their own religious identities for further rhetorical and interactional purposes, such as claiming the relevance of religion to particular conversational settings (or topics) and avoiding (being perceived to be) boasting. Further research could therefore explore not only when, where, and how but also—and particularly—*why* everyday folk choose discursively to construe their religious identities. This line of questioning has been pursued extensively in relation to politicians and other public figures, but very little attention has been paid to everyday interactions in which religious identity is discursively construed. Yet, the discursive construal of religious identity in everyday settings is critically important because our increasingly connected and diverse world now brings together people with multiple (including conflicting) religious identities—not only in families and neighbourhoods, but also around controversial social issues in which both religious and nonreligious people may be heavily invested. Several of my informants expressed both pleasure in, and appreciation for, the opportunity to discuss their religious commitments in the non-adversarial environment provided by my research interviews. Harry, for instance, remarked that he felt "good proud to be able to express myself." Barbara went further, explaining that:

> it's good to communicate that I think and get it out it's almost a cathartic experience I think
> for some people because we tend to like I said it's difficult to talk about sometimes we tend

to bundle it all up because we don't want to offend people or we don't want to look stupid or we don't want to you know be perceived as being weird or different.

Finding constructive ways to talk across our differences and understanding better the interpersonal, social, and political roles played by discursive construals of religious identity are key challenges for both researchers and individuals. The mainstream media are also implicated here, given their often reductionistic and discriminatory coverage of diverse (and particularly minority) religious groups.

Further Reading

Heather, N. (2000). *Religious language and critical discourse analysis: Ideology and identity in Christian discourse today*. Peter Lang.

This book is one of the earliest discourse analytic studies of religious identity. It draws on Theo van Leeuwen's work on the representation of social actors, which is an important discourse analytic framework with great relevance to religious identity.

Jule, A. (Ed.). (2006). *Gender and religious identity: Women in discourse*. Palgrave Macmillan.

This book explores discursive construals of religious identity in relation to gender and addresses a variety of religious traditions.

Power, K. (2012). Investigating religious "identity": The promise and problem of discourse analytic methods for religious studies inquiries. *Fieldwork in Religion, 8*(1), 7–26.

This article discusses how and why discourse analytic methods are useful for investigating religious identity, as well as the limitations of this method.

Prakash Kapoor, C., & Misra, I. (2017). Religious identity: A missing link in identity discourse. *Indian Journal of Social Science and Organizational Behaviour, 6*(1–2), 7–15.

This article brings a non-western perspective to the study of religious identity, while exploring what it means for religion to be conceptualized as an "identity" and positioning this inquiry in relation to social psychology.

Thumma, S. (1991). Negotiating a religious identity: The case of the gay evangelical. *Sociological Analysis, 52*(4), 333–347.

This article explores a specific religious identity in which elements that are often stereotypically depicted as incompatible intersect. Although it is not a discourse analytic study, it nevertheless raises important questions around categorization, identity negotiation, and intersectionality.

References

Antaki, C. & Widdicombe, S. (1998). Identity as an Achievement and as a Tool. In C. Antaki & S. Widdicombe (Eds.), *Identities in talk*, 1–14. SAGE.

Baron, A. (2004). "I'm a woman but I know God leads my way": Agency and Tzotzil evangelical discourse. *Language in Society, 33*(2), 249–283.

Barsalou, L.W. (1983). Ad hoc categories. *Memory and Cognition, 11*(3), 211–227.

Bauer, M.W. & Aarts, B. (2000). Corpus Construction: a Principle for Qualitative Data Collection. In M.W. Bauer & G. Gaskell (Eds.), *Qualitative researching with text, image and sound: A practical handbook*, 19–37. SAGE.

Bechhofer, F., McCrone, D., Kiely, R., & Stewart, R. (1999). Constructing national identity: Arts and landed elites in Scotland. *Sociology, 33*(3), 515–534.

Bibby, R.W. (1999). Multiculturalism in Canada: A Methodologically Inadequate Political Virtue. *DISKUS Web Edition, 5*. http://web.uni-marburg.de/religionswissenschaft/journal/diskus/bibby.html

Chandrasegaran, A. & Kong, K.M.C. (2006). Stance-taking and stance-support in students online forum discussion. *Linguistics and Education, 17*(4), 374–390.

Davie, G. (2006). The future of religion and its implications for the social sciences. In A. von Harskamp, M. Klaver, J. Roeland, & P. Versteeg (Eds.), *Playful religion: Challenges for the study of religion*, 137–149. Eburon.

Day, A. (2009). Believing in belonging: an ethnography of young people's constructions of belief. *Culture and Religion, 10*(3), 263–278.

Droogers, A. ([1995] 2006). Identity, Religious Pluralism and Ritual in Brazil: Umbanda and Pentecostalism. In A. von Harskamp, M. Klaver, J. Roeland, & P. Versteeg (Eds.), *Playful religion: Challenges for the study of religion*, 27–45. Eburon.

Du Bois, J.W. (2007). The stance triangle. In R. Englebretson (Ed.), *Stancetaking in discourse: Subjectivity, evaluation, interaction*, 139–182. John Benjamins Publishing Company.

Fairclough, N. (2003). *Analyzing discourse: Textual analysis for social research*. Routledge.

Fitzgerald, R. & Housley, W. (2002). Identity, categorization and sequential organization: the sequential and categorial flow of identity in a radio phone-in. *Discourse & Society, 13*(5), 579–602.

Geertz, C. (1979). From the Native's Point of View: On the Nature of Anthropological Understanding. In P. Rabinow & W.M. Sullivan (Eds.), *Interpretive social science: A reader*, 225–241. University of California Press.

Glaser, B.G. & Strauss, A.L. (1967). *The discovery of grounded theory*. Aldine.

Godlove, T.F. (2000). Religious Discourse and First Person Authority. In R.T. McCutcheon (Ed.), *The insider/outsider problem in the study of religion*, 164–178. Cassell.

Grad, H. & Martín Rojo, L. (2008). Identities in discourse: An integrative view. In R. Dolón & J. Todolí (Eds.), *Analysing identities in discourse*, 3–28. John Benjamins Publishing Company.

Harding, S.F. (2000). *The book of Jerry Falwell: Fundamentalist Language and Politics*. Princeton University Press.

Heather, N. (2000). *Religious language and critical discourse analysis: Ideology and identity in Christian discourse today.* Peter Lang.

Hervieu-Léger, D. (2000). *Religion as a chain of memory*. Translated by S. Lee. Polity Press.

Hester, S. (1992). Recognising references to deviance in referral talk. In G. Watson & R.M. Sieler (Eds.), *Text in Context: Contributions to Ethnomethodology*, 156–174. SAGE.

Jayyusi, L. (1984). *Categorization and the moral order*. Routledge & Kegan Paul.

Jenkins, R. ([1996] 2004). *Social identity*, 2nd edition. Routledge.

Jucker, A.H., Smith, S.W., & Lüdge, T. (2003). Interactive Aspects of Vagueness in Conversation. *Journal of Pragmatics, 35*(12), 1737–1769.

Jule, A. (Ed.). (2006). *Gender and religious identity: Women in discourse*. Palgrave Macmillan.

Lincoln, B. (2000). Culture. In W. Braun & R.T. McCutcheon (Eds.), *Guide to the Study of Religion*, 409–422. Cassell.

Lyon, D. (2000). Introduction. In D. Lyon & M. Van Die (Eds.), *Rethinking church, state, and modernity: Canada between Europe and America*, 3–19. University of Toronto Press.

Martin, D. (2000). Canada in Comparative Perspective. In D. Lyon & M. Van Die (Eds.), *Rethinking Church, State, and Modernity: Canada between Europe and America*, 23–33. University of Toronto Press.

O'Donnell-Trujillo, N. & Adams, K. (1983). Heheh in Conversation: Some Coordinating Accomplishments of Laughter. *The Western Journal of Speech Communication, 47*(2), 175–191.

Ochs, E. (1992). Indexing Gender. In A. Duranti & C. Goodwin (Eds.), *Rethinking Context: Language as an Interactive Phenomenon*, 335–358. Cambridge University Press.

Power, K. (2012). Investigating religious "identity": The promise and problem of discourse analytic methods for religious studies inquiries. *Fieldwork in Religion, 8*(1), 7–26.

Power, K. (2014). Talking sexuality–Religious identity construction in rural Canada. In H. Shipley (Ed.), *Globalized religion and sexual identity: Contexts, contestations, voices*, 62–85. Brill.

Power, K. (2016). Charity chicks: a discourse-analytic study of religious self-identification by rural Canadian Mormon women. In B.R. Lee & T.T.-l. Woo (Eds.), *Canadian women shaping diasporic religious identities*, 139–194. Wilfred Laurier University Press.

Prakash Kapoor, C. & Misra, I. (2017). Religious identity: A missing link in identity discourse. Indian Journal of Social Science and Organizational Behaviour, 6(1–2), 7–15.

Rambo, L.R. (1993). *Understanding religious conversion*. Yale University Press.

Sacks, H. (1979). Hotrodder: A Revolutionary Category. In G. Psathas (Ed.), *Everyday Language: Studies in Ethnomethodology*, 7–14. Irvington Press.

Sacks, H. (1992). *Lectures on conversation, 1*. Basil Blackwell.

Sacks, H. ([1972] 1986). On the analyzability of stories told by children. In J.J. Gumperz & D. Hymes (Eds.), *Directions in sociolinguistics: The ethnography of communication*, 325–345. Basil Blackwell.

Sayer, A. (2003). *Restoring the moral dimension in social scientific accounts: A qualified ethical naturalist approach.* International Association for Critical Realism Annual Conference, Amsterdam. www.lancaster. ac.uk/fass/resources/sociology-online-papers/papers/sayer-restoring-the-moral-dimension.pdf

Schegloff, E.A. (1999). Naivety vs. Sophistication or Discipline vs. Self-Indulgence: A Rejoinder to Billig. *Discourse & Society, 10*(4), 577–582.

Schegloff, E.A. (2007). A tutorial on membership categorization. *Journal of Pragmatics, 39*(3), 462–482.

Thumma, S. (1991). Negotiating a religious identity: The case of the gay evangelical. *Sociological Analysis, 52*(4), 333–347.

Watson, D.R. (1978). Categorisation, authorisation and blame-negotiation in conversation. *Sociology, 12*(1), 105–113.

Watson, D.R. (1987). Interdisciplinary considerations in the analysis of pro-terms. In G. Button & J.R.E. Lee (Eds.), *Talk and Social Organisation*, 261–289. Multilingual Matters.

Wetherell, M. (Ed.). (1996). *Identities, groups and social issues.* SAGE.

Wodak, R. (2004). National and transnational identities. European and other identities constructed in interviews with EU-officials. In R.K. Herrmann, T. Risse, & M.B. Brewer (Eds.), *Transnational identities. Becoming European in the EU*, 97–128. Rowman & Littlefield.

Woodhead, L. (1999). Theology and the Fragmentation of the Self. *International Journal of Systematic Theology, 1*(1), 53–72.

Zimmerman, D.H. (1998). Identity, Context and Interaction. In C. Antaki & S. Widdicombe (Eds.), *Identities in talk*, 87–106. SAGE.

28

CONVERSION NARRATIVES

Kumaran Rajandran

Introduction and Background

Conversion is defined distinctly among religions and no single definition captures the various aspects involved (Rambo & Farhadian, 2014). It may be intra-religious (e.g., Martin Luther from Catholic Christian to Protestant Christian) or inter-religious (e.g., Jewish Saul to Christian Paul) but a clear criterion is a movement among faith systems (Rambo, 1993). Conversion is never a neutral act (Rambo & Farhadian, 2014) because it simultaneously creates boundaries of belonging and non-belonging. It is gradual or swift (Jindra, 2011) but always involves a personal transformation in religion. The transformation reorients individual life (Hobbs, 2021; Kling, 2014) and leaves lifelong implications (Hindmarsh, 2014). It provides an identity-giving experience because the new religion shapes converts' attitude and behavior.

The experience of conversion, manifested in language, is termed conversion narratives (Carl, 2009; Stromberg, 2014). The earliest are recorded in *Confessions* by St. Augustine (fourth century CE) although for Kling (2014), these narratives are modern and represent a fraction of conversion to Christianity, as most people throughout history did not document their conversion. Conversion narratives are documented across religions (Linge, 2023) although the literature is focused on Christianity in multiple spatiotemporal contexts. Besides studies on conversion to Catholicism (Carl, 2009), Evangelicalism (Kling, 2014), Lutheranism (Carl, 2009), and Puritanism (Kling, 2020), there exist studies on the Bahá'í Faith (Jindal, 2011), Hinduism (Singh, 2018), and Islam (Burhani, 2020; Casey, 2019; Linge, 2023; van Nieuwkerk, 2014). Most research considers varieties of Christianity and inter-religious narratives severely outweigh intra-religious narratives.

Research on conversion is primarily conducted in anthropology, history, psychology, sociology, and theology. Although the experience of conversion is mediated by language (Stromberg, 2014), the contribution of linguistics remains minimal (Hobbs, 2021). van Noppen coined the terminology theolinguistics in 1981 (Crystal, 2018). It acknowledges language as part of sacred meaning making in multiple contexts, such as conversion (Hobbs, 2021). Language 'makes' converts (Rambo & Farhadian, 2014) as choosing language features can represent converts' experience of conversion. Language analyses can disclose the nature of religious change and the relationship between religion and identity (Stromberg, 2014). A caveat is that analyses are not studying the reality of conversion but rather its linguistic manifestation.

DOI: 10.4324/9781003301271-31

Existing research has examined genre, theme, and grammatical and lexical choices in conversion narratives. The genre has the communicative purpose of describing how/why conversion happened. Rambo's (1993) seminal study lists the stages of conversion, which may be mapped onto a genre's stages (Bhatia, 2004). Conversion involves a context (macro and micro), crisis (catalyst for conversion), quest (searching for purpose), encounter (knowing advocates of the new religion), interaction (trying the new religion), commitment (adopting the new religion), and consequences (impact of conversion on various aspects of life).

Conversion narratives use characteristic stages, establishing a beginning, middle, and end (Kling, 2014, 2020). In an evangelical conversion narrative, Kling (2014) finds that the beginning is where converts do not know God, the middle is critical because it enables a transition, and the end grants a sense of peace. Singh (2018) notes two stages in Swami Shraddhanand's autobiography. They contrast life before and after joining the Arya Samaj (a reformist Hindu organization), and parallel uncertainties emerging and being resolved. The stages point towards a climax, such as enlightenment in Buddhism and forgiven sins in Christianity (Hindmarsh, 2014). The stages are the 'location' of plot, actors, causality, and temporality (Linge, 2023). Causality gives factors in favor of the religion embraced, becoming apologia for cognitive and emotive transformations (Hindmarsh, 2014). Temporality distinguishes the life lived in the past and present, often presenting destructive to righteous transformations (Stromberg, 2014).

The theme in conversion narratives justifies the reasons causing movement among faith systems (Hobbs, 2021; Jindra, 2011). Various reasons motivate conversion, but intellectual or mystical reasons are commonly reported. From previous research, versions of Christianity, Hinduism, or Islam provide logical/scientific or inexplicable/otherworldly reasons for conversion. The reasons frame a push-pull strategy. It contrasts the old and new faiths, and prompts a change in converts. For instance, Kling (2014) identifies narratives of forsaking other deities, embracing Christ and incorporation in a new community among early Christian converts while Casey (2019) observes narratives of awakening, continuity, and return to Islam among present-day Muslim converts.

The genre and theme deploy a range of grammatical and lexical resources. Grammatical choices involve the passive voice (e.g., And it came upon me that…), presuming the silent workings of divinity (Stromberg, 2014). The tense also shifts, where past tense characterizes previous beliefs and practices, but present tense indicates contemporary and general beliefs and practices. Converts being the narrator, first-person pronouns (I) and determiners (my) are abundant. They are their own agent because their actions and decisions propel conversion (Linge, 2023). But they are also a patient because multiple agents facilitate their conversion. Divine agency predominates Christian and Muslim narratives (Casey, 2019; Hindmarsh, 2014). For instance, people are God's instruments, and Jesus, family, acquaintances, or even devotional literature (Carl, 2009; Leone, 2014) are potent agents in Catholic conversion narratives. This agency guides and inspires converts.

Lexical choices activate words and phrases in the repository of a particular religion. The adoption of vocabulary in a sacred language (e.g., Arabic, Sanskrit) or typical vernacular vocabulary marks cognizance of the religion and solidarity. Carl (2009) notes adjectives to judge the value of Catholicism and Lutheranism (e.g., holy Carmelite scapular, condemnable Lutheran error) while Kling (2020) finds a pre-set script of phrases from evangelical subculture in Puritan conversion narratives (e.g., hunger for God's word). This lexis invokes qualities of the old and new religions respectively (Hindmarsh, 2014), and create moral standards because converts choose the 'better' religion and can be presumed to imbibe desirable values.

The abstract nature of religion invites metaphors (Pihlaja, 2013). Carl (2009) and Stromberg (2014) observe journey metaphors about reaching Christianity, where salvation replaces sin. Carl (2009) and Hobbs (2021) mention life and death, and light and dark metaphors about changing undesirable to desirable qualities (e.g., darkness of Catholicism, great light of the Lutheran faith). Similarly, Singh (2018) finds light and dark metaphors characterizing Swami Shraddhanand's discovery of a 'pure' Hinduism.

Conversion narratives may mention a concept/persona/scripture/structure or introduce their words using direct/indirect speech or nominalization to share the legitimacy of the voice of religion. Sacred legitimation (Hobbs, 2021) imprints the authority of persona (e.g., Jesus, Muhammad, saints) (Carl, 2009; Stromberg, 2014) or scripture (e.g., Bible, Quran, Vedas). For instance, Muslim televangelists reinforce their authority by relating their dream about Prophet Muhammad or citing him (Burhani, 2020). The revoicing reinforces their position as teachers of religion. It justifies actions and decisions taken because divine sanction is provided. The revoicing sacralizes the profane and the present is interpreted in terms of the eternal. The conversion is unique but also part of a grander divine event, making it seem inevitable.

Using a repertoire of language features, conversion narratives convey an autobiography of religious transformation (Linge, 2023). The insider perspective is provided as converts are simultaneously author, narrator, and protagonist (Hindmarsh, 2014). They depict a presumably authentic religious identity to an audience (Casey, 2019), but this identity is subjective because their narratives are retrospective and reconstructive. Converts speak after conversion and reinterpret past activities through present convictions (van Nieuwkerk, 2014). It reveals the way that converts perceive themselves and the way that they want others to perceive them. These narratives explain and justify conversion, creating a linear sequence that culminates in religious transformation. They can serve multiple purposes but van Nieuwkerk (2014) states that conversion narratives are a preaching genre, to introduce the faith to non-members and to maintain or strengthen the faith of members. The narratives may become vectors of ideologies, and condition attitude and behavior toward a religion.

The focus of the present chapter is Hinduism, a category which spans a broad faith system with four major denominations named Śaiva, Śākta, Smarta, and Vaiṣṇava. Vaiṣṇavism is a significant denomination and its four major sampradāyas (lineages/traditions) are Brahmā, Kumara, Rudra, and Śrī. Every sampradāya is comprised of multiple branches, and one branch in the Brahmā sampradāya is linked to Caitanya (1486–1534), who introduced the public congregational chanting of the mantra *Hare Kṛṣṇa Hare Kṛṣṇa, Kṛṣṇa Kṛṣṇa Hare Hare, Hare Rāma Hare Rāma, Rāma Rāma Hare Hare* in fifteenth-century Bengal. He also composed the Śikṣāṣṭakam, eight prayer verses in Sanskrit condensing his teachings. These teachings propounded the philosophy of acintya bhedābheda tattva (inconceivable difference in non-difference), centered on bhakti (devotion) to Rādhā-Kṛṣṇa.

Bhakti became the motivational basis for his community, which expanded in the modern Indian states of Odisha, Uttar Pradesh, and West Bengal. The origin and center being Bengal, Caitanya's teachings came to be termed Gauḍīya (Bengal) Vaiṣṇavism. After Caitanya's death, his disciples codified and expanded Gauḍīya Vaiṣṇavism, primarily the Six Gosvāmīs in the sixteenth century. Gauḍīya Vaiṣṇavism declined in the seventeenth and eighteenth centuries but it was revived in the twentieth century under Bhaktivinoda Ṭhākura and Bhaktisiddhānta Saraswatī, whose disciple was Bhaktivedānta Svāmī Prabhupāda (1896–1977). Prabhupāda discharged his guru's (spiritual master's) instruction to preach in the West. He migrated to New York City in 1965 and founded the International Society for Kṛṣṇa Consciousness (ISKCON), often named the Hare Kṛṣṇas, in 1966.

Prabhupāda (1994) did not claim ISKCON to be a Hindu organization because the terminology 'Hinduism' is absent in scriptures, but ISKCON now considers itself an organization representing (Gauḍīya) Vaiṣṇavism (ISKCON, 2020). ISKCON expanded in Canada, the United Kingdom, the

United States, and other countries during Prabhupāda's lifetime although it was labeled a counter-culture organization in the 1960s and 1970s (Ullman, 1988). Prabhupāda's death in 1977 started a decay, which worsened in the 1980s as monetary and sexual scandals were revealed (Rochford, 2013). Surprisingly, since the 1990s, ISKCON has reinvented itself. Its isolationist tendencies have been replaced by flexibility and modernity, and ISKCON survived and flourished in the 2000s (Dwyer & Cole, 2013). Its global spread in six decades is evidenced by centers, educational institutions, farms, temples, and restaurants on every continent.

ISKCON actively converts Hindus and non-Hindus to Vaiṣṇavism although Hinduism has displayed divergent tendencies on conversion throughout its history. Modern Hinduism purport-edly discourages people converting to or from it (Sharma, 2012, p. 129). It does not seem to be a proselytizing religion, converting others to its exclusive and exclusionary membership (Sharma, 2012, 2014). Yet, Hindu scriptures and other literature describe intra/inter-religious conversion (e.g., from Buddhist/Jain to Śaiva/Vaiṣṇava and from Śaiva/Smarta to Vaiṣṇava). Continuing this practice, certain Hindu lineages/traditions across denominations proselytize and practice conversion (Sharma, 2014). Conversion is related to dīkṣā (initiation), where an individual formally joins a denomination (Sharma, 2012).

Gauḍīya Vaiṣṇavism has proselytized since its start because Caitanya traveled the north, east and south of India to spread bhakti to Hindus and non-Hindus. He predicted the chanting of the names of Kṛṣṇa in villages and towns of the world (Caitanya-bhāgavata, 2008, 3.4.126). ISKCON considers itself instrumental in realizing his prediction and has remained an intensely proselytizing organization (Karapanagiotis, 2020, 2021). Among its seven objectives, the first is to propagate spiritual knowledge to society, the knowledge being Gauḍīya Vaiṣṇavism. Consequently, ISKCON inspires and guides individuals towards initiation. New followers are called bhakta (for males) or bhaktin (for females), meaning devotee. After initiation, they are given an initiated name and the surname Dāsa (for males) or Devī Dāsī (for females). These names are employed in a religious context and would not replace their legal names.

'I Was Looking for Kṛṣṇa': Conversion Narratives of ISKCON Followers

ISKCON has produced videos of individuals describing their conversion. They have been posted on some ISKCON-linked websites and YouTube. The format is consistent, where a seated/standing individual faces the camera and reveals their participation in ISKCON. The videos share the communicative purpose of describing how/why conversion happened, and hence fit the genre of conversion narratives. Ten narratives were randomly selected to be analyzed, as listed in Table 28.1. The names of the individuals were anonymized by acronyms. They have received dīkṣā (initiation), which can be taken as conversion to Gauḍīya Vaiṣṇavism. These individuals speak in English, but they may not be first language speakers of the language. They live in the Americas and Asia, where the majority of ISKCON followers are located.

The videos were analyzed with a theolinguistic orientation, to focus on conversion as sacred meaning making (Hobbs, 2021). Theolinguistics is method agnostic because it does not favor specific approaches (Crystal, 2018; Hobbs, 2021). A study should employ suitable approaches to achieve its research objectives. This is informed by a review of approaches utilized on similar texts, the availability of items in texts to be analyzed by these approaches, the components of these approaches to adopt/adapt, and perhaps researcher competence. The present chapter deployed conversion motifs (Lofland & Skonovd, 1981) and membership categorization analysis (MCA) (Sacks, 1995; Stokoe, 2012) to understand the conversion narratives of ISKCON followers.

Table 28.1 Selected conversion narratives

No.	Name	Gender	Country
1	GS	M	Philippines
2	L	F	USA
3	MY	F	Ecuador
4	N	M	USA
5	NK	F	India
6	NU	M	Brazil
7	PS	F	Peru
8	RP	F	China
9	SB	M	Chile
10	SK	M	Argentina

Conversion narratives display a motif or a convert's subjective perception of conversion. Lofland and Skonovd (1981) propose six motifs or prototypes about how/why conversion happened. The motifs are termed affectional, coercive, experimental, intellectual, mystical, and revivalist (Lofland & Skonovd, 1981). These are broad and defined separately but may share overlaps because conversion may be traced to more than one prototype. Their use is responsive to spatiotemporal and cultural traits, and the preference of religious groups (Lofland & Skonovd, 1981). Affectional emphasizes personal attachment or strong liking, and participation precedes belief (1); coercive means a forced conversion (2); experimental involves curiosity and trying, and participation precedes belief (3); intellectual is motivated by individual investigation regarding alternative or new concepts, and belief precedes participation (4); mystical encapsulates non-logical experiences, involving emotional arousal to intensify belief (5); and revivalist is characterized by ecstatic group emotions, and participation precedes belief (6). The motifs emphasize an individual's perception of conversion. The emphasis is achieved by organizing their perception using membership categorization devices (MCDs), which involve membership categories (Sacks, 1995).

An MCD recognizes categories as part of a collective category (e.g., father and mother are part of the MCD 'family') and categories can be part of various MCDs (Sacks, 1995; Stokoe, 2012). Categories are not pre-constituted or static but develop in situational contexts as interaction unfolds. Moreover, they can be openly stated, or insinuated by category-relevant features (Schegloff, 2007; Stokoe, 2012). Categories become a short-cut in communication and package knowledge about members, their activities, and predicates (Stokoe, 2012). The packaging can expand or narrow a category and include or exclude social actors. Therefore, the choice of categories makes the 'right' resonances and inferences (Housley & Fitzgerald, 2015; Stokoe, 2012) and goes beyond categorizing because moral judgments are implied.

Several terminologies from Stokoe (2012) are utilized to identify where categorization transpires in conversion narratives. Category-bound activities are activities linked to categories (e.g., Mothers [category] take care of children [activity]). Category-tied predicates specify characteristics of categories (e.g., This mother [category] cares for [predicate] her children). Standardized relational pairs are categories denoting duties and obligations (e.g., teacher-student, neighbor-neighbor). Duplicative organizations are categories in a unit (e.g., father and mother in a family; center and defender in a football team). Positioned categories are categories in a hierarchical relationship (e.g., child and adult, where an adult is chided if behaving like a child).

For analysis, I transcribed the spoken language in the videos. The transcripts were analyzed in terms of conversion motifs and MCD. Close readings of the transcripts identified the motifs in the videos. The readings coded words/phrases about how/why conversion happened, and matched these language features to motifs, as indicated by Lofland and Skonovd (1981). The motifs imbue sense in conversion using local categories (Housley & Fitzgerald, 2015). An inventory of explicit and implicit mentions of categories, and their category-resonant activities and predicates was built (Stokoe, 2012). Individuals orient to/from the categories, which reveals the practice of describing their conversion. Cumulatively, the motifs and categories display the individual's understanding of becoming/being a Vaiṣṇava, as exemplified in Extracts 1–15 below.

The conversion narratives record a spiritual autobiography about conversion to Vaiṣṇavism. Religious groups may prefer selected motifs (Lofland & Skonovd, 1981) and the analysis suggests that ISKCON followers prefer experimental and intellectual motifs. Although individual experience rarely fits one sole motif, one motif dominates the moment of narration. The performance of category-relevant activities (Schegloff, 2007), which receive positive predicates, evidence a shift in categories from non-Vaiṣṇava to Vaiṣṇava, as demonstrated in Extracts 1–4.

Extract 1

> Then he said me but if you want to be a devotee, you have to look like a devotee. I said ok, I want to look like a devotee. Ok you have to shave hair, use white clothes, ok, no problem. I was by this time long hair, you know, dreadlocks and like this. So I came straight away, I went to this barber shop, I cut my hair, I leave my śikhā [tuft of hair on head], I became a vegetarian straight away. So this was, this was from one minute to the other. (SK)

Extract 2

> So I went there of course and everything was so beautiful, the music, the food, kīrtan [devotional music], the smell. It creates a huge impression in my heart…and I liked the music so much, and this I think it was very, very important for me in the spiritual life. (SB)

Through the experimental motif, individuals sample an aspect of Vaiṣṇava practice, namely books, clothing, food, or music. ISKCON has cultivated these practices since its inception, and they have become linked to its public perception (Dwyer & Cole, 2013). In Extract 1, SK adopted clothing ('shave hair…white clothes') and eating ('vegetarian') habits, and in Extract 2, SB enjoyed 'the music, the food, kīrtan [devotional music]'. Their activities prioritize the agency of self because SK and SB participated actively ('I said…I want…I was…I came…I went…I cut…I leave…I became' in Extract 1, 'I went…I liked…I think' in Extract 2). The use of the first-person pronoun marks their actions and decisions to participate in Vaiṣṇava practice.

The practice receives favorable predication because certain words/phrases evoke the right resonances (Housley & Fitzgerald, 2015; Stokoe, 2012). In Extract 1, SK introduces implicit evaluation with 'ok no problem', 'straight away' and 'from one minute to the other'. In Extract 2, SB presents explicit evaluation with 'so beautiful', 'huge impression', 'so much' and 'very, very important'. The two individuals value participation positively and it is part of a pull strategy. It signals a shift in categories from non-Vaiṣṇava to Vaiṣṇava, where SK reports a swift shift, but SB has a gradual shift to Vaiṣṇava practice.

Extract 3

Um, I remember I was, I was kind of a spiritual seeker, I was looking for spiritual life, I was going to churches and I was Jewish. So I was, I was looking for Kṛṣṇa, or looking for God. And I went so many different places but I couldn't find anyone serious about God or anyone who could answer my questions. But when I came in contact with the devotees then immediately all my questions became answered. (L)

Extract 4

But I didn't choose to become a devotee until I was about 15 or 16 years old and I came to Vṛndāvan to do Bhakti-Śāstrī [scriptural study program] and then through the study of Śrīla Prabhupād's books and through the association of devotees. (N)

Through the intellectual motif, individuals comprehend Vaiṣṇava philosophy, as ISKCON answers their spiritual questions. The unfamiliarity of the philosophy is absent, and its potential receives focus. In Extract 3, L is a 'spiritual seeker', 'looking for spiritual life' and recognizes ISKCON 'answer[ing] my questions', and in Extract 4, N studied 'Bhakti-Śāstrī' [scriptural study program] and 'Śrīla Prabhupād's books'. Their activities prioritize the agency of self because L and N indicate their quest using journey metaphors ('I was looking...I couldn't find...I came in contact' in Extract 3, 'I didn't choose...I came' in Extract 4). The use of the first-person pronoun marks their actions and decisions to believe in Vaiṣṇava philosophy.

The philosophy receives favorable predication because certain words/phrases evoke the right resonances (Housley & Fitzgerald, 2015; Stokoe, 2012). In Extract 3, L designates other faith categories, namely Christianity ('churches') and Judaism ('Jewish'). But these categories receive a negative evaluation because they were not 'serious about God' and they did not 'answer my questions'. The conjunction 'But' introduces a contrast and 'immediately all my questions became answered' shows a positive evaluation of the philosophy taught by ISKCON. Similarly in Extract 4, 'Bhakti-Śāstrī' and 'Śrīla Prabhupād's books' are a positive evaluation of the philosophy in the program and books. The exposure influenced N's choice to 'become a devotee'. L and N value the philosophy positively and it is also part of a pull strategy. It signals a shift in categories from non-Vaiṣṇava to Vaiṣṇava because Vaiṣṇava philosophy provided existential explanations.

Extract 5

I was a person, uh, who, who was very low, like ah, had a nature of complaining and depressing nature. But when I came to ISKCON, I learn a lot of things, uh, like basic thing which I really learn was selflessness and how we can live a happy life by actually giving and not just by taking. (NK)

Extract 6

Um, I'm married. I live in New Jersey with my wife Tulsi, um, and my parents. And um, I love to read, I love to do kīrtan, um, I love to preach when I can, I love to go on Harinām sankīrtan [public chanting] in the streets. (N)

Before converting, ISKCON followers are reported to have chaotic lives or emotional troubles but conversion produced improvements (Ullman, 1988). NK in Extract 5 negatively predicates her non-Vaiṣṇava self in the past as 'low', 'nature of complaining and depressing nature' and using the conjunction 'But', she positively predicates her Vaiṣṇava self in the present as 'learn a lot of things...selflessness...live a happy life'. The contrast from negative to positive evaluation is corresponded by a movement from past tense ('I was...had') to present tense ('I learn... we can live'), linking personal improvement to temporal change. This sequence is common in conversion narratives, where past and present are contrasted in favor of the religion embraced (Hindmarsh, 2014).

These improvements are infrequent in the conversion narratives because ISKCON followers have extended beyond the counterculture crowd (Dwyer & Cole, 2013). It is a mature organization and people become followers to complement their stable lives. N in Extract 6 says 'I'm married. I live in New Jersey with my wife Tulsi...and my parents', and these activities imply stability. It is enhanced by being an ISKCON follower because he reads, does kīrtan, preaches and does Harinām sankīrtan [public chanting]. He repeats the verb 'love' four times in the present tense, which designates the value of the activities to his daily life. But these activities may be conditioned by other factors, as indicated by the dependent clause 'when I can'.

From Extracts 1–6, the activities and predicates render the 'Vaiṣṇava' MCD desirable because the religion has changed the lives of the individuals. The habitus of Vaiṣṇavism is developing, and its beliefs and practices shape their attitude and behavior. The MCD is also embodied in clothing, which visibly manifests their religion. Their forehead is anointed by tilak (sandalwood paste) and they wear tulasī (Holy Basil) necklaces. These two are exclusive symbols of Vaiṣṇavism and indicate their surrender to God. They also wear traditional Indian clothing and although it is not religion-centered, the clothing further marks developing a new habitus.

Besides the category of Vaiṣṇava, individuals can be part of other categories, making overlaps probable (Schegloff, 2007). These categories are complementary as they facilitate becoming/ being a Vaiṣṇava. Two other MCD, education and family, encourage socialization in the habitus of Vaiṣṇavism. Cultural schema presumes their supportive roles in the lives of individuals, and it is reproduced in the narratives.

Extract 7

> I was a student at the State University of New York in Buffalo, New York, and um, one devotee, Rupanuga Prabhu, he had a class on *Bhagavad Gītā* at my university and um, some of my friends were going and chanting Hare Kṛṣṇa. (L)

Extract 8

> At that time, I'm a student in a university and devotees come to the English Corner and to ah, introduce the philosophy of Kṛṣṇa consciousness to us. (RP)

The first MCD of education evokes the categories of students and teachers. Extracts 7–8 use the noun 'student', and L and RP are university students because L was at 'the State University of New York' and RP was 'in a university'. Education presumes category-relevant academic activities (Schegloff, 2007), which do not have to be explicated. Preachers ('one devotee, Rupanuga Prabhu' in Extract 7, 'devotees' in Extract 8) preached to L and RP. This institutes a standardized relational pair of student and teacher but repurposed for religion, particularly as preacher and proselyte.

The 'class' in Extract 7 and 'English Corner' in Extract 8 further demonstrate the repurposing of academic activities. The spaces are utilized to teach and learn, and the preachers and proselytes make Vaiṣṇavism seem part of academic study. ISKCON has preached at universities since its early days (Rochford, 2013) and the preaching enables individuals to learn about Vaiṣṇavism. Being a student developed the Vaiṣṇava identity of L and RP because their universities inadvertently fostered spiritual education despite being institutions of secular education.

Extract 9

> Now, uh, I and my husband, uh, who is also a devotee, we regularly come to city nearby every weekend to organize uh, younger, uh, devotees and those who are interested in Kṛṣṇa consciousness to come to our house and to um, gain prasādam [sanctified food], lecture and the chanting. (RP)

Extract 10

> And at that time my mother she was very sick, she had cancer. So she called me one day and said you know I think you should go to India. There you will find your spiritual path. (SB)

The MCD of family evokes the categories of child, parent, and spouse. Mentioning one implies the other, where RP is a wife because she has a 'husband' in Extract 9 and SB is a son because he has a 'mother' in Extract 10. The determiner 'my' confirms RP being a wife and SB being a son. This duplicative organization establishes members as part of a beneficial unit (Stokoe, 2012). RP and her husband organize gatherings together, as indicated by the pronoun 'we'. Their domestic space ('our house') is also a devotional space because it hosts 'prasādam [sanctified food], lecture and the chanting'. SB's mother initiated his exploration because she 'called' him and encouraged him to 'go to India' despite her bad health ('very sick...cancer'). She enabled devotion to start, as marked by the metaphor 'your spiritual path'. Being a family member developed the Vaiṣṇava identity of RP and SB because the family supports belief and participation.

From Extracts 7–10, Vaiṣṇava identity is complemented by education and family. The categories of student, wife, and son are expanded to adjust to the religion. ISKCON followers are not world-denying. Rather, they can be educated and have families because their activities as student or family member develop their faith. Because individuals are presumptive representatives of their roles (Schegloff, 2007), ISKCON followers 'fit' typical social roles, making ISKCON seem more mainstream.

Extract 11

> So very soon after that, one devotee approach me. Actually I thought he was going to sell something, I don't know what. So I was trying to sneak out of him, I was, I was trying to escape from him because I didn't like salesman. But he was very determined and he catch me and he just uh, he showed me this book, actually I was, I had read Prabhupād's book *Coming Back* years ago and I thought it was very

interesting but I never met a devotee...And he, he preached to me so much. He was very, very much giving. He told me so many things. We spoke about one hour, just there, under the scorching sun. (MY)

Individual agency is noted in the categories but it is partial because multiple agents facilitate religious transformation (Hindmarsh, 2014). Preachers are instrumental to ISKCON. They introduce Vaiṣṇavism to L and RP in Extracts 7 ('one devotee, Rupanuga Prabhu') and 8 ('devotees'). Similarly in Extract 11, a preacher ('one devotee') sold a book and taught the proselyte (MY). The preacher established contact, and her activities of initial evasion ('trying to sneak out...trying to escape...I didn't like salesman') became activities of reciprocation because she found a book 'very interesting' and spoke to the preacher 'about one hour...under the scorching sun'.

The preaching surpassed temporal and climatic conditions, which imply her interest. It is predicated positively, as in 'very determined', 'preached to me so much', 'very, very much giving' and 'told me so many things'. This positive evaluation is intensified by 'very' and 'so' because she found the quality of preaching extraordinary. The preaching is reconfigured in the present because the pivotal encounter introduced MY to Vaiṣṇavism.

The preacher and proselyte in Extracts 7, 8, and 11 constitute a standardized relational pair (Stokoe, 2012) because the two require one another for a 'transaction', where the preacher explains and the proselyte hears. This dyad suggests knowledge and non-knowledge, and a book ('*Bhagavad Gītā*' in Extract 7, '*Coming Back*' in Extract 11) is a medium to transfer knowledge from preacher to proselyte. It helps to start and sustain preaching because MY found '*Coming Back*' 'very interesting' and her interest motivated the preacher to continue speaking.

Extract 12

When, when the first day I met my guru mahārāj, he actually came to ah, a program and he saw me singing. And then he say, he told me you were singing with foreign bands, now sing for Kṛṣṇa. (MY)

Extract 13

I'm regularly learning, on a regular basis because transformation of heart is not easy. It is a process, that is what His Holiness Radhanath Swami Mahārāj says. It is a slow process and uh, with gradual, gradual chanting of Hare Kṛṣṇa mahā-mantra... our heart, which is contaminated because of our past deeds gets purified slowly and steadily. (NK)

Extract 14

The first book that I got is *Chant and Be Happy* by A.C. Bhaktivedānta Svāmī Prabhupād...so I was easily captivated by the book. And then from then I, uh, you know, I bought and I, uh, borrow a lot of Bhaktivedānta Prabhupād books, BBT, and uh, the rest is history. (GS)

Another agent is a guru (spiritual master), either the one who initiated the individual or Prabhupāda, who although not alive, is termed the Founder-Ācārya (Founder-Preceptor) of ISKCON. A spiritual master has disciples, and the two represent a standardized relational pair

(Stokoe, 2012). This guru-disciple dyad is rooted in Hindu doctrine and is an institutionalized relationship. A guru instructs their disciples about Vaiṣṇava beliefs and practices, and the disciples are expected to fulfil these instructions.

While MY receives a direct instruction from 'my guru mahārāj' to 'sing for Kṛṣṇa' in Extract 12, 'what His Holiness Radhanath Swami Mahārāj says' is an indirect instruction for NK's 'transformation of heart' in Extract 13. MY and NK accept their guru's instructions, which are not predicated because these are taken for granted as positive. GS in Extract 14 did not meet Prabhupāda but his books provide instructions about Vaiṣṇavism. GS was 'easily captivated' and bought and borrowed 'a lot of...books', predicating Prabhupāda's positive impact.

The references to gurus via their words or works are intertextual. The activities of singing (Extract 12), self-transformation (Extract 13), and reading (Extract 14) can be traced to a guru's sanction and acquire sacred legitimation (Hobbs, 2021). These activities become spiritual because their performance fulfils a guru's instructions and therefore helps the spiritual development of MY, NK, and GS. It is evidence of discipleship and evokes moral judgments about MY, NK, and GS being ideal disciples.

Extract 15

> By Kṛṣṇa's arrangement, I catch this Katwa local train...this train station by Kṛṣṇa's arrangement was Navadvip station...this was, this was from one minute to the other. And then by Kṛṣṇa's mercy you know, I was in the hands of many Prabhupād disciples. (SK)

God is the ultimate agent who leads the convert towards conversion (Leone, 2014). In Extract 15, 'Kṛṣṇa' modifies the nouns 'arrangement' and 'mercy' as SK claims divine inspiration to take the train, to stop at Navadvip, and to meet ISKCON followers ('many Prabhupād disciples'). The activities are chance or random but are considered providential as they resulted in conversion. SK was not exercising his own volition but was an instrument of God. Conversion changed him and the activities contributing to it are 'converted', acquiring a new significance. These past activities are reinterpreted through present convictions as evidence of divine agency. The other individuals in the videos did not mention God. Unlike Christian and Muslim narratives (Carl, 2009; Casey, 2019), divine agency is absent perhaps because it is presumed to reside in preachers and gurus as divine instruments.

From Extracts 1–15, the individuals construct a testimony about their conversion. The new religion influences activities and predicates, and it designates a boundary of who they are not and who they are. It also overlaps with time, as they were non-Vaiṣṇavas in the past but Vaiṣṇavas in the present. This self-categorization shows the development of the habitus of Vaiṣṇavism because its beliefs and practices are becoming ingrained in their lives. Conversion becomes an identity-giving experience, and it has shaped their attitude and behavior.

The conversion narratives can serve multiple purposes. They record a conversion for the individual and for ISKCON, articulating it discursively. It marks a personal transformation in religion, which gives a new layer of identity to an individual and provides new devotees to validate the ISKCON objective of propagating Gauḍīya Vaiṣṇavism. These narratives become a tangible repository of conversion as videos can be viewed online across place and time. Consequently, the conversion transcends the individual and ISKCON, and can impact other people's experience of Vaiṣṇavism. The existing narratives become a model for future narratives (Leone, 2014). Other individuals may change or maintain the motifs or categories, reflecting their own conversion. The conversion narratives as repository and model create an archive of texts documenting religious history. This does not need to mean a centralized archive but instead the conversion narratives become part of the multiple genres portraying ISKCON in particular and Hinduism in general. It also captures a shared experience, which, reiterated across place and time, solidifies the community of followers (Hobbs, 2021).

The videos in Table 28.1 are hosted online in some ISKCON-linked websites and YouTube. They expose the public to Vaiṣṇavism, an inadvertent audience of its beliefs and practices (Karapanagiotis, 2020). The conversion narratives could be considered a preaching genre because a solution to people's spiritual quest is provided. The narratives may persuade others to ultimately join ISKCON. Indeed, ISKCON is intensifying endeavors to interest more people besides Indians in India and the diaspora to join it (Karapanagiotis, 2021). The individuals in conversion narratives (Table 28.1) represent different ethnicities/nationalities. Their presence may mitigate the 'foreign' aspects of ISKCON and Vaiṣṇavism, portraying that anyone can be a Vaiṣṇava. Incorporating these narratives in preaching implies diversity in ISKCON. It should resonate with an online audience, which is obviously diverse, and amplify the persuasion in conversion narratives.

Conversion narratives concretize the concept of yukta vairāgya or practical renunciation. It means using materials in the world to evangelize (Karapanagiotis, 2021), such as narratives, videos, and online platforms. Conversion narratives form part of the genres to induce public interest in Gauḍīya Vaiṣṇavism. They are about one convert but help to make more converts. Hence, the motifs and categories reflect the wider ideology of ISKCON and serve an evangelical purpose. As van Nieuwkerk (2014) states, conversion narratives are a preaching genre. Their use can bolster preaching, as do public chanting, and food and book distribution, activities vigorously cultivated by ISKCON.

Implications and Future Directions

This chapter develops the literature on Hindu, particularly Vaiṣṇava, conversion narratives. The conversion motifs (Lofland & Skonovd, 1981) and membership categories (Sacks, 1995; Stokoe, 2012) are useful approaches to understand the identity-giving experience of conversion. They locate conversion as linguistic phenomenon, identifying language features about how/why conversion happened. Language is crucial in representing conversion, and selected motifs and categories emerge in conversion narratives. The motifs and categories can engage any linguistic feature, which can serve a religious purpose, given the right context (Hobbs, 2021).

Other discursive approaches may reveal different characteristics of conversion narratives. Genre analysis can determine the structure, and propose the obligatory and optional stages of these narratives (Bhatia, 2004). The stages demonstrate which information is common to religious transformation, and which information augments it. Every stage deploys lexicogrammatical choices and Systemic Functional Linguistics (Halliday & Matthiessen, 2014) can identify the function of these choices in construing, evaluating and organizing the narratives. A Transitivity analysis studies the construal of entities and events, an Appraisal analysis identifies the positive/negative, explicit/implicit values ascribed to them, and a Theme analysis traces their use from the start to the end of conversion narratives. These studies can be enriched by corpus linguistics, by creating a corpus to generate frequencies, keywords and concordances. The corpus can reveal patterns in language use, characteristic to these narratives.

Besides denotative choices, figurative choices, notably metaphors, are commonly utilized in conversion narratives. Conceptual Metaphor analysis (Lakoff & Johnson, 2003) can explore embodied conceptions about conversion. The types of metaphors, and the target and source domains may reveal physical/cultural groundings of conversion. Other analyses may employ critical approaches, studying conversion narratives as vectors of ideologies, investigatating the perspectives and meanings excluded/included, and how/why exclusion/inclusion transpires. The discursive approaches proposed can be enriched with insights from anthropology, history, psychology, sociology, or theology. Their contribution triangulates method or data on the multifaceted nature of conversion.

Conversion involves a shift of categories from X to Y religion, but multiple categories and agents enable the shift. Their contribution must be better comprehended, to be supportive of converts. Religious groups should be aware of such categories or agents, to maintain converts' interest and to enable their development as faith members. Moreover, the religious 'market' is competitive and saturated. It exhibits a cornucopia of discourses to induce interest in a religion. While multiple genres are recruited in preaching, conversion narratives can build a desirable representation of a religion. Religious groups should deploy suitable language features in these narratives as part of their evangelical drive.

Future directions of research are promising. Research on Hindu conversion narratives is scarce as Hinduism is mostly not considered a proselytizing religion (Sharma, 2012, 2014). Research can enhance the literature and study the conversion narratives of Śaiva, Śākta or Smarta denominations, or other branches of Vaiṣṇavism. Older narratives are chronicled in Hindu scriptures and other literature, and newer narratives are shared on social media sites, video hosting sites, and websites. These texts establish the basis for intra-religious comparison. Scholars can develop a body of work on Hindu narratives, inspired by the fecund research on Christian narratives.

Most research on conversion narratives tends to be religion specific. An inter-religious comparison would underscore specific beliefs and practices and explore (dis)similarities. Comparison can first be extended to 'Dharmic' religions (Buddhism, Jainism, Sikhism) which share cultural and philosophical contexts with Hinduism, and later 'Abrahamic' religions (Christianity, Islam, Judaism), which encounter Hinduism in India and other parts of the world. It could produce novel findings for the language of conversion and may develop a typology of intra/inter-religious conversion narratives.

These narratives are available in various languages but those in English are often studied, perhaps reflecting the origin of scholars although it privileges the conversion experience in a dominant global language. Research is language-heavy, and it examines the capacity of language to convey religious transformation. But the narratives are a multimodal phenomenon, where body language, facial expressions, gestures, colors, and images are employed with language. These modes co-construct the representation of conversion and their semiotic labor should be acknowledged. Future research requires a move from theolinguistics to theosemiotics, where the multimodal features of conversion are analyzed.

Conversion is dynamic and does not end at the moment of conversion as converts continue adopting the beliefs and practices of their new religion. The adoption may stimulate post-conversion narratives, making motifs and categories open to change. Moreover, converts are diverse, and research should engage sociodemographic variables like age, class, ethnicity, gender, nationality, and sexuality. These variables are prominent in present-day conversations on religion and may impact the experience in the narratives.

Conversion narratives inadvertently privilege converts because their experience is the object of research. But these narratives are available to a multitude of listeners/readers. The motifs and categories evoked may influence their own conversion. While producers (converts) are studied, the consumers (audience) should also be involved, to balance the research agenda and to recognize their contribution to interpreting conversion. Although conversion is almost always linked to religion, it exists in domains where a movement among faith systems is probable (Lyons, Hasell, Tallapragada, & Jamieson, 2019). For instance, individuals may 'convert' to buying a product/ service, and to favoring a party/politician, which is examined in Corporate Communication and Political Communication respectively. Existing research may favor the explicit religious language of world religions but implicit religious language extends beyond religion (Hobbs, 2021). Conversion narratives in secular domains should be explored, as like religion, they are able to reorient individual life and leave lifelong implications.

These proposals require a richer examination of the context of conversion (Kling, 2020). Context is always mentioned but it is the immediate context while the wider social context is elided or presumed. Conversion varies by person, place, and time, and therefore its representation is produced and consumed under concrete historical conditions (Hindmarsh, 2014). Elucidating these conditions enriches understanding the language about how/why individuals/groups change faith systems. Ultimately, conversion and language constitute a virtuous circle (Leone, 2014). Converts describe conversion using language, which promotes new conversion, which new converts describe using language, *ad infinitum*.

Further Reading

Dwyer, G. & Cole, R. (2013). Introduction. In G. Dwyer & R. Cole (Eds.), *Hare Krishna in the modern world*, 7–10. Arktos Media Ltd.
Interviews leading members in ISKCON and reviews their opinions about the organization's history and its endeavor to remain relevant for the future.
Hobbs, V. (2021). *An introduction to religious language*. Bloomsbury.
Describes various linguistic approaches to study the language of religion, mainly Christianity.
Karapanagiotis, N. (2021). *Branding bhakti.* Indiana University Press.
Explores rebranding strategies by ISKCON to interest new, non-Indian followers.
Kling, D. (2020). *A history of Christian conversion*. Oxford University Press.
Surveys the factors influencing individuals/groups to convert to Christianity across spatiotemporal contexts.
Rambo, L. & Farhadian, C. (2014). *The Oxford handbook of religious conversion*. Oxford University Press.
Provides an overview of conversion, using approaches in various disciplines and examining the perspectives of major religions.

References

Bhatia, V. (2004). *Worlds of written discourse*. Continuum.
Burhani, A. (2020). Muslim televangelists in the making: Conversion narratives and the construction of religious authority. *The Muslim World, 110*(2), 154–175.
Caitanya-bhāgavata. (2008). *Verse 3.4.126*. Retrieved 15 November 2022 from www.wisdomlib.org/hinduism/book/chaitanya-bhagavata/d/doc1110286.html
Carl, G. (2009). Catholic-Lutheran-Catholic: Strategies of justification and conceptions of the self in the conversion narratives of Johannes Ferdinand Franz Weinberger (1687–90). *The Medieval History Journal, 12*(2), 327–353.
Casey, P. (2019). Conversion to Islam: Narratives of awakening, continuity, and return. *Sociological Forum, 34*(3), 752–773.
Crystal, D. (2018). Whatever happened to theolinguistics? In P. Chilton & M. Kopytowska (Eds.), *Religion, language and the human mind*, 3–18. Oxford University Press.
Dwyer, G. & Cole, R. (2013). Introduction. In G. Dwyer & R. Cole (Eds.), *Hare Krishna in the modern world*, 7–10. Arktos Media Ltd.

Halliday, M. & Matthiessen, C. (2014). *Halliday's introduction to functional grammar*, 4th edition. Routledge.

Hindmarsh, B. (2014). Religious conversion as narrative and autobiography. In L. Rambo & C. Farhadian (Eds.), *The Oxford handbook of religious conversion*, 343–368. Oxford University Press.

Hobbs, V. (2021). *An introduction to religious language*. Bloomsbury Academic.

Housley, W. & Fitzgerald, R. (2015). Introduction to membership categorization analysis. In R. Fitzgerald & W. Housley (Eds.), *Advances in membership categorization analysis*, 1–22.

ISKCON. (2020). *ISKCON*. Retrieved 15 November 2022 from www.iskcon.org

Jindra, I. (2011). How religious content matters in conversion narratives to various religious groups. *Sociology of Religion*, *72*(3), 275–302.

Karapanagiotis, N. (2020). Automatic rituals and inadvertent audiences: ISKCON, Krishna and the ritual mechanics of Facebook. In X. Zeiler (Ed.), *Digital Hinduism*, 51–67. Routledge.

Karapanagiotis, N. (2021). *Branding bhakti*. Indiana University Press.

Kling, D. (2014). Conversion to Christianity. In L. Rambo & C. Farhadian (Eds.), *The Oxford handbook of religious conversion*, 598–631. Oxford University Press.

Kling, D. (2020). *A history of Christian conversion*. Oxford University Press.

Lakoff, G. & Johnson, M. (2003). *Metaphors we live by*. University of Chicago Press.

Leone, M. (2014). Religious conversion and semiotic analysis. In L. Rambo & C. Farhadian (Eds.), *The Oxford handbook of religious conversion*, 369–400. Oxford University Press.

Linge, M. (2023). Muslim narratives of desistance among Norwegian street criminals: Stories of reconciliation, purification and exclusion. *European Journal of Criminology*, *20*(2), 568–585.

Lofland, J. & Skonovd, N. (1981). Conversion motifs. *Journal for the Scientific Study of Religion*, *20*(4), 373–385.

Lyons, B., Hasell, A., Tallapragada, M. & Jamieson, K. (2019). Conversion messages and attitude change: Strong arguments, not costly signals. *Public Understanding of Science*, *28*(3), 320–338.

Pihlaja, S. (2013). Truck stops and fashion shows: A case study of the discursive performance of Evangelical Christian group affiliation on YouTube. In M. Gillespie, D. Herbert & A. Greenhill (Eds.), *Social media and religious change*, 165–184. De Grutyer.

Prabhupāda, B. (1994). *The science of self-realization*. Bhaktivedānta Book Trust.

Rambo, L. (1993). *Understanding religious conversion*. Yale University Press.

Rambo, L. & Farhadian, C. (2014). Introduction. In L. Rambo & C. Farhadian (Eds.), *The Oxford handbook of religious conversion*, 1–24. Oxford University Press.

Rochford, B. (2013). Sociological reflections on the history and development of the Hare Krishna movement. In G. Dwyer & R. Cole (Eds.), *Hare Krishna in the modern world*, 11–35. Arktos Media Ltd.

Sacks, H. (1995). *Lectures on conversation*. Blackwell.

Schegloff, E. (2007). A tutorial on membership categorization. *Journal of Pragmatics*, *39*(3), 462–482.

Sharma, A. (2012). *Problematizing religious freedom*. Springer.

Sharma, A. (2014). Hinduism and conversion. In L. Rambo & C. Farhadian (Eds.), *The Oxford handbook of religious conversion*, 429–443. Oxford University Press.

Singh, M. (2018). 'A question of life and death': Conversion, self and identity in Swami Shraddhanand's autobiography. *South Asia: Journal of South Asian Studies*, *41*(2), 452–467.

Stokoe, E. (2012). Moving forward with membership categorization analysis: Methods for systematic analysis. *Discourse Studies*, *14*(3), 277–303.

Stromberg, P. (2014). The role of language in religious conversion. In L. Rambo & C. Farhadian (Eds.), *The Oxford handbook of religious conversion*, 117–139. Oxford University Press.

Ullman, C. (1988). Psychological well-being among converts in traditional and nontraditional religious groups. *Psychiatry*, *5*(3), 312–322.

van Nieuwkerk, K. (2014). "Conversion" to Islam and the construction of a pious self. In L. Rambo & C. Farhadian (Eds.), *The Oxford handbook of religious conversion*, 667–686. Oxford University Press.

29

COGNITIVE METAPHOR AND RELIGION

Peter Richardson

Introduction and Background

Religious discourse rarely involves believers offering opinions about the existence of a God or ultimate reality, but rather is more often about believers expressing their perceived experience of such a reality. These experiences often relate to sophisticated and highly abstract mental states and perceptions, so it is not surprising to find that a prominent role is played by figurative language. However, the use of figurative language raises important questions. Consider the examples of an Evangelical Christian believer saying, "I felt something of God's presence coming into my heart", to describe the perception of the commencement of an intimate, personal relationship (Miah, 2020) or a Zen Buddhist, upon experiencing awakening, exclaiming, "every single thing disappeared in a dazzling stream of illumination ... For a fleeting eternity I was alone" (Kapleau, 2000, p. 53). Are these descriptions of a similar type of experience, or are these very different conceptualizations that suggest distinct ways of being religious? To address this question, we will explore the cognitive dimension of metaphor use and how it interacts with the broader cognitive aspects of religious language.

There is widespread agreement among scholars from a variety of different fields that metaphor plays an important part in religious language (Chilton & Kopytowska, 2018; Pihlaja 2014; Soskice 1985). There is also general agreement that figurative language can reveal people's attitudes and that it is useful when talking about abstract topics (Cameron, 2011). What is still contested is the precise nature and role of the cognitive dimension of metaphor, or what has become known as *conceptual metaphor* (Gibbs, 2017). *Cognitive linguistics* is an approach to language that begins with the premise that our acquisition and use of language is connected to the mind's general cognitive abilities and conceptual structures. In short, this means that cognitive linguists examine language by exploring how concepts are organized and connected to words, phrases, and grammatical constructions. Another key concern is the notion of *embodied cognition*, or the influence that having a human body and physically interacting with our environments has on the way we think.

When it comes to the use of figurative language in religious discourse and texts, we immediately notice both the incredible diversity of metaphors employed and the fact that certain metaphors occur across multiple traditions. One reason for this is that, in the same way that all brains have many structural similarities, our bodies also have many similarities in form and motor functions.

DOI: 10.4324/9781003301271-32

This means that we have certain shared domains of knowledge that are often an important part of the human experience, either in terms of being highly salient or oft-repeated activities, or very important or frequently encountered objects or aspects of our environments (Lakoff, 1999). Cognitive linguists would argue that when we come to express our more abstract beliefs and experiences, we create *cross-domain mappings* between a more concrete, physical domain of knowledge, such as the experience of grabbing and holding something, and a more abstract domain of knowledge, such as understanding something. This particular mapping is then referred to as UNDERSTANDING IS GRASPING with both the *source domain* (GRASPING) and the *target domain* (UNDERSTANDING) capitalized using small caps to mark them as conceptual domains.

Cognitive linguists refer to the above mapping as one example of a *primary metaphor* or a metaphor that is more fundamentally embodied than others, with the source domain being directly derived from the experience of using our sensorimotor system (Grady, 1997). Some more key primary metaphors are included below along with some examples of their use from contemporary religious writers:

PURPOSES ARE DESTINATIONS

"Only a very few start this journey with God as the object."

(Rohr, 2019, p. 75)

"What you keep in front of you, you're moving toward."

(Osteen, 2014, p. 10)

KNOWING IS SEEING

"The light of boundless compassion not only illuminates our existential reality of karmic evil, but its warm rays and nurturing power transforms it completely into the highest good."

(Unno, 2002, p. 123)

CAUSES ARE PHYSICAL FORCES

"All of a sudden, something began to stir within me, something began to push me, to prompt me."

(Merton, 2015, p. 215)

STRUCTURE IS PHYSICAL STRUCTURE

"No robes, no titles, just an appreciation for a method of training that seemed to have the trappings of a religion, but at its foundation held something more."

(Williams, 2000, p. 4)

INTIMACY IS CLOSENESS

"... asking the Father, my Father and His, to receive me into His infinite and special love ... the love of those creatures who are drawn to Him in and with the power of His own love for Himself."

(Merton, 2015, p. 225)

Over time, these primary metaphors then serve as the basis for the formation of more complex mappings. A popular example of this would be THEORIES ARE BUILDINGS, for eample, "But like most Beatles myths, this theory collapses when you examine it ..." from the COCA corpus (Davies,

2008) being formed from a combination of the primary metaphors PERSISTING IS REMAINING ERECT and STRUCTURE IS PHYSICAL STRUCTURE (Gibbs, 2005, p. 117).

When we take a closer look at figurative language, we also see a *schematicity hierarchy* in operation, which means that figurative language makes use of different levels of abstractness and specificity (Kövecses, 2015; 2020). At the most abstract level is the notion of *schemas*, which can be viewed as fundamental organizational frameworks for structuring our thoughts. Schemas cover notions such as something being contained within something else or a part of a whole, or viewing objects as near or far or in the center or at the periphery (Evans, 2019, pp. 225–236). One other schema that is particularly important for religious language is referred to as the *source-path-goal schema*. Whenever we find ourselves thinking about some aspect of our life in terms of an initial condition, a current condition, and a destination we are purposefully heading towards, we are making use of this schema (Lakoff, 1999, pp. 32–34). Religious language usually revolves around identifying some form of a problem (it may be a metaphysical problem, such as sin or the Buddhist notion of life's inherent unsatisfactoriness, or it may be a physical problem, such as the need for personal success, health, or a good harvest) which requires specific solutions (for example, Christ's death or detachment from desire or the repetition of a ritual). This problem-solution framework requires goal-based ways of thinking, which is one reason why the source-path-goal schema underpins so many different types of religious language (Richardson, 2012; Richardson, Mueller, & Pihlaja, 2021, pp. 40–42).

Another reason for the pervasiveness of the source-path-goal schema is the fact that it underpins those metaphors that use purposeful movement as their source domain. Domains are viewed as networks of information that are fairly schematic in their structure, but more detailed than schemas (Kövecses, 2020, pp. 56–58). The highly productive LIFE IS A JOURNEY conceptual metaphor is a clear example of a domain mapping that adds more detail to its underlying source-path-goal schema, as we see in this extract from a book by a well-known US Evangelical,

> You are on the road to discovering your special story. But to be sure you are on the right road, God provides an important road sign you ought not to ignore: the wise counsel of other people.
>
> (Jeffress, 2018, p. 49)

We have so far discussed schemas and domains, but to make sense of all the information in this example, we also need to draw on other levels along a hierarchy of schematicity. The JOURNEY domain provides us with the notion of an individual moving from point A to point B to reach a specific destination for a specific purpose. The reference to a road sign when giving advice about being a Christian adds an extra layer of specificity and detail to this relatively abstract mapping. One approach within cognitive linguistics, known as *extended conceptual metaphor theory* (Kövecses, 2020), uses the term *frames* (Fillmore, 1982) to capture this less abstract level on the schematicity hierarchy. When we consider the above example, we can see two frame mappings that add an extra level of detail: THE CHRISTIAN LIFE IS A JOURNEY ALONG A ROAD and GOD'S GUIDANCE IS A ROAD SIGN.

To complete this analysis, we need to also briefly discuss the bottom level which has the most specificity. Over the last 20 years, many scholars within applied linguistics have emphasized the fluid, dynamic nature of language (Cameron, 2011; Gibbs & Cameron, 2008). They have pointed out that the words and constructions we choose are heavily influenced by our culture and speech communities in the form of the previous texts and interactions we have encountered. In addition to this, we are continually adapting what we say and how we say it to fit with what has just been said by other interlocutors in the current conversation. This fluidity and dynamic interconnectedness in language use requires choices to be made in working memory (rather than long-term memory). This is achieved by the continual construction and updating of *mental spaces* (Fauconnier & Turner, 2002). These make use of entrenched, abstract mappings like the ones we have discussed above, but they combine and add detail to them in a way that uniquely suits them to the communicative purposes within the present discourse stream (Kövecses, 2020, p. 57). This constant engagement with more abstract mappings then feeds back into the way these mappings are structured. This means that over time old frame and domain mappings may be reshaped in addition to new mappings being created to fit new contexts.

Returning to our example above, it is possible to analyze it as a series of mental spaces or a type of scenario (Musolff, 2004) where Christians are faced with a series of potential paths from which they must choose the one correct path leading to their destination. To ensure that Christians find the correct path and move in the appropriate direction, God provides road signs that can be followed, with one of these signs corresponding to the importance of listening to the good advice provided by other Christians. As we have seen, this scenario makes use of several established schemas, domains, and frames, but this exact arrangement is unique to Jeffress and put together during the process of writing to fit a particular purpose at a specific point in his book.

This series of choices raises an important question: what is the advantage of using figurative language in these types of statements? One answer is that it allows the believer to think about highly abstract topics often connected to the positing of invisible forces in a form that is more concrete, tangible, and easy to grasp and visualize (Charteris-Black, 2016). This does not just apply to the readers and discourse participants who are exposed to figurative language, but also to the users themselves. The conceptual frameworks beneath figurative language have been shown to structure the way we look at and interact with the world, even when we are not consciously aware of each mapping (Gibbs, 2017, pp. 104–221). The use of embodied metaphor also triggers perceptual simulations relating to the source domain's physical domain. When people hear or use language related to physical actions, there is similar activation in the brain as there would be if the physical action were being performed:

Mirror neurons associated with grasping become active when people see others grasping objects, when they imagine grasping objects, or when they hear the verb grasp, to take one instance. Thus, people understand abstract verb meaning (e.g. to grasp the concept) by simulating sensorimotor actions.

(Gibbs, 2017, p. 456)

In other words, metaphor shapes not only our conceptualization but also our experience. This brings us back to the notion of embodied cognition: physical language, including many mappings involved in metaphorical language, are intimately connected to the perception of doing something in the world.

(Littlemore, 2019, pp. 15–16)

Particular schemas and mappings also have their own unique impact. For example, the use of the source-path-goal schema and the LIFE IS A JOURNEY mapping construes Evangelical Christianity as a concrete, physical endeavor with an objective that can only be achieved via a single route. This naturally fits with and consolidates the perception within conservative Evangelical Christianity that there is only one truth, which is not just absolute and objective, but also tangible and able to be personally experienced. The other critical feature of figurative language is its remarkable plasticity. For example, while it is true that the LIFE IS A JOURNEY mapping has such a key role in expressing and consolidating absolute forms of belief, it is also just as essential in the expression of inclusivist and pluralistic forms of belief. As an example of the latter, consider the use of figurative language in the following extract from a book introducing Contemplative Studies (Komjathy, 2018, p. 6):

> Contemplatives and contemplative communities, and members of any culture more generally, inhabit different worlds, at least cognitively speaking. In theological terms, one is confronted with diversity and plurality. It is possible that different contemplative practices derive from, orient one toward, and/or lead to experiences of different realities. That is, reality may be plural rather than singular, multiple rather than unified.

The use of *from*, *toward*, and *lead to* figuratively construct the image of different spatially located realities. Particular practices can be originally located in one of these realities, and/or turn practitioners in their direction, and/or facilitate their movement towards them. The use of *orient one toward* and *lead to* suggests the figurative construal of the practice as an agent (i.e., personification) and, in the case of *lead to*, a sense of shared movement with the direction controlled by the practice (Richardson, 2012). In a similar manner to the Jeffress quote, the passage expertly employs movement metaphors to help the reader visualize an abstract set of propositions and relationships in concrete, tangible terms. However, in this case, we are being encouraged to view reality as clearly pluralistic rather than linear and absolute.

It is also possible to connect the metaphor usage here to a broader cognitive framework underpinning the paragraph. As we have noted, the representation of different realities as inhabiting different spatial locations consolidates and reinforces the non-figurative conceptions of diversity and plurality. These conceptions reveal one aspect of the author's framework, or system, for structuring his beliefs about reality. The above analysis outlines how figurative language plays an important part in this framework, although the role is often to express or consolidate key non-figurative aspects. To capture how figurative language interacts with these broader cognitive aspects, it is necessary to introduce the cognitive linguistic notion of *idealized cognitive models* (ICMs).

ICMs can be defined as frame-like structures for organizing our knowledge of a particular aspect of the world. They can be viewed as gestalts based on schemas and organized as propositions or metonymic or metaphorical mappings (Lakoff, 1987, p. 68). One popular example that has often been used to illustrate a propositional ICM is our understanding of the word *mother*. Lakoff (1987) has argued that the word appears to be very straightforward in meaning but is in fact comprised of a cluster of ICMs, such as (p. 74):

The birth model: The person who gives birth is the mother.

The genetic model: The female who contributes the genetic material is the mother.

The nurturance model: The female adult who nurtures and raises a child is the mother of that child.

These ICMs, grouped together, contribute to our total knowledge of what a mother is. In addition, if we were to explore in detail the experiences and feelings of a particular individual over the course of their life, what usually emerges is that, out of all the possible mother ICMs, there is a "strong pull to view one as the most important" (Lakoff, 1987, p. 75). Once we have developed a particular way of looking at and thinking about the world, there is a tendency (that we may or may not resist) to perceive an ICM as a direct way of perceiving reality (Al-Zahrani, 2008). It is important to note at this point that ICMs are involved in structuring every aspect of our lives, to the point where it is possible to talk about a driving ICM or a Sunday ICM (Littlemore, 2015, p. 13). These daily-life scripts or frameworks are unlikely to become sources of tension when we become aware of ICMs that differ from our own. However, other types of ICMs that structure our cherished beliefs and connect to experiences that have evoked strong feelings can generate a strong pull over time, and even an aversion to competing ICMs.

This brings us to the ICMs that structure religious language. We have already briefly discussed a conservative Evangelical use of movement metaphors to reinforce an exclusivist (there is only one truth) belief system and the use above of spatial metaphors to reinforce a pluralistic belief system. These can be viewed as ICMs within an ICM cluster of possible systems. They form part of a network that involves descriptions about how the world is organized and works and how a divine entity interacts with that world (doctrine), in addition to frameworks of behavior in terms of how an adherent should or should not act in the world (rules and guidelines) or precisely what to do within the religious realm to achieve certain effects (ritual). Religious language is often structured according to particular system ICMs, but there are others that are equally as important. ICMs have been previously discussed in relation to religious beliefs (Richardson, Mueller, & Pihlaja, 2021), but there has yet to be a systematic attempt to identify the key ICMs that could account for religious language in general and the role that metaphor plays in their expression. The analysis in the section below is an initial attempt to fill that gap.

The Role of Movement and Containment Metaphors in Relationship and State ICMs in Religious Language

One way to get at the differences between the various ways of being religious is to examine how ICM networks interact with each other in texts and stretches of discourse, which networks are being foregrounded, which ones are being backgrounded, and what metaphoric mappings are being used to structure them. This section compares the description of experiencing the initial stages of enlightenment by Adyashanti, a prominent Zen Buddhist teacher, with a conversion experience by an Evangelical Christian. I chose Zen Buddhism and Evangelical Christianity because Zen, in contrast to Christianity, is usually viewed as a religion that does not emphasize a relationship with a divine being. I chose to focus on Adyashanti's account of his initial experience of enlightenment and an Evangelical conversion experience because both experiences were preceded by some level of desperation and emotional discomfort; in addition, both experiences also involved a particular moment that marked a substantial breakthrough emotionally, intellectually, and cognitively.

Let us begin with Adyashanti's account. The *Metaphor Identification Procedure* or MIP (Pragglejaz, 2007) was used to identify metaphorical lexical units. The steps in the procedure include identifying lexical units that have a physical, concrete usage in some contexts, but a more abstract, less concrete usage in the text being analyzed. For example, "shifted" can be used to denote the change in location of a physical object, but in the passage below, it is being used to describe the more abstract change in a viewpoint. Using MIP, all metaphorical lexical items have been underlined:

And just as I began to try to meditate, to try to calm my mind, all of a sudden—from my guts, not from my head, but from deep down within me—something yelled out inside me: "I can't do this anymore! I can't do it! I don't know how to <u>break through</u>! I don't know how to stop struggling. I don't know how to stop striving. I can't do this!" That was the moment. That was the moment that everything began to change. I didn't know it at the time, but everything I'd ever done <u>in</u> my life up until that moment had prepared me to realize that I was powerless, because I was <u>trapped in</u> a certain view of things ... But <u>in</u> that moment where I realized there was literally nothing I could do, everything changed. All of a sudden, my view of everything <u>shifted</u>. Almost like <u>flipping over a card or coin</u>, everything that I ever thought or felt, everything that I could remember, everything in that moment literally disappeared. I was finally alone. And in this aloneness, I had no idea what I was, or where I was, or what was happening. All I knew was that I had <u>hit</u> the <u>end</u> of some imaginary <u>road</u>. I'd <u>come to</u> some <u>brick wall</u> and found myself suddenly <u>on the other side</u> of it, where the <u>brick wall</u> actually disappeared. And then this great revelation occurred where I realized that I was both nothing and everything, simultaneously.

(Adyashanti, 2013, pp. 167–168)

This account primarily consists of an idealized narrative reconstruction of various mental states. Raw mental states and immediate emotion responses are not ICMs, but they become ICMs when they are reconstructed from memory and organized into a narrative arc that fits within a particular belief community. These may include organized reconstructions of peace, love, forgiveness, guilt, bliss, or even the experience of subdoxastic states, such as nonconceptual awareness. In this case, various mental states and emotional responses are being used to present an idealized event model for a shift from negative states associated with trying to achieve ego dissolution through self-effort to a non-dualistic state that is characterized as both nothingness and all-encompassing oneness. One more important component of Adyashanti's account is a developing series of system ICMs. The relationship between the state and system ICMs has been represented in diagrammatic form below in Figure 29.1.

In the first part of the event model, strong mental states are suggested by references to his attempts to calm his mind and his feelings of exasperation and desperation at his inability to continue. These references are also closely connected to a system ICM network, explicitly represented

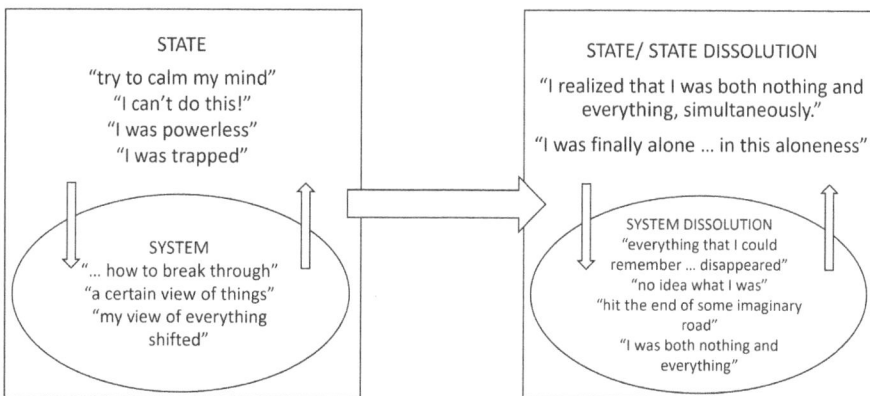

Figure 29.1 Adyashanti's Enlightenment Event model

in the references to a "view of things" and a "view of everything", which is related to trying to achieve the dissolution of the sense of self through self-effort. This is metaphorically structured by two mappings: ACHIEVING SOMETHING IS BREAKING THROUGH AN OBSTACLE and INCOR-RECT/UNSUITABLE BELIEFS ARE TRAPS. These two metaphorical mappings are key as they set up a force-dynamic struggle (Talmy, 2000) involving one force, the self's effort (referred to as an agonist), attempting to overcome a competing force tendency (referred to as an antagonist) in the form of the trap or obstacle's structural integrity.

The second part of the event model, introduced through "my view of everything shifted", utilizes another movement mapping: CHANGING BELIEFS IS CHANGING POSITION/ORIENTATION. The references to disappearance and nothingness suggest a notion of nonconceptual awareness, while the descriptions of aloneness, realization, and pervading unity still suggest some type of state. However, the language of not knowing, disappearance, and the paradoxicality of nothing-ness yet absolute oneness suggests the dismantling of any sense of a system. These key notions of disappearance and coming to an end of a former way of being are visualized through the metaphor-ical images provided by "hit the end of some imaginary road" and Adyashanti's relocation to the other side of a wall and, along with everything else, its subsequent disappearance. At a more sche-matic level of domains, this grouping is underpinned by a common mapping that connects coming to the end of a path on to completing something, or something finishing, or no longer being usable. There are then two more mappings at the more detailed level of frames: THE DISAPPEARANCE OF AN OBSTACLE IS THE CESSATION OF SELF-EFFORT and THE DISAPPEARANCE OF OBJECTS IS THE CESSATION OF DUALISTIC THINKING. The road's end and the wall's disappearance (rather than collapse) are crucial as they solve the force-dynamic competition through dissolution of both the self and self-effort, rather than through one force overcoming the other (which would signal the triumph of the self, not its dissolution). It is important to add that these overlapping notions of soli-tariness, nothingness, oneness, and disappearance of objects representing the cessation of dualistic thinking can be commonly found in Zen Buddhist accounts of an initial experience of enlighten-ment, providing justification for treating these as constituting an established ICM network. Some examples have been included below from three separate testimonials:

Ding, dong! The clock chimed. This alone *is*! This alone *is*! There's no reasoning here.

(Kapleau, 2000, p. 232)

Abruptly the pains disappear, there's only Mu! Each and every thing is Mu. "Oh, it's *this*!" I exclaimed, reeling in astonishment, my mind a total emptiness.

(Kapleau, 2000, p. 264)

At last it dawned on me: *there is Nothing to realize*!

(Kapleau, 2000, p. 277)

We can therefore summarize Adyashanti's account in idealized Buddhist terms as a move from a system of self-effort that is causing suffering to a non-dualistic state involving the dissolution of system thinking and the experience of nothingness and unity. It makes use of a state and system ICM network structured by CONTAINER and PATH schemas while simultaneously attempting to subvert them through depictions of a non-dualistic state. Keep in mind that what we are analyzing here is the structuring of idealized cognitive models. We are not concerned with truth claims, but only with recovering how Adyashanti conceptualizes and presents his reconstructed perceptions of a particular highly meaningful experience. In other words, Adyashanti is relating an experience of being in a state of absolute desperation and psychological torment, where the experience of nothingness, aloneness, and oneness is perceived as the necessary solution.

In the above analysis of Adyashanti's experience, there is no reference at all to relationship ICMs. This does not mean that Adyashanti does not make use of relationship language and patterns of interacting agency. Consider the example below from the same book that contains the account of his initial enlightenment experience:

> What if you found out that the way spirit wanted to manifest through you was as a simple, ordinary person, but a person with great love … What if that were the way life wanted to manifest through you?
>
> (Adyashanti, 2013, p. 198)

"Spirit" and "you" in addition to "life" and "you" are being set up as two interacting pairs with "you" being construed as the patient (the participant being acted upon) in both cases. Regardless of whether "spirit' and "life" are considered metaphorical or metonymic, it is clear that the excerpt is an example of relationship language. This fits with the point that all religious language at some point draws on all three aspects of being religious. However, it is still valuable to look for patterns of foregrounding and backgrounding accompanied by developing metaphor usage at different points in a discourse stream or a text. It is also important to find analogous moments in different religious adherents—in this case, a period of psychological torment preceding a particular watershed moment—and to track and discuss key similarities and differences.

Let us therefore now turn to the analysis of an Evangelical Christian's conversion experience. The extract, from the popular British Evangelical newspaper, *The Evangelical Times*, has been included below:

> I had my own business. I travelled. I had friends, and outwardly was 'doing okay', but inwardly I had arrived at a place where peace didn't seem to exist. Towards my friends and family my face was false, a mask that I hid behind. I would laugh and smile and joke around; I was very good at this deception … My mind was so distorted and tormented by this time, that I was looking for a way out. I wanted oblivion and played with the idea that a bottle of sleeping pills may give me the peace I longed for. But even that road held no escape. How could I bring such devastation on my family? I was trapped, with no way out. Little did I know then that my idea of a way out would have held no peace. And little did I know then what awaited God's perfect timing in my life. That perfect timing came one cold, snowy morning, before the house where I was staying at the time stirred. Halfway across the world in Vancouver (British Columbia), Canada, I got down on my knees and asked a God I didn't even know existed to prove himself to me, because I was desperate. This bit is hard to write, even now after 35 years or so of my life. The memory of first meeting that divine love, a love that transcends time, a love that entered my soul so deeply, a love that knew the number of hairs I have on my head, moves me to tears.
>
> (Davis, 2018)

In contrast to Adyashanti's account, Davis's account is focused primarily on a relationship ICM network, although a state ICM network also plays an important role. A relationship ICM can be defined as a conceptual framework that organizes, underpins, and motivates language where the believer is acted upon and in interaction with an agent. The agent may be some form of a divine

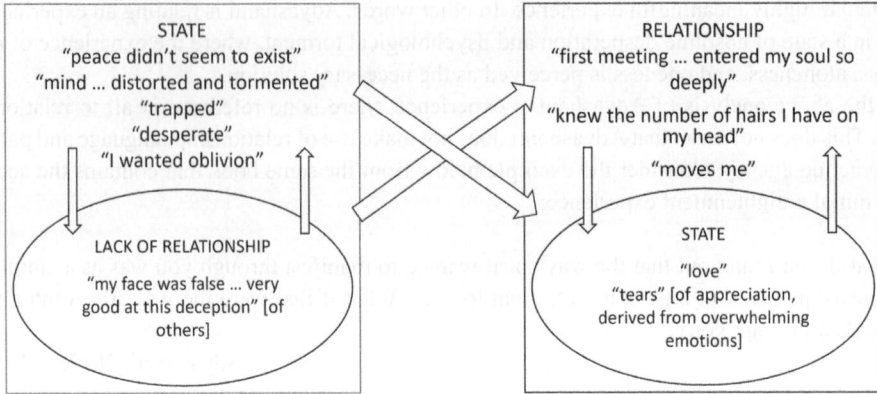

Figure 29.2   Davis's Conversion Event model

being or reality or a metaphysical construct that is being figuratively represented as an agent, such as life or the universe, or a key non-metaphysical member of the adherent's belief community, such as a prophetic figure.

In this account, system ICMs are almost completely absent within the event model. Davis does reject the idea of suicide on the grounds that her parents would be devastated, which suggests either a moral framework that includes familial duty or responsibility or possibly just an expression of love and therefore empathy for her parents. Another possible example of system language is the later reference to not knowing whether God existed, the request to prove his existence, and the belief that divine love transcends time and has intimate knowledge of believers, although this also overlaps with relationship language. Due to the lack of a clear trajectory for system language, it has been omitted from the diagram below in Figure 29.2.

The state ICM network involves a dramatic shift from a negatively evaluated set of states characterized by desperation and the sense of being trapped (THE EXPERIENCE OF NEGATIVE EMOTIONS IS A TRAP) to a positively evaluated set of states. The experience of this state of lack of peace is figuratively construed as a location that can be travelled to ("I had arrived at a place"), and also away from, although with great difficulty ("even that road held no escape"). This absence of peace leads to the need to hide the absence from others, expressed through the mapping NOT SHOWING YOUR TRUE FEELINGS IS WEARING A MASK, which denotes the perception of a lack of a true relationship in her life. The desire for death represents the level of her desperation, to the point where she wishes for the absolute absence of states and relationships.

The relationship ICM network is represented as situated within the state ICM network in the pre-conversion section of the event model but becomes primary in the post-conversion section. The reason for this is that in the first section, mental states are construed as causing dysfunctional relationships, but in the second section, the new relationship with the divine results in new mental states. However, the use of the concept LOVE as a CHARACTERISTIC FOR PERSON metonymy sets up a very close connection between the relationship and state ICMs, and it also denotes an agency pattern that conveys an intimate personal relationship. This relationship is constructed through the source domain of SPATIAL PROXIMITY and the primary metaphorical mapping INTIMACY IS CLOSENESS, beginning with the notion of meeting and proceeding to the figurative construal of the divine entity entering her, "a love that entered my soul so deeply". This conception of personal intimacy is then further reinforced by the highly detailed knowledge that the divine entity has of the author (in contrast to the deceiving of others that characterized the first part of the event model) and the intense emotional effect of the relationship expressed through the movement metaphor, "moves me to tears".

This figurative conception of the divine entity entering the believer represents an established relationship ICM in Evangelical conversion experiences, either in the form of the divine entity entering the person or entering their life. Another very common component of Evangelical conversion experiences is the pre-conversion state being characterized by an absence of peace (as we see in this event model), and the post-conversion state being characterized by the experience of peace (not stated in this event model). We can see these components in the examples below:

> At that moment in time my life was eternally changed. The peace of God entered my heart, mind, and soul.
>
> (Edwards, 2021)

> When they talked about Jesus it was as if they knew him personally. They too had found what my brother had found: peace, love, and forgiveness in Jesus ... I asked Jesus to forgive me and save me ... there is nothing that compares with that moment when he came into my life in June 1979.
>
> (Wighton, 2021)

> I begged God to forgive me, to take my heart and make it new. I pleaded with Christ to come into my life and make me a new creation in him.
>
> (Kulczycka, 2020)

It is important to note that one unusual feature of the conversion account we are analyzing in this section is that a system ICM network does not have a key role. The majority of Evangelical conversion accounts also contain a process of awareness of a particular conception of sin, guilt over sin, repentance, and an experience of being forgiven (as we see in the last two extracts above) that connects to a sophisticated doctrinal framework.

Returning to the analysis of Davis's conversion account, it is possible to summarize this conversion event model as a move from a state of extreme desperation, dysfunctional, distant relationships, and the absence of peace to a state of love characterized by a functional, deeply personal and intimate relationship. CONTAINER and PATH schemas played a crucial role in expressing this event model, as they did in the Adyashanti account, although the PATH schema was used in a very different way. In Adyashanti, movement metaphors were used to represent reaching the end of a dualistic framework, while for Davis, movement metaphors were used in a sense to reinforce dualism by initiating an intimate, personal relationship between two entities.

This analysis suggests that the above accounts are composed of different combinations of three organizing components: states, relationships, and systems. When one or two of these are foregrounded in certain patterns, they can represent ways of being religious that are uniquely suited to address the acute need for a particular way of being for a certain type of adherent at a specific point in time. This suggests that figurative language is very important in expressing and consolidating the idealized cognitive models structuring these accounts.

Implications and Future Directions

Analyzing religious language in terms of combinations of ICMs opens up several possibilities for future research related to the cognitive dimension of figurative language. First, identifying how particular forms of conceptual metaphors express and consolidate specific combinations of ICMs over different contexts allows for a deeper level of analysis than is possible from analyzing figurative language in isolation. This is because it involves a more holistic analysis that connects figurative and non-figurative cognitive components, thereby encouraging the researcher to look for the relationship between them. This opens up another layer of analysis that could be useful when comparing the language of believers from the same belief community and across different belief communities. Lakoff (1987) also always intended ICMs to be multi-faceted frameworks drawing on not just metaphor, but also metonymy and image schemas intertwined with typicality effects. Their use therefore encourages researchers to produce truly multi-level analyses that integrate the tracking of conceptual metaphors with other key elements of a cognitive linguistic analysis.

Secondly, when analyzing conversion or realization accounts, the identification of metaphor within a framework of ICMs provides another layer of analysis for examining the language before, during, and after the transitional moment. This raises an interesting research question. Is there usually a close, interconnected relationship between the need or the problem in the pre-breakthrough language and the solution or new way of being established after the breakthrough moment? If it is possible to identify and track particular relationships between these different segments of the event model, it may be possible to generate hypotheses as to why particular types of believers are drawn to specific ways of being religious. The idea that almost all religions posit some type of fundamental problem and solution is well-known within religious studies, but what requires more research is whether believers with particular needs, problems, and inclinations are drawn to ways of being religious that offer the possibility of specific solutions or answers.

One question that the analysis in the previous section raises is why researchers of religion should be particularly interested in the interplay between systems, states, and relationships. To begin to answer this from a cognitive linguistic perspective, it is useful to begin with Sweetser and DesCamp's (2014) discussion of what motivates some of the key conceptual metaphors in religion, such as GOD IS FATHER. They note that a significant influence on our way of thinking about human-divine relationships is the shared experience of vulnerability as an infant and the nurturance and support received by a caregiver. Given the importance of these experiences, it is no surprise that mappings such as INTIMACY IS CLOSENESS and AFFECTION IS WARMTH are viewed as primary metaphors in cognitive linguistics while also playing an important role in many types of religious language. Sweetser and DesCamp (2014) also go on to talk about the importance of our early experiences of positive and negative assessments of situations, how we associate particular feelings with these assessments, and how these experiences later form the basis of our moral frameworks. When all this is put together, the crucial importance for religious belief of the interaction between relationships, states or feelings, and systems becomes apparent. When exploring different ways of being religious, for example someone talking about being led by the spirit, someone describing the performance of a ritual in order to receive some benefit, or a dharma talk about the dissolution of the ego and the experience of enlightenment, an examination of how each of these three elements are being backgrounded, foregrounded, connected, and mapped provides a useful starting point for any comparative analysis.

The importance of analyzing the interplay between these three aspects may also contribute to the ongoing debate of whether there is a common core in religious or spiritual experience in general or specific definitions of mystical language in particular (cf. Hood & Chen, 2015). For those scholars that support the idea of a common core, it is often argued, for example, that complex relationship language or doctrinal and ritualistic systems are later interpretative additions to a purer experiential core that revolves around key states or insights, such as an experience of undifferentiated unity or ego dissolution (Hood & Chen, 2013; Stace, 1960). However, it is possible that scholars supporting the common core hypothesis are utilizing data collection methods that encourage the selection of particular features from a more complex and variable range of experiences (Taves, 2020). If close analyses of ICM networks and associated conceptual metaphors can demonstrate and track the importance of specific types of systems or detailed relationship language for particular individuals, communities, and contexts, this may call into question the idea that such elements are on the periphery of a believer's experience. It may be possible that there are multiple interacting key components (rather than just one core) that move through certain patterns for specific ways of being religious. If this is the case, these components would have both non-metaphorical and metaphorical elements, with the metaphorical elements playing a key role at the level of conceptualizing, consolidating, and concretizing religious experience (not just interpreting it). Far more extensive analyses of larger samples of texts and discourse than the samples above are required to investigate these issues further.

Further Reading

Chilton, P. & Kopytowska, M. (Eds.). (2018). *Religion, language, and the human mind*. Oxford University Press.
This volume is particularly important for two reasons: it brings together a collection of analyses on a wide array of religious texts that include Christianity, Judaism, Islam, Buddhism, and Hinduism, while also attempting in its introduction to provide a much-needed bridge between cognitive linguistics and the Cognitive Science of Religion.
Charteris-Black, J. (2004). *Corpus approaches to critical metaphor analysis*. Palgrave Macmillan.
This book provides a comprehensive comparative analysis of conceptual metaphors in the Bible and the Quran, in addition to introducing a rigorous methodology for identifying and exploring metaphors in religious texts.
Charteris-Black, J. (2017). *Fire metaphors: Discourses of awe and authority*. Bloomsbury Academic.
This book examines how a single source domain is used across a wide range of religious texts that encompass Judaism, Christianity, Zoroastrianism, and Hinduism.
Pihlaja, S. (Ed.). (2017). *Metaphor and the Social World, Special Issue: Metaphor in Religion and Spirituality*, 7(1).
This collection of articles offers perspectives on metaphor usage in religious language from both cognitive linguistic researchers and those outside of the field. This allows readers to see how cognitive linguistic analyses of figurative language can be situated within analyses that originate from other discourse analytic approaches.
Richardson, P., Mueller, C. M., & Pihlaja, S. (2021). *Cognitive linguistics and religious language: An introduction*. Routledge.
This book assumes no prior knowledge of cognitive linguistics and the notion of conceptual metaphor and provides a clear but more detailed explanation to many of the topics discussed in this chapter.

References

Adyashanti (2013). *Falling into grace*. Sounds True.
Al-Zahrani, A. (2008). Darwin's metaphors revisited: Conceptual metaphors, conceptual blends, and idealised cognitive models in the theory of evolution. *Metaphor and Symbol, 23(*1), 50–82.
Cameron, L. J. (2011). *Metaphor and reconciliation: The discourse dynamics of empathy in post-conflict conversations*. Routledge.
Charteris-Black, J. (2016). *Fire metaphors: Discourses of awe and authority*. Bloomsbury Academic.
Chilton, P. & Kopytowska, M. (Eds.). (2017). *Religion, language, and the human mind*. Oxford University Press.

Davies, M. (2008) The Corpus of Contemporary American English (COCA). www.english-corpora.org/coca/.

Evans, V. (2019). *Cognitive linguistics: A complete guide*. Edinburgh University Press.

Fauconnier, G. & Turner, M. (2002). *The way we think: Conceptual blending and the mind's hidden complexities*. Basic Books.

Fillmore, C. (1982). Frame semantics. In Linguistic Society of Korea (Ed.), *Linguistics in the Morning Calm*, 111–35. Hanshin.

Gibbs, R.W. Jr. (2017). *Metaphor wars: Conceptual metaphors in human life*. Cambridge University Press.

Gibbs, R.W. Jr. (2005). *Embodiment and cognitive science*. Cambridge University Press.

Gibbs, R.W. Jr. & Cameron, L. J. (2008). The social-cognitive dynamics of metaphor performance. *Cognitive Systems Research*, *9*(1–2), 64–75.

Grady, (1997). Theories are buildings revisited. *Cognitive Linguistics*, *8*, 267–90. Cambridge University Press.

Hood, R.W. & Chen, Z. (2015). Mystical, Spiritual, and Religious Experiences. In Paloutzian, R.F. & Park, C.L. (Eds.), *Handbook of the psychology of religion and spirituality, second edition*, 422–440. Guilford.

Hood, R.W. & Chen, Z. (2013). The social scientific study of Christian mysticism. In J.A. Lamm (Ed.), *The Wiley-Blackwell companion to Christian mysticism*, 577–591. Wiley-Blackwell.

Jeffress, R. (2018). *Choosing the extraordinary life: God's seven secrets for success and significance*. Baker Books.

Kapleau, P. (2000). *The three pillars of Zen: Teaching, practice, and enlightenment*. Anchor Books.

Komjathy, L. (2018). *Introducing contemplative studies*. Wiley-Blackwell.

Kövecses, Z. (2020). *Extended conceptual metaphor theory*. Cambridge University Press.

Kövecses, Z. (2015). *Where metaphors come from: Reconsidering context in metaphor*. Oxford University Press.

Lakoff, G. (1987). *Women, fire, and dangerous things: What categories reveal about the mind*. University of Chicago Press.

Lakoff, G. & Johnson, M. (1999). *Philosophy in the flesh: The embodied mind and its challenge to Western thought*. Basic Books.

Littlemore, J. (2015). *Metonymy: Hidden shortcuts in language, thought and communication*. Cambridge University Press.

Littlemore, J. (2019). *Metaphors in the mind: Sources of variation in embodied metaphor*. Cambridge University Press.

Merton, T. (2015). *The seven storey mountain, centenary edition*. SPCK classics.

Musolff, A. (2004). *Metaphor and political discourse: Analogical reasoning in debates about Europe*. Palgrave Macmillan.

Osteen, J. (2014). *You can you will: 8 undeniable qualities of a winner*. Large Print Edition. FaithWords.

Pihlaja, S. (2014). *Antagonism on YouTube: Metaphor in online discourse*. Bloomsbury.

Pihlaja, S. (Ed.) (2017). *Metaphor and the Social World, Special Issue: Metaphor in Religion and Spirituality*. *7*(1).

Pragglejaz Group (2007). MIP: A method for identifying metaphorically used words in discourse. *Metaphor and Symbol*, *22*(1), 1–39.

Richardson, P. (2012). A closer walk: A study of the interaction between metaphors related to movement and proximity and presuppositions about the reality of belief in Christian and Muslim testimonials. *Metaphor and the Social World*, *2*(2), 233–261.

Richardson, P., Mueller, C.M., & Pihlaja, S. (2021). *Cognitive linguistics and religious language: An introduction*. Routledge.

Rohr, R. (2019). *The universal Christ: How a forgotten reality can change everything we see, hope for and believe*. SPCK.

Soskice, J.M. (1985). *Metaphor and religious language*. Oxford University Press.

Stace (1960). *Mysticism and philosophy*. Lippincott.

Sweetser, E.E. & DesCamp, M.T. (2014). Motivating Biblical metaphors for God: Refining the cognitive model. In B. Howe & J.B. Green (Eds.), *Cognitive linguistic explorations in Biblical Studies*, 7–23. De Gruyter.

Talmy, L. (2000). *Towards a cognitive semantics*, *2*. MIT Press.

Taves, A. (2020). Mystical and other alterations in sense and self: An expanded framework for studying nonordinairy experiences. *Perspectives on psychological science*, *15*(3), 1–22.

Unno, T. (2002). *Shin Buddhism: Bits of rubble turn into gold*. Doubleday.

Williams, A.K. (2000). *Being black: Zen and the art of living with fearlessness and grace*. Penguin Compass.

Testimonials from the Evangelical Times

22 November 2018: Jackie Davis
Overwhelmed by God's love
www.evangelical-times.org/overwhelmed-by-gods-love/

26 November 2021: Yvonne Edwards
Rescued from a life of drink and cocaine
www.evangelical-times.org/rescued-from-a-life-of-drink-and-cocaine/

25 November 2021: Terry Wighton
From crime to Christ
www.evangelical-times.org/from-crime-to-christ-2/

18 November 2020: Victoria Kulczycka
I was an actress in a hit US TV show, but there was still a void within me
www.evangelical-times.org/i-was-an-actress-in-a-hit-us-tv-show-but-there-was-still-a-void-within-me/

18 November 2020: Akik Miah
Practising Islam was simply our way of life. Then I found Christ.
www.evangelical-times.org/practising-islam-was-simply-our-way-of-life-then-i-found-christ/

30
RELIGIOUS RITUAL AND LANGUAGE IN THE LOCAL COMMUNITY

Andrey Rosowsky

Introduction and Background

There are a number of terms denoting the language variety that is used for ritual or liturgical purposes. When this variety is a distinct language, usually archaic and text-dependent (see Bennett, this volume)—rather than only a special variety of an existing standard language, such as the variety of English that is sometimes used in High Anglican or post-Vatican II Catholic services—the terms 'liturgical' (Rosowsky, 2008), 'sacred' (Bennett, 2017), or 'religious classical' (Fishman, 1989) can be found. In this chapter, I will follow Bennett (2017) and use 'sacred language' for a religious language variety that (a) is invariably archaic and ancient, (b) is centred on a sacred text and primarily used for ritual, and (c) has long since been abandoned as a spoken register.

A number of sociolinguists (Ferguson, 1982; Fishman, 1989; Rosowsky, 2008; Safran, 2008) have observed how, in conditions of *diaspora* where minority languages face attrition from a majority language, but where a sacred language is part of that community's *linguistic repertoire* (Gumperz & Hymes, 1972; Busch, 2012), it is the maintenance of that sacred language that is privileged through community efforts and community funding, even to the extent of the community minority or heritage language shifting to the majority language for most functions and in most, if not all, domains. Although a number of terms can be found in the research literature for denoting the vernacular of a diasporic community—for example, 'community language', 'heritage language', 'minority language'—in this chapter, I will use 'heritage language' for the (usually) spoken variety that a minority community lays claim to regardless of their proficiency in that language—which can range from fully conversant to symbolic allegiance only—and which forms part of their linguistic repertoires along with the sacred language where that is present.

The maintenance of the sacred language within the community is often ensured through the establishment of weekend and after-school supplementary education where children follow a systematic programme of sacred language acquisition (Rosowsky, 2008; Schachter, 2010; Miller, 2010). Such programmes allow children to acquire at least a 'minimal' (Safran, 2008, p. 186) proficiency in decoding and memorisation, sufficient to allow the performance of regular rituals such as daily or weekly prayer and recitation of sacred texts. Occasionally, these programmes include efforts to maintain the heritage minority language, but evidence shows that it is the acquisition of

DOI: 10.4324/9781003301271-33

the sacred language that is protected whilst heritage minority languages regularly undergo shift to the majority language (Fishman, 1991).

Sacred language acquisition takes place in a diverse range of faith contexts and a full list might include Amish children learning Lutheran German, Buddhist children learning one or more of the sacred languages linked to their faith, or Russian Orthodox children using a variety of Church Slavonic. However, in practice, apart from the special circumstances of the Amish, other faiths often restrict the acquisition and practice of the sacred language to their clerics and scholars. Such is generally the case with Buddhism where, although some children may acquire a sacred language, they usually only do so if they are living as child monks (Parkes, 2022).

Similarly, in Orthodox and some Roman Catholic traditions (pre-Vatican II, for example), only the clergy would have significant proficiency in the sacred language and congregations would usually be 'silent observers' (Prusak, 2010) uttering only occasional responses in the sacred language. This 'bystander' effect constituted one of the drivers for the reform of the Roman Catholic liturgy at Vatican II (1962–1965) where an important objective was to make ritual more engaging for the congregation and a move to the use of the vernaculars instead of Latin was considered a key element (Paton, 2013). The type of sacred language acquired and *regularly* used by worshippers as an integral part of their faith practices is what Bennett calls a *demotic* sacred language. The sacred language used, in the main, by clerics and scholars is what he calls a *hieratic* sacred language (see chapter by Bennett in this volume).

Interestingly, a sacred language can move from a demotic mode to a hieratic one. Before the 1917 revolution in Russia, it was more usual for children to acquire Church Slavonic, but this practice ended abruptly at that point and now Church Slavonic is almost always a hieratic sacred language. There are some signs that a lay revival is taking place since the end of the Soviet Union though it is perhaps too early to evaluate its extent (Uvarova, 2017).

Demotic sacred languages in the present era are best represented by the two monotheist faiths of Judaism and Islam where the requirement for children to acquire the faiths' sacred languages is much more bound up with individual religious identity and practice. It is therefore quite usual, given the need to have at least minimal proficiency in the sacred language to meet the requirements of worship, to find Jewish and Muslim supplementary schools in most diasporic contexts. For a Muslim child, this minimal requirement would be the ability to decode the Qur'an and then learn and memorise enough text to perform adequately the canonical prayer. This might be the limit of proficiency for the rest of their lives. Others may go on to develop and extend their proficiency, but these are generally in the minority (Rosowsky, 2021). In Jewish supplementary schools, a similar programme exists. Children are led to acquiring the ability to decode Biblical Hebrew, thus enabling them to take part in the rite of passage of the Bar Mitzvah (Bat Mitzvah), where being able to decode a short section of the Torah in front of the congregation is required, as well as in other canonical practices. Again, memorisation plays a part in children learning some basic prayers which are needed to participate in ritual. This might be the limit of the acquired proficiency for Jewish children and their lives as Jewish adults. As with Muslim children, some may go on to develop and extend this proficiency, but most do not (Schachter, 2010).

Research into sacred language acquisition, like research into language and religion more generally, is relatively recent but a modest body of work is now emerging that shares both theoretical and methodological perspectives, enough at least to justify a circumscribed field of study. Fishman (1989) was an early observer of how what he called 'religious classicals' can be understood as 'special' additional minority languages noting their distinctive features (archaic and ancient, text-based, linked to ritual) and their apparent staying power in minority language contexts. Drawing on Ferguson (1982), he was one of the first to notice how minority language communities privilege their sacred language over their minority spoken vernaculars. In addition to the sacred languages mentioned above, Fishman listed Ecclesiastical Greek, Coptic, and Latin, all of which probably fall into the category of hieratic sacred language acquisition and practice for elites such as priests and clerics rather than constituting a rite of passage for young people into the respective faiths, as is the case with Muslim and Jewish children. In the twenty-first century, a series of edited volumes advocating a *sociology of language and religion* has sought to capture the state of play regarding the sociological study of language and religion (Omoniyi & Fishman, 2006; Omoniyi, 2010; Pandharipande et al., 2019) and each has included chapters relating to sacred language practices. Rosowsky (2006a) begins what would become a series of publications on what he then called 'liturgical literacy' with a chapter that accounts for how Muslim children in a small town in the north of England acquire their sacred language through the presence of supplementary schools he calls 'mosque schools'. Incidentally, we sometimes find in the literature the term 'madrassa' or 'madrassah'. Although this is the unproblematic translation for 'school' in Arabic, in certain contexts, it has acquired an occasional (often-undeserved) pejorative connotation (Seddon, 2004). I have always sought to avoid this by using 'mosque school', recognising the fact that most such establishments are part of a mosque. Pandharipande (2006) shows how language practices in the United States Hindu diaspora, as with language practices in Hinduism in general, lay less stress on the sacred language relative to the languages of the wider setting, in this case English. Whereas *satsang* (a form of teaching in the presence of a guru) can be conducted in a range of languages including English, she also shows how there remains a modicum of sacred language practice in *puja* practices. For example, certain *puja* such as *Hanuman Chalisa* uses Sanskrit, though other languages, including English, can be used for other *puja* (see also Pandharipande, 2018).

Spolsky (2010), in an account of both the changing and non-changing nature of sacred language practice in Judaism over the past 3000 years, shows how the evolving sociolinguistic ecology in which the Jewish community found itself (either over time or through displacement) affected both the status and nature of the sacred language. For instance, whereas once Aramaic was once used widely as the community's vernacular and in texts as a gloss for those who no longer knew Hebrew, it came over time to take on a sanctity of its own (Fishman calls this process 'co-sanctification', 2006) and came to be used in some ritual practices (the Jewish mourning prayer, the Kaddish, is usually performed in Aramaic). Another example of linguistic co-sanctification can occur when certain language varieties are used in special domains and for particular functions such as devotional poetry and song. Rosowsky (2020) shows how the formal and performative practice of reciting or singing devotional verses can share partially in the sanctity of the sacred language which is often present in the same setting. In this way, certain formulaic expressions in Classical Arabic can frame the performance of an ode in Urdu to the extent that the ode itself becomes a sanctified text and is treated with an almost equal degree of reverence and esteem.

Kaur and David (2019) in their quantitative study reveal how in Singapore the sacred text of the Sikhs, the Sri Guru Granth Sahib, is no longer understood by 85 per cent of the Sikhs they surveyed. The text is therefore often experienced in the temple in an *ultralingual* way with participants either experiencing the sacred language sonically or relying on translations. I use the term *ultralingual* to denote language experience where the referential sense of the text (it's usually a text, even when experienced orally) is partially or fully absent. Ultralingual practice is regularly associated with sacred text practice (Rosowsky, 2021). As with most sacred text settings, in Sikhism, proficiency in the sacred language is generally the preserve of the priests. This example of ultralingualism has two causes—one is the general lack of understanding of the variety of Classical Punjabi in which the Sri Guru Granth Sahib is composed and the other is the more general language shift to English which has happened to the Sikh community's spoken vernacular, Punjabi, in Singapore.

The text of the Sri Guru Granth Sahib is actually composed in a number of language varieties. Although most of the text is in Classical Punjabi and Hindi, there are elements of Lahnda, Prakrits, Apabhramsa, Sanskrit, Sindhi, and Persian, all written in a script known as Gurmukhi.

Other bodies of research include Rosowsky's (2008) ethnographic study of a Muslim community in the UK which explores the interrelationship between community language practices and sacred language practice. Carried out at the beginning of the twenty-first century, the study reveals how language shift in the community more generally was beginning to impact upon sacred text acquisition in the mosque school. Specifically, children were shifting to English from their heritage language, and this had implications for how they were taught the sacred language by their teachers who were largely recruited from their homeland. In 2021, Rosowsky demonstrated how in the space of two decades, the English language was now dominant in mosque schools (if not in mosques) and that pedagogies have had to alter as the sacred language was now being taught through the medium of English.

A corresponding body of work by Moore (2006, 2013) has researched in detail how young Cameroonian Muslims acquire their sacred language. She helps make an important distinction between prayer and ritual uttered or experienced in a sacred language (in Classical Arabic) and prayer in a vernacular mode (Fulfude), which is the personal prayer uttered by the plaintive and which can be carried out in any language. Her studies allow us to observe that sacred language practices among Fulfude-speaking Muslims in Cameroon have a very similar pattern of sacred language/vernacular demarcation to those of migrant Pakistani-heritage Muslims in the UK (Rosowsky, 2008) who may use Urdu, Punjabi, Bengali (or any South Asian language used in the community), or even English for personal prayer.

Another important research perspective on sacred language practice is a performative one. What I call ultralingual practice attunes closely to research carried out in the verbal arts and performance. Bauman (1975) shows how verbatim oral performance often emphasises form over content with performers focusing their attention on the form and structure of their utterances. Although Bauman was writing about verbal art more generally, and had little to say about religious texts, his identification of two dominant characteristics in verbal performance help in an understanding of the value of sacred text recitation. On the one hand, verbal art performance demands attention from both performer and audience to the way language is presented often to the peripherisation of referential meaning. This entails an emphasis on accurate rendition of verbal utterances in terms of pronunciation and recitation conventions. This 'getting it right' aspect is added to by an enhanced concentration on communicative skill or beauty.

The other dominant characteristic, which is evoked by the first, is the enhancement of experience of the audience. The latter experiences the performance not only through an intellectual and semantic understanding of what is performed—if this understanding is available—but is also emotionally moved by the communicative power and/or beauty of the performed utterances. Sacred text practice always involves the first of these characteristics and often the second. Rosowsky (2013) explores the performative nature of much sacred language practice and shows how young Muslims who embrace the performative nature of their practices are able to articulate the value of reading or reciting in such a way. In an important sense, the performative aspect of sacred language practice is what moves it away from deficit concepts of reading and pejorative accusations of rote learning (Cherti & Bradley, 2011). Reciting or memorising (or performing) a sacred text is as much part of worship as prayer and other ritual (see Mueller, this volume).

Very recent linguistic research has seen to position sacred language acquisition and practice *as language practice per se* among a much wider range of linguistic and cultural activity both religious and non-religious (Rosowsky, 2021). The linguistic phenomenon of using language (reading, reciting, listening, even pseudo-speaking) without any grasp of referential meaning is perhaps sur-prisingly rather widespread. In the world of music this is common. Singers from all musical genres can find themselves singing in languages unknown to them and audiences listen, often happily, with the same degree of ignorance. The 2003 Eurovision Song Contest entry from Belgium was a song composed in a language unknown to both performer and audience. That did not seem to pre-vent it coming an impressive second. Music is a rich source of what I call *ultralingual* performance but there are other contexts too. Sacred language practice can often share in this *ultralingual* char-acteristic with both performers (reciters, readers, singers) and listeners (teachers, fellow students, congregations) unable to access referential meaning. Much is sometimes made of this phenom-enon being simply an initial stage in the learning of the sacred language and that comprehension comes later but research shows that such *ultralingual* performance becomes the reality for most participants and remains so for the rest of their lives (Rosowsky, 2008).

Religious Ritual and Language in Local Communities

Liddicoat's (2012) work on religious language policy identifies two obvious orientations in lan-guage use in religious contexts. He calls these the 'sacral-' and 'comprehensibility-' orientations. The former represents language belief and practice where a sacred language lies at the heart of the faith in question. As we have seen already, examples are numerous—though within individual faiths the fate of the sacred language can vary. For centuries, Latin was very much understood as a sacred language for the Roman Catholic Church. With Vatican II this ended, and vernaculars took its place. In Liddicoat's terms, this was a move from the 'sacral-' to the 'comprehensibility-' orientations (2012, p. 122). However, within the Catholic Church this distinction, one might argue, has perhaps not been as fully resolved as it was in the move to the vernaculars in the sixteenth-century Reformation (though even here the vernaculars of the time have sometimes evolved into a quasi-sacred (or co-sanctified) language of their own). The last-but-one Pope, Benedict XVI, attempted to loosen some of the restrictions on the use of Latin as a liturgical language placed upon it at Vatican II (Kizcek, 2009). The present Pope, Francis, has re-imposed these restrictions (Hebert, 2022).

The fate of sacred languages in their respective faith communities is a varied one. In Islam, for example, there has been little movement if any towards replacing the sacred language with a ver-nacular even though vernaculars have accompanied it throughout its history. Much of this comes down to language belief. Classical Arabic (and a particular variety of it), emically understood as the revealed language of the Qur'an and, as God's speech, is immutable. In Judaism, a similar language belief prevails. Despite the Jewish community shifting from vernacular Hebrew to other vernaculars millennia ago, the sacred language has been retained for purposes of ritual and reli-gious scholarship. Its re-vernacularisation as a living language in present-day Israel is yet another stage in its story as a sacred language and incidentally constitutes one of the most successful instances of reversing language shift the world has known (Fishman, 1991).

By contrast, in Hinduism, although Sanskrit is understood as a sacred language and shares in the features of other sacred languages (ancient and archaic, related to text and scripture, no longer spoken), there has been a much greater acceptance of other languages for ritual purposes. As Pandharipande shows above (2006), this multilingual approach to ritual now includes English. In Fishman's *Decalogue* of precepts for a sociology of language and religion (2006), his fourth precept is that a consequence of convergence with the vernacular together with the activity of translation sometimes leads to the vernaculars acquiring a 'degree of sanctity of their own' (p.17). Hoenes del Pinal (2016) writes of how the use of the vernacular Q'eqchi' in the local Catholic

Church in Guatemala has gradually evolved into an almost sanctified variety serving as a barrier to the encroachment of Spanish and accruing to itself in the process notions of piety and sacredness which the colonial language is deemed to lack. Other examples of sanctified languages used specifically for ritual and in other religiously defined domains include the particularly formal registers of Standard English used in the English-speaking High Anglican and Catholic Churches. Although not strictly speaking 'sacred' languages, these varieties still must be acquired by those using them along with the conventions as to when and where they would be used.

Pedagogy in contemporary faith-based supplementary schools is often based on a loose alliance of traditional and modern methodologies. In conditions of diaspora, the latter have become more prominent (Rosowsky, 2006b). The most common and significant factor in teaching the sacred language is the decision about through which vernacular instruction takes place. In English-speaking settings of the Jewish diaspora, the sacred language is generally taught through the medium of English as the non-Haredi Jewish community has long since shifted to English as a first language. For the Haredi community in the diaspora, Yiddish has generally been retained as a first language though Haredi communities in Israel have begun to shift to vernacular Hebrew as a first language (Spolsky, 2010). In *chedarim* (the Hebrew word used for a school where religious knowledge is acquired roughly equivalent to a 'Sunday School' in Christian contexts and a 'mosque school' in Islamic ones) in the US and in the UK, teachers use bilingual English-Hebrew teaching materials to induct children into the Hebrew language. All instruction is generally in English.

One cause of disagreement is the trend in some *chedarim* to employ transliterated texts to facilitate learning of the sacred text (Miller, 2010). In terms of language belief, such a development moves the community away from an understanding that the Hebrew script itself is as sacred as the language it represents. A similar concern is found in Islamic settings where transliteration has now become a regular feature of teaching materials. As a strategy for teaching the Arabic script it has merits, particular for children who have begun to acquire literacy in the majority language. The fear expressed by some is that transliteration becomes a barrier rather than a stepping stone to acquiring the original script. As the teaching of writing is not usually a regular aspect of sacred language acquisition, children (and adults) make recourse to transliteration more readily in this mode (Rosowsky, 2010).

The language, therefore, used to instruct children can change quite rapidly in conditions of diaspora. As mentioned above, in some Muslim communities in the UK the medium of instruction has changed within a relatively short period of two decades. Where once the sacred language was mediated through a heritage language such as Urdu, Punjabi, Bengali (or even Arabic), the overwhelming evidence shows that English is now the preferred language for instruction— though in some settings, depending on the language of the teacher, this might also be a case of codeswitching or translanguaging (Rosowsky, 2021). This appears to be the case even in mosque settings where adults are still addressed (in sermons for example) in the heritage languages.

Personnel can also be a factor in the language used for teaching the sacred language. This factor has two dimensions. One is that language shift has happened almost fully with the younger, third, and now fourth generations of Muslims in the UK. This means that the most readily available language for teaching for both students and children is English. Second, the younger generation is generally more formally educated than are their elders with a larger percentage of young Muslims proceeding to higher education than was the case with their parents and grandparents. However, Muslim representation in UK higher education is not all that it should or could be as recent research has indicated (Stevenson, 2018). As a result of this change in teacher profile, teachers are now being recruited to mosque schools who are first language English speakers (sometime with only a modicum of knowledge of their heritage language) and who have been educated through the mainstream school system, allowing them insight into and experience of a range of pedagogical strategies not usually available to hitherto more traditional teachers (often recruited from the community's heartlands back home). Despite some tension between parents wanting a more traditional approach to learning the sacred language (usually consisting of a wish to have this receive 100 per cent attention) and teachers wanting to teach more generally about the religion, this reflects a more contemporary approach to sacred language acquisition and although acquisition of the sacred language is not necessarily at risk, there is some movement towards a comprehensibility-orientation (Liddicoat, 2012).

The remainder of this chapter will attempt to illustrate some of the themes and issues identified in the previous sections. Taking as an example the multilingual communities of the South Asian diaspora in the West, qualitative data (interview transcripts) will be shared that illustrate the diverse language patterns and behaviours present when a sacred language, Qur'anic Arabic, is added to individuals' already complex linguistic repertoires. Using the sociolinguistic framework of *language shift* and *reversing language shift*, analysis shows that such communities tend to foreground sacred languages over any *minority* (*heritage*) languages that may be available. Specifically, I show how a Pakistani-heritage community in the north of the UK invests significant time in and resources to the acquisition and practices associated with the sacred language of the Qur'an and how this contrasts favourably with community efforts to maintain its heritage languages (spoken Punjabi and Urdu). Data is presented from both the beginning of the century and more recently to show how language shift has happened with heritage language whilst the sacred language retains a relatively secure and unendangered status within the community's linguistic repertoire.

Twenty years ago (Rosowsky, 2008), when questioned about the teaching of their sacred language in their local mosque school, two parents offered the following comments with a similar sentiment (all names are pseudonyms):

I think myself, if children go to the mosque, they should read in Arabic and also in English as well. They should understand what is the meaning of this word. I mean, if they are reading that, and they don't understand, they don't know what is the meaning of this, they are just wasting time. We want proper teachers, qualified teachers, who can teach these children born in this country. (Munir)

Because most of the kids ... are very fluent in English and were born here and most of the kids speak English and some of them have difficulty understanding Mirpuri or Urdu. Even Urdu. Mainly Urdu they have difficulty understanding it. I mean if they don't understand it, how are they going to learn? (Wajib)

NB 'Mirpuri' is used here by the parent to denote a variety of Punjabi spoken in the Mirpur region of north-eastern Pakistan, the heartlands of most of the original Pakistani settlers to the UK in the 1950–1970s (Lothers & Lothers, 2012).

Twenty years later (Rosowsky, 2021) a mosque school teacher could say:

[the children] enjoy going for the fact that [the teacher] was teaching in English. It might not have been the best English in the world, but it was English. And he could understand you as well. He might not have been the best person to express himself in English but he could understand you. (Suhai)

These two extracts encapsulate the language shift affecting the community more generally and its particular impact on sacred language acquisition. On the one hand, teaching in English is now considered a more effective way of getting children to acquire the sacred language. On the other, the use of English is recognising a need for greater comprehensibility in matters of religious knowledge. The sacral/comprehensibility distinction is still present but manifests itself in a changed sociolinguistic context.

In 2001, four of the five teachers working in Town A's local mosques had been recruited from 'back home' and had been educated in Pakistan seminaries. Two were graduates of the Faculties of Religious Sciences (*Dar ul-Uloom*) in Faisalabad and Islamabad. One was a graduate and doctor of the Faculty of Religious Sciences of the University of Karachi and the fourth was from the Faculty of Religious Sciences, Delhi. They were undoubtedly well qualified to teach the sacred language but could only do so through the medium of their first languages (Urdu, Pushto, and Gujerati). Their relatively isolated existence in the local community also meant that learning English was not a priority or had not yet reached a level suitable for teaching with it in the mosque school. Children at that time were largely experiencing shift to English and even their heritage language (variously called 'Mirpuri' or, more linguistically correct, Pothwari or Pahari) was a spoken vernacular that was often not shared with their teachers.

> Our imam is only speaking Urdu. And it should be in English. (Munir, parent)
> They're preaching in Urdu…Urdu is not our language…Urdu is not the language of my children…although it is a beautiful language… . (Wajib, parent)
> The first thing is language…most teachers speak Urdu… .and the children do not understand it. (Mufti Siddiq, teacher)

These comments contrast starkly with the current generation of mosque school teachers who are often graduates and if not first language speakers are nevertheless fluent English speakers.

> And so what you're getting, the biggest change, is you're getting more professionals in these fields, so people who are teachers, people who work in fields that are deemed as professionals are coming into, bringing that experience, into the madrassahs. (Ali, mosque schoolteacher)

NB Ali' and his colleagues use the term 'madrassa' for their mosque school and indeed this is the term used emically by the community. I prefer the term 'mosque school' for the reason provided earlier.

> [W]e've been through the schooling system. That's unique. We relate with the kids. They can't get away with being what we've been through. We see what they see. We've done what they are doing. … 'Don't tell me about Facebook. I know more than you do'. 'How dare you. Twitter? How come you don't follow that?' ''Stazi' [roughly equivalent to 'Sir' in a mainstream school setting], you're on Twitter?!' I know more games than they do. That kind of stuff is different. This was not there in the past. (Ali, mosque schoolteacher)

These two quotations from Ali, a teacher in a contemporary mosque school, contrast starkly with how sacred language teachers were only twenty years earlier. The emergence of this new generation of teachers fully conversant both linguistically and culturally with the lives of their young students has resulted in a degree of convergence between traditional mosque school instruction and more 'liberal' approaches to sacred language acquisition.

In other contemporary mosque settings, alongside the sacred language of the Qur'an, children are sometimes inducted into co-sanctified (Fishman, 2006) language varieties. As with their sacred language acquisition, this can happen ultralingually even when the language varieties concerned are related to their heritage languages. Language shift has often replaced these languages with English and has left only a minimal or even merely symbolic attachment to the heritage languages. We find therefore children reciting in literary Urdu, Classical Punjabi (a literary variety of Punjabi often found in Shahmukhi script but often transliterated in diaspora contexts) and, more rarely, Persian. To the Western ear, much devotional verse recitation sounds like singing. However, emically, such verse is usually understood as 'reading'. These co-sanctified varieties are generally linguistically distant from any spoken associated varieties such as spoken Punjabi or Urdu and are characterised, as are most literary registers, by greater complexity in the lexicon and in the use of poetic and archaic syntax. These sanctified texts are used in formal devotional performances and sometimes given as much reverence as that given to sacred text recitation itself. Much of that repertoire is inaccessible from a referential meaning point of view. However, such is the nature of ultralingual performance that inaccessibility for many merely adds to the otherworldly quality of the devotional performance.

> We know the naat [a devotional poem that is usually in Urdu, Classical Punjabi or, more rarely, Persian] but we don't know what it means. [They are important] because they are for the Prophet.
> You get the feelings, special feelings through the words that you can't get in English. Maybe in 50 years or so there will be a poet who writes naat in English…. that when people read it they will feel that love coming out of the words…. but you can't get in English at the moment what you get in Urdu or Arabic. (Shahid, 23, naat performer)

These two quotations encapsulate two important and characteristic orientations when performing ultralingually. On the one hand, there is a clear awareness among many young performers of these devotional texts that referential meaning is inaccessible. However, as with ultralingual recitation of the Qur'an, this does not appear to evoke feelings of incongruity and discomfiture. On the other hand, there is a sense articulated here that such lack of understanding not only does not detract from engagement but possibly adds to an 'otherworldly' or 'spiritual' experience ('love coming out of the words') and that a fully comprehensible utterance as might be the case in English would itself detract from such experience ('you can't get it in English').

Implications and Future Directions

Future research hopefully will continue to plot the contrasting patterns of language maintenance and language shift with respect to the acquisition of the sacred language. With the Jewish and Muslim diasporas settled all over the globe, the linguistic repertoires in which the sacred language takes its place are diverse. The usual language shift pattern should mean that majority languages will eventually displace any minority heritage languages (in Jewish *chedarim* this mostly happened some time ago—apart from in Haredi communities which retain Yiddish). This has implications for pedagogy for it should explore how the sacred language in the diasporas is now regularly taught through the *majority* language rather than through the community heritage languages (in the case study in this chapter, through English rather than through spoken Punjabi, Urdu, Sylheti, or Bengali). There is already evidence that sacred language teaching materials are widely available for children using the majority languages rather than the heritage languages of their parents and grandparents in a range of online sites, including YouTube videos and varying levels of formal instructional sites.

A perusal of any of these resources will also reveal that a wealth of sacred language teaching material is now available online and digitally. In terms of pedagogy, future research should explore both the use of digital technologies and online contexts for the acquisition of sacred languages. In Rosowsky (2021), I briefly describe how one mosque school is using digital technology (laptop and data projector) to support the acquisition of Qur'anic Arabic. This is a field of research which requires more extensive exploration and would complement research carried out into online and digital pedagogies more widely. Although there is substantial research being carried out into online religion (see Campbell, 2013), as yet only a small number of publications has extended this research into religion and language in online settings. Rosowsky (2018) presents an attempt to open up this field but little has appeared that focuses on sacred language acquisition. Pandharipande in the same volume shares data that suggests that sacred languages in the Hindu diaspora remain of the hieratic variety (for clerics and scholars) whilst Hindu worshippers in general embrace vernaculars more readily (as has been the case in India itself) for ritual purposes facilitated by the move to online religion.

Bennett's (this volume) distinction between demotic and hieratic sacred languages deserves to be explored and fleshed out with further examples. Of particular interest perhaps is the phenomenon of a once demotic sacred language becoming hieratic. This is the case with Church Slavonic in the twentieth and twenty-first centuries where the sacred language has become predominantly the preserve of clerics and scholars whilst the congregations are now restricted to the vernacular. The opposite is also possible. For millennia Biblical Hebrew was a hieratic sacred language known mainly to rabbis and scholars. The re-vernacularisation of Hebrew in the twentieth century has brought the sacred language to the people (at least in Israel), albeit it now takes its place alongside spoken varieties of Hebrew as well as the Biblical variety.

Although not discussed above, as language shift proceeds, the access to traditionally co-sanctified varieties for devotional purposes may recede and the emergence of English may be more widely used leading to perhaps an Islamic-oriented variety of English for devotional purposes in a similar way to how a devotional variety of English (often termed the 'King James Bible' variety of English) is evident in many English-speaking Christian congregations. Although we are no longer in a time where translation of sacred texts is considered anathema by some, there is still debate over the most appropriate form of English to be used for Muslim texts and discourse. Depending on the origin of certain Muslim communities, different varieties of English appear to mediate certain rituals and can find themselves into translations of texts and ritual formulae. Thus, there are South Asian varieties of English which can find their way into written translations of originally Arabic religious texts whereas one can also find other instances of English translation of Arabic text which tend to draw more readily on traditionally academic conventions (Rosowsky, 2018). Similarly, certain doctrinal differences within Islam can lead to preferred lexical choices in English which often betray an individual's stance. Whether this will lead to competing varieties of Islamic English is unclear.

Berglund and Gent's (2018) work in the field of education is also potentially fruitful when exploring sacred language acquisition practices in Muslim supplementary schools (2018). They show how such practices can have important influences on pedagogical and learning practices in mainstream school settings. In particular, they show how memorisation practices in the supplementary schools lead to learning dividends in mainstream learning. One of their findings, for example, shows how "the skill of memorization where what we refer to here as liturgical literacy is experienced as transferable to mainstream schooling thus helping students to master a variety of school subjects". The value of transferability from the supplementary to the mainstream setting is communicated strongly in this work and is something that is worth developing further. Complementing this finding is the observation drawn by Gent (2011) that the Qur'an should be as much understood "as an aural experience as … a written text" (p. 13). Their work in general situates sacred language acquisition in the field of 'new literacies' (Street, 2003) with 'liturgical' or 'sacred text' literacy being but one of a number of complementary literacies in the lives of these young people.

There are, therefore, a number of aspects regarding sacred language acquisition within community practices that would benefit from further study and exploration. I end this chapter with a set of questions that might inform such work:

- What evidence is there of other *demotic* sacred languages apart from the two most evident examples in Islam and Judaism?
- When sacred language acquisition takes place in contexts of language shift, how does the transition from teaching through the heritage language to teaching through the majority language manifest itself? Materials? Personnel? Technology? Other language practices such as code-switching and translanguaging?
- How are the increasingly available digital resources for sacred language use affecting sacred language acquisition and practice?
- How might sacred language acquisition pedagogy influence mainstream school practices and vice versa?
- Is there any evidence that an Islamic variety of English is developing akin to the variety of English used in High Anglican and Roman Catholic rituals and other religious settings?

Further Reading

Baker, J.N. (1993) The Presence of the Name: Reading Scripture in an Indonesian Village. In J. Boyarin (Ed.), *The Ethnography of Reading*, 98–138. University of California Press.
This ethnographic study accounts for how sacred language acquisition leads to an 'apprehending of' to words rather than comprehending of them in the referential sense.
Berglund, J. & Gent, B. (2018) Memorization and focus: important transferables between supplementary Islamic education and mainstream schooling. *Journal of Religious Education*, 66(2), 125–138.
This UK-based pedagogical study shows how sacred language acquisition complements mainstream school learning.
Liddicoat, A.J. (2012). Language planning as an element of religious practice. *Current Issues in Language Planning*, 13(2), 121–144.
In this article, the sacral-orientation-/comprehensibility-orientation distinction in religious language practice is explored.
Moore, L.C. (2006) Learning by heart in Qur'anic and public schools in northern Cameroon. *Social Analysis: The International Journal of Cultural and Social Practice*, 50(3), 109–126. Berghahn Journals.
This article explores sacred language acquisition and practice in a multilingual context.
Rosowsky, A. (2015) Faith Literacies. *The Routledge handbook of literacy studies*. Routledge.
An introduction to the topic of sacred language acquisition and practice.

References

Bauman, R. (1975). Verbal Art as Performance. *American Anthropologist*, *77*, 290–311.

Bennett, B. (2017). *Sacred languages of the world: An introduction*. Wiley.

Berglund, J. & Gent, B. (2018). Memorization and focus: important transferables between supplementary Islamic education and mainstream schooling. *Journal of Religious Education*, *66*(2), 125–138.

Busch, B. (2012). The Linguistic Repertoire Revisited. *Applied Linguistics*, *33*(5), 503–523.

Campbell, H. (2013) *Digital religion: Understanding religious practice in new media worlds*. Routledge

Cherti, M. & Bradley, L. (2011). *Inside madrassas: Understanding and engaging with British-Muslim faith supplementary schools*. Institute for Public Policy Research.

Ferguson, C.A. (1982). Religious factors in language spread. In R.L. Cooper (Ed.), *Language Spread: Studies in Diffusion and Social Change*, 95–106. Indiana University Press.

Fishman, J.A. (1989). *Language and identity in minority sociolinguistic perspective*. Multilingual Matters.

Fishman, J.A. (1991). *Reversing language shift: Theoretical and empirical foundations of assistance to threatened languages*. Multilingual Matters.

Fishman, J.A. (2006). A Decalogue of basic theoretical perspectives for a sociology of language and religion. In T. Omoniyi & J.A. Fishman (Eds.), *Explorations in the sociology of language and religion*, 13–25. John Benjamins Publishing Company.

Gent, B. (2011). The world of the British hifz class student: observations, findings and implications for education and further research. *Journal of Religious Education*, *33*(1), 3–15.

Gumperz, J.J. & Hymes, D. (Eds.). (1972). *Directions in sociolinguistics—the ethnography of communication*. Holt, Rinehart & Winston.

Hebert, P. (2022). La Réforme Liturgique, Histoire et Perspectives. *Nouvelle Revue Théologique*, *144*, 395–406.

Hoenes del Pinal, E. (2016). From Vatican II to speaking in tongues: theology and language policy in a Q'eqchi'-Maya Catholic parish. *Language Policy*, *15*, 179–197.

Kaur, S. & David, M.K. (2019). Language shift but religious and cultural maintenance: a study of the Punjabi Sikh community in Petaling Jaya. Selangor, Malaysia. In R.V. Pandharipande, M. Eisenstein Ebsworth & M.K. David (Ed.), *Language maintenance, revival and shift in the sociology of religion*, 98–113. Multilingual Matters

Kiczek, S. A. (2009). Pope Benedict XVI's Summorum Pontificum: Reconciling Conflicting Values. *Journal of Religious and Theological Information*, *8*(1–2), 37–64.

Lothers, M. & Lothers, L. (2012). *Mirpuri immigrants in England: a sociolinguistic survey*. SIL International.

Miller, H. (2010). Supplementary Jewish education in Britain: facts and issues of the cheder system. *International Journal of Jewish Education Research*, *2010*(1), 95–115.

Moore, L.C. (2006) Learning by heart in Qur'anic and public schools in northern Cameroon. *Social Analysis: The International Journal of Cultural and Social Practice*, *50*(3), 109–126.

Moore, L.C. (2013). Qur'anic school sermons as a site for sacred and second language socialisation. *Journal of Multilingual and Multicultural Development*, *34*(5), 445–458.

Omoniyi, T. (Ed.). (2010). *The sociology of language and religion: Change, conflict and accommodation*. Palgrave Macmillan.

Omoniyi, T. & Fishman, J.A. (Eds.). (2006). *Explorations in the sociology of language and religion*. John Benjamins Publishing Company.

Pandharipande, R.V. (2006). Ideology, authority and language choice: Language of religion in South Asia. In T. Omoniyi & J.A. Fishman (Eds.), *Explorations in the sociology of language and religion*, 141–164. John Benjamins Publishing Company.

Pandharipande, R.V. (2018). Online Satsang and online Puja: Faith and language in the era of Globalization. In A. Rosowsky (Ed.), *Faith and language practices in digital spaces*, 185–208. Multilingual Matters.

Pandharipande, R.V., Eisenstein Ebsworth, M., & David, M.K. (Eds.). (2019). *Language maintenance, revival and shift in the sociology of religion*. Multilingual Matters

Parkes, D.W. (2022). Bringing Child Buddhist Monks into the Alternative Care Conversation: Reflections on an Under-considered Group of Children. *Institutionalised Children Explorations and Beyond*, *9*(1), 60–71.

Paton, I. (2013). *Sacrosanctum Concilium*: Fifty years on. *The Expository Times*, *125*(4), 157–166.

Prusak, B.P. (2010). Getting the History Right. *Commonweal,* 2 September. Retrieved 5 December 2022 from www.commonwealmagazine.org/getting-history-right

Rosowsky, A. (2006a). The role of liturgical literacy in UK Muslim communities. In T. Omoniyi & J.A. Fishman (Eds.), *Explorations in the sociology of language and religion*, 309–324. John Benjamins Publishing Company.

Rosowsky, A. (2006b). 'I used to copy what the teachers at school would do'. Cross-cultural Fusion: the role of older children in community literacy practices. *Language and Education*, *20*(6), 529–542.

Rosowsky, A. (2008). *Heavenly readings: Liturgical literacy in a multilingual context*. Multilingual Matters.

Rosowsky, A. (2010). 'Writing it in English': script choices among young multilingual Muslims in the UK. *Journal of Multilingual and Multicultural Development*, *31*(2), 163–179.

Rosowsky, A. (2013). Religious classical practice: Entextualisation and performance. *Language and Society*, *42*(3), 307–330

Rosowsky, A. (2018). *Faith and language practices in digital spaces*. Multilingual Matters.

Rosowsky A. (2020). Singing in My Language(s): How Religious Verse and Song Contribute to Minority Language Maintenance. In R.V. Pandharipande, M. Eisenstein Ebsworth & M.K. David (Eds.), *Language maintenance, revival and shift in the sociology of religion*, 33–50. Multilingual Matters.

Rosowsky, A. (2021). *The performance of multilingual and 'ultralingual' devotional practices by young British Muslims*. Multilingual Matters

Safran, W. (2008). Language, ethnicity and religion: a complex and persistent linkage. *Nations and Nationalism*, *14* (1), 171–190.

Schachter, L. (2010). Why Bonnie and Ronnie can't 'read' (the Siddur). *Journal of Jewish Education*, *76*, 17–91.

Seddon, M.S. (2004). Muslim Communities in Britain: A Historiography. In M.S. Seddon, D. Hussain, & N. Malik (Eds.), *British Muslims between assimilation and segregation: Historical, legal and social realities*, 1–42. The Islamic Foundation.

Spolsky, B. (2010). Jewish Religious Multilingualism. In T. Omoniyi (Ed.), *The sociology of language and religion: Change, conflict and accommodation*, 14–28. Palgrave Macmillan.

Stevenson, J. (2018). *Muslim Students in UK higher education: Issues of inequality and inequity*. The Bridge Institute for Research and Policy.

Street, B. (2003). What's "new" in New Literacy Studies? Critical approaches to literacy in theory and practice. *Current Issues in Comparative Education*, *5*(2), 77–91.

Uvarova, I,Y. (2017). Методика преподавания церковнославянского языка в светской и воскресной школах (из опыта работы по авторской программе «Красота славянской письменности» (Church Slavic Teaching Methodology in Secular and Sunday schools). Retrieved 5 December 2022 from https://mroc.pravobraz.ru/uvarova-metodika-krasota-slavyanskoj-pismennosti/

INDEX